Lecture Notes in Computer Science 2384

Edited by G. Goos, J. Hartmanis, and J. van Leeuwen

T0134696

Springer
Berlin
Heidelberg
New York
Barcelona
Hong Kong
London
Milan
Paris
Tokyo

Lecture Notes in Computer Science 2384
Edited by G. Goos, J. Hartmanis, and J. van Leeuwen

Springer
Berlin
Heidelberg
New York
Barcelona
Hong Kong
London
Milan
Paris
Tokyo

Lynn Batten   Jennifer Seberry (Eds.)

Information Security and Privacy

7th Australasian Conference, ACISP 2002
Melbourne, Australia, July 3-5, 2002
Proceedings

Springer

Series Editors

Gerhard Goos, Karlsruhe University, Germany
Juris Hartmanis, Cornell University, NY, USA
Jan van Leeuwen, Utrecht University, The Netherlands

Volume Editors

Lynn Batten
Deakin University, Rusden Campus
Burwood Road, Melbourne, Victoria, Australia
E-mail: lmbatten@deakin.edu.au

Jennifer Seberry
University of Wollongong, Department of Computer Science
Northfields Avenue, Wollongong, NSW, Australia
E-mail: jennifer.seberry@uow.edu.au

Cataloging-in-Publication Data applied for

Die Deutsche Bibliothek - CIP-Einheitsaufnahme

Information security and privacy : 7th Australasian conference ; proceedings
/ ACISP 2002, Melbourne, Australia, July 3 - 5, 2002. Lynn Batten ; Jennifer
Seberry (ed.). - Heidelberg ; New York ; Barcelona ; Hong Kong ; London ;
Milan ; Paris ; Tokyo : Springer, 2002
    (Lecture notes in computer science ; Vol. 2384)
    ISBN 3-540-43861-0

CR Subject Classification (1998): E.3, K.6.5, D.4.6, C.2, E.4, F.2.1, K.4.1

ISSN 0302-9743
ISBN 3-540-43861-0 Springer-Verlag Berlin Heidelberg New York

Springer-Verlag Berlin Heidelberg New York
a member of BertelsmannSpringer Science+Business Media GmbH

http://www.springer.de

© Springer-Verlag Berlin Heidelberg 2002
Printed in Germany

Typesetting: Camera-ready by author, data conversion by PTP Berlin, Stefan Sossna e. K.
Printed on acid-free paper   SPIN 10870504   06/3142   5 4 3 2 1 0

Preface

The Seventh Australasian Conference in Information Security and Privacy (ACISP) was held in Melbourne, 3–5 July, 2002. The conference was sponsored by Deakin University and iCORE, Alberta, Canada and the *Australian Computer Society*.

The aims of the *annual* ACISP conferences have been to bring together people working in different areas of computer, communication, and information security from universities, industry, and government institutions. The conferences give the participants the opportunity to discuss the latest developments in the rapidly growing area of information security and privacy.

The reviewing process took six weeks and we heartily thank all the members of the program committee and the external referees for the many hours of valuable time given to the conference.

The program committee accepted 36 papers from the 94 submitted. From those papers accepted 10 papers were from Australia, 5 each from Korea and USA, 4 each from Singapore and Germany, 2 from Japan, and 1 each from The Netherlands, UK, Spain, Bulgaria, and India. The authors of every paper, whether accepted or not, made a valued contribution to the conference.

In addition to the contributed papers, we were delighted to have presentations from the Victorian Privacy Commissioner, Paul Chadwick, and eminent researchers Professor Hugh Williams, Calgary, Canada, Professor Bimal Roy, ISI, Kolkota, India (whose invited talk was formally referred and accepted by the program committee), and Dr Hank Wolfe from Otago, New Zealand.

In addition we would like to thank Beom Sik Song, Willy Susilo, and especially Ken Finlayson for the vast work they put into getting this volume together in the time available.

July 2002

Lynn Batten
Jennifer Seberry

ACISP 2002

July 3-5, 2002, Melbourne, Australia

General Chair

Lynn Batten, Deakin University, Australia

Program Co-chairs

Lynn Batten, Deakin University, Australia
Jennifer Seberry, University of Wollongong, Australia

Program Committee

Colin Boyd	Queensland University of Technology, Australia
Mike Burmester	Florida State University, USA
Ed Dawson	Queensland University of Technology, Australia
Cunsheng Ding	University of Science & Technology, Hong Kong
Paul England	Microsoft, USA
Dieter Gollman	Microsoft, United Kingdom
Thomas Hardjono	VeriSign, USA
Kathy Horadam	RMIT, Australia
Kwangjo Kim	ICU, South Korea
Lars Knudsen	Technical University of Denmark, Denmark
Keith Martin	Royal Holloway, United Kingdom
Atsuko Miyaji	JAIST, Japan
Sangjae Moon	Kyungpook National University, South Korea
Yi Mu	Macquarie University, Australia
Eiji Okamoto	Toho University, Japan
Josef Pieprzyk	Macquarie University, Australia
Greg Rose	QUALCOMM, Australia
Rei Safavi-Naini	University of Wollongong, Australia
Qing Sihan	Academy of Science, China
John Snare	Adacel, Australia
Vijay Varadharajan	Macquarie University, Australia
Hugh Williams	University of Calgary, Canada
Yuliang Zheng	University of North Carolina, USA

External reviewers

Joonsang Baek, Monash University, Australia
Asha Baliga, RMIT University, Australia
Niklas Borselius, Royal Holloway, United Kingdom
Serdar Boztas, RMIT University, Australia
Laurence Bull, Monash University, Australia
Bernard Colbert, Telstra Research Laboratories, Australia
Robert Coulter, Deakin University, Australia
Ken Finlayson, Wollongong University, Australia
Goichiro Hanaoka, University of Tokyo, Japan
Marie Henderson, RMIT University, Australia
Matt Henricksen, QUT, Australia
Yvonne Hithchenson, QUT, Australia
Hartono Kurino, Wollongong University, Australia
Hiroaki Kikuchi, Japan
Jun Kogre, Fujitsu, Japan
Tanja Lange, Ruhr University, Germany
Bill Millan, QUT, Australia
Kenji Ohkuma, Toshiba, Japan
Marcus Peinado, Microsoft, USA
Ian Piper, Wollongong University, Australia
Chengxi Qu, University of New England, Australia
Matt Robshaw, Royal Holloway, United Kingdom
Nickolas Sheppard, Wollongong University, Australia
Igor Shparlinski, Macquarie University, Australia
Leonie Simpson, QUT, Australia
Masakazu Soshi, JAIST, Japan
Ron Steinfeld, Monash University, Australia
Karolyn Sprinks, Wollongong University, Australia
Willy Susilo, Wollongong University, Australia
Mitsuru Tada, Chiba University, Japan
Kapali Viswanthan, QUT, Australia
Yejing Wang, Wollongong University, Australia
Huaxiong Wang, Macquarie University, Australia
Tianbing Xia, Wollongong University, Australia
Masato Yamamichi, Japan
Jin Yuan, Hong Kong University of Science and Technology
Fangguo Zhang, ICU, Korea
Xianmo Zhang, Macquarie University, Australia

Table of Contents

Cryptanalysis I

Elliptic Curves

AES

Security Management

Authentication

Invited Talk

Oblivious Transfer

Cryptanalysis II

Dealing with Adversaries

A New Distributed Primality Test for Shared RSA Keys Using Quadratic Fields

Ingrid Biehl and Tsuyoshi Takagi

Technische Universität Darmstadt, Fachbereich Informatik,
Alexanderstr. 10, D-64283, Darmstadt, Germany
ttakagi@cdc.informatik.tu-darmstadt.de

Abstract. In the generation method for RSA-moduli proposed by Boneh and Franklin in [BF97] the partial signing servers generate random shares p_i, q_i and compute as candidate for an RSA-modulus $n = pq$ where $p = (\sum p_i)$ and $q = (\sum q_i)$. Then they perform a time-consuming distributed primality test which *simultaneously* checks the primality both of p and q by computing $g^{(p-1)(q-1)} = 1 \bmod n$. The primality test proposed in [BF97] cannot be generalized to products of more than two primes. A more complicated one for products of three primes was presented in [BH98].

In this paper we propose a new distributed primality test, which can *independently* prove the primality of p or q for the public modulus $n = pq$ and can be easily generalized to products of arbitrarily many factors, i.e., the Multi-Prime RSA of PKCS #1 v2.0 Amendment 1.0 [PKCS]. The proposed scheme can be applied *in parallel* for each factor p and q. We use properties of the group $Cl(-8n^2)$, which is the class group of the quadratic field with discriminant $-8n^2$.

As it is the case with the Boneh-Franklin protocol our protocol is $\lfloor \frac{k-1}{2} \rfloor$-private, i.e. less than $\lfloor \frac{k-1}{2} \rfloor$ colluding servers cannot learn any information about the primes of the generated modulus. The security of the proposed scheme is based on the intractability of the discrete logarithm problem in $Cl(-8n^2)$ and on the intractability of a new number theoretic problem which seems to be intractable too.

Keywords: Distributed RSA, primality test, parallel computation, quadratic fields.

1 Introduction

In recent literature the usage of distributed digital signature schemes is discussed as cost-friendly alternative for high security trust center applications. This allows to get rid of expensive measures to serve for the organizational security of a single signing server as it is the common practice in today's realizations. Even for the process of the generation of the secret keys, methods are known which allow a distributed computation among so-called partial signing servers, which guarantee the correctness of the result while preventing single parties from learning something about the secret keys.

L. Batten and J. Seberry (Eds.): ACISP 2002, LNCS 2384, pp. 1–16, 2002.
© Springer-Verlag Berlin Heidelberg 2002

Here we consider the case of the generation of RSA-like moduli which is part of the distributed generation process of RSA keys. The distributed RSA-modulus generation by Boneh-Franklin in [BF97] consists of two steps. In the first step each server $i(i = 1, 2, ..., k)$ generates shares p_i, q_i of numbers p, q where $n = pq$ is a candidate for an RSA-modulus. The shares have to be kept secret while all servers generate the common public modulus $n = pq = (\sum_i p_i)(\sum_i q_i)$ by means of the so-called BGW protocol [BGW88], which is proved to leak no information about the shares p_i, q_i and about p, q apart from the value n as far as less than $\lfloor \frac{k-1}{2} \rfloor$ parties collude.

To come to an RSA-modulus, p and q have to be primes. If one of them is composite the whole process has to be restarted again. Thus the expected number of repetitions is approximately ℓ^2, if p and q are ℓ-bit numbers. To check the primality in the second step a distributed primality test has to be engaged, which checks simultaneously the primality of p and q. Thus, the costs for the primality check of each candidate pair and the expected number of repetitions to find a correct RSA-modulus are the reason for the considerable running time of this approach.

In more details the test has the following form: At first trial division is made to eliminate candidate pairs, which contain small divisors. Then the candidate pair is checked by means of the Fermat test, i.e. an integer $g \in \mathbb{Z}/n\mathbb{Z}$ is randomly chosen and the servers work together to check whether $g^{n+1} \equiv \prod_i g^{p_i+q_i} \bmod n$. To do so $g^{p_i+q_i} \bmod n$ is locally computed by server S_i and is sent to the other servers. The secret shares $p_i, q_i(i = 1, 2, ..., k)$ are not revealed. Notice that $g^{n+1} \equiv \prod_i g^{p_i+q_i} \bmod n$ is equivalent to $g^{(p-1)(q-1)} \equiv 1 \bmod n$ since $(p-1)(q-1) = n+1-\sum p_i - \sum q_i$. Since there are integers which pass this Fermat test with high probability even if they are composite, in a last step Boneh and Franklin engage a Fermat test in a more complicated group to cope with these cases. The whole test is a probabilistic test and it has to be iterated to guarantee with high probability that $n = pq$ is a product of two primes. If the primality test fails, then the whole procedure starting with the choice of distributed p and q has to be repeated.

After generating shared primes p_i, q_i, a public exponent e and secret shares d_i of a secret exponent $d = (\sum_i d_i)$ with $ed \equiv 1 \bmod (p-1)(q-1)$ are distributively computed. Catalo et al. proposed an efficient protocol to compute a sharing of d [CGH00]. Then the partial signing servers easily can sign messages m by individually publishing $s_i = m^{d_i} \bmod n$. Verification is done as usual by checking whether $(\prod_i s_i)^e \equiv m \bmod n$. Miyazaki et al. proposed a protocol to achieve a k-out-of-n threshold signature for $k < n$ [MSY01], which is based on the Simmons' protocol-failure of RSA cryptosystem. A similar construction was used for the distributed RSA, but it requires a trusted dealer and strong primes for its security proof [Sho99]. Dåmgard and Koprowski dropped the conditions, namely that the modulus must be a product of safe primes and that a trusted dealer generates the keys [DK01]. Recently, Fouque and Stern proposed a distributed RSA key generation for any type of RSA modulus [FS01]. We can combine these results to our proposed distributed primality test and construct a distributed RSA cryptosystem.

Contribution of This Paper

In this paper we give a new distributed primality test which can *independently* prove the primality of p or q for the public modulus $n = pq$. The new distributed primality test is based on the ideal arithmetic of non-maximal quadratic orders of quadratic fields. We use the map between two different class groups of non-maximal orders, namely $Cl(-8n^2)$ and $Cl(-8q^2)$. The kernel of the map φ_p : $Cl(-8n^2) \rightarrow Cl(-8q^2)$ is a cyclic group with order $p - (-2/p)$, where $(\cdot/p)$ is the Jacobi symbol modulo p. We give an algorithm, which distributively generates an ideal $\mathfrak{p}$ in the kernel of the map φ_p. Then we can check the primality of p by checking whether $\mathfrak{p}^{p \pm 1} \stackrel{?}{=} 1 \in Cl(-8n^2)$. Analogously we check the primality of q. Thus the proposed scheme can be applied *in parallel* for each factor p and q.

The security of the proposed distributed primality test depends on the discrete logarithm problem in $Cl(-8n^2)$ and a number theoretic problem, which can be characterized as follows and which seems to be intractable: find p or q given pairs of ideals $(\mathfrak{a}_1, \mathfrak{a}_2)$ and $(\mathfrak{b}_1, \mathfrak{b}_2)$ in $\mathcal{O}_{-8n^2}$, where $\widetilde{\varphi_p}(\mathfrak{a}_1) = \mathfrak{a}_1 \mathcal{O}_{-8q^2}$, $\widetilde{\varphi_p}(\mathfrak{a}_2) = \mathfrak{a}_2 \mathcal{O}_{-8q^2}$ are equivalent with exactly one reduction step in $\mathcal{O}_{-8q^2}$ and $\widetilde{\varphi_q}(\mathfrak{b}_1) = \mathfrak{b}_1 \mathcal{O}_{-8p^2}$, $\widetilde{\varphi_q}(\mathfrak{b}_2) = \mathfrak{b}_2 \mathcal{O}_{-8p^2}$ are equivalent with exactly one reduction step in $\mathcal{O}_{-8p^2}$.

To check a factor it is sufficient to do this test once. Thus the new test is a good candidate for a more efficient practical test compared to the well-known tests published so far. As another advantage the proposed distributed primality test can be easily generalized to products of different form, for example to products $n = p_1 p_2 p_3$ for primes p_1, p_2, p_3. We can apply it to the Multi-Prime RSA of PKCS # 1 v2.0 Amendment 1.0 [PKCS]. This extension appears more natural and efficient than the method proposed by Boneh and Horwitz in [BH98].

As in the Boneh-Franklin method we assume the servers to be honest but curious, i.e. they follow honestly the protocol but may try to deduce information about the factors of the candidate RSA-modulus by means of the exchanged information. Moreover we suppose that there is a secure communication channel between each pair of parties. Although our method can be generalized we concentrate for reason of simplicity on an k-out-of-k scheme, i.e. all k servers are needed to generate and test a candidate RSA-modulus. As it is the case with the Boneh-Franklin protocol our protocol is $\lfloor \frac{k-1}{2} \rfloor$-private, i.e. less than $\lfloor \frac{k-1}{2} \rfloor$ colluding servers cannot learn any information about the primes of the generated modulus.

In Section 2 we sketch the method of Boneh and Franklin. In Section 3 we present a new distributed multiplication method DistMult which is a variant of the BGW method and allows to distributively compute the product of arbitrarily many shared integers. This protocol will serve as a subroutine in our primality test. In Section 4 we will introduce as necessary basics ideals of quadratic orders and prove the mentioned properties of the maps φ_p. Then we present in Section 5 the new distributed primality test and analyze it.

2   RSA-Modulus Generation by Boneh-Franklin

In this section we sketch the distributed generation of an RSA-modulus by k servers as it is proposed by Boneh-Franklin in [BF97]. Let $S_i(i = 1, 2, ..., k)$ be the servers which are connected to each other by means of a secure channel. The server S_i locally generates two random integers p_i, q_i, and keeps them secret. Then all of them work together to generate and publishes the modulus $n = pq$ with $p = \sum_i p_i, q = \sum_i q_i$ by means of the BGW protocol [BGW88], which does not reveal any information about the partial shares $p_i, q_i(i = 1, 2, ..., k)$ or about p or q. The BGW protocol (adapted from protocols proposed in [BGW88]) and thus the Boneh-Franklin protocol is at most $\lfloor \frac{k-1}{2} \rfloor$-private, i.e. any coalition of $\lfloor (k-1)/2 \rfloor$ servers cannot learn any information which cannot be directly derived by n and their own shares.

In the following we will present a similar protocol, which allows to compute (additive) shares of the product of two (additively) shared numbers p, q.

After generation of the composite modulus in the protocol by Boneh and Franklin trial division is applied with primes up to some not too large bound B. Then the distributed Fermat primality test is applied: for a random element g in $\mathbb{Z}/n\mathbb{Z}$ it is checked whether $g^{n+1} \overset{?}{\equiv} \prod_i v_i \bmod n$, where $v_i \equiv g^{p_i+q_i} \bmod n$ and v_i is locally computed and published by the server S_i. Since $n+1-\sum_i(p_i+q_i) = (p-1)(q-1)$ the test is equivalent to the test of $g^{(p-1)(q-1)} \equiv 1 \bmod n$. As this relation might hold although n is not of the correct form it has to be repeated several times for different g. Unfortunately there are composite numbers n which are not the product of two primes but always pass the distributed Fermat test (for all g) though. Accordingly to Boneh and Franklin the probability to get such an integer is very small.

Apart from these rare exceptions the probability for g to lead to an accepting test is at most $1/2$ if n is not of the correct form. Thus it is sufficient to repeat the test t times to guarantee with probability $1 - 1/2^t$ that the found number is of the correct form.

The security of the test is based on the intractability of the discrete logarithm problem: To compute the shares p_i, q_i one has to solve the discrete logarithm problem for v_i which is supposed to be an intractable problem. Therefore, this distributed primality test is computationally secure and no server S_i can learn information about the shares p_j, q_j $(j = 1, 2, ..., k, j \neq i)$.

3   Distributive Multiplication of Shared Integers

We present a new variant of the BGW protocol, which is used in Section 5.

Algorithm 1 (DistMult)
Input: A prime $r > pq$ and $r > k$. Each party S_i has shares p_i, q_i $(i = 1, ..., k)$ such that $p \equiv \sum_i p_i \bmod r, q \equiv \sum_i q_i \bmod r$.
Output: Each party has a share w_i $(i = 1, ..., k)$ such that $pq \equiv \sum_i w_i \bmod r$.

1. Let $i = 1, 2, ..., k$ and $l = \lfloor \frac{k-1}{2} \rfloor$. The party S_i generates random polynomials $f_i(x), g_i(x) \in \mathbb{Z}_r[x]$ of degree l with $f_i(0) \equiv p_i \bmod r, g_i(0) \equiv q_i \bmod r$, a random polynomial $h_i(x) \in \mathbb{Z}_r[x]$ of degree $2l$ and keeps these polynomials secret. Moreover it sets $w_i \equiv -h_i(0) \bmod r$ as share.
2. For $j = 1, 2, ..., k$ each party S_i computes $p_{i,j} \equiv f_i(j) \bmod r, q_{i,j} \equiv g_i(j) \bmod r, h_{i,j} \equiv h_i(j) \bmod r$ and sends $p_{i,j}, q_{i,j}, h_{i,j}$ to party j for all $j \neq i$.
3. Each party S_i computes

$$n_i \equiv \left(\sum_{j=1}^{k} p_{j,i} \right) \left(\sum_{j=1}^{k} q_{j,i} \right) + \left(\sum_{j=1}^{k} h_{j,i} \right) \bmod r. \qquad (1)$$

Then party S_i sends n_i to the first party S_1.
Notice that for $t(x) \equiv ((\sum f_j) * (\sum g_j) + (\sum h_j))(x) \bmod r$ follows: t has degree $2l$ and $n_i \equiv t(i) \bmod r$.
4. Since $k \geq 2l + 1$ the first party S_1 knows enough interpolation points to interpolate $t(x)$. Thus it computes $w_1 \equiv t(0) - h_1(0) \bmod r$ by

$$w_1 \equiv \left(\sum_{i=1}^{k} n_i \cdot \left(\prod_{j \neq i} \frac{j}{j-i} \right) \right) - h_1(0) \bmod r. \qquad (2)$$

The protocol is correct since

$$\sum_i w_i \equiv (t(0) - h_1(0)) + \sum_{i=2}^{k} (-h_i(0))$$

$$\equiv \left(\sum_i f_i(0) \right) \left(\sum_i g_i(0) \right) + \left(\sum_i h_i(0) \right) - \left(\sum_i h_i(0) \right)$$

$$\equiv (\sum_i p_i)(\sum_i q_i)$$

$$\equiv pq \bmod r.$$

The protocol is l-private since less than $l + 1$ colluders won't learn any information on any of the used polynomials (compare Shamirs secret sharing method) and each set of $k - 1$ numbers appears with the same probability as set of $k - 1$ output shares. Thus it is $\lfloor \frac{k-1}{2} \rfloor$-private and one can prove the following theorem:

Proposition 1. *Any coalition of at most $\lfloor \frac{k-1}{2} \rfloor$ parties can simulate the transcript of the DistMult protocol, thus the DistMult protocol is $\lfloor \frac{k-1}{2} \rfloor$-private.*

Please notice that the protocol can be modified to compute $pq \bmod a$ for some arbitrary integer a. To do so it has to be applied for each prime divisor r of a and the results have to be combined by the usual methods of Chinese remaindering and Hensel lifting. Even if the prime factorization of a is not known the protocol can be applied and either works or leads to a refinement of the factorization of a. In the latter case it has to be restarted with the newly improved

partial factorization. Thus this method terminates and causes at most $O(\log|a|)$
restarts.

Moreover, the protocol can repeatedly be applied to compute the product of
arbitrarily many factors $m = g_1 \ldots g_c$ supposed there is a prime $r > m$ and each
factor g_j is shared among the parties by shares $g_j^{(i)}$ such that $\sum_i g_j^{(i)} \equiv g_j \bmod r$.
Using a tree-like multiplication sequence one needs about $O(\log c)$ applications
of the above protocol.

In the original BGW protocol the product value is publicly known after the
protocol. Obviously this can be achieved by publishing all w_i in the DistMult
protocol.

4   Mathematical Backgroud

4.1   Quadratic Order

In this section we will explain the arithmetic of ideals of quadratic orders which
we will use in this paper. A more comprehensive treatment can be found in
[Cox89].

A *discriminant* Δ is a non-square integer such that $\Delta \equiv 0, 1 \bmod 4$. It is
called *fundamental* if $\Delta \equiv 1 \bmod 4$ and is square-free, or $\Delta/4 \equiv 2, 3 \bmod 4$ and is
square-free. In this paper we use only negative discriminants. The *quadratic field*
of discriminant Δ is $\mathbb{Q}(\sqrt{\Delta}) = \mathbb{Q} + \sqrt{\Delta}\mathbb{Q}$. The *quadratic order* of discriminant
Δ is $\mathcal{O}_\Delta = \mathbb{Z} + \frac{\Delta + \sqrt{\Delta}}{2}\mathbb{Z}$. Every element $\alpha \in \mathcal{O}_\Delta$ can be represented as $\alpha = (x + y\sqrt{\Delta})/2$ for some $x, y \in \mathbb{Z}$. Every ideal $\mathfrak{a}$ of $\mathcal{O}_\Delta$ can be represented by

$$\mathfrak{a} = m\left(a\mathbb{Z} + \frac{b + \sqrt{\Delta}}{2}\mathbb{Z}\right), \tag{3}$$

where $m \in \mathbb{Z}$, $a \in \mathbb{Z}_{>0}$, and $b \in \mathbb{Z}$ such that $b^2 \equiv \Delta \pmod{4a}$ [BW88]. When
a is a prime integer, then we call $\mathfrak{a}$ a *prime ideal*. The *norm* of an ideal $\mathfrak{a}$ is
defined by $N(\mathfrak{a}) = aq^2$. A *fractional ideal* $\mathfrak{a}$ of $\mathcal{O}_\Delta$ is a subset of $\mathbb{Q}(\sqrt{\Delta})$ of the
form $\mathfrak{a} = q\left(a\mathbb{Z} + \frac{b + \sqrt{\Delta}}{2}\mathbb{Z}\right)$, where $q = m/d \in \mathbb{Q}$ and a, b, and m satisfy the
criteria in equation (3). Then (q, a, b) is called the *standard representation* of
ideal $\mathfrak{a}$. If $q = 1$ holds for an ideal $\mathfrak{a}$, then the ideal $\mathfrak{a}$ is called *integral*. If $q = 1$
holds for an ideal $\mathfrak{a}$, then $\mathfrak{a}$ is said to be *primitive* and in that case we represent
$\mathfrak{a}$ by (a, b). For two given ideals $\mathfrak{a}, \mathfrak{b}$, we can compute their product $\mathfrak{a}\mathfrak{b}$ which
needs $O((\log(\max\{N(\mathfrak{a}), N(\mathfrak{b})\}))^2)$ bit operations (see, for example, [BW88]). A
fractional ideal $\mathfrak{a}$ of $\mathcal{O}_\Delta$ is *invertible* if there exits another fractional ideal $\mathfrak{b}$ such
that $\mathfrak{a}\mathfrak{b} = \mathcal{O}_\Delta$. The set of invertible ideals is $\mathcal{I}_\Delta$. For an element $\gamma \in \mathbb{Q}(\sqrt{\Delta})$,
the ideal $\mathfrak{a}$ generated by γ is called a *principal* ideal. We denote it by $\mathfrak{a} = (\gamma)$ or
$\mathfrak{a} = \gamma\mathcal{O}_\Delta$ and then γ is called the *generator* of the principal ideal $\mathfrak{a}$. The set of
principal ideals is denoted by $\mathcal{P}_\Delta$.

Two fractional ideals $\mathfrak{a}$ and $\mathfrak{b}$ of $\mathcal{O}_\Delta$ are called *equivalent* (i.e. $\mathfrak{a} \sim \mathfrak{b}$) if there
is $\alpha \in \mathbb{Q}(\sqrt{\Delta})$ such that $\mathfrak{a} = \alpha\mathfrak{b}$. The *class group* $Cl(\Delta)$ of the quadratic order

$\mathcal{O}_\Delta$ is defined as $Cl(\Delta) = \mathcal{I}_\Delta / \mathcal{P}_\Delta$ with respect to the equivalent relation $\sim$. If $\mathfrak{a}$ is a fractional ideal then we denote by $[\mathfrak{a}]$ the corresponding class. For a primitive ideal $\mathfrak{a}$ in $\mathcal{I}_\Delta$, we say that $\mathfrak{a} = (a, b)$ is *reduced* if $|b| \leq a \leq c = (b^2 - \Delta)/4a$ and additionally $b \geq 0$ if $a = c$ or $a = |b|$. There is only one reduced ideal in every equivalence class. For a primitive ideal $\mathfrak{a}$ we denote by $Red_\Delta(\mathfrak{a})$ the uniquely determined reduced ideal equivalent to $\mathfrak{a}$. Define the *reduction operator* $\rho_\Delta((a, b)) = (\frac{b^2 - \Delta}{4a}, -b)$ for primitive ideals $\mathfrak{a} = (a, b)$. One can prove that for $\mathfrak{a}' = \rho_\Delta(\mathfrak{a})$ that $\mathfrak{a}^{-1} * \mathfrak{a}'$ is principal. Then one can compute $Red_\Delta(\mathfrak{a})$ by $O(\log^2 N(\mathfrak{a}))$ repeated applications of ρ_Δ (see [BB97]).

Every non-fundamental discriminant Δ can be represented by $\Delta = \Delta_1 f^2$, where Δ_1 is the fundamental discriminant and f is a positive integer called the *conductor* (we write Δ_f instead of $\Delta_1 f^2$). Moreover, the order $\mathcal{O}_\Delta = \mathbb{Z} + f\mathcal{O}_{\Delta_1}$ is called *non-maximal order* with conductor f and $\mathcal{O}_{\Delta_1}$ is called the *maximal order*. For a quadratic order $\mathcal{O}_\Delta$ with conductor f, we say that a non-zero fractional ideal $\mathfrak{a}$ is *prime* to f if the denominator and the numerator of $N(\mathfrak{a})$ are relatively prime to f. For a fractional principal ideal $\gamma\mathcal{O}_\Delta$ ($\gamma \in \mathbb{Q}(\Delta)$), we define: $\gamma\mathcal{O}_\Delta$ is *prime to* f if the denominator and the numerator of $N(\gamma)$ are relative prime to f. We denote the subgroup of all fractional ideals prime to f by $\mathcal{I}_\Delta(f)$. The subset of $\mathcal{I}_\Delta(f)$ which is generated by the principal ideals $\gamma\mathcal{O}$ ($\gamma \in \mathbb{Q}(\Delta)$), whose norm is relative prime to f, is a subgroup of $\mathcal{I}_\Delta(f)$ and is denoted by $\mathcal{P}_\Delta(f)$. It is well known that any ideal class in $Cl(\Delta)$ contains an ideal prime to the conductor f. One can prove that $Cl(\Delta) \overset{\sim}{\to} \mathcal{I}_\Delta(f)/\mathcal{P}_\Delta(f)$.

4.2   The Idea of a New Primality Test

Let Δ_{fg} be the non-fundamental discriminant $\Delta_1(fg)^2$. The relationship of ideals in the order tower of $\mathcal{O}_{\Delta_{fg}} \subset \mathcal{O}_{\Delta_f} \subset \mathcal{O}_{\Delta_1}$ plays the main role in our proposed distributed primality test. There is a nice structure in the relationship between $Cl(\Delta_{fg})$ and $Cl(\Delta_f)$, namely:

Proposition 2. *Consider the map* $\varphi_g : Cl(\Delta_{fg}) \to Cl(\Delta_f)$ *with* $\varphi_g([\mathfrak{a}]) = [\mathfrak{a}\mathcal{O}_{\Delta_f}]$ *then*

$$\#Ker(\varphi_g) = g \prod_{p|g} \left(1 - \left(\frac{\Delta_f}{p}\right)\right)\frac{1}{p}.$$

Especially, if g is prime and $\left(\frac{\Delta_f}{g}\right) = -1$ then $\#Ker(\varphi_g) = g + 1$.

Proposition 3. *Define* $\varphi_g^{-1} : Cl(\Delta_f) \to Cl(\Delta_{fg})$ *by* $\varphi_g^{-1}([\mathfrak{A}]) = [\mathfrak{A} \cap \mathcal{O}_{fg}]$. *Then it follows for all $\mathfrak{a} \in \mathcal{I}_{\Delta_{fg}}$ and $[\mathfrak{b}] = \varphi_g^{-1}(\varphi_g([\mathfrak{a}]))$ that $[\mathfrak{a}][\mathfrak{b}]^{-1} \in Ker(\varphi_g)$.*

We want to use this for a new primality check for g: The idea is to compute a kernel element $[\mathfrak{p}]$ of φ_g and then to check whether $[\mathfrak{p}^{\#Ker(\varphi_g)}]$ is principal. Thus we have to explain a method to compute such a kernel element.

Since $Cl(\Delta) \overset{\sim}{\to} \mathcal{I}_\Delta(d)/\mathcal{P}_\Delta(d)$ for arbitrary discriminant Δ and integer d and this isomorphism is a holomorphism with respect to ideal multiplication, one can compute with ideals in $\mathcal{I}_{\Delta_{fg}}(fg)$ resp. in $\mathcal{I}_{\Delta_f}(fg)$ instead of computing with elements in $Cl(\Delta_{fg})$ resp. $Cl(\Delta_f)$.

Proposition 4. *Consider a fundamental discriminant Δ_1 and non-fundamental discriminants $\Delta_{fg} = \Delta_1(fg)^2$ and $\Delta_f = \Delta_1 f^2$. The map $\widetilde{\varphi_g} : \mathcal{I}_{\Delta_{fg}}(fg) \to \mathcal{I}_{\Delta_f}(fg)$ with $\mathfrak{a} \mapsto \widetilde{\varphi_g}(\mathfrak{a}) = \mathfrak{a}\mathcal{O}_{\Delta_f}$ is an isomorphism. The inverse of this map is $\widetilde{\varphi_g}^{-1} : \mathcal{I}_{\Delta_f}(fg) \to \mathcal{I}_{\Delta_{fg}}(fg)$ with $\mathfrak{A} \mapsto \widetilde{\varphi_g}^{-1}(\mathfrak{A}) = \mathfrak{A} \cap \mathcal{O}_{\Delta_{fg}}$.*

For proofs of the above propositions see [Cox89]. Thus we can use $\widetilde{\varphi_g}$ (resp. $\widetilde{\varphi_g}^{-1}$) as a substitute for φ_g (resp. φ_g^{-1}) as defined above. Thus our strategy to compute a kernel element is: choose $\mathfrak{a} \in \mathcal{I}_{\Delta_{fg}}(fg)$, set $\mathfrak{A} = \widetilde{\varphi_g}(\mathfrak{a}) \in \mathcal{I}_{\Delta_f}(fg)$, apply the reduction operator to get $\mathfrak{A}' = \rho_{\Delta_f}(\mathfrak{A})$ and go back to $\mathcal{I}_{\Delta_{fg}}(fg)$ by computing $\mathfrak{b} = \widetilde{\varphi_g}^{-1}(\mathfrak{A}')$. Then one can prove the following

Proposition 5. *Consider a fundamental discriminant Δ_1 and non-fundamental discriminants $\Delta_{fg} = \Delta_1(fg)^2$ and $\Delta_f = \Delta_1 f^2$. Let $\mathfrak{a} \in \mathcal{I}_{\Delta_{fg}}(fg)$ and $\rho_{\Delta_f}(\widetilde{\varphi_g}(\mathfrak{a})) \in \mathcal{I}_{\Delta_f}(fg)$ and*

$$\mathfrak{b} = \widetilde{\varphi_g}^{-1}(\rho_{\Delta_f}(\widetilde{\varphi_g}(\mathfrak{a})))$$

then $[\mathfrak{a}\mathfrak{b}^{-1}]$ is a non-trivial element of $Ker(\varphi_g)$.

For a proof of Proposition 5, see the appendix. Finally we explain how one efficiently computes $\widetilde{\varphi_g}$ and $\widetilde{\varphi_g}^{-1}$: By the standard representation of an ideal, we have the relationship $\mathfrak{a}\mathcal{O}_{\Delta_f} = (a\mathbb{Z} + \frac{b+g\sqrt{\Delta_f}}{2}\mathbb{Z})(\mathbb{Z} + \frac{\Delta_f+\sqrt{\Delta_f}}{2}\mathbb{Z})$. Then we obtain a practical algorithm to compute $\widetilde{\varphi_g}$ as follows:

Algorithm 2 (GoToOrder$_f$)
Input: the discriminant Δ_{fg}, the integer g, and a primitive ideal $\mathfrak{a} = (a, b) \in \mathcal{I}_{\Delta_{fg}}(fg)$ prime to fg
Output: A ideal $\mathfrak{A} = \widetilde{\varphi_g}(\mathfrak{a}) = (A, B) \in \mathcal{I}_{\Delta_f}(fg)$.

1. $A \leftarrow a$
2. $b_{\mathcal{O}} \leftarrow \Delta_{fg} \bmod 2$
3. Find $\mu, \lambda \in \mathbb{Z}$ with $1 = \mu g + \lambda a$ using the extended Euclidean algorithm.
4. $B \leftarrow b\mu + ab_{\mathcal{O}}\lambda \bmod 2a$, $(-A \leq B < A)$

We discuss the inverse map of GoToOrder$_f$: Here, we represent a primitive ideal $\mathfrak{A}$ in $\mathcal{I}_{\Delta_f}(fg)$ by the standard representation: $\mathfrak{A} = (A\mathbb{Z} + \frac{B+\sqrt{\Delta_f}}{2}\mathbb{Z})$. $\mathcal{O}_{\Delta_{fg}} = \mathbb{Z} + \frac{\Delta_{fg}+g\sqrt{\Delta_f}}{2}\mathbb{Z}$. The ideal $\widetilde{\varphi_g}^{-1}(\mathfrak{A})$ is represented as $\mathfrak{A} \cap \mathcal{O}_{\Delta_{fg}} = (A\mathbb{Z} + \frac{B+\sqrt{\Delta_f}}{2}\mathbb{Z}) \cap (\mathbb{Z} + \frac{\Delta_{fg}+g\sqrt{\Delta_f}}{2}\mathbb{Z})$. In this intersection the smallest rational integer obviously is A, and the element $\frac{B+\sqrt{\Delta_f}}{2}x$ ($x \in \mathbb{Z}$) must satisfy $g|x$. Thus $\mathfrak{a} = \widetilde{\varphi_g}^{-1}(\mathfrak{A})$ is a primitive ideal with $N(\mathfrak{A}) = N(\mathfrak{a})$, and the standard representation $\widetilde{\varphi_g}^{-1}(\mathfrak{A}) = (a\mathbb{Z} + \frac{b+\sqrt{\Delta_{fg}}}{2}\mathbb{Z})$ can be computed by $a = A$, $b \equiv Bg$ (mod $2a$). As we showed above, the practical algorithm to compute the map $\widetilde{\varphi_g}^{-1}$ is as follows:

Algorithm 3 (GoToOrder$_{fg}$)
Input: A primitive ideal $\mathfrak{A} = (A, B) \in \mathcal{I}_{\Delta_f}(fg)$, the integer g
Output: A primitive ideal $\mathfrak{a} \in \mathcal{I}_{\Delta_{fg}}(fg)$ such that $\widetilde{\varphi_g}^{-1}(\mathfrak{A}) = \mathfrak{a} = (a, b)$.

1. $a \leftarrow A$,
2. $b \leftarrow Bg \bmod 2a$, $(-a \leq b < a)$
3. RETURN (a, b)

5   The New Distributed Primality Test

In this section we present a new distributed primality test for $n = pq$. Assume that each partial signing server S_i $(i = 1, 2, ..., k)$ has secret shares p_i, q_i, where $p = \sum_i p_i$, $q = \sum q_i$. The proposed distributed primality test consists of three steps. In the first step we compute the common modulus $n = pq$ using the Dist-Mult protocol from the partial shares $p_i, q_i, (i = 1, 2, ..., k)$. Thus our scheme is at most $\lfloor \frac{k-1}{2} \rfloor$-private. Let $\Delta = -8n^2$ be the public discriminant of the quadratic order $\mathcal{O}_\Delta$. Note that the class number of the maximal order $\mathcal{O}_{-8}$ of $\mathcal{O}_{-8n^2}$ is one. All servers know the discriminant Δ. In the second step, we distributively compute a non-trivial kernel element $[\mathfrak{p}] \in Cl(\Delta)$ of $\varphi_q : Cl(\Delta) \to Cl(\Delta/q^2)$ without publishing Δ/q^2 or q. Thus we have to invent a distributed version of the algorithms GoToOrder$_{fg}$ and GoToOrder$_g$.

For reason of simplicity we consider here the case that $p, q \equiv -1 \bmod 8$. Then the order of the kernel can be proved to be $q + 1$. Thus, we can check in the third step as distributed primality test whether $[\mathfrak{p}^{q_k+1} \prod_{i=1,2,..,k-1} \mathfrak{p}^{q_i}] \stackrel{?}{=} 1$ in the common class group $Cl(\Delta)$.

The first step to generate the common discriminant Δ is as follows:

Generation of the public discriminant Δ: Each party $S_i(i = 2, ..., k)$ generates two random integers p_i, q_i with $p_i, q_i \equiv 0 \bmod 8$ and keeps them secret. Here we assume each integer p_i, q_i has the same bit-length l/k. Moreover party S_1 generates p_1, q_1 of bitlength l/k with $p_1 \equiv -1 \bmod 8$ and $q_1 \equiv -1 \bmod 8$. By means of the DistMult protocol using a prime $r > pq$ the product $n = pq$ is distributively generated and published, where $p = \sum_{i=1}^k p_i$ and $q = \sum_{i=1}^k q_i$. Let $\Delta = -8n^2$.

5.1   Distributed Generation of a Kernel Element

Let $\Delta = -8n^2$ be the public discriminant of the quadratic order $\mathcal{O}_\Delta$. We describe how to distributively generate a non-trivial kernel element $[\mathfrak{p}]$ of $Cl(\Delta) \to Cl(\Delta/q^2)$. The distributed generation has 4 steps. In the first step we choose a common prime ideal $\mathfrak{a} \in \mathcal{O}_\Delta$. In the second step we distributively compute $\mathfrak{A} = \text{GoToOrder}_p(\mathfrak{a})$. In the third step we compute $\rho_{\Delta/q^2}(\mathfrak{A})$, i.e. we switch from the ideal $\mathfrak{A}$ to $\mathfrak{A}'$ which is equivalent to $\mathfrak{A}$ in $Cl(\Delta/q^2)$. In the fourth step we distributively compute $\mathfrak{a}_{new} = \text{GoToOrder}_{pq}(\mathfrak{A}')$. Finally we obtain the kernel element $[\mathfrak{p}]$ by computing $\mathfrak{p}Red_\Delta(\mathfrak{a}_{new}\mathfrak{a}^{-1})$. We describe the algorithm in the following:

1. **Pick up an ideal** $\mathfrak{a} \in \mathcal{O}_\Delta$: The first server generates a prime $a \in \mathbb{Z}$ such that $0 < a < \sqrt{\Delta}$. Then it checks whether $\gcd(a, \Delta) = 1$ and $\left(\frac{\Delta}{a}\right) = 1$ hold. If not, it repeats this step.
   Then it generates $b \in \mathbb{Z}$ such that $b^2 \equiv \Delta \bmod 4a$ and publishes $\mathfrak{a} = (a, b) \in \mathcal{O}_\Delta$.

2. **Distributed** $\mathsf{GoToOrder}_p$: Each server S_i computes $\lambda_a \equiv \Delta^{-1} \bmod a$.
   It sets $w_i = -8np_i \in \mathbb{Z}$ as share of $-8p^2 q = \sum_{j=1}^{k} w_j \in \mathbb{Z}$ and $\lambda_i = \lambda_a w_i \bmod a$ as share of $\lambda = \sum_{j=1}^{k} \lambda_j \bmod a$. Then $1 \equiv \lambda q \bmod a$.
   It locally computes an integer B_i with $B_i \equiv b\lambda_i \bmod 2a$ and keeps it secret. Then the ideal $\mathfrak{A} = (A, B)$ is an image of $\mathsf{GoToOrder}_p(\mathfrak{a}) = \widetilde{\varphi_q}(\mathfrak{a})$, i.e. $\mathfrak{A} = \mathfrak{a}\mathcal{O}_{-8p^2}$, where $A = a \in \mathbb{Z}$ and $B = \sum_{i=1}^{k} B_i \in \mathbb{Z}$.

3. **Distributed reduction operator in** $\mathcal{O}_{-8p^2}$:
   a) The first server chooses and publishes some prime $r > (4k^2 + 8)\Delta^2 > B^2 + 8p^2$. All servers $(i = 1, 2, ..., k)$ distributively compute shares $m_i \bmod r$ of $B^2 = \sum_{i=1}^{k} m_i \bmod r$ and shares $z_i \bmod r$ of $-8p^2 = \sum_{i=1}^{k} z_i \bmod r$ by means of the DistMult protocol. Each server secretly holds the shares $m_i \bmod r$ and $z_i \bmod r$.
   b) Each server S_i locally computes $m_i + z_i \bmod r$ and broadcasts this value to the other servers. Thus $B^2 + 8p^2 \bmod r$ is public while p and B are secret. Since $r > B^2 + 8p^2$ the integer $B^2 + 8p^2$ is uniquely determined by $B^2 + 8p^2 \bmod r$.
   c) The first server computes $C = (B^2 + 8p^2)/4A \in \mathbb{Z}$ and check whether $\gcd(C, \Delta) = 1$ holds. If a non-trivial $(\neq 1, 2)$ factor is found the whole generation of the composite modulus has to be repeated.
   d) Each server S_i $(i = 1, 2, ..., k)$ puts $A = C \in \mathbb{Z}$, $B_i = -B_i \in \mathbb{Z}$. Note that the ideal $\mathfrak{A}' = (A, B)$ is $\rho_{-8p^2}(\widetilde{\varphi_q}(\mathfrak{a}))$.

4. **Distributed** $\mathsf{GoToOrder}_{pq}$:
   a) Each server sets $a_{new} = A$.
   b) All servers $(i = 1, 2, ..., k)$ distributively compute and publish an integer b_{new} with $b_{new} \equiv (\sum_{i=1}^{k} B_i)(\sum_{i=1}^{k} q_i) \bmod a_{new}$ using the DistMult protocol. Thus they know the public ideal $\mathfrak{a}_{new} = (a_{new}, b_{new}) = \widetilde{\varphi_q}^{-1}(\mathfrak{A}')$.

5. **Computing a kernel element**: Each server computes $\mathfrak{p} = Red_\Delta(\mathfrak{a}_{new}\mathfrak{a}^{-1})$.

In the first step a prime ideal $\mathfrak{a}$ in $\mathcal{O}_\Delta$ is chosen whose norm is smaller than $\sqrt{\Delta}$. To do so one generates a prime a such that $a < \sqrt{\Delta}$, $\left(\frac{\Delta}{a}\right) = 1$ and solve b such that $b^2 \equiv \Delta \bmod 4a$. Then $\mathfrak{a} = (a, b)$ is a prime ideal in $\mathcal{O}_\Delta$ (see Section 4.1). By checking the condition $\gcd(\Delta, a) = 1$, one knows that the ideal $\mathfrak{a}$ is prime to conductor pq and one can map it to the order $\mathcal{O}_{\Delta/q^2}$. In the second step, $\mathsf{GoToOrder}_p(\mathfrak{a})$ is to be computed. Since $\Delta \equiv 0 \bmod 2$, $(A, B) = \mathfrak{A} = \mathsf{GoToOrder}_p(\mathfrak{a})$ can be computed $A = a, B = b\lambda \bmod 2a$ where $\lambda \equiv q^{-1} \bmod a$. This is done as follows: All servers have to compute λ with only the secret knowledge of p_i $(i = 1, 2, ..., k)$ but without the knowledge of p. To do so they publicly compute $\lambda_a \equiv \Delta^{-1} \bmod a$ with the public discriminant Δ. Since there is a representation $1 = -8(pq)^2\lambda_a + \mu a = (-8np\lambda_a)q + \mu a$ for an integer μ it follows that $q^{-1} \equiv (-8np\lambda_a) \bmod a$. Thus $\lambda_i = \lambda_a w_i = -8np_i\lambda_a$ is a share of $\lambda =$

$\sum_{i=1}^{k} \lambda_i$ with $1 = \lambda q + \mu a$. Thus one can distributively compute $\mathsf{GoToOrder}_p(\mathfrak{a})$ by computing secretly $B_i \equiv b\lambda_i \bmod 2a$ by each server S_i. The non-published corresponding ideal $\mathsf{GoToOrder}_p(\mathfrak{a})$ then is (A, B) with $B = \sum_{i=1}^{k} B_i$. In the third step one switches from the ideal $\mathfrak{A}$ to the ideal $\mathfrak{A}'$ in the equivalent class of $Cl(\Delta/q^2)$. We choose the ideal which is obtained with exactly one reduction step, i.e. such that $\mathfrak{A}' = (C, -B)$ where $C = (B^2 - \Delta/q^2)/4A$. Here $(B^2 - \Delta/q^2) = B^2 + 8p^2$ is computed by means of the $\mathsf{DistMult}$ protocol. The ideal $\mathfrak{A}'$ is published. In the fourth step, the servers distributively compute $(a_{new}, b_{new}) = a_{new} = \mathsf{GoToOrder}_{pq}(\mathfrak{A}') = \widetilde{\varphi_q}^{-1}(\mathfrak{a}')$. This is calculated by $a_{new} = A, b_{new} \equiv (\sum_{i=1}^{k} B_i)(\sum_{i=1}^{k} q_i) \bmod a_{new}$ using the $\mathsf{DistMult}$ protocol.

Here note that $a_{new} = \widetilde{\varphi_q}^{-1}(\rho_{-8p^2}(\widetilde{\varphi_q}(\mathfrak{a})))$ holds. Since $C = (B^2 - \Delta/q^2)/4A$ is relatively prime to $\Delta = -8n^2$ in the protocol, $N(B - \sqrt{-8p^2})$ is also relatively prime to Δ and $\rho_{-8p^2}(\widetilde{\varphi_q}(\mathfrak{a})) \in \mathcal{I}_{-8p^2}(pq)$. Thus we can apply Proposition 5 to get the following lemma as result:

Lemma 1. *Let $\mathfrak{a}$ and a_{new} be the output from the protocol above and $\mathfrak{p} = Red_\Delta(a_{new}\mathfrak{a}^{-1})$. Then $[\mathfrak{p}]$ is a non-trivial kernel element of the map $\varphi_q : Cl(-8n^2) \to Cl(-8p^2)$.*

5.2 Distributed Primality Test for q

In this section we propose a distributed primality test which proves the primality of q. Let $[\mathfrak{p}]$ be a non-trivial kernel of map $\varphi_q : Cl(-8n^2) \to Cl(-8p^2)$. The protocol is explained in the following:

1. Each server $i(i = 2, ..., k - 1)$ computes $\mathfrak{u}_i = \mathfrak{p}^{q_i}$ in $\mathcal{O}_\Delta$ and sends it to the first server.
2. The first server computes $\mathfrak{u}_1 = \mathfrak{p}^{q_1+1}$ in $\mathcal{O}_\Delta$ and checks whether $\prod_{i=1}^{k} \mathfrak{u}_i = 1$. If not, $q(= \sum_{i=1}^{k} q_i)$ is not a prime number.

Lemma 2. *Let $q \equiv -1 \bmod 8$. If q is a prime number then $\prod_{i=1}^{k} \mathfrak{u}_i = 1$. If q is composite, then the test rejects with probability at least $1 - 1/s$, where s is the largest prime divisors of $\#Ker(\varphi_q)$.*

Proof. (Sketch) All kernel elements will appear in the protocol with almost the same probability. Assume q is a prime number. The order of $Ker(\varphi_q)$ is given by $q - \left(\frac{-8p^2}{q}\right) = q - \left(\frac{-2}{q}\right) = q - \left(\frac{-1}{q}\right) \cdot \left(\frac{2}{q}\right) = q + 1$ which can be proven for $q \equiv -1 \bmod 8$ by Gauss' lemma. This proves the first statement.

Next, assume n is not of the correct form. We consider the subgroup $G = \{g \in Ker(\varphi_q) ; g^{q+1} = 1\}$ of $Ker(\varphi_q)$ whose elements are a bad choice for the test.

Since the kernel is a cyclic group one can prove that $\#G = \gcd(\#Ker(\varphi_q), q + 1)$ and thus the probability to get a kernel element $\mathfrak{p} \in G$ (which does not help to detect the compositeness of q) for testing the primality of q is bounded by

$\frac{\gcd(\#Ker(\varphi_q),q+1)}{\#Ker(\varphi_q)}$. Let $q = \prod_i r_i^{e_i}$ be the prime decomposition of the prime candidate q, then the order of $Ker(\varphi_q)$ is given by $\prod_i r_i^{e_i-1}(r_i \pm 1)$ (see proposition 2) where the sign $\pm$ depends on the quadratic residuosity of -2 modulo r_i. Let s be the largest prime of $\#Ker(\varphi_q)$. We have two cases $s = r_i$ or $s|(r_i \pm 1)$ for some i. In the first case, assume that $s = r_i$ for some i, then $s|q$ and $s \nmid (q+1)$. Thus the probability to get a kernel element $\mathfrak{p} \in G$ for testing the primality of q is bounded by $\frac{\gcd(\#Ker(\varphi_q),q+1)}{\#Ker(\varphi_q)} \le 1/s$. Now consider the second case that $s \ne r_i$ for all i and $s|(r_i \pm 1)$ for some i. If $s \nmid (q+1)$ then again we know that the probability to get a kernel element $\mathfrak{p} \in G$ for testing the primality of q is at most $1/s$. On the other hand if $s|(q+1)$ then $0 = q+1 \equiv 1 \pm \prod_{i \ne j} r_j^{e_j} \bmod s$. Thus this may only happen if $\prod_{i \ne j} r_j^{e_j} \equiv \pm 1 \bmod s$.

Since each r_j is a prime different from s for all j, we can assume that $r_j \bmod s$ is a random number for all j. Therefore in this case too and thus in all cases the probability to get $\mathfrak{p} \in G$ as proof for the primality of q is bounded by $\frac{1}{s}$.

6   Efficiency Considerations

Let t be the largest prime divisor of q, then we have the following prime decomposition $q = t^e \prod_i t_i^{e_i}$, where $t_i < t$. At first we consider the case of $e = 1$. The order of $\#Ker(\varphi_q)$ is given by $(t \pm 1) \prod_i t_i^{e_i-1}(t_i \pm 1)$, where the sign $\pm$ depends on the quadratic residuosity of -2 modulo t or t_i. From lemma 2 we can estimate the succeeding probability of the primality test, if we estimate the probability of the smoothness of $\#Ker(\varphi_q)$. The probability that for a given random integer a the largest prime divisor t of a is not larger than $a^{1/6}$ bits is 0.0000196 [Rie94, pp.163] independently of the size of the random integer. Thus for a random 512-bit integer q the probability is at least 0.0000196 that the largest prime divisor t is at most $q^{1/6} \sim 85.17$ bits. Moreover we assume that for a random 85-bit prime t the integer $t \pm 1$ behaves like a random 85-bit integer.[1] Then, the probability that the largest prime divisor of $t \pm 1$ is smaller than $(t \pm 1)^{1/6} \sim 14.19$ bits again is 0.0000196. Therefore, the above primality test proves the primality of q with probability at least $(1 - 1/2^{14.19})(1 - 0.0000196)(1 - 0.0000196) > (1 - 1/10^4)$. In the case of $e > 1$ (with respect to $q = t^e \prod_i t_i^{e_i}$), we have $t|(\#Ker(\varphi_q))$. Then we do not have to care about the probability of the smoothness of $t \pm 1$ and the succeeding probability of the proposed primality test is higher. We stress that this estimate is pessimistic. A more detailed analysis has to take into account not only the largest prime divisor of q but all of them.

To come to a similar minor error probability in the Boneh-Franklin primality test one has to repeat the test about 14 times (since the error probability in each repetition is bounded by $1/2$). Since the operations in our new primality test are

---

[1] This assumption was confirmed by experimental results using the LiDIA-library [LiDIA]: In over 1,000,000 random 100-bit prime t, 423 were found with the property that $t - 1$ was a 20-bit smooth number. Thus the ration is about $0.000423 \sim 10^{-3.37}$. This corresponds to the ratio of 20-bit smooth numbers under all 100-bit numbers which is $10^{-3.45}$ accordingly to the list in [Rie94, pp.163].

very simple apart from two applications of the BGM protocol the new test may be an efficient new alternative compared to the Boneh-Franklin protocol.

Moreover we can come to a more practical method by using a discriminant Δ which is the product of lots of candidate primes, testing each after the other until one has found two primes among them. With high probability one will find at least two primes of bit length l if the parties distributively multiply about l candidates of bit length l. Thus they have to do l times the above primality test compared to the expected number of l^2 repetitions of the Boneh-Franklin method. Unfortunately taking Δ as a product of l candidate primes will lead to bit length l^2 for the numbers one has to cope with. Thus asymptotically there is no efficiency gain in theory if we consider the needed bit operations. Nevertheless the amount of communication between the parties is reduced since distributive multiplication of about l integers can be done with $\log l$ calls of DistMult and we have to manage only l distributed primality tests.

7   Security of the Proposed Scheme

As introduced by Boneh and Franklin we assume that all parties honestly follow the protocol (*honest but curious* scenario). Since we engage the DistMult protocol our protocol at best is $\lfloor \frac{k-1}{2} \rfloor$-private, i.e. collusions of at most $\lfloor \frac{k-1}{2} \rfloor$ servers learn no information about the factors of the computed n.

But there is a major difference between our protocol and the protocol proposed by Boneh and Franklin. Indeed in the protocols for the generation of kernel elements of the maps φ_q and φ_p information is published which cannot be computed by a small subgroup of the servers.

A pair of ideals $(\mathfrak{a}_1, \mathfrak{a}_2)$ and a pair of ideals $(\mathfrak{b}_1, \mathfrak{b}_2)$ are distributively computed and published where $\widetilde{\varphi_p}(\mathfrak{a}_1), \widetilde{\varphi_p}(\mathfrak{a}_2)$ are equivalent with exactly one reduction step in $\mathcal{O}_{-8q^2}$ and $\widetilde{\varphi_q}(\mathfrak{b}_1), \widetilde{\varphi_q}(\mathfrak{b}_2)$ are equivalent with exactly one reduction step in $\mathcal{O}_{-8p^2}$.

E. Jaulmes and A. Joux show in [JJ99] that given at least two pairs which are equivalent with exactly one reduction step in the same order either $\mathcal{O}_{-8q^2}$ or $\mathcal{O}_{-8p^2}$ will allow with non-negligible probability to compute q resp. p but they stress that there seems to be no way to do this if only one such pair is given. Thus it is important not to start the distributed computation of a kernel element twice. But one may assume that the following problem is an intractable problem:

Computation of divisors of the conductor (CDC): Let $\Delta = -8p^2q^2$. Given two pairs of ideals $(\mathfrak{a}_1, \mathfrak{a}_2) \in \mathcal{O}_\Delta$ and $(\mathfrak{b}_1, \mathfrak{b}_2) \in \mathcal{O}_\Delta$ where $\widetilde{\varphi_p}(\mathfrak{a}_1), \widetilde{\varphi_p}(\mathfrak{a}_2)$ are equivalent with exactly one reduction step in $\mathcal{O}_{-8q^2}$ and $\widetilde{\varphi_q}(\mathfrak{b}_1), \widetilde{\varphi_q}(\mathfrak{b}_2)$ are equivalent with exactly one reduction step in $\mathcal{O}_{-8p^2}$. Compute p and q.

Moreover one can prove that the new distributed protocol does not lack any information apart from two pairs of ideals with the mentioned property:

Lemma 3. *Suppose $n = pq$ with (secret) primes $p, q \equiv -1$ mod 8 is given. Let $\Delta = -8p^2q^2$. Moreover suppose a pair of ideals $(\mathfrak{b}_1, \mathfrak{b}_2) \in \mathcal{O}_\Delta$ as lacked by the* *protocol is given where* $\widetilde{\varphi_p}(\mathfrak{b}_1), \widetilde{\varphi_p}(\mathfrak{b}_2)$ *are equivalent with exactly one reduction step in* $\mathcal{O}_{-8p^2}$. *If the discrete logarithm problem in* $Cl(\Delta)$ *is intractable then for any coalition of* $t \leq \lfloor \frac{k-1}{2} \rfloor$ *parties there is a simulator for the view of this coalition in the protocol for primality testing* q.

Proof. (Sketch) First we sketch that the view of the t colluding parties, in the protocol part for the generation of the kernel element $\mathfrak{p} = Red_\Delta(\mathfrak{a}_{new}\mathfrak{a}^{-1}) = Red_\Delta(\mathfrak{b}_2\mathfrak{b}_1^{-1})$ can be simulated. The ideal $\mathfrak{b}_1$ is used instead of the randomly picked ideal in step 1 of the primality test. Step 2 can be done as in the protocol. Step 3 can be simulated accordingly to the simulability of the DistMult protocol. The value of C is set to the first coefficient of $\mathfrak{b}_2$. This corresponds to the identical situation in the protocol's run which generates $(\mathfrak{b}_1, \mathfrak{b}_2) \in \mathcal{O}_\Delta$ as $(\mathfrak{a}, \mathfrak{a}_{new})$. In step 4 the view of the run of the DistMult protocol can be simulated again accordingly to the properties of the DistMult protocol and the real protocol would deliver $\mathfrak{b}_{new}$, the second coefficient of $\mathfrak{b}_2$. Thus the simulation may use this value.

Finally we have to show that the view of the distributed primality test for q can be simulated. The coalition knows values p_i, q_i for t indices i, thus the corresponding ideals are $\mathfrak{u}_i = \mathfrak{p}^{q_i}$ as in the real protocol. The resting ideals $\mathfrak{u}_j$ apart from one, say $\mathfrak{u}_1$, are chosen randomly from the set $\{\mathfrak{p}^x : 0 \leq x \leq B\}$ where B is some number much larger than $q+1$. Then $\mathfrak{u}_1$ is set to $(\prod_{l=2}^k \mathfrak{u}_i)^{-1}$. Since the discrete logarithm problem is assumed to be intractable the distribution of the sets $\{\mathfrak{u}_i\}$ generated in the protocol cannot be distinguished from the distribution of the sets generated by this simulator.

Thus the protocol is secure if the discrete logarithm problem in $Cl(\Delta)$ and the CDC-problem are intractable.

Theorem 1. *If the discrete logarithm problem in* $Cl(\Delta)$ *and the CDC-problem are intractable then the proposed distributed protocol for the generation and test of a composite integer* $n = pq$ *with* p, q *prime is* $\lfloor \frac{k-1}{2} \rfloor$*-private, i.e. if all parties follow honestly the protocol even a coalition of up to* $\lfloor \frac{k-1}{2} \rfloor$ *curious parties will not learn any information about the prime divisors of* n.

References

[BB97]   I. Biehl and J. Buchmann, "An analysis of the reduction algorithms for binary quadratic forms", Technical Report No. TI-26/97, Technische Universität Darmstadt, (1997).

[BGW88]   M. Ben-Or, S. Goldwasser and A. Wigderson, "Completeness theorems for non-cryptographic fault tolerant distributed computation", STOC, (1988), pp.1-10.

[BF97]   D. Boneh and M. Franklin, "Efficient generation of shared RSA keys", CRYPTO '97, LNCS 1294, (1997), Springer, pp.425-439.

[BH98]   D. Boneh and J. Horwitz, "Generating a product of three primes with an unknown factorization", The third Algorithmic Number Theory Symposium, ANTS III, LNCS 1423, (1998), Springer, pp.237-251.

[BW88]   J. Buchmann and H. C. Williams, "A key-exchange system based on imaginary quadratic fields", Journal of Cryptology, 1, (1988), Springer, pp.107-118.

[CGH00]   D. Catalano, R. Gennaro, S. Halevi, "Computing Inverses over a Shared Secret Modulus," EUROCRYPT 2000, LNCS 1807, (2000), pp.190-206.

[Cox89]   D. A. Cox: *Primes of the form $x^2 + ny^2$*, John Wiley & Sons, New York, (1989).

[DK01]   I. Dåmgard and M. Koprowski, "Practical Threshold RSA Signatures without a Trusted Dealer," EUROCRYPT 2001, LNCS 2045, (2001), pp.152-165.

[FS01]   P.-A. Fouque and J. Stern, "Fully Distributed Threshold RSA under Standard Assumptions," ASIACRYPT 2001, LNCS 2248, (2001), pp.310-330.

[Jac99]   M. J. Jacobson, Jr., "Subexponential Class Group Computation in Quadratic Orders", PhD Thesis, Technical University of Darmstadt, (1999).

[JJ99]   E. Jaulmes and A. Joux, "A NICE cryptanalysis", EUROCRYPT 2000, LNCS 1807, (2000), pp.382-391.

[LiDIA]   LiDIA - A library for computational number theory. Technische Universität Darmstadt, Germany.

[MSY01]   S. Miyazaki, K. Sakurai, and M. Yung, "On Distributed Cryptographic Protocols for Threshold RSA Signing and Decrypting with No Dealer," IEICE Transaction, Vol.E84-A, No.5, (2001), pp.1177-1183.

[Rie94]   H. Riesel, *Prime Numbers and Computer Methods for Factorization*, Second Edition, Prog. in Math. 126, Birkhäuser, 1994.

[PKCS]   PKCS, Public-Key Cryptography Standards, RSA Laboratories, http://www.rsasecurity.com/rsalabs/pkcs/index.html.

[Sho99]   V. Shoup, "Practical Threshold Signatures," Eurocrypt 2000, LNCS 1807, (2000), pp.207-220.

A   Proof of Proposition 5

5 Proposition Consider a fundamental discriminant Δ_1 and non-fundamental discriminants $\Delta_{fg} = \Delta_1(fg)^2$ and $\Delta_f = \Delta_1 f^2$. Let $\mathfrak{a} \in \mathcal{I}_{\Delta_{fg}}(fg)$ and $\rho_{\Delta_f}(\widetilde{\varphi_g}(\mathfrak{a}))) \in \mathcal{I}_{\Delta_f}(fg)$ and

$$\mathfrak{b} = \widetilde{\varphi_g}^{-1}(\rho_{\Delta_f}(\widetilde{\varphi_g}(\mathfrak{a})))$$

then $[\mathfrak{a}\mathfrak{b}^{-1}] \in Ker(\varphi_g)$ and $[\mathfrak{b}\mathfrak{a}^{-1}]$ is a non-trivial.

Proof. Let $\widetilde{\varphi_g}(\mathfrak{a}) = \mathfrak{A} = A\mathbb{Z} + \frac{B+\sqrt{\Delta_f}}{2}\mathbb{Z}$ then $\rho_{\Delta_f}(\widetilde{\varphi_g}(\mathfrak{a})) = \mathfrak{A}' = \frac{B^2-\Delta_f^2}{4A}\mathbb{Z} + \frac{-B+\sqrt{\Delta_f}}{2}\mathbb{Z}$. The ideals $\mathfrak{A}$ and $\mathfrak{A}'$ are equivalent to each other and

$$\mathfrak{A}(B - \sqrt{\Delta_f}) = \mathfrak{A}'(2A) \tag{4}$$

holds. $N(B - \sqrt{\Delta_f})$ is relatively prime to q by the assumption. Thus the ideals in equation (4) can be mapped to the order $\mathcal{O}_{\Delta_{fg}}$. We have the relationship

$a\widetilde{\varphi_g}^{-1}(B - \sqrt{\Delta_f}) = b\widetilde{\varphi_g}^{-1}(2A)$ and $[ba^{-1}] = [\widetilde{\varphi_g}^{-1}(B - \sqrt{\Delta_f})(\widetilde{\varphi_g}^{-1}(2A))^{-1}]$. Here $\widetilde{\varphi_g}^{-1}(2A)$ is a principal ideal since $\widetilde{\varphi_g}^{-1}(2A) = (2A)\mathcal{O}_{\Delta_f} \cap \mathcal{O}_{\Delta_{f_g}} = (2A)\mathcal{O}_{\Delta_{f_g}}$. If $\widetilde{\varphi_g}^{-1}(B - \sqrt{\Delta_f})$ is not a principal ideal, then $[ba^{-1}]$ is a non-trivial kernel element. Notice that the standard representation of a principal ideal $(B - \sqrt{\Delta_f})\mathcal{O}_{\Delta_{f_g}}$ is $2(\frac{B^2 - \Delta_f}{4}\mathbb{Z} + \frac{-B + \sqrt{\Delta_f}}{2}\mathbb{Z})$ and $\gcd(\frac{B^2 - \Delta_f}{4}, q) = 1$ holds. Using algorithm GoToOrder$_{pq}$, we obtain the standard representation:

$$\widetilde{\varphi_g}^{-1}(B - \sqrt{\Delta_f}) = 2\left(\frac{B^2 - \Delta_f}{4}\mathbb{Z} + \frac{E + \sqrt{\Delta_f}}{2}\mathbb{Z}\right),$$

where $E \equiv -Bg \bmod \frac{B^2 - \Delta_f}{4}$. Recall B is defined by $(g^{-1} \bmod A) \cdot A \bmod 2A$ for large integers A, g, thus $\frac{B^2 - \Delta_f}{4} \neq 1$ holds. Consequently $\widetilde{\varphi_g}^{-1}(B - \sqrt{\Delta_f})$ is not a principal ideal and thus $[ba^{-1}]$ is a non-trivial kernel element.

Security Analysis and Improvement of the Global Key Recovery System

Yanjiang Yang, Feng Bao, and Robert H. Deng

Laboratories for Information Technology
21 Heng Mui Keng Terrace, Singapore 119613
{yanjiang, baofeng, deng}@lit.org.sg

Abstract. Key recovery is a technology that allows the owner of encrypted data or a trusted third party to recover encrypted data, mostly by reconstructing lost decryption key. In [HLG99], Harn *et al* proposed a Global Key Recovery System (GKRS) that combines the functions of the key recovery authorities and the public key certification authorities (CAs). Among other features, user-dominance, i.e., a user is allowed to select his own public-private key pair and especially a public element for verifying the validity of the public-private key pair, is considered extremely important by [HLG99] for wide acceptance of GKRS. In this paper, we attack the RSA version of GKRS by showing that its user-dominant feature and the corresponding key verification scheme employed by the CAs allow for fraud by users against CAs. We then propose an improvement to the original GKRS. The improved system makes the probability of user fraud negligibly small.

1. Introduction

With the advent of e-commerce over both public and private networks, strong encryption systems are broadly deployed to protect valuable and confidential data from offensive eavesdropping, interception, theft and many other sinister threats. Strong encryption technology, by its definition, makes it extremely difficult for anyone except the designated users who have the right decryption key to obtain/recover the original data from encrypted traffic/data.

The objective of a key escrow system is to provide encryption of user traffic such that the session/decryption keys used for traffic encryption are available to authorised third parties (e.g., law enforcement agencies) under special circumstances, such as in the event of a court order. This grants third parties which have monitored user traffic the capability to decrypt such traffic. On the other hand, a key recovery system allows a legitimate party (e.g., owner of encrypted data or owner's organisation) to recover the original data from encrypted data following loss of keying material or destruction of keying material due to equipment failure or malicious activities. From technical point of view, there is no evident difference between key recovery and key escrow. So throughout the paper, we will use the terms "key recovery" and "key escrow" in a broad sense and obscure the distinctions between them.

Considerable effort has gone into the design of key escrow/recovery systems (see for examples, Mic93, KL94, FY95, LWY95, KP98, HLG99, VBD99, and NVBD00).

L. Batten and J. Seberry (Eds.): ACISP 2002, LNCS 2384, pp. 17–24, 2002.
© Springer-Verlag Berlin Heidelberg 2002

In this paper, we focus on the Global Key Recovery System (GKRS) proposed by Harn, Lin and Gong [HLG99]. GKRS recovers a user's private key of a public key cryptosystem. This private key can then be used to produce digital signatures or decrypt random session keys. GKRS makes use of a multisignautre algorithm to combine the functions of certification authorities (CAs) and key recovery authorities; therefore, the system can be implemented within CA infrastructures. Among other features, user-dominance, i. e., a user is allowed to select his own public-private key pair as well as a public element used for verifying the validity of the public-private key pair, was considered by [HLG99] as an extremely important factor for wide acceptance of GKRS. In GKRS, a user can select a public-private key pair in either RSA scheme or discrete-logarithm based scheme. In this paper, we attack the RSA version of GKRS by showing that its user-dominant feature and the associated key verification method open a door for fraud by users against CAs. We then propose an improved GKRS which makes the probability of such fraud arbitrarily small.

The rest of the paper is organised as follows. In section 2 we review GKRS as originally proposed in [HLG99]. Section 3 presents our attack to GKRS and Section 4 shows our improved system. Finally, Section 5 contains some concluding remarks.

2.   Review of GKRS

Operations in GKRS can be divided into two phases, private key deposition and certificate generation [HLG99]. To simplify the notations throughout the paper, we will assume that a user selects two CAs, CA_1 and CA_2, as his public-key certification and private key recovery authorities. Generalisation to the cases of more than two CAs is straightforward.

2.1 Private Key Deposition

A user computes a RSA modulus $n = pq$ and $\phi(n) = (p-1)(q-1)$, where p and q are two large secret primes. Let e and d be the user's public key and private key, respectively, where ed mod $\phi(n) = 1$. The user splits d into d_1 and d_2 such that $d = d_1 + d_2$ mod $\phi(n)$ and computes

$$v_1 = \alpha^{d_1} \bmod n$$

$$v_2 = \alpha^{d_2} \bmod n$$

where α is an element in Z_n^* with a large order. The user then submits (m, d_1, α) to CA_1 and (m, d_2, α) to CA_2, where

$$m = (n, e, CA_1, v_1, CA_2, v_2)$$

For this submission, we point out that as v_1 and v_2 (contained in m) are sent to CA_1 and CA_2 respectively, the user may take a chance to send CA_1 and CA_2 different v_1's and v_2's in order to cheat. If this is the case, it would make no sense for the proposed GKRS, both the RSA scheme and the Discrete-logarithm based scheme. Fortunately, in the certificate generation phase, CA_i signs m to generate certificate for the user's public key, excluding such a cheating.

Upon receiving (m, d_i, α), CA_i checks the validity of the user's public-private key pair by determining whether

$$v_i = \alpha^{d_i} \bmod n$$

$$(v_1 v_2)^e \bmod n = \alpha$$

If both conditions hold, then CA_i is convinced that the user has correctly deposited his private key d_i share and that the user's public key matches his private key.

2.2 Certificate Generation

In this second phase, the CAs collaboratively generate a certificate for the user's public key $m = (n, e, CA1, v_1, CA2, v_2)$ using the multisignature scheme presented in [KL94]. Let P be a large prime and G a primitive element of $GF(P)$. Both P and G are made public. CA_i has a private key x_i and a corresponding public key y_i in the multisignature scheme, where x_i is randomly selected from $GF(P)$ and where

$$y_i = G^{x_i} \bmod P$$

The collective public key of the two CAs is

$$y = y_1 y_2 \bmod P$$

To generate a certificate for the user's public key, CA_i computes

$$r_i = G^{k_i} \bmod P$$

and sends it to the other CA, where k_i is a random element from $GF(P)$ and kept secret. Each CA_i then computes a commitment value

$$r = r_1 r_2 \bmod P$$

Upon the successful validity verification of the user's public-private key pair, CA_i, using its private key x_i and k_i, computes

$$s_i = x_i H(m) - k_i r \bmod (P-1)$$

where $H()$ is an one-way hash function. Note that CA_i signs $m = (n, e, CA1, v_1, CA2, v_2)$, preventing the user from cheating as sending CA_1 and CA_2 different v_1's and v_2's. Finally, CA_i returns its partial signature (r_i, s_i) to the user.

Once the user receives each partial signature (r_i, s_i), he verifies their validity by checking

$$y_i^{H(m)} = r_i^r G^{s_i} \bmod P$$

If all partial signatures are valid, the certificate on the user's public key is (r, s), where $s = s_1 + s_2$ mod $P-1$. Certification verification can be done by anyone by checking

$$y^{H(m)} = r^r G^s \bmod P$$

3. Security Analysis of GKRS

Recall that the user-dominant feature of GKRS implies that a user is free to select his own public-private key pair and the element α without intervention of CAs. In this section, we attack GKRS by showing that this user-dominant feature and the way α is used in checking the validity of a user's public-private key pair allow the user to cheat CAs. In particular, a malicious user can deposit shares of an invalid private key to CAs without being detected. As far as CAs are concerned, it is inadvisable for them to place complete trust in the GKRS key verification method.

In what follows, $ord(\alpha)$ denotes the order of α, $\varphi(n) = (p-1)(q-1)$, $\lambda(n) = lcm(p-1, q-1)$, where $n = pq$ is a RSA modulus. The following facts from number theory will be used in our discussion.

Proposition 1: Given $\varphi(n)$ or $\lambda(n)$ and its factorization, it is easy to determine $ord(\alpha)$ where $\alpha \in Z_n^*$; while without knowing the factorization of $\varphi(n)$ or $\lambda(n)$, it is hard to find $ord(\alpha)$.

In the following attack we will demonstrate that, in GKRS, a user can deposit shares of an invalid private key d' which is different from his true private key d and get a certificate for his true public key from the CAs, where $ed = 1$ mod $\lambda(n)$. The attack works as follows:

1. Without loss of generality, a user first fixes a prime τ and chooses primes p_1 and q_1 such that $p = 2p_1\tau + 1$ and $q = 2q_1\tau + 1$ are large primes.
2. The user computes the RSA modulus $n = pq$ and $\lambda(n) = lcm(p-1, q-1) = 2p_1q_1\tau$. From **Proposition 1**, the user can find an element α in Z_n^* with $ord(\alpha) = \tau$ easily. To find such a α, he first finds an element $g \in Z_n^*$ whose order is $\lambda(n)$. This is easy as nearly half of the elements in Z_n^* are of order $\lambda(n)$ and since the user knows $\lambda(n)$ and its factorization. Then he sets

$$\alpha = g^{2p_1q_1} \bmod n$$

   It is obvious that α has order τ.
3. The user computes his genuine public-private key pair e and d, where ed mod $\lambda(n) = 1$. Then he computes a fake private key d' such that $d' = e^{-1}$ mod $\tau \neq e^{-1}$ mod $\lambda(n)$. Obviously, $d' \neq d$.
4. Next, the user splits d' into d_1 and d_2 such that $d' = (d_1 + d_2)$ mod τ, computes

$$v_1 = \alpha^{d_1} \bmod n$$

$$v_2 = \alpha^{d_2} \bmod n$$

and submits (m, d_1, α) to CA_1 and (m, d_2, α) to CA_2, where $m = (n, e, CA1, v_1, CA2, v_2)$.

After receiving (m, d_i, α), CA_i performs validity check by determining whether

$$v_i = \alpha^{d_i} \bmod n$$

$$(v_1 v_2)^e \bmod n = \alpha$$

Since $ord(\alpha) = \tau$ and $ed' = 1 \bmod \tau$, we have

$$(v_1 v_2)^e \bmod n = \alpha^{ed'} \bmod n = \alpha^{c\tau+1} \bmod n = \alpha$$

where c is an integer. Undoubtedly, the verification is passed and the CAs are fooled into believing that d' is the user's valid private key corresponding to the public key e and will issue the certificate for e.

The flaw of the verification scheme in the original GKRS is due to the following implicit assumption: if the verification

$$(v_1 v_2)^e \bmod n = \alpha^{e(d_1+d_2)} \bmod n = \alpha$$

holds for α, then $e(d_1+d_2) = 1 \bmod \lambda(n)$ is true. This assumption, however, is wrong as can be observed from the following proposition.

Proposition 2: Let $n = pq$, $\lambda(n) = lcm(p-1, q-1)$, $\varphi(n) = (p-1)(q-1)$, where p and q are two large secret primes. Let e and d be elements in $[1, n-1]$. Further let $d = d_1 + d_2 \bmod \lambda(n)$, $\alpha \in Z_n^*$, such that

$$v_1 = \alpha^{d_1} \bmod n$$

$$v_2 = \alpha^{d_2} \bmod n$$

Then

$$(v_1 v_2)^e \bmod n = \alpha^{e(d_1+d_2)} \bmod n = \alpha^{ed} \bmod n = \alpha$$

implies $e(d_1+d_2) = ed = 1 \bmod \lambda(n)$ (and $ed = 1 \bmod \varphi(n)$) only if $ord(\alpha) = \lambda(n)$.

Proof: If $ord(\alpha) = \lambda(n)$, then $\alpha^{ed} = \alpha$ implies that $ed = c_1\lambda(n) + 1$ (where c_1 is an integer) which in turn implies that $ed = 1 \bmod \lambda(n)$. Note that $\lambda(n)$ is the maximum order for any element in Z_n^*. Now consider the case where $ord(\alpha) < \lambda(n)$. We can select e and d such that $ed = 1 \bmod ord(\alpha) \neq 1 \bmod \lambda(n)$. Then it follows that

$$\alpha^{ed} \bmod n = \alpha^{c_2 ord(\alpha)+1} \bmod n = \alpha$$

(where c_2 is an integer) but $ed = 1 \bmod \lambda(n)$ does not hold. □

In the original GKRS, there is no provision for the CAs to check the order of α (disclosing the order of α may cause n being factorized easily); they just accept whatever value of α supplied by the user. As a result, the system is vulnerable to our attack.

4. Improvement of GKRS

From **Proposition 2**, it is clear that to counter our attack to the original GKRS, the CAs must have great confidence that the α used in the key verification scheme is of order $\lambda(n)$. From **Proposition 1**, however, we see that it is hard for CAs to find the order of α since they know neither $\lambda(n)$ nor the factorization of $\lambda(n)$. In the original GKRS, the value of α is solely supplied by the user. Central to our improved GKRS is that we exclude the absolute control of α by the user and we employ a sequence of "random" αs in the key verification process, in an effort to dramatically reduce the probability of cheating by users.

In our improved GKRS, a user computes p, q, n, $\lambda(n)$, e, d, d_1, and d_2 as in the original GKRS and then submits (m, d_1) to CA_1 and (m, d_2) to CA_2, where $m = (n, e, CA1, CA2)$.

Upon receiving the user's submission, CA_i chooses αs to conduct verification. It is desirable for CA_i to choose a sequence of random αs that are uniformly distributed over Z_n^*. To this end, CA_i resorts to a hash function $H()$ with $|H()| = |n|$. However, we know that n is usually 1024 bits long; whereas, output of those commonly used hash functions is far less than 1024 bits. Take SHA for example, its output is 160 bits long. A simple way to obtain such a $H()$ is as follows.

Let $h()$ be a commonly used one-way hash function, say MD5 or SHA, and define

$$h^1() = h()$$
$$h^i() = h(h^{i-1}())$$
$$H() = (h()\|h^2()\|h^3()\|h^4()\|h^5() \|h^6()\|h^7()) \bmod n$$

To make $|H()| = |n|$, approximately $(1024/160 \cong 7)$ outputs of $h()$ are concatenated (\|\|) modulo n.

Then αs are computed as

$$\alpha_1 = H(n, r)$$
$$\alpha_2 = H(\alpha_1)$$
$$\cdots$$
$$\alpha_l = H(\alpha_{l-1})$$

where l is a security parameter and r is the commitment value computed jointly by CA_1 and CA_2 (see Section 2.2). Note that the computation of r is independent of user's input; therefore, it can be pre-computed off-line. CA_i computes

$$v_{i,j} = \alpha_j^{d_i} \bmod n, \quad \text{for } j = 1, 2, \ldots, l$$

and broadcast them to the other CA. Next, CAi performs the validity check of the keys by determining whether

$$(v_{1,j}v_{2,j})^e \bmod n = \alpha_j, \text{ for } j = 1, 2, \ldots, l$$

CAs will accept the shares of the user's private key and issue a certificate for the public key only if all the l checks are positive; otherwise, the user's submission is rejected.

There can be variations to the above improved GKRS. For example, instead of letting CAs compute α_j and

$$v_{i,j} = \alpha_j^{d_i} \bmod n, \text{ for } j = 1, 2, ..., l$$

such computations can be carried out by the user and then the user publishes α_j's and $v_{i,j}$'s to public.

From theoretical point of view, our improved GKRS can not guarantee 100% fraud-resistance. However, we prove in the following that the chances left for a user to cheat can be made negligible.

Suppose $g \in Z_n^*$ is of order $\lambda(n)$ and $W = \{g^k : 0 \le k < \lambda(n)\}$ is the group generated by g, then we know that

$$ord(g^k) = \lambda(n)/gcd(\lambda(n), k)$$

This implies that an element g^k in W is of order $\lambda(n)$ if and only if $gcd(k, \lambda(n)) = 1$. So the number of elements whose order equals to $\lambda(n)$ is $\varphi(\lambda(n))$, and a randomly selected element has a probability of $\varphi(\lambda(n))/\lambda(n)$ of being order $\lambda(n)$.

From **Proposition 2** and our improved verification scheme, we know that CAs are able to detect key fraud as long as one of the α_j's, $j = 1, 2, ..., l$, has order $\lambda(n)$. Note that since α_j's are computed as a sequence of input-output to an one-way hash function, and since the initial input (n, r) to the hash function are contributed independently by the user and the CAs, α_j's can be regarded as a sequence of random numbers. Therefore, the probability of a key fraud attempted by a user being undetected is approximately given by

$$Pud = (1-\varphi(\lambda(n))/\lambda(n))^l$$

As an example, let us consider the attack presented in Section 3, where the user selected parameters are $p = 2p_1r+1$, $q = 2q_1r+1$, $n = pq$ and $\lambda(n) = lcm(p-1, q-1) = 2p_1q_1r$. Then we have $\varphi(\lambda(n))/\lambda(n) = \varphi(2p_1q_1r)/2p_1q_1r = (2-1)(p_1-1)(q_1-1)(r-1)/2p_1q_1r \cong \frac{1}{2}$, and Pud $= (1-1/2)^l$. For $l = 60$, $Pud \cong 8.7\times10^{-19}$. In other words, CAs has an overwhelming probability of $(1-8.7\times10^{-19})$ to detect the user's fraud.

5. Conclusion

The GKRS proposed in [HLG99] combines the functions of public key certification and key recovery authorities. The system recovers a user's private key that is used to generate digital signatures or to encrypt session keys. Operations in GKRS are carried out in two phases. In the private key deposition phase, a user generates his public-private key pair and deposits the public key, shares of the private key, and some other public parameters to CAs. In the certificate generation phase, each CA verifies the validity of the public-private key pair based on the public parameters supplied by the user. The CAs accept the shares of the private key for deposition and issue a public key certificate only if keys are checked being valid. In this paper, we showed that the key verification process in GKRS is not secure and vulnerable for attack. We demonstrated how a malicious user can deposit an invalid private key without being detected and in return get a certificate for a public key which corresponds to private key different from the one being deposited. We then introduced an improvement to the original GKRS key verification scheme and showed that the probability of cheating by a user in the improved system can be made arbitrarily small.

References

[FY95]   Y. Frankel and M. Yung, *Escrow Encryption System Visited: Attack, Analysis and Designs*. Advances in Cryptology, Crypto '95, LNCS 0963, Springer-Verlag, pp. 222-235, 1995.

[HLG99]   L. Harn, H. Y. Lin and G. Gong, *A Global Key Recovery System*, Proceedings of the International Workshop on Cryptographic Techniques & E-Commerce, Hong Kong, pp.81-85, 1999.

[KL94]   J. Kilian and T. Leighton, *Failsafe Key Escrow*, Technical Report 636, MIT Lab, for Computer Science, 1994.

[KP98]   J. Kilian and E. Petrank, *Identity Escrow*, Advances in Cryptology, Crypto '98, LNCS 1462, 1998.

[LWY95]   A. K. Lenstra, P. Winkler, Y. Yacobi, *A Key Escrow System with Warrant Bounds*, Adances in Cryptology, Crypto '95, LNCS 963, pp. 197-207, 1995

[Mic93]   S. Micali, *Fair Public-Key Cryptosystems*, Technical Report 579, MIT Lab, for Computer Science, 1993.

[NVBD00] J. G. Nieto, K. Viswanathan, C. Boyd and E. Dawson, *Key Recovery System for the Commerical Environment*, Security and Privacy (ACISP '2000), Springer-Verlag, pp.149-162, 2000.

[VBD99]   K. Viswanathan, C. Boyd and E. Dawson, *Publicly Verifiable Key Escrow with Limited Time Span*, Information Security and Privacy (ACISP '99), LNCS 1587, Springer-Verlag, pp.36-51, 1999.

The LILI-II Keystream Generator

A. Clark[1], Ed Dawson[1], J. Fuller[1], J. Golić[2], H-J. Lee[3], William Millan[1],
S-J. Moon[4], and L. Simpson[1]

[1] Information Security Research Centre,
Queensland University of Technology,
GPO Box 2434, Brisbane, Queensland 4001, Australia
{aclark, dawson, fuller, millan, simpson }@isrc.qut.edu.au
[2] GEMPLUS, Rome CryptoDesign Center, Technology R&D,
Via Pio Emanuelli, 00413 Rome, Italy
jovan.golic@gemplus.com
[3] School of Internet Engineering, Dongseo University
San 69-1, Churye-2Dong, SaSang-Ku, Pusan 617-716, Korea
hjlee@dongseo.ac.kr
[4] School of Electronic and Electrical Engineering
Kyungpook National University, 1370,
Sankyuk-dong, Taegu 702-701, Korea.
sjmoon@knu.ac.kr

Abstract. The LILI-II keystream generator is a LFSR based synchronous stream cipher with a 128 bit key. LILI-II is a specific cipher from the LILI family of keystream generators, and was designed with larger internal components than previous ciphers in this class, in order to provide increased security. The design offers large period and linear complexity, is immune to currently known styles of attack, and is simple to implement in hardware or software. The cipher achieves a security level of 128 bits.

1 Introduction

Many keystream generator designs are based on shift registers, both for the simplicity and speed of Linear Feedback Shift Register (LFSR) implementation in hardware and for the long period and good statistical properties LFSR sequences possess. To make use of the good keystream properties while avoiding the inherent linear predictability of LFSR sequences, many constructions introduce nonlinearity, by applying a nonlinear function to the outputs of regularly clocked LFSRs or by irregular clocking of the LFSRs [17].

However, keystream generators using regularly clocked LFSRs are susceptible to correlation attacks, including fast correlation attacks, a concept first introduced in [16]. As a means of achieving immunity to these correlation attacks, keystream generators consisting of irregularly clocked LFSRs were proposed. These keystream generators are also susceptible to certain correlation attacks, such as the generalised correlation attack proposed in [8]. As correlation attacks have been successful against keystream generators based on the single design

L. Batten and J. Seberry (Eds.): ACISP 2002, LNCS 2384, pp. 25–39, 2002.

principles of either a nonlinear function of regularly clocked LFSR sequences [19, 18] or on irregular clocking of LFSRs [8,20], both of these approaches are combined for the LILI keystream generators, a family of keystream generators first introduced in [21].

LILI-II is a specific cipher from the LILI family of keystream generators. The development of LILI-II was motivated by the response to the LILI-128 keystream generator, included as a stream cipher candidate for NESSIE [6]. Although the design for the LILI keystream generators is conceptually simple, it produces output sequences with provable properties with respect to basic cryptographic security requirements. Hypothesised attacks on LILI-128, and the request for a re-keying proposal prompted a review of the LILI-128 parameters to ensure provable security properties could be maintained while achieving an effective key size of 128 bits. LILI-II is slightly less efficient in software than LILI-128 mainly due to the larger LFSRs and larger Boolean function which are used in the design to increase security. However, in hardware LILI-II offers the same high speed as LILI-128.

We now briefly summarise the security claims for LILI-II. Firstly, the period at around $2^{128} \cdot 2^{127} = 2^{255}$ greatly exceeds 2^{128}, and exceeds the length of any practical plaintext, rendering any attacks based on the period infeasible. Secondly, the linear complexity is conjectured to be at least 2^{175}, so that at least 2^{176} consecutive bits of known plaintext are required for the Berlekamp-Massey attack. This is an infeasible amount of text to collect. Thirdly, the $127 + 128 = 255$ bit state size renders any of the general time-memory-data tradeoff attacks infeasible. Additionally, we conjecture that the complexity of divide and conquer attacks on LILI-II exceeds 2^{128} operations, and requires a substantial amount of known keystream bits. Taken together, these results indicate that LILI-II is a secure synchronous stream cipher, in that there are no currently known attacks on the cipher which are more feasible than exhaustive key search.

2   Description of LILI-II Keystream Generator

The LILI-II keystream generator is a simple and fast keystream generator using two binary LFSRs and two functions to generate a pseudorandom binary keystream sequence. Both of the LFSRs in LILI-II use the Galois configuration rather than the more common Fibonacci style, although there is no security difference as the state cycle structures of these two LFSR styles have identical properties. This design decision is motivated by the observation that although the two LFSR styles are equally efficient in hardware, the Galois style LFSR is faster in software.

The structure of the LILI keystream generators is illustrated in Figure 1. The components of the keystream generator can be grouped into two subsystems based on the functions they perform: clock control and data generation. The LFSR for the clock-control subsystem is regularly clocked. The output of this subsystem is an integer sequence which controls the clocking of the LFSR within the data-generation subsystem. If regularly clocked, the data-generation subsystem is a simple nonlinearly filtered LFSR [17] (nonlinear filter generator).

The state of LILI-II is defined to be the contents of the two LFSRs. The functions f_c and f_d are evaluated on the current state data, and the feedback bits are calculated. Then the LFSRs are clocked and the keystream bit is output. At initialisation the 128 bit key and a publicly known 128 bit initialisation vector are combined to form the initial values of the two shift registers. For efficiency,this initialisation process uses the LILI-II structure itself, and can also be used for re-keying. All valid keys produce different keystreams and there are no known weak keys.

The LILI keystream generators may be viewed as clock-controlled nonlinear filter generators. Such a system, with the clock control provided by a stop-and-go generator, was examined in [7]. However, the use of stop-and-go clocking produces repetition of the nonlinear filter generator output in the keystream, which may permit attacks. This system is an improvement on that proposal, as stop-and-go clocking is avoided. For LILI keystream generators, $LFSR_d$ is clocked at least once and at most d times between the production of consecutive keystream bits. For LILI-II, $d = 4$, so $LFSR_d$ is clocked at most four times between the production of consecutive keystream bits.

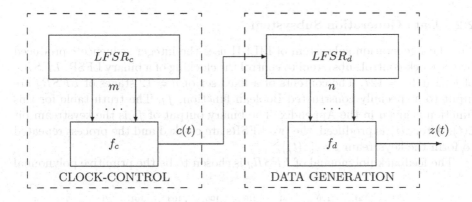

Fig. 1. Overview of LILI keystream generators.

2.1   Clock Control Subsystem

The clock-control subsystem of LILI-II uses a pseudorandom binary sequence produced by a regularly clocked LFSR, $LFSR_c$, of length 128 and a function, f_c, operating on the contents of $m = 2$ stages of $LFSR_c$ to produce a pseudorandom integer sequence, $c = \{c(t)\}_{t=1}^{\infty}$. The feedback polynomial of $LFSR_c$ is chosen to be the primitive polynomial

$$x^{128} + x^{126} + x^{125} + x^{124} + x^{123} + x^{122} + x^{119} + x^{117} + x^{115} + x^{111} + x^{108}$$
$$+x^{106} + x^{105} + x^{104} + x^{103} + x^{102} + x^{96} + x^{94} + x^{90} + x^{87} + x^{82} + x^{81}$$
$$+x^{80} + x^{79} + x^{77} + x^{74} + x^{73} + x^{72} + x^{71} + x^{70} + x^{67} + x^{66} + x^{65} + x^{61}$$
$$+x^{60} + x^{58} + x^{57} + x^{56} + x^{55} + x^{53} + x^{52} + x^{51} + x^{50} + x^{49} + x^{47} + x^{44}$$
$$+x^{43} + x^{40} + x^{39} + x^{36} + x^{35} + x^{30} + x^{29} + x^{25} + x^{23} + x^{18} + x^{17} + x^{16}$$
$$+x^{15} + x^{14} + x^{11} + x^{9} + x^{8} + x^{7} + x^{6} + x^{1} + 1$$

and the initial state of $LFSR_c$ can be any state except the all zero state. It follows that $LFSR_c$ produces a maximum-length sequence of period $P_c = 2^{128} - 1$.

At time instant t, the contents of stages 0 and 126 of $LFSR_c$ are input to the function f_c and the output of f_c is an integer $c(t)$, such that $c(t) \in \{1, 2, 3, 4\}$. The function f_c is given by

$$f_c(x_0, x_{126}) = 2(x_0) + x_{126} + 1.$$

This function was chosen to be a bijective mapping so that the distribution of integers $c(t)$ is close to uniform. Thus $c = \{c(t)\}_{t=1}^{\infty}$ is a periodic integer sequence with period equal to $P_c = 2^{128} - 1$.

2.2   Data Generation Subsystem

The data-generation subsystem of LILI-II uses the integer sequence c produced by the clock-control subsystem to control the clocking of a binary LFSR, $LFSR_d$, of length $L_d = 127$. The contents of a fixed set of $n = 12$ stages of $LFSR_d$ are input to a specially constructed Boolean function, f_d. The truth table for this function is given in the Appendix. The binary output of f_d is the keystream bit $z(t)$. After $z(t)$ is produced, the two LFSRs are clocked and the process repeated to form the keystream $z = \{z(t)\}_{t=1}^{\infty}$.

The feedback polynomial of $LFSR_d$ is chosen to be the primitive polynomial

$$x^{127} + x^{121} + x^{120} + x^{114} + x^{107} + x^{106} + x^{103} + x^{101} + x^{97} + x^{96} + x^{94}$$
$$+x^{92} + x^{89} + x^{87} + x^{84} + x^{83} + x^{81} + x^{76} + x^{75} + x^{74} + x^{72} + x^{69} + x^{68}$$
$$+x^{65} + x^{64} + x^{62} + x^{59} + x^{57} + x^{56} + x^{54} + x^{52} + x^{50} + x^{48} + x^{46} + x^{45}$$
$$+x^{43} + x^{40} + x^{39} + x^{37} + x^{36} + x^{35} + x^{30} + x^{29} + x^{28} + x^{27} + x^{25} + x^{23}$$
$$+x^{22} + x^{21} + x^{20} + x^{19} + x^{18} + x^{14} + x^{10} + x^{8} + x^{7} + x^{6} + x^{4} + x^{3} + x^{2} + x + 1$$

and the initial state of $LFSR_d$ is not permitted to be the all zero state. Then $LFSR_d$ produces a maximum-length sequence of period $P_d = 2^{127} - 1$, which is a Mersenne Prime.

The 12 inputs to f_d are taken from the $LFSR_d$ positions (0, 1, 3, 7, 12, 20, 30, 44, 65, 80, 96, 122), which form a full positive difference set (see [11]). The function selected for f_d is balanced, highly nonlinear and has first order correlation immunity. The function f_d has nonlinearity of 1992, and an algebraic order of 10. The truth table of the Boolean function f_d is given in Hex in the Appendix. A function with these properties was selected in order to provide greater security against possible attacks (see Section 4).

2.3   Key Loading and Re-keying

In some communication systems, errors occur which require that the entire message be re-sent. When a synchronous stream cipher such as LILI-II is used, then security requires that a different keystream sequence be used. To achieve this, a re-keying algorithm is used to combine the secret key, k, with v_i, the 128-bit initialisation vector for the ith re-keying. If the initialisation vector has length less than 128 bits, then multiple copies of the vector will be concatenated, repeated and truncated as required, to form a 128-bit vector. Typically the v_i sequence is publicly known, thus introducing security concerns. The existence of re-keyed messages allows the possibility for attacks based on the re-keying. These scenarios have subtle differences as described below.

If only a single segment of keystream is known, (no re-keying occurs) then to break a particular instance of the cipher, the cryptanalyst must recover the initial internal state S_0, using knowledge of the structure of the keystream generator and some amount of the keystream, z. Attacks based on this scenario are discussed in Section 4. No attack which is better than exhaustive key search has been identified.

In contrast, with resynchronisation occurring, the cryptanalyst has access to related keystreams produced under the same k and for different but known v_i, typically sequential or differing in only a few bits. The cryptanalyst's task is then to recover k, given a set of (v_i, z_i) pairs. For security in this scenario, it is required that the re-keying process should does not leak information about the key k.

We now describe the proposed method for initial key loading and for re-keying of the LILI-II keystream generator. The process to generate the initial state for the keystream generator uses the generator itself twice. The starting state of $LFSR_c$ is obtained by XORing the two 128-bit binary strings k and v_i. The starting state of $LFSR_d$ is obtained by deleting the first bit of k and the last bit of v_i, and XORing the two resulting 127-bit binary strings. Now the cipher is run to produce an output string of length 255 bits. For the second application of the cipher, the first 128 bits of this output string are used to form the initial state of $LFSR_c$, and the remaining 127 bits are used to form the initial state of $LFSR_d$. The cipher is run again to produce an output string of length 255 bits. The output from this second application is used to form the initial state of the keystream generator when we begin keystream production. As previously, the first 128 bits form the initial state of $LFSR_c$, and the remaining 127 bits form the initial state of $LFSR_d$.

By employing the LILI-II algorithm itself, we take advantage of both the known security properties of the algorithm and also its fast implementation. Due to the high security of LILI-II we conclude that the best attack in the re-keying scenario is exhaustive key search.

3   Keystream Properties

Several properties of pseudorandom binary sequences are considered basic security requirements: a sequence that does not possess these properties is generally considered unsuitable for cryptographic applications. Basic requirements for pseudorandom binary sequences are a long period, high linear complexity and good statistics regarding the distribution of zeroes and ones in the output. High linear complexity avoids an attack using the Berlekamp-Massey [15] algorithm.

Using the results from [21] it can be shown that for the keystream of LILI-II:

· the period is $(2^{128} - 1) * (2^{127} - 1)$,

· the linear complexity is at least 2^{175}, and

· the ratio of ones to zeroes is $\frac{2^{126}}{2^{126}-1} \approx 1$.

4   Possible Attacks

A number of attacks should be considered with respect to the LILI-II keystream generator. These are known-plaintext attacks conducted under the standard assumption that the cryptanalyst knows the complete structure of the generator, and the secret key is only the initial states of the component shift registers. The attacks we consider here are only in the no-rekeying scenario. In the re-keying scenario, there may be some related key attack like that suggested in [3], however the high security of the re-keying algorithm we have proposed prevents any rekeying attack from being effective.

Firstly, a general cryptanalytic attack on stream ciphers known as a T/M/D (time/memory/data) tradeoff attack is discussed in relation to LILI-II. Alternatively, for keystream generators based on more than one LFSR where the key consists of the initial states of the LFSRs, such as the LILI-II generator, divide-and-conquer attacks targeting individual LFSRs should be considered. For these attacks, the given keystream is viewed as an irregularly decimated version of a nonlinearly filtered $LFSR_d$ sequence, with the decimation under the control of $LFSR_c$. For divide and conquer attacks, we deal firstly with attacks that target $LFSR_d$, and then with those attacks that target $LFSR_c$. We shall describe these attacks in relation to the general LILI keystream generator as described in [21], and point out why such attacks are not feasible for LILI-II.

4.1   Time/Memory/Data Tradeoff Attacks

The objective of the time-memory tradeoff attacks is to recover the internal state at a known time. The attacks are conducted in two stages. During a preprocessing phase, the cryptanalyst constructs a lookup table, mapping possible internal states to prefixes of the corresponding output keystreams. In the real time phase of the attack, the cryptanalyst takes a segment of known keystream and tries to find the corresponding internal state, by searching through the lookup table.

In [3] Babbage described time-memory tradeoff attacks against LILI-128 with complexity less than 2^{128}. As mentioned in Section 1, LILI-II is designed to overcome these attacks through the use of longer LFSRs providing a 255 bit internal state, rather than the 128 bits of LILI-128. We analyse LILI-II in relation to the time-memory tradeoff attacks below.

Let S, M, T, P and D denote the cardinality of the internal state space, the memory (in binary words of size equal to $\log_2 S$), the computational time (in table lookups), the precomputation time (in table lookups), and the amount of data (without re-keying, this is the length of known keystream), respectively.

For the time-memory attacks described in [2,12] $T \cdot M = S$, $P = M$ and $D = T$. For example, a $2^{128}.2^{127} = 2^{255}$ tradeoff could be used although, as this requires time equivalent to exhaustive key search, and an excessive amount of memory and known keystream, such an attack is certainly not feasible. The more general time-memory-data tradeoff [4] asserts that $T \cdot M^2 \cdot D^2 = S^2$, $P = S/D, D^2 \leq T$. This decreases D at the cost of increasing P. For example, one may choose $M = D = S^{1/3}$ and $T = P = S^{2/3}$, but for LILI-II, with $S = 255$, this gives $M = D = 2^{85}$ and $T = P = 2^{170}$, clearly worse than exhaustive key search. Alternatively, to reduce the time required (with a corresponding reduction in D), we can increase the amount of memory required, and obtain, for example, $M = 2^{127}$, $D = 2^{64}$ and $T = 2^{128}$, although this is still no better than exhaustive search, and requires an excessive amount of memory. The tradeoffs permitted by this attack result in either M or T being in excess of 2^{128}, when applied to LILI-II.

In any case, the use of the initialisation scheme (the key-loading/re-keying algorithm) to expand the 128-bit secret key into a 255 bit initial state renders the time-memory attacks on LILI-II infeasible, as their performance is at best, no better than exhaustive key search.

4.2   Attacks on Irregularly Clocked $LFSR_d$

Suppose a keystream segment of length N is known, say $\{z(t)\}_{t=1}^N$. This is a decimated version of a segment of length M of the underlying regularly clocked nonlinearly filtered $LFSR_d$ sequence, $g = \{g(i)\}_{i=1}^M$, where $M \geq N$. The objective of correlation attacks targeting $LFSR_d$ is to recover the initial state of $LFSR_d$ by identifying the segment $\{g(i)\}_{i=1}^M$ that $\{z(t)\}_{t=1}^N$ was obtained from through decimation, using the correlation between the regularly clocked sequence and the keystream, without knowing the decimating sequence.

For clock-controlled shift registers with constrained clocking (so that there is a fixed maximum number of times the data shift register may be clocked before an output bit must be produced), correlation attacks based on a constrained Levenshtein distance and on a probabilistic measure of correlation are proposed in [8] and [9], respectively, and further analysed in [10]. These attacks could be adapted to be used as the first stage of a divide-and-conquer attack on LILI-II. The rest of this section describes how such an attack would be performed.

For a candidate initial state of $LFSR_d$, say $\{\hat{d}(i)\}_{i=1}^{L_d}$, use the known $LFSR_d$ feedback function to generate a segment of the $LFSR_d$ sequence, $\{\hat{d}(i)\}_{i=1}^{M+L_d-1}$, for some $M \geq L_d$. Then use the known filter function f_d to generate a segment of length M of the output of the nonlinear filter generator when regularly clocked, $\{\hat{g}(i)\}_{i=1}^{M}$. A measure of correlation between $\{\hat{g}(i)\}_{i=1}^{M}$ and $\{z(t)\}_{t=1}^{N}$ is calculated (either the Constrained Levenshtein Distance (CLD) [8], or the Probabilistic Constrained Edit Distance (PCED) [9]) and the process repeated for all $LFSR_d$ initial states.

In either case, the attack is considered successful if only a few initial states are identified. As the correlation attack based on the PCED takes into account the probability distribution of the decimating sequence, it is statistically optimal and may be successful in cases where the embedding attack based on the CLD is not, such as for larger values of m. The value of M is a function of N and m. If $M = 2^m \times N$, then the probability of not identifying the correct $LFSR_d$ initial state is zero.

The second stage of a divide-and-conquer attack on the generator is the recovery of the initial state of the second shift register. This can be performed as in [20]. From the calculation of the edit distance (either CLD or PCED) between $\{\hat{g}(i)\}_{i=1}^{M}$ and $\{z(t)\}_{t=1}^{N}$, form the edit distance matrix, and use this to find possible edit sequences. From each possible edit sequence, form a candidate integer sequence $\{\hat{c}(t)\}_{t=1}^{N}$. From this, the underlying binary sequence $\{\hat{a}(t)\}_{t=1}^{N}$ and hence the candidate initial state of $LFSR_c$ can be recovered. To determine whether the correct initial states of both LFSRs have been recovered, use both candidate initial states to generate a candidate keystream and compare it with the known keystream segment.

To conduct either of these correlation attacks requires exhaustive search of the $2^{127} - 1$ $LFSR_d$ initial states. For each $LFSR_d$ initial state, the attacks require calculation of either the CLD or the PCED, with computational complexity $O(N(M - N))$. Finally, further computational complexity is added in finding the corresponding $LFSR_c$ initial state. For either correlation attack, the minimum length of keystream required for a successful attack on $LFSR_d$ is linear in L_d, but exponential or even super-exponential in 2^m (see [10]). For $m = 2$, the required keystream length [23] is prohibitively large.

This is supported by the work of Chambers and Gollmann [5] on embedding, which indicates embeddings for $d > 3$ require impractically long output sequences. The LILI class of ciphers uses $d = 4$. The complexity of such an attack on LILI-II is $(2^{127} - 1)$ multiplied by the complexity of computing the correlation measure, with the additional complexity of recovering the corresponding $LFSR_c$ state. That is, the performance of divide and conquer attacks which target $LFSR_d$ are much worse than exhaustive key search.

4.3   Attacks Targeting $LFSR_c$

A possible approach to attacking the proposed generator is by targeting the clock-control sequence produced by $LFSR_c$. Guess an initial state of $LFSR_c$, say $\{\hat{a}(t)\}_{t=1}^{L_c}$. Use the known $LFSR_c$ feedback function and the function f_c to generate the decimating sequence $\{\hat{c}(t)\}_{t=1}^{N}$ for some $N \geq L_c$. Then position the known keystream bits $\{z(t)\}_{t=1}^{N}$ in the corresponding positions of $\{\hat{g}(i)\}_{i=1}^{\infty}$, the nonlinear filter generator output when regularly clocked. At this point we have some (not all consecutive) terms in the nonlinear filter generator output sequence and are trying to reconstruct a candidate initial state for $LFSR_d$.

Note that the amount of trial and error involved in guessing the initial state of $LFSR_c$ is the same as for guessing the secret key. Thus, the performance of any divide and conquer attack targeting $LFSR_c$ will be worse than exhaustive key search. Nevertheless, we outline several ways such an attack could proceed.

Consistency Attack. One method is to use the known filter function f_d to write equations relating terms in the underlying $LFSR_d$ sequence to terms in $\{\hat{g}(i)\}_{i=1}^{\infty}$. Reject the guessed initial state $\{\hat{c}(t)\}_{t=1}^{L_c}$ when the equations are inconsistent. This is a generalisation of the linear consistency test [22]. The feasibility of such an approach depends on the number of inputs to f_d, on the tap positions producing these inputs and on some properties of f_d such as its nonlinearity and order of correlation immunity. For example, this attack is complicated if the tap positions are chosen according to a full positive difference set (see [11]), as in the case of LILI-II.

Attacks on Regularly Clocked $LFSR_d$. An alternative approach is to use a correlation attack on the nonlinear filter generator [18] to recover a linear transform of the $LFSR_d$ sequence, and then recover the $LFSR_d$ initial state. However, this is complicated by not having consecutive terms in the regularly clocked nonlinear filter generator sequence. The feasibility of such an attack primarily depends on the use of a feedback polynomial of $LFSR_d$ that is of low weight or has low weight polynomial multiples and on the nonlinearity of f_d.

The feedback polynomial of $LFSR_d$ has been selected so that it does not have low-weight polynomial multiples of relatively small degrees, in order to avoid the vulnerability to fast correlation attacks on $LFSR_d$ when regularly clocked.

An alternative correlation attack on a (regularly clocked) nonlinear filter generator which could be applied at this point is the conditional correlation attack [1], with a difference that the known output bits are not consecutive. The feasibility of such an attack depends on the number of inputs to the filter function and on the tap positions. The use of a full positive difference set for the tap positions, as suggested in [11], and of a filter function with correlation-immunity order greater than zero renders this attack infeasible. The number and positions of taps for the filter function, f_d, have been chosen to ensure resistance to the attacks discussed in Section 4.3. This was the motivation for our choice of 12 inputs from tap positions which do form a full positive difference set.

Finally, the inversion attack [11] can be adapted to deal with the case of non-consecutive output bits, but the associated branching process is then super-critical, because more than one bit has to be guessed at a time. As a consequence, the computational complexity may be prohibitively high even if the tap positions are not spread across the $LFSR_d$ length.

Jönsson and Johansson's Attack. In [13], a divide and conquer attack on the LILI-128 stream cipher was proposed. The attack involved guessing an initial state for $LFSR_c$, and then solving the remaining $LFSR_d$ with the clocking known. This is a fast correlation attack, that is not based on iterative probabilistic decoding, and as such does not require the available keystream bits to be consecutive.

Applying any of the approaches discussed above requires exhaustive search over the $LFSR_c$ initial state space and additional computation for each candidate $LFSR_c$ state. Thus, all of these attacks are worse than exhaustive search on the 128-bit secret key.

4.4 Summary of Security Claims

In this section we summarise the claims we make for the security of LILI-II. Firstly, the period at around 2^{255} is sufficiently large. Secondly the linear complexity is conjectured to be at least 2^{175}, so that at least 2^{176} consecutive bits of known plaintext are required for the Berlekamp-Massey attack. This is an infeasible amount of text to collect. Thirdly, we conjecture that the complexity of divide and conquer attacks on LILI-II is in excess of 2^{128} operations, and additionally these attacks require knowledge of a large amount of keystream. The best known attack is therefore conjectured to be exhaustive search on the 128-bit key. This indicates that LILI-II is a secure synchronous stream cipher.

5 Efficiency and Implementation

5.1 Software Efficiency

The current software implementation of LILI-II runs at 6.07 Mbps on a 300MHz Pentium III using Borland C++ 5.5, and 3.75 Mbps on a 450MHz SPARCv9 using gcc 2.95.3. In comparison, implementations of LILI-128 achieved speeds of 6.65 MHz and 4.12 MHz under the respective conditions.

There are several internal differences between the implementation of LILI-128 and that of LILI-II. These differences include using Galois structure (rather than traditional Fibonacci style), for the LFSR state transitions, the increase in the size of the registers and increasing the number of inputs to the filter function from 10 to 12. These aspects have different effects on the speed of the design in software.

The use of Fibonacci style LFSRs is traditional in stream ciphers. In this style, the feedback polynomial selects a set of bits which are added mod 2 (XOR) to create the feedback bit which is shifted in to the LFSR. In contrast, the Galois style checks the value of the bit shifted out and if it is 1 then a constant vector (the feedback polynomial) is XORed in to the LFSR. These two styles can be seen as the time reversal of each other. Their state sequences have the same period. We believe that there is no security difference between the methods, so we choose to use the Galois style as it is faster in software.

The length of the $LFSR_c$ and $LFSR_d$ are increased from 39 and 89 bits to 128 bits and 127 bits, respectively. These structures now take 4 words each (on 32-bit processors). The clocking of the LFSRs will take more operations due to the extra words. This slight speed reduction compared to LILI-128 is unavoidable, but will be less of a problem when implemented on processors with 64 or 128 bit words. LILI-II will be slightly faster on those processors.

The most efficient way to implement the shifting of multiple-word LFSRs requires every second word to be physically reversed and shifted the other way. This removes the need for an extra shift per word to properly place the bit shifting between words. This reversal was taken into account during the design of the boolean function input assembly.

An interesting part of the implementation is the selection of bits from $LFSR_d$ as input to the Boolean function. We have chosen a full positive difference set (FPDS) to describe the bit positions selected, as this maximised resistance to correlation attacks. However, each bit must be selected by a logical mask and shifted to the desired position for input to a look-up-table. This means up to two operations per bit are required to assemble the 12-bit boolean function input value. By careful analysis of the chosen FPDS and given the abovementioned word reversal implementation style, we were able to slightly reduce the number of operations to assemble the value for input to the filter function. However the overall speedup from this optimisation is only about 2%.

5.2   Hardware Efficiency

The basic approach to the hardware design of LILI-II does not differ significantly from that proposed for LILI-128. Both ciphers can run at the clock speed with very small space required. The timing is simulated using a Max+plus II from the ALTERA Co., the logic circuit is implemented for an FPGA device (EPF10K20RC240-3), and the throughput stability is analysed up to a rate of 50 Mbps (ie. higher than the T3 rate at 45 Mbps, plus the maximum delay routine in the proposed design was below 20ns) with a 50MHz system clock, We have translated/simulated our VHDL design for Lucent's ASIC device (LV160C, 1.3 micrometer CMOS and 1.5V technology) and it can achieve a throughput of about 500 Mbps with a 0.13 micrometer semiconductor for the maximum path delay below 1.8ns.

Since the LILI-II cipher is a clock-controlled keystream generator, the keystream data rate is degraded in a clock-synchronised hardware logic design. Basically the clock-controlled $LFSR_d$ in the LILI-II cipher requires clocking at up to 4 times the rate of the $LFSR_c$. If the same clock is selected for both then the system throughput will be lowered. Accordingly, we propose a 4-bit parallel $LFSR_d$ where each register bit includes four variable data routines for feedback or shifting within the $LFSR_d$. After shifting $LFSR_d$, output sequences are generated using the nonlinear filter function from the 12 input taps in FPDS structure. The primitive polynomials require only some XOR operations. The data required to store the 12-input Boolean function is four times the space required for the 10-bit function of LILI-128, however at 512 bytes, this is still no problem even for memory-tight applications.

In the design for hardware, we have used an idea about the parallel structure of LFSR, from [14]. In most clock-synchronised logic designs, the feedback/shift in each register is implemented by a synchronised system clock to stabilise the hardware. However, since $LFSR_d$ in LILI-II requires many (1 to 4) clocks within a system clock period, this is a serious drawback. A frequency multiplier has been suggested to solve this problem, yet this is inappropriate for high-speed communications due to the small margin in a clock time interval. Accordingly, a 4-bit parallel $LFSR_d$ where each register has four variable data routines within the $LFSR_d$ was used. Note that the $LFSR_c$ and f_c can be easily implemented using a general shift register with feedback and a full adder device. Whereas each register in the 127-stage $LFSR_d$ represented by $d_0, d_1, ... d_{126}$ can randomly jump 1-4 registers from right to left according to the output of f_c. This $LFSR_d$ can be implemented using 127 D flip-flops and 127 multiplexors (4-1 MUX). For example the d_{122} register can select a 1-bit input d_{123+f_c} from the 4-bit registers d_{123} through d_{126}, where the selection signal is the output of f_c, implemented using a 1-bit full adder. As the $LFSR_d$ feedback polynomial is fixed, the four feedback logics can be precalculated from that vector, as linear functions of the current state.

6   Conclusion

In this paper, the LILI-II keystream generator, intended for use in stream cipher applications, is proposed. The design is simple: the generator is based on two binary LFSRs and uses two combining functions. The security of this keystream generator has been investigated with respect to currently known styles of attack. With the chosen parameters, LILI-II provides the basic security requirements for cryptographic sequences, such as a long period and high linear complexity. Also, LILI-II is immune to current known-plaintext attacks, conducted under the assumption that the cryptanalyst knows the entire structure of the generator and also the 128-bit initialisation vector. The 128-bit secret key is used only to form the initial states of the two LFSRs, using the re-keying algorithm outlined. We conjecture that the fastest possible attack on LILI-II is exhaustive key search.

The use of both nonlinear combining functions and irregular clocking in LFSR based stream ciphers is not a novel proposal, and has been employed in previous constructions. However, in this proposal the two approaches are combined in a manner that produces output sequences with provable properties with respect to basic cryptographic security requirements and also provides security against currently known cryptanalytic attacks.

The design is transparent, relying on basic known results in LFSR theory. In addition, LILI-II is easy to implement in software or hardware and, as it employs only simple components, can be implemented efficiently on any platform. The cipher is especially efficient in hardware. Our demonstration software implementation of LILI-II runs at approximately ninety percent of the speed that LILI-128 achieves, while giving far greater security. The speed we obtain in software is still fast enough for most applications, and the very fast hardware speed is sufficient even for applications requiring both high speed and high security.

Finally, the designers would like to state that no weakness has been deliberately inserted into the LILI-II design.

References

1. R. Anderson. Searching for the Optimum Correlation Attack. In *Fast Software Encryption - Leuven'94*, volume 1008 of *Lecture Notes in Computer Science*, pages 137–143. Springer–Verlag, 1995.

2. S. Babbage. A space/time tradeoff in exhaustive search attacks on stream ciphers. European Convention on Security and Detection, IEE Conference Publication No. 408, May 1995.

3. S. Babbage. Cryptanalysis of LILI-128. Available at *https://cosic.esat.kuleuven.ac.be/nessie/reports/extwp3-001-2.pdf*

4. A. Biryukov and A. Shamir. Cryptanalytic time/memory/data tradeoffs for stream ciphers. In *Advances in Cryptology - ASIACRYPT 2000*, volume 1976 of *Lecture Notes in Computer Science*, pages 1–13. Springer–Verlag, 2000.

5. W.G. Chambers and D. Gollmann. Embedding attacks on step[1..D] clock-controlled generators. Electronics Letters, vol.36 pp.1771-1773, 2000.

6. E. Dawson, A. Clark, J. Golić, W. Millan, L. Penna and L. Simpson. The LILI-128 Keystream Generator. Available at *https://www.cosic.esat.kuleuven.ac.be/nessie/workshop/submissions.html*.

7. C. Ding, G. Xiao and W. Shan. *The Stability Theory of Stream Ciphers*. Volume 561 of *Lecture Notes in Computer Science*. Springer–Verlag, 1991.

8. J. Dj. Golić and M. J. Mihaljević. A Generalised Correlation Attack on a Class of Stream Ciphers Based on the Levenshtein Distance. *Journal of Cryptology*, vol. 3(3), pp. 201–212, 1991.

9. J. Dj. Golić and S. Petrović. A Generalised Correlation Attack with a Probabilistic Constrained Edit Distance. In *Advances in Cryptology - EUROCRYPT'92*, volume 658 of *Lecture Notes in Computer Science*, pages 472–476. Springer–Verlag, 1992.

10. J. Dj. Golić and L. O'Connor. Embedding and Probabilistic Correlation Attacks on Clock-Controlled Shift Registers. In *Advances in Cryptology - EUROCRYPT'94*, volume 950 of *Lecture Notes in Computer Science*, pages 230–243. Springer–Verlag, 1994.

11. J. Dj. Golić. On the Security of Nonlinear Filter Generators. In *Fast Software Encryption - Cambridge'96*, volume 1039 of *Lecture Notes in Computer Science*, pages 173–188. Springer–Verlag, 1996.

12. J. Dj. Golić. Cryptanalysis of Alleged A5 stream cipher. In *Advances in Cryptology - EUROCRYPT'97*, volume 1233 of *Lecture Notes in Computer Science*, pages 239–255. Springer–Verlag, 1997.

13. F. Jönsson and T. Johansson A Fast Correlation Attack on LILI-128. *http://www.it.lth.se/thomas/papers/paper140.ps*

14. H-J. Lee and S-J. Moon Parallel Stream Cipher for Secure High-Speed Communications. *Signal Processing*, vol. 82, no. 2, pp. 137-143, 2002.

15. J. Massey. Shift-Register Synthesis and BCH Decoding. *IEEE Trans. Inform. Theory*, IT-15:122-127, January 1969.

16. W. Meier and O. Staffelbach. Fast Correlation Attacks on Certain Stream Ciphers. *Journal of Cryptology*, vol. 1(3), pp. 159–167, 1989.
17. R. Rueppel. *Analysis and design of stream ciphers*. Springer–Verlag, Berlin, 1986.
18. M. Salmasizadeh, L. Simpson, J. Dj. Golić and E. Dawson. Fast Correlation Attacks and Multiple Linear Approximations. In *Information Security and Privacy - Nepean '97*, volume 1270 of *Lecture Notes in Computer Science*, pages 228–239. Springer–Verlag, 1997.
19. T. Siegenthaler. Decrypting a Class of Stream Ciphers Using Ciphertext Only. *IEEE Trans. Computers*, vol. C-34(1), pp. 81–85, 1985.
20. L. Simpson, J. Dj. Golić and E. Dawson. A Probabilistic Correlation Attack on the Shrinking Generator. In *Information Security and Privacy - Brisbane '98*, volume 1438 of *Lecture Notes in Computer Science*, pages 147–158. Springer–Verlag, 1998.
21. L. Simpson, E. Dawson, J. Dj. Golić and W. Millan. LILI Keystream Generator. *Proceedings of the Seventh Annual Workshop on Selected Areas in Cryptology - SAC'2000*, volume 2012 of *Lecture Notes in Computer Science*, pages 248–261, Springer–Verlag, 2000.
22. K. C. Zeng, C. H. Yang and T. R. N. Rao. On the Linear Consistency Test (LCT) in Cryptanalysis with Applications. In *Advances in Cryptology - CRYPTO'89*, volume 434 of *Lecture Notes in Computer Science*, pages 164–174. Springer–Verlag, 1990.
23. M. Živković. An Algorithm for the Initial State Reconstruction of the Clock-Controlled Shift Register. *IEEE Trans. Inform. Theory*, vol. IT-37, pp. 1488–1490, Sept. 1991.

Appendix

Output Boolean Function for LILI-II Stream Cipher

This is the truth table (in hex) of the output function f_d:

C22C2CC22CC2C22CC22C2CC2C22C2CC2
C22CC22C2CC22CC2C22CC22CC22CC22C
C2C22C2C2C2CC2C2C2C22C2CC2C22C2C
C2C2C2C22C2C2C2CC2C2C2C2C2C2C2C2
CC2222CC22CCCC22CC2222CCCC2222CC
CC22CC2222CC22CCCC22CC22CC22CC22
CCCC22222222CCCCCCCC2222CCCC2222
CCCCCCCC22222222CCCCCCCCCCCCCCCC
A44A4AA44AA4A44AA44A4AA4A44A4AA4
A44AA44A4AA44AA4A44AA44AA44AA44A
A4A44A4A4A4AA4A4A4A44A4AA4A44A4A
A4A4A4A44A4A4A4AA4A4A4A4A4A4A4A4
AA4444AA44AAAA44AA4444AAAA4444AA
AA44AA4444AA44AAAA44AA44AA44AA44
AAAA44444444AAAAAAAA4444AAAA4444
AAAAAAAA444444446886866886686886
6886866868886686886688686688668

68866886688668866868868686866868
68688686686886866868686886868686
68686868686868686688886688666688
66888866668888666686668888668866
66886886688668866668888888886666
66668888666688886666666688888888
0EE0E00EE00E0EE00EE0E00E0EE0E00E
0EE00EE0E00EE00E0EE00EE00EE00EE0
0E0EE0E0E0E00E0E0E0EE0E00E0EE0E0
0E0E0E0EE0E0E0E000EEEE00EE0000EE
00EEEE0000EEEE0000EE00EEEE00EE00
4000AEEEE6EE0800CAA028CAC642424E
C2CA26C88C626C842206C26CC4AAAC84
22C8EA0A2866404E2286286868668628
EC84022E84642EA8C86422C42A2C8AC6

The Boolean Function has 12 inputs and these properties:
Balanced, CI(1), Order=10, Nonlinearity=1992, No Linear Structures.

A Secure Re-keying Scheme with Key Recovery Property

Hartono Kurnio[1], Rei Safavi-Naini[1], and Huaxiong Wang[2]

[1] Centre for Computer Security Research
School of Information Technology and Computer Science
University of Wollongong
Wollongong, NSW 2522, AUSTRALIA
{hk22, rei}@uow.edu.au
[2] Department of Computing
Macquarie University
Sydney, NSW 2109, AUSTRALIA
hwang@ics.mq.edu.au

Abstract. A commonly used solution for controlling access to information in a multicast group is to encrypt the data using a group key (session key). The group key is only known by users in the group, but not others. A multicast group is dynamic in the sense that group memberships changes in each session. To start a new session, the session key must be updated through a *re-keying* scheme. In this paper we propose a re-keying scheme for multiple user revocation and multiple user join. Our construction employs logical key hierarchy in conjunction with one-way hash chain to achieve higher efficiency. We prove that our scheme satisfies *forward secrecy*, *backward secrecy* and *forward-backward secrecy*. We also provide key recovery property which gives a system the ability to recover a session key using the previous and future session keys. We show security of the system.

1 Introduction

Sending a message from a sender to a group of users can be over a *unicast, broadcast* or *multicast* channel. Using unicast channel requires the sender to send a separate copy of the message to each user in the group, while using broadcast channel results in a copy of the message to be sent to all users. With multicast channel, the sender sends the message only once and the multicast-enabled routers forward the message to all users who have subscribed to the *multicast group*, hence minimizing the number of copies that traverses the network. This results in a more efficient usage of bandwidth and so multicast is the preferred mode of communication for most group communication services such as distributing stock-quotes, pay-TV and tele-conferencing.

In many applications such as pay-TV and private tele-conferencing using multicast channel, access to the data must be restricted. The standard technique to provide access control is to maintain a *group key* that is known to all

L. Batten and J. Seberry (Eds.): ACISP 2002, LNCS 2384, pp. 40–55, 2002.
© Springer-Verlag Berlin Heidelberg 2002

users in the multicast group, but is unknown to non-group users. Group communication is encrypted using the group key. The main challenge in securing multicast communication is to ensure that only group users have access to the group key while the group membership changes: that is, new users join the group or existing users leave (revoked) the group. These changes require the group key to be changed. A multicast *re-keying* scheme is an algorithm to securely and efficiently update the group key. Efficiency of a re-keying scheme is measured in terms of the cost of communication, size of the key storage for the users and the group controller, and computation cost. Minimizing the cost of re-keying while maintaining security is the main goal of multicast re-keying systems.

Another important problem in multicast communication is reliability. Since multicasting is an unreliable mode of communication, packets may be lost during the communication. If a packet containing key updating information is lost, authorised receivers may not be able to calculate the session key. This may influence re-keying and so the re-keying system must be resilient if packet loss occurs.

1.1   Related Work

There has been several approaches to forming authorised subgroups including (i) *Broadcast Encryption* (ii) *Secret Sharing* (iii) *Logical Key Hierarchy.*

Broadcast encryption schemes are introduced by Fiat and Naor [9] and enable a single source to securely broadcast to an arbitrary and dynamically changing subset of users from a larger group $\mathcal{U}$ of users. Such mechanism can be used to send a group key to a subset of users and so revoke any number of users while the system remains secure against collusion of at most t revoked users. The communication cost of the scheme proposed in [9], assuming the existence of one-way functions, is $\mathcal{O}(t^2 n \log^2 t)$ while the storage cost of a user is $\mathcal{O}(tn^2 \log t)$ keys, where $n = |\mathcal{U}|$. Blundo et al. [3,4] and Stinson et al. [22] studied broadcast encryption in unconditionally secure model and gave lower and upper bounds on the cost of communication and user key storage. Luby and Staddon [13] showed the trade-off between the number of users' keys and the cost of communication. Other works on broadcast encryption include [11,1,20,15]. The main drawback of using broadcast encryption schemes to re-keying problem is that they provide security against collusion of up to t users where the parameter t significantly influences the efficiency of the schemes.

Using secret sharing schemes to establish a group key is independently proposed by Anzai et al. [2] and Naor et al. [16]. They used Shamir's secret sharing scheme [21] with threshold $t + 1$ to revoke up to t users while remaining secure against collusion of all revoked users. The scheme requires a user to store only one key and the cost of communication is equivalent to t keys. A generalisation of the scheme to cater for revocation of any number of users is proposed in [12]. The main drawback of this approach is that users are required to perform relatively large number of modular exponentiations.

A scheme based on logical key hierarchy is independently proposed by Wallner et al. [23] and Wong et al. [24]. The scheme uses tree structure to efficiently update a group key in order to revoke or join users. When applied to a group of n users, the scheme requires a group controller to store $\frac{dn-1}{d-1}$ keys and a user to store $\log_d n + 1$ keys. Revocation of a single user has communication cost equivalent to $d \log_d n - 1$ keys, where d is the degree of the tree (scheme [23] uses $d = 2$, i.e., binary tree). The communication cost is reduced to $(d-1) \log_d n$ keys in [14,6]. The trade-off between communication cost and key storage of group controller and users is further studied in [7]. The schemes are initially designed to support revocation or join of a single user, but they can be repetitively used to revoke or join multiple users. Thus a trivial method of revoking or joining k users has communication cost equivalent to $k(d-1) \log_d n$ keys. Chang et al. [8] focused on the problem of multiple user revocation and applied boolean function minimization technique to binary trees to minimize the cost of communication. In their scheme, the user storage is $\log_d n$ keys and the storage of the group controller is reduced to $\log_d n$ keys. The main shortcoming of the scheme is that collusion of two users can reveal all system keys.

Reliable re-keying systems have been studied by a number of authors. Wong and Lam [25] used error-correcting codes to construct re-keying packets. A re-keying packet is split into p packets using a scheme such as Rabin's IDA [18], Reed-Solomon codes, or Digital Fountain codes [5]. When a user receives any q packets, he can reconstruct the re-keying packet. Perrig et al. [17] addressed reliability by using short 'hint' messages. The hint is appended to the re-keying packet and used to verify the validity of a group key. Their method allows a trade-off between communication cost and computation cost of the user.

1.2   Our Work

In this paper we consider re-keying problem, and propose a re-keying scheme to provide multiple user revocation and user join. Our construction is based on the logical key hierarchy approach and uses a one-way hash chain to provide fast re-keying. One-way hash chains have been previously used in other security schemes such as micropayment systems and high-speed signature schemes. We use the hash chain to generate all the keys of a user from a seed value, hence reducing the storage cost of the user. The logical tree in our scheme does not need to be full or balanced and there is no limit on the number of users who can be revoked or join the group, or on size of the collusion. In fact, we prove that our scheme satisfies the requirement of strong security as defined in section 2. The scheme improves Wallner et al.'s scheme by reducing the cost of communication by a factor 2. For multiple user revocation or join, the scheme's cost of communication is less than the trivial scheme (see section 3). A user's cost of computation is equivalent to u symmetric key decryption together with v hashing where $u + v \leq \log_d n$. The required storage for the group controller is $\frac{dn-1}{d-1}$ keys and for a user is $\log_d n + 1$ keys, assuming a tree of degree d which is full and balanced. The scheme also provides key recovery that allows the key for one session to be recovered from the key of the future sessions combined with those of the past sessions. This property increases the reliability of the system and ensures that the re-keying will succeed even if the re-keying packet is lost.

Organisation of the paper. Section 2 describes the model and defines security properties of a re-keying scheme. Section 3 gives a new re-keying scheme based on logical key hierarchy. Section 4 applies the re-keying scheme to multicast group and proves its security properties. Section 5 describes a key recovery method that can be embedded in the re-keying scheme. Section 6 concludes the paper.

2 Model

We consider the scenario where there is a set $\mathcal{U}$ of users and a group controller GC[1]. A user holds a unique set $\mathcal{K}(U) \subseteq \mathcal{K}$ of keys, where $\mathcal{K}$ is the set of keys in the system. By *dynamic* we mean that group memberships changes in each session. In a session i, the group consists of a set $\mathcal{M}_i = \{U_1, \ldots, U_{n_i}\} \subseteq \mathcal{U}$ of users sharing a session key (group key) $K_{s_i} \in \mathcal{K}$. A user $U \notin \mathcal{M}_i$ does not know the session key K_{s_i}. To start a new session, a *re-keying* system will be used.

Group Operations. Re-keying consists of two group operations.

- *User revocation.* A subset $\mathcal{R}_i \subseteq \mathcal{M}_i$ of users is revoked from $\mathcal{M}_i$ resulting in a new session consisting of $\mathcal{M}_{i+1} = \mathcal{M}_i \setminus \mathcal{R}_i$ sharing a new session key $K_{s_{i+1}}$.
- *User join.* A subset $\mathcal{J}_i \subseteq (\mathcal{U} \setminus \mathcal{M}_i)$ of users join $\mathcal{M}_i$ resulting in a new session consisting of $\mathcal{M}_{i+1} = \mathcal{M}_i \cup \mathcal{J}_i$ sharing a new session key $K_{s_{i+1}}$.

System Operation. During the initial session $i = 0$, GC generates the keys $\mathcal{K}$ and sends a subset $\mathcal{K}(U) \subseteq \mathcal{K}$ of keys to user $U \in \mathcal{M}_0$[2] via a secure unicast channel. In all subsequent sessions, GC manages re-keying by sending a re-keying message $\mathcal{M}_{rkey}$ over an insecure multicast channel. A user $U \in \mathcal{M}_{i+1}$ uses his set of keys $\mathcal{K}(U)$ and the re-keying message $\mathcal{M}_{rkey}$ to calculate the new session key K_{i+1}.

Security Properties. We assume adversaries are passive and computationally bounded. A multicast re-keying scheme may provide one of the following types of security.

Definition 1. *A re-keying protocol provides forward secrecy if for any session i, collusion of users in $Tot(\mathcal{R}_i) = \cup \mathcal{R}_a, \mathcal{R}_a \subseteq \mathcal{M}_a$, where $0 \le a \le i$, cannot distinguish a session key K_{s_b}, where $b \ge i + 1$ from a random string, provided that $Tot(\mathcal{R}_i) \cap \mathcal{M}_b = \emptyset$.*

Definition 2. *A re-keying protocol provides backward secrecy if for any session j, collusion of users in $Tot(\mathcal{J}_j) = \cup \mathcal{J}_a, \mathcal{J}_a \subseteq (\mathcal{U} \setminus \mathcal{M}_a)$, where $a \ge j$, cannot distinguish a session key K_{s_b}, where $0 \le b \le j$ from a random string, provided that $Tot(\mathcal{J}_j) \cap \mathcal{M}_b = \emptyset$.*

---

[1] Although GC may be a member of the group, that is $\mathsf{GC} \in \mathcal{M}$, we assume $\mathsf{GC} \notin \mathcal{M}$ in this paper.

[2] Without loss of generality, we may assume $\mathcal{M}_0 = \mathcal{U}$.

Definition 3. *A re-keying protocol provides forward-backward secrecy if for any sessions i and j, where $i < j$, collusion of users in $Tot(\mathcal{R}_i, \mathcal{J}_j) = (\cup \mathcal{R}_a) \cup (\cup \mathcal{J}_b), \mathcal{R}_a \subseteq \mathcal{M}_a$ and $\mathcal{J}_b \subseteq (\mathcal{U} \setminus \mathcal{M}_b)$, where $0 \leq a \leq i$ and $b \geq j$, cannot distinguish a session key K_{s_c}, where $i + 1 \leq c \leq j$ from a random string, provided that $Tot(\mathcal{R}_i, \mathcal{J}_j) \cap \mathcal{M}_c = \emptyset$.*

In the above definitions, in the case of forward secrecy the adversaries are the revoked users and it is required that the collusion of all adversaries from preceding sessions cannot obtain the key for subsequent sessions. Backward secrecy includes joined users and it is required that the collusion of all adversaries from subsequent sessions cannot obtain any preceding session key. Forward-backward secrecy considers collusion of both revoked and joined users and assures the collusion cannot discover session keys where they do not have memberships.

Key Recovery

We also consider key recovery in the system. This allows a legitimate user to recover a lost session key in a subsequent session. That is, a session key K_{s_i} can be recovered in any of the future sessions $s_{i+1}, \ldots, s_{i+t}$ (t is a pre-defined system parameter) provided the user is in all these sessions. To provide key recovery, the re-keying message contains additional information $\mathcal{M}_{rec}$ that allows legitimate users to recover the session key. Key recovery should not breach the security property of re-keying. That is the security properties given in definitions 1, 2 and 3 must remain valid. This is captured in the following definition.

Definition 4. *A key recovery scheme provides (i) forward secrecy, (ii) backward secrecy, or (iii) forward-backward secrecy if it satisfies definitions 1, 2, or 3, respectively. In (iii), it is required that $j \geq i + 2t$.*

3   A LKH Re-keying Scheme

In this section we propose a LKH re-keying scheme that uses one-way hash chain for updating group key in user revocation and join operations.

Definition 5. *A logical key hierarchy (LKH) is a tree where each node logically corresponds to a key and each leaf logically corresponds to a user. A user knows the keys of nodes along the path from the user's leaf to the root.*

Let $\mathcal{M} = \{U_1, \ldots, U_n\}$ be the set of users and T be a tree with n leaves. Nodes of the tree are divided into *internal nodes* and *leaves*. Each node is given a label $I_w^{(l)}$ and a key $K_w^{(l)}$, called *node key*, where l is the level of the node and w is a unique number identifying the node. Node keys are divided into *internal keys* and *leaf keys*. Each leaf corresponds to a user U. Let s_U be the level of the leaf attached to user U. Node labels are public while node keys are kept secret. For a user U, let $\mathcal{N}(U) = \{I_w^{(0)}, \ldots, I_w^{(s_U)}\}$ be the set of nodes along the path from his corresponding leaf to the root. The user holds the set $\mathcal{K}(U) = \{K_w^{(0)}, \ldots, K_w^{(s_U)}\}$ of node keys along the path. In other words, $\mathcal{K}(U) = \{K_w^{(l)} \mid I_w^{(l)} \in \mathcal{N}(U)\}$. All users have a common internal key called *root key* $K_w^{(0)}$. Figure 1 shows an

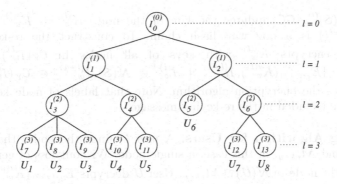

Fig. 1. A tree structure for 8 users

example of a tree structure for 8 users where the secret keys of U_1 are $\mathcal{K}(U_1) = \{K_0^{(0)}, K_1^{(1)}, K_3^{(2)}, K_7^{(3)}\}$.

A re-keying scheme based on the logical key hierarchy updates the root key $K_w^{(0)}$ by updating a subset $\mathcal{K}(\mathcal{S})$ of internal keys that include the root key $K_w^{(0)} \in \mathcal{K}(\mathcal{S})$ to a subset $\mathcal{K}'(\mathcal{S})$ of new keys. The basic method of updating the internal keys based on LKH can be found in Wallner *et al.* [23].

We employ one-way hash chain to increase efficiency of re-keying. We discuss re-keying *single-*$\mathcal{K}(\mathcal{S})$ for a single user revocation or join, and only state our results for multiple user revocation or join.

Definition 6. *A $h^v(x)$, where $h()$ is a one-way hash function, is a one-way hash chain when the function h is applied v times to an argument x. The result will be denoted as $h^v(x)$, where $h^v(x) = \underbrace{h(h(\ldots(h(x))\ldots))}_{v\ times}$. When $v = 0$, $h^0(x) = x$.*

We assume the function $h()$ is cryptographically secure. For example, we can use the one-way hash function in [19,26,10].

Single-$\mathcal{K}(\mathcal{S})$

First we consider the special case where $\mathcal{K}(\mathcal{S}) = \{K_w^{(0)}, \ldots, K_w^{(s)}\}$ for all levels s, $s < max\{s_U : U \in \mathcal{M}\}$. The set $\mathcal{K}(\mathcal{S})$ contains at most only one node key at each level. Let $\mathcal{N}(\mathcal{S}) = \{I_w^{(l)} \mid K_w^{(l)} \in \mathcal{K}(\mathcal{S})\}$ be the set of nodes corresponding to keys in $\mathcal{K}(\mathcal{S})$ and let $\mathcal{N}(\mathcal{S})^{(l)}$ be the set of nodes at level l of $\mathcal{N}(\mathcal{S})$. Note that $\mathcal{N}(\mathcal{S})^{(l)}$ contains only a single node. Let $\mathcal{C}(I_w^{(l)})$ be the set of nodes having parent $I_w^{(l)}$ (the nodes are at level $l + 1$). For a node $I_w^{(l)} \in \mathcal{N}(\mathcal{S})$, the set $\mathcal{C}(I_w^{(l)})$ can be partitioned into two subsets $\mathcal{C}_X(I_w^{(l)})$ and $\mathcal{C}_Y(I_w^{(l)})$ where $\mathcal{C}_X(I_w^{(l)}) = \mathcal{C}(I_w^{(l)}) \cap \mathcal{N}(\mathcal{S})^{(l+1)}$ consists of nodes in $\mathcal{C}(I_w^{(l)})$ that their corresponding keys must be changed, while $\mathcal{C}_Y(I_w^{(l)}) = \mathcal{C}(I_w^{(l)}) \setminus \mathcal{C}_X(I_w^{(l)})$ contains the rest of the nodes in $\mathcal{C}(I_w^{(l)})$. Note that $\mathcal{C}_X(I_w^{(l)})$ contains only a node.

Re-keying Algorithm for GC. GC chooses a random number $r \in_R \{0,1\}^b$, where b is the security parameter. For level $l = s, \ldots, 0$ and a node

$I_w^{(l)} \in \mathcal{N}(\mathcal{S})^{(l)}$, GC updates the key of the node $K_w^{(l)}$ to $K_w'^{(l)} = h^{s-l}(r)$ where $h^{s-l}()$ is a one way hash chain. To construct the re-keying message, GC encrypts $K_w'^{(l)}$ with keys of all nodes in $\mathcal{C}_Y(I_w^{(l)})$. That is, $\mathcal{M}_{rkey} = \{E_{K_w^{(l+1)}}(K_w'^{(l)}), I_w^{(l+1)} \mid I_w^{(l)} \in \mathcal{N}(\mathcal{S}), I_w^{(l+1)} \in \mathcal{C}_Y(I_w^{(l)})\}$ where $E()$ denotes the encryption algorithm. Note that labels of node keys used to encrypt are included in the re-keying message.

Re-keying Algorithm for Users. A user U finds the nodes that are both in $\mathcal{N}(U)$ and $\mathcal{M}_{rkey}$, in this case, a single node. Without loss of generality, let $I_w^{(y+1)}$ be the node in $\mathcal{N}(U) \cap \mathcal{M}_{rkey}$. User U decrypts $E_{K_w^{(y+1)}}(K_w'^{(y)}) \in \mathcal{M}_{rkey}$ using his node key $K_w^{(y+1)} \in \mathcal{K}(U)$ to update $K_w^{(y)} \in \mathcal{K}(U)$. That is, $K_w'^{(y)} = D_{K_w^{(y+1)}}(E_{K_w^{(y+1)}}(K_w'^{(y)}))$ where $D()$ denotes the decryption algorithm. User U needs to update keys of node $I_w^{(y)}$ and all its ancestors, i.e., $I_w^{(y-1)}, \ldots, I_w^{(0)}$. Thus for level $l = y - 1, \ldots, 0$ and every node $I_w^{(l)} \in \mathcal{N}(U)$, user U updates the node key $K_w^{(l)}$ to $K_w'^{(l)} = h^{y-l}(K_w'^{(y)})$ where $h^{y-l}()$ is a one way hash chain.

Theorem 1. *Let the tree T be a full and balanced tree of degree d. Then updating single-$\mathcal{K}(\mathcal{S})$ requires (i) communication cost equivalent to at most $(d-1)\log_d n + 1$ keys and (ii) user computation cost equal to a single decryption plus at most $\log_d n - 1$ hashing.*

The basic algorithm described above can be extended to revoke or join multiple users. We use *multi-$\mathcal{K}(\mathcal{S})$* to denote the re-keying operation required in this case. Note that in this case, s is the level of the deepest node in $\mathcal{N}(\mathcal{S})$ and $|\mathcal{N}(\mathcal{S})^{(l)}| \geq 1$. Table 1 gives an algorithm for GC to generate the re-keying message $\mathcal{M}_{rkey}$ and table 2 shows how legitimate users can update their keys. The details are omitted due to the lack of space.

Theorem 2. *Assume T is a full, balanced tree of degree d, updating multi-$\mathcal{K}(\mathcal{S})$ requires (i) communication cost of at most $n + \sum_{e=1}^{\log_d n - 1} d^e(1 - \frac{1}{d})$ keys and (ii) user computation cost of u decryption operations and v hashing where $u + v \leq \log_d n$.*

Note that the communication cost of $n + \sum_{e=1}^{\log_d n - 1} d^e(1 - \frac{1}{d})$ keys is for the worst case where all internal keys have to be updated. The following shows that even in the worst case, the multicast length of our scheme is less than the multicast length of the trivial scheme. Observe that using the trivial scheme needs multicast length of $n + \frac{n}{d}(d-1)(\log_d n - 1)$ keys. Hence,

$$n + \sum_{e=1}^{\log_d n - 1} d^e\left(1 - \frac{1}{d}\right) < n + \frac{n}{d}(d-1)(\log_d n - 1)$$

$$\sum_{e=1}^{\log_d n - 1} d^e < n(\log_d n - 1)$$

Table 1. Re-keying algorithm to generate $\mathcal{M}_{rkey}$

---

(1) $\mathcal{M}_{rkey} = \emptyset$
(2) for $l = s$ to 0 do
(3)   for all $I_w^{(l)} \in \mathcal{N}(\mathcal{S})^{(l)}$ do
(4)   if $\mathcal{C}_X(I_w^{(l)}) = \emptyset$ do
(5) $K_w'^{(l)} \in_R \{0,1\}^b$
(6) $\mathcal{M}_{tmp} = \{E_{K_w'^{(l+1)}}(K_w'^{(l)}), I_w^{(l+1)} \mid I_w^{(l+1)} \in \mathcal{C}_Y(I_w^{(l)})\}$
(7)   else do
(8) $K_w'^{(l)} = h(K_{w'}'^{(l+1)})$ where $I_{w'}^{(l+1)} \in_R \mathcal{C}_X(I_w^{(l)})$
(9) $\mathcal{M}_{tmp} = \{E_{K_w'^{(l+1)}}(K_w'^{(l)}), I_w^{(l+1)} \mid I_w^{(l+1)} \in \mathcal{C}_X(I_w^{(l)}) \setminus \{I_{w'}^{(l+1)}\}\} \cup$
                $\{E_{K_w'^{(l+1)}}(K_w'^{(l)}), I_w^{(l+1)} \mid I_w^{(l+1)} \in \mathcal{C}_Y(I_w^{(l)})\}$
(10)   end
(11) $\mathcal{M}_{rkey} = \mathcal{M}_{rkey} \cup \mathcal{M}_{tmp}$
(12)   end
(13) end

Theorem 3. *The re-keying scheme satisfies the following properties:*
(i) All users calculate the same new root key.
(ii) A user U can only find the new keys for $\mathcal{K}(U) \cap \mathcal{K}(\mathcal{S})$ but not any other new key.
(iii) A passive adversary who knows the keys in $\mathcal{K}(\mathcal{S})$ cannot discover any new key in $\mathcal{K}'(\mathcal{S})$.
(iv) A passive adversary who knows new keys in $\mathcal{K}'(\mathcal{S})$ cannot discover any key in $\mathcal{K}(\mathcal{S})$.

Proof is omitted due to limitation of space.

Table 2. Re-keying algorithm to update user keys

---

(1) for $l = s_U - 1$ to 0 do
(2)   for a pair $I_w^{(l)}, I_w^{(l+1)} \in \mathcal{N}(U)$ do
(3)   if $I_w^{(l+1)} \in \mathcal{M}_{rkey}$ and $K_w^{(l+1)} \to K_w'^{(l+1)}$ do
(4) $K_w'^{(l)} = D_{K_w'^{(l+1)}}(E_{K_w'^{(l+1)}}(K_w'^{(l)}))$ where $E_{K_w'^{(l+1)}}(K_w'^{(l)}) \in \mathcal{M}_{rkey}$
(5)   else if $I_w^{(l+1)} \in \mathcal{M}_{rkey}$ and $K_w^{(l+1)} \not\to K_w'^{(l+1)}$ do
(6) $K_w'^{(l)} = D_{K_w^{(l+1)}}(E_{K_w^{(l+1)}}(K_w'^{(l)}))$ where $E_{K_w^{(l+1)}}(K_w'^{(l)}) \in \mathcal{M}_{rkey}$
(7)   else if $I_w^{(l+1)} \notin \mathcal{M}_{rkey}$ and $K_w^{(l+1)} \to K_w'^{(l+1)}$ do
(8) $K_w'^{(l)} = h(K_w'^{(l+1)})$
(9)   end
(10)   end
(11) end

---

4   Group Operations

4.1   System Initialisation

A multicast group is initialised in session 0. Let $\mathcal{M}_0 = \{U_1, \ldots, U_{n_0}\}$. GC constructs a tree structure with n_0 leaves, gives a unique label $I_w^{(l)}$ to each node, attachs a randomly generated key $K_w^{(l)} \in_R \{0,1\}^b$ to each node $I_w^{(l)}$, and corresponds each leaf to a user. GC publishes the tree structure (node labels and users' positions) in a public bulletin board and keeps all node keys secret. GC sends to user U, a set $\mathcal{K}(U)$ of node keys along the path from U's leaf to the root over a secure unicast channel. The cardinality of $\mathcal{K}(U)$ is the height of U's leaf. Each user U holds the set $\mathcal{K}(U)$ as his secret keys. The root key, shared by all users, is the session key K_{s_0}. Hence assuming a full and balanced tree of degree d, GC has to store $\frac{d n - 1}{d-1}$ keys and a user has to store $\log_d n + 1$ keys.

4.2   User Revocation

Suppose in session $i+1$ a set $\mathcal{R}_i \subseteq \mathcal{M}_i$ of users are revoked and $\mathcal{M}_{i+1} = \mathcal{M}_i \backslash \mathcal{R}_i$. Session key K_{s_i} must be updated to $K_{s_{i+1}}$ such that only users in $\mathcal{M}_{i+1}$ know the updated key.

Group Controller. GC does the following.

1. Updates the tree structure by pruning leaves corresponding to all users in $\mathcal{R}_i$. Observe that the resulting tree may have some redundant internal nodes. To increase efficiency, GC may remove the redundant nodes by pruning internal nodes having only one child by replacing the parent with the child, and pruning the internal nodes having no child. As a result, GC also removes keys of redundant nodes from his storage and rearranges the levels of affected nodes and keys in the updated tree. Let the updated tree be denoted by T'. GC publishes T' in a public bulletin board.
2. Updating the session key K_{s_i} to $K_{s_{i+1}}$ (updating root key) requires all internal keys belonging to the users in $\mathcal{R}_i$ to be updated. With respect to the updated tree T', let $\mathcal{K}(\mathcal{R}_i) \subseteq \bigcup_{U \in \mathcal{R}_i} \mathcal{K}(U) \backslash \{K_w^{(s_U)}\}$ be the set of internal keys that need to be updated. GC performs re-keying scheme in section 3 with $T = T'$ and $\mathcal{K}(\mathcal{S}) = \mathcal{K}(\mathcal{R}_i)$.

User. Users in $\mathcal{M}_{i+1}$ do the following.

1. Each affected user $U \in \mathcal{M}_{i+1}$ removes the redundant nodes and keys from $\mathcal{N}(U)$ and $\mathcal{K}(U)$, respectively, and rearranges the levels of the affected nodes and keys.
2. Each user $U \in \mathcal{M}_{i+1}$ receives the re-keying message $\mathcal{M}_{rkey}$ and performs the re-keying scheme in section 3 to update the keys in $\mathcal{K}(U) \cap \mathcal{K}(\mathcal{R}_i)$ and obtains the session key $K_{s_{i+1}}$.

An example. Suppose $\mathcal{R}_i = \{U_3, U_5, U_6\}$ in figure 1 are revoked from the group.

1. GC updates the tree structure as shown in figure 2 where nodes $I_2^{(1)}, I_4^{(2)}, I_5^{(2)}$, $I_9^{(3)}, I_{11}^{(3)}$ have been pruned. Nodes in dashed line are the affected nodes and they have been rearranged to new levels. Keys of the grey coloured nodes are required to be updated, that is, $\mathcal{K}(S) = \{K_3^{(2)}, K_1^{(1)}, K_0^{(0)}\}$. The result of re-keying is, $K_3'^{(2)} = r, K_1'^{(1)} = h^1(r), K_0'^{(0)} = h^2(r)$ and $\mathcal{M}_{rkey} = \{E_{K_7^{(3)}}(K_3'^{(2)}), I_7^{(3)}, E_{K_8^{(3)}}(K_3'^{(2)}), I_8^{(3)}, E_{K_{10}^{(2)}}(K_1'^{(1)}), I_{10}^{(2)}, E_{K_6^{(1)}}(K_0'^{(0)}), I_6^{(1)}\}$.

2. After decryption, users U_1 and U_2 will have $K_3'^{(2)}$ from $\mathcal{M}_{rkey}$ and calculate $K_1'^{(1)} = h^1(K_3'^{(2)}), K_0'^{(0)} = h^2(K_3'^{(2)})$. User U_4 will have $K_1'^{(1)}$ from $\mathcal{M}_{rkey}$ and calculate $K_0'^{(0)} = h^1(K_1'^{(1)})$. Users U_7 and U_8 will have $K_0'^{(0)}$ from $\mathcal{M}_{rkey}$ and the session key is $K_{s_{i+1}} = K_0'^{(0)} = h^2(r)$.

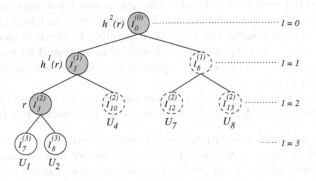

Fig. 2. Updated tree T' when revoking users U_3, U_5 and U_6

In the light of theorem 3, part (iii), we have

Theorem 4. *User revocation provides forward secrecy in the sense of definition 1.*

4.3   User Join

Assume a set $\mathcal{J}_i \subseteq (\mathcal{U} \setminus \mathcal{M}_i)$ of users are to join in session i, resulting in a new session $i + 1$ with $\mathcal{M}_{i+1} = \mathcal{M}_i \cup \mathcal{J}_i$. The session key K_{s_i} must be updated to $K_{s_{i+1}}$ such that users in $\mathcal{J}_i$ cannot obtain the session key K_{s_i}. Let $|\mathcal{J}_i| = m$.

Group Controller. GC does the following.

1. Updates the tree structure by adding m new leaves to the tree. The new leaves can be simply attached to the existing internal nodes, or GC may create new internal nodes in order to attach the new leaves. A new internal node replaces an existing leaf and the leaf becomes the child of the node. GC then rearranges the levels of the affected nodes and keys in the updated tree T', and publishes T' in a public bulletin board.

2. Produces a randomly chosen key for each new leaf, and associates each new user $U \in \mathcal{J}_i$ to a new leaf. GC then securely sends the key associated to a user to him over a unicast channel. Let the leaf key of the user U be $K_w^{(s_U)}$.

3. With respect to the updated tree T', let $\mathcal{N}(\mathcal{J}_i) = \bigcup_{U \in \mathcal{J}_i} \mathcal{N}(U) \setminus \{I_w^{(s_U)}\}$ be the set of internal nodes belonging to the new users. Updating the session key K_{s_i} to $K_{s_{i+1}}$ (updating root key) requires the internal keys corresponding to all nodes in $\mathcal{N}(\mathcal{J}_i)$ to be updated. GC performs the re-keying scheme in section 3 with $T = T'$ and $\mathcal{K}(\mathcal{S}) = \{K_w^{(l)} \mid I_w^{(l)} \in \mathcal{N}(\mathcal{J}_i)\}$.

User. Users in $\mathcal{M}_{i+1}$ do the following.

1. Before re-keying, each new user $U \in \mathcal{J}_i$ only knows $\mathcal{N}(U)$, but not $\mathcal{K}(U) \setminus \{K_w^{(s_U)}\}$. User U performs the re-keying operation described in section 3 to obtain the updated keys in $\mathcal{K}(U)$ and the new session key $K_{s_{i+1}}$.

2. Each affected user $U \in \mathcal{M}_i$ adds the new nodes (new ancestors of the U's leaf) to $\mathcal{N}(U)$ and rearranges the level of his leaf and leaf key. Note that the user does not know the keys corresponding to the new nodes. The user performs the re-keying operation described in section 3 to update the keys in $\mathcal{K}(U) \cap \mathcal{K}(\mathcal{J}_i)$ (to obtain the updated keys of the new nodes) and obtain the session key $K_{s_{i+1}}$.

3. The rest of the users in $\mathcal{M}_i$ perform the re-keying scheme of section 3 to update the keys in $\mathcal{K}(U) \cap \mathcal{K}(\mathcal{J}_i)$ and obtain the session key $K_{s_{i+1}}$.

Note that unlike the other proposed schemes where to join a new user U, GC must send all the keys in $\mathcal{K}(U)$ to U through a secure unicast channel, the join operation in our scheme requires GC to send only the leaf key to U through a secure unicast channel. The new user obtains other keys through the re-keying (multicast channel).

An example. Suppose $\mathcal{J}_i = \{U_9, U_{10}\}$ join the group in figure 1.

1. GC updates the tree structure to figure 3 where two new leaves $I_{15}^{(3)}, I_{16}^{(3)}$ and a new internal node $I_{14}^{(2)}$ (nodes with bold line) have been added. The node with dashed line is the affected node and has been rearranged to the new level. Keys of the grey coloured nodes are required to be updated, that is, $\mathcal{K}(S) = \{K_{14}^{(2)}, K_6^{(2)}, K_2^{(1)}, K_0^{(0)}\}$. The result of re-keying is, $K_{14}'^{(2)} = r_1, K_6'^{(2)} = r_2, K_2'^{(1)} = h^1(r_1), K_0'^{(0)} = h^2(r_1)$ and $\mathcal{M}_{rkey} = \{E_{K_5^{(3)}}(K_{14}'^{(2)}), I_5^{(3)}, E_{K_{15}^{(3)}}(K_{14}'^{(2)}), I_{15}^{(3)}, E_{K_{12}^{(3)}}(K_6'^{(2)}), I_{12}^{(3)}, E_{K_{13}^{(3)}}(K_6'^{(2)}), I_{13}^{(3)},$
   $E_{K_{16}^{(3)}}(K_6'^{(2)}), I_{16}^{(3)}, E_{K_6'^{(2)}}(K_2'^{(1)}), I_6^{(2)}, E_{K_1^{(1)}}(K_0'^{(0)}), I_1^{(1)}\}$.

2. After decryption, users $U_1, \ldots, U_5$ will have $K_0'^{(0)}$, users U_6 and U_9 will have $K_{14}'^{(2)}$ and will calculate $K_2'^{(1)} = h^1(K_{14}'^{(2)}), K_0'^{(0)} = h^2(K_{14}'^{(2)})$, and users U_7, U_8, U_{10} will have $K_6'^{(2)}$ and $K_2'^{(1)}$ and will calculate $K_0'^{(0)} = h^1(K_2'^{(1)})$. The session key will be $K_{s_{i+1}} = K_0'^{(0)} = h^2(r_1)$.

In the light of theorem 3, part (iv), we have

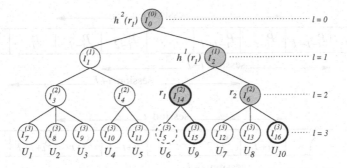

Fig. 3. Updated tree T' when joining new users U_9 and U_{10}

Theorem 5. *User join provides backward secrecy in the sense of definition 2. Furthermore, user revocation together with user join provide forward-backward secrecy in the sense of definition 3.*

5   Key Recovery

Multicasting is an unreliable mode of communication and may result in loss of packets. If the packet that carries the re-keying information is lost, legitimate users will not be able to compute the group key. In this section, we propose a solution to increase reliability of re-keying messages. The basic idea is to allow legitimate users to recover the group key from his previous session keys. More specifically, in each session i, legitimate users can recover t previous session keys $K_{s_{i-1}}, \ldots, K_{s_{i-t}}$. A straightforward approach to provide such property is to give $K_{s_{i-1}}, \ldots, K_{s_{i-t}}$ in session i encrypted with the session key K_{s_i}. It is easy to show that this satisfies the security requirement of forward secrecy, but does not satisfy the security requirements of backward secrecy and forward-backward secrecy in definition 4.

Our proposed key recovery technique is as follows. A key K is broken into two values P and S. For each session key, the value P is part of the re-keying message in t subsequent sessions while the value of S is part of the re-keying message in the t preceding sessions. More specifically, for a key K_i in session i, P_i is given in sessions $a, i+1 \leq a \leq i+t$ and S_i is given in sessions $b, i-t \leq b \leq i-1$. Therefore, computing (recovering) the key K_i needs a pair P_i and S_i, where P_i and S_i can be obtained in a session i_p and a session i_s, respectively, for any $i-t \leq i_s < i < i_p \leq i+t$. This implies that the key K_i can be recovered in any session $i+1, \ldots, i+t$. In general, there will be a set $\mathcal{P}_i = \{P_{i-1}, \ldots, P_{i-t}\}$ and a set $\mathcal{S}_i = \{S_{i+1}, \ldots, S_{i+t}\}$ given in session i[3] and as a result, it is possible to compute (recover) t preceding session keys $K_{i-1}, \ldots, K_{i-t}$. The snapshot of sets $\mathcal{P}$ and $\mathcal{S}$ in multiple sessions is given below.

In practice, the value S may be chosen randomly and the value P can be computed from K and S, that is, $P = K \oplus S$ where $\oplus$ denotes Exclusive

---

[3] This is not the case for the first t sessions ($i = 1, \ldots, t$).

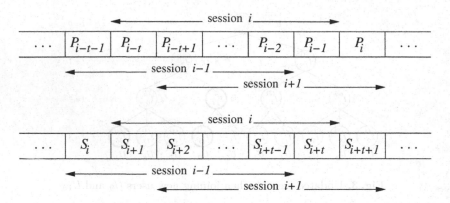

Fig. 4. The sets $\mathcal{P}$ and $\mathcal{S}$ in sessions $i-1, i$, and $i+1$

OR operation. This is possible since for a key K_i in session i, S_i is given in sessions before session i and P_i is given in sessions after session i. Thus, after obtaining S_i and P_i, it is easy to compute $K_i = S_i \oplus P_i$. In general, the set $\mathcal{S}$ contains random values and the set $\mathcal{P}$ contains values that are computed. Observe that for a session i, set $\mathcal{P}_i$ inherits $t-1$ elements from set $\mathcal{P}_{i-1}$, that is, $\mathcal{P}_i \cap \mathcal{P}_{i-1} = \{P_{i-2}, \ldots, P_{i-t}\}$, and the element P_{i-1} is computed from $P_{i-1} = K_{i-1} \oplus S_{i-1}$. Also, the set $\mathcal{S}_i$ inherits $t-1$ elements from set $\mathcal{S}_{i-1}$, that is, $\mathcal{S}_i \cap \mathcal{S}_{i-1} = \{S_{i+1}, \ldots, S_{i+t-1}\}$, and the element S_{i+t} will be randomly generated.

We can incorporate the key recovery method above in the re-keying system. The result will be a system with the ability to not only update the session keys, but also recover previous session keys that are lost, while maintaining all the security properties. To do so, GC multicasts a key recovery message $\mathcal{M}_{rec}$ in addition to a re-keying message $\mathcal{M}_{rkey}$. Suppose an update to the multicast group $\mathcal{M}_i$ is required.

Group Controller. GC does the following.

- Performs the re-keying algorithm and multicasts $\mathcal{M}_{rkey}$.
- Generates the set $\mathcal{S}_{i+1} = \{S_{i+2}, \ldots, S_{i+t+1}\}$ and computes the set $\mathcal{P}_{i+1} = \{P_i, \ldots, P_{i-t+1}\}$ where $\forall P_a \in \mathcal{P}_{i+1}, P_a = K_{s_a} \oplus S_a$. Then, GC multicasts a key recovery message $\mathcal{M}_{rec} = \{E_{K_{s_{i+1}}}(\mathcal{S}_{i+1} \cup \mathcal{P}_{i+1})\}$.

User. Each user $U \in \mathcal{M}_{i+1}$ does the following.

- Receives $\mathcal{M}_{rkey}$ and performs the re-keying algorithm to obtain $K_{s_{i+1}}$.
- Receives $\mathcal{M}_{rec}$ and decrypts $D_{K_{s_{i+1}}}(\mathcal{M}_{rec})$ to obtain the sets $\mathcal{S}_{i+1}$ and $\mathcal{P}_{i+1}$. User U may recover the previous session keys $K_{s_i}, \ldots, K_{s_{i-t+1}}$ by computing $K_{s_a} = P_a \oplus S_a$ where $P_a \in \mathcal{P}_b$ for $i-t+1 \le a \le i, a+1 \le b \le i+1$, and $S_a \in \mathcal{S}_b$ for $i-t+1 \le a \le i, a-t \le b \le a-1$. User U may retain $\mathcal{S}_{i+1}$ to be used in subsequent sessions.

Theorem 6. *Recovering t previous session keys requires (i) message length of $2t$ keys and (ii) a legitimate user to calculate t XOR operations.*

Theorem 7. *The key recovery scheme provides (i) forward secrecy, (ii) backward secrecy, or (iii) forward-backward secrecy in the sense of definition 4.*

Proof (sketch). (i) Observe that the colluding users in $Tot(\mathcal{R}_i)$ know the values $S_0, \ldots, S_{i+t}$ and $P_0, \ldots, P_{i-1}$. The collusion may recover $K_0, \ldots, K_{i-1}$, but not $K_i, \ldots, K_{i+t}$ since they do not know the values $P_i, \ldots, P_{i+t}$.
(ii) Without loss of generality, let the collusion be $Tot(\mathcal{J}_j) = \cup \mathcal{J}_a, \mathcal{J}_a \subseteq (\mathcal{U} \setminus \mathcal{M}_a)$, where $j \le a \le q$ for any $q > j$. Observe that users in $Tot(\mathcal{J}_j)$ know the values $S_{j+2}, \ldots, S_{q+t+1}$ and $P_{j+1-t}, \ldots, P_q$. The collusion may recover $K_{j+2}, \ldots, K_q$, but not $K_{j+1-t}, \ldots, K_{j+1}$ since they do not know the values $S_{j+1-t}, \ldots, S_{j+1}$.
(iii) Let $j = i + 2t$. Users in $Tot(\mathcal{R}_i)$ know the values $S_0, \ldots, S_{i+t}$ and $P_0, \ldots, P_{i-1}$. Users in $Tot(\mathcal{J}_j)$ know the values $S_{i+2t+2}, \ldots, S_{q+t+1}$ and $P_{i+1+t}, \ldots, P_q$ for any $q > j$. The collusion cannot recover $K_i, \ldots, K_{i+2t+1}$ which means cannot recover $K_i, \ldots, K_{j+1}$. Observe that if $j < i + 2t$, collusion of users in $Tot(\mathcal{R}_i) \cup Tot(\mathcal{J}_j)$ may recover some $K_{i+1}, \ldots, K_j$. $\square$

Since efficiency and recovery capability depends on t, in practice we must choose t considering the network rate of packet loss. t can be dynamically chosen to suit network condition.

6   Conclusions and Further Discussions

Observe that in the description above, we allowed one operation in a session: either user revocation or user join. To increase efficiency we may consider user revocation and join at the same time.

Suppose in session i, GC needs to revoke a set of users $\mathcal{R}_i$ and join a set of new users $\mathcal{J}_i$. To obtain the new session key $K_{s_{i+1}}$, first GC removes leaves of the revoked users and the redundant internal nodes, then adds the new internal nodes and the new leaves, and rearranges the levels of the affected nodes and keys to form T'. GC then performs the re-keying operation with $T = T'$ and $\mathcal{K}(\mathcal{S}) = \mathcal{K}(\mathcal{R}_i) \cup \mathcal{K}(\mathcal{J}_i)$. Users do the necessary adjustment to their nodes and keys, and perform re-keying operation to update (obtain) their keys including the session key $K_{s_{i+1}}$.

We considered the re-keying problem for dynamic group in multicast environments with unreliable communication. We proposed a re-keying scheme that can be used for multiple user join and revocation. We proved the security of the scheme and showed that compared to the trivial scheme, it has a better communication efficiency. The re-keying has also less computation compared to other known methods. We also considered the problem of reliability of re-keying when the packets can be lost and proposed a key recovery method that allows the keys for t previous sessions be calculated, hence providing robustness against loss of packets. We evaluated security and efficiency of the resulting method.

References

1. M. Abdalla, Y. Shavitt and A. Wool. Towards Making Broadcast Encryption Practical. *Financial Cryptography '99, Lecture Notes in Computer Science 1648*, pages 140-152, 1999.
2. J. Anzai, N. Matsuzaki and T. Matsumoto. A Quick Group Key Distribution Scheme with "Entity Revocation". *Advances in Cryptology – ASIACRYPT '99, Lecture Notes in Computer Science 1716*, pages 333-347, 1999.
3. C. Blundo and A. Cresti. Space Requirements for Broadcast Encryption. *Advances in Cryptology – EUROCRYPT '94, Lecture Notes in Computer Science 950*, pages 287-298, 1994.
4. C. Blundo, L. A. Frota Mattos and D. Stinson. Trade-offs Between Communication and Storage in Unconditionally Secure Systems for Broadcast Encryption and Interactive Key Distribution. *Advances in Cryptology – CRYPTO '96, Lecture Notes in Computer Science 1109*, pages 387-400, 1996.
5. J. W. Byers, M. Luby, M. Mitzenmacher and A. Rege. A Digital Fountain Approach to Reliable Distribution of Bulk Data. *Proceedings of the ACM SIGCOMM '98*, 1998.
6. R. Canetti, J. Garay, G. Itkis, D. Micciancio, M. Naor and B. Pinkas. Issues in Multicast Security: A Taxonomy and Efficient Constructions. *Proceedings of INFOCOM '99*, pages 708-716, 1999.
7. R. Canetti, T. Malkin and K. Nissim. Efficient Communication-Storage Tradeoffs for Multicast Encryption. *Advances in Cryptology – EUROCRYPT '99, Lecture Notes in Computer Science 1592*, pages 459-474, 1999.
8. I. Chang, R. Engel, D. Kandlur, D. Pendarakis and D. Saha. Key Management for Secure Internet Multicast Using Boolean Function Minimization Techniques. *Proceedings of INFOCOM '99*, pages 689-698, 1999.
9. A. Fiat and M. Naor. Broadcast Encryption. *Advances in Cryptology – CRYPTO '93, Lecture Notes in Computer Science 773*, pages 480-491, 1994.
10. FIPS 180-1. Secure Hash Standard. *NIST, US Department of Commerce, Washington D.C.*, April 1995.
11. R. Kumar, S. Rajagopalan and A. Sahai. Coding Constructions for Blacklisting Problems Without Computational Assumptions. *Advances in Cryptology – CRYPTO '99, Lecture Notes in Computer Science 1666*, pages 609-623, 1999.
12. H. Kurnio, R. Safavi-Naini and H. Wang. Efficient Revocation Schemes for Secure Multicast. *Information Security and Cryptology – ICISC 2001, Lecture Notes in Computer Science 2288*, pages 160-177, 2002.
13. M. Luby and J. Staddon. Combinatorial Bounds for Broadcast Encryption. *Advances in Cryptology – EUROCRYPT '98, Lecture Notes in Computer Science 1403*, pages 512-526, 1998.
14. D. A. McGrew and A. T. Sherman. Key Establishment in Large Dynamic Groups Using One-Way Function Trees. *Manuscript*, 1998.
15. D. Naor, M. Naor and J. Lotspiech. Revocation and Tracing Schemes for Stateless Receivers. *Advances in Cryptology – CRYPTO 2001, Lecture Notes in Computer Science 2139*, pages 41-62, 2001.
16. M. Naor and B. Pinkas. Efficient Trace and Revoke Schemes. *Financial Cryptography 2000, Lecture Notes in Computer Science 1962*, pages 1-20, 2001.
17. A. Perrig, D. Song and J. D. Tygar. ELK, a New Protocol for Efficient Large-Group Key Distribution. *IEEE Symposium on Security and Privacy 2001*, pages 247-262, 2001.

18. M. O. Rabin. The Information Dispersal Algorithm and Its Applications. *Sequences: Combinatorics, Compression, Security and Transmission*, pages 406-419, 1990.

19. R. Rivest. The MD5 Message Digest Algorithm. *RFC 1321*, April 1992.

20. R. Safavi-Naini and H. Wang. New Constructions for Multicast Re-keying Schemes Using Perfect Hash Families. *7th ACM Conference on Computer and Communication Security*, ACM Press, pages 228-234, 2000.

21. A. Shamir. How to Share a Secret. *Communications of the ACM* **22**, pages 612-613, 1979.

22. D. R. Stinson and T. van Trung. Some New Results on Key Distribution Patterns and Broadcast Encryption. *Designs, Codes and Cryptography* **15**, pages 261-279, 1998.

23. D. M. Wallner, E. J. Harder and R. C. Agee. Key Management for Multicast: Issues and Architectures. *Internet Draft (draft-wallner-key-arch-01.txt), ftp://ftp.ietf.org/internet-drafts/draft-wallner-key-arch-01.txt*.

24. C. K. Wong, M. Gouda and S. S. Lam. Secure Group Communication Using Key Graphs. *Proceedings of SIGCOMM '98*, pages 68-79, 1998.

25. C. K. Wong and S. S. Lam. Keystone: A Group Key Management Service. *International Conference on Telecommunications, ICT 2000*, 2000.

26. Y. Zheng, J. Pieprzyk and J. Seberry. HAVAL - A One-Way Hashing Algorithm with Variable Length of Output. *Advances in Cryptology – AUSCRYPT '92, Lecture Notes in Computer Science 718*, pages 83-104, 1993.

Modelling Trust Structures for Public Key Infrastructures[*]

Marie Henderson[1], Robert Coulter[2][**], Ed Dawson[1], and Eiji Okamoto[3]

[1] Information Security Research Centre, Queensland University of Technology
marie@serc.rmit.edu.au, e.dawson@qut.edu.au
[2] School of Computing and Mathematics, Deakin University
shrub@deakin.edu.au
[3] Institute of Information Sciences and Electronics, University of Tsukuba
okamoto@is.tsukuba.ac.jp

Abstract. The development of Public Key Infrastructures (PKIs) is highly desirable to support secure digital transactions and communications throughout existing networks. It is important to adopt a particular trust structure or PKI model at an early stage as this forms a basis for the PKI's development. Many PKI models have been proposed but use only natural language descriptions. We apply a simple formal approach to describe the essential factors of a PKI model. Rule sets for some PKI models are given and can be used to distinguish and classify the different PKI models. Advantages for this approach with conglomerate PKIs, those that are built from multiple distinct PKI models, are discussed.

1 Introduction

Public key cryptography has now matured to the point of being widely used in real world applications. The security services supported by public key cryptography include authentication, confidentiality, integrity and non-repudiation. Combining public key cryptography with other cryptographic mechanisms (such as symmetric cryptography) provides the most practical and efficient cryptographic solution for securing modern communications. This is the reason organisations are now applying public key cryptography.

With public key cryptography each entity has a public key, which is available to all entities, and a private key, which is protected from disclosure and whose use is limited to the owner. With symmetric cryptography the difficulty is to transport the keys while preserving confidentiality. With public key cryptography confidentiality is not required for the public key but rather a guarantee of authenticity (to protect against masquerade attacks etc.). Trusted authorities called Certification Authorities (CAs) provide such guarantees by issuing

[*] Research sponsored by the Telecommunications Advanced Organisation (TAO) of Japan.
[**] This author was funded by a QUT postdoctoral research fellowship.

L. Batten and J. Seberry (Eds.): ACISP 2002, LNCS 2384, pp. 56–70, 2002.
© Springer-Verlag Berlin Heidelberg 2002

certificates which link the public key to other data in the certificate. The certificate data may be identity information (as with the X.509 standard [9]) or authorisations (as with SPKI [4]), and other information. An entity may prove their association with the public key of a certificate by using their private key to digitally sign a random challenge or other communication.

The term Public Key Infrastructure (PKI) is used to cover the management and distribution of public keys and associated data. A simple public key exchange could consist of two entities, Alice and Bob, who meet and exchange public key values. In a global setting, such as the Internet, it is impossible for all parties to exchange public keys in this way, motivating the use of intermediary CAs. In this case it will be necessary to use multiple CAs to service the large community of users. The structuring of the relationships between these CAs becomes an important issue for constructing a PKI. Basically, the CA structuring reflects how the CAs issue certificates. A number of generic structuring models have been proposed, some of which we will discuss. We will refer to these structuring models as *PKI models*. The term trust models is also used as the PKI model describes how trust is referenced within the PKI. In a PKI a *trust anchor* is any CA (or rather their certificate or public key) which is trusted without the trust being referenced through the PKI certificates. An example is in a hierarchy PKI model where the top most CA, sometimes called the *root CA*, is the trust anchor for the PKI. The public keys of trust anchors must be obtained out-of-band. Further references and background information on PKI and the related cryptographic security services can be found in [8].

In this article we give formal descriptions for PKI models, focusing on those that look to achieve broad coverage (i.e. they service a large user community or cross national or organisational boundaries). In [13] and [6] informal descriptions for some PKI models are given. However, the main focus of [6] is to outline weaknesses of existing PKI solutions and provide some currently feasible remedies. In this article we focus on the PKI models and so exclude such areas from consideration (the interested reader can refer to [6]). In Section 2 we provide a brief overview of some existing PKI models. We also include a PKI model from [13] as this incorporates an approach distinct from PKI models considered elsewhere. In Section 3 we give a formal description of PKI models from Section 2. We explain how this improves upon the natural language description and also discuss the new PKI models of [13]. In Section 4 we consider issues facing the development of a global PKI, the most challenging setting for establishing a PKI. We give a useful mechanism for joining multiple PKIs which is motivated by our analysis of PKI models in Section 3. Concluding remarks are made in Section 5.

2   Existing PKI Models

The consideration of PKI models has often been confused with certificate standards. For example, many regard the X.509 standard as being synonymous with a hierarchical PKI model. However this is not the case. In fact this scenario was deliberately avoided by the authors of X.509 as it would severely restrict the flexibility of the standard to adapt to different requirements. The choice of PKI model is largely independent of the certificate structure, although it may place certain requirements for additional information to be carried by the certificate. Past and present attempts to develop workable (broad coverage) PKI models include, but are not limited too, the following PKI models. Our choice is motivated by the fact that this collection of PKI models represents a useful sample set for our development in Section 3 and discussion in Section 4.

Pretty Good Privacy (PGP)

PGP [14] is an unregulated PKI where each entity controls which public keys they trust. It is used by individuals to encrypt and digitally sign electronic mail messages and files. We shall refer to PGP-like PKI models as *mesh* models (mesh models are also known as webs of trust or the user centric trust model). Figure 1 depicts a mesh model with five entities.

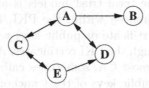

Fig. 1. A five entity incomplete mesh model

PGP is anarchic by design. This means that even though PGP may be used widely, it does not scale well or lend itself to large deployments.

Privacy Enhanced Mail (PEM)

PEM was developed by the Internet Engineering Task Force (IETF) to secure Internet email. The PKI model adopted consisted of a (global) *hierarchy* model with a single trust anchor (the Internet Policy Registration Authority), a lower layer of policy CAs, and lower level CAs. Figure 2 depicts a simple hierarchy with a total of four levels.

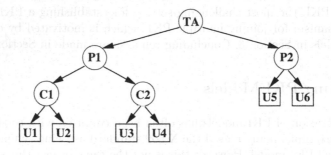

Fig. 2. A hierarchy model

Of the four associated documents, Part II specifies the supporting PKI model [10]. The certificate structure adopted was the X.509 version 1 certificate format. Each policy CA published and registered with the trust anchor a policy statement covering all lower certificates. All PEM CAs adhered to name subordination rules based on the X.500 naming scheme. For a variety of reasons, PEM was never widely adopted and has been replaced by the IETF with PKIX [7] which does not mandate a PKI model.

ICE-TEL Project

The now finished ICE-TEL project employed a PKI model where hierarchies were joined using X.509 cross certificates between the trust anchors[1] merged with PGP (as individual users control their own set of trusted public keys [2]). We shall refer to such PKI models as a *web of hierarchies* model. Each user keeps a set of trusted public keys of users and certificates of trust anchors. The hierarchies operate using X.509 version 3 certificates and each separate hierarchy is referred to as a *security domain*. The trust anchors can construct cross certificates between the hierarchies and X.509 extensions are used in the usual way to control the trust relationship extension into other security domains. Users may also place limits on the number of cross certificates they will accept in a certificate path. Security domains of higher trust may reside within the structure of a lower security domain but not conversely. The ICE-TEL PKI covered a number of European countries but was primarily focused on servicing the academic and research community. Note that the utilisation of the university based academic and research community follows the early evolution of the Internet. Figure 3 depicts a simple mesh of three hierarchies (with trust anchors T1, T2 and T3) one of which is a sub-hierarchy of another (T2 is below C2) and a single external user, X, trusted by U6.

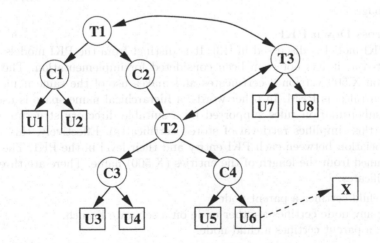

Fig. 3. An example ICE-TEL model

---

[1] the ICE-TEL project used the term trust points instead of trust anchors

Bridge CA

A Bridge CA (BCA) acts as a hub CA for a number of different PKIs. Each PKI joins to the BCA through their own Principal CA (PCA). The PCA may coincide with PKI trust anchors (for example, in a hierarchy the PCA is normally the trust anchor). Figure 4 depicts five PCAs joined through a BCA. The PCAs would be in turn joined to their respective PKIs.

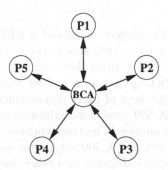

Fig. 4. A Bridge CA model joining five PKIs

Using BCAs (in place of bilateral arrangements between separate PKIs) can decrease the total number of cross certificates required to join the PKIs. The BCA does not become a trust anchor for any of the PKIs as it is not directly trusted by any of the PKI entities. Rather trust is referenced from internal PKI trust anchors. The United States federal PKI (FPKI) project is attempting to join together multiple PKIs set up under separate federal agency programs using bridge CAs. See [8, Chapter 16] for further information or the steering committee home page [5].

Up-Cross-Down PKI

This PKI model is discussed in [13]. It is distinct from the PKI models already presented as it has not even been considered for implementation. The PKI is based on X.509 version 3 certificates and makes use of the same name subordination rules as PEM. In other words, a hierarchical name space is used with name subordination rules supported by a suitable directory structure such as X.500 (this simplifies retrieval of stored certificates). Effectively, this imposes an association between each PKI entity and their level in the PKI. The level is determined from the length of the entities (X.500) name. There are three types of certificates:

Up: a child certifies a parent node.
Cross: any node certifies another node on a separate branch.
Down: a parent certifies a child node.

In the basic system any user will progress up through the name space until a least common ancestor or cross certificate to an ancestor of the target name is found. The certificate path contains either:

- the certificates up to the least common ancestor and the certificates down to the required certificate, or
- the certificates up to the cross certificate, the cross certificate, and then those down to the required certificate.

The name subordination rules disallow lower level entities from creating certificates for higher level entities unless for the unique entity that has created a certificate for them. Cross certificates at the same level are allowed. Figure 5 depicts a simple up-cross-down model with three levels.

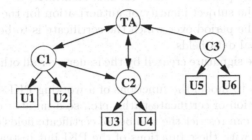

Fig. 5. An up-cross-down model with three levels

3   A Formalisation of PKI Models

Natural language is very flexible and expressive but lacks precision. Unambiguous descriptions are supported through the use of formal languages. The use of formal methods to support the clear specification of PKI processes has been used in [11,12,3]. In this section we shall take a formal approach to precisely describe some of the basic PKI models that have been proposed (specifically, we consider the PKI models presented in the previous section). This is not intended to replace the existing natural language descriptions but to help clarify the distinguishing features. This approach has limitations. For example, the scope of coverage for certificate contents must be restricted to enable a concise description. However, such limitations still affect natural language descriptions (descriptions of PKI models normally only include the certificate contents required for the description). Overall, our descriptions are comparable and improve clarity and analysis methods. We shall take the following approach:

> A PKI model consists of a set of certificates which adhere to a given set of rules. It is not just the certificates that distinguish the PKI model but also the rules that govern the construction of certificate paths or, equivalently, the issuance of certificates.

Indeed, it is possible to derive from a given set of certificates different PKI models as the certificates do not supply all information about how the PKI is structured: this must come also from rules describing acceptable certificate paths.

The most detailed definition of a certificate (and the best known) is given in the ITU-T X.509 standard [9]. X.509 gives an extensive description of a certificate's contents and processing rules. In [12] formal methods are applied to analyse these processing rules for the IETF PKIX standard [7]. In this article we do not require as detailed an examination of the contents of a certificate, rather we use a high level description of some generic certificate data fields, similar to that given in [11]:

- **issuer**: the issuer identity.
- **public key**: the public key value for this identifier.
- **identifier**: the subject identity or authorisation for the public key.
- **use-period**: the period over which the certificate is to be used.
- **data**: additional data fields.
- **signature**: the signature created by the issuer over all other certificate data.

In [11] the focus is to model the functions of a working PKI such as issuance of certificates, validation of certificate paths, etc., so a number of certificate fields were required. We can restrict the number of certificate fields even further as we are not concerned with these functions of the PKI but instead with static PKI models or structuring rules. Nonetheless, it is useful to have this basic description of the certificate data fields. The relationship between our approach and that of [11] is discussed again at the end of this section.

We begin our development with some high level definitions for fundamental sets (or types):

- **ENT**: represents the set of PKI entities (these are PKI members that are either people, machines or processes, etc.),
- **ID**: the set of all PKI identifiers (e.g. for authorisations or to simply denote a public key),
- **DATA**: the set of all additional certificate data, and
- **CERT**: the set of all PKI certificates.

We assume that a certificate is the tuple (x, y, z) where $x \in$ ENT, $y \in$ ENT $\cup$ ID, and $z \in$ DATA. The set ENT$\cap$ID is assumed to be empty. This allows certificates to exist in the PKI that connect public keys to identities *or authorisations*. We use the set DATA to cover all additional certificate data not relevant to the immediate discussion (such as public key value, period of certificate use, policies, signature etc.). Then, as in [12], the certificate contents can be later extended, as desired. This gives the scope to cover further PKI operations or processing if desired. Simply, we have

$$\text{CERT} \subseteq \text{ENT} \times (\text{ENT} \cup \text{ID}) \times \text{DATA}. \tag{1}$$

As in [11], we use the following functions to obtain the component values from a certificate $C \in$ CERT given by $C = (x, y, z)$:

$$I(C) = x, \; S(C) = y, \text{ and } D(C) = z.$$

Loosely, these functions may be interpreted to return the *issuer* of the certificate, $I(C)$, the *subject* of the certificate, $S(C)$, and the remaining *data* of the certificate, $D(C)$, respectively. From a set of PKI certificates the set of all certificate paths can be constructed. Let seq CERT be the set of all sequences of certificates from CERT. For example, if CERT $= \{(a, b, c), (x, y, z)\}$ then

$$\text{seq CERT} = \{\langle\rangle, \langle(a, b, c)\rangle, \langle(x, y, z)\rangle, \langle(a, b, c), (x, y, z)\rangle, \langle(x, y, z), (a, b, c)\rangle\}$$

where $\langle\rangle$ is the empty sequence and $\langle C_1, \dots, C_n \rangle = \{(1, C_1), \dots, (n, C_n)\}$. We shall also use the sequence join function:

$$\langle X_1, \dots, X_m \rangle ^\frown \langle Y_1, \dots, Y_n \rangle = \langle X_1, \dots, X_m, Y_1, \dots, Y_n \rangle.$$

Let $\#(A)$ denote the number of elements in the set A. Next we construct the set of all certificate paths, CERT_PATH, of a PKI from the set seq CERT:

$$\text{CERT\_PATH} = \{(1, cert) \mid cert \in \text{CERT}\} \cup$$
$$\{s \in \text{seq CERT} \mid \#(s) \geq 2 \wedge S(s(i)) = I(s(i+1)), 1 \leq i \leq \#(s) - 1\}$$

Thus the set CERT_PATH contains all single certificate sequences and all longer sequences of certificates from CERT for which the issuer of each certificate in the sequence is the same as the subject of the previous certificate. There are, of course, equivalent definitions. We call $p \in$ CERT_PATH a *loop* of certificates if $S(p(\#(p))) = I(p(1))$, i.e. if the subject of the last certificate is also the issuer of the first certificate. Note that for a loop of certificates $\langle C_1, C_2, \dots, C_k \rangle \in$ CERT_PATH, there will be k certificates paths in CERT_PATH given by $\langle C_i, C_{i+1}, \dots, C_{i+k} \rangle$ for $i = 1, \dots, k$ that are also loops.

Let $\mathbb{P}(X)$ represent the power set of a set X (i.e. the set containing all subsets of X). We shall use the functions *ancestor* : ENT $\to \mathbb{P}(\text{ENT})$ given by:

$$ancestor(x) = \{y \in \text{ENT} \mid \exists\, cert \in \text{CERT} \bullet S(cert) = x \wedge I(cert) = y\}$$

and *des_set* : ENT $\to \mathbb{P}(\text{ENT} \cup \text{ID})$ given by:

$$des\_set(x) = \{z \in \text{ENT} \cup \text{ID} \mid \exists\, path \in \text{CERT\_PATH}, (i, k \in \{1, \dots, \#(path)) \bullet$$
$$I(path(i)) = x \wedge S(path(k)) = z \wedge k \geq i\}$$

The first function, *ancestor*, returns the set of entities who have issued a certificate to the given entity, $x \in$ ENT. The second function, *des_set*, returns the set of all entities or identifiers that the given entity's, $x \in$ ENT, certificate's have been used to certify in any certificate path. Note that the second function will only count once any descendants originating from certificate loops.

Further set definitions that we shall use in our descriptions are as follows:

- CA a subset of ENT of special authorities, known as Certification Authorities (CAs), who manage certificates.
- TA a subset of CA, known as Trust Anchors.
- BCA a element of CA known as a Bridge CA.
- PCA a special subset of CA known as Principal CAs.

We are now ready to begin our description of the PKI models given in Section 2. We note that the rules listed do not form a unique set of rules for each model, i.e. many equivalent rule sets can be given.

A: The Mesh Model (PGP)

The mesh model follows PGP as it is unregulated (see Section 2) but allows the incorporation of CAs (PGP has also moved towards utilising CAs in later versions). The mesh provides a limiting case for our analysis, in one sense, as there are no rules applied to the construction of certificate paths, i.e. all certificate paths are acceptable.

B: The Hierarchical Model (PEM)

We consider a hierarchical model with a single trust anchor, as proposed with the PEM project.

B1: $\forall\, cert \in$ CERT $\bullet\; I(cert) \in$ CA

B2: $\#(\text{TA}) = 1$

B3: $\forall\, p \in$ CERT_PATH $\bullet\; I(p(1)) \in$ TA

B4: $\forall cert \in$ CERT $\bullet\; \#(ancestor(S(cert))) = 1$

Rule B1 states that all certificates are issued by CAs. Rule B2 states that there is a single trust anchor. Rule B3 states that all certificate paths begin with a certificate issued by the trust anchor. Rule B4 ensures that for each certificate subject there is a unique issuer (we have assumed that trust anchors have issued self signed certificates - a common PKI practice). Again, the hierarchy is another limiting case in the sense that each entity has only a single certification path. In this regard, the hierarchy is the most regulated PKI model.

C: The Web of Hierarchies Model (ICE-TEL)

The hierarchical model can be extended to cover a collection of cross certifying trust anchors and individual users building limited PGP-like relationships as implemented with the ICE-TEL project. Basically the trust anchors are not limited in regards to the certificate paths constructed between them, i.e. the certificate paths between trust anchors are constructed along the lines of the mesh model. The rules of the hierarchy model shall be enforced for descendants of a trust anchor whom are not themselves trust anchors[2] unless they are single

---

[2] In the terminology of [2] trust anchors define separate *security domains* so that each security domain employs a hierarchical PKI model. However, as each security domain is controlled by a single trust anchor, there is a one-to-one correspondence between these sets. In this case there is no need for us to make a distinction.

end user public keys trusted by individual users. To keep things simple we shall use the certificate structure to model this exchange of public keys. The issuer of such certificates shall be the entity who has chosen to trust them and they shall use as the subject of the certificate the special identifier pub_key $\in$ ID. User limits on the number of acceptable cross certificates in a certificate path does not affect the set of constructible certificate paths (except from their perspective). Therefore this does not affect the PKI model so we do not consider it further. These requirements are reflected in the following rules:

C1: $\forall\, cert \in$ CERT $\bullet$ $(I(cert) \in$ CA$) \vee (I(cert) \notin$ CA $\wedge S(cert) =$ pub_key$)$

C2: TA $\neq \emptyset$

C3: $\forall\, p \in$ CERT_PATH $\bullet$ $I(p(1)) \in$ TA $\vee (I(p(1)) \notin$ CA $\wedge \#(p) = 1)$

C4: $\forall\, cert \in$ CERT $\bullet$ $S(cert) \notin$ TA $\Rightarrow \#(ancestor(cert)) = 1$

The first rule, C1, states that only CAs issue certificates with the exception of certificates identifying public keys and in this case such certificates are not issued by CAs. Rule C2 ensures that the set of trust anchors, TA, is non-empty (distinguishing this model from the mesh model). Rule C3 states that all certificate paths begin with a certificate issued by a trust anchor or are a single certificate path. Rule C4 guarantees that for each subject of a certificate, who is not a trust anchor, there is a unique issuer. These rules can be modified to exclude public keys. However, we have included this aspect to completely describe the ICE-TEL model as given in [2].

D: The Bridge CA Model (FPKI)

The Bridge CA model is not a stand alone PKI model but, as described in Section 2, is used to join a number of other PKIs using a single BCA and PCAs for each of the joined PKIs. Therefore, no restrictions are placed on the joined PKIs in regards to the models they employ, except that they have a single PCA. We need to define a set of PKIs $\{$PKI$_1, \ldots ,$PKI$_k\}$ which are joined via the BCA. For PKI$_i$, $1 \leq i \leq k$, the full set of certificate paths are given by CERT_PATH$_i$, the set of acceptable certificate paths is given by ACC_PATH$_i$ (i.e. those that satisfy the rules for the PKI$_i$ model), the set of entities is given by ENT$_i$, the set of trust anchors is given by TA$_i$, and the PCAs are given by PCA$_i$. Also, $data_{iBCA}$ represents the additional data in the certificate issued by PCA$_i$ to BCA whereas $data_{BCAi}$ represents the additional data in the certificate issued by BCA to PCA$_i$. The certificate paths of the entire PKI are described by the following rules:

D1: BCA $\notin \bigcup_{i=1}^{k}$ ENT$_i$

D2: ENT $= \{$BCA$\} \bigcup (\cup_{i=1}^{k}ENT_i)$

D3: $\forall i \in \{1, \ldots , k\} \bullet$ PCA$_i \in$ CA$_i$

D4: ACC_PATH $= \left(\bigcup_{i=0}^{k}$ ACC_PATH$_i \right)$

$\bigcup_{\substack{i,j=0 \\ i \neq j}}^{k} \Big(\{p_i \in$ ACC_PATH$_i | S(p_i(\#(p_i))) =$ PCA$_i\}$

$^\frown \{(\#(p_i) + 1, PCA_i,$ BCA$, data_{iBCA}), (\#(p_i) + 2, BCA, PCA_j, data_{BCAj})\}$

$^\frown \{p_j \in$ CERT_PATH$_j | I(p_j(1)) =$ PCA$_j\}\Big)$

The first rule states that the BCA is not an entity in any of the joined PKIs (so trivially can not be a trust anchor for any PKI). Rule D2 determines the entity set. Rule D3 ensures that the PCA for each PKI is a CA of the PKI. The rule D4 gives all certificate paths: those from the joined PKIs and the new certificate paths which pass through the BCA from a PCA of one PKI to the PCA of another PKI.

E: The Up-Cross-Down Model
The only restriction placed on certificate paths by this PKI model is that of the name subordination rules from the X.500 naming scheme, see [8]. We may represent this by assigning a level to each CA in CA and requiring that a lower level CA can only issue a single certificate to a higher level CA. Let $level : CA \rightarrow \{1, \dots, n\}$ be the function mapping each CA of the PKI to their level within the PKI (that is to say their depth in the name subordination hierarchy). Here n is the maximum length of any CA name. It is not clearly stated in [13] that only certificates issued by CAs are acceptable. However, we shall assume that this is the case here.

E1: $\forall\, cert \in \text{CERT} \bullet (level(I(cert)) - level(S(cert))) \in \{0, \pm 1\}$

E2: $\forall x \in \text{ENT} \bullet \#\{cert \in \text{CERT}|S(cert) = x \wedge level(I(cert)) > level(x)\} = 1$

E3: $\forall x \in \text{ENT} \bullet (\exists\, c_1 \in \text{CERT} \bullet I(c_1) = x \wedge level(S(c_1)) > level(x)) \Rightarrow$
$(\exists\, c_2 \in \text{CERT} \bullet I(c_2) = S(c_1) \wedge S(c_2) = I(c_1))$

E4: $\forall\, cert \in \text{CERT} \bullet (I(cert) \wedge S(cert)) \notin \text{ENT}$

The first rule, E1, states that for any certificate the maximum distance between the level of the issuer and the level of the subject is one. Rule E2 ensures that for any entity there is exactly one certificate issued from a higher level with that entity as the subject. The rule E3 states that for any entity there is at most one certificate with a subject from a higher level which has been issued by this entity, and that subject is the unique issuer from E2. Finally E4 ensures that entities whom are not CAs can not issue certificates to each other. These rules are implied by the name subordination rules.

Discussion
The first two PKI models are simple to describe and are generally well understood. However, our descriptions make their distinctions clear: the mesh model has no rules restricting the creation of certificate paths while the hierarchical model has the most restrictive set of certification path rules. The models following these are more difficult to describe. For example, it is not a simple matter to determine the essential features of the ICE-TEL model from [2] and [13] does not clearly outline all of the up-cross-down model features. This is not a specific criticism of these articles but a general criticism of the natural language description method for PKI models. Our method provides an unambiguous description, requiring only minimal additional technical knowledge of the reader to understand the language used. As the audience must already be exposed to the general (technical) PKI area we do not think that this is an unrealistic expectation.

In [13], another PKI model is presented, called the flexible-bottom-up PKI. This is the advocated PKI model from [13] and is developed from the up-cross-down PKI model. It employs the name constraints extension from X.509 within the up-cross-down model framework to add flexibility by circumventing the tight name subordination rules. Effectively, the rules E1, E2 and E3 would no longer apply and we are left with the mesh model[3]. When restrictive name constraints are imposed as in [13], it is similar to "pruning" in the mesh model and eventually the up-cross-down model is obtained. Finally, we note that both the up-cross-down and flexible-bottom-up models seem to necessarily impose that a single certificate policy is enforced throughout the entire PKI, especially if policy constraints are applied. The situation in regards to other X.509 extensions needs to be clarified given that the name constraints extension is being used.

As mentioned above, a formal description for the hierarchy model is already given in [11]. However, the focus of [11] is more on the operations of the PKI (for example, joining new members, revocation, etc.). In [11] the hierarchy rules enforced certain restrictions on the operations. Our results can be used to extend to other PKI models: we take a static view of the acceptable PKI certificate paths and define the PKI by the rules that are applied but this can be used to state that at all times the structuring rules of PKI must hold no matter how the certificate sets are varied (and thus extend the scope of [11]).

We explain further: to determine a legitimate certificate path there are two processes to be performed, path discovery and path processing. The path discovery algorithm returns all the possible paths, perhaps subject to some limits set by the certificate requester. The path processing algorithm determines that validity of each given path in regards to signature validation, policies, path restrictions imposed by CAs, etc. The models given here do not cover these operations of a PKI but rather the structuring rules. They can be used to determine whether a given alteration (addition of a new certificate or deletion of a certificate from the PKI) is acceptable. Also, if certificates carry PKI model identifiers then this would enable the optimal path discovery algorithm to be used. This gives the optimal solution to the path discovery problem. This is particularly advantageous when a single PKI is made up of a number of distinct PKI models all joined together as in the Bridge CA model.

4   Prospectives for a Global PKI

The example PKI models we introduced in Section 2 were selected as they provide a good sample set for our development in Section 3. However, they are all intended to be broad coverage PKIs or, in other words, service large user communities. In this section we consider implications for the development of a global PKI, based on previous experience. We propose adoption of a classification system for PKI models, based on formal descriptions (or rule sets). Firstly,

---

[3] It is noted in [13] the flexible-bottom-up model is, in the limiting case, no different from the mesh model.

we consider the past attempts to develop a PKI model suitable for the global situation, focusing on those models from Section 2.

Existing Experience

Attempts to construct a global PKI have so far not progressed to an actual realisation of a workable global PKI. Many problems have been identified, which are usually operational (i.e. certificate management etc.). For example, operational issues have convinced the PKI community that the mesh model is not an acceptable basis for a global PKI while the hierarchy model has problems with placing significant control and dependence on a single root CA. The ICE-TEL project met with some success (at least compared to previous projects) but was limited to a community of users comfortable with electronic communications technology and collaborations spanning institutional and national boundaries. An important aspect was the acceptance that users can control the public keys they trust (another capability existing in this community). The FPKI project seems to have been developed as the pragmatic solution to join together a wide number of U.S. federal agencies with existing commitments to pilot PKI projects. It is now being offered as a PKI solution for e-commerce security. This is important as the global PKI is itself likely to be built from the ground up in an unplanned (and unstructured) way (much like the development of the internet). The PKI models from [13] do not seem that distant from the mesh model when viewed in regards to the rules imposed on certificate path construction. However, they may be a possible next step from the bridge CA model to join a number of BCAs in a more manageable way then using a mesh model.

Desired Characteristics

At the highest level, we believe the wish list of characteristics for a global PKI would include the following:

1. the PKI should be connected,
2. the PKI should support multiple trust requirements,
3. the PKI should be flexible, to incorporate different user community needs.

Although a user will not have the need to securely communicate, with all other users it is not possible *a priori* to determine the subset of users they will ever communicate with motivating the first selection. The reasons for choosing two and three are similar to each other (flexibility) but as the implementation mechanics may be different, we differentiate between them. It is becoming widely accepted that trust identifiers should form part of a certificate (indicating the strength of management procedures employed). International codification of trust levels would make such certificates useful to a broader number of applications.

Future Perspectives

As PKI implementers have already experienced, development of technology outpaces the development of policy so the pragmatic solution will succeed (this seems to be the case with the FPKI). In this case it is unlikely that a connected PKI will ever be achieved. The best solution seems to incorporate a Bridge CA model with the ICE-TEL acknowledgement that users can decide to accept certificates (or public keys). This gives a flexible solution where trust can be managed by end users. In this case the Global Internet Trust Register [1] provides an important end user service. The Bridge CA model allows joined PKIs to select their own internal PKI model. As the global PKI develops it may be necessary to further expand the BCA into a structured mesh model, along the lines of the up-cross-down or flexible-bottom-up models. These add flexibility while maintaining some structure.

In this case the global PKI will be a complex interconnection of multiple PKIs employing distinct PKI models to match their business needs. We refer to such PKIs as *conglomerate* PKIs. Given this view of the global PKI future, it is useful to place identifiers in certificates which state the PKI model that is used for the descendants of a given certificate. This would allow further refinement of the set of acceptable certificate paths. Suppose MODEL_m, $m \in \{1, \ldots, n\}$, is the PKI model identifier used for PKI_i for $i \in \{1, \ldots, k\}$.

D6 $\forall cert \in \text{CERT} \bullet I(cert) \in des\_set(\text{PCA}_i) \Rightarrow \text{MODEL}_m$

The PKI model identifier can map to the set of rules (from Section 3 or rule sets developed elsewhere) which describe the acceptable certificate paths. The PKI model identifier would also allow the selection of the most efficient certificate path discovery algorithm in a straight forward way leading to an optimal path discovery algorithm.

5   Conclusions

We have used a very simple, general description to accommodate the different PKI models based on the restrictions placed on acceptable certificate paths (concerned with structuring). Our description does not rely on natural language alone but is supported by the use of formal language. The methods employed are easily accessible to a general audience with some technical skill but no more than would be expected in the general PKI area. In this way, ambiguities or omissions in the descriptions are avoided and clarity achieved. Using this basis, we have considered several existing PKIs. Our PKI model development has led to the idea of using PKI model identifiers in certificates when joining multiple PKIs employing different PKI models into a conglomerate PKI. This provides a way to achieve optimal path discovery algorithms across conglomerate PKIs. Combining our work with the results of [11] gives further benefits of extending results for PKI operations to the models described here. Finally, we motivate our direction for stricter definitions (and classification) of PKI models by arguing that the conglomerate PKI structure is most likely for the global situation.

References

1. R. Anderson, B. Crispo, J. Lee, C. Manifavas, V. Matyas, F. Petitcolas, *The Global Internet Trust Register*, MIT Press, 1999.

2. D. W. Chadwick, A. J. Young, and N. K. Cicovic, *Merging and extending the PGP and PEM trust models: the ICE-TEL trust model*, IEEE Network, **11(3)**, 16–24, 1997.
3. Defense Information Systems Agency, *State Analysis of Certification Path Processing Procedures*, June 2000.
   http://www-pki.itsi.disa.mil/certpathproc.htm
4. C. Ellison, B. Frantz, B. Lampson, R. Rivest, B. Thomas, and T. Ylonen, *SPKI Certificate Theory*, Request for Comment 2693, September 1999.
   ftp://ftp.isi.edu/in-notes/rfc2693.txt
5. Federal Public Key Infrastructure Steering Committee
   http://www.cio.gov/fpkisc/
6. M. Henderson, M. Burmester, E. Dawson, and E. Okamoto, *Weaknesses in Public Key Infrastructures*, Proceedings of the First Workshop on Information Security Applications (WISA 2000), November 2000, 53–66.
7. R. Housley, W. Ford, T. Polk, and D. Solo, *Internet X.509 Public Key Infrastructure Certificate and CRL Profile* Request for Comment 2459, 1999.
   http://www.ietf.org/html.charters/pkix-charter.html.
8. R. Housley and T. Polk, *Planning for PKI: Best Practices Guide for Deploying Public Key Infrastructure*, John Wiley and Sons, 2001.
9. ITU-T Recommendation X.509, *Information Technology - Open Systems Interconnection - The Directory: Authentication Framework*, June 1997 (equivalent to ISO/IEC 9594-8, 1997).
   http://www.imc.org/ietf-pkix/mail-archive/msg04337.html)
10. S. Kent, *Privacy Enhancement for Internet Electronic Mail, Part II: Certificate-Based Key Management*, Request for Comment 1422, February 1993.
    http://www.ietf.org/rfc/rfc1422.txt?number=1422
11. C. Liu, M. Ozols, M. Henderson, and T. Cant, *A State-Based Model for Certificate Management Systems*, Public Key Cryptography: Third International Workshop on Practice and Theory in Public Key Cryptography (PKC 2000), Lecture Notes in Computer Science, **1751**, 2000, 75–92.
12. M. Ozols, M. Henderson, C. Liu, and T. Cant, *The PKI Specification Dilemma: A Formal Solution*, Proceedings of the 5th Australasian Conference on Information Security and Privacy (ACISP 2000), Lecture Notes in Computer Science, **1841**, 2000, 206–219.
13. R. Perlman, *An Overview of PKI Trust Models*, IEEE Network, **13(6)**, 38–43, 1999.
14. P. R. Zimmermann, *The Official PGP User's Guide*, MIT Press, Cambridge, Massachussets, 1995.

Size of Broadcast in Threshold Schemes with Disenrollment

S.G. Barwick[1], W.-A. Jackson[1], Keith M. Martin[2], and Peter R. Wild[2]

[1] Department of Pure Mathematics, University of Adelaide, Adelaide 5005, Australia.
[2] Information Security Group, Royal Holloway, University of London, Egham, Surrey
TW20 0EX, U.K.

Abstract. Threshold schemes are well-studied cryptographic primitives
for distributing information among a number of entities in such a way
that the information can only be recovered if a threshold of entities co-
operate. Establishment of a threshold scheme involves an initialisation
overhead. Threshold schemes with disenrollment capability are threshold schemes that enable entities to be removed from the initial threshold scheme at less communication cost than that of establishing a new
scheme. We prove a revised version of a conjecture of Blakley, Blakley,
Chan and Massey by establishing a bound on the size of the broadcast
information necessary in a threshold scheme with disenrollment capability that has minimal entity information storage requirements. We also
investigate the characterisation of threshold schemes with disenrollment
that meet this bound.

1 Introduction

Since 1979 there has been a considerable amount of research concerning threshold
schemes [1,10]. These are cryptographic primitives that enable a piece of secret
data to be shared among a number of entities in such a way that the data can
only be recovered if a certain pre-determined number of these entities co-operate.
There are numerous areas of both cryptography and network security where this
type of primitive has proven useful. In cryptography, applications have included
component-wise protection of high level cryptographic keys, distributed trust
of key recovery information, and controlled access to important security codes,
as well as being the enabling primitive behind the whole field of cryptographic
research known as *threshold cryptography*. In network security, threshold schemes
have been applied to applications requiring a high degree of fault-tolerance,
where rather than directly protecting secret datum, they ensure that a particular
outcome is guaranteed so long as a threshold of channels are available for use.
For further discussion of applications see [12].

In its most abstract sense, we say that in a (t, n)-*threshold scheme*, a *secret*
is distributed by a trusted *dealer* among n *participants* (or *shareholders*) by
securely giving each participant a private *share* such that

L. Batten and J. Seberry (Eds.): ACISP 2002, LNCS 2384, pp. 71–88, 2002.

1. any t shares uniquely determine the secret;
2. no $t - 1$ or fewer shares uniquely determine the secret.

A (t, n)-threshold scheme is called *perfect* if $t - 1$ or fewer shares do not provide any additional information about the secret other than any information that is already publicly known. This concept of "not providing any additional information" implies that perfect threshold schemes only make sense when discussed in an information theoretic security environment. Indeed throughout this paper we will make no cryptographic computational assumptions, and will discuss only solutions that offer unconditional security. For the rest of the paper, even when not stated explicitly, the threshold schemes discussed are perfect.

It is clear from the above model that because the dealer must use a secure channel to distribute the initial shares, the initialisation of a threshold scheme is a relatively expensive process. After this initial distribution of the shares of a (t, n)-threshold scheme, it is possible that a share becomes compromised either by being accidentally disclosed, deliberately revealed by a malicious participant, or deliberately revealed by the dealer because the participant is no longer deemed trustworthy. By publicly revealing a share, the threshold scheme effectively becomes a $(t - 1, n - 1)$-threshold scheme. In all three cases, rather than suffer this reduction from t to $t - 1$ in the effective threshold, it is preferable that the initial threshold level of t is maintained. We thus seek to *disenroll* the participant whose share has been compromised by converting the (t, n)-threshold scheme to a $(t, n - 1)$-threshold scheme.

An obvious method of disenrolling a participant is to establish a new $(t, n-1)$-threshold scheme. However, the underlying assumption we make throughout this paper is that the dealer no longer has access to the expensive secure channels used to distribute the initial shares. Even if such channels are available, we will assume that the dealer prefers to use less expensive insecure channels, should such an option exist. A threshold scheme is said to have *disenrollment capability* if it *is* possible for the dealer to disenroll participants by distributing information using insecure channels. The messages sent to achieve this disenrollment are generally referred to as *broadcasts*, and we reasonably assume that a broadcast is public knowledge.

Threshold schemes with disenrollment capability were first discussed in [2,7]. Blakley *et al* [2] established a lower bound on the size of a participant's share in a threshold scheme with disenrollment capability and gave several examples of implementations of schemes that attain this bound. They observed that one such scheme, from [7], could be modified to further reduce the size of the broadcasts and made a conjecture concerning the minimum possible size of the broadcasts in any threshold scheme with disenrollment capability. The modified scheme achieves this conjectured minimum.

In this paper we show that this conjecture, as stated, is not true. Nevertheless, a revised statement is true, and in proving it we also establish a partial characterisation of schemes attaining the bound. We show that for a large class of parameters, the modified scheme referred to above is essentially the only way of achieving the minimum broadcast size. For the remaining parameter sets, an implementation of the scheme from [7] with modified broadcasts again achieves the minimum, but there are also other examples.

We note some other related works. Disenrollment for secret sharing schemes (threshold schemes with a more general access structure) was discussed in [7]. In [3] a model for more general types of change to the access structure of a secret sharing scheme was considered. In [5,9] techniques for changing access structure through the use of secure channels between participants (but not involving the dealer) were presented, and in [8] the problem of changing access structure without the help of the dealer or secure channels was described. Finally, in [14] schemes for the simultaneous disenrollment of more than one participant were exhibited, as well as schemes for different threshold scheme parameter changes. For a mathematical introduction to the whole problem of secret sharing, see [13].

The paper is organised as follows. In Section 2 we consider threshold schemes with disenrollment and present the revised bound, as well as providing an example that shows that the bound is tight. In Section 3 we prove that the revised bound holds. In Section 4 we present a partial characterisation of schemes that attain this bound. In the final section we make some concluding remarks.

2 Threshold Schemes with Disenrollment

We begin by describing a suitable information theoretic model for a perfect (t, n)-threshold scheme, first used by Karnin $et\ al$ [6]. We use Shannon's entropy function [11] and model the secret, and each share held by a participant, as random variables that take a finite set of values. For a brief introduction to entropy and its basic properties, see Appendix A.

We can now express the two properties of a perfect threshold scheme, informally described in Section 1, in the following way:

Definition 1. Let $1 \leq t \leq n$. A $perfect\ (t, n)$-$threshold\ scheme$ is a collection of random variables $(K, S_1, \ldots, S_n)$ such that for any $\{i_1, \ldots, i_u\} \subseteq \{1, \ldots, n\}$,

1. $H(K \mid S_{i_1}, \ldots, S_{i_u}) = 0$ if $u \geq t$;
2. $H(K \mid S_{i_1}, \ldots, S_{i_u}) = H(K)$ if $u < t$.

Example 1. Shamir's polynomial scheme. The following perfect (t, n)-threshold scheme was described in [10]. Let $K, S_1, \ldots, S_n$ all take values from $\mathbf{Z}_q$ (the unique finite field of size q), for some prime $q > n$. Let $x_1, \ldots, x_n$ be n distinct non-zero elements of $\mathbf{Z}_q$, where x_i is publicly known and associated with S_i. The dealer randomly chooses a polynomial $f(x)$ of degree at most $t - 1$, with coefficients from $\mathbf{Z}_q$, and gives $f(x_i)$ as a share to the participant associated with S_i. The secret is taken to be $f(0)$. Each polynomial is uniquely determined by any t points on it, and so it follows that the secret is uniquely determined by any t shares (and the public knowledge of the values x_i). Indeed, by Lagrange interpolation, for any subset $T = \{i_1, \ldots, i_t\} \subseteq \{1, \ldots, n\}$ of t indices corresponding to participants there exists a vector $\mathbf{c}_T = (c_1, \ldots, c_n) \in \mathbf{Z}_q^n$, uniquely determined by the values $x_{i_1}, \ldots, x_{i_t}$, such that, $c_i = 0$ for $i \notin T$ and $f(0) = \sum_{l=1}^{t} c_{i_l} f(x_{i_l})$. (We remark that the vectors $\{c_T \mid T \subseteq \{1, \ldots, n\}, |T| = t\}$ span an $(n - t + 1)$-dimensional subspace of $\mathbf{Z}_q^n$ – a fact that is relevant to the discussion in Section 5.) That fewer than t participants obtain no information about the secret is easily verified, since each value of $\mathbf{Z}_q$ occurs equally often as a value taken at 0 by the polynomials determined by $t - 1$ or fewer shares.

Assume now that one share in the (t, n)-threshold scheme has become compromised. Since this share can be assumed to be publicly known it follows that any $t - 1$ of the remaining shares now suffice to uniquely determine the secret. The effective threshold to determine the secret has thus decreased to $t - 1$. A (t, n)-threshold scheme with disenrollment capability is a procedure for avoiding this threshold decrease by using another secret and modifying the shares through the use of broadcasts. It follows that, in any (t, n)-threshold scheme with disenrollment capability, the new secret after disenrollment must be independent of the old secret, otherwise $t - 1$ participants could determine some information about it (the two independent secrets may however be linked to the same outcome - for example the secrets may be linked to an access code; after disenrollment the old secret is simply disabled, and the new secret enabled, as a permission to activate the access code).

A (t, n)-threshold scheme for which L successive disenrollments can be conducted is said to have L-*fold* disenrollment capability. The end result of such a scheme is a $(t, n - L)$-threshold scheme and $L + 1$ independent secrets are used during the successive disenrollments. In a scheme with L-fold disenrollment capability, we model the successive secrets as random variables $K_0, \ldots, K_L$. If l, $(1 \leq l \leq L)$, participants corresponding to indices $j_1, \ldots, j_l$ have been successively disenrolled, we model the broadcast relating to new secret K_l by the random variable $B_{(j_1, \ldots, j_l)}$. We denote by $\mathcal{X}(n, l)$ the collection of all sequences $(j_1, \ldots, j_l)$, where $j_1, \ldots, j_l$ are distinct integers between 1 and n. We denote the set of shares that may be held by the ith participant (the set of values taken by S_i) by $[S_i]$. Similarly we denote the set of broadcasts corresponding to $B_{(i_1, \ldots, i_l)}$ by $[B_{(i_1, \ldots, i_l)}]$ and the set of secrets corresponding to K_l by $[K_l]$.

We are now ready to formalise the notion of a threshold scheme with L-fold disenrollment capability:

Definition 2. Let $1 \leq L \leq n - t$. A perfect (t, n)-threshold scheme with L-*fold disenrollment capability* is a collection of random variables

$$(K_0, \ldots, K_L, S_1, \ldots, S_n, \{B_{(j_1, \ldots, j_l)} \mid (j_1, \ldots, j_l) \in \mathcal{X}(n, l), 1 \leq l \leq L\})$$

such that

1. $(K_0, S_1, \ldots, S_n)$ is a perfect (t, n)-threshold scheme;

and for $l = 1, \ldots, L$, any $(j_1, \ldots, j_l) \in \mathcal{X}(n, l)$ corresponding to l successively disenrolled participants, and any $\{i_1, \ldots, i_u\} \subseteq \{1, \ldots, n\}$ with $\{i_1, \ldots, i_u\} \cap \{j_1, \ldots, j_l\} = \emptyset$, it holds that

2. $H(K_l \mid S_{i_1}, \ldots, S_{i_u}, B_{(j_1)}, \ldots, B_{(j_1,\ldots,j_l)}) = 0$ if $u \geq t$;
3. $H(K_l \mid S_{i_1}, \ldots, S_{i_u}, S_{j_1}, \ldots, S_{j_l}, B_{(j_1)}, \ldots, B_{(j_1,\ldots,j_l)}) = H(K_l)$ if $u < t$.

The second condition (2.) says that the first l broadcasts and the shares of t participants who have not been disenrolled determine the lth secret. The third condition (3.) says that the first l broadcasts, the shares of the disenrolled participants and the shares of less than t participants who have not been disenrolled provide no additional information about the lth secret other than the information that is publicly known. Note that by (2.), the shares of a group of at most $t - 1 + l$ participants do not determine K_l. However, we do not place any restrictions on a group of at least $t + l$ participants constructing secret K_l before the lth disenrollment. It is assumed that such an activity would be rendered meaningless by the application. Should this be a potential problem, then a threshold scheme with disenrollment capability should not be used, as a stronger model is necessary.

The following two examples of (t, n)-threshold schemes with L-fold disenrollment capability were described in [2]. In each case we assume that the disenrolled participants correspond, in sequence, to $S_{j_1}, \ldots, S_{j_L}$.

Example 2. This scheme was referred to in [2] as the modified Martin scheme. We will call it the *advanced share technique.*

1. For each i $(1 \leq i \leq n)$, let $S_i = (S_i^0, S_i^1, \ldots, S_i^L)$, where for each l $(0 \leq l \leq L)$ $(K_l, S_1^l, \ldots, S_n^l)$ is a perfect $(t + l, n)$-threshold scheme.
2. Initially the effective (t, n)-threshold scheme used is $(K_0, S_1^0, \ldots, S_n^0)$.
3. At the lth disenrollment, broadcast the shares held by the (successively disenrolled) shareholders corresponding to $S_{j_1}, \ldots, S_{j_l}$ in scheme $(K_l, S_1^l, \ldots, S_n^l)$. The effective $(t, n - l)$-threshold scheme used is $(K_l, S_1^l, \ldots, S_n^l)$ with l of the shares public.

Example 3. This scheme was referred to in [2] as the Brickell-Stinson scheme. We will call it the *advanced key technique.*

1. For each i $(1 \leq i \leq n)$, let $S_i = (S_i^0, R_i^1, \ldots, R_i^L)$, where $(K_0, S_1^0, \ldots, S_n^0)$ is a perfect (t, n)-threshold scheme and all the R_i^l represent random variables such that $p_{R_i^l}$ is uniform and $[S_i^l] = [S_i^0]$ is an additive group.
2. Initially the effective (t, n)-threshold scheme used is $(K_0, S_1^0, \ldots, S_n^0)$.
3. At the lth disenrollment, let $(K_l, S_1^l, \ldots, S_n^l)$ be a (t, n)-threshold scheme and, for any $i \in \{1, \ldots, n\} \backslash \{j_1, \ldots, j_l\}$, where the disenrolled shareholders correspond to $S_{j_1}, \ldots, S_{j_l}$, broadcast $R_i^l + S_i^l$. The effective $(t, n - l)$-threshold scheme used is $(K_l, S_1^l, \ldots, S_n^l)$ with l of the shares unknown.

Thus, the advance share technique involves equipping the participants with a series of independent shares for a sequence of threshold schemes with increasing threshold parameters. Disenrollment of a participant involves the dealer broadcasting enough information that the next threshold scheme in the sequence can be used. On the other hand, the advance key technique involves issuing each participant with a sequence of "cryptographic keys". Disenrollment of a participant involves the dealer broadcasting the new shares, encrypted by the appropriate one-time pad encryption key, to the remaining participants.

For simplicity we will assume throughout the rest of the paper that $H(K_0) = \cdots = H(K_L) = k$ in any scheme that we consider. We will also abbreviate the set of random variables previously listed as

$$(K_0, \ldots, K_L, S_1, \ldots, S_n, \{B_{(j_1, \ldots, j_l)} \mid (j_1, \ldots, j_l) \in \mathcal{X}(n, l), 1 \le l \le L\})$$

by $(\mathbf{K}, \mathbf{S}, \mathbf{B})$.

Blakley $et\ al$ [2] proved the following lower bound on the size of the share that each participant must hold in a perfect (t, n)-threshold scheme with L-fold disenrollment capability.

Theorem 1. Let $(\mathbf{K}, \mathbf{S}, \mathbf{B})$ be a perfect (t, n)-threshold scheme with L-fold disenrollment capability. Then, for $i = 1, \ldots, n$, $H(S_i) \ge (L+1)k$.

Both the advanced share technique and the advanced key technique can meet the bounds in Theorem 1 with equality. We say that a (t, n)-threshold scheme with L-fold disenrollment capability that meets this bound is *share minimal*. The following conjecture was made in [2] concerning an equivalent lower bound on the size of broadcasts.

Conjecture 1. Let $(\mathbf{K}, \mathbf{S}, \mathbf{B})$ be a perfect (t, n)-threshold scheme with L-fold disenrollment capability. Then, for $l = 1, \ldots, L$, we have, for any $(j_1, \ldots, j_l) \in \mathcal{X}(n, l)$, that $H(B_{(j_1, \ldots, j_l)}) \ge lk$.

This conjecture is not true as stated since it is always possible to have broadcast size k at the expense of very large share size. This is achieved by issuing each shareholder in advance with a share of a one-time pad encrypted secret in every possible $(t, n - l)$-threshold scheme that could result after any sequence of disenrollments. To enable a particular $(t, n - l)$-threshold scheme it suffices for the dealer to broadcast the appropriate key to decrypt the secret. Since each secret has size k we need only a key of size k for the encryption to ensure that there is no information leakage and so in each case $H(B_{(j_1, \ldots, j_l)}) = k$. Thus Conjecture 1 only makes sense if the size of each share is restricted to take the minimal size, as follows.

Conjecture 2. Let $(\mathbf{K}, \mathbf{S}, \mathbf{B})$ be a share minimal (t, n)-threshold scheme with L-fold disenrollment capability. Then, for $l = 1, \ldots, L$, we have, for any $(j_1, \ldots, j_l) \in \mathcal{X}(n, l)$, that $H(B_{(j_1, \ldots, j_l)}) \ge lk$.

Conjecture 2 is based on an assumption that the advanced share technique yields a scheme with minimal size of broadcasts as well as minimal shares. However, we see that Conjecture 2 is also not true, as stated, since the advanced key technique provides a counterexample when $L > n/2$. In this case, for any l with $n/2 < l \le L$, we can obtain $H(B_{(j_1, \ldots, j_l)}) = (n - l)k < lk$. In fact, in Example 4, we show that when $n < 2l + t - 1$ it is possible to broadcast less information than the disenrolled participants' shares in the lth scheme of the advanced share technique so that any t of the remaining $n - l < l + t - 1$ participants can determine K_l. Only the equivalent of $n - t + 1 - l < l$ shares is required to be broadcast in order that t of the remaining participants can determine K_l.

Even for $n \geq 2L + t - 1$, if the advanced share technique is used as stated in Example 2, except that the broadcast for the lth disenrollment is accompanied by some advance information concerning the $(l+1)^{th}$ broadcast, then Conjecture 2 also fails to hold. The bound for the lth broadcast is not guaranteed to hold unless preceding $l - 1$ broadcasts meet a minimality condition. More precisely, if we broadcast, at the lth disenrollment, the shares held by the shareholders corresponding to $S_{j_1}, \ldots, S_{j_l}$ in schemes $(K_l, S_1^l, \ldots, S_n^l)$ and $(K_{l+1}, S_1^{l+1}, \ldots, S_n^{l+1})$ then it suffices to broadcast the share held by the shareholder corresponding to $S_{j_{l+1}}$ in scheme $(K_{l+1}, S_1^{l+1}, \ldots, S_n^{l+1})$ to conduct the $(l+1)^{th}$ disenrollment.

These observations suggest that a somewhat more complex result concerning the size of broadcasts holds. In this paper we show that the correct bound is given in the following theorem:

Theorem 3.1 *Let* $(\mathbf{K}, \mathbf{S}, \mathbf{B})$ *be a share minimal* (t, n)*-threshold scheme with* L*-fold disenrollment capability. Then, for* $m = 1, \ldots, L$,

$$\sum_{l=1}^{m} H(B_{(j_1, \ldots, j_l)}) \geq \sum_{l=1}^{m} \min(l, n - t + 1 - l)k$$

for all $(j_1, \ldots, j_m) \in \mathcal{X}(n, m)$.

We prove Theorem 2 later, but first note that the following example shows that this bound can be attained.

Example 4. Let $q > n$ be a prime. Let $x_1, \ldots, x_n$ be distinct non-zero elements of $\mathbf{Z}_q$. For $l = 0, \ldots, L$ let f_l be a random polynomial of degree at most $l + t - 1$ with coefficients in $\mathbf{Z}_q$. The secret corresponding to K_l is $f_l(0)$ and the share corresponding to S_i is $(f_0(x_i), \ldots, f_L(x_i))$. This sets up a threshold scheme with L-fold disenrollment capability based on the advanced share technique using Shamir's polynomial scheme. (See Examples 2 and 3.) Let m be an integer such that $1 \leq m \leq L$. Let $\mathcal{J}$ be the subspace of $\mathbf{Z}_q^{m+t}$ spanned by the vectors $(1, x_{j_l}, x_{j_l}^2, \ldots, x_{j_l}^{m+t-1})$ for $l = 1, \ldots, m$ and let $\mathcal{I}$ be the subspace spanned by the vectors $(1, x, x^2, \ldots, x^{m+t-1})$ for $x \in \{0, x_1, \ldots, x_n\} \backslash \{x_{j_1}, \ldots, x_{j_m}\}$. The dimension of $\mathcal{J}$ is m and the dimension of $\mathcal{I}$ is $\min(n + 1 - m, m + t)$. Let $\mathcal{B}$ be a basis for $\mathcal{J} \cap \mathcal{I}$ and put $b = |\mathcal{B}|$. Then $b = \min(n + 1 - m - t, m)$. For $u = 1, \ldots, b$, let $(d_1^u, \ldots, d_m^u)$ be linearly independent elements of $\mathbf{Z}_q^m$, such that

$$d_1^u(1, x_{j_1}, \ldots, x_{j_1}^{m+t-1}) + \ldots + d_m^u(1, x_{j_m}, \ldots, x_{j_m}^{m+t-1})$$

belongs to $\mathcal{B}$. When participants corresponding to indices $j_1, \ldots, j_m$ have successively been disenrolled the broadcast is

$$\left(\sum_{l=1}^{m} d_l^1 f_m(x_{j_l}), \ldots, \sum_{l=1}^{m} d_l^b f_m(x_{j_l}) \right).$$

Since, for any $\{i_1, \ldots, i_t\} \subseteq \{1, \ldots, n\} \backslash \{j_1, \ldots, j_m\}$, the vectors

$$(1, x_{i_1}, x_{i_1}^2, \ldots, x_{i_1}^{m+t-1}), \ldots, (1, x_{i_t}, x_{i_t}^2, \ldots, x_{i_t}^{m+t-1})$$

together with $\mathcal{J} \cap \mathcal{I}$ span $\mathcal{I}$, this broadcast together with the shares of the corresponding participants determines K_m. However, no $t - 1$ of the remaining participants, together with the broadcasts and, possibly, the shares of the disenrolled participants, can determine K_m. This is because the broadcasts are determined by the shares of the m disenrolled participants and the shares of any set of $m + t - 1$ participants do not give any information about K_m. Note that when $b = m$ then $\mathcal{J} \subseteq \mathcal{I}$ and, for $u = 1, \ldots, m$, we may choose $d_u^u = 1$ and $d_i^u = 0$ for $i \neq u$. The broadcast is then $(f_m(x_{j_1}), \ldots, f_m(x_{j_m}))$ as for the advanced share technique, Example 2.

3   Bounding the Size of Broadcast Messages

In this section we prove Theorem 2. We use an inductive technique, and so first prove the result for the case $t = 1$.

Throughout the following lemmas, let $(\mathbf{K}, \mathbf{S}, \mathbf{B})$ be a perfect $(1, n)$-threshold scheme with L-fold disenrollment capability. We begin with several technical lemmas. These lemmas use standard information theoretic manipulations to obtain entropy and mutual information relationships that are required as steps in the main proof.

Lemma 1. *Let* $j_1, \ldots, j_L, i$ *be distinct elements of* $\{1, \ldots, n\}$ *and suppose that the indices* $j_1, \ldots, j_L$ *correspond to* L *successively disenrolled participants. Then, for* $l = 0, \ldots, L$,

(i) $I(K_l; S_{j_1}, \ldots, S_{j_l}, B_{(j_1)}, \ldots, B_{(j_1, \ldots, j_l)}, K_0, \ldots, K_{l-1}) = 0$
(ii) $I(K_l; S_i \mid B_{(j_1)}, \ldots, B_{(j_1, \ldots, j_l)}, K_0, \ldots, K_{l-1}) = H(K_l)$
(iii) $I(K_l; S_i \mid S_{j_1}, \ldots, S_{j_l}, B_{(j_1)}, \ldots, B_{(j_1, \ldots, j_l)}, K_0, \ldots, K_{l-1}) = H(K_l)$
(iv) $H(S_i \mid S_{j_1}, \ldots, S_{j_l}, B_{(j_1)}, \ldots, B_{(j_1, \ldots, j_l)}, K_0, \ldots, K_{l-1})$
       $= k + H(S_i \mid S_{j_1}, \ldots, S_{j_l}, B_{(j_1)}, \ldots, B_{(j_1, \ldots, j_l)}, K_0, \ldots, K_l)$
       $\geq (L + 1 - l)k$, *with equality if* $H(S_i) = (L + 1)k$.

Proof. See Appendix B.

Lemma 2. *Let* $i_1, \ldots, i_{L+1}$ *be distinct elements of* $\{1, \ldots, n\}$. *Then, for* $l = 0, \ldots, L$,

(i) $H(K_l \mid S_{i_1}, \ldots, S_{i_l}, K_0, \ldots, K_{l-1}) = k$
(ii) $H(S_{i_{l+1}} \mid S_{i_1}, \ldots, S_{i_l}, K_0, \ldots, K_l) \geq (L - l)k$.

Proof. See Appendix C.

Lemma 3. *Let* $j_1, \ldots, j_L, j_{L+1}$ *be distinct elements of* $\{1, \ldots, n\}$ *and suppose that the indices* $j_1, \ldots, j_L$ *correspond to* L *successively disenrolled participants. Then, for* $l = 0, \ldots, L$, *if* $H(S_{j_{l+1}}) = (L + 1)k$,

$$H(S_{j_{l+1}} \mid B_{(j_1)}, \ldots, B_{(j_1, \ldots, j_l)}, K_0, \ldots, K_l) \leq (L - l)k.$$

Proof. See Appendix D.

The first stage in proving Theorem 2 requires treatment of the degenerate case $t = 1$. The proof involves repeated technical manipulations of the related entropy expressions and we state it in full in the appendix.

Lemma 4. *Let* $(\mathbf{K}, \mathbf{S}, \mathbf{B})$ *be a share minimal* $(1, n)$-*threshold scheme with* L-*fold disenrollment capability. Then for* $m = 1, \ldots, L$,

$$\sum_{l=1}^{m} H(B_{(j_1, \ldots, j_l)}) \geq \sum_{l=1}^{m} \min(l, n - l)k$$

for all $(j_1, \ldots, j_m) \in \mathcal{X}(n, m)$.

Proof. See Appendix E.

We are now ready to prove Theorem 2, the main result.

Theorem 2. *Let* $(\mathbf{K}, \mathbf{S}, \mathbf{B})$ *be a share minimal* (t, n)-*threshold scheme with* L-*fold disenrollment capability. Then, for* $m = 1, \ldots, L$,

$$\sum_{l=1}^{m} H(B_{(j_1, \ldots, j_l)}) \geq \sum_{l=1}^{m} \min(l, n - t + 1 - l)k$$

for all $(j_1, \ldots, j_m) \in \mathcal{X}(n, m)$.

Proof. Let $i_1, \ldots, i_{t-1}$ be distinct elements of $\{1, \ldots, n\}$ and let $i_t, \ldots, i_n$ be chosen such that $\{i_1, \ldots, i_n\} = \{1, \ldots, n\}$. Let $(s_1, \ldots, s_{t-1}) \in [S_{i_1}] \times \ldots \times [S_{i_{t-1}}]$ have non-zero probability. We claim that

$$(K_0', \ldots, K_L', S_{i_t}', \ldots, S_{i_n}', \{B_{(i_{t+j_1}, \ldots, i_{t+j_l})}' \mid (j_1, \ldots, j_l) \in \mathcal{X}(n - t + 1, l), 1 \leq l \leq L\})$$

is a perfect $(1, n - t + 1)$-threshold scheme with L-fold disenrollment capability, where, for a random variable X, we write X' for the random variable with $[X'] = [X]$ such that, for $x \in [X']$ the probability $p_{X'}(x)$ equals the conditional probability $p_{X S_{i_1} \ldots S_{i_{t-1}}}(x \mid s_1, \ldots, s_{t-1})$ of x given $s_1, \ldots, s_{t-1}$.

Indeed, for $l = 0, \ldots, L$, since $H(K_l \mid S_{i_1}, \ldots, S_{i_{t-1}}) = H(K_l) = k$, we have $H(K_l') = k$. Also, for $l = 1, \ldots, L$, we have, for any $(j_1, \ldots, j_l) \in \mathcal{X}(n, l)$ and $(h_1, \ldots, h_u) \in \mathcal{X}(n - t + 1, u)$ with $\{i_1, \ldots, i_{t-1}, i_{t-1+h_1}, \ldots, i_{t-1+h_u}\} \cap \{j_1, \ldots, j_l\} = \emptyset$, that

$$H(K_l' \mid S_{i_{t-1+h_1}}', \ldots, S_{i_{t-1+h_u}}', B_{(j_1)}', \ldots, B_{(j_1, \ldots, j_l)}') = 0 \text{ if } u \geq 1,$$

since

$$H(K_l \mid S_{i_1}, \ldots, S_{i_{t-1}}, S_{i_{t-1+h_1}}, \ldots, S_{i_{t-1+h_u}}, B_{(j_1)}, \ldots, B_{(j_1, \ldots, j_l)}) = 0 \text{ if } u \geq 1.$$

Similarly, (in the case that $u = 0$), we have

$$H(K_l' \mid S_{j_1}', \ldots, S_{j_l}', B_{(j_1)}', \ldots, B_{(j_1, \ldots, j_l)}') = H(K_l').$$

This establishes our claim.

Now, for $l = 1, \ldots, L$, we have that, for any distinct elements $j_1, \ldots, j_l$ chosen from the set $\{1, \ldots, n\} \setminus \{i_1, \ldots, i_{t-1}\}$, $H(B_{(j_1, \ldots, j_l)}) \geq H(B'_{(j_1, \ldots, j_l)})$. By Lemma 4, we also have that $H(B'_{(j_1, \ldots, j_l)}) \geq \sum_{l=1}^{m} \min(l, n - t + 1 - l)k$. Since $i_1, \ldots, i_{t-1}$ are arbitrary we have established the bound.

We thus now have two separate bounds on important parameters in a threshold scheme with disenrollment capability. Firstly a bound on the size of shares, given by Theorem 1, which is met when the scheme is share minimal. Next we have a bound on the size of broadcast message for share minimal schemes, given by Theorem 2. We will now consider threshold scheme with disenrollment capability that are both share minimal and meet the bound of Theorem 2. Since these schemes satisfy both bounds we will refer to them as being *optimal*. In the next section we present a partial characterisation of optimal threshold schemes with disenrollment capability.

4   Characterising Optimal Schemes

In this section we present a partial characterisation of optimal (t, n)-threshold schemes with disenrollment capability. The motivation for this is to study to what extent the known techniques for disenrollment already discussed in this paper might be effectively the only way of conducting a disenrollment. As in the previous section, we proceed by applying an inductive argument, beginning with the degenerate case $t = 1$. We begin with a useful technical lemma.

Lemma 5. *Let $(\mathbf{K}, \mathbf{S}, \mathbf{B})$ be an optimal $(1, n)$-threshold scheme with L-fold disenrollment capability, and $i_1, \ldots, i_{L+1}$ be distinct elements of $\{1, \ldots, n\}$. Then, for $m = 0, \ldots, L$, we have that*

$$H(S_{i_1}, \ldots, S_{i_{m+1}}, K_0, \ldots, K_m) \geq \left((L+1)(m+1) - \frac{(m+1)m}{2}\right)k.$$

Further, if equality holds then, for $l = 0, \ldots, m$,

$$H(K_l \mid S_{i_1}, \ldots, S_{i_{l+1}}, K_0, \ldots, K_{l-1}) = 0.$$

Proof. We have

$$
\begin{aligned}
&H(S_{i_1}, \ldots, S_{i_{m+1}}, K_0, \ldots, K_m) \\
&= \sum_{l=0}^{m} \big(H(S_{i_{l+1}} \mid S_{i_1}, \ldots, S_{i_l}, K_0, \ldots, K_{l-1}) \\
&\qquad\qquad + H(K_l \mid S_{i_1}, \ldots, S_{i_{l+1}}, K_0, \ldots, K_{l-1}) \big) \\
&\text{(by the chain rule)} \\
&\geq \sum_{l=0}^{m} H(S_{i_{l+1}} \mid S_{i_1}, \ldots, S_{i_l}, K_0, \ldots, K_{l-1})
\end{aligned}
$$

$$\geq \sum_{l=0}^{m} H(S_{i_{l+1}} \mid S_{i_1}, \ldots, S_{i_l}, B_{(i_1)}, \ldots, B_{(i_1, \ldots, i_l)}, K_0, \ldots, K_{l-1})$$

$$\geq \sum_{l=0}^{m} (L + 1 - l)k$$

(by Lemma 1(iv))

$$= \left((L+1)(m+1) - \frac{(m+1)m}{2}\right)k$$

and the result follows.

The inequality given in this lemma specifies the minimum total entropy required to be held by $m+1$ participants in a $(1,n)$-threshold scheme with L-fold disenrollment capability. Ostensibly such a scheme might require $m+1$ participants to hold total entropy $(m+1)(L+1)k$ as each of the participants' shares must have entropy $H(S_i) \geq (L+1)k$ by the bound of Blakley et al [2]. However there may be redundancy in the collection of shares held by the $m+1$ participants. With threshold $t = 1$ the share S_1 (which determines K_0) may determine $H(K_0) = k$ bits of each of $S_2, \ldots, S_n$. And when the participant corresponding to S_1 is disenrolled, S_1 does not determine the k bits of S_2 that determine (together with the broadcast) K_1, while S_2 may determine k bits of each of $S_3, \ldots, S_n$. And so on. Thus $(m + (m - 1) + \ldots + 1)k = \frac{(m+1)m}{2}k$ bits of the $m+1$ shares may be determined by other bits. When equality holds the scheme must be share minimal and this redundancy must hold. Thus one participant determines K_0, two determine K_1 and so on. The lemma below shows that, in the case of threshold $t = 1$, provided no more than half the participants are disenrolled, when the scheme is optimal then equality does hold, the secret is shared by perfect threshold scheme with threshold one more than the number of disenrolled participants. Further, the broadcasts provide the same information about the next secret as the do the shares of the disenrolled participants. Thus the scheme is essentially the advanced share technique for these secrets.

Lemma 6. Let $(\mathbf{K}, \mathbf{S}, \mathbf{B})$ be a share minimal $(1, n)$-threshold scheme with L-fold disenrollment capability such that for some m, $1 \leq m \leq L$, $(\mathbf{K}, \mathbf{S}, \mathbf{B})$ is an optimal $(1, n)$-threshold scheme with m-fold disenrollment capability. Then, for $l = 0, \ldots, \alpha - 1$, $(K_l, S_1, \ldots, S_n)$ is a perfect $(l + 1, n)$-threshold scheme, where $\alpha = \min(m, \lfloor \frac{n+1}{2} \rfloor)$.

Proof. Let $i_1, \ldots, i_\alpha$ be any α distinct elements of $\{1, \ldots, n\}$ and let l be such that $0 \leq l \leq \alpha - 1$. Since equality holds in the bound Lemma 4, we see from the step involving the application of Lemma 2 in the proof that

$$H(S_{i_1}, \ldots, S_{i_\alpha}, K_0, \ldots, K_{\alpha-1}) = \sum_{l=0}^{\alpha-1} (k + (L - l)k)$$

$$= \left(\alpha(L+1) - \frac{\alpha(\alpha-1)}{2}\right)k,$$

so that $H(K_l \mid S_{i_1}, \ldots, S_{i_{l+1}}, K_0, \ldots, K_{l-1}) = 0$ by Lemma 5. Thus

$$H(K_0, \ldots, K_l \mid S_{i_1}, \ldots, S_{i_{l+1}})$$

$$= \sum_{h=0}^{l} H(K_h \mid S_{i_1}, \ldots, S_{i_{l+1}}, K_0, \ldots, K_{h-1})$$

(by the chain rule)

$$\leq \sum_{h=0}^{l} H(K_h \mid S_{i_1}, \ldots, S_{i_{h+1}}, K_0, \ldots, K_{h-1}) = 0.$$

Hence

$$H(K_l \mid S_{i_1}, \ldots, S_{i_{l+1}}) \leq H(K_0, \ldots, K_l \mid S_{i_1}, \ldots, S_{i_{l+1}}) = 0.$$

Also, by Lemma 1(i),

$$H(K_l \mid S_{i_1}, \ldots, S_{i_l}, B_{(i_1)}, \ldots, B_{(i_1, \ldots, i_l)}, K_0, \ldots, K_{l-1}) = H(K_l).$$

So $H(K_l \mid S_{i_1}, \ldots, S_{i_l}) = H(K_l)$. This establishes the result.

We now extend Lemma 6 to the general case by induction as before. Thus, for arbitrary threshold t, provided fewer than $\lfloor \frac{n-t+2}{2} \rfloor$ participants are disenrolled and the scheme is optimal, the sharing of the secret is essentially the advanced share technique.

Theorem 3. *Let $(\mathbf{K}, \mathbf{S}, \mathbf{B})$ be a share minimal (t, n)-threshold scheme with L-fold disenrollment capability such that for for some m, $1 \leq m \leq L$, $(\mathbf{K}, \mathbf{S}, \mathbf{B})$ is an optimal (t, n)-threshold scheme with m-fold disenrollment capability. Then, for $l = 0, \ldots, \alpha - 1$, $(K_l, S_1, \ldots, S_n)$ is a perfect $(l+t, n)$-threshold scheme, where $\alpha = \min(m, \lfloor \frac{n-t+2}{2} \rfloor)$.*

Proof. By Lemma 6 we have that, for $l = 0, \ldots, \alpha - 1$, $(K'_l, S'_{i_t}, \ldots, S'_{i_n})$ is a perfect $(l + 1, n - t + 1)$-threshold scheme. Thus, for any $(h_1, \ldots, h_u) \in \mathcal{X}(n - t + 1, u)$,

$$H(K'_l \mid S'_{i_{t-1+h_1}}, \ldots, S'_{i_{t-1+h_u}}) = 0 \text{ if } u \geq l + 1$$

and

$$H(K'_l \mid S'_{i_{t-1+h_1}}, \ldots, S'_{i_{t-1+h_u}}) = H(K'_l) \text{ if } u < l + 1.$$

Since this is true for all choices of $s_1, \ldots, s_{t-1}$ with $p_{S_{i_1} \ldots S_{i_{t-1}}}(s_1, \ldots, s_{t-1}) \neq 0$, we have

$$H(K_l \mid S_{i_1}, \ldots, S_{i_{t-1}}, S_{i_{t-1+h_1}}, \ldots, S_{i_{t-1+h_u}}) = 0 \text{ if } u \geq l + 1$$

and

$$H(K_l \mid S_{i_1}, \ldots, S_{i_{t-1}}, S_{i_{t-1+h_1}}, \ldots, S_{i_{t-1+h_u}}) = H(K_l) \text{ if } u < l + 1.$$

Hence, since $i_1, \ldots, i_{t-1}$ are arbitrary, $(K_l, S_1, \ldots, S_n)$ is a perfect $(t + l, n)$-threshold scheme.

5   Further Remarks

We have established a lower bound on the size of a broadcast message in threshold schemes with disenrollment capability, finally answering a long standing open question posed in [2]. Further, we have shown that this bound is tight and we have a partial characterisation of schemes that meet the bound in terms of the effective secret sharing schemes that are used.

We note that $\sum_{l=1}^{m} H(B_{(j_1,\ldots,j_l)}) = \sum_{l=1}^{m} \min(l, n-t+1-l)k$ for $m = 1, \ldots, L$ if and only if $H(B_{(j_1,\ldots,j_l)}) = \min(l, n-t+1-l)k$ for $l = 1, \ldots, L$. Thus if the scheme is optimal and $n \geq 2L+t-1$ then equality holds in the bounds on the size of a broadcast conjectured by Blakley et al [2]. Our characterisation shows that a scheme meeting these bounds must have been established using the advanced share technique.

However, when $n < 2L + t - 1$, the appropriate bound is our revised bound. In Example 4 we presented a scheme meeting this bound that uses the advanced share technique with modified broadcasts. There is also another method by which we may meet the bound. We note the following modification of an advanced key technique to obtain a reduction in the size of the broadcasts which is optimal also. Thus the partial characterisation given in Theorem 3 is the best possible result for a characterisation that determines the effective secret sharing schemes uniquely.

With reference to Examples 1 and 3, suppose that, for $i = 1, \ldots, n$, $[S_i^0] = \mathbf{Z}_q$, for some prime $q > n$, and we implement each scheme $(K_l, S_1^l, \ldots, S_n^l)$, $1 \leq l \leq L$, using Shamir's polynomial scheme. Suppose that participants corresponding to indices $j_1, \ldots, j_L$ are successively disenrolled. For $l = 1, \ldots, L$, the $\binom{n-l}{t}$ vectors $\mathbf{c}_T$, for T a t-subset of $\{1, \ldots, n\}\backslash\{j_1, \ldots, j_l\}$, span a $(n - t + 1 - l)$-dimensional subspace of $\mathbf{Z}_q^n$. Let $\mathbf{b}_1, \ldots, \mathbf{b}_{n-t+1-l}$ be a basis for this subspace and, for $i = 1, \ldots, n - t + 1 - l$, put $\mathbf{b}_i = (b_1^i, \ldots, b_n^i)$. (Note that, for $i = 1, \ldots, n - t + 1 - l$, we have $b_j^i = 0$ for all $j \in \{j_1, \ldots, j_l\}$.) When the lth participant is disenrolled, we broadcast the $n - t + 1 - l$ elements

$$\left(\sum_{i=1}^{n} b_i^1 (r_i^l + s_i^l), \ldots, \sum_{i=1}^{n} b_i^{n-t+1-l} (r_i^l + s_i^l) \right)$$

where, for $i = 1, \ldots, n$, the value taken by R_i^l is r_i^l and the value taken by S_i^l is s_i^l.

It follows that, for any subset $T = \{i_1, \ldots, i_t\} \subseteq \{1, \ldots, n\}\backslash\{j_1, \ldots, j_l\}$ of t distinct indices with corresponding vector $\mathbf{c}_T$, the value $\sum_{h=1}^{t} c_{i_h}(r_{i_h}^l + s_{i_h}^l)$ is public knowledge. Thus the participants corresponding to these indices can use their shares to evaluate $\sum_{h=1}^{t} c_{i_h} r_{i_h}^l$ and so determine the value $\sum_{h=1}^{t} c_{i_h} s_{i_h}^l$ taken by K_l.

It is clear that an optimal scheme may be implemented by using the advanced share technique with respect to the lth effective scheme, $l = 1, \ldots, \min(L, \lfloor \frac{n-t+2-L}{2} \rfloor)$, and using either the advanced share technique or the advanced key technique, with respect to the remaining effective schemes.

References

1. G. R. Blakley. Safeguarding cryptographic keys. *Proceedings of AFIPS 1979 National Computer Conference*, 48 (1979) 313–317.
2. B. Blakley, G.R. Blakley, A.H. Chan and J.L. Massey. Threshold schemes with disenrollment. In *Advances in Cryptology - CRYPTO'92, LNCS 740* Springer-Verlag, Berlin (1993) 540–548.
3. C. Blundo, A. Cresti, A. De Santis and U. Vaccaro. Fully dynamic secret sharing schemes. In *Advances in Cryptology - CRYPTO '93, LNCS 773*, Springer, Berlin (1993) 110–125.
4. T.M. Cover and J.A. Thomas. *Elements of Information Theory*, John Wiley & Sons, New York (1991).
5. Y. Desmedt and S. Jajodia. Redistributing secret shares to new access structures and its applications. Preprint (1997).
6. E.D. Karnin, J.W. Greene and M.E. Hellman. On secret sharing systems. *IEEE Trans. on Inf. Th.*, 29 (1983) 35–41.
7. K.M. Martin. Untrustworthy participants in perfect secret sharing schemes. In *Cryptography and Coding III*, (M.J. Ganley, Ed.) Clarendon Press, Oxford (1993) 255–264.
8. K.M. Martin, J. Pieprzyk, R. Safavi-Naini and H. Wang. Changing thresholds in the absence of secure channels. In *Information Security and Privacy - ACISP'99, LNCS 1587*, Springer, Berlin (1999) 177–191.
9. K.M. Martin, R. Safavi-Naini and H. Wang. Bounds and techniques for efficient redistribution of secret shares to new access structures. *The Computer Journal*, 42, No.8 (1999) 638–649.
10. A. Shamir. How to share a secret. *Communications of the ACM*, 22 (1979) 612–613.
11. C.E. Shannon. Communication theory of secrecy systems. *Bell System Tech. Journal*, 28 (1949) 656–715.
12. G. J. Simmons. An introduction to shared secret and/or shared control schemes and their application. In *Contemporary Cryptology*, 441–497. IEEE Press, (1991).
13. D.R. Stinson. An explication of secret sharing schemes. *Des. Codes Cryptogr.*, 2 (1992) 357–390.
14. Y. Tamura, M. Tada and E. Okamoto. Update of access structure in Shamir's (k, n)-threshold scheme. *Proceedings of The 1999 Symposium on Cryptography and Information Security*, Kobe, Japan, January 26–29, (1999).

Appendix A: Entropy Basics

We present a brief description of the basic properties of entropy used throughout this paper. If X is a random variable that takes values in the finite set $[X]$ and p_X is the corresponding probability distribution then the entropy of X is

$$H(X) = - \sum_{x \subset [X]} p_X(x) \log p_X(x).$$

The entropy $H(X)$ measures the average uncertainty of X. It follows that $0 \leq H(X) \leq \log |[X]|$, where $H(X) = 0$ when X takes one value with certainty, and $H(X) = \log |[X]|$ when each value is equi-probable. Given a second random variable Y that takes values in the finite set $[Y]$ and a joint probability distribution p_{XY} (with corresponding entropy denoted $H(X,Y)$), the *conditional entropy* $H(X|Y)$ is defined as

$$H(X|Y) = - \sum_{y \in [Y]} \sum_{x \in [X]} p_Y(y) p_{XY}(x|y) \log p_{XY}(x|y)$$

where for $x \in [X]$ and $y \in [Y]$, $p_{XY}(x|y)$ denotes the conditional probability of x given y. The conditional entropy measures the average uncertainty of X given the value taken by Y. It can be shown that $H(X,Y) = H(X) + H(Y|X)$ and that $0 \leq H(X|Y) \leq H(X)$. The quantity $H(X) - H(X|Y)$ is often conveniently abbreviated to $I(X;Y)$ and is referred to as the *mutual information* between X and Y. Similarly, if Z is another random variable that takes values in the finite set $[Z]$ then $0 \leq H(X|Y,Z) \leq H(X|Y)$ and the *conditional mutual information* between X and Y given Z is $I(X;Y|Z) = H(X|Z) - H(X|Y,Z)$ (where the definition of $H(X|Y,Z)$ uses the joint probability distribution p_{YZ}). It is easy to show that $I(X;Y) = I(Y;X)$ and $I(X;Y|Z) = I(Y;X|Z)$. It is simple to extend these definitions to several random variables. For example, if $X_1, \ldots, X_n$ are random variables such as X then we have the *chain rule* that $H(X_1 \ldots X_n) = \sum_{i=1}^{n} H(X_i|X_1, \ldots, X_{i-1})$. There is a similar chain rule for mutual information. For details and more properties of entropy, see a general background text such as [4].

Appendix B: Proof of Lemma 1

Proof. (i) This is contained in Lemma 5 of Blakley *et al* [2].
(ii) This is contained in Lemma 6 of Blakley *et al* [2].
(iii) We have that

$$I(K_l; S_i \mid S_{j_1}, \ldots, S_{j_l}, B_{(j_1)}, \ldots, B_{(j_1,\ldots,j_l)}, K_0, \ldots, K_{l-1})$$
$$= I(K_l; S_i, S_{j_1}, \ldots, S_{j_l}, B_{(j_1)}, \ldots, B_{(j_1,\ldots,j_l)}, K_0, \ldots, K_{l-1})$$
$$-I(K_l; S_{j_1}, \ldots, S_{j_l}, B_{(j_1)}, \ldots, B_{(j_1,\ldots,j_l)}, K_0, \ldots, K_{l-1}) \text{ (by chain rule)}$$
$$= I(K_l; S_i, S_{j_1}, \ldots, S_{j_l}, B_{(j_1)}, \ldots, B_{(j_1,\ldots,j_l)}, K_0, \ldots, K_{l-1}) \text{ (by (i))}$$
$$= H(K_l) - H(K_l \mid S_i, S_{j_1}, \ldots, S_{j_l}, B_{(j_1)}, \ldots, B_{(j_1,\ldots,j_l)}, K_0, \ldots, K_{l-1})$$
$$= H(K_l),$$

since $H(K_l \mid S_i, S_{j_1}, \ldots, S_{j_l}, B_{(j_1)}, \ldots, B_{(j_1,\ldots,j_l)}, K_0, \ldots, K_{l-1})$
$$\leq H(K_l \mid S_i, B_{(j_1)}, \ldots, B_{(j_1,\ldots,j_l)}) = 0 \text{ (by condition 2 of Definition 2.)}$$

(iv) We have (by repetition of the argument)

$$H(S_i \mid S_{j_1}, \ldots, S_{j_l}, B_{(j_1)}, \ldots, B_{(j_1,\ldots,j_l)}, K_0, \ldots, K_{l-1})$$
$$= I(S_i; K_l \mid S_{j_1}, \ldots, S_{j_l}, B_{(j_1)}, \ldots, B_{(j_1,\ldots,j_l)}, K_0, \ldots, K_{l-1})$$
$$+H(S_i \mid S_{j_1}, \ldots, S_{j_l}, B_{(j_1)}, \ldots, B_{(j_1,\ldots,j_l)}, K_0, \ldots, K_l)$$
$$= k + H(S_i \mid S_{j_1}, \ldots, S_{j_l}, B_{(j_1)}, \ldots, B_{(j_1,\ldots,j_l)}, K_0, \ldots, K_l)$$
$$\text{(by (iii))}$$
$$\geq k + H(S_i \mid S_{j_1}, \ldots, S_{j_l}, S_{j_{l+1}}, B_{(j_1)}, \ldots, B_{(j_1,\ldots,j_l)}, B_{(j_1,\ldots,j_{l+1})}, K_0, \ldots, K_l)$$

$$\vdots$$
$$= (L + 1 - l)k + H(S_i \mid S_{j_1}, \ldots, S_{j_L}, B_{(j_1)}, \ldots, B_{(j_1, \ldots, j_L)}, K_0, \ldots, K_L)$$
$$\geq (L + 1 - l)k.$$

If $H(S_i) = (L + 1)k$ then equality holds throughout the above calculation for $l = 0$ and the result follows.

Appendix C: Proof of Lemma 2

Proof. We have

$$H(K_l \mid S_{i_1}, \ldots, S_{i_l}, K_0, \ldots, K_{l-1}) \leq H(K_l) = k$$

and $H(K_l \mid S_{i_1}, \ldots, S_{i_l}, K_0, \ldots, K_{l-1})$

$$\geq H(K_l \mid S_{i_1}, \ldots, S_{i_l}, B_{(i_1)}, \ldots, B_{(i_1, \ldots, i_l)}, K_0, \ldots, K_{l-1})$$
$$= H(K_l) - I(K_l; S_{i_1}, \ldots, S_{i_l}, B_{(i_1)}, \ldots, B_{(i_1, \ldots, i_l)}, K_0, \ldots, K_{l-1})$$
$$= H(K_l) = k \quad \text{(by Lemma 1(i))}$$

Thus $H(K_l \mid S_{i_1}, \ldots, S_{i_l}, K_0, \ldots, K_{l-1}) = k$. Also, $H(S_{i_{l+1}} \mid S_{i_1}, \ldots, S_{i_l}, K_0, \ldots, K_l)$

$$\geq H(S_{i_{l+1}} \mid S_{i_1}, \ldots, S_{i_l}, B_{(i_1)}, \ldots, B_{(i_1, \ldots, i_l)}, K_0, \ldots, K_l)$$
$$\geq (L - l)k \quad \text{(by Lemma 1(iv))}.$$

Appendix D: Proof of Lemma 3

Proof. We have (by repetition of the argument)

$$H(S_{j_{l+1}}) = I(S_{j_{l+1}}; K_0) + H(S_{j_{l+1}} \mid K_0)$$
$$= k + H(S_{j_{l+1}} \mid K_0)$$
$$\quad \text{(by Lemma 1(ii))}$$
$$\geq k + H(S_{j_{l+1}} \mid B_{(j_1)}, K_0)$$
$$= k + I(S_{j_{l+1}}; K_1 \mid B_{(j_1)}, K_0) + H(S_{j_{l+1}} \mid B_{(j_1)}, K_0, K_1)$$
$$= 2k + H(S_{j_{l+1}} \mid B_{(j_1)}, K_0, K_1)$$
$$\quad \text{(by Lemma 1(ii))}$$
$$\vdots$$
$$= (l + 1)k + H(S_{j_{l+1}} \mid B_{(j_1)}, \ldots, B_{(j_1, \ldots, j_l)}, K_0, \ldots, K_l)$$

and the result follows.

Appendix E: Proof of Lemma 4

Proof. Let $(j_1, \ldots, j_m) \in \mathcal{X}(n, m)$ and $(i_1, \ldots, i_\alpha) \in \mathcal{X}(n, \alpha)$ be such that

$$\{i_l, \ldots, i_\alpha\} \cap \{j_1, \ldots, j_{\hat{l}}\} = \emptyset \qquad \text{for } l = 1, \ldots, \alpha \tag{1}$$

where $\hat{l} = \min(m, n - \alpha + l - 1)$. We have

$$\sum_{l=1}^{m} H(B_{(j_1, \ldots, j_l)}) + (m + 1)k$$

$$= \sum_{l=1}^{m} H(B_{(j_1, \ldots, j_l)}) + \sum_{l=0}^{m} H(K_l)$$

$$\geq H(B_{(j_1)}, \ldots, B_{(j_1, \ldots, j_m)}, K_0, \ldots, K_m)$$

$$= H(B_{(j_1)}, \ldots, B_{(j_1, \ldots, j_m)}, K_0, \ldots, K_m, S_{i_1}, \ldots, S_{i_\alpha})$$
$$\quad - H(S_{i_1}, \ldots, S_{i_\alpha} \mid B_{(j_1)}, \ldots, B_{(j_1, \ldots, j_m)}, K_0, \ldots, K_m)$$

$$\geq H(S_{i_1}, \ldots, S_{i_\alpha}, K_0, \ldots, K_m)$$
$$\quad - H(S_{i_1}, \ldots, S_{i_\alpha} \mid B_{(j_1)}, \ldots, B_{(j_1, \ldots, j_m)}, K_0, \ldots, K_m)$$

$$= \sum_{l=0}^{\alpha-1} \bigl(H(K_l \mid S_{i_1}, \ldots, S_{i_l}, K_0, \ldots, K_{l-1})$$

$$\qquad + H(S_{i_{l+1}} \mid S_{i_1}, \ldots, S_{i_l}, K_0, \ldots, K_l) \bigr)$$

$$\quad + \sum_{l=\alpha}^{m} H(K_l \mid S_{i_1}, \ldots, S_{i_\alpha}, K_0, \ldots, K_{l-1})$$
$$\quad - H(S_{i_1}, \ldots, S_{i_\alpha} \mid B_{(j_1)}, \ldots, B_{(j_1, \ldots, j_m)}, K_0, \ldots, K_m)$$
$$\text{(by the chain rule)}$$

$$\geq \sum_{l=0}^{\alpha-1} (k + (L - l)k) + \sum_{l=\alpha}^{m} k$$
$$\quad - H(S_{i_1}, \ldots, S_{i_\alpha} \mid B_{(j_1)}, \ldots, B_{(j_1, \ldots, j_m)}, K_0, \ldots, K_m)$$
$$\text{(by Lemma 2)}$$

$$= (m + 1)k + \sum_{l=1}^{\alpha} (L - \alpha + l)k$$
$$\quad - H(S_{i_1}, \ldots, S_{i_\alpha} \mid B_{(j_1)}, \ldots, B_{(j_1, \ldots, j_m)}, K_0, \ldots, K_m)$$

$$\geq (m + 1)k + \sum_{l=1}^{\alpha} (L - \alpha + l)k$$

$$\quad - \sum_{l=1}^{\beta} H(S_{i_l} \mid B_{(j_1)}, \ldots, B_{(j_1, \ldots, j_{n-\alpha+l-1})}, K_0, \ldots, K_{n-\alpha+l-1})$$

$$\quad - \sum_{l=\beta+1}^{\alpha} H(S_{i_l} \mid B_{(j_1)}, \ldots, B_{(j_1, \ldots, j_m)}, K_0, \ldots, K_m)$$
$$\text{where } \beta = \max(0, m - n + \alpha)$$
$$\text{(since } n - \alpha + l - 1 < m \text{ for } l \leq m + n - \alpha)$$

$$\geq (m+1)k + \sum_{l=1}^{\alpha}(L-\alpha+l)k$$

$$- \sum_{l=1}^{\beta}(L-n+\alpha-l+1)k$$

$$- \sum_{l=\beta+1}^{\alpha}(L-m)k$$

(since, by (1), we can apply Lemma 3,
as $\min(m, n-\alpha+l-1) = n-\alpha+l-1$ for $l \leq m-n+\alpha$
and $\min(m, n-\alpha+l-1) = m$ for $l \geq m-n+\alpha+1$)

$$= (m+1)k + \sum_{l=1}^{\beta}(n-2\alpha-1+2l)k + \sum_{l=\beta+1}^{\alpha}(m-\alpha+l)k$$

$$= (m+1)k + \sum_{l=1}^{m}\min(l, n-l)k.$$

The last equality follows by counting, firstly by columns and secondly by rows, the number of points of the 2-dimensional integer lattice bounded by the quadrangle with vertices $A = (\alpha+1-\gamma, \gamma), B = (\alpha, 1), C = (\alpha, m)$ and $D = (m+\alpha+1-2\gamma, m)$, where $\gamma = \min(m, \frac{n}{2})$. (Note that $D = (\beta+1, m)$. Also, $D = A$ if $\alpha = m$, so that $ABCD$ is a triangle.) Thus the bound is established.

Requirements for Group Independent Linear Threshold Secret Sharing Schemes*

Brian King

Purdue School of Engineering and Technology, IUPUI campus
briking@iupui.edu

Abstract. In a t out of n threshold scheme, any subset of t or more participants can compute the secret key k, while subsets of $t-1$ or less participants cannot compute k. Some schemes are designed for specific algebraic structures, for example finite fields. Whereas other schemes can be used with any finite abelian group. In [24], the definition of group independent sharing schemes was introduced. In this paper, we develop bounds for group independent t out of n threshold schemes. The bounds will be lower bounds which discuss how many subshares are required to achieve a group independent linear threshold scheme. In particular, we will show that our bounds for the $n-1$ out of n threshold schemes are tight for infinitely many n.

Keywords: *secret sharing, linear secret sharing, threshold cryptography, group independent linear threshold schemes, monotone span programs, and bounds on share size.*

1   Introduction

Secret sharing is important in the cases where a secret needs to be distributed over a set of n participants so that only authorized subsets of participants can recover the secret. A setting where the authorized sets consists of all subsets of t or more is called a t out of n threshold secret sharing scheme. Some threshold schemes are constructed for certain algebraic structures, such as fields, groups, semi-groups, etc. Shamir's scheme [27] provides an efficient way to construct t out of n threshold sharing over a field. However, in many cases the setting of the secret space is not a field, for example in RSA [26]. In some cases when the secret space is not a field, it is possible to embed the secret within a field and share it out using Shamir's secret sharing scheme. In threshold cryptography, for example threshold signature sharing [6,12], the participants are not reconstructing a secret but a function of the secret (for example a signature). In such cases, one cannot embed the secret within a field, and must utilize the algebraic structure for which the secret space resides. When developing RSA threshold signature schemes an alternative to Shamir's scheme must be used. Some of these alternatives rely on tailoring the scheme to this algebraic setting [18,19]. Other alternatives introduced the concept of developing threshold schemes which can be used over

---

* This work was partially funded by NSF grant CCR-9508528.

L. Batten and J. Seberry (Eds.): ACISP 2002, LNCS 2384, pp. 89–106, 2002.

any finite abelian group, see [11,14]. A third alternative described how threshold sharing can be achieved over any finite group [13], even non abelian groups, this can as well be used with abelian groups.

The group independent sharing schemes in [11,14] provide zero-knowledge threshold sharing. Thus not only do they provide a method for threshold RSA sharing, but as well, the only known method to achieve zero-knowledge RSA threshold sharing. Group independent sharing is important as well, for the following observation. New public key paradigms are constantly being developed, group independent sharing schemes provides the most secure way to develop sharing schemes for these new public key alternatives.

Our intent is to provide lower bounds for the number of subshare in *group independent linear threshold schemes - GILTS*. A considerable amount of work on creating bounds for secret sharing schemes has been generated. Using entropy, Karnin, Greene, and Hellman [22], were able to develop an upper bound on the size of n given an ideal[1] t out of n threshold scheme. In [3], Blackburn, Burmester, Desmedt, and Wild developed an upper bound on the size of n given a perfect t out n threshold scheme. In addition, they developed a lower bound on share expansion for a t out of n threshold scheme. This implies a bound on the size of shares, and in the case of a 2 out of n threshold scheme their bound is tight. Our work is an extension of the Blackburn et. al. work, since they have created bounds for t out of n threshold scheme's which can be applied in group independent threshold schemes. Our bound for a t out of n threshold scheme is an improvement on their bound whenever $t \geq \frac{n+1}{2}$. Other work involving bounds on secret sharing schemes, typically involved creating upper bounds on information rate for example see [4,5,7,9,28]. A lower bound on the number of subshares, immediately implies an upper bound on the average information rate, in the cases where each participant's share space is equal to $\mathcal{K}^{a_i}$ where $\mathcal{K}$ is the set of secrets and a_i is a positive integer (which is the setting in which we will work). However, all of [4,5,7,9,28] are working with general secret sharing with some monotone access structure, whereas we are working with t out of n threshold sharing. The problem of developing lower bounds on the number of subshares for general secret sharing is quite different than the emphasis of this paper. For a lower bound on share size of general secret sharing may be high due to the existence of a certain access structures.

In [21], Karchmer and Wigderson introduced the notion of monotone span programs and its connection to secret sharing schemes. Within [21], the authors established lower bounds concerning the size of monotone span program for Boolean function which have at least t ones, which immediately implied lower bounds on number of shares distributed to participants in a t out of n threshold scheme defined over a finite field. Their bounds include, but are not limited to: a tight bound of a 2 out of n scheme which indicated that the number of shares is $n \log_2 n$ and an asymptotic bound on the $n - 1$ out of n scheme expressed,

---

[1] The information rate for participant P_i is the ratio of the number of bits in the secret to the number of bits in a share $\overline{s}_i$. A sharing scheme is called ideal if the information rate for each participant is 1.

using complexity notation, as $O(n \log_2 n)$. Here they established that the optimal monotone span program for Boolean functions which have at least $n - 1$ ones satisfied that the program size was $\leq 2n \log_2 n$ (see Theorem 12 in [21]). Thus implying the big O bound. However, the Karchmer and Wigderson bound does not imply that there cannot be an $n-1$ out of n with share size less than $n \log_2 n$. Within this paper we prove that $n \log_2 n$ is the lower bound. In addition our work is developed within a broader context. That is if we extend the notion of *monotone span programs* over a field to *monotone span programs defined over free abelian group*, then we provide lower bounds for monotone span programs over "free abelian groups" which compute Boolean functions which have at least t ones.

In [24], the definition of a group independent sharing scheme was introduced. In addition to providing the definition, [24] explored what the amount of randomness was needed to generate group independent sharing schemes. Some of the randomness bounds developed, were dependent on the number of subshares distributed to the participants.

Organization of this paper is as follows. We first provide some background material. We review the definition of a GILTS as given in [24], and review pertinent GILTS results. We then describe a lemma which allows a participant to reorganize their subshares. (This reorganization provides us a representation for which it is easier to develop our lower bounds on share size.) We then develop our lower bounds. Throughout the paper we provide examples of what we mean by a t out of n GILTS, as well as an example of reducing a matrix to Smith-normal form. (In some cases, these examples have been moved to the appendix.)

2   Definitions and Notation

$M_{m \times n}(\mathbf{Z})$ represents the set of all m by n matrices with integer entries. If A is a matrix, it's transpose will be denoted by A^T. A row (column) operation of type I is a row (column) interchange. A row (column) operation of type II is a row (column) multiplied by a nonzero constant. A row (column) operation of type III is a row (column) multiplied by a nonzero constant added to another row (column) leaving this result in the second row (column). The rank of a matrix is the number of linearly independent rows within the matrix. If $x_1 \ldots x_n$ are vectors then a linear combination is $\sum_{i=1}^{n} \lambda_i x_i$ where $\lambda_i \in \mathbf{Z}$. $GL(n, \mathbf{Z})$ will denote the group with respect to matrix multiplication of all $n \times n$ nonsingular integer matrices (see [25]). All row vectors will be denoted as x. If A is a matrix where A is partitioned by $A = [A_1 | A_2 | \cdots | A_n]$ and x is a row of A, then x has a partition, which we represent as $x = (x_1, x_2, \ldots, x_n)$. Column vectors will be denoted by $\overline{x}$. The exponent of a group G is the smallest positive integer a such that $a \cdot g$ is the identity for all elements $g \in G$.[2] The set Γ of all sets of t or more participants is called the access structure. Because every set of t or more

---

[2] If G is an multiplicative group then the exponent is the smallest positive integer a such that $g^a = e$ for all $g \in G$.

participants contains a set of precisely t participants, we will use Γ_0 to represent those sets which contain exactly t participants.

Definition 1. [14,15] A linear secret sharing scheme is one in which for each set $B = \{i_1, \ldots i_t\}$ of t participants, the secret k can be written as $k = \sum_{j=1}^t \psi_{B,i_j}(\bar{s}_{i_j})$ where ψ_{B,i_j} is a homomorphism from participant P_{i_j}'s share space $\mathcal{S}_{i_j}(+)$ to the keyspace $\mathcal{K}(+)$.

This can be algebraically represented as:

$$\begin{bmatrix} \psi_{B_1,1} & \psi_{B_1,2} & \cdots & \psi_{B_1,n} \\ \psi_{B_2,1} & \psi_{B_2,2} & \cdots & \psi_{B_2,n} \\ \vdots & \vdots & & \vdots \\ \psi_{B_{|\Gamma|},1} & \psi_{B_{|\Gamma|},2} & \cdots & \psi_{B_{|\Gamma|},n} \end{bmatrix} \begin{bmatrix} \bar{s}_1 \\ \bar{s}_2 \\ \vdots \\ \bar{s}_n \end{bmatrix} = \begin{bmatrix} k \\ k \\ \vdots \\ k \end{bmatrix}$$

where $\psi_{B_i,j} \cdot \bar{s}_j$ represents $\psi_{B_i,j}(\bar{s}_j)$.

There are many examples of threshold schemes which are linear, including [3, 14,22,27]. In [11,14], the secret space was a module (finite abelian group), and the scalars belonged to the set of integers $\mathbf{Z}$. Thus the scheme itself can be written in the form of a matrix, with integer entries, the column matrix that would be multiplied to this integer matrix would be the shares (entries belonging to the module). The number of rows of this integer matrix would be at least $\binom{n}{t}$. Note that there is no requirement that the integer entries in this matrix are either 0,1, or -1. In fact in [14], the integer entries most certainly take on other values.

2.1 Definition of a t out of n Group Independent Linear Threshold Sharing Scheme

As introduced in [24], a group independent linear threshold sharing scheme is defined as:

Definition 2. [24] Let $\mathbf{K} = \{\mathcal{K}|\mathcal{K}$ is a finite abelian group$\}$. A group independent t out of n linear threshold scheme or GILTS is an ordered pair $(\Psi, \mathcal{S})$ such that:
(1) For each $\mathcal{K} \in \mathbf{K}$ and for each $i = 1, \ldots, n$ there corresponds a sharespace $S_{i,\mathcal{K}}$. We write $\mathcal{S}_i = \{S_{i,\mathcal{K}} : \mathcal{K} \in \mathbf{K}\}$ and $\mathcal{S} = (\mathcal{S}_1, \mathcal{S}_2, \ldots, \mathcal{S}_n)$.
(2) For all $B \in \Gamma_0$ and for all i there exists a function $\psi_{B,i}$ such that for all $\mathcal{K} \in \mathbf{K}$, $\psi_{B,i} : S_{i,\mathcal{K}} \longrightarrow \mathcal{K}$ is a homomorphism. Further, for all $k \in \mathcal{K}$, shares $\bar{s}_i$ belonging to $S_{i,\mathcal{K}}$ are distributed to participant P_i such that $\forall B \in \Gamma_0$, $k = \sum_{i \in B} \psi_{B,i}(\bar{s}_i)$,
   (i) $Prob(\mathbf{k} = k | \bar{s}_{i_1} = \bar{s}_{i_1}, \ldots, \bar{s}_{i_{t-1}} = \bar{s}_{i_{t-1}}) = Prob(\mathbf{k} = k)$, and
   (ii) $Prob(\mathbf{k} = k | \bar{s}_{i_1} = \bar{s}_{i_1}, \ldots, \bar{s}_{i_t} = \bar{s}_{i_t}) = 1$.

Ψ is used to represent $[\psi_{B,i}]_{i=1,\ldots,n;B \in \Gamma_0}$.

Example 1. [17] A group independent 2 out of 3 threshold scheme.
Let k represent an indeterminate for which once a group $\mathcal{K}$ is chosen, will be replaced by the secret. Let r_1 and r_2 represent indeterminates for which once $\mathcal{K}$ is

fixed, will be selected randomly from $\mathcal{K}$ to achieve Definition 2 (2)(i) and (2)(ii). For all $\mathcal{K} \in \mathbf{K}$, define $S_{1,\mathcal{K}} = \mathcal{K}$ and $S_{i,\mathcal{K}} = \mathcal{K} \times \mathcal{K}$ for $i=2, 3$. There are 3 sets which belong to Γ_0. Define $\psi_{\{1,2\},1}(x) = x$, $\psi_{\{1,3\},1}(x) = x$, $\psi_{\{1,2\},2}(x_1, x_2) = x_1$, $\psi_{\{2,3\},2}(x_1, x_2) = x_2$ $\psi_{\{1,3\},3}(x_1, x_2) = x_1$, and $\psi_{\{2,3\},2}(x_1, x_2) = x_2$. For $i \notin B$, $B \in \Gamma_0$, define $\psi_{B,i}(x) = 0$.

Shares will be distributed as follows: P_1 has 1 subshare with $\overline{s}_1 = k - r_1$, P_2 has 2 subshares with $\overline{s}_2 = [r_1, k - r_2]^T$, and P_3 has 2 subshares with $\overline{s}_3 = [r_1, r_2]^T$. Once a group $\mathcal{K}$ is fixed, and the secret k is selected, assuming that the distribution of the secrets is uniform over $\mathcal{K}$, we randomly and independently select r_1 and r_2 from $\mathcal{K}$. We satisfy Definition 2 due to the one-time pad. Of course there is a simpler representation of Ψ so that $\Psi[\overline{s}_1, \overline{s}_2, \overline{s}_3]^T = [k, k, k]^T$. That is,

$$
\begin{bmatrix} 1 & 1 & 0 & 0 & 0 \\ 1 & 0 & 0 & 1 & 0 \\ 0 & 0 & 1 & 0 & 1 \end{bmatrix} \begin{bmatrix} \overline{s}_1 \\ \overline{s}_2 \\ \overline{s}_3 \end{bmatrix} = \begin{bmatrix} k \\ k \\ k \end{bmatrix}.
$$

2.2   Assumptions Made

We adopt similar assumptions that were made in [24], they are summarized as follows.

– We assume that $S_{i,\mathcal{K}}$ is the direct product $\mathcal{K}^{a_i}$, since this is the only method known to achieve group independent sharing (here $S_{i,\mathcal{K}}$ denotes participant P_i's share space and $\mathcal{K}$ is the keyspace, a_i is some positive integer).
– It is assumed that $\psi_{B,i}$ is a row matrix (with a_i columns) of integers (i.e. P_i possesses subshares which belong to the keyspace), such that $\psi_{B,i}(\overline{s}_i) = \psi_{B,i} \cdot \overline{s}_i$ where the latter is a scalar dot product between an integer vector and a vector containing group entries.
– Let Ψ describe a group independent t out of n threshold scheme. Then Ψ is a matrix belonging to $M_{\mu \times \mathcal{T}}(\mathbf{Z})$, where μ represents the number of rows of Ψ and $\mathcal{T} = \sum_{i=1}^{n} a_i$. Shares are distributed to the n participants (which we collectively represent by $\overline{s}$) such that

$$
\Psi \overline{s} = \overline{k} \text{ where } \overline{k} = [\alpha_1 k, \alpha_2 k, \ldots, \alpha_\mu k]^T, \tag{1}
$$

and α_i is either 0 or 1. When $\alpha_i = 1$, this row describes how the set of participants (those with nonzero entries) can compute k. [3]
– For each i, $\overline{s}_i$ denotes the share distributed to P_i. This share consists of a_i subshares, the jth subshare of participant P_i will be denoted by $s_{i,j}$. It is assumed that all subshares are used in Ψ. As $s_{i,j}$ must be used in Ψ there exists a row ψ in Ψ such that the coefficient in j^{th} column $\psi_{B,i}$ is nonzero.

---

[3] To reduce the amount of randomness needed, one may want to introduce additional dependencies in Ψ. Such a dependency is introduced when an $\alpha_i = 0$. To illustrate this we provide two examples in the appendix, see Examples 8 and 9.

- Although the description of a GILTS may resemble sharing schemes over a field, recall that we are working with finite abelian groups. The tools that can be used when working with a field are much broader than the tools that we can employ. For example, in a field all $n \times n$ matrices of full rank are nonsingular. One must be careful when working with finite abelian groups, for an integer scalar applied to a group element represents repeated computations with the group element. Thus all scalars must be integers, as well, as all matrices must have integer entries. Further an invertible matrix, should satisfy that its inverse has integer entries. This restricts row/column operations on matrices to those of type I and/or III.
- It is permitted to perform row (column) operation of type II as long as we restrict ourselves to multiplying the row (column) by the scalar -1. If a group $\mathcal{K}$ is fixed then one will be permitted to multiply rows (columns) by other nonzero scalars. (For example, if the fixed group $\mathcal{K}$ has a prime exponent, then the entries in Ψ are reduced modulo the exponent, belong to a field. In this case one can use any nonzero field element as a scalar and perform row/column operations of type II.) Lastly, there will be occasions when we do use row operations of type II with integer scalars, but in those cases, the inverse of the matrix will not be relevant and will not be used.
- Many of our results for a GILTS (group independent linear threshold scheme) are developed using familiar mathematical tools like reduction to Smith-normal form, reduction to Gauss-Jordan form, etc. Often these tools are applied to the general representation of Ψ, at other times these tools are applied to the scheme where a group $\mathcal{K}$ has been adopted.[4] Note that any lower bound required by a group $\mathcal{K}$ implies a lower bound for the GILTS. It is important to realize the consequence of the implementation of these tools. For example, reduction to Smith-normal form may be different dependent on whether it is applied to the general Ψ or $\Psi_{\mathcal{K}}$, the result of adopting the group $\mathcal{K}$. We always use a subscript $\mathcal{K}$ to indicate that the matrices will be reduced modulo the exponent of $\mathcal{K}$.

2.3   Reduction to Smith-Normal Form

An important tool will be the reduction to Smith-normal form on a matrix (for more information see [1,20,23]). Its use in this context for secret sharing was made in [15]. In this section, we survey the results given in [15] and [24].

Suppose that Ψ is reduced to Smith-normal form. Then there exists $U \in GL(\mu, \mathbf{Z})$ and $V \in GL(\sum a_i, \mathbf{Z})$ such that $U\Psi V = D$ where

$$D = \begin{bmatrix} D_l & 0 \\ 0 & 0 \end{bmatrix}$$

where D_l is a square diagonal $l \times l$ matrix with nonzero integer entries d_i along the diagonal, called the invariant factors, and satisfy $d_i | d_{i+1}$. U and V are nonsingular matrices which have integer entries, and l is the rank of Ψ. Observe

---

[4] In such cases we will use a subscript of $\mathcal{K}$, for example $\Psi_{\mathcal{K}}$ would represent the scheme Ψ when group $\mathcal{K}$ has been adopted.

that U can be interpreted as a series of row operations of types I and/or III, and V can be interpreted as a series of column operations of type I and/or III that are performed on Ψ to reduce it to D. Since the ring $\mathbf{Z}$ is a principal ideal domain, the invariant factors of Ψ are unique, up to sign, we assume without loss of generality that all invariant factors are positive.

Then $U\Psi VV^{-1}\overline{s} = U\overline{k}$. Hence $DV^{-1}\overline{s} = U\Psi VV^{-1}\overline{s} = U\overline{k}$. Consider the first l rows of the column matrix $U\overline{k}$. Each row can be interpreted as an integer $\sum_j \alpha_j u_{ij}$ applied to k. It follows then that $d_i|(\sum_j \alpha_j u_{ij})$. Since $d_i|\sum_{j=1}^{\mu} \alpha_j u_{ij}$ (for $i = 1, \ldots, l$), we can divide each of the first l rows by the corresponding d_i and still retain the form of an integer matrix. It follows then that we have

$$\begin{bmatrix} I_{l \times l} & 0_{l \times (\mathcal{T}-l)} \\ 0_{(\mu-l) \times l} & 0_{(\mu-l) \times (\mathcal{T}-l)} \end{bmatrix} V^{-1}\overline{s} = [k\frac{\sum_{i=1}^{\mu} \alpha_i u_{1i}}{d_1}, \ldots, k\frac{\sum_{i=1}^{\mu} \alpha_i u_{li}}{d_l}, 0, \ldots, 0]^T.$$

Recall $\mathcal{T} = \sum_{i=1}^{n} a_i$. Let $R = \sum a_i - l$, and let $r_1, \ldots, r_R$ be chosen uniformly at random from denote $\mathcal{K}$. Then

$$V^{-1}\overline{s} = [k\frac{\sum_{i=1}^{\mu} \alpha_i u_{1i}}{d_1}, \ldots, k\frac{\sum_{i=1}^{\mu} \alpha_i u_{li}}{d_l}, r_1, \ldots, r_R]^T.$$

Therefore

$$\overline{s} = V[\frac{\sum_{i=1}^{\mu} \alpha_i u_{1i}}{d_1}k, \ldots \frac{\sum_{i=1}^{\mu} \alpha_i u_{li}}{d_l}k, r_1, \ldots, r_R]^T. \tag{2}$$

Represent V as $V = [X|Y]$, where X is a $\sum a_i \times l$ matrix (which is formed by using the first l columns of V). Then $\overline{s}$ can be represented as

$$\overline{s} = C[k, r_1, \ldots, r_R]^T, \tag{3}$$

where $C = \left[X \cdot [\frac{\sum_{i=1}^{\mu} \alpha_i u_{1i}}{d_1}, \ldots, \frac{\sum_{i=1}^{\mu} \alpha_i u_{li}}{d_l}]^T | Y \right]$. Consequently the total number of subshares $\sum a_i$ can be expressed as $R+l$. R is the number of random elements required, and l is the rank of Ψ.

Let the rank of Ψ be denoted by l. Then there exists a matrix $U_1 \in GL(\mu, \mathbf{Z})$ (which can be interpreted as a series of row operations of types I and/or III) such that

$$U_1\Psi\overline{s} = U_1\overline{k} = [k, 0, \ldots, 0]^T. \tag{4}$$

We will represent $U_1\Psi$ by

$$U_1\Psi = [\boldsymbol{y}_1, \ldots, \boldsymbol{y}_l, 0, \ldots, 0]^T. \tag{5}$$

The following results were established in [24].

- For each $i = 1, \ldots, n$, either the rank of A_i equals the size of $\overline{s}_i$ or participant P_i can reduce his share size to the rank of A_i. That is, participant P_i can form share $\overline{s}'_i$, which is of size equal to rank of A_i, and P_i can form a new submatrix A'_i of rank equal to the rank of A_i such that $A_i\overline{s}_i = A'_i\overline{s}'_i$.

– For each $i = 1, \ldots, n$, C_{P_i} denotes those rows of C which pertain to participant P_i. Then for each i, either the rank of C_{P_i} equals a_i or it is possible to replace $\overline{s}_i$ by a share $\overline{s}'_i$ whose size is equal to rank of C_{P_i}.

The matrix A_i represents the manner in which participant P_i computes a partial secret using his subshares. The matrix C_{P_i} represents the manner in which the distributor (or dealer) forms the subshares for participant P_i. What we see is that the rank of both matrices can be assumed to be equal, otherwise there exists some dependency either in the way P_i computes partial secrets or in the way the distributor forms the subshares. In this case, it is possible to reduce share size, which removes the dependency. In [16], it was noted that within the Desmedt-Frankel scheme [14] there exists dependencies in the matrix which described the manner in which the partial secret were computed. Hence the authors were able to reduce the share size by one-half. From now on we assume that rank of $A_i =$ rank of $C_{P_i} = a_i$.

3 A Lemma That Allows Us to Reorganize Shares

We now describe an equivalent representation of shares distributed to participants in a GILTS. This representation aids us in creating lower bounds on the number of subshares. The motivation for this is as follows: in our effort to find lower bounds, it would be preferable if each participant (belonging to a given $B \in \Gamma_0$) would use exactly one of their subshares when they participate in the reconstruction of k. However, this is probably not true. In fact it is possible that when subshares are dealt out, a participant may always have to use more than one of their subshares during reconstruction. This lemma will imply that a participant can reorganize their subshares, so that for a certain collection of their subshares, for each subshare in this collection they are guaranteed that there exists a $B \in \Gamma_0$ such that the participant uses only that subshare during the reconstruction (the dealer is not needed to perform the reorganization).

For each i, reduce A_i to Smith-normal form: $U_{A_i} A_i V_{A_i} = D_{A_i}$ where D_{A_i} is a matrix with zeros off the diagonal, and the diagonal is $(d_{i1}, \ldots, d_{ia_i}, 0, \ldots, 0)$. For each i, A_i has rank a_i, and the invariant factors d_{ij} of A_i, satisfy $d_{ij}|d_{ij+1}$. Let ρ_i denote the largest integer (less than or equal to the rank of A_i), such that $d_{i\rho_i} = 1$. The proof is provided in the appendix.

Lemma 3. *Let $\Psi = [A_1| \cdots |A_n]$ be a GILTS. Then it is possible to replace A_i by A'_i and $\overline{s}_i$ by $\overline{s}'_i$ where the matrices have equal rank and the shares have equal size respectively, such that (1) $A_i \overline{s}_i = A'_i \overline{s}'_i$ and (2) there exists a series of row interchanges U' such that*

$$U'A'_i = \begin{bmatrix} I_{\rho_i \times \rho_i} & 0 \\ Y & Z \end{bmatrix}.$$

Remark. $I_{\rho_i \times \rho_i}$ is the identity matrix. Observe that participant P_i has rearranged his subshares so that ρ_i of participant P_i's subshares are such that for each of these subshares there exists a row of Ψ where P_i uses only that subshare during the reconstruction of the secret key k.

3.1   Definition of G, S, G_i, and S_i

Let $\mathbf{Z}^T = \{\boldsymbol{x} : \boldsymbol{x} = (\xi_1, \xi_2, \ldots, \xi_T) \text{ where } \xi_i \in \mathbf{Z})\}$, define $G = \{\boldsymbol{x} \in \mathbf{Z}^T : \boldsymbol{x} \cdot \overline{s} = 0\}$. Then G is an additive abelian group. An alternate but equivalent definition of G which uses the row matrices $\{\boldsymbol{y}_i : i = 2, \ldots, l\}$ defined by equation (5) (observe that $\boldsymbol{y}_1$ is omitted) is:

$$G = \{\boldsymbol{x} \in \mathbf{Z}^T : \boldsymbol{x} = \sum_{i=2}^{l} \theta_i \boldsymbol{y}_i \ \theta_i \in \mathbf{Z}\}. \tag{6}$$

The threshold scheme Ψ maps $\mathbf{Z}^T \longrightarrow < k, r_1, \ldots, r_R >$ by a homomorphism φ. [5] This follows implicitly from equation (3), by defining $\varphi(\boldsymbol{x}) = \boldsymbol{x} \cdot \overline{s}$. G is the kernel of the homomorphism φ.

Define $S = \{\boldsymbol{x} \in \mathbf{Z}^T : \boldsymbol{x} \cdot \overline{s} = k\}$. Then S is a coset of G, since $S = \boldsymbol{y}_1 + G$, where $\boldsymbol{y}_1$ is defined by equation (5). For each $\boldsymbol{x} \in \mathbf{Z}^T$, one can partition $\boldsymbol{x}$ into n blocks in the same manner as the matrix Ψ is partitioned into n blocks, i.e. $\Psi = [A_1| \cdots |A_n]$. Thus $\boldsymbol{x} = (\boldsymbol{x}_1, \boldsymbol{x}_2, \ldots, \boldsymbol{x}_n)$

For each $i = 1, \ldots, n$, define $G_i = \{\boldsymbol{x} \in G : \boldsymbol{x}_i = \boldsymbol{0}\}$. Observe that G_i is a subgroup of G. Similarly, define $S_i = \{\boldsymbol{x} \in S : \boldsymbol{x}_i = \boldsymbol{0}\}$. Then S_i is a coset of G_i.

3.2   Consequences of the Reorganization of Shares

Let $\Psi = [A_1| \cdots |A_n]$ be a GILTS. We will assume that each participant P_i has applied Lemma 3 to A_i.

Recall that ρ_i represents the number of invariant factors of A_i which are 1. Then by Lemma 3, for each $j = 1, \ldots, \rho_i$, there exists a $\boldsymbol{x} \in S$, such that block i of $\boldsymbol{x}$ denoted by $\boldsymbol{x}_i$, satisfies $\boldsymbol{x}_i = (0, \ldots, 0, 1, 0, \ldots, 0)$ where the 1, as illustrated, occurs in the jth position and the zeros occur in all other positions. Since S is a coset of G, it follows that for any $\boldsymbol{x} \in S$, $S = \boldsymbol{x} + G$. In addition, in a t out of n threshold scheme with $t < n$, each participant P_i does not participate in at least one set of t participants. Hence there exists a $\boldsymbol{z} \in S$ such that $\boldsymbol{z}_i = (0, \ldots, 0)$. Observing that $S = \boldsymbol{z} + G$, we see that for each $j = 1, \ldots, \rho_i$ there exists an $\boldsymbol{x}' \in G$ such that $\boldsymbol{x}_i' = (0, \ldots, 0, 1, 0, \ldots, 0)$ with a 1 in the jth position. Since $\boldsymbol{z} + \boldsymbol{x}' = \boldsymbol{x} \in S$ we have the property that $\forall j = 1, \ldots, \rho_i$ there exists an $\boldsymbol{x} \in S$ such that $\boldsymbol{x}_i = (0, \ldots, 0, 1, 0, \ldots, 0)$ where 1 is in the jth position.

3.3   A Comment on the Group G, Once a Group $\mathcal{K}$ Is Selected

The group G as described is infinite. Once a group $\mathcal{K}$ is chosen to use in Ψ, then the entries in Ψ can be reduced modulo the exponent $e_{\mathcal{K}}$ of $\mathcal{K}$. We will represent this "reduced" Ψ by $\Psi_{\mathcal{K}}$. We then apply the technique of reducing the rank of A_i to the rank of C_{P_i} as well as Lemma 3. to $\Psi_{\mathcal{K}}$. Apply the Smith-normal reduction to $\Psi_{\mathcal{K}}$, for the fixed group $\mathcal{K}$. Then rearrange the shares of P_i for all i, develop groups $G_{\mathcal{K}}$, $G_{i,\mathcal{K}}$ (for all i), and develop $S_{\mathcal{K}}$ and $S_{i,\mathcal{K}}$ (for all i). (We use

---

[5] $< k, r_1, \ldots, r_R >$ denotes the free abelian group.

a subscript of $\mathcal{K}$ to remind the reader that these groups and cosets are dependent on the group $\mathcal{K}$ that is adopted.) The group $G_\mathcal{K}$ differs from the group G (the group generated by Ψ) by the fact that $G_\mathcal{K}$ is finite, that the entries of $x \in G_\mathcal{K}$ are simply the entries of $x \in G$ reduced modulo the exponent $e_\mathcal{K}$, and that the θ_i that describe $G_\mathcal{K}$ in equation (6) belong to $\mathbf{Z}_{e_\mathcal{K}}$.

3.4   An Observation When $\mathcal{K}$ Has a Prime Exponent

Suppose $\mathcal{K}$ has an exponent $e_\mathcal{K}$ equal to prime p. Then $|G_\mathcal{K}| = p^{l-1}$. This follows from equation (6) and applying a modular reduction mod p to the θ_i.

For each participant P_i, let $a_{i,\mathcal{K}}$ denote the number of invariant factors of the original A_i (the A_i of the Ψ which has not been reduced modulo the exponent of $\mathcal{K}$) which are relatively prime with p. Thus $1 \leq a_{i,\mathcal{K}} \leq a_i$. Observe that if there exists an invariant factor of A_i which is not relatively prime with p, then (since p is prime) there will be a subshare that is NOT used in the threshold scheme for group $\mathcal{K}$. So $a_{i,\mathcal{K}}$ can be interpreted as the number of subshares participant P_i uses in the group $\mathcal{K}$. Since $\mathcal{K}$ has a prime exponent, the entries in Ψ belong to a field.[6] So we are allowed to use row operations of type II. Apply Smith-normal form to $A_{i,\mathcal{K}}$ (A_i with entries reduced modulo p), noting that we are now working with field $\mathcal{K}$. Thus all invariant factors are 1. For each $i = 1, \ldots, n$, and for each $j = 1, \ldots, a_{i,\mathcal{K}}$, there exists an $x \in G_\mathcal{K}$, such that $x_i = (0, \ldots, 0, 1, 0, \ldots, 0)$ where the 1 occurs in the jth position. It follows then that for all $w = 0, 1, 2, \ldots, p-1$, there exists an $x' \in G_\mathcal{K}$, such that $x_i' = (0, \ldots, 0, w, 0, \ldots, 0)$, i.e. $x + x + \cdots x \in G_\mathcal{K}$. As $G_\mathcal{K}$ is closed over all convex combinations, for each $w_1, w_2, \ldots, w_{a_{i,\mathcal{K}}} \in \{0, 1, 2, \ldots, p-1\}$, there exists an $x \in G_\mathcal{K}$, such that $x_i = (w_1, w_2, \ldots, w_{a_{i,\mathcal{K}}})$. Recall there exists a $z \in S_\mathcal{K}$ such that $z_i = (0, \ldots, 0)$.[7] As $S_\mathcal{K} = z + G_\mathcal{K}$, we see that for all $w_1, w_2, \ldots, w_{a_{i,\mathcal{K}}} \in \{0, 1, 2, \ldots, p-1\}$, there exists an $x \in S_\mathcal{K}$, such that $x_i = (w_1, w_2, \ldots, w_{a_{i,\mathcal{K}}})$.

$G_{i,\mathcal{K}}$ is a subgroup of $G_\mathcal{K}$. By the above argument, we see that the *index* of $G_{i,\mathcal{K}}$ in $G_\mathcal{K}$ is $p^{a_{i,\mathcal{K}}}$. That is $|G_\mathcal{K}|/|G_{i,\mathcal{K}}| = p^{a_{i,\mathcal{K}}}$. Therefore $|G_\mathcal{K}| = p^{a_{i,\mathcal{K}}}|G_{i,\mathcal{K}}|$. Of particular interest is the case when the prime p is 2. That is, when group $\mathcal{K}$ has exponent 2, the above equation reduces to

$$|G_\mathcal{K}| = 2^{a_{i,\mathcal{K}}}|G_{i,\mathcal{K}}|. \tag{7}$$

4   Our Bounds

Theorem 4. *For any finite abelian group $\mathcal{K}$ adopted in GILTS Ψ,*

$$(n-t)\binom{n}{t} \leq \sum_{i=1}^{n} |G_{i,\mathcal{K}}| \leq (n-t)|G_\mathcal{K}|.$$

---

[6] Computations are in $\mathbf{Z}_p$ rather than in $\mathbf{Z}$.
[7] The existence of z follows from the fact that $n \geq t+1$.

Proof. Let $\mathcal{K}$ be any finite abelian group used in Ψ.

For each $\boldsymbol{x} \in G_{\mathcal{K}}$, define the set $\mathcal{H}_x = \{i : \boldsymbol{x}_i = \boldsymbol{0}\}$. Thus $|\mathcal{H}_x|$ represents the number of participants who do not contribute a share to $\boldsymbol{x}$. Then $\sum_{\boldsymbol{x} \in G_{\mathcal{K}}} |\mathcal{H}_x|$ represents the "total number" of times participants do not contribute to some $\boldsymbol{x} \in G_{\mathcal{K}}$. By the definition of $G_{i,\mathcal{K}}$, $|G_{i,\mathcal{K}}|$ represents the number of times participant P_i does not contribute a share to some $\boldsymbol{x} \in G_{\mathcal{K}}$. Consequently $\sum_{\boldsymbol{x} \in G_{\mathcal{K}}} |\mathcal{H}_x| = \sum_{i=1}^{n} |G_{i,\mathcal{K}}|$.

For each $\boldsymbol{x} \in S_{\mathcal{K}}$, define the set $\mathcal{L}_x = \{i : \boldsymbol{x}_i = \boldsymbol{0}\}$. Thus $|\mathcal{L}_x|$ represents the number of participants who do not contribute a share to $\boldsymbol{x}$. $\sum_{\boldsymbol{x} \in S_{\mathcal{K}}} |\mathcal{L}_x|$ represents the total number of times participants do not contribute to some $\boldsymbol{x} \in S_{\mathcal{K}}$. By a similar argument, $\sum_{\boldsymbol{x} \in S_{\mathcal{K}}} |\mathcal{L}_x| = \sum_{i=1}^{n} |S_{i,\mathcal{K}}|$. Recalling that $S_{i,\mathcal{K}}$ is a coset of $G_{i,\mathcal{K}}$, we have $|S_{i,\mathcal{K}}| = |G_{i,\mathcal{K}}|$. Therefore $\sum_{\boldsymbol{x} \in S_{\mathcal{K}}} |\mathcal{L}_x| = \sum_{i=1}^{n} |G_{i,\mathcal{K}}|$.

We will now create bounds for $\sum_{\boldsymbol{x} \in S_{\mathcal{K}}} |\mathcal{L}_x|$. Observe that there exists $\binom{n}{t}$ sets B which contain t and only t participants. Therefore there exists at least $\binom{n}{t}$ elements x of $S_{\mathcal{K}}$ for which $|\mathcal{L}_x| \geq (n-t)$. Hence $(n-t)\binom{n}{t} \leq \sum_{\boldsymbol{x} \in S_{\mathcal{K}}} |\mathcal{L}_x|$.

Now we find an upper bound for $\sum_{\boldsymbol{x} \in S_{\mathcal{K}}} |\mathcal{L}_x|$. Since $\Psi_{\mathcal{K}}$ represents a t out of n threshold scheme, any set of participants which can calculate the secret k, needs to have at least t people participate. Therefore at most $n - t$ participants will not contribute. The number $\sum_{\boldsymbol{x} \in S_{\mathcal{K}}} |\mathcal{L}_x|$ represents the sum total of all nonparticipants over all $B \in \Gamma$ (i.e. each set of participants which can calculate the secret k). Consequently, $\sum_{\boldsymbol{x} \in S_{\mathcal{K}}} |\mathcal{L}_x| \leq (n-t)|S_{\mathcal{K}}|$. Hence $(n-t)\binom{n}{t} \leq \sum_{\boldsymbol{x} \in S_{\mathcal{K}}} |\mathcal{L}_x| \leq (n-t)|S_{\mathcal{K}}|$. From our above comments and due to the fact that $|S_{\mathcal{K}}| = |G_{\mathcal{K}}|$, $(n-t)\binom{n}{t} \leq \sum_{i=1}^{n} |G_{i,\mathcal{K}}| \leq (n-t)|G_{\mathcal{K}}|$.

Theorem 5. *For a GILTS described by Ψ satisfying Definition 2 the size of the shares distributed satisfy*

$$\sum_{i=1}^{n} a_i \geq \left\lceil n \log_2\left(\frac{n}{n-t}\right) \right\rceil.$$

Proof. If Ψ is a GILTS, then Ψ is a secure t out of n threshold scheme for all groups which have exponent 2. We now develop a lower bound on the sum of shares that are needed when we are working with a group $\mathcal{K}$ which has exponent of 2. Since $\mathcal{T} = \sum_i a_i \geq$ the number of shares of $\overline{s}$ used in groups with exponent 2, we will have developed the lower bound for $\sum a_i$. Let $\mathcal{T}_{\mathcal{K}} = \sum_{i=1}^{n} a_{i,\mathcal{K}}$, then $\mathcal{T} \geq \mathcal{T}_{\mathcal{K}}$.

Assume group $\mathcal{K}$ which has exponent 2. Recall that under this situation we can use equation (7), $|G_{i,\mathcal{K}}| = \frac{|G_{\mathcal{K}}|}{2^{a_{i,\mathcal{K}}}}$, where $a_{i,\mathcal{K}} \leq a_i$. Therefore

$$\sum_{i=1}^{n} |G_{i,\mathcal{K}}| = \sum_{i=1}^{n} \frac{|G_{\mathcal{K}}|}{2^{a_{i,\mathcal{K}}}} = |G_{\mathcal{K}}| \sum_{i=1}^{n} \frac{1}{2^{a_{i,\mathcal{K}}}}.$$

Using Theorem 4, we have

$$\sum_{i=1}^{n} |G_{i,\mathcal{K}}| = |G_{\mathcal{K}}| \sum_{i=1}^{n} \frac{1}{2^{a_{i,\mathcal{K}}}} \leq (n-t)|G_{\mathcal{K}}|.$$

Therefore

$$\sum_{i=1}^{n} \frac{1}{2^{a_{i,\kappa}}} \leq (n-t).$$

A well known result [10], is that the arithmetic mean is greater than or equal to the geometric mean. Consequently,

$$\sqrt[n]{\frac{1}{2^{a_{1,\kappa}}} \cdot \frac{1}{2^{a_{2,\kappa}}} \cdots \frac{1}{2^{a_{n,\kappa}}}} \leq \frac{\sum_{i=1}^{n} \frac{1}{2^{a_{i,\kappa}}}}{n}.$$

Hence

$$\prod_i 2^{a_i} \geq \prod_i 2^{a_{i,\kappa}} = (\prod_i 2^{-a_{i,\kappa}})^{-1} \geq (n^{-1} \sum_i 2^{-a_{i,\kappa}})^{-n} \geq ((n-t)/n)^{-n}$$

and so $\sum_{i=1}^{n} a_i \geq \left\lceil n \log_2(\frac{n}{n-t}) \right\rceil$.

Theorem 6. *Let Ψ represent a $n-1$ out of n GILTS, and $\sum a_i$ represents the number of subshares. Then $\sum_{i=1}^{n} a_i \geq \lceil n \log_2 n \rceil$.*

Proof. This result follows from Theorem 5, and taking $t = n-1$.

As described in [13], there exists $n-1$ out of n threshold schemes with a total of subshares equal to $n \log_2 n$, for $n = 2^1, 2^2, 2^3, \ldots$. Thus our lower bound in Theorem 6 is tight for infinitely many n.

Observe that the proof to Theorem 5 could be used to establish bounds for threshold schemes defined over fields of characteristic 2. As we have noted earlier, Karchmer and Wigderson [21] introduced the notion of span programs and monotone span programs. For a review of span programs see [2,21]. A span program is a matrix M over a field F with rows labeled by literals $\{x_1, \ldots, x_n\}$. The size of the program is the number of rows of M. A span programs accepts an assignment if and only if the all-ones row is a linear combination of the rows whose labels are consistent with the assignment. A monotone span program has only positive literals to represent the row labels. (The monotone span model can be used to describe secret sharing.) In [21], the authors described monotone span programs which compute Boolean functions which accept at least t ones, such functions we will denote by T_t^n. (A monotone span program which can compute at least t ones, can be used to describe a t out of n threshold scheme.) In particular, Karchmer and Wigderson derived bounds concerning the size of such monotone span programs. For example they showed that the smallest sized monotone span program for T_2^n was $\geq n \log_2 n$ and the smallest sized monotone span program for T_{n-1}^n was $O(n \log_2 n)$. Our work shows that the $n \log_2 n$ bound is an actual lower bound and not just an asymptotic bound of a monotone span program for T_{n-1}^n. Recently Cramer and others [8] have developed bounds, as well as constructed sharing schemes that satisfy these bounds, of montone span programs over a ring that compute T_t^n.

Every t out of n threshold scheme contains t out of $t+1$ schemes, when $n \geq t+1$. Suppose Ψ defines a t out of n GILTS. Consider the $t+1$ participants which have the $t+1$ smallest number of sub shares. Assume without loss of generality that these participants are $P_1, \ldots, P_{t+1}$. Restricting the sharing scheme to these $t+1$ results in a t out of $t+1$ GILTS. So $\sum_{i=1}^{t+1} a_i \geq (t+1) \lceil \log_2(t+1) \rceil$. Therefore their average share size is $\geq \log_2(t+1)$. For the remaining $n-t$ participants each of their shares must exceed or equal the average $\log_2(t+1)$, and so we have the following.

Corollary 7. *Let Ψ represent a t out of n GILTS where $\sum a_i$ represents the number of subshares. Then $\sum_{i=1}^{n} a_i \geq n \lceil \log_2(t+1) \rceil$.*

Remark. If $n \geq t+1$ then $t+1 \geq \frac{n}{n-t}$. Therefore the lower bound described above is better than the bound in Theorem 5. In [3], the bound that Blackburn et. al. established on share expansion implied that $\sum_i a_i \geq n \log_2(n - (t-2))$. Thus our bound is an improvement on their bound whenever $t+1 \geq n - (t-2)$. That is, when $t \geq \frac{n+1}{2}$.

4.1 Some Observations

These lower bounds concerning the share size do not assume anything about the distribution of the shares. For example we do not assume that each share is of the same size. However there appears to be a "penalty" if one purposely distributes the shares unevenly. For example suppose we have a 7 out of 9 GILTS, then by Theorem 7, $\sum a_i \geq 9 \cdot \log_2 8 = 27$. Suppose we purposely distribute a share that consists of only one subshare to a participant. Let's assume that participant is P_1. Consider the participant who possesses the largest number of subshares (we assume without loss of generality that it is P_2). Now $\{P_1, P_3, \ldots, P_9\}$ represent 8 participants. Hence they can be viewed as a 7 out of 8 GILTS. Thus $a_1 + \sum_{i=3}^{9} a_i \geq 8 \log_2 8 = 24$. Therefore $\sum_{i=3}^{9} a_i \geq 24 - 1 = 23$. Since the size of s_2 must exceed the average, we have $a_2 \geq 23/7$. Hence $a_2 \geq 4$. Consequently $\sum_{i=1}^{9} a_i \geq 24 + 4 = 28 > 27$. Thus this example illustrates that if a share of size 1 is dealt out, there appears to be a penalty (that is a penalty in terms of the application of our bounds).

Let the term *optimal GILTS* refer to a GILTS which uses a minimal number of subshares and the term *efficient GILTS* refer to a GILTS which uses a minimal amount of randomness. Then the bound in [3] implies that the scheme in [13] will construct an optimal 2 out of n GILTS (for infinitely many n). Our bound implies that the scheme in [13] will construct an optimal $n-1$ out of n scheme (for infinitely many n, whenever $n = 2^j$). An example of an optimal 3 out of 4 GILTS is provided in the appendix. See Example 10.

5 Conclusion

We have developed lower bounds for group independent linear threshold schemes. These bounds address the minimal number of required subshares to achieve Definition 2. We have observed that for the $n-1$ out of n threshold schemes, the bound on the share size is tight for infinitely many n. Because $\sum_i a_i = R + l$, bounds on R and l are important. However, because $\sum_i a_i$ is dependent on both, the minimal $\sum a_i$ will not necessarily occur when both R and l are minimal. The generation of random elements represents a significant computational requirement. Randomness in a GILTS has been discussed in [24], but further work remains. For example, will *efficient GILTS* always be optimal? Example 1 is optimal. Because $\sum a_i = 5 = \lceil 3 \log_2 3 \rceil$. (This follows from both our bound and [3]'s bound.) It can easily be proven that Example 1 is efficient. Example 8 in the appendix is an optimal 2 out of 4 GILTS, but it is not efficient. This is proven by Example 9 in the appendix, which is both optimal and efficient. Some questions:

(1) In our attempt to describe group independent linear sharing we assumed that each homomorphism $\psi_{B,i}$ was a row of integers. All known group independent schemes are of this form. Does there exist a group independent scheme not of this form?

(2) Is it possible to establish tight lower bounds on rank l and randomness R for all t out of n threshold scheme?

(3) Do all optimal group independent t out of n threshold scheme have invariant factors equal to 1? One can perform Smith-normal form on matrix C described in equation (3), are all invariant factors of C equal to 1, when the group independent threshold scheme is efficient?

(4) Many of the optimal schemes described in this paper are such that the integer entries of Ψ is 0,1, or -1. Is this true in general for all optimal schemes? It is known that in the GILTS defined in [14], there exist integer entries in Ψ that are neither 0,1 nor -1. Does this imply that one can apply reduction to Ψ to significantly reduce the share size?

The author wishes to thank the reviewers for their suggestions.

References

1. W. Adkins and S. Weintrab. *Algebra, an approach via module theory.* Springer-Verlag, NY, 1992.
2. A. Beimel, A. G'al, and M. Paterson. Lower bounds for monotone span programs. *Computational Complexity,* 6(1):29–45, 1997.
3. S. Blackburn, M. Burmester, Y. Desmedt, and P. Wild. "Efficient Multiplicative Sharing schemes". In *Advances in Cryptology - Eurocrypt '96, LNCS 1070,* pp. 107-118, Springer-Verlag, 1996.
4. C. Blundo, A. De Santis, A.G. Gaggia, and U. Vaccaro. "New Bounds on the Information rate of Secret Sharing Schemes". In *IEEE Trans. on Inform. Theory,* 41, no. 2, pp. 549-554, 1995.
5. C. Blundo, A. De Santis, R. De Simone,, and U. Vaccaro. "Tight Bounds on the Information rate of secret Sharing Schemes". In *Design, Codes and Cryptography,* 11, pp. 107-122, 1997.
6. C. Boyd, Digital Multisignatures, *Cryptography and coding,* Clarendon Press, 1989, pp 241-246.
7. R.M. Capocelli, A. De Santis, L. Gargano, and U. Vaccaro, "On the Size of Shares for secret Sharing Schemes" In *Journal of Cryptology,* 6, pp. 157-167, 1993.

8. R. Cramer. *Personal communication*
9. L. Csirmaz. "The Size of a Share Must Be large". In *Journal of Cryptology*, 10, pp. 223-231, 1997.
10. N. De Lillo. *Advanced Calculus with applications*. MacMillan, NY, 1982.
11. A. De Santis, Y. Desmedt, Y. Frankel, and M. Yung. "How to share a function". In *Proceedings of the twenty-sixth annual ACM Symp. Theory of Computing (STOC)*, pp. 522-533, 1994.
12. Y. Desmedt. Society and group oriented cryptography: a new concept. In *Advances of Cryptology- Crypto '87*
13. Y. Desmedt, G. Di Crescenzo, and M. Burmester. "Multiplicative non-Abelian sharing schemes and their application to threshold cryptography". In *Advances in Cryptology - Asiacrypt '94, LNCS 917.* pp. 21-32, Springer-Verlag, 1995.
14. Y. Desmedt and Y. Frankel. "Homomorphic zero-knowledge threshold schemes over any finite Abelian group". In *Siam J. Disc. Math. vol 7, no. 4* pp. 667-679, SIAM, 1994.
15. Y. Desmedt and S. Jajodia. Redistributing secret shares to new access structures and its applications. Tech. Report ISSE-TR-97-01, George Mason University, July 1997 ftp://isse.gmu.edu/pub/techrep/97.01.jajodia.ps.gz
16. Y. Desmedt, B. King, W. Kishimoto, and K. Kurosawa, "A comment on the efficiency of secret sharing scheme over any finite Abelian group", In *Information Security and Privacy*, ACISP'98 (Third Australasian Conference on Information Security and Privacy), LNCS 1438, 1998, 391-402.
17. Y. Frankel, Y. Desmedt, and M. Burmester. " Non-existence of homomorphic general sharing schemes for some key spaces", in *Advances of Cryptology- Crypto '92*, 740 ,1992 pp 549-557
18. Y. Frankel, P. Gemmel, P. Mackenzie, and M. Yung. "Optimal-Resilience Proactive Public-key Cryptosystems". In *Proc. 38th FOCS*, IEEE, 1997, p. 384-393.
19. R. Gennaro, S. Jarecki, H. Krawczyk, and T. Rabin. "Robust and efficient sharing of RSA functions". In *Advances of Cryptology-Crypto '96*, LNCS 1109, Springer Verlag, 1996, p. 157-172.
20. T. Hungerford. *Algebra.* Springer-Verlag, NY, 1974.
21. M. Karchmer and A. Wigderson. On span programs In *Proc. of 8th annual Complexity Theory Conference,* pp 102-111, 1993.
22. E. Karnin, J. Greene, and M. Hellman. "On secret sharing systems." In *IEEE Trans. Inform. Theory, 29(1),* pp. 35-41, 1983.
23. H.L. Keng. *Introduction to Number Theory.* Springer Verlag, NY 1982
24. B. King. "Randomness Required for Linear Threshold Sharing Schemes Defined over Any Finite Abelian Group". In *ACISP 2001.* pp. 376-391.
25. R. Lidl and G. Pilz. *Applied Abstract Algebra.* Springer Verlag, NY 1984
26. R. Rivest, A. Shamir, and L. Adelman, A method for obtaining digital signatures and public key cryptosystems, *Comm. ACM,* 21(1978), pp 294-299.
27. A. Shamir, How to share a secret, *Comm. ACM,* 22(1979), pp 612-613.
28. M. van Dijk. "A Linear Construction of Secret Sharing Schemes". In *Design, Codes and Cryptography 12*, pp. 161-201, 1997.

6 Appendix

6.1 Examples Concerning the Introduction of Dependencies between Shares

For many threshold schemes, we will see that some additional dependencies may need to be introduced.

Example 8. [13] Consider the following 2 out of 4 scheme, such that each participant is given 2 shares. Participant P_i is given share $\overline{s}_i$ such that s_{i1} and s_{i2} are defined by the following table.

s_{11}	s_{12}	s_{21}	s_{22}	s_{31}	s_{32}	s_{41}	s_{42}
$k-r_2$	$k-r_1$	$k-r_2$	r_1	r_2	$k-r_3$	r_2	r_3

For all $\mathcal{K} \in \mathbf{K}$, let $S_{i,\mathcal{K}} = \mathcal{K}^2$. k represents the secret, r_1, r_2, r_3 represent three random elements that will be chosen from the finite Abelian group uniformly random. Here $-r$ represents the inverse of r. Each row represents one of the $\binom{4}{2}$ sets B (sets of cardinality 2) and indicates how that set can compute the secret. The corresponding Ψ will be

$$\Psi = \begin{bmatrix} 1 & 0 & 0 & 0 & 1 & 0 & 0 & 0 \\ 1 & 0 & 0 & 0 & 0 & 0 & 1 & 0 \\ 0 & 0 & 1 & 0 & 1 & 0 & 0 & 0 \\ 0 & 0 & 1 & 0 & 0 & 0 & 1 & 0 \\ 0 & 1 & 0 & 1 & 0 & 0 & 0 & 0 \\ 0 & 0 & 0 & 0 & 0 & 1 & 0 & 1 \end{bmatrix}$$

So we have $\Psi \overline{s} = [k, k, \ldots, k]^T$, and $\sum a_i = 8$.

Example 9. [13] One can easily see that to have two distinct random elements r_2 and r_3 is not necessary. We can choose $r_1 = r_3$ and still achieve Definition 2.

s_{11}	s_{12}	s_{21}	s_{22}	s_{31}	s_{32}	s_{41}	s_{42}
$k-r_2$	$k-r_1$	$k-r_2$	r_1	r_2	$k-r_1$	r_2	r_1

It can easily be established that this scheme is as secure as the first example. The share size is the same as before, but to create a more *efficient* scheme (i.e. reduce the amount of randomness), we have increased the rank of Ψ (this was done by introducing an additional dependency between shares). The corresponding Ψ will be

$$\Psi = \begin{bmatrix} 1 & 0 & 0 & 0 & 1 & 0 & 0 \\ 1 & 0 & 0 & 0 & 0 & 1 & 0 \\ 0 & 0 & 1 & 0 & 1 & 0 & 0 \\ 0 & 0 & 1 & 0 & 0 & 0 & 1 & 0 \\ 0 & 1 & 0 & 1 & 0 & 0 & 0 \\ 0 & 0 & 0 & 0 & 0 & 1 & 0 & 1 \\ 0 & 0 & 0 & 1 & 0 & 0 & 0 & -1 \end{bmatrix},$$

where $\Psi\bar{s} = [k,k,k,k,k,k,0]^T$. This last row of Ψ is needed. This row infers that the second share of P_2 is the same as the second share of P_4. (i.e. $r_1 = r_3$.) Note, the reader may ask why there do not exist other rows that describe dependencies. For example, $s_{11} = k - r_2 = s_{21}$. However, by performing row operations of type III on Ψ, one would discover that this dependency is revealed.

Example 10. [13] A 3 out of 4 GILTS. Let s_{ij} denote the jth subshare of participant P_i in the table below.

s_{11}	s_{12}	s_{21}	s_{22}	s_{31}	s_{32}	s_{41}	s_{42}
r_1	r_3	r_2	r_4	$k - r_1 - r_2$	$k - r_3 - r_4$	$k - r_1 - r_2$	$k - r_3 - r_4$

Here k denotes the secret key, and r_i denotes the independently chosen, uniform random elements. In a 3 out of 4 GILTS, the minimal share size is $4\log_2 4 = 8$. Then this scheme can be expressed as:

$$\Psi = \begin{bmatrix} 1 & 0 & 1 & 0 & 1 & 0 & 0 & 0 \\ 1 & 0 & 1 & 0 & 0 & 0 & 1 & 0 \\ 0 & 1 & 0 & 0 & 0 & 1 & 0 & 1 \\ 0 & 0 & 0 & 1 & 0 & 1 & 0 & 1 \end{bmatrix}$$

where $\Psi\bar{s} = [k,k,k,k]^T$.

6.2 Proof to Lemma 3

For each i, reduce A_i to Smith-normal form: $U_{A_i} A_i V_{A_i} = D_{A_i}$ where D_{A_i} is a matrix with zeros off the diagonal, and the diagonal is $(d_{i1}, \ldots, d_{ia_i}, 0, \ldots, 0)$. For each i, A_i has rank a_i, and the invariant factors d_{ij} of A_i, satisfy $d_{ij}|d_{ij+1}$. We assume that all invariant factors are positive.

To prove Lemma 3 we first establish two lemmas as stated below.

Lemma 11. *Let $\Psi = [A_1|\cdots|A_n]$ be a GILTS, then for all $i = 1,\ldots,n$, the first invariant factor d_{i1} of A_i is 1.*

Proof. This follows from the following argument. If $d_{i1} \neq 1$, then consider the threshold scheme Ψ applied with the group $\mathbf{Z}_{d_{i1}}$ (integers modulo d_{i1}). A_i is a matrix that can be reduced (modulo d_{i1}) to a zero matrix (that is, $D_{A_i} = 0$, and $A_i = U_{A_i}^{-1} D_{A_i} V_{A_i}^{-1}$). Hence P_i does not contribute any shares in computing the secret key. However there exists sets B (of t participants), belonging to Γ_0, containing P_i. This would violate security condition (2)(i) of Definition 2 (since $t - 1$ or less participants can compute the secret key). Therefore at least one of the invariant factors is 1. Hence $d_{i1} = 1$.

Let ρ_i denote the largest integer (less than or equal to the rank of A_i), such that $d_{i\rho_i} = 1$.

Lemma 12. *Let $\Psi = [A_1|\cdots|A_n]$ be a GILTS. Then it is possible to replace A_i by A_i' and $\bar{s}_i$ by $\bar{s}'_i$ where the matrices have equal rank and the shares have equal size respectively, such that (i) $A_i\bar{s}_i = A_i'\bar{s}'_i$ and (ii) there exists a series of row interchanges U' such that*

$$U'A_i' = \begin{bmatrix} I_{\rho_i \times \rho_i} & X' \\ Y' & Z' \end{bmatrix}.$$

Proof. $U_{A_i} A_i V_{A_i} = D_{A_i}$. We define $A_i'' = U_{A_i}^{-1} D_{A_i}$ and $\overline{s}_i'' = V_{A_i}^{-1} \overline{s}_i$. Then $A_i'' \overline{s}_i'' = A_i \overline{s}_i$.

Observe that the first ρ_i columns of D_{A_i} are 1 along the diagonal. Thus the first ρ_i columns of A_i'' are determined by row operations of type I or III performed on these 1's. Consider the submatrix, of A_i'', which consists of the first ρ_i columns, denote this by $A_i''|_{1...\rho_i}$. Since this matrix has rank ρ_i, there exist ρ_i rows of $A_i''|_{1...\rho_i}$, which are linearly independent. Assume without loss of generality that these rows were the first ρ_i rows of $A_i''|_{1...\rho_i}$. (Otherwise perform row interchanges on $A_i''|_{1...\rho_i}$ to place ρ_i linearly independent rows in the first ρ_i rows.) Then $A_i''|_{1...\rho_i} = \begin{bmatrix} X \\ Y \end{bmatrix}$. Here X is a ρ_i by ρ_i matrix, which consists of ρ_i linearly independent rows. Hence X^{-1} exists and $X^{-1} \in GL(\rho_i, \mathbf{Z})$.

Now $A_i'' = \begin{bmatrix} X & Z_1 \\ Y & Z_2 \end{bmatrix}$. Define $A_i' = \begin{bmatrix} I_{\rho_i \times \rho_i} & Z_1 \\ YX^{-1} & Z_2 \end{bmatrix}$ (note Y is a $(\mu - \rho_i) \times \rho_i$ matrix).

Let $\overline{s}_{i_1...\rho_i}''$ denote the first ρ_i subshares of $\overline{s}''$. Then $Y \overline{s}_{i_1...\rho_i}'' = YX^{-1} X \overline{s}_{i_1...\rho_i}''$. Define $\overline{s}'_{i_1...\rho_i} = X \overline{s}_{i_1...\rho_i}''$ and $\overline{s}'_{i_{\rho_i+1}...a_i} = \overline{s}_{i_{\rho_i+1}...a_i}''$. Then

$$A_i' \overline{s}'_i = \begin{bmatrix} I_{\rho_i \times \rho_i} & Z_1 \\ YX^{-1} & Z_2 \end{bmatrix} \begin{bmatrix} X & 0_{\rho_i \times (a_i - \rho_i)} \\ 0_{(a_i - \rho_i) \times \rho_i} & I_{(a_i - \rho_i) \times (a_i - \rho_i)} \end{bmatrix} \overline{s}'' = A_i'' \overline{s}'' = A_i \overline{s}_i.$$

Proof to Lemma 3

Proof. Let us assume that A_i is already in the form described by Lemma 12. Further we will assume that row interchanges are not needed. Thus $A_i = \begin{bmatrix} I_{\rho_i \times \rho_i} & X' \\ Y' & Z' \end{bmatrix}$.

Since $I_{\rho_i \times \rho_i}$ is an identity matrix, there exists a series of column operations of type III, which can be represented by V_1, such that

$$A_i V_1 = \begin{bmatrix} I_{\rho_i \times \rho_i} & 0 \\ Y' & Z'' \end{bmatrix}.$$

Since $V_1^{-1} \in GL(a_i, \mathbf{Z})$, we have $A_i V_1 V_1^{-1} \overline{s}_i = A_i \overline{s}_i$. Set $A_i' = A_i V_1$ and $\overline{s}'_i = V_i^{-1} \overline{s}_i$.

Efficient Sharing of Encrypted Data*

Krista Bennett, Christian Grothoff, Tzvetan Horozov, and Ioana Patrascu

S³ lab and CERIAS,
Department of Computer Sciences, Purdue University
{klb,grothoff,horozov,patrascu}@cs.purdue.edu
http://www.gnu.org/software/GNUnet/

Abstract. This paper describes the design of a censorship-resistant distributed file sharing protocol which has been implemented on top of GNUnet, an anonymous, reputation-based network. We focus on the encoding layer of the GNUnet file-sharing protocol which supports efficient dissemination of encrypted data as well as queries over encrypted data. The main idea advocated in this paper is that simple cryptographic techniques are sufficient to engineer an efficient data encoding that can make it significantly harder to selectively censor information. Our encoding allows users to share files encrypted under descriptive keys which are the basis for querying the network for content. A key property of our encoding is that intermediaries can filter invalid encrypted replies without being able to decrypt the query or the reply. Files are stored in small chunks which are distributed and replicated automatically by the GNUnet infrastructure. Additionally, data files may be stored in plaintext or encrypted form or as a combination of both and encrypted on demand.

1 Introduction

Internet censorship can appear in many forms. Whether it is government regulation aimed to stifle political dissent or a campaign orchestrated by pressure groups against opponents, a common feature of all forms of censorship is that each must identify objectionable information and prevent its sharing. The goal of our research is to study requirements and design a censorship-resistant file-sharing protocol. In this paper, we focus on the design of the encoding layer of such a protocol and briefly describe a prototype implementation that we have realized on top of the GNUnet networking infrastructure [1].

Keeping published documents available in the face of powerful adversaries requires an array of techniques. Censorship can be enacted in many ways, such as sweeping through users hard drives to discover objectionable content, filtering user queries to catch requests, and even denial of service attacks against servers providing storage for the documents. Our goal is to design a file-sharing protocol that protects against all of these attempts to limit the free flow of information. In particular, both content and queries should always be encrypted; furthermore,

---

* Portions of this work were supported by sponsors of CERIAS

L. Batten and J. Seberry (Eds.): ACISP 2002, LNCS 2384, pp. 107–120, 2002.
© Springer-Verlag Berlin Heidelberg 2002

servers as well as all intermediate hosts should be oblivious of the data they are actually storing such that they can neither be singled out for attack nor held liable in a court of law.

To address this challenge, we have implemented a censorship-resistant file-sharing protocol on top of the GNUnet anonymous reputation-based network. Our system protects servers and users through an original encryption scheme. The design of the cipher was motivated by the idea of a wide area distributed network where many parties want to share data. Identical data may be inserted by many independent parties at any time. Some users may want to keep a copy of their files in plaintext on their drive – and may not want to waste space on a second, encrypted copy – while others must always keep all the data in encrypted form. Files are identified by keywords and retrieved by issuing queries for all documents matching a given keyword. Some complex queries, such as boolean formulas over keywords, should also be supported.

This paper focuses on the content and query encryption techniques used within GNUnet. Other aspects such as host discovery, host authentication, and the GNUnet economic reputation-trading model (to prevent denial of service attacks) will not be addressed here.

The GNUnet encryption scheme is remarkable in that it allows identical files encrypted under different keys to yield the same ciphertext, modulo a small block of metadata. These files can then be split into small blocks and distributed (and replicated if need be) across hosts in a GNUnet system to balance load. The network can thus automatically optimize the storage requirements of a document even if multiple users insert the same files under different search keys at different times. Another implication is that a document can be entered under many search keys at little cost in space. The overhead in space of our scheme is less than 4% of the plaintext size, with one 1KB per additional copy of the file. The scheme is based on hash trees [6] and allows swarm distribution [7]. Encryption speed is about 3MB/sec and decryption is a bit slower, about 350KB/sec, as our decryption code is multi-threaded and has to deal with file fragments being returned by different hosts out-of-order.

The remainder of the paper is organized as follows. Section 2 begins by listing the requirements of file-sharing protocols and motivating our choices. Then, in Section 3, we contrast this work with other censorship-resistant systems having similar goals. Section 4 describes the details of the GNUnet encoding scheme. Finally, Section 5 describes some possible attacks.

2   Requirements for Censorship-Resistant File-Sharing

This section briefly describes the requirements for a censorship-resistant file-sharing protocol. These requirements will then be used to drive our design and, in section 3, to assess the appropriateness of related systems.

We start with a scenario that tries to highlight a common use-case for such a protocol:

Suppose that *Alice* inserts a file *F* containing the text of Salman Rushdie's Satanic Verses in the network under the keyword `"satanicverses"`, and the same file is independently inserted by *Bob* under keyword `"rushdie's verses"`. Furthermore, *Alice* decides to keep file *F* in plaintext on her drive and is not willing to dedicate space for a second, encrypted copy on the drive. *Bob* on the other hand, lives under an oppressive regime and is afraid of being caught with the file, so he wants to make sure that the file cannot be found on his drive. Thus he encrypts the file, and his computer starts to distribute pieces of the file all over the network. What we want to be able to do is to have a user *Carol* perform a query `"satanicverses"` AND `"rushie's verses"` and retrieve the file *F*, potentially retrieving a few pieces from the copy that *Bob* inserted and distributed as well as a few other pieces that *Alice* contributed. *Alice* should not have to perform encryption on the pieces of *F* that *Carol* obtained from other parts of network. In this case, the encryption of *F* guarantees that participating servers can claim ignorance about the contents of *F*.

We now turn to the requirement placed on a file-sharing protocol that could support the above use case.

2.1 Plausible Deniability

In order to protect intermediaries, it is desirable that these hosts be unable to discover what they are sending. Servers must be able to deny knowledge of the content they store or transport. Intermediate and responding hosts should neither be able to find out what the query is about nor what the contents of the data returned are. Many modern systems [3] overcome this by hashing the query and searching for the hash, which does not reveal the original keyword.

Additionally, content migration is used both to ensure that the original sender cannot be located as well as to distribute the load. The host that initially inserted the content can then forget the "key" and claim ignorance, even if the content is still stored locally; as long as the adversary has not performed full traffic analysis, it remains plausible that content could have come from another node.

In GNUnet, users are anonymous. Thus, our encoding scheme is aimed at protecting the *servers*, not the individuals requesting the data. Servers must be able to deny knowledge of the content they index, store or transport.

If hosts are unable to see which content they are serving, they cannot exercise editorial control by selectively deleting or modifying content. Exercising editorial control implies liability for content. A lack of editorial control usually relieves the provider from responsibility for the nature of the data served.[1]

---

[1] In *Stratton Oakmont v. Prodigy*, an Internet provider was found liable for hosting a bulletin-board where offensive messages had been posted. This is because the provider had hired individuals to exercise editorial control over content. If the provider had merely published messages from users without interference, the provider would probably not have been held accountable[10].

2.2   Content Retrieval

Searching for a file by a unique keyword creates a problem. The user needs some means of actually obtaining the keyword in the first place. If no secrecy is required, this problem is equivalent to using a search engine to obtain URLs from keywords on the World Wide Web.

The problem we try to solve is that of allowing complex searches without exposing the search-string to the network. If the query consists of several keywords, an obvious approach is to search for each of the keywords, download and decrypt all matching files, and then compare their contents. This is clearly impractical. An ideal system would support regular expressions for queries and return only all files that exactly match the regular expression.

2.3   File Distribution Mechanism

In order to be able to move content from host to host in the network, it is desirable that large files can be split. Fine-grained pieces of data are quickly moved from site to site. If it were necessary to transfer large files *as a whole* for a valid transfer to occur, incomplete transfers would result in a huge waste of resources.

Additionally, we want to be able to combine identical files from different sources as illustrated in the motivating example and to allow each source to specify its individual list of keywords for the file.

2.4   Scalability

Naturally, in order for a file-sharing system to scale, the overhead of the encoding should be small. The size of an encoded file should not be significantly larger than the original file. The memory requirements to encrypt or decrypt a file should also be minimal.

Finally, users should be able to store a file in plaintext on their local drive (perhaps because they are using it), without doubling space requirements; the encoding should allow files to be served that are stored locally in plaintext without requiring the storage of a second copy in encrypted form.[2] In addition to the fact that users may assemble the same file using parts from different servers, this storage option requires the ability to encrypt small parts from the middle of the file. For efficiency, this should of course not require reading (or even encrypting) any other part of the file. To the best of our knowledge, GNUnet is the first system that allows this kind of random access on-demand encryption for arbitrary parts of a file.

---

[2] This would of course reduce deniability; however, we value giving users the choice between efficiency and security.

3   Related Work

Censorship-resistant publishing systems are commonly based on three techniques:

1. replication, to ensure that a document is not lost if a single copy is destroyed;
2. distribution, to keep content available if a site goes down;
3. encryption, to prevent servers from exercising editorial control over the content they store.

All systems differ widely in their specific implementations of these three building blocks. While GNUnet also chooses a unique approach to replication and distribution, we do not discuss these aspects in this paper, including the description of related work. Instead, we focus solely on encryption.

3.1   Freenet

The main content encoding scheme used in *Freenet* [2,4] uses the hash of the content as the key (CHK). Other key types indirect to content-hash keys. *Freenet* has several different types of keys. The different key types are used to allow additional features such as content signing, personal namespaces or splitting of content. While this encryption scheme yields the same encrypted data for independent encryptions, it has some disadvantages.

One disadvantage of *Freenet* is that it does not allow direct sharing of files from the local drive without encrypting and inserting them first. Thus, to keep content easily accessible on the host, a node operator must keep a local copy of the unencrypted file in addition to the encrypted content in the *Freenet* database.

Freenet also requires unique keys which may be non-trivial to guess. As collisions for keys are not allowed, multiple results can never be found. If an attacker inserts meaningless data under common keywords, *Freenet* will preserve this content because it is frequently requested and make it impossible to use that keyword for useful data. A solution to the problem of finding keywords is approached by the use of keyservers which provide indices to all known keys. The disadvantage of these keyservers is that they must be maintained; in reality, they often index content which is no longer available.

The CHK encoding does not allow for file completion with content from truncated files. In distributed systems, aborted downloads for large files are fairly frequent. Because the hash of the file is different if even one single bit was not transferred, the entire transfer becomes useless if not completed.

3.2   Mojo Nation

Mojo Nation is a distributed file-sharing system based on micropayments. This system first breaks the original file into several pieces (the larger the file, the greater the number of pieces). Each piece is then broken into eight blocks, any four of which are sufficient to reconstruct the original piece. These data blocks are hashed to generate a unique identity tag. This tag is then later used to retrieve the blocks. A *sharemap* or *Dinode* is used to reconstruct the file.

This protocol distinguishes strictly between searching and downloading. This makes it easy for the system to censor certain queries. While this is an intended feature of the Mojo Nation system, it is unacceptable for GNUnet.

3.3 Free Haven

In Free Haven, documents are split into n shares which are distributed over a number of servers. Any k out of n shares are sufficient to reconstruct the entire document [8]. To retrieve a document, the user must obtain the key that was used to sign the document from some source outside the Free Haven network. The user then forwards the key to the server which encrypts and sends its share of the document.

Because shares are stored in plaintext (only the transfer is encrypted), hosts can exercise editorial control over content. Also, the k out of n share reconstruction scheme does not allow reconstruction of a file by mixing shares from independent insertions (see section 4.2).

The requirement that the users obtain Free Haven keys from other sources makes it impossible to search the network. Furthermore, these keys consist of random bits instead of guessable keywords. While this is desirable if content in the network is meant to be accessed only by authorized parties, it is a drawback in a system where files are intended to be publicly available.

3.4 Tangler

The Tangler network [6] is a system where new content is entangled with old content. This entanglement introduces a dependency that makes it impossible to retrieve the new content if the other content that it was entangled with is lost. While this makes it impossible to censor specific content without losing unrelated content (since the entanglement pairs are chosen randomly), this process *at least* doubles the amount of data that must be transported by the network.

Furthermore, outdated or unpopular content cannot be removed because of the entanglement scheme. Tangler's approach is quite radical as it not only disallows selective removal of content (censorship), but any removal. The Tangler protocol also makes unreasonable assumptions, such as extremely high availability of servers and synchronous decisions in a distributed network. The paper notes that the network will probably not scale.

3.5 Publius

Publius [5] is a static network that uses Rabin's file splitting algorithm [8] to distribute an encrypted file to n servers. The key used to encrypt the file can be used to retrieve the shares. The servers can not decrypt the file as the key is never entirely revealed to them.

Publius keys are random strings. The system does not provide any search mechanism and expects the users to obtain the keys from an alternate source.

3.6   Summary

Figure 1 compares the different systems discussed in this section. The most important questions are:

- Are servers prevented from decrypting the content?
- Can content inserted by independent sources be joined?
- Can content be encrypted on-demand?
- Is content split into smaller pieces?
- Is the method of encrypting the content reasonable for the goal of being censorship-resistant?
- Is a boolean search possible? (AND, OR, XOR, NOT, etc.)
- Is a search with regular expressions possible?
- Can there be different files matching the same keyword?
- How much data must be transferred per file as a multiple of the actual file size (not counting indirections due to anonymity provisions)?

System	Freenet	Mojo Nation	Free Haven	Tangler	Publius	GNUnet
server can decrypt	no	yes	no	yes	no	no
joins content	yes	yes	no	no	no	yes
on-demand encryption	no	no	no	no	no	yes
content splitting	yes	yes	yes	yes	yes	yes
censorship-resistant	yes	no	yes	yes	yes	yes
boolean search	no	yes	no	no	no	yes
regex	no	no	no	no	no	no
key collisions	no	yes	no	no	no	yes
network overhead	≈ 1	≈ 1	≈ 1	≈ 2	≈ 1	≈ 1

Fig. 1. Quick Comparison.

4   GNUnet Content Representation

The design of GNUnet storage and content distribution attempts to achieve several goals:

1. Deniability for all participants;
2. Distribution of content and load;
3. Efficiency in terms of space and bandwidth.

In this section, we describe an encoding scheme for content that achieves all three goals. While the receiver can decrypt the file, none of the intermediaries can discern its contents. Additionally, the query is sent encrypted; thus, the other hosts on the network cannot compute what the user is looking for. Some minor goals have also influenced our design. First of all, we wanted to be able to perform boolean queries of the form $a \, AND \, b$, without revealing a or b. Secondly, we require content migration to be simple and fast, making it easier for GNUnet to migrate (or copy) files, thus achieving distribution and redundancy.

The remainder of this section describes how these goals are achieved by our approach. In part 4.1 we describe how files are split into *GBlocks*, which are easier to migrate. Part 4.2 describes how the *GBlocks* are encrypted in order to make it impossible for the intermediaries to determine what they are storing or serving. Part 4.3 describes how the user can query for content without exposing the (plaintext) query or the corresponding content. The following description summarizes the full scheme that we develop in this section:

1. The user gives the local GNUnet node the content C, a list of keywords K and a description D (and optionally the pseudonym P) to use.
2. GNUnet breaks C into blocks B_i, each of size 1k, and computes the hash values $H_i = H(B_i)$ and $H_i^2 = H(H(B_i))$. Random padding is added if needed.
3. Each block is then encrypted, yielding $E_i = E_{H_i}(B_i)$.
4. GNUnet stores E_i under the name H_i^2.
5. If C was larger than 1k (and thus there is more than one H_i), GNUnet groups up to 51 H_i values together with a CRC32 of the original data to form a new block of size 1k. Random padding is added if needed. Each new 1k block obtained in this manner is then processed as in step 2.
6. If the size of C was smaller than 1k (and thus there is only one hashcode H_1), GNUnet builds a root-node containing H_1, the description D, the original length of C, a CRC checksum, and optionally the pseudonym P and a signature. The total size of the root node must be less than 1k in size (the length of the description may be shortened as needed). The resulting root-node R is then padded and encrypted once for *each* keyword K yielding $R_K = E_{H(K)}(R)$.
7. Finally, for each K, the result R_K is stored under $H(H(K))$.

The space m required for a file of size n is

$$m \leq n + 1k \cdot \sum_{i=0}^{\lfloor log_{51} \lceil \frac{n}{1k} \rceil \rfloor} 51^i$$

$$\approx 1.02 \cdot n.$$

4.1   *GBlocks*

In order to be able to migrate large files and to distribute load on the network, GNUnet splits large files into many small files called *GBlocks*. There are 3 types of *GBlocks*: *IBlocks*, *DBlocks* and *RBlocks*. Similar to UNIX INodes, *IBlocks* are special indirection-blocks which encode how the leaf-nodes of the file tree (the *DBlocks*) can be reassembled into the original file (see figure 2).

Splitting large files makes content migration inexpensive. Without splitting these files, it is unlikely that a node would be able to find another host that

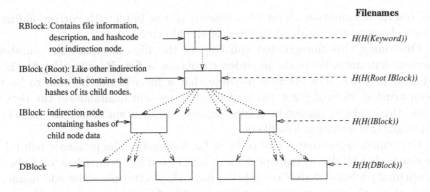

Fig. 2. Encoding of the entire file

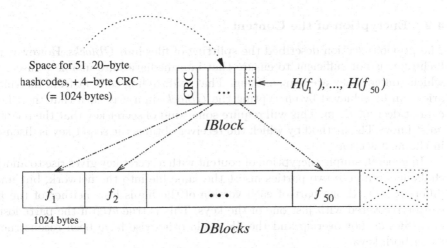

Fig. 3. Encoding of the 1k blocks

is willing (or able) to provide enough space. The traffic burst that this transfer would impose on the network is impractical, as both nodes would become very busy for a long time. Storing a large file on a single host also fails to facilitate distribution of load when a user requests this large file.

The size of all types of *GBlocks* in GNUnet is normalized to 1k. Thus, a 50k file will be split into 50 *DBlocks* f_i of length 1k each. Then, 50 RIPE-MD-160 hashcodes of the *DBlocks* are composed to form an *IBlock* $H(f_1), \ldots, H(f_{50})$, which is stored with all the other *GBlocks* (see figure 3). *GBlocks* that are less than 1k in length are padded with random information. *IBlocks* can store up to 51 hashcodes ($51 * 20\,bytes = 1020\,bytes$) and one CRC32 checksum.

Larger files require multiple levels of indirection. A special *RBlock* on top of the file tree contains the length of the file, a description and the hashcode of the topmost *IBlock*. In this way, the user can download a single 1k *GBlock* and obtain information about the contents of the full-length corresponding file before choosing to download the rest of the file tree.

Obviously, this fine-grained splitting of the files increases the number of queries that must be made in order to obtain a file. Because the file is distributed in parts, it is entirely possible that a file will not be able to be fully reconstructed, even if some parts of the file are still available on the network. While this problem cannot be solved entirely, duplication of files in the network will make this situation less likely.

One could argue that a size of 1k is far too small. The rationale behind this file size is that UDP, the transport mechanism used by GNUnet has (on Ethernet) an optimal packet size that is slightly above 1k. As GNUnet must add headers to the packets, the size approximates this number. Furthermore, many file systems can be formatted with a block-size of 1k.

4.2   Encryption of the Content

The previous section described the splitting of files into *GBlocks*. However, this technique is not sufficient to ensure that intermediaries are unable to ascertain which content they are transmitting. That said, hiding content from intermediaries can be achieved by encrypting the *GBlocks* in a way such that their hosts cannot decrypt them. This will require some kind of secret key that the recipient must know. The method by which the receiver obtains the secret key is discussed in the next section.

In general, simple encryption of content with a secret key gives rise to another challenge. Suppose two parties insert the same file into the network, but under different keys. If one part of each version of the file is lost, neither of the files can be recovered with just one of the keys. This is true even if the parts lost in both files do not overlap and the file could otherwise have been reconstructed using both keys.

GNUnet encodes *GBlocks* in a special way that makes it possible to reassemble parts of two identical files that were inserted under different secret keys without anyone but the recipient even knowing that the *GBlocks* were related.

The key idea here is to use the hash of each *GBlock* as its key. More precisely, GNUnet encodes a 1k block B with the hash of B, $H(B)$. A RIPE-MD-160 hash provides 128 bits for a symmetric cipher, and another 32 bits for the initialization vector. Because the hashcode cannot be retrieved from the encrypted file $E_{H(B)}(B)$, intermediaries cannot decrypt the content. However, even with this scheme in place, two identical plaintexts that were inserted independently will have the same keys (except for the root node) and thus yield the same encrypted ciphertexts.

For the *RBlock*, a slightly different scheme is used to allow queries. Here, the user specifies the secret keys. These differing secret keys are used only to encrypt the *RBlocks*. Any of these keys can then be used to decrypt the entire file. A small problem arises from *GBlocks* that need to be padded to achieve the size of 1k. In order to avoid identical content being hashed to different values, only the actual data is hashed, not the random padding.

The encryption scheme for the *RBlock* is similar to the scheme used in *Freenet*; both use the hash of the keyword. However, our keywords are free-form and we only use them to encrypt the *RBlock*. The rest of the file is encrypted differently.

4.3 Queries

The scheme described so far leaves one question open: how to query for data. If the files were stored under the hash-codes of the original data, intermediaries could decrypt them. However, storing more than a single value per *DBlock* in the *IBlocks* would be inefficient.

In GNUnet, a block B is stored as $E_{H(B)}(B)$ under the name $H(H(B))$. Because H is a one-way function, the intermediaries cannot obtain the original hashcode from the filename. However, other nodes can compute $H(H(B))$ given $H(B)$.

The *RBlock* R of a file stores the hashcode $H(B)$ of the root *IBlock* B, which is then encrypted with $H(K)$ (where K is a user-supplied keyword). $E_{H(K)}(R)$ (the encrypted root node) is then stored under $H(H(K))$. When a user searches for K, his client will send a request for $H(H(K))$ and decrypt the returned result with $H(K)$. No other node in the network can obtain any information about the data transferred except by guessing the keyword K (or by knowing the exact file that is returned, which usually implies that this node originally inserted the file). Although a dictionary attack is thus possible, such an attack can be avoided by carefully choosing K.

This scheme has another advantage. It allows users to specify boolean queries of the form $a\,AND\,b$. GNUnet will then search for a and for b and return only those files that match both queries. Content providers can insert content under many keywords without using significantly more storage space, as only one extra *RBlock* per keyword is required. This allows users to search for content efficiently.

4.4 On-Demand Encoding

If the user intends to keep the file in plaintext on the local drive, the file can be indexed and encrypted on-demand. In that case, the insertion process will compute the hashes of each *GBlock* and store the hash together with the address of the *GBlock* in GNUnets database. The *IBlocks* and the *RBlock* are processed as usual. The size of the *IBlocks* and the hashes in the database is about 5% of the total filesize.

If GNUnet is searched for any of the *GBlocks*, it can locate the corresponding 1k block of the original file, compute its hash, encrypt it and send it out. GNUnet is not required to read any other GBlock from the original file.

4.5 Avoiding Content from Malicious Hosts

As mentioned before, the actual query for a datum matching Q is hidden by hashing Q first. As $H(Q)$ is used as the key for the decryption, $H(H(Q))$ is the obvious choice for the published query. However, this approach has a small problem.

If N matches the query Q, the encoded node $E_{H(Q)}(N)$ no longer has $H(Q)$. Thus, intermediaries that do not know $H(Q)$ cannot verify that this node matches the query at all. A malicious node could return random data to any query $H(H(Q))$, claiming that the extraneous data matches the query. The receiver would then have to propagate a message back through the query chain that the original sender was malicious. As intermediaries cannot keep track of earlier connections for a long time, this feedback may not reach the malicious node. Thus, a malicious node could actually improve its reputation by sending out meaningless data to the network. This would be unfortunate for reputation-based systems like GNUnet or Mojo Nation [7].

This problem is prevented in GNUnet by using $H(H(H(Q)))$ for the query. The sender must then provide $H(H(Q))$ to demonstrate that the sender actually has matching data. Because the sender cannot guess $H(H(Q))$, it can be assumed that the sender had matching content at some point. Of course, this cannot prevent malicious hosts from inserting bad data in general. Malicious nodes could *guess* that the keyword K is frequently used and just compute $H(H(K))$ and $H(H(H(K)))$, returning their useless data once a matching query comes by. However, this is similar to inserting extraneous data under that keyword into the network. Because no software can distinguish valuable content from worthless content in general, this is not a design flaw. Still, it demonstrates that the problem of content moderation is not entirely solved with this approach. The triple-hash scheme simply makes it harder to reply to arbitrary queries with random data; it cannot prevent users from inserting such data under popular keys.

5   Discussion

Splitting files into many small pieces might be perceived as having a negative effect on the preservation of data. If only one of the small pieces is lost, the larger file can no longer be reconstructed. Thus, many other systems strive to keep files intact. GNUnet guards against the loss of files by replicating the data. Small files (*GBlocks*) are quickly migrated from host to host; thus, they are cheaply replicated and thereby kept available.

The real issue with small blocks is the high number of queries that are required to find all the pieces in a distributed network. However, smaller blocks improve the load-balancing capabilities of the network [8,7].

For GNUnet, we chose a very small granularity of 1k. While the encoding scheme described basically allows any granularity, this size is admittedly quite small. While this is an implementation detail, this allows GNUnet to duplicate blocks at a negligible cost per block. Duplicating a file with several megabytes of data in a single transaction, on the other hand, is both much more costly and more likely to fail.

Small blocks also allow GNUnet to operate with very limited memory, which may be of note for embedded devices. Additionally, any request in GNUnet can be answered using a single ethernet frame.

The encoding described above is open to two kinds of attacks. The most obvious attack is that of an adversary guessing the keyword and thus being able to decrypt the file. As users must have a way to decrypt the file solely by means of the keyword (which is also a guess), this cannot be avoided.

Another attack occurs when the attacker guesses the exact contents of the file (or at least the exact contents of an incriminating part). The attacker can then encode the file to see if the encrypted file matches the encoding that he is trying to break. This is possible because we wanted different keys to result in the same ciphertext. The attack requires a fair amount of knowledge on the part of the attacker. In fact, the attack is equivalent to one where an attacker inserts content into the network and waits for a another user to try retrieve it. This kind of attack is extremely hard to avoid, since GNUnet depends upon users providing content.

Both attacks fail to thwart the stated goal of the GNUnet encoding scheme, which is to prevent intermediaries from being able to exercise editorial control over content. While hosts can theoretically be forced to censor well-known keywords and files, they are unable to censor new keywords or unknown content. As small changes to the content or keyword are sufficient to make a detection impossible, censorship should be impractical.

The guessing attack described does provide the opportunity for limited forms of censorship. A server can create a "blacklist" of keywords or files and from these keywords (or the blocks of the files) compute the names of the corresponding blocks. Matching blocks could then be filtered out. It should be noted, however, that guessing the keyword or the exact contents of the file are the only way to distinguish blocks. In encrypted form, all types of blocks are indistinguishable.

6   Conclusion

We have described an encoding scheme that is able to produce the same ciphertext (with the exception of a 1k *RBlock*) for the encryption of a file X with two different keys K_a and K_b. We illustrated that this scheme allows boolean searches without exposing the keys. We have shown that the ciphertext is not significantly larger than the plaintext. Arbitrary pieces of the ciphertext can be generated from plaintext without reading unrelated parts of the plaintext. While dictionary attacks on the password and known plaintext attacks on the ciphertext are possible, they are harmless with respect to the goal of deniability.

In the future, remote searches in encrypted data deserve further attention. An interesting technique that allows word-based searching in a document without ever exposing the contents or the keyword is described in [9]. The technique is not vulnerable to guessing attacks but requires the data to be split at (key)word boundaries at encryption time. Like the approach described in this paper, [9] requires exact matches. Keyword extraction and approximate keyword matching are performed by modern search engines and should be a goal for secure searches in the future.

GNUnet is free software and part of the GNU project. The GNUnet code is approximately 19.000 lines of C code and is available on our webpage. The GNUnet server uses about about 2 MB of memory under GNU/Linux.

Acknowledgments. The authors wish to thank the members of the Secure Software Systems Lab for helpful discussions, Jan Vitek for support and editing, Jens Palsberg for encouragement and Mikhail Atallah for supporting unusual ideas for class projects.

References

1. K. Bennett, C. Grothoff, T. Horozov, I. Patrascu, and T. Stef. Technical report.
2. I. Clarke. A distributed decentralised information storage and retrieval system, 1999.
3. I. Clarke, O. Sandberg, B. Wiley, and T. Hong. Freenet: A distributed anonymous information storage and retrieval system. In *Proc. of the ICSI Workshop on Design Issues in Anonymity and Unobservability*. International Computer Science Institute, 2000.
4. Steven Hazel. Libfreenet, a case study in horrors incomprehensible to the mind of man, and other secure protocol design mistakes., Feb. 2002.
5. Aviel D. Rubin Marc Waldman and Lorrie Faith Cranor. Publius: A robust, tamper-evident, censorship-resistant, web publishing system. In *Proc. 9th USENIX Security Symposium*, pages 59–72, August 2000.
6. David Mazieres Marc Waldman. Tangler: A censorhip-resistant publishing system based on document entanglements. 2001.
7. Mojo Nation. Technology overview, Feb. 2000.
8. Michael O. Rabin. Efficient dispersal of information for security, load balancing, and fault tolerance. *Journal of the ACM*, 36(2):335–348, 1989.
9. Dawn Xiaodong Song, David Wagner, and Adrian Perrig. Practical techniques for searches on encrypted data. In *IEEE Symposium on Security and Privacy*, pages 44–55, 2000.
10. Stratton Oakmont vs Prodigy Services Company, 1995 N.Y. Misc. Lexis 229, (N.Y. Sup. Ct. Nassau Co., 1995).

Cheating Prevention in Linear Secret Sharing

Josef Pieprzyk and Xian-Mo Zhang

Centre for Advanced Computing – Algorithms and Cryptography
Department of Computing
Macquarie University
Sydney, NSW 2109, AUSTRALIA
{josef,xianmo}@ics.mq.edu.au

Abstract. Cheating detection in linear secret sharing is considered. The model of cheating extends the Tompa-Woll attack and includes cheating during multiple (unsuccessful) recovery of the secret. It is shown that shares in most linear schemes can be split into subshares. Subshares can be used by participants to trade perfectness of the scheme with cheating prevention. Evaluation of cheating prevention is given in the context of different strategies applied by cheaters.

Keywords: Cryptography, Secret Sharing, Linear Secret Sharing Schemes, Cheating Detection, Cheating Identification.

1   Introduction

Secret sharing was introduced by Shamir [14] and Blakley [3]. The main purpose of secret sharing is to allow a group of participants to own a secret. The secret is typically divided into shares and each principal has at least one share of the secret. The ownership is collective, i.e. to recover the secret, a big enough subgroup of participants must get together and pool their shares. The collection of all subsets of participants authorised to recover the secret, is called the access structure. Ito, Saito and Nishizeki [9] showed that there is a perfect secret sharing for any access structure. Benaloh and Leichter [2] and Simmons, Jackson and Martin [15] showed alternative constructions for perfect secret sharing.

Tompa and Woll [16] demonstrated that Shamir threshold secret sharing can be subject to cheating by one or more dishonest participants. At the pooling time, instead of valid shares, dishonest participants submit modified shares to the combiner who recovers the matching polynomial. Knowing an invalid secret returned from the combiner, dishonest participants can correct it and recover the valid secret while honest ones are left with the invalid secret. In order to prevent cheating, Tompa and Woll [16] suggested to make x co-ordinates of the polynomial secret.

2   Results Achieved

The work generalises the TW attack for the broader class of linear secret sharing and defines a new repeat recovery attack (RR attack). In the attack, it is assumed

L. Batten and J. Seberry (Eds.): ACISP 2002, LNCS 2384, pp. 121–135, 2002.

that the currently active group is engaged in precisely two unsuccessful secret recovery attempts. The RR attack works even if the underlying matrix and shares are secret.

Linear secret sharing is introduced and it is shown that shares can be easily and efficiently converted into independent pieces (sub-shares). The model is applicable to many known secret sharing schemes including the Shamir scheme [14], the modular scheme [1], and the Karnin-Greene-Hellman scheme [10]. We demonstrate how the linear secret sharing with sub-shares can be used to combat cheating.

3   Model of Cheating

Consider a group of n participants $\mathcal{P} = \{P_1, \ldots, P_n\}$. Given any $GF(q)$. Denote $\mathcal{S} = GF(q)$ as the set of secrets, $\mathcal{S}_i$ – the set of shares assigned to the participant P_i, and Γ – an access structure which consists of all subsets of participants who are able to recover the secret by pooling their shares together. Secret sharing scheme is a collection of two algorithms: distribution algorithm and recovery algorithm. The distribution algorithm also called the dealer is a probabilistic algorithm which takes access structure Γ, the secret $s \in \mathcal{S}$ and a random string $r \in \mathcal{R}$ as an input and assigns shares $s_i \in \mathcal{S}_i$ to participants P_i; $i = 1, \ldots, n$. This can be written as: $D_\Gamma : \mathcal{S} \times \mathcal{R} \to \mathcal{S}_1 \times \mathcal{S}_2 \times \cdots \times \mathcal{S}_n$.

For a given access structure Γ, the recovery algorithm (also called combiner) is a deterministic algorithm and accepts shares from participants and recovers the secret $s \in \mathcal{S}$ only when the currently active collection $\mathcal{A} \in \Gamma$ of participants belongs to the access structure. Otherwise, the algorithm fails with an overwhelming probability. So knowing the active set $\mathcal{A} \subset \Gamma$ and the corresponding set of shares $\mathcal{S}_\mathcal{A}$, the recovery algorithm is $R_\Gamma : 2^{\mathcal{S}_\mathcal{A}} \to \mathcal{S}$, where $2^{\mathcal{S}_\mathcal{A}}$ stands for the collection of all subsets of shares that exist for the group $\mathcal{A}$.

Threshold schemes constitute a very interesting class of secret sharing schemes. Their access structure is particularly simple as any t out of n participants are able to run successfully the recovery algorithm. The access structure of a (t, n) threshold scheme is $\Gamma = \{\mathcal{A} : |\mathcal{A}| = t\}$, where $|\mathcal{A}|$ stands for cardinality of the set $\mathcal{A}$ and $\mathcal{A} \subset \mathcal{P}$.

Definition 1. *A linear (t, n) threshold scheme is a scheme for which the distribution algorithm has the form*

$$(s_1, \ldots, s_n) = (r_1, \ldots, r_t)A \tag{1}$$

where A is a $t \times n$ matrix with entries from $GF(q)$, whose any $(t \times t)$ matrix is nonsingular, and each column is assigned to each share, i.e. $s_i \leftrightarrow \eta_i$ where η_i is a column vector of A. The vector $r = (r_1, \ldots, r_t)$ is selected at random so $r_i \in_R GF(q)$ for $i = 1, \ldots, t$. The secret $s = \sum_{i=1}^{t} r_i$. Shares s_i are secret and known to their owners P_i while the matrix A is public. The recovery algorithm collects t shares and a corresponding $(t \times t)$ matrix and recovers the secret by solving an appropriate collection of linear equations.

3.1   The TW Attack on Linear Secret Sharing

Tompa and Woll [16] showed that a dishonest participant can modify their share in such a way that the secret can be recovered only by the cheater leaving others with an invalid value. The attack was shown for the Shamir scheme and can be easily modified for any linear scheme. For the sake of clarity, assume that participants use the linear (t, n) threshold scheme whose distribution algorithm is defined by Equation (1). We also assume that the $(n \times t)$ matrix A is publicly known. In Shamir schemes, this translates into the assumption that x co-ordinates of underlying polynomial $f(x)$ assigned to participants are public. Let $\mathcal{A} = \{P_1, \ldots, P_t\}$ be the currently active group of participants who wish to reveal the secret and P_1 be a cheater.

During the pooling time, each participant P_i; $i \neq 1$, submits their correct share s_i. The cheater P_1 gives $\tilde{s}_1 = s_1 - \alpha$ where $\alpha \in_R GF(q)$ is a random integer. The recovery algorithm takes shares and solves

$$(r_1, r_2, \ldots, r_t) = (\tilde{s}_1, s_2, \ldots, s_t) A_{\mathcal{A}}^{-1} \tag{2}$$

where $A_{\mathcal{A}}$ is a $t \times t$ matrix derived from A by removing all columns for participants not in $\mathcal{A}$. By design, the matrix $A_{\mathcal{A}}$ is nonsingular so the vectors $(r_1, \ldots, r_t)$ have a unique solution. Let it be $(\tilde{r}_1, \ldots, \tilde{r}_n)$. The recovery algorithm outputs an invalid secret

$$\tilde{s} = \sum_{i=1}^{t} \tilde{r}_i.$$

We follow Tompa and Woll and claim that P_1 can recover the valid secret while others are left with the invalid one $\tilde{s}$. To do so the cheater must know the currently active group (the matrix $A_{\mathcal{A}}$). Note that

$$(\tilde{r}_1, \tilde{r}_2, \ldots, \tilde{r}_t) = (s_1 - \alpha, s_2, \ldots, s_t) A_{\mathcal{A}}^{-1}$$
$$= (s_1, s_2, \ldots, s_t) A_{\mathcal{A}}^{-1} - (\alpha, 0, \ldots, 0) A_{\mathcal{A}}^{-1}$$

The cheater can easily compute an error vector $\Delta = (\delta_1, \ldots, \delta_t)$ caused by the modification of his share by α. So if

$$(\delta_1, \delta_2, \ldots, \delta_t) = (\alpha, 0, \ldots, 0) A_{\mathcal{A}}^{-1}$$

then the cheater can recover the valid secret

$$s = \tilde{s} + \sum_{i=1}^{t} \delta_i = \sum_{i=1}^{t} (\tilde{r}_i + \delta_i)$$

by adding the correction $\Delta = (\delta_1, \ldots, \delta_t)$. Note that even when the recovery algorithm outputs the vector $\tilde{r} = (\tilde{r}_1, \ldots, \tilde{r}_t)$, none of the active participants is able to detect cheating as $\tilde{r} A_{\mathcal{A}}$ gives the correct share for all active (and honest) participants. The modification done by the cheater is obviously undetectable by honest participants.

A secret sharing may offer a different degree of protection against cheaters applying the TW attack. In general, a cheating participant P_1 can try to achieve the following goals:

- G1 - the cheater wants to recover the valid secret while the honest participants are unable to detect cheating,
- G2 - the cheater wants to recover the valid secret while the honest participants are able to detect cheating.

3.2   Practicality of One-Time Recovery

In the unconditionally secure setting, it is customary to assume that secret sharing is designed for a single recovery of the secret. We argue that this assumption does not hold in many practical situations. In particular, consider the following arguments.

Concurrent recovery. Given a group holding a secret using (t, n) where t is smaller than $\frac{n}{2}$. The necessity of recovery of the secret is in many cases triggered by an event that is observed independently by all members of the group (say, a stock exchange crash). It should be no surprise to see more than one subgroup attempting to recover the secret roughly at the same time. There is no facility built in secret sharing to prevent multiple key recovery. Even if it was one, it would mean that recovery would go ahead only after checking whether the secret had not been reconstructed by any subgroup. This is clearly unreasonable and it will not work in cases when there some members of the group are not contactable or simply ceased to exist.

Proxy recovery. Multiple recovery can be put into a good use in the case when the combiner is not trusted. Consider first the case where the TW attack can be actually useful in preventing the combiner from leaking the recovered secret to outsiders. The combiner is normally implemented as a computer program which is run under a watchful eye of a trusted operating system and using underlying secure communication infrastructure to collect shares from participants. Even if the participants are aware about security gaps in the implementation of the combiner, they may still be tempted to use it as it offers communication and computing facilities that otherwise may not be readily available. Assume that the group delegates a member who is entrusted by the group to act on their behalf. Note that this member is the real combiner who is using untrusted one to quickly and efficiently use the (insecure) infrastructure. All participants submit their shares to the untrusted combiner except the delegated member who submits an incorrect share. The combiner recovers an incorrect secret and communicates it to the group (and leaks it to outsiders). Only the delegated member is able to recover the secret. Note that in the unconditionally secure setting, participants may use the untrusted combiner because of the accessible communication infrastructure (they obviously could use authenticated broadcasting). In the conditionally secure setting, participants may use untrusted combiner as a powerful (and insecure) server. A multiple recovery could be useful if the participants are allowed to lie about their shares by "small" modification of their shares.

Multiple recoveries. Multiple recovery can be used to get rid of combiner altogether and the secret reconstruction can then be seen as a probabilistic game with participants broadcasting their shares distorted by a small "noise". It is expected that if the entropy of noise is appropriately selected then the participants have advantage over outsiders in finding the secret from many "noisy" recoveries. Note that they know precise values of their individual shares while outsiders do not.

3.3   A Repeat-Recovery Attack

To make the presentation clearer, we assume that the currently active subset of participants is $\mathcal{A} = \{P_1, \ldots, P_t\}$ from which P_1 is a cheater and $P_2, \ldots, P_t$ are honest. To prevent cheating, the dealer has distributed pairs (s_i, η_i) secretly to each participant. In the repeat-recovery (RR) attack, any unsuccessful attempt in secret recovery provides the cheater information about the secret. From a point of view of the cheater, the matrix $A_{\mathcal{A}}$ is seen as

$$(\eta_1, \eta_2, \ldots, \eta_t)$$

where vectors $\eta_2, \ldots, \eta_t$ are unknown. The recovery algorithm collects pairs (s_i, η_i), constructs the matrix $A_{\mathcal{A}}$, computes its inverse $A_{\mathcal{A}}^{-1}$ and computes the secret $s = \sum_{i=1}^{t} r_i$ where

$$(r_1, r_2, \ldots, r_t) = (s_1, s_2, \ldots, s_t) A_{\mathcal{A}}^{-1}$$

The secret is sent back to active participants via secure channels.

In the RR attack, the cheater modifies his share and sends the pair $(s_1 + \alpha_1, A_1)$ where $\alpha_1 \in_R GF(q)$. Honest participants provide their pairs. The recovery algorithm computes

$$(r_1^{(1)}, r_2^{(1)}, \ldots, r_t^{(1)}) = (s_1 + \alpha_1, s_2, \ldots, s_t) A_{\mathcal{A}}^{-1}$$
$$= (s_1, s_2, \ldots, s_t) A_{\mathcal{A}}^{-1} + (\alpha_1, 0, \ldots, 0) A_{\mathcal{A}}^{-1}$$

The invalid secret $s' = \sum_{i=1}^{t} r_i^{(1)}$ is returned to all active participants. Next the cheater publicly acknowledges that he has made a mistake while sending the share and asks for another try. In the second attempt, the cheater modifies his share using $\alpha_2 \in_R GF(q)$ and sends $(s_1 + \alpha_2, A_1)$ to the combiner. The recovery algorithm again computes the vector r which is

$$(r_1^{(2)}, r_2^{(2)}, \ldots, r_t^{(2)}) = (s_1 + \alpha_2, s_2, \ldots, s_t) A_{\mathcal{A}}^{-1}$$
$$= (s_1, s_2, \ldots, s_t) A_{\mathcal{A}}^{-1} + (\alpha_2, 0, \ldots, 0) A_{\mathcal{A}}^{-1}$$

The second invalid secret is $s'' = \sum_{i=1}^{t} r_i^{(2)}$. After getting it, the cheater can write a system of two equations with four known integers: s', s'', α_1 and α_2. The system has the form:

$$s' = \sum_{i=1}^{t} r_i^{(1)} = s + \sum_{i=1}^{t} (\alpha_1, 0, \ldots, 0) \eta_i^*$$

$$s'' = \sum_{i=1}^{t} r_i^{(2)} = s + \sum_{i=1}^{t} (\alpha_2, 0, \ldots, 0) \eta_i^*$$

where η_i^* is the i-th column of the matrix $A_{\mathcal{A}}^{-1}$. If the first equation is multiplied by α_2 and the second by α_1, then the cheater obtains:

$$\alpha_2 s' = \alpha_2 s + \sum_{i=1}^{t}(\alpha_1\alpha_2, 0, \ldots, 0)\eta_i^*$$

$$\alpha_1 s'' = \alpha_1 s + \sum_{i=1}^{t}(\alpha_1\alpha_2, 0, \ldots, 0)\eta_i^*$$

The secret is

$$s = \frac{\alpha_2 s' - \alpha_1 s''}{\alpha_2 - \alpha_1}$$

The cheater now knows the secret. The above considerations are summarised in the following theorem.

Theorem 1. *Given (t, n) threshold linear secret sharing with the matrix A. Let each participant be assigned her secret pair (s_i, η_i) where s_i is her share and η_i is the column vector of A assigned to P_i (see Equation (1)). Assume that after having collected t pairs (s_i, η_i), the recovery algorithm returns the secret to all active participants via secure channels. Let P_1 be a cheater who modifies his shares by choosing two random modifications α_1 and α_2 ($\alpha_1 \neq \alpha_2$). Then the cheater is able to recover the secret after two unsuccessful attempts. Honest participants do not have any information about the secret except the information provided by the combiner.*

The only point we have not proved is the last statement. From an honest participant point of view, invalid secrets s' and s'' are random variables controlled by random variables α_1 and α_2, respectively. If α_1 and α_2 are two random variables ($\alpha_1 \neq \alpha_2$) selected from all nonzero elements of $GF(q)$, then so are s' and s''. The only information accessible to honest participants is that the valid secret must be different from both s' and s''.

How we can prevent linear secret sharing against the new attack ? The general rule is *Do not give the cheater another chance.* More precisely, the RR attack works only if the same matrix $A_{\mathcal{A}}$ is used twice by the recovery algorithm. To thwart the RR attack, it is enough to replace a single participant by a new one. This changes the matrix and the cheater is unable to recover the valid secret.

Assume that participants have agreed for multiple recovery of the secret. Again the currently active group is $\mathcal{A} = \{P_1, \ldots, P_\ell\}$ where P_1 is cheating and other participants are honest. The cheater may have the following goals:

- Goal $G1_{RR}$ – recovery of the valid secret while the cheater does not mind to be identified by the honest participants,
- Goal $G2_{RR}$ – recovery of the valid secret while the cheater wants to remain unidentified.

3.4   Previous Works

The Tompa-Woll attack put the cheating problem in the spot-light. The suggestion of making x co-ordinates secret does not really address the problem but rather removes the main incentive behind cheating. We are interested in cheating detection in the unconditionally secure setting. Rabin and Ben-Or [13] used a system of linear equations to validate shares before they are passed into the combiner. Carpentieri in [5] constructed a similar scheme but with shorter shares. Carpentieri, De Santis and Vaccaro [6] argued that share expansion is unavoidable to detect cheating. They proved that any (t, n) threshold scheme must have the size of share bigger by $\log \frac{1}{\varepsilon}$ than the size of the secret to detect cheating with the probability better than $1 - \varepsilon$.

Note that all solutions for cheating detection presented in the literature suffer from a dramatic share expansion. So dramatic, in fact, that their practicality is questionable. Note that the Rabin and Ben-Or solution requires $(3n - 2)$ additional elements of the length of the secret per participant. Carpentieri managed to reduce this to $t + 2(n - 1)$ elements where t is the threshold parameter and n is the number of participants in the group. The underlying secret sharing is perfect and unconditionally secure. Some other methods of cheating detection are considered in [4,7,8,12].

The solution we propose does not need any share expansion and in fact, can be applied to any linear secret sharing (including Shamir secret sharing). This claim seems to be in odds with the finding of Carpentieri at al [6]. The solution is built on the observation (see [11]) that it is possible to design Shamir secret sharing with divisible shares. The divisibility of shares allowed the authors of [11] to increase the effective threshold of secret sharing. Here we are using it to trade perfectness of the scheme with the cheating detection. In other words, if participants do not care about cheating, they treat their shares as atomic - the scheme is perfect. If however, they choose to detect cheating, they donate a part of their sub-shares to the combiner leaving some sub-shares to verify the correctness of the returned structure. Note that in our solution, the cheating detection is done individually by active participants after the combiner has returned the secret together with additional information to the participants.

4   Linear Secret Sharing with Sub-shares

Consider an ideal and linear (t, n) threshold scheme and P_i holds the share s_i. Assume that $S = S_i = GF(q)$ for $i = 1, \ldots, n$. Shares held by participants are normally atomic – either withheld or given out in their totality. Suppose further that $GF(q) = GF(p^v)$, σ be a root of a primitive polynomial $p(y) = a_0 + a_1 y + \cdots + a_{v-1} y^{v-1} + y^v$ of degree v over $GF(p)$. Then any element in $\tau \in GF(p^v)$ can be expressed as $\tau = b_0 + b_1 \sigma + \cdots + b_{v-1} \sigma^{v-1}$ where each $b_j \in GF(p)$. We call the vector $(b_0, b_1, \ldots, b_{v-1})$ the *vector representation* of τ.

Now consider a (t, n) threshold scheme described by Equation (1). This equation can be equivalently presented as

$$(\varepsilon_1, \ldots, \varepsilon_{nv}) = (\rho_1, \ldots, \rho_{vt})B \tag{3}$$

where $\varepsilon = (\varepsilon_1, \ldots, \varepsilon_{nv})$ and $\tau = (\rho_1, \ldots, \rho_{tv})$ are created from vectors $(s_1, \ldots, s_n)$ and $(r_1, \ldots, r_t)$ respectively by replacing each entry by its vector representations, and B is an $tv \times nv$ matrix over $GF(p)$ obtained from the matrix A in the following way. We take the unit vector $\rho^{(i)} = (0, \ldots, 0, 1, 0, \ldots, 0)$ which has all zero co-ordinates except the i-th co-ordinate that is "1". Next we find the vector $r^{(i)}$ such that $r^{(i)}$ and $\rho^{(i)}$ present the same integer, in other words, $r^{(i)} = (r_1, \ldots, r_t)$ where each $r_j \in GF(p^v)$, and $\rho^{(i)} = (\rho_1, \ldots, \rho_{tv})$ where each $\rho_j \in GF(p)$, satisfy $\sum_{j=1}^{t} r_j q^{t-j} = \sum_{j=1}^{tv} \rho_j p^{tv-j}$ where $q = p^v$. Then we compute $s^{(i)} = r^{(i)} A$. The vector $s^{(i)}$ is translated into its equivalent $\varepsilon^{(i)}$ – this is the i-th row of B. If we continue this process for all unit vectors $\rho^{(i)}$; $i = 1, \ldots, vt$, we get explicit form of the matrix B with tv rows and nt columns. So we have proved the following.

Lemma 1. *Given a perfect and linear (t, n) threshold scheme whose shares are computed according to Equation (1) where A is the $t \times n$ matrix over $GF(q) = GF(p^v)$, then shares can be equivalently computed by Equation (3) where B is the $tv \times nv$ matrix over $GF(p)$, obtained from the matrix A.*

We further notice that the matrix B in (3) can also be constructed immediately from the matrix A as follows. Define a $v \times v$ matrix D over $GF(p)$ such that:

$$D = \begin{bmatrix} 0 & 1 & 0 & \cdots & 0 & 0 \\ 0 & 0 & 1 & \cdots & 0 & 0 \\ \vdots & \vdots & \vdots & & \vdots & \vdots \\ 0 & 0 & 0 & \cdots & 0 & 1 \\ -a_0 & -a_1 & -a_2 & \cdots & -a_{v-2} & -a_{v-1} \end{bmatrix} \tag{4}$$

Lemma 2. *Let σ be a root of a primitive polynomial $p(y) = a_0 + a_1 y + \cdots + a_{v-1} y^{v-1} + y^v$ of degree v over $GF(p)$. Then $(c_0 + c_1 \sigma + \cdots + c_{v-1} \sigma^{v-1})(b_0 + b_1 \sigma + \cdots + b_{v-1} \sigma^{v-1}) = (d_0 + d_1 \sigma + \cdots + d_{v-1} \sigma^{v-1})$, where each b_j, c_j and d_j are elements in $GF(p)$, if and only if*

$$(c_0, c_1, \ldots, c_{v-1})(b_0 I_v + b_1 D + \cdots + b_{v-1} D^{v-1}) = (d_0, d_1, \ldots, d_{v-1})$$

where D has been defined in (4) and I_v denotes the $v \times v$ identity matrix.

We reconsider a (t, n) threshold scheme described by Equation (1). Due to Lemma 2, Equation (1) can be equivalently presented as

$$(\varepsilon_1, \ldots, \varepsilon_{nv}) = (\rho_1, \ldots, \rho_{tv})B \tag{5}$$

where $\varepsilon = (\varepsilon_1, \ldots, \varepsilon_{nv})$ and $\tau = (\rho_1, \ldots, \rho_{tv})$ are created from vectors $(s_1, \ldots, s_n)$ and $(r_1, \ldots, r_t)$ respectively by replacing each entry by its vector representations, and B is an $tv \times nv$ matrix over $GF(p)$ obtained from the matrix A by changing σ^i into the matrix D^i ($\sigma^0 = 1$ and $D^0 = I_v$ is the $v \times v$ identity matrix).

A (t, n) Shamir Secret Sharing with v Sub-shares ([11])

Let sub-shares be chosen from $GF(p)$ and create shares with v elements. A single
share consists of v sub-shares. The group $\mathcal{P} = \{P_1, \ldots, P_n\}$ collectively holds
the secret.

Dealer

- chooses at random a polynomial $f(x)$ of degree $tv - 1$ with elements from
  $GF(p)$,
- defines the secret $s = (f(-v), \ldots, f(-1))$,
- communicates shares $s_i = (\varepsilon_{i,1}, \ldots, \varepsilon_{i,v})$ to the participant P_i via a secure
  channel, where $\varepsilon_{i,j} = f(x_{i,j})$ and $x_{i,j}$ are public co-ordinates assigned to P_i.

Combiner

- is activated by a subgroup $\mathcal{A} \subseteq \mathcal{P}$,
- collects t shares (or alternatively tv sub-shares) from a currently active group
  $\mathcal{A}$, applies the Lagrange interpolation and recovers the polynomial $f(x)$,
- recovers the secret $s = (f(-v), \ldots, f(-1))$ and distributes it to the group $\mathcal{A}$
  via secure channels.

5   Cheating Detection in Linear Secret Sharing with Sub-shares

If a linear (t, n) threshold scheme allows to use sub-shares, there are new possibilities for cheating prevention including the following:

1. non-atomic submission of shares with public matrix B. A participant pools
   a collection of sub-shares leaving the unused ones for verification purposes,
2. non-atomic submission of shares with partially secret matrix B. A participant submits sub-shares whose corresponding columns of matrix B are public. The columns related to sub-shares used by the participants for verification purposes, are private,
3. submission of sub-shares with secret matrix B.

The linear (t, n) threshold scheme with v sub-shares assigned to each participant according to Formula (3) allows to trade cheating detection ability with
the threshold value ℓ. In particular,

- the threshold value is $\ell = t$, then the participants pool all their sub-shares so
  they collectively provide tv sub-shares (or alternatively t shares) and recover
  the secret. In this case there is no cheating detection,
- the threshold value $\ell > t$ and each participant submits k sub-shares such
  that $\ell k = tv$. A participant can use $v - k$ unused sub-shares for verification
  of the recovered secret.

Before we describe the new scheme, we introduce the following notation. Given
a linear secret sharing scheme (t, n) with v sub-shares assigned to participants
according to Formula (3). Then

(a) B denotes a $tv \times nv$ matrix such that any $tv \times tv$ sub-matrix (obtained by removing the suitable number of columns) is nonsingular,

(b) B_{P_i} denotes a $tv \times v$ sub-matrix of B that contains columns corresponding to all sub-shares assigned to the participant P_i,

(c) $B_{\mathcal{A}}$ denotes a $tv \times av$ sub-matrix of B that contains all columns corresponding to the group $\mathcal{A}$ of a participants,

(d) $B_{\mathcal{A}(k)}$ denotes a $tv \times ak$ sub-matrix of $B_{\mathcal{A}}$ that is obtained by removing $(v - k)$ columns corresponding to participant $P_i \in \mathcal{A}$. This matrix defines columns related to sub-shares provides by the participants of the group $\mathcal{A}$.

A (ℓ, n) Secret Sharing with Cheating Detection

Dealer

- constructs a (t, n) Shamir secret sharing with v sub-shares such that there is an integer k $(k < v)$ such that $k\ell = tv$. The scheme is described by Formula (3) where P_i is assigned a share $s_i = (\varepsilon_{(i-1)v+1}, \ldots, \varepsilon_{iv})$ which consists of v sub-shares. All sub-shares create the vector $\varepsilon = (\varepsilon_1, \ldots, \varepsilon_{nv})$. The vector $\rho = (\rho_1, \ldots, \rho_{tv})$ is typically selected at random while the secret $s = (\rho_1, \ldots, \rho_v)$,

- communicates the shares to participants via confidential channel (the matrix B is public).

Combiner

- is activated by a collection $\mathcal{A}$ of ℓ active participants,
- collects k sub-shares from each participant $P_i \in \mathcal{A}$ and determines the matrix $B_{\mathcal{A}(k)}$,
- computes the vector $\rho = (\rho_1, \ldots, \rho_{tv})$,
- communicates the vector ρ to active participants via secure channel.

Verification - Each participant $P_i \in \mathcal{A}$

- takes the vector ρ and checks

$$(\varepsilon_{(i-1)v+1}, \ldots, \varepsilon_{iv}) \overset{?}{=} (\rho_1, \ldots, \rho_{tv}) B_{P_i}$$

If the check holds, the participant computes the secret from the vector ρ. Otherwise, P_i aborts the scheme and announces a cheating attempt to the other participants.

Lemma 3. *Given a system of n equations in t unknowns $(n \geq t)$ generated from a linear (t, n) threshold scheme described by*

$$(\alpha_1, 0, \ldots, 0, \alpha_{t+1}, \ldots, \alpha_n) = (r_1, r_2, \ldots, r_t) A$$

where co-ordinates $\alpha_2 = 0, \ldots, \alpha_t = 0$. Assume also that the solution for the vector $r = (r_1, \ldots r_t)$ is different from zero. Then co-ordinates $\alpha_1, \alpha_{t+1}, \ldots, \alpha_n$ are different from zero.

A cheating participant clearly controls his own sub-shares but has no influence on the sub-shares owned by the other active participants. Unlike in the original TW attack, the cheater this time has a limited knowledge about which sub-shares are actually submitted to the combiner. As a result, he does not know which columns of the matrix $B_{\mathcal{A}}$ are used by the combiner. In other words, the cheater knows $B_{\mathcal{A}}$ but does not know $B_{\mathcal{A}(k)}$. In general, a cheating participant P_1 can try to achieve the following goals:

- G1 – the cheater wants to recover the valid vector ρ (or the valid secret) while leaving the honest participants with the invalid vector ρ that passes the verification for all honest participants $P_2, \ldots, P_\ell$,
- G2 – the cheater wants to recover the valid vector ρ (or the valid secret) while leaving the honest participants with the invalid vector ρ that fails verification for some honest participants,

Theorem 2. *Given (ℓ, n) secret sharing with cheating detection based on (t, n) scheme with v sub-shares. Assume that the active group $\mathcal{A} = \{P_1, \ldots, P_\ell\}$ includes a single cheater P_1. Then P_1 attains the goal*

- *G1 only if $\lambda = v$, where $\lambda = \frac{k\ell - 1}{\ell - 1}$,*
- *G2 if $k \leq \lambda < v$ and the probability of success is smaller than or equal to*

$$\binom{\lambda}{k}^{\ell-1} \Big/ \binom{v}{k}^{\ell-1}$$

Assume that there are multiple cheaters who collectively create a group $\mathcal{B} = \{P_1, \ldots, P_m\}$ within the group $\mathcal{A} = \{P_1, \ldots, P_\ell\}$. The cheaters now control mk positions. They also know the a part of the matrix B which corresponds to the currently active group $\mathcal{A}$. By a manipulation of their own mk sub-shares they can easily target any $tv - 1$ sub-shares of honest participants so they will not change their values after cheating (see Lemma (3)). Note that the parameter

$$\lambda = \frac{k\ell - 1}{\ell - m}$$

denotes the average numbers of zeroes available for the group to be added to honest participant contributions. The conclusions obtained in Theorem 2 are still valid after rather trivial adjustments.

6   Prevention against the RR Attack

Consider a (ℓ, n) secret sharing with cheating detection. Assume that participants have agreed for multiple recovery of the secret. Again the currently active group is $\mathcal{A} = \{P_1, \ldots, P_\ell\}$ where P_1 is cheating and other participants are honest. The cheater may have the following goals:

- Goal G1$_{RR}$ – recovery of the valid vector ρ (and the secret) while the cheater does not mind to be identified by the honest participants,

- Goal $G2_{RR}$ – recovery of the valid vector ρ (and the secret) while the cheater wants to remain unidentified.

Honest participants are likely to have a single goal in mind, namely, they wish to detect cheating and identify the cheater so they can create a new active group without the cheater and recover the secret.

To achieve their goals both parties may choose different strategies. The cheater may use

- Strategy $S1_c$ – the cheater modifies the sub-share vector ε by designing a vector α of the length ℓv with $k\ell - 1$ zeros distributed evenly among $\ell - 1$ honest participants. The vector α is fixed for the duration of all recoveries. At the pooling stage, the cheater selects her k sub-shares at random.
- Strategy $S2_c$ – as the strategy $S1_c$ except the cheater chooses α independently for each recovery.

Honest participants may apply

- Strategy $S1_h$ – for each recovery, an honest participant chooses at random k sub-shares.
- Strategy $S2_h$ – for the first recovery, an honest participant chooses at random k sub-shares and then keeps re-sending them for other recoveries.

Note that if the cheater applies the strategy $S2_c$ while honest ones behave according to the strategy $S2_h$, then the cheater will always succeed (recovers the correct vector ρ and the secret) while the honest ones have no knowledge about the secret. In other words, the cheater applies the RR attack and achieves $G1_{RR}$. Clearly, the honest participants are able to identify the cheater.

It is most likely that both parties (the honest participants and the cheater) will use strategies $S1_h$ and $S1_c$, respectively. As the two strategies are identical we call them the strategy $S1$. To achieve the goal $G2_{RR}$, the cheater must use this strategy so her behaviour is identical to behaviour of honest participants. On the other hand, honest participants are discouraged to use the strategy $S2_h$ as this strategy makes them vulnerable to the RR attack.

So all participants use the strategy $S1$ and obviously, they agreed for multiple recovery. In practice, however, it is reasonable to assume that after two unsuccessful recoveries, some participants may not wish to take part in further attempts or more likely, the active group may wish to replace some participants by the new ones. In any case, every unsuccessful recovery reveals an incorrect vector ρ' which permits active participants to recover the vector ε' (by multiplying ρ' by the public B_A). A part of ε' corresponding to P_i contains at last k sub-shares that have been indeed submitted by them the other $v - k$ vary depending on how particular participants selected their sub-shares.

A probabilistic model of multiple recovery can be as follows. Given a field $GF(q)$ from which all sub-shares are chosen and a fixed and unknown vector $\beta = (\beta_1, \ldots, \beta_v)$ (it contains all sub-shares of a given participant whose sub-shares are to be identified); $\beta_i \in GF(q)$. To identify the vector, one queries a probabilistic oracle (the combiner). For each enquire, the oracle returns a vector $\gamma = (\gamma_1, \ldots, \gamma_v)$ which

– contains at least k correct co-ordinates. The oracle selects randomly one pattern of k correct co-ordinates out of $\binom{v}{k}$ possible ones.

– contains at most $v - k$ co-ordinates which are chosen randomly, uniformly and independently from the set $GF(q)$.

Note that each co-ordinate in the vector β is in fact, a random variable X with the probability distribution of the following form:

$$P(X = a) = \begin{cases} \frac{k}{v} + (1 - \frac{k}{v})\frac{1}{q} & \text{if } a \text{ is the correct sub-share;} \\ (1 - \frac{k}{v})\frac{1}{q} & \text{otherwise.} \end{cases}$$

To justify this, it is enough to observe that the given co-ordinate with the correct sub-share occurs $\binom{v-1}{k-1} / \binom{v}{k} = \frac{k}{v}$ times assuming the the oracle chooses k out of v position at random. The correct sub-share may also happen if the co-ordinate has not been chosen and the correct sub-share has been selected from $GF(q)$. The wrong value of sub-share occurs when the co-ordinate has not been selected to the subset of k out of v correct sub-shares and the random element tossed from all $GF(q)$ is different from the correct sub-share.

Identification of correct sub-shares can be accomplished using standard statistical tools such as hypothesis testing. We can put forward two hypotheses related to the binary random variable $X \in \{0, 1\}$. The first one

$$H_0 \mapsto P(X = a) = \begin{cases} \frac{k}{v} + (1 - \frac{k}{v})\frac{1}{q} & \text{if } a = 0; \\ (1 - \frac{k}{v})\frac{q-1}{q} & \text{otherwise.} \end{cases}$$

and its alternative

$$H_1 \mapsto P(X = a) = \begin{cases} (1 - \frac{k}{v})\frac{1}{q} & \text{if } a = 0; \\ \frac{k}{v} + (1 - \frac{k}{v})\frac{q-1}{q} & \text{otherwise.} \end{cases}$$

7   Conclusions

Tompa and Woll were first to demonstrate how a dishonest participant can cheat others during the recovery of secret. The TW attack is applicable if the recovery algorithm is run once only. We have argued that in many applications the assumption about single recovery is not reasonable and there is no mechanism incorporated into secret sharing which would prevent it from multiple recoveries. If we allow multiple recoveries than a new threat called the repeat recovery attack emerges. Unlike the TW attack, the RR attack can be successful even if the x co-ordinates are secret. Note that this is a surprising result as the cheater does not have any information about x co-ordinates while being able to determine the valid secret ! The RR attack can be put to a good use so an active group can recover secret after the combiner has been compromised. A trusted participant plays the role of combiner using the compromised combiner.

A (ℓ, n) secret sharing scheme with cheater detection is built on the basis of (t, n) threshold scheme with v sub-shares. Unlike in standard secret sharing, participants are expected to split their sub-shares into two subsets. One subset is submitted to the combiner while the other is left for verification purposes. The combiner returns the vector ρ (instead of the recovered secret) which further is used by participants to check its validity. The sharing scheme with cheater detection has the following properties:

- The scheme can be used as a standard (t, n) secret sharing with atomic shares.
- Cheating according to the TW attack (the goal G1) is only successful if the parameters $v = \lambda$ (λ specifies the number of sub-shares per participants which could be manipulated by cheater by putting zeroes in her α vector). For any $v > \lambda$, the goal G1 cannot be achieved.
- The recovery of the valid secret by the cheater while the honest participants detect cheating (the goal G2) can be achieved with the probability of guessing the subset of sub-shares submitted to the combiner.

The secret sharing scheme with cheater detection is also investigated in the context of the RR attack. We argued that if the cheater wishes not to be identified then she must fix her (modified) sub-shares for the duration of multiple recoveries. The cheater and honest participants are now trying to identify their sub-shares. This scenario resembles the TW attack if the number of recoveries is big enough so everybody can correctly identify sub-shares. Note, however, that honest participants may wish to refuse to participate after some number of recoveries when the probability of guessing of correct secret by the cheater becomes too high.

Acknowledgement. The work was partially supported by Australian Research Council grant A00103078.

References

1. C. Asmuth and J. Bloom. A modular approach to key safeguarding. *IEEE Transactions on Information Theory*, IT-29 No. 2:208–211, 1983.
2. J. Benaloh and J. Leichter. Generalised secret sharing and monotone functions. In S. Goldwasser, editor, *Advances in Cryptology - CRYPTO'88*, LNCS No. 403, pages 27–36. Springer-Verlag, 1988.
3. G. R. Blakley. Safeguarding cryptographic keys. In *Proc. AFIPS 1979 National Computer Conference*, pages 313–317. AFIPS, 1979.
4. E.F. Brickell and D.R. Stinson. The detection of cheaters in threshold schemes. In S. Goldwasser, editor, *Advances in Cryptology - CRYPTO'88*, LNCS No. 403, pages 564–577. Springer-Verlag, 1988.
5. M. Carpentieri. A perfect threshold secret sharing scheme to identify cheaters. *Designs, Codes and Cryptography*, 5(3):183–187, 1995.
6. M. Carpentieri, A. De Santis, and U. Vaccaro. Size of shares and probability of cheating in threshold schemes. In T. Helleseth, editor, *Advances in Cryptology - EUROCRYPT'93*, LNCS No. 765, pages 118–125. Springer, 1993.

7. H. Ghodosi, J. Pieprzyk, R. Safavi-Naini, and H. Wang. On construction of cumulative secret sharing. In C. Boyd and E. Dawson, editor, In *Proceedings of the Third Australasian Conference on Information Security and Privacy (ACISP'98)*, LNCS No. 1438, pages 379–390. Springer-Verlag, 1998.

8. H. Lin, and L. Haen. A generalised secret sharing scheme with cheater detection. In H. Imai, R. Rivest, and T. Matsumoto, editor, In *Proceedings of ASIACRYPT'91*, LNCS No. 739, pages 149-158. Springer-Verlag, 1993.

9. M. Ito, A. Saito, and T. Nishizeki. Secret sharing scheme realizing general access structure. In *Proceedings IEEE Globecom '87*, pages 99–102. IEEE, 1987.

10. E.D. Karnin, J.W. Greene, and M.E. Hellman. On secret sharing systems. *IEEE Transactions on Information Theory*, IT-29:35–41, 1983.

11. K. Martin, J. Pieprzyk, R. Safavi-Naini, and H. Wang. Changing thresholds in the absence of secure channels. In *Proceedings of the Fourth Australasian Conference on Information Security and Privacy (ACISP'99)*, LNCS No. 1587, pages 177–191. Springer-Verlag, 1999.

12. W. Ogata and K. Krurosawa. Optimum secret shares scheme secure against cheating. In U. Maurer, editor, *Advances in Cryptology - EUROCRYPT'96*, LNCS No. 1070, pages 200–211.

13. T. Rabin and M. Ben-Or. Verifiable secret sharing and multiparty protocols with honest majority. In *Proceedings of 21st ACM Symposium on Theory of Computing*, pages 73–85, 1989.

14. A. Shamir. How to share a secret. *Communications of the ACM*, 22:612–613, November 1979.

15. G.J. Simmons, W. Jackson, and K. Martin. The geometry of shared secret schemes. *Bulletin of the ICA*, 1:71–88, 1991.

16. M. Tompa and H. Woll. How to share a secret with cheaters. *Journal of Cryptology*, 1(2):133–138, 1988.

Note on Fast Computation of Secret RSA Exponents

Wieland Fischer and Jean-Pierre Seifert

Infineon Technologies Corporation
Security & ChipCard ICs
Technology & Innovations
D-81609 Munich
Germany
{wieland.fischer,jean-pierre.seifert}@infineon.com

Abstract. Today's cryptography using RSA is faced with the problem of increased bit length and so called fast on-card key generation — both for security reasons. These two requirements often constitute a problem on existing cards as their arithmetic coprocessors are most often designed for a fixed bit length which is not suited for latest security demands. While the main problem, the overcoming of the computational limitations of the cards coprocessor can in principle be solved via recent efficient algorithms, the subproblem of computing the secret RSA exponents cannot be solved satisfactory by these algorithms. This is due to the fact that the key generation, including the secret RSA exponent, is done during the *card personalization* in the fab where production times are very costly. This article proposes a very simple, natural and efficient solution to this problem. Namely, computing the secret RSA exponent d via the Chinese Remainder Theorem (CRT) wrt. $p-1$ and $q-1$ where p and q denote the two secret primes of the the public modul N. We stress that it is impossible to use the CRT in a straightforward way, as $p-1$ and $q-1$ are not relatively prime. Nevertheless the solution to this problem is natural and very simple. However, as we have not found anywhere in the literature a hint on this very practical result, we felt to share it with the community.

Moreover, we present another method to compute efficiently secret RSA exponents d for certain short public keys e which we have not seen so far in the public literature.

Keywords: Carmichael's λ-function, Chinese Remainder Theorem, Key generation, RSA, Secret exponent, Short public key.

1 Introduction

Recently we have seen some progress on integer factorization [C$^+$] which currently demands for higher RSA bit length, as RSA is still the most popular industrial used signature scheme. However, with the increased use of RSA on the other hand in daily life (for, e.g., in smart cards, trusted platform modules)

L. Batten and J. Seberry (Eds.): ACISP 2002, LNCS 2384, pp. 136–143, 2002.
© Springer-Verlag Berlin Heidelberg 2002

we also see a demand for the so called on-card or on-board key-generation. Unfortunately, these two requirements lead to an unsatisfactory situation of the system issuer (for, e.g., the card industry) as the usual arithmetic coprocessors were most often designed for a 1024-bit range (or even only a 512-bit range) which is, as said above, not any longer state of the art.

This situation is due to the fact that, say 2048-bit RSA, cannot be handled efficiently on such cards directly. Only with some work-around this situation becomes a manageable task on a 1024-bit coprocessor. Namely, as it is now folklore knowledge, one can use for the RSA signature the CRT, thus resulting in nearly only 1024-bit operations, see [CQ]. To keep the RSA verification also relatively simple, one uses most often as public exponent the fourth Fermat number, which results in only a few 2048-bit modular multiplications. Only recently it was shown how to reduce efficiently such modular 2048-bit multiplications to 1024-bit modular multiplications, see for, e.g., [HP,Pai]. Nevertheless, it remains the costly key-generation consisting of finding the two primes and the secret exponent, while the public exponent is already fixed. Clearly, finding 1024-bit primes is feasible on a 1024-bit coprocessor. But, finding the secret exponent, the inverse to the public exponent, modulo some number around 2048-bits is a time consuming task on a 1024-bit coprocessor. Although it could be done in principle by the techniques developed in [HP,Pai] the costs for such a task are tremendously and unacceptable high for the card issuer, as this inversion is done during the card personalization in the fab, meaning that the production time of one card takes too long.

To overcome this computational bottleneck this article proposes a very simple, natural and efficient solution to this problem. Namely, computing the secret RSA exponent d via the Chinese Remainder Theorem wrt. $p-1$ and $q-1$ where p and q denote the two secret primes of the the public modulus N. We stress that it is impossible to use the CRT in a straightforward way, as $p-1$ and $q-1$ are not relatively prime. Nevertheless our solution to this problem is natural and very simple.

Despite intensive checking the literature on cryptography we have not found anywhere in the classical literature such as [Kob94,Kob99,RSA,MvOV,Sch], even a hint on this practical result concerning this easy way of computing the secret RSA exponent. Therefore, we felt to write down this short note and to share this practical simple result, which might be also of some general interest.

In addition to this method to compute the secret key d with the help of the CRT out of $d_p := d \bmod p - 1$ and $d_q := d \bmod q - 1$, we will present another method applicable under certain circumstances. This method is especially suited for the computation of secret keys d for public keys e being a small prime number, e.g., F_4.

The article is organized as follows. In the next section we state the pretty unknown version of the generalized CRT. In section 3 we show how to use this generalized CRT in order to compute the secret RSA exponent via the generalized CRT. Hereafter, we present a novel method to compute the private exponent d, which is efficiently and indeed possible if e is a short prime number. Finally, in the conclusions we also give a practical application where it is really necessary to have the full secret exponent d instead of only having d_p and d_q, as it is typically when using RSA in the CRT mode.

2   Generalized Chinese Remainder Theorem

Although the CRT is well known, the version of the generalized CRT, where the moduli are not necessarily coprime, is less known. For instance, Knuth [Knu] mentions this generalized form only in the exercises. Although the generalized chinese remainder theorem is also valid for more than two moduli, we only state the generalized form in the version of two moduli which is exactly what we need.

Theorem 1. *Let m_1 and m_2 be positive integers and $m = \mathrm{lcm}(m_1, m_2)$. Let u_1 and u_2 be arbitrary integers. There exists exactly one integer u that satisfies the conditions*

$$0 \leq u < m, \qquad u \equiv u_1 \pmod{m_1}, \qquad u \equiv u_2 \pmod{m_2},$$

provided that

$$u_1 \equiv u_2 \pmod{\gcd(m_1, m_2)}.$$

Although the proof is already known due to Gauss [Ga], and also a constructive proof was later given by Fraenkel [Fr], we will present in the appendix a proof. Furthermore, it follows from the constructive proofs and immediately from proposition 2 within the appendix (see also [BS,Knu]) that the aforesaid integer u can be computed similar to H. L. Garner's algorithm as described in [MvOV] or [Knu] and especially in our case as follows.

For the integers u_1, u_2 and m_1, m_2 define

$$v_1 := u_1 \pmod{m_1}$$
$$v_2' := u_2 - v_1.$$

Afterwards, compute via the extended Euclidean algorithm integers x and y satisfying

$$x\,m_1 + y\,m_2 = \gcd(m_1, m_2) =: g.$$

Finally,

$$u = v_1 + \left(\frac{x\,v_2'}{g} \left(\bmod \frac{m_2}{g}\right) \right) m_1. \tag{1}$$

3 Computing Secret RSA Exponents via CRT

We briefly recall for the sake of completeness the definition of the RSA public-key cryptography system. First, one chooses randomly two primes p and q and defines $N := pq$ as the public modul. In addition to this public modul one chooses an $e \in (\mathbb{Z}/\phi(N))^*$, the public exponent, where $\phi(N) = (p-1)(q-1)$. Hereafter, one computes the secret exponent d satisfying $ed \equiv 1 \pmod{\lambda(N)}$ with $\lambda(N) = \mathrm{lcm}(p-1, q-1)$.

We now show how to use the constructive version of the generalized CRT in order to compute a secret RSA exponent.

Proposition 1. *For $N = pq$ an RSA modulus and $e \in (\mathbb{Z}/\phi(N))^*$ a public exponent, the unique secret exponent d (mod $\lambda(N)$) can be computed via the generalized CRT wrt. $(p-1)$ and $(q-1)$.*

Proof. We have to show how to compute a d satisfying

$$ed \equiv 1 \pmod{\lambda(N)}$$

with

$$\lambda(N) = \mathrm{lcm}(p-1, q-1) = \frac{(p-1)(q-1)}{\gcd(p-1, q-1)}$$

using Theorem 1 with respect to the moduli $p-1$ and $q-1$. Thus, we first compute integers d_p and d_q satisying

$$e\,d_p \equiv 1 \pmod{(p-1)} \quad \text{and} \quad e\,d_q \equiv 1 \pmod{(q-1)},$$

which exist as $e \in (\mathbb{Z}/p-1)^*$ and $e \in (\mathbb{Z}/q-1)^*$. This is due to the fact that $e \in (\mathbb{Z}/\phi(N))^*$. Now, we will prove that d_p and d_q indeed satisfy the necessary requirement

$$d_p \equiv d_q \pmod{\gcd(m_1, m_2)}.$$

This can be seen as follows. For $\gcd(p-1, q-1) = g$, $\overline{(p-1)}\,g = p-1$, and $\overline{(q-1)}\,g = q-1$ we have

$$d_p \equiv e^{-1} \pmod{\overline{(p-1)}\,g} \quad \text{and} \quad d_q \equiv e^{-1} \pmod{\overline{(q-1)}\,g},$$

which after reducing g results in

$$d_p \equiv e^{-1} \pmod{g} \quad \text{and} \quad d_q \equiv e^{-1} \pmod{g}$$

and proves the aforesaid requirement to apply Theorem 1. Now, simply use Formula (1) to compute the unique d satisfying

$$ed \equiv 1 \pmod{\lambda(N)}.$$

$\square$

4   The Case of Short Prime e

We will now present an efficient method to compute the private key d for a public key e which is applicable for the case of e being a small prime with $\gcd(\varphi(N), e) = 1$.

Our task is to solve the equation

$$d\, e = 1 \bmod \varphi(N),$$

for a given prime e, which is equivalent to find the unique integer $d \in \{0, \dots, \varphi(N) - 1\}$ such that

$$d\, e + x\, \varphi(N) = 1,$$

for some x. Note that $x \in \{-e + 1, \dots, 0\}$. We now reduce the last equation mod e, obtaining the new modular equation

$$x\, \varphi(N) = 1 \bmod e,$$

and then subtracting e such that $-e < x < 0$. Thus, we are left with the problem to compute the inverse of $\varphi(N)$ mod e. This can be easily done by a short exponentiation mod e, i.e.,

$$x = \varphi(N)^{e-2} \bmod e.$$

So, we eventually have simply to compute

$$d := \frac{(1 - x\, \varphi(N))}{e}.$$

This method is especially pleasant on smart card IC implementations which are optimized towards a physical secure and efficient modular exponentiation, cf. [CKN,HJMS,HP]. Thus, in order to make the final division secure against the afore mentioned side-channel attacks, we propose the following algorithm to compute $Q := \lfloor A/B \rfloor$, for A and B numbers of bitlength n_A and n_B.

First, choose a positive integer $s \geq n_A + 2 - 2n_B$. Hereafter, we set $A' := 2^s A$, $B' := 2^s B$ and $B'' := B' + 1$. Now, compute $R_1 := A' \bmod B'$ and $R_2 := A' \bmod B''$. Finally, the result is given by

$$Q := R_1 - R_2 \bmod B''.$$

This is especially on dedicated hardware, cf. [HP], very interesting as this hardware is optimized towards security and efficient modular arithmetic.

5   Conclusions

In this article we have shown how to compute the full unique secret exponent d via the CRT wrt. $p - 1$ and $q - 1$ out of d_p and d_q. One could argue that, when using RSA in the CRT mode we are only interested in having d_p and

d_q and as well p and q as this is enough for RSA signatures and so there is no interest in efficiently computing d out of d_p and d_q. However, when using RSA in CRT mode one has to incorporate countermeasures against so-called differential fault attacks due to Boneh, DeMillo and Lipton [BDL]. Unfortunately, one very efficient popular countermeasure against this side-channel-attack on RSA with CRT (due to Shamir [Sha]) needs the full secret exponent d to detect this kind of attack, cf. [JPY]. Moreover, Shamir's countermeasure cannot be changed trivially to work when using only d_p and d_q — it heavily depends on the knowledge of the full secret exponent d. Thus, given only d_p and d_q and as well p and q, Shamir's countermeasures can still be efficiently implemented using our method to compute d out of d_p and d_q via the generalized CRT.

Also, we have presented a physical secure method to compute the secret key d in the case for appropriately chosen public keys e, as given in most practical applications.

It is our hope and feeling that there are more applications of our methods to compute the secret RSA exponents, maybe our ideas will be fruitful for other areas.

References

[BS]   E. Bach, J. Shallit, *Algorithmic Number Theory*, MIT Press, Cambridge MA, 1996.

[BDL]   D. Boneh, DeMillo, R. Lipton, "On the Importance of Eliminating Errors in Cryptographic Computations" *Journal of Cryptology* **14**(2):101-120, 2001.

[CKN]   J.-S. Coron, P. Kocher and D. Naccache, *Statistics and secret leakage*, Proc. of Financial Cryptography '00, pp. ?-?, 2000.

[C$^+$]   S. Cavallar *et alii*, *Proc. of EUROCRYPT '00*, Springer LNCS, vol. 1807, pp. 1-19, 2000.

[CQ]   C. Couvreur, J.-J. Quisquater, "Fast decipherment algorithm for RSA public-key cryptosystem", *Electronics Letters* **18**(21):905-907, 1982.

[Fr]   A. S. Fraenkel, "New proof of the generalized Chinese Remainder Theorem", *Proc. Amer. Math. Soc.* **14**:790-791, 1963.

[Ga]   C. F. Gauss, *Disquisitiones Arithmeticae*, G. Fleischer, Leipzig, 1801.

[HP]   H. Handschuh, P. Pailler, "Smart Card Crypto-Coprocessors for Public-Key Cryptography", *CryptoBytes* **4**(1):6-11, 1998.

[HJMS]   E. Hess, N. Janssen, B. Meyer, T. Schütze, "Information leakage attacks against smart card implementations of cryptographic algorithms and countermeasures", *Proc. of EUROSMART-Security-Conference 2000*, pp. 53-64, 2000.

[JPY]   M. Joye, P. Pailler, S.-M. Yen, "Secure Evaluation of Modular Functions", *Proc. of 2001 International Workshop on Cryptology and Network Security*, pp. 227-229, 2001.

[Knu]   D. E. Knuth, *The Art of Computer Programming, Vol.2: Seminumerical Algorithms*, 3rd ed., Addison-Wesley, Reading MA, 1999.

[Kob94] N. Koblitz, *A Course in Number Theory and Cryptography*, Springer, Berlin, 1994.

[Kob99] N. Koblitz, *Algebraic Aspects of Cryptography*, Springer, Berlin, 1999.

[MvOV]   A. J. Menezes, P. van Oorschot, S. Vanstone, *Handbook of Applied Cryptography*, CRC Press, New York, 1997.

[Pai]   P. Pailler, "Low-cost double size modular exponentiation or how to stretch
         your cryptocoprocessor", *Proc. of Public Key Cryptography '99*, Springer
         LNCS, vol. 1560, pp. 223-234, 1999.

[RSA]   R. Rivest, A. Shamir, L. Adleman, "A method for obtaining digital signatures
         and public-key cryptosystems", *Comm. of the ACM* **21**:120-126, 1978.

[Sch]   B. Schneier, *Applied Cryptography*, John Wiley & Sons, New York, 1996.

[Sha]   A. Shamir, "Method and Apparatus for protecting public key schemes from
         timing and fault attacks", U.S. Patent Number 5,991,415, November 1999.

Appendix

For the rest of the appendix we denote for $a, b \in \mathbb{N}$ with $g := \gcd(a, b)$ $a =: a' \cdot g$
and $b =: b' \cdot g$.

Lemma 1. *The sequence of $\mathbb{Z}$-algebras*

$$0 \longrightarrow \frac{ab}{g}\mathbb{Z}/ab\mathbb{Z} \stackrel{i}{\longrightarrow} \mathbb{Z}/ab\mathbb{Z} \stackrel{\mathrm{pr}}{\longrightarrow} \mathbb{Z}/a\mathbb{Z} \times \mathbb{Z}/b\mathbb{Z} \stackrel{\delta}{\longrightarrow} \mathbb{Z}/g\mathbb{Z} \longrightarrow 0$$

with the canonical maps i, pr *and*

$$\delta(u \bmod a\mathbb{Z}, v \bmod b\mathbb{Z}) := v - u \bmod g\mathbb{Z}$$

is exact.

Proof. Exactness at $\frac{ab}{g}\mathbb{Z}/ab\mathbb{Z}$ is clear since i is injective. Exactness at $\mathbb{Z}/ab\mathbb{Z}$
follows from that fact that $\mathrm{pr}(u \bmod ab\mathbb{Z}) = (0, 0)$ iff $a|u$ and $b|u$, i.e., $u \in$
$\frac{ab}{g}\mathbb{Z}/ab\mathbb{Z}$. Exactness at $\mathbb{Z}/g\mathbb{Z}$ follows since δ is surjective. Exactness at $\mathbb{Z}/a\mathbb{Z} \times$
$\mathbb{Z}/b\mathbb{Z}$ is seen as follows. The sequence is obviously a complex at $\mathbb{Z}/a\mathbb{Z} \times \mathbb{Z}/b\mathbb{Z}$
as $\delta \circ \mathrm{pr} = 0$. Finally, by virtue of Euler's equation, saying that for a finite
complex of finite groups, the alternating product of the group orders is equal
to the alternating product of the homology group orders, the exactness follows
from the fact, that

$$\#(\frac{ab}{g}\mathbb{Z}/ab\mathbb{Z}) \cdot \#(\mathbb{Z}/a\mathbb{Z} \times \mathbb{Z}/b\mathbb{Z}) = \#(\mathbb{Z}/ab\mathbb{Z}) \cdot \#(\mathbb{Z}/g\mathbb{Z}).$$

$\square$

Remark 1. If $g = 1$ then we get the classical CRT, namely the isomorphism
$\mathbb{Z}/ab\mathbb{Z} \cong \mathbb{Z}/a\mathbb{Z} \times \mathbb{Z}/b\mathbb{Z}$ via the canonical projection. Furthermore the sequence
from above immediately transforms into the short exact sequence

$$0 \longrightarrow \mathbb{Z}/\frac{ab}{g}\mathbb{Z} \stackrel{\mathrm{pr}}{\longrightarrow} \mathbb{Z}/a\mathbb{Z} \times \mathbb{Z}/b\mathbb{Z} \stackrel{\delta}{\longrightarrow} \mathbb{Z}/g\mathbb{Z} \longrightarrow 0$$

Now, denote by $\sigma_a \colon \mathbb{Z}/a\mathbb{Z} \to \mathbb{Z}$ and $\sigma_b \colon \mathbb{Z}/b\mathbb{Z} \to \mathbb{Z}$ any sections of the canonical projections $\mathbb{Z} \to \mathbb{Z}/a\mathbb{Z}$ and $\mathbb{Z} \to \mathbb{Z}/b\mathbb{Z}$.

Proposition 2. *Let x, $y \in \mathbb{Z}$ be integers such that $xa + yb = g$. Then, the map*

$$\sigma \colon \mathbb{Z}/a\mathbb{Z} \times \mathbb{Z}/b\mathbb{Z} \longrightarrow \mathbb{Z}/\frac{ab}{g}\mathbb{Z}$$

given by

$$\sigma(\alpha, \beta) = \sigma_a(\alpha) + xa' \cdot (\sigma_b(\beta) - \sigma_a(\alpha)) \bmod \frac{ab}{g}\mathbb{Z}$$

is a section of pr *over* $\ker(\delta)$, *i.e.,*

$$\mathrm{pr} \circ \sigma|_{\ker(\delta)} = \mathrm{id}_{\ker(\delta)}.$$

Proof. Let $(\alpha, \beta) \in \ker(\delta)$. Since $(\alpha, \beta) = (\sigma_a(\alpha) \bmod a\mathbb{Z}, \sigma_b(\beta) \bmod b\mathbb{Z})$ we know

$$\sigma_b(\beta) - \sigma_a(\alpha) \equiv 0 \bmod g\mathbb{Z},$$

i.e., $g \mid (\sigma_b(\beta) - \sigma_a(\alpha))$. We yet have to prove that $\sigma(\alpha, \beta) \bmod a\mathbb{Z} = \alpha$ and $\sigma(\alpha, \beta) \bmod b\mathbb{Z} = \beta$ holds. This follows as

$$\begin{aligned}
\sigma(\alpha, \beta) &= \sigma_a(\alpha) + xa'(\sigma_b(\beta) - \sigma_a(\alpha)) \\
&= \sigma_a(\alpha) + xa \cdot \frac{\sigma_b(\beta) - \sigma_a(\alpha)}{g} \\
&\equiv \sigma_a(\alpha) \bmod a\mathbb{Z} \\
&= \alpha.
\end{aligned}$$

and

$$\begin{aligned}
\sigma(\alpha, \beta) &= \sigma_a(\alpha) + xa'(\sigma_b(\beta) - \sigma_a(\alpha)) \\
&= \sigma_a(\alpha) + xa \cdot \frac{\sigma_b(\beta) - \sigma_a(\alpha)}{g} \\
&\equiv \sigma_a(\alpha) + g \cdot \frac{\sigma_b(\beta) - \sigma_a(\alpha)}{g} \bmod b\mathbb{Z} \\
&\equiv \sigma_a(\alpha) + (\sigma_b(\beta) - \sigma_a(\alpha)) \bmod b\mathbb{Z} \\
&\equiv \sigma_b(\beta) \bmod b\mathbb{Z} \\
&= \beta.
\end{aligned}$$

$\square$

Remark 2. Since

$$\begin{aligned}
xa'(\sigma_b(\beta) - \sigma_a(\alpha)) &= a\left(x \cdot \frac{\sigma_b(\beta) - \sigma_a(\alpha)}{g}\right) \\
&\equiv a\left(x \cdot \frac{\sigma_b(\beta) - \sigma_a(\alpha)}{g} + \gamma b'\right) \bmod \frac{ab}{g}\mathbb{Z},
\end{aligned}$$

for all $\gamma \in \mathbb{Z}$, one can first reduce the value in the large brackets modulo b' before computing $\sigma(\alpha, \beta)$. If σ_a and σ_b are the usual sections, e.g., $\sigma_a \colon \mathbb{Z}/a\mathbb{Z} \to \{0, 1, \ldots, a - 1\}$, then the computed value $\sigma(\alpha, \beta)$ will also be reduced.

Better than BiBa: Short One-Time Signatures with Fast Signing and Verifying

Leonid Reyzin and Natan Reyzin

Boston University
111 Cummington St.
Boston, MA 02215
reyzin@cs.bu.edu
http://www.cs.bu.edu/~reyzin

Abstract. One-time signature schemes have found numerous applications: in ordinary, on-line/off-line, and forward-secure signatures. More recently, they have been used in multicast and broadcast authentication. We propose a one-time signature scheme with very efficient signing and verifying, and short signatures. Our scheme is well-suited for broadcast authentication, and, in fact, can be viewed as an improvement of the BiBa one-time signature (proposed by Perrig in CCS 2001 for broadcast authentication).

1 Introduction

In [Per01], Perrig proposes a one-time signature scheme called "BiBa" (for "Bins and Balls"). BiBa's main advantages are fast verification and short signatures. In fact, to the best of our knowledge, BiBa has the fastest verification of all currently-known one-time signature schemes. These desirable properties allow Perrig to design a stream authentication scheme with small communication overhead and fast authentication of each packet (also called BiBa in [Per01]).

BiBa's main disadvantage is the time required to sign a message, which is longer than in most previously proposed one-time signature schemes. We present a simpler one-time signature scheme that maintains BiBa's advantages and removes its main disadvantage. Specifically, in our scheme verifying is as fast as in BiBa, and signing is even faster than verifying. The key and signature sizes are slightly improved, as well (for the same security level).

Like BiBa, our signature scheme can be used r times, instead of just once, for small values of r (in both schemes, security decreases as r increases), which is essential for its use in the stream authentication scheme of [Per01]. The security of our scheme relies only on complexity-theoretic assumptions, and does not require the use of random oracles. This is in contrast to BiBa, in which the use of random oracles seems essential.

We present our scheme in two parts. In Section 2, we slightly generalize a scheme proposed by Bos and Chaum [BC92]), providing a tradeoff that allows us to decrease signature size and verification time at the expense of increasing the

L. Batten and J. Seberry (Eds.): ACISP 2002, LNCS 2384, pp. 144–153, 2002.
© Springer-Verlag Berlin Heidelberg 2002

public key length. The resulting scheme is not, however, as efficient as we wish. Thus, in Section 3, we present our most efficient construction (named "HORS," for reasons to be explained), whose security is based on stronger assumptions. In HORS, signing requires just one hash function evaluation, and verifying requires 17 hash function evaluations for a high level of security.

1.1 Prior Work

One-time signatures based on the idea of committing to secret keys via one-way functions were proposed independently by Lamport [Lam79] and (in an interactive setting) by Rabin [Rab78]. Various improvements were proposed by Meyer and Matyas [MM82, pages 406–409], Merkle [Mer82], Winternitz (as cited in [Mer87]), Vaudenay [Vau92] (in an interactive setting), Bos and Chaum [BC92], and Even, Goldreich and Micali [EGM96]. Bleichenbacher and Maurer considered generalization of the above work in [BM94,BM96a,BM96b].

Perrig's BiBa [Per01], however, appears to be the first scheme whose primary design goal was fast signature verification (while Bleichenbacher and Maurer concern themselves with "optimal" one-time signature schemes, their notion of optimality translates into fast key generation, rather than efficient signing or verifying). Our scheme preserves BiBa's verifying efficiency, dramatically increases its signing efficiency, and slightly decreases the sizes of BiBa's keys and signatures.

1.2 Applications of One-Time Signatures

One-time signatures have found applications in constructions of ordinary signature schemes [Mer87,Mer89], forward-secure signature schemes [AR00], online/off-line signature schemes [EGM96], and stream/multicast authentication [Roh99], among others. We note that our scheme fits well into all of these applications, including, in particular, the BiBa broadcast authentication scheme of [Per01]. In fact, the BiBa broadcast authentication scheme itself would need no modifications at all if our signature scheme was substituted for the BiBa signature scheme.

2 The Construction Based on One-Way Functions

The construction presented in this section relies solely on one-way functions for its security. It is a simple generalization of the construction of Bos and Chaum [BC92], which, in turn, is a generalization of Lamport's construction [Lam79]. As stated above, this scheme is mainly of theoretical interest due to performance considerations. However, it is a stepping stone to our ultimate signature scheme, and thus we present it first.

PRELIMINARIES. To build a scheme to sign b-bit messages[1], pick t and k such that $\binom{t}{k} \geq 2^b$. (Naturally, there are multiple possible choices for t and k, and, in fact, a trade-off between them. We note that the public key size will be linear in t, and the signature size and verification time will be linear in k).

Let T denote the set $\{1, 2, \ldots, t\}$.

Let S be a bijective function that, on input m, $0 \leq m < \binom{t}{k}$, outputs the m-th k-element subset of the T (of course, there are many possibilities for S; we do not care how S is chosen as long as it is efficiently implementable and bijective). Our proposal for implementing S is contained in Section 2.1.

Let f be a one-way function operating on l-bit strings, for a security parameter l.

THE SCHEME. To generate a key pair given the security parameter 1^l, generate t random l-bit quantities for the secret key: $SK = (s_1, \ldots, s_t)$. Compute the public key as follows: $PK = (v_1, \ldots, v_t)$, where $v_1 = f(s_1), \ldots, v_t = f(s_t)$.

To sign a b-bit message m, interpret m as an integer value between 0 and $2^b - 1$, and let $\{i_1, \ldots, i_k\}$ be the m-th k-element subset of T (found using the function S). Reveal the values $s_{i_1}, \ldots, s_{i_k}$ as the signature.

To verify a signature $(s'_1, s'_2, \ldots, s'_k)$ on a message, again interpret m as an integer value between 0 and $2^b - 1$, and let $\{i_1, \ldots, i_k\}$ be the m-th k-element subset of T. Verify that $f(s'_1) = v_{i_1}, \ldots, f(s'_t) = v_{i_t}$.

EFFICIENCY. Key generation requires t evaluations of the one-way function. The secret key size is lt bits, and the public key size is $f_l t$ bits, where f_l is the length of the one-way function output on input of length l. The signature is kt bits long.

The signing algorithm takes as long as running time of the algorithm for S: the time required to find the m-th k-element subset of a t-element set. Our implementations of S, in Section 2.1, have running time $O(tk \log^2 t)$, or $O(k^2 \log t \log k)$ with some precomputation. The verifying algorithm takes the same amount of time, plus k evaluations of the one-way function.

We note that [BC92] proposed essentially the same scheme, with the restriction that $k = t/2$. Such choice minimizes the public key size. Our goal (and the goal of BiBa), however, is to minimize the signature size while keeping the public key size reasonable.

SECURITY. Because each message corresponds to a different k-element subset of the set T, it is trivial to prove that, in order to existentially forge a signature on a new message after a one-time adaptive chosen message attack, the forger would have to invert the one-way function f on at least one of the $t - k$ values in the public key for which the corresponding value in the secret key has not been revealed. Thus, the security of the signature scheme is reduced to the one-wayness of f.

---

[1] In order to sign arbitrary-length messages, one can use the standard technique of applying a collision-resistant hash function to the message and then signing the resulting hash value.

If longer messages are being hashed down to b bits before being signed, then the security relies not only on the one-wayness of f, but also on the collision-resistance of the hash function.

2.1   The Selection Algorithms

Here we present two algorithms that, on input m, $0 \le m < \binom{t}{k}$, output the m-th k-element subset of T, where $T = \{1, 2, \ldots, t\}$. The first algorithm is due to Bos and Chaum [BC92]; the second one, to the best of our knowledge, is new.

Algorithm 1. The first algorithm is based on the following equation:

$$\binom{t}{k} = \binom{t-1}{k-1} + \binom{t-1}{k}.$$

In other words, if the last element of T belongs to the subset, then there are $t - 1$ elements remaining from which $k - 1$ need to be chosen. Otherwise, there are $t - 1$ elements remaining from which k need to be chosen.

Thus, on input (m, k, t), the algorithm checks if $m < \binom{t-1}{k-1}$. If so, it adds t to the output subset, and recurses on $(m, k - 1, t - 1)$. Else, it adds nothing to the output subset, and recurses on $\left(m - \binom{t-1}{k-1}, k, t - 1\right)$. Note that $\binom{t}{k}$ can be precomputed once and for all, and then at each recursive level, the algorithm simply needs to do one division and one multiplication to compute $\binom{t-1}{k-1} = k\binom{t}{k}/t$, plus possibly one subtraction to compute $\binom{t-1}{k} = \binom{t}{k} - \binom{t-1}{k-1}$.

Thus, the cost per recursive level is one multiplication of an $O(k \log t)$-bit number by an $O(\log k)$-bit number, followed by one division of an $O(\log k + k \log t)$-bit number by an $O(\log t)$-bit number, for a total of $O(k \log k \log t) + O((\log k + k \log t)(\log t)) = O(k \log^2 t)$. There are t levels, for the total cost of $tk \log^2 t$.

Algorithm 2. The second algorithm is slightly more complicated, and is based on the following equation:

$$\binom{t}{k} = \binom{\lceil t/2 \rceil}{0}\binom{\lfloor t/2 \rfloor}{k} + \binom{\lceil t/2 \rceil}{1}\binom{\lfloor t/2 \rfloor}{k-1} + \ldots + \binom{\lceil t/2 \rceil}{k}\binom{\lfloor t/2 \rfloor}{0}$$

$$= \sum_{i=0}^{k} \binom{\lceil t/2 \rceil}{i}\binom{\lfloor t/2 \rfloor}{k-i}.$$

In other words, if k elements are selected from T, then, for some i, i elements come from the first half of T, and $k - i$ elements come from the second half of T.

Thus, on input (m, k, t), the algorithm finds j ($0 \le j \le k$) such that

$$\sum_{i=0}^{j-1} \binom{\lceil t/2 \rceil}{i}\binom{\lfloor t/2 \rfloor}{k-i} \le m, \text{ but } \sum_{i=0}^{j} \binom{\lceil t/2 \rceil}{i}\binom{\lfloor t/2 \rfloor}{k-i} > m.$$

Then let $m' = m - \sum_{i=0}^{j-1} \binom{\lceil t/2 \rceil}{i} \binom{\lfloor t/2 \rfloor}{k-i}$; let $m_1 = m' \operatorname{div} \binom{\lceil t/2 \rceil}{j}$ and $m_2 = m' \bmod \binom{\lceil t/2 \rceil}{j}$ (where div stands for integer division, and mod stands for the remainder). The algorithm recurses on $(m_1, j, \lceil t/2 \rceil)$ and $(m_2, j, \lfloor t/2 \rfloor)$. It then combines the subsets that the two recursive calls return.

If t is a power of two, and k is not too large, then it is possible to precompute $\binom{t/2^a}{b}$, for all $a < \log t$ and $b < k$ (this would be $O(k \log t)$ values, for $O(k^2 \log^2 t)$ bits). The recursive calls form a binary tree with of depth $\log t$. The cost of each invocation within this binary tree is dominated by multiplications of precomputed values of the form $\binom{t/2^a}{b}$; moreover, there are at most as many multiplications as the size of the subset that the particular invocation is looking for. Note that the sum of the sizes of subsets across each *level* of the binary tree is at most k. Hence, summing up over all $\log t$ levels, there are a total of $O(k \log t)$ multiplications of $O(k \log t)$-bit values. Thus, the computational cost is $O(k^2 \log^2 t)$.

Moreover, for a random m, the expected depth of the tree is actually $O(\log k)$ (because, intuitively, the subset is likely to be divided fairly evenly between the two halves of T). Therefore, the expected running time for a random m is actually $O(k^2 \log t \log k)$.

Finally, we note that, in practice, it is better to change the order in which the sum is computed: instead of going from $i = 0$ to k, it is better to start with $i = k/2$ and go in both directions (to 0 and to k). This is so because we are likely to stop sooner, because k is more likely to be split evenly. Moreover, it is more efficient to have the base case of $k = 1$ than $k = 0$. Our implementation of this algorithm (based on Wei Dai's Crypto++ library for multiprecision arithmetic) takes .09 milliseconds on a 1700 MHz Pentium 4 for $t = 1024$, $k = 16$, and a random m.

3   Construction Based On "Subset-Resilient" Functions

This section presents our most efficient construction.

In the above scheme, the function S makes it *impossible* to find two distinct messages that will result in the same k-element subset of T (because S is bijective, it guarantees that such two messages do not exist). To improve efficiency, we propose to replace S with a function H that provides no such iron-clad guarantee, but merely makes it *infeasible* to find two such messages. Moreover, we will relax the requirement that the subset of T corresponding to each message contain *exactly* k elements, and rather require it to contain *at most* k elements. The requirement on H now will be that it is infeasible to find two messages, m_1 and m_2, such that $H(m_2) \subseteq H(m_1)$.

This relaxation of the requirements allows us to consider using a single public key to provide not one, but several signatures. If the signer provides up to r signatures, then, for the scheme to be secure, it should be infeasible to find $r + 1$ messages $m_1, m_2, \ldots, m_{r+1}$ such that $H(m_{r+1}) \subseteq H(m_1) \cup H(m_2) \cup \ldots \cup H(m_r)$.

Using H instead of S also allows us to remove the restrictions on message length, and with it the need for collision-resistant hashing in order to sign longer messages.

It should be clear how to formalize the precise requirements on H in order to prove security of our one-time signature scheme (naturally, in order for the requirements to be meaningful, H has to be selected at random from a family of functions, and which particular H is chosen should be part of the public key). We do so in Appendix A. We note that the formalizations are different depending on whether the adversary for the signature scheme is allowed a chosen message attack or a random message attack. We also note that if H is modeled as a random oracle, then it trivially satisfies the definitions.

THE EFFICIENT SCHEME. We propose using a cryptographic hash function *Hash*, for example SHA-1 [NIS95] or RIPEMD-160 [DBP96], to construct H as follows:

1. split the output of the hash function into k substrings of length $\log t$ each;
2. interpret each $(\log t)$-bit substring as integer written in binary;
3. combine these integers to form the subset of T of size at most k.

We believe that such H satisfies our definition (it certainly does if the cryptographic hash function is modeled as a random oracle).

Such construction of H results in the scheme we call HORS (for "Hash to Obtain Random Subset"). We present it in Figure 1. HORS possesses extremely efficient signing, requiring just one evaluation of the cryptographic hash function, and efficient verifying, requiring one evaluation of the hash function in addition to k evaluations of the one-way function f. (We note that in every signature scheme used in practice, both signing and verifying always require at least one evaluation of a cryptographic hash function if the messages are long.)

The use of cryptographic hash function with 160-bit outputs results in practically convenient parameters. One can take $k = 16$ and $t = 2^{10} = 1024$, or $k = 20$ and $t = 2^8 = 256$. We analyze the security of these specific parameters in the Section 4.

SECURITY. The security proof for this scheme follows directly from subset-resilience of the hash function, as defined in Appendix A, and one-wayness of f. Specifically, the signatures are existentially unforgeable against r-time chosen-message (or random-message) attacks (in the sense of [GMR88]) if the hash function is r-subset-resilient (or, respectively, r-target-subset-resilient) and f is one-way. The proof trivially reduces a signature forgery to a break of the one-way function or the hash function, depending on whether the forgery uses a new element of T or only re-uses the ones already revealed during the attack.

The exact security against non-adaptive chosen-message attack is analyzed in the next section.

Key Generation
    Input: Parameters l, k, t
        Generate t random l-bit strings $s_1, s_2, \ldots, s_t$
        Let $v_i = f(s_i)$ for $1 \le i \le t$
    Output: $PK = (k, v_1, v_2, \ldots, v_t)$ and $SK = (k, s_1, s_2, \ldots, s_t)$

Signing
    Input: Message m and secret key $SK = (k, s_1, s_2, \ldots, s_t)$
        Let $h = Hash(m)$
        Split h into k substrings $h_1, h_2, \ldots, h_k$, of length $\log_2 t$ bits each
        Interpret each h_j as an integer i_j for $1 \le j \le k$
    Output: $\sigma = (s_{i_1}, s_{i_2}, \ldots, s_{i_k})$

Verifying
    Input: Message m, signature $\sigma = (s_1', \ldots, s_k')$, public key $PK = (k, v_1, \ldots, v_t)$
        Let $h = Hash(m)$
        Split into k substrings $h_1, h_2, \ldots, h_k$, of length $\log_2 t$ bits each
        Interpret each h_j as an integer i_j for $1 \le j \le k$
    Output: "accept" if for each j, $1 \le j \le k$, $f(s_j') = v_{i_j}$; "reject" otherwise

Fig. 1. *HORS one-time signature scheme, where f is a one-way function and Hash is a hash function. Both f and Hash may be implemented using a standard hash function, such as SHA-1 or RIPEMD-160. Suggested parameter values are $l = 80$, $k = 16$ and $t = 1024$, or $l = 80$, $k = 20$ and $t = 256$.*

4   Comparison with BiBa

BiBa requires about $2t$ calls to the random oracle for signing messages, while, in contrast, HORS requires only one call to H. Verification in BiBa requires k calls to the one-way function f, just like in HORS. However, BiBa verification also requires k calls to the random oracle, while HORS requires only one call to H. Thus, our scheme is significantly more efficient in signing and slightly more efficient in verifying.

Another advantage of HORS is that slightly smaller values of t and k can be used to achieve the same security levels (or, alternatively, more security can be obtained from the same values of t and k), as shown below.

One cannot compare the security of our scheme directly to the security of BiBa, because BiBa relies on the assumption that *Hash* is a random oracle, whereas HORS does not. Therefore, for a fair comparison, we have to make the same assumptions as [Per01] makes: that *Hash* is a random oracle. Given this, we analyze the exact security of HORS against r-non-adaptive-message attack: that is, just like [Per01], we assume that the adversary obtains signatures on r messages of its choice (but the choice is independent of *Hash*), and then tries to forge a signature on a any new message m of its choice. We are interested in the probability that the adversary is able to do so without inverting the one-way function f. It is quite easy to see that this probability is at most $(rk/t)^k$ for each invocation of *Hash*, i.e., the probability that after rk elements of T are fixed, k elements chosen at random are a subset of them.

In other words, we get $k(\log t - \log k - \log r)$ bits of security. Thus, we use $k = 16$, $t = 1024$ and $r = 1$, then the security level is 2^{-96}. After four signatures are given, the probability of forgery is 2^{-64}. This is in contrast to 2^{-58} for Perrig's scheme with the same parameters (see Section 5 of [Per01]). Alternatively, we could reduce the size of the public key $t = 790$ to match the 2^{-58} security level.

For the example of $k = 20$ and $t = 256$, our security level is 2^{-73} if $r = 1$ and 2^{-53} if $r = 2$.

We note that the above does not analyze the security of HORS against *adaptive* chosen-message attacks, where the adversary gets to decide the messages on which to obtain signatures *after* evaluating *Hash* on multiple messages. The security of HORS against such an attack is lower than above (because, similarly to the "birthday paradox," the adversary has a higher chance of being able to choose the $r+1$ messages such that the union of the subsets corresponding to the first r of them covers the subset corresponding the last one). However, HORS is more secure against such an attack than BiBa is. A precise analysis will be provided in the full version of this paper.

Acknowledgments. We are thankful to Kevin Fu and Michael Freedman for helpful discussions, to Wei Dai for his Crypto++ library, and to Jonathan Katz for pointing us to the [BC92] paper.

References

[AR00]   Michel Abdalla and Leonid Reyzin. A new forward-secure digital signature scheme. In Tatsuaki Okamoto, editor, *Advances in Cryptology—ASIACRYPT 2000*, volume 1976 of *Lecture Notes in Computer Science*, pages 116–129, Kyoto, Japan, 3–7 December 2000. Springer-Verlag. Full version available from the Cryptology ePrint Archive, record 2000/002, http://eprint.iacr.org/.

[BC92]   Jurjen N. E. Bos and David Chaum. Provably unforgeable signatures. In Ernest F. Brickell, editor, *Advances in Cryptology—CRYPTO '92*, volume 740 of *Lecture Notes in Computer Science*, pages 1–14. Springer-Verlag, 1993, 16–20 August 1992.

[BM94]   Daniel Bleichenbacher and Ueli M. Maurer. Directed acyclic graphs, one-way functions and digital signatures. In Yvo G. Desmedt, editor, *Advances in Cryptology—CRYPTO '94*, volume 839 of *Lecture Notes in Computer Science*, pages 75–82. Springer-Verlag, 21–25 August 1994.

[BM96a]   Daniel Bleichenbacher and Ueli M. Maurer. On the efficiency of one-time digital signatures. In Kwangjo Kim and Tsutomu Matsumoto, editors, *Advances in Cryptology—ASIACRYPT '96*, volume 1163 of *Lecture Notes in Computer Science*, pages 145–158, Kyongju, Korea, 3–7 November 1996. Springer-Verlag.

[BM96b]   Daniel Bleichenbacher and Ueli M. Maurer. Optimal tree-based one-time digital signature schemes. In Claude Puech and Rüdiger Reischuk, editors, *Symposium on Theoretical Aspects of Computer Science*, volume 1046 of *Lecture Notes in Computer Science*, pages 363–374. Springer-Verlag, 1996.

[DBP96]   Hans Dobbertin, Antoon Bosselaers, and Bart Preneel. RIPEMD-160: A strengthened version of RIPEMD. In D. Gollmann, editor, *Fast Software Encryption. Third International Workshop Proceedings*. Springer-Verlag, 1996.

[EGM96]   Shimon Even, Oded Goldreich, and Silvio Micali. On-line/off-line digital signatures. *Journal of Cryptology*, 9(1):35–67, Winter 1996.

[GMR88]   Shafi Goldwasser, Silvio Micali, and Ronald L. Rivest. A digital signature scheme secure against adaptive chosen-message attacks. *SIAM Journal on Computing*, 17(2):281–308, April 1988.

[Lam79]   Leslie Lamport. Constructing digital signatures from a one way function. Technical Report CSL-98, SRI International, October 1979.

[Mer82]   Ralph C. Merkle. *Secrecy, Authentication, and Public Key Systems*. UMI Research Press, 1982.

[Mer87]   Ralph C. Merkle. A digital signature based on a conventional encryption function. In Carl Pomerance, editor, *Advances in Cryptology— CRYPTO '87*, volume 293 of *Lecture Notes in Computer Science*, pages 369–378. Springer-Verlag, 1988, 16–20 August 1987.

[Mer89]   Ralph C. Merkle. A certified digital signature. In G. Brassard, editor, *Advances in Cryptology—CRYPTO '89*, volume 435 of *Lecture Notes in Computer Science*, pages 218–238. Springer-Verlag, 1990, 20–24 August 1989.

[MM82]   Carl H. Meyer and Stephen M. Matyas. *Cryptography: A New Dimension in Computer Data Security*. John Wiley & Sons, 1982.

[NIS95]   *FIPS Publication 180-1: Secure Hash Standard*. National Institute of Standards and Technology (NIST), April 1995. Available from http://csrc.nist.gov/fips/.

[Per01]   Adrian Perrig. The BiBa one-time signature and broadcast authentication protocol. In *Eighth ACM Conference on Computer and Communication Security*, pages 28–37. ACM, November 5–8 2001.

[Rab78]   Michael O. Rabin. Digitalized signatures. In Richard A. Demillo, David P. Dobkin, Anita K. Jones, and Richard J. Lipton, editors, *Foundations of Secure Computation*, pages 155–168. Academic Press, 1978.

[Roh99]   Pankaj Rohatgi. A compact and fast hybrid signature scheme for multi-cast packet authentication. In *Sixth ACM Conference on Computer and Communication Security*, pages 93–100. ACM, November 1999.

[Vau92]   Serge Vaudenay. One-time identification with low memory. In P. Camion, P. Charpin, S. Harari, and G. Cohen, editors, *Proceedings of EUROCODE '92*, Lecture Notes in Computer Science, pages 217–228. Springer-Verlag, 1992.

A   Definitions of Subset-Resilience

Let $\mathcal{H} = \{H_{i,t,k}\}$ be a family of functions, where $H_{i,t,k}$ maps an input of arbitrary length to a subset of size at most k of the set $\{0, 1, \ldots, t-1\}$. (Note that for each t and k, $\mathcal{H}$ contains a number of functions, which are indexed by i.) Moreover, assume that there is a polynomial-time algorithm that, given $i, 1^t, 1^k$ and M, computes $H_{i,t,k}(M)$.

Definition 1. *We say that $\mathcal{H}$ is r-subset-resilient if, for every probabilistic polynomial-time adversary A,*

$$\Pr_i \left[(M_1, M_2, \ldots, M_{r+1}) \leftarrow A(i, 1^t, 1^k) \right.$$

$$\left. s.t. \ H_{i,t,k}(M_{r+1}) \subseteq \bigcup_{j=1}^{r} H_{i,t,k}(M_j) \right] < negl(t,k).$$

Fix a distribution D on the space of all inputs to H (i.e., on the space of messages).

Definition 2. *We say that $\mathcal{H}$ is r-target-subset-resilient if, for every probabilistic polynomial-time adversary A,*

$$\Pr_i \left[M_1, M_2, \ldots, M_r \overset{R}{\leftarrow} D; \ M_{r+1} \leftarrow A(i, 1^t, 1^k, M_1, \ldots, M_r) \right.$$

$$\left. s.t. \ H_{i,t,k}(M_{r+1}) \subseteq \bigcup_{j=1}^{r} H_{i,t,k}(M_j) \right] < negl(t,k).$$

Note that subset-resilience is a stronger property than target-subset-resilience. The former is needed to prove security of our scheme against adaptive chosen message attacks, while the latter suffices for random message attacks.

For $r = 1$, the above definitions can be realized using only collision-resilient hash families. Namely, if $\mathcal{H}$ is a collision-resilient hash function family, and S is the subset-selection algorithm of Section 2, then $\{H(S)\}_{H \in \mathcal{H}}$ is a 1-subset-resilient family. Similarly, if $\mathcal{H}$ is target-collision-resilient (a.k.a. "universal one-way"), then $\{H(S)\}_{H \in \mathcal{H}}$ is 1-target-subset-resilient.

For $r > 1$, realizing the above definitions using only common complexity-theoretic assumptions (without random oracles) is an open problem. We believe, however, that it is reasonable to assume that selecting subsets via cryptographic hash functions, such as SHA-1 or RIPEMD-160, will satisfy these definitions for small values of r.

Cryptanalysis of Stream Cipher COS (2, 128) Mode I

Hongjun Wu and Feng Bao

Laboratories for Information Technology
21 Heng Mui Keng Terrace, Singapore 119613
{hongjun,baofeng}@lit.org.sg

Abstract. Filiol and Fontaine recently proposed a family of stream ciphers named COS. COS is based on nonlinear feedback shift registers and was claimed to be highly secure. Babbage showed that COS (2, 128) Mode II is extremely weak. But Babbage's attack is very expensive to break the COS (2, 128) Mode I (the complexity is around 2^{52}). In this paper, we show that the COS (2, 128) Mode I is very weak. Secret information could be recovered easily with about 2^{16}-bit known plaintext.

1 Introduction

Filiol and Fontaine recently designed a family of stream ciphers called COS [3, 4,5]. The COS (2, 128) is with two 128-bit internal registers. Two versions of COS (2,128) are available: Mode II and the more secure Mode I. In [1], Babbage showed that the COS (2, 128) Mode II is too weak and the secret information could be recovered easily from a short piece of key stream. Babbage's attack also reduced the complexity of the COS (2, 128) Mode I to 2^{64}. In [2], Babbage's improved attack reduced the complexity of the COS (2, 128) Mode I to 2^{52}.

In this paper, we show that the COS (2, 128) Mode I could be broken with a short plaintext in negligible time. In average about 2^{16}-bit known plaintext is required in the attack. The time required is about 15 milliseconds on Pentium IV.

This paper is organized as follows. Section 2 introduces the COS (2, 128) stream cipher. The attack against the COS (2, 128) Mode I is given in Section 3. Section 4 concludes this paper.

2 COS Stream Cipher

We give only a brief introduction to the COS (2, 128). This version of COS cipher is with two 128-bit registers, L_1 and L_2, as the initial states. We will ignore the key setup of COS (since the key setup has no effect on our attack) and only introduce the key stream generation process.

Let $L_1 = L_{10} \parallel L_{11} \parallel L_{12} \parallel L_{13}$, $L_2 = L_{20} \parallel L_{21} \parallel L_{22} \parallel L_{23}$, where $\parallel$ indicates concatenation and each L_{ij} is a 32-bit word. At the ith step, the output key stream is generated as:

L. Batten and J. Seberry (Eds.): ACISP 2002, LNCS 2384, pp. 154–158, 2002.
© Springer-Verlag Berlin Heidelberg 2002

1. Compute clocking value d.
   a) Compute $m = 2 \times (L_{23} \mathbin{\&} 1) + (L_{13} \mathbin{\&} 1)$ where $\&$ is the binary AND operator.
   b) $d = C_m$, where $C_0 = 64$, $C_1 = 65$, $C_2 = 66$, $C_3 = 64$.
2. If i is even, clock L_1 d times; otherwise, clock L_2 d times.
3. Let $H_i = H_{i0} \parallel H_{i1} \parallel H_{i2} \parallel H_{i3}$, where $H_{i0} = L_{20} \oplus L_{12}$, $H_{i1} = L_{21} \oplus L_{13}$, $H_{i2} = L_{22} \oplus L_{10}$, $H_{i3} = L_{23} \oplus L_{11}$.
4. For Mode II, the output for the ith step is given as H_i.
5. For Mode I, compute $j = (L_{13} \oplus L_{23}) \mathbin{\&} 3$, $k = (L_{10} \oplus L_{20}) \gg 30$. If $j = k$, then let $k = j \oplus 1$. The output for the ith step is given as $H_{ij} \parallel H_{ik}$.

Two feedback boolean functions are used, $f9a$ for L_1 and $f9b$ for L_2. They use bits $2, 5, 8, 15, 26, 38, 44, 47, 57$ of L_1 and L_2 as input. These two functions are available at [3].

3   Cryptanalysis of COS

In this section we show that the COS $(2, 128)$ Mode I is very weak. Subsection 3.1 gives a brief introduction to our attack while the detailed attack is given in Subsection 3.2. The experiment result is given in Subsection 3.3.

3.1   The Basic Idea of Our Attack

Let us take a look at any four consequent steps starting with an odd step. L_1 is clocked at the second and forth steps; L_2 is clocked at the first and third steps.

	Step 1		Step 2		Step 3		Step 4	
L_1	b	a	c	b'	c	b'	d	c'
L_2	x	w	x	w	y	x'	y	x'

Fig. 1. Four Steps (starting with an odd step) of COS $(2, 128)$

In Fig. 1, a, b, b', c, c' and d are 64-bit words of L_1 at the end of a step; w, x, x', y are 64-bit words of L_2 at the end of a step. According to the key stream generation process, b' may be the same as b; or b' may be obtained by right shifting b one (or two) bit position and with the most significant one (or two) bit of b being filled with unknown value. The same applies to c' and c.

The value of (c, b') could be recovered if the following two conditions are satisfied:

Condition 1. The outputs at the first, second, third and forth steps are given as $b \oplus w$, $c \oplus w$, $b' \oplus y$ and $c' \oplus y$ respectively, i.e., (j, k) is $(2, 3)$ or $(3, 2)$ at Step 1 and Step 2 and $(1, 0)$ or $(0, 1)$ at Step 3 and Step 4.

Condition 2. One of b' and c' is not the same as b and c respectively, and b' and c' are not obtained by right shifting b and c (respectively) by the same position.

From Condition 1, we could obtain the values of $b \oplus c$ and $b' \oplus c'$ from the output key stream of these four steps. Once Condition 1 and Condition 2 are satisfied, it is trivial to compute (c, b').

In the next subsection, we will illustrate the idea above in detail and give the estimated results.

3.2   The Detailed Attack

Before introducing the attack in detail, we give the following two observations:

Observation 1. For the COS $(2, 128)$ Mode I, at each step the probability that (j, k) is $(2, 3)$ is 2^{-3}. The same probability holds for (j, k) being $(3, 2)$, $(1, 0)$, $(0, 1)$.

Observation 2. At the ith step, if j is 0 or 2, the clocking value at the next step is 64. If j is 1 or 3, the clocking value at the next step is 65 or 66.

These two observations are trivial according to the specifications of the COS cipher.

We now list in Table 1 those 16 cases that satisfy Condition 1. According to Observation 1, each case appears with probability 2^{-12}.

Table 1. (j, k) values for those 16 cases satisfying Condition 1

	Step 1	Step 2	Step 3	Step 4
Case 1	(2,3)	(2,3)	(0,1)	(0,1)
Case 2	(2,3)	(2,3)	(0,1)	(1,0)
Case 3	(2,3)	(2,3)	(1,0)	(0,1)
Case 4	(2,3)	(2,3)	(1,0)	(1,0)
Case 5	(2,3)	(3,2)	(0,1)	(0,1)
Case 6	(2,3)	(3,2)	(0,1)	(1,0)
Case 7	(2,3)	(3,2)	(1,0)	(0,1)
Case 8	(2,3)	(3,2)	(1,0)	(1,0)
Case 9	(3,2)	(2,3)	(0,1)	(0,1)
Case 10	(3,2)	(2,3)	(0,1)	(1,0)
Case 11	(3,2)	(2,3)	(1,0)	(0,1)
Case 12	(3,2)	(2,3)	(1,0)	(1,0)
Case 13	(3,2)	(3,2)	(0,1)	(0,1)
Case 14	(3,2)	(3,2)	(0,1)	(1,0)
Case 15	(3,2)	(3,2)	(1,0)	(0,1)
Case 16	(3,2)	(3,2)	(1,0)	(1,0)

However, not all those 16 cases satisfy Condition 2. According to Observation 2, Cases 1, 2, 5, 6 do not satisfy Condition 2 since $b' = b$ and $c' = c$; Cases 11, 12, 15, 16 satisfy Condition 2 with probability 0.5; the other eight cases all satisfy Condition 2. Thus for every four steps starting with an odd step, Conditions 1 and 2 are satisfied with probability $10 \times 2^{-12} \approx 2^{-8.7}$. To determine the value of L_1, this attack requires the output of about 820 steps in average.

In the following we estimate the amount of (c, b') being produced in each case, and show how to filter the wrong values of (c, b'). We illustrate Case 4 as an example: at Step 2 L_1 is clocked for 64 times $(b = b')$; at Step 4 L_1 is clocked 65 or 66 steps. So 6 values of (c, b') are generated for every four steps starting with an odd step. For each pair of (c, b'), the values of w and y of L_2 could be obtained. Since L_2 is clocked for only 64 times at Step 3, the 7 least significant bits of y are generated from w. So the wrong (c, b') could pass this filtering process with probability 2^{-7}.

The further filtering is carried out at Step 5 and Step 6. Let $d = d_0 \parallel d_1$, $c = c_0' \parallel c_1'$, $e = e_0 \parallel e_1$, $d' = d_0' \parallel d_1'$, $z = z_0 \parallel z_1$, $y = y_0' \parallel y_1'$ where d_0, d_1, c_0', c_1', e_0, e_1, d_0', d_1', z_0, z_1, y_0' and y_1' are 32-bit words. In Fig. 2, for each (c, b'), there are 6 values for (d, c', e, d') (L_1 is clocked 65 or 66 times at Step 4 and is clocked 64 or 65 or 66 times at Step 6). The L_2 is clocked 65 or 66 times at Step 5, so there are 6 possible values for y'. Now if any one of j or k is equal to 2 or 3 in Sep 4 or 5, then for the right (c, b'), at least one of $d_0 \oplus y_0'$, $d_1 \oplus y_1'$, $e_0 \oplus y_0'$ and $e_1 \oplus y_1'$ appears in the output. Otherwise, j and k could only be 0 or 1 at Step 4 and Step 5, the output of Step 5 is $(c_0' \oplus z_0) \parallel (c_1' \oplus z_1)$ or $(c_1' \oplus z_1) \parallel (c_0' \oplus z_0)$, that of Step 6 is $(d_0' \oplus z_0) \parallel (d_1' \oplus z_1)$ or $(d_1' \oplus z_1) \parallel (d_0' \oplus z_0)$. By xoring the outputs of Step 5 and 6 (taking into the considering whether (j, k) is $(1, 0)$ or $(0, 1)$), the right (c, b') should generate $c_0' \oplus d_0'$ and $c_1' \oplus d_1'$. The wrong (c, b') could pass this filtering process with probability $6 \times 6 \times 8 \times 2^{-32} \approx 2^{-23.8}$.

	Step1		Step2		Step3		Step4		Step5		Step6	
L_1	b	a	c	b'	c	b'	d	c'	$d_0 \parallel d_1$	$c_0' \parallel c_1'$	$e_0 \parallel e_1$	$d_0' \parallel d_1'$
L_2	x	w	x	w	y	x'	y	x'	$z_0 \parallel z_1$	$y_0' \parallel y_1'$	$z_0 \parallel z_1$	$y_0' \parallel y_1'$

Fig. 2. The 6 Steps (starting with an odd step) of COS $(2, 128)$

So for every 4 steps starting with an odd step, a correct (c, b') is generated with probability 2^{-12} and a wrong (c, b') is generated with probability $6 \times 2^{-7} \times 2^{-23.8} \approx 2^{-28.2}$.

We list in Table 2 the probabilities that right and wrong (c, b') are generated for any 4 steps starting with an odd step.

So for any 4 steps starting with an odd step, a correct (c, b') is generated with probability $2^{-8.7}$ and a wrong one is generated with probability $2^{-23.6}$. It is obvious that only the correct (c, b') could pass the filtering process. Once (c, b') is determined, it is easy to recover L_2 from the values of w and y.

3.3   Experiment Result

We implemented an attack that uses only the Case 4. In average, our program recovers L_1 in about 15 milliseconds on PC (Pentium IV 1.7GHz) with the outputs of about 2^{13} steps. The COS program provided by the COS designers [3,4] is used in our experiment.

Table 2. The probabilities that correct and wrong L_1 being generated

	Correct L_1 Prob.	Wrong L_1 Prob.
Case 1	0	–
Case 2	0	–
Case 3	2^{-12}	$2^{-30.8}$
Case 4	2^{-12}	$2^{-28.2}$
Case 5	0	–
Case 6	0	–
Case 7	2^{-12}	$2^{-28.2}$
Case 8	2^{-12}	$2^{-25.6}$
Case 9	2^{-12}	$2^{-31.8}$
Case 10	2^{-12}	$2^{-29.2}$
Case 11	2^{-13}	$2^{-30.4}$
Case 12	2^{-13}	$2^{-26.8}$
Case 13	2^{-12}	$2^{-29.2}$
Case 14	2^{-12}	$2^{-26.6}$
Case 15	2^{-13}	$2^{-27.8}$
Case 16	2^{-13}	$2^{-25.2}$

4   Conclusions

In this paper, we showed that the stream cipher COS $(2, 128)$ Mode I is extremely weak and should not be used.

References

1. S.H. Babbage, "The COS Stream Ciphers are Extremely Weak",
   http://eprint.iacr.org/2001/078/
2. S.H. Babbage, "Cryptanalysis of the COS (2,128) Stream Ciphers",
   http://eprint.iacr.org/2001/106/
3. E. Filiol and C. Fontaine, "A New Ultrafast Stream Cipher Design: COS Ciphers",
   http://www-rocq.inria.fr/codes/Eric.Filiol/English/COS/COS.html
4. E. Filiol and C. Fontaine, "A New Ultrafast Stream Cipher Design: COS Ciphers",
   in *Proceedings of the 8th IMA Conference on Cryptography and Coding*, LNCS 2260, pp. 85-98.
5. E. Filiol, "COS Ciphers are not "extremely weak"! — the Design Rationale of COS Ciphers", http://eprint.iacr.org/2001/080/

The Analysis of Zheng-Seberry Scheme

David Soldera[1], Jennifer Seberry[1], and Chengxin Qu[2]

[1] Centre for Computer Security Research
University of Wollongong, NSW 2522, Australia
jennie@uow.edu.au
[2] School of Mathematical and Computer Science
University of New England, Armidale, NWS 2531, Australia
cxqu@turing.une.edu.au

Abstract. The Zheng-Seberry (ZS) encryption scheme was published in 1993 and was one of the first practical schemes that was considered secure against a chosen ciphertext adversary. This paper shows some problems that the semantic security of the one-way hash variant of the ZS scheme is insecure on some special circumstances. Attempts to modify the ZS scheme resulted on an El-Gamal variant that is provably secure in the random oracle model.

1 Introduction

In 1993 Zheng-Seberry [9] presented a paper introducing three new public-key encryption schemes that were efficient and considered secure against a chosen ciphertext adversary, under some assumptions. Since then much progress has made in the area of provable security for public-key cryptosystems, from those that use the Random Oracle (RO) model [2] to the scheme by Cramer-Shoup (CS) [4] that is provably secure using standard public key cryptography assumptions.

Using the RO model or standard assumptions represent opposite ends of the provable security spectrum. The RO model yields extremely efficient schemes yet practical implementations using hash functions fall short of actual RO's. Using standard assumptions gives us tremendous confidence in security yet schemes are still too inefficient for the majority of practical implementations.

The hardness of the Diffie-Hellman decision problem is essentially equivalent to the semantic security of basic El-Gamal encryption scheme [5]. The basic El-Gamal scheme is completely insecure against adaptive chosen ciphertext attack. This new Secure El-Gamal scheme was born out of the OWH variant of the original ZS scheme, since as shall be seen in section 2.2 it is insecure against a chosen ciphertext adversary (CCA). Securing the ZS scheme meant providing a proof for security and the best proof (in that it requires the least assumptions) was that by Cramer-Shoup. Unfortunately the CS proof cannot easily be used to prove the security of Secure El-gamal. So section 3 presents the new Secure El-Gamal scheme, and a proof of security which borrows many parts of the CS proof. Unfortunately the proof still needs to rely on the random oracle model, but encouragingly, it only relies on it in a minimal way.

L. Batten and J. Seberry (Eds.): ACISP 2002, LNCS 2384, pp. 159–168, 2002.

It has become standard practice that the level of security required for a public-key cryptosystem is indistinguishability of encryptions, IND, (equivalently semantic security or non-malleability) against an adaptive chosen ciphertext adversary (CCA2), for formal definitions see [1]. The basic idea behind an IND-CCA2 adversary is that they are given access to an encryption and decryption oracle, they then choose two messages, one of which gets encrypted (they do not know which). They are then presented with the ciphertext of the encrypted message and asked to determine which of the two messages was encrypted. They must succeed with probability non-negligibly better than 0.5. The only restriction is the adversary may not query the decryption oracle with the challenge ciphertext.

2   Original ZS

The ZS paper presented three variants of an El-Gamal like cryptosystem. The three variants were described as 'immunising' the cryptosystem against a CCA2 adversary. The variants incorporated a one-way hash function (OWH), a universal hash function and a digital signature.

2.1   ZS-OWH

The ZS-OWH variant is presented below.

ZS-OWH
Preliminaries: Consider message of length n, a one-way hash function H with output length k_0 and a PRNG G with output length $n + k_0$. Operations are modulo p and there is a generator g.
Key Generation: Private key is $x_R \in GF(p)$ and public key is $y_R = g^{x_R} \mod p$.
Encryption; 1, $x \in_R [1, p-1]$ 2, $z = G(y_R^x)_{[1K\,(n+k_0)]}$ 3, $t = H(m)$ 4, $c_1 = g^x$ 5, $c_2 = z \oplus (m||t)$ Ciphertext is (c_1, c_2)
Decryption: 1, $z' = G(c_1^{x_R})_{[1K\,(n+k_0)]}$ 2, $w = z' \oplus c_2$ 3, $m = w_{[1...n]}$ 4, $t' = w_{[(n+1)K(n+k_0)]}$ If $H(m) = t'$, then output m else output $\emptyset$.

The security of ZS-OWH depends on the hardness of Diffie-Hellman one way problem.

2.2   Breaking ZS-OWH in IND-CCA2 Sense

"Due to the involvement of $t = H(m)$, the creation of the ciphertext is apparently impossible without the knowledge of x and m. .... This motivates us to introduce a notion called $sole - samplable$ space." ([9], pg. 721)

If the authors had to pick an assumption in the ZS paper that ultimately turned out to be incorrect, the above assumption would be an appropriate choice. As it turns out an adversary can create a new ciphertext from an existing ciphertext, if the message in the existing ciphertext is known.

To see how this is achieved consider the last part of the ciphertext,

$$c_2 = z \oplus (m||t) = z \oplus (m||H(m)),$$

which just depends on the message. So if the message is known, this part of the ciphertext can be recreated. If the adversary wishes to replace the message m with another message m', this can be achieved via:

$$
\begin{aligned}
c_2' &= c_2 \oplus (m||H(m)) \oplus (m'||H(m')) \\
&= z \oplus (m||H(m)) \oplus (m||H(m)) \oplus (m'||H(m')) \\
&= z \oplus [(m||H(m)) \oplus (m||H(m))] \oplus (m'||H(m')) \\
&= z \oplus (m'||H(m')),
\end{aligned}
$$

in which $[(m||H(m)) \oplus (m||H(m))] = 0$ due to Boolean addition.

The new ciphertext is (c_1, c_2') and the adversary is successful in manipulating the cryptosystem.

This attack can be used by a CCA2 adversary to defeat IND and the adversary succeeds 100% of the time. In this situation the adversary does not know which of two messages, m_0 or m_1, has been encrypted, but they know one of them has been. Let the encrypted message be m_b where $b \in [0, 1]$. The adversary uses the above attack by setting $m = m_0$ and $m' = m_1$ and creates a new cryptogram via:

$$
\begin{aligned}
c_2' &= c_2 \oplus [m_0||H(m_0)] \oplus [m_1||H(m_1)] \\
&= z \oplus [m_b||H(m_b)] \oplus [m_0||H(m_0)] \oplus [m_1||H(m_1)] \\
&= z \oplus [m_{\neg b}||H(m_{\neg b})]
\end{aligned}
$$

Hence the adversary creates a new ciphertext (c_1, c_2'), which is a valid ciphertext for the message that was not encrypted in the challenge ciphertext. Since the adversary is a CCA2 adversary, and the new ciphertext is not the challenge ciphertext, they may query the decryption oracle with it. The decryption oracle will dutifully return the message that was not encrypted, m_b, and the adversary makes their choice for b as corresponding to the message not returned by the decryption oracle.

The ZS-OWH scheme is largely of theoretical value to the cryptographic community, so while breaking the scheme does not have many practical implications, it is still of theoretical use. This break highlights the importance of adding random information to the check on the message, as shall be shown. Also, as recently as EUROCRYPT 2000, a paper [6] made reference to the ZS paper with the implication being it was secure, under some assumptions. So this attack means ZS-OWH now needs to be added to the list of schemes that were considered secure but turned out to be insecure.

This attack on ZS-OWH is a very trivial one and as could be expected a trivial change to the scheme thwarts this attack. By simply creating a new variable $r = y_R^x$ and changing $t = H(m||r)$, then the attack no longer works. The change incorporates some randomness into the hash calculation and thus defeats the above attack as the adversary can no longer create the concatenation of message and hash because the adversary does not know the random information. This change defeats the above attack, but of course does not prove the security of the scheme.

This change was borrowed from an authenticated-encryption version of ZS-OWH by Zheng [8], however Zheng stresses that the changes made are only needed for the new scheme proposed and that the original scheme is secure.

3   Secure El-Gamal

The attack and the repair of the original ZS-OWH leaves a rather large question mark over its security. Securing the original ZS-OWH scheme led to a new El-Gamal variant. Great efforts were made to prove the security of this new variant using the CS proof and thus derive a scheme that was secure under some reasonable assumptions, but without using the RO model. Unfortunately, this goal was not realised, but encouragingly the proof does not heavily rely on the RO model.

Secure El-Gamal
Preliminaries: Consider messages of length $n - k_0$, a random oracle H with output length k_0. Operations are modulo p where $p = 2q + 1$ (q is a prime) and a generator g of order q.
Key Generation: Private key is $x_R \in GF(p)$ and public key is $y_R = g^{x_R} \bmod p$.
Encryption: Encrypt message m as follows;   1, $x \in_R [1, p-1]$ 2, $r = y_R^x$ 3, $t = H(m||r)$ 4, $c_1 = g^x$ 5, $c_3 = r \cdot (m||t)^2$ Ciphertext is (c_1, c_3).
Decryption: 1, $r' = c_1^{x_R}$ 2, $w = \sqrt{\frac{c_3}{r'}}$ (choose square root that yields the correct hash)   3, $m = w_{[1\cdots(n-k_0)]}$ 4, $t' = w_{[(n-k_0+1)Kn]}$ If $H(m||r') = t'$, then output m, else output $\emptyset$.

The differences between this and the original El-Gamal scheme is the addition of the hash appended to the message, and the squaring of the message and hash to convert them into a quadratic residue (this makes it an element of the quadratic residues of $GF(p)$, the group of order q). Note that in step 2 of the decryption, if neither square root yields a correct hash then the output is $\emptyset$.

The proof relies on the difficulty of the Decision Diffie-Hellman Problem (DDHP), the definition of which, from Cramer-Shoup, is given below.

Definition 1. - *([4], pg. 16) Let G be a group of large prime order q. Consider the following two distributions:*

- *the distribution R of random quadruples $(g_1, g_2, u_1, u_2) \in G^4$;*
- *the distribution D of quadruples $(g_1, g_2, u_1, u_2) \in G^4$, where g_1, g_2 are random, and $u_1 = g_1^r$ and $u_2 = g_2^r$ for random $r \in Z_q$.*

An algorithm that solves the DDHP is a statistical test that can effectively distinguish between these two distributions. For a given quadruple coming from one of the two distributions, it should output 0 or 1 and there should be a non-negligible difference between the probability that it outputs 1 given an input from R and the probability that it outputs 1 given an input from D. The decision Diffie-Hellman problem is hard if there is no such polynomial-time statistics test.

The construction of the proof is as follows. It is assumed an adversary that can break the cryptosystem in the IND-CCA2 sense exists, and then it is shown how this adversary can unwittingly be used to help solve what is considered a computationally unfeasible problem, in this case the DDHP. The construction of the proof can be seen in Figure 1.

The input to the proof are quadruples coming from either D or R (but not both). These go to a constructed simulator, which is responsible for, the creation of keys, simulation of an encryption oracle and simulation of a decryption oracle. The IND-CCA2 adversary receives all its information, including oracle queries, from the simulator.

The proof runs as follows. A quadruple is input. The simulator creates a valid secret key (once only) and the public key, which is passed to the IND-CCA2 adversary. The adversary runs its first stage A_1 and produces two messages m_0 and m_1. Then it passes the two messages to the simulated encryption oracle. The simulated encryption oracle chooses a random bit $b \in [0, 1]$, encrypts m_b and passes the challenge ciphertext back to the adversary. The adversary cannot see the simulator's choice for b.

The adversary then runs its second stage, A_2, on the challenge ciphertext and outputs its guess, b', for the random bit. Both the simulator and the adversary pass b and b' respectively to a distinguisher that outputs 1 if $b = b'$ otherwise 0.

Consider the case when the input comes from R, the simulator is unable to create a valid ciphertext (as the relation that quadruples from D have, are not present in quadruples from R). This fact will be crucial in showing the adversary cannot succeed in guessing b with any advantage. Alternatively, when the input comes from D, then the simulator creates a perfectly valid ciphertext and the adversary can guess the bit b with an advantage.

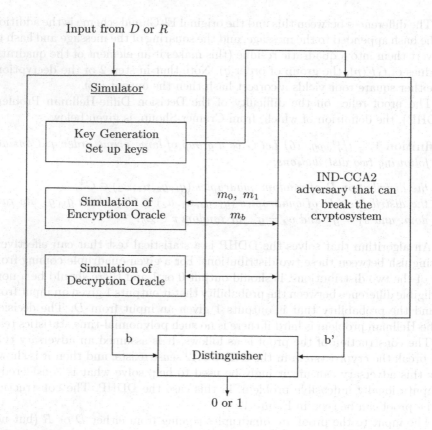

Fig. 1. Graphical representation for the construction of the Secure El-Gamal proof.

Hence by observing the distribution of 0's and 1's that are output by the distinguisher, it can be determined which distribution the quadruples are coming from. If the quadruples are coming from R then 1's will occur with probability 0.5 and 0's with probability 0.5. The adversary will only be correct half the time, as it has no advantage. If the quadruples come from D then the adversary has an advantage and 1's will occur with probability $0.5 + \varepsilon$ (where ε is the adversary's non-negligible advantage) and 0's with probability $0.5 - \varepsilon$.

Hence, by observation of the output distribution, one has a statistical test for the DDHP.

The construction of the proof is relatively simple, however there are several properties that must hold for the proof to be valid.

- The simulator must create a valid ciphertext if the quadruple comes from D and an invalid ciphertext if the quadruple comes from R.

- When the quadruple comes from D the joint distribution of the adversary's view and the random bit b must be statistically indistinguishable from that in an actual attack.
- When the quadruple comes from R the distribution of the random bit b must be (essentially) independent from the adversary's view.

Theorem 1. *Secure El-Gamal is secure against adaptive chosen ciphertext attack in the Random Oracle model assuming that the Diffie-Hellman decision problem is hard in the group $GF(p)$.*

The proof of security is for a scheme that is slight variant of the El-Gamal scheme described above, but the two schemes are interchangeable. The scheme used in the proof has an extra part to the ciphertext, c_2. A ciphertext from the El-Gamal scheme (above) can be transformed into one for this scheme (in the proof) by $(c_1, c_3) \rightarrow (c_1, c_2, c_3 \times c_2)$. The transformation back is obvious.

First the simulator is described. On input the quadruple (g_1, g_2, c_1, c_2) the simulator generates a random private key $x_R \in_R GF(p)$ and outputs the public key as $y_R = g^{x_R}$.

The simulator simulates the encryption oracle as follows. On input two messages m_0 and m_1 it selects a random bit $b \in [0, 1]$ and computes:

$$r = c_1^{x_R}$$
$$c_3 = (r \times c_2) \times (m_b \| H(m_b \| r))^2$$

The simulated encryption oracle outputs (c_1, c_2, c_3), where c_1 and c_2 come from the input quadruple to the simulator.

The simulator simulates the decryption oracle as follows. On input (c_1, c_2, c_3) it computes:

$$r = c_1^{x_R}$$
$$w = \sqrt{\frac{c_3}{(r \times c_2)}} \quad \text{(choose the square root that yields the correct hash)}$$
$$m = w_{[1 \cdots (n-k_0)]}$$

If the simulated decryption oracle outputs m, else it outputs $\emptyset$.

The aim now is to show that when the input comes from D the simulator simulates the encryption and decryption oracles perfectly (probabilistically) and the advantage of the adversary is apparent at the distinguisher. Alternatively, if the input comes from R then the output of the simulated encryption oracle will not be a valid ciphertext in the sense that .

It is also important to note that since the DDHP is hard for the adversary they cannot even find out any partial information about the secret key that could be used to determine b.

The theorem follows from the following two lemmas.

Lemma 1. - *When the simulator's input comes from D, the joint distribution of the adversary's view and the hidden bit b is statistically indistinguishable from that in the actual attack.*

In this case it is clear the output of the simulated encryption oracle has the right form as

$$c_1^{x_R} c_2 = (g_1^x)^{x_R} g_2^x = (g_1^{x_R})^x g_2^x = y_R^x g_2^x$$

which is equivalent to the output of the actual encryption oracle. Similarly, the simulated decryption oracle will accept all valid ciphertexts.

It remains to be shown that all invalid ciphertexts are rejected with overwhelming probability. If an invalid ciphertext (in the sense that $\log_{g_1} c_1 \neq \log_{g_2} c_2$) is presented as a query to the decryption oracle it will be rejected as the resulting r will not be correct for recovering m from c_3. More importantly the invalid ciphertext will not pass the check involving the random oracle (H). By using a random oracle it is ensured that the hash is completely non-malleable and no partial information is leaked.

Lemma 2. - *When the simulator's input comes from R, the distribution of the hidden bit is (essentially) independent from the adversary's view.*

First it will be shown that no partial information about b is leaked from just the challenge ciphertext, this essentially is showing IND-CPA security. Then it will be shown that there is only a negligible chance that the simulated decryption oracle gives the adversary any information about b. Since an IND-CCA2 adversary that cannot gain any information from a decryption oracle is equivalent to an IND-CPA adversary, the lemma is proven.

It has been shown that assuming DDHP the El-Gamal cryptosystem is secure in the sense of IND-CPA [3,7]. To show the IND-CPA security of this scheme it will be shown how to convert an El-Gamal challenge ciphertext into one for this scheme. First a second generator needs to be created, if p is of the form $p = 2q + 1$, then there are $q - 1$ generators. Hence by considering powers of g_1 a second generator of the form $g_2 = g_1^w$ can be found in polynomial time, with w known. So g_2^x can be calculated as $(g_1^x)^w$. So an El-Gamal challenge ciphertext can be transformed into a Secure El-Gamal challenge ciphertext as

$$(g_1^x, y_R^x \times m_b) \rightarrow (g_1^x, g_2^x, (y_R^x g_2^x) \times m_b).$$

It should be noted that the message is a different size to a message in an actual Secure El-Gamal challenge ciphertext. However this is not an issue, if p is an n bit prime, and the hash function outputs 128 bits, then the chances that two messages chosen at random do not differ in the first $n - 128$ bits is $\frac{n}{2} - 128$, which is negligible for suitable large n. The absence of the appended hash is irrelevant since the use of a random oracle ensures no information about m is leaked to an IND-CPA adversary. Also, without access to a decryption oracle there is no need for a correct hash value to be present in the ciphertext.

The simulated decryption oracle still needs to reject all invalid ciphertexts, otherwise relevant information will be leaked. A valid ciphertext is (c_1, c_2, c_3), an invalid one is (c_1', c_2', c_3'). There are two cases to consider.

1) $(c_3) = (c_3')$. If this happens with non-negligible probability then the random oracle must not be one way since c_1' and c_2' will create a different r (as they

are different from c_1 and c_2) and this will cause decryption to a different message and hash. If the hash check passes, then the hash has been created without knowledge of the message.

2) $(c_1, c_2) = (c'_1, c'_2)$. With $c_3 \neq c'_3$, then the adversary has to replace the message and hash in c_3 to create c'_3. They can't just replace the message as if the hash check passes then a collision has been found. They can't replace the hash, or the message and hash, as without complete knowledge of r the correct hash cannot be calculated, and if it could then a collision could be found.

Using a random oracle means that one-wayness and collision-freeness cannot be defeated, in fact no partial information is leaked about the pre-image of the hash. Thus, the simulated decryption oracle will reject all invalid ciphertexts, except with negligible probability.

Hence if the DDHP is a computationally unfeasible problem then an IND-CCA2 attacker for Secure El-Gamal cannot exist.

4   Conclusion

This paper has shown that the one-way hash variant of the scheme by Zheng-Seberry [9] is insecure in the sense of IND against a chosen ciphertext adversary.

A new scheme was created, called Secure El-Gamal, that was shown to be provably secure in the random oracle model.

Acknowledgments. Breaking the Zheng-Seberry scheme was discovered during discussions with Associate Professor Josef Pieprzyk. Also, the authors wish to thanks Dr David Pointcheval for his help in verifying the proof of Secure El-Gamal.

References

[1] M. Bellare, A. Desai, D. Pointcheval and P. Rogaway, *Relations among notions of security for public-key encryption schemes* CRYPTO'98. LNCS 1462, pg 26-45. Springer-Verlag, California, 1998.

[2] M. Bellare and P. Rogaway, *Optimal asymmetric encryption - how to encrypt with RSA* EUROCRYTP'94. LNCS 950, pg 92-111. Springer-Verlag, 1994.

[3] D. Boneh, *The decision Diffie-Hellman problem*, Third Algorithmic Number Theory Symposium (ANTS)LNCS 1423, Springer-Verlag, 1998..

[4] R. Cramer and V. Shoup, *A practical public key cryptosystem provably secure against adaptive chosen ciphertext attack*, CRYPTO'98. LNCS 1462, pg 13-25. Springer-Verlag, California, 1998.

[5] T. El Gamal, *A public key cryptosystem and signature schme based on discrete logarithms*, IEEE Trans. Inform. Theory, 31:469-472, 1985.

[6] V. Shoup, *Using hash functions as a hedge against chosen ciphertext attack* EUROCRYPT'00. LNCS 1807, pg 275-288. Springer-Verlag, 2000.

[7] Y. Tsiounis and M. Yung, *"On the security of El-Gamal based encryption,* PKC'98. LNCS 1431, Spinger-Verlag, Japan, 1998.

[8] Y. Zheng, *Improved public key cryptosystems secure against chosen ciphertext attacks*, Technical Report 94-1, University of Wollongong, 1994.

[9] Y. Zheng and J. Seberry, *Immunizing public key cryptosystems against chosen ciphertext attacks*, IEEE Journal on Selected Areas in Communications, 1993. 11(5): p. 715-724.

Cryptanalysis of Stream Cipher Alpha1

Hongjun Wu

Laboratories for Information Technology
21 Heng Mui Keng Terrace, Singapore 119613
hongjun@lit.org.sg

Abstract. Komninos, Honary and Darnell recently proposed stream cipher Alpha1. Alpha1 is based on A5/1 and is claimed to be much safer than A5/1. However Alpha1 is insecure: a 29-bit feedback shift register could be recovered with about 3000 known plaintext bits with $O(2^{29})$ operations. The rest of the message could be recovered in the broadcast application in which the same message is encrypted with different keys.

1   Introduction

The stream cipher Alpha1 [6] was proposed recently to strengthen A5/1. A5/1 is used to protect the mobile communication privacy and is with extremely simple structure: three LFSRs (64 bits in total) are used and the output is obtained by XORing the most significant bits of those registers. The LFSRs go/stop according to the majority rule: each register provides one bit (clocking tap) and the majority bit is computed. The registers whose clocking taps agreeing with the majority bit are clocked.

There have been several attacks on A5/1 [1,5,3,4]. The real time known-plaintext cryptanalysis of A5/1 were given by Biryukov, Shamir and Wagner [4] by exploiting two major weaknesses of A5/1: the relatively small number of internal states (2^{64}) and the poor choice of the clocking taps. As a cipher with small number of internal states, A5/1 is vulnerable to the general time-memory tradeoff attack on stream ciphers (which is discovered independently by Golic [5] and Babbage [2]). The poor choice of clocking taps enables special states being accessed easily and the efficiency of the time-memory tradeoff attack can be improved significantly.

To strengthen A5/1, Komninos, Honary and Darnell proposed Alpha1. Alpha1 is with four LFSRs (128 bits in total). Three registers go/stop according to two groups of clocking taps while one register is regularly clocked. The attacks against A5/1 seem no longer applicable to Alpha1. Unfortunately, an additional binary AND operation is used in Alpha1 in order to achieve high linear complexity. This AND operation causes a disaster to Alpha1: the combination of the output of those irregularly clocked LFSRs is not uniformly distributed. The statistical information could be applied to recover the register which is regularly clocked. The design of Alpha1 reminds us that it is dangerous to modify the internal structure of a cipher.

L. Batten and J. Seberry (Eds.): ACISP 2002, LNCS 2384, pp. 169–175, 2002.

After recovering the regularly clocked register, information of the message is leaked. If a message is encrypted with a number of different keys and those ciphertext are known (in some broadcast applications), the rest of the message could be recovered. If a message is longer than $2^{29} - 1$ bits and is encrypted with different keys, the ciphertext only attack is applicable to recover the message.

This paper is organized as follows. Section 2 introduces the Alpha1 stream cipher. The attack against Alpha1 is given in Section 3. The message recovery in the broadcast application is studied in Section 4. Section 5 concludes this paper.

2   Stream Cipher Alpha1

Alpha1 is built from four short linear feedback shift registers (LFSRs) of lengths $29, 31, 33$ and 35 bits, which are denoted as R_1, R_2, R_3 and R_4 respectively. Four primitive polynomials $p_1(x)$, $p_2(x)$, $p_3(x)$ and $p_4(x)$ are used for R_1, R_2, R_3 and R_4 respectively. They are given in Table 1.

Table 1. Primitive Polynomials

$p_1(x)$	$x^{29} + x^{27} + x^{24} + x^8 + 1$
$p_2(x)$	$x^{31} + x^{28} + x^{23} + x^{18} + 1$
$p_3(x)$	$x^{33} + x^{28} + x^{24} + x^4 + 1$
$p_4(x)$	$x^{35} + x^{30} + x^{22} + x^{11} + x^6 + 1$

We denote R_1, R_2, R_3 and R_4 as

$$R_1 = \sum_{i=0}^{28} R_{1,i} \cdot x^i, \qquad R_2 = \sum_{i=0}^{30} R_{2,i} \cdot x^i$$

$$R_3 = \sum_{i=0}^{32} R_{3,i} \cdot x^i, \qquad R_4 = \sum_{i=0}^{34} R_{4,i} \cdot x^i$$

The output y of Alpha1 is given as

$$y = R_{1,28} \oplus R_{2,30} \oplus R_{3,32} \oplus R_{4,34} \oplus (R_{2,30} \ \& \ R_{3,32})$$

where '$\&$' is the binary AND operator.

R_1 is shifted every clock cycle. R_2, R_3 and R_4 are clocked in a stop/go fashion according to the following majority rule: R_2 is clocked if $R_{2,10}$ agrees with the majority bit of $(R_{2,10}, R_{3,22}, R_{4,11})$ and $R_{2,21}$ agrees with the majority bit of $(R_{2,21}, R_{3,10}, R_{4,24})$; R_3 is clocked if $R_{3,22}$ agrees with the majority bit of $(R_{2,10}, R_{3,22}, R_{4,11})$ and $R_{3,10}$ agrees with the majority bit of $(R_{2,21}, R_{3,10}, R_{4,24})$; R_4 is clocked if $R_{4,11}$ agrees with the majority bit of $(R_{2,10}, R_{3,22}, R_{4,11})$ and $R_{4,24}$ agrees with the majority bit of $(R_{2,21}, R_{3,10}, R_{4,24})$. We list in Table 2 all the 16 cases that R_2, R_3 and R_4 stop/go. The designers of Alpha1 listed only 13 cases and estimated wrongly that each R_2, R_3 and R_4 move with probability $\frac{7}{13}$ [6]. We need to mention here that those 16 cases do not occur independently. We will discuss the probabilities of those cases in Section 3.

Table 2. Registers (R_2, R_3, R_4) Being Shifted At One Clock Cycle

	Condition 1	Condition 2	Registers Being Shifted
Case 1	$R_{2,10} = R_{3,22} \neq R_{4,11}$	$R_{2,21} = R_{3,10} \neq R_{4,24}$	R_2, R_3
Case 2	$R_{2,10} = R_{3,22} \neq R_{4,11}$	$R_{2,21} \neq R_{3,10} = R_{4,24}$	R_3
Case 3	$R_{2,10} = R_{3,22} \neq R_{4,11}$	$R_{2,21} = R_{4,24} \neq R_{3,10}$	R_2
Case 4	$R_{2,10} = R_{3,22} \neq R_{4,11}$	$R_{2,21} = R_{3,10} = R_{4,24}$	R_2, R_3
Case 5	$R_{2,10} \neq R_{3,22} = R_{4,11}$	$R_{2,21} = R_{3,10} \neq R_{4,24}$	R_3
Case 6	$R_{2,10} \neq R_{3,22} = R_{4,11}$	$R_{2,21} \neq R_{3,10} = R_{4,24}$	R_3, R_4
Case 7	$R_{2,10} \neq R_{3,22} = R_{4,11}$	$R_{2,21} = R_{4,24} \neq R_{3,10}$	R_4
Case 8	$R_{2,10} \neq R_{3,22} = R_{4,11}$	$R_{2,21} = R_{3,10} = R_{4,24}$	R_3, R_4
Case 9	$R_{2,10} = R_{4,11} \neq R_{3,22}$	$R_{2,21} = R_{3,10} \neq R_{4,24}$	R_2
Case 10	$R_{2,10} = R_{4,11} \neq R_{3,22}$	$R_{2,21} \neq R_{3,10} = R_{4,24}$	R_4
Case 11	$R_{2,10} = R_{4,11} \neq R_{3,22}$	$R_{2,21} = R_{4,24} \neq R_{3,10}$	R_2, R_4
Case 12	$R_{2,10} = R_{4,11} \neq R_{3,22}$	$R_{2,21} = R_{3,10} = R_{4,24}$	R_2, R_4
Case 13	$R_{2,10} = R_{3,22} = R_{4,11}$	$R_{2,21} = R_{3,10} \neq R_{4,24}$	R_2, R_3
Case 14	$R_{2,10} = R_{3,22} = R_{4,11}$	$R_{2,21} \neq R_{3,10} = R_{4,24}$	R_3, R_4
Case 15	$R_{2,10} = R_{3,22} = R_{4,11}$	$R_{2,21} = R_{4,24} \neq R_{3,10}$	R_2, R_4
Case 16	$R_{2,10} = R_{3,22} = R_{4,11}$	$R_{2,21} = R_{3,10} = R_{4,24}$	R_2, R_3, R_4

3   Cryptanalysis of Alpha1 – Recover R_1

In this section, we show that R_1 could be determined with about 3000 known plaintext bits by exploiting the non-uniform distribution of the output of R_2, R_3 and R_4. We write the Alpha1 output y alternatively as

$$y = R_{1,28} \oplus (R_{2,30}|R_{3,32}) \oplus R_{4,34}$$

where '$|$' is the binary inclusive OR operator. Let

$$y' = (R_{2,30}|R_{3,32}) \oplus R_{4,34},$$

then

$$y = R_{1,28} \oplus y'.$$

Denote the output of Alpha1 as Y and let the sequences consisting of y' and $R_{1,28}$ be Y' and Y'' respectively. Obviously $Y = Y' \oplus Y''$. Since R_1 is clocked regularly, there are only 2^{29} possible values for Y''. If the bits of Y' are not uniformly distributed, those statistical properties could be used to recover Y'' ($= R_1$). We will show below that 00, 01, 10 and 11 in Y' are not uniformly distributed.

We start with computing the probabilities of those 16 cases. By analyzing Table 2, we know that: if Case 2 or 5 appears, only Case 1, 2, 5 and 6 may appear in the next clock cycle and each one appears with equal probability $\frac{1}{4}$; if Case 3 or 9 appears, only Case 1, 3, 9 and 11 may appear in the next clock cycle and each one appears with equal probability $\frac{1}{4}$; if Case 7 or 10 appears, only Case 6, 7, 10 and 11 may appear in the next clock cycle and each one appears with equal probability $\frac{1}{4}$; if Case 1, 4, 6, 8, 11, 12, 13, 14, 15 or 16 appears, in the next clock cycle each of those 16 cases appears with equal probability $\frac{1}{16}$. These 16 cases form a Markoff Chain. We compute the steady state probabilities and list them in Table 3.

Table 3. The Probability of Each Case

	Probability		Probability
Case 1	$\frac{3}{28}$	Case 9	$\frac{2}{28}$
Case 2	$\frac{2}{28}$	Case 10	$\frac{2}{28}$
Case 3	$\frac{2}{28}$	Case 11	$\frac{3}{28}$
Case 4	$\frac{1}{28}$	Case 12	$\frac{1}{28}$
Case 5	$\frac{2}{28}$	Case 13	$\frac{1}{28}$
Case 6	$\frac{3}{28}$	Case 14	$\frac{1}{28}$
Case 7	$\frac{2}{28}$	Case 15	$\frac{1}{28}$
Case 8	$\frac{1}{28}$	Case 16	$\frac{1}{28}$

At the ith clock cycle, if Case 1, 4 or 13 appears, only R_2 and R_3 are clocked, (y_i', y_{i-1}') would be 00, 01, 10, 11 with probability $\frac{5}{16}, \frac{3}{16}, \frac{3}{16}, \frac{5}{16}$ respectively; if Case 2, 3, 5 or 9 appears, only one of R_2 and R_3 is clocked, (y_i', y_{i-1}') would be 00, 01, 10, 11 with probability $\frac{3}{8}, \frac{1}{8}, \frac{1}{8}, \frac{3}{8}$ respectively; if Case 6, 7, 8, 10, 11, 12, 14, 15 or 16 appears, R_4 is clocked and R_2 or R_3 may be clocked, (y_i', y_{i-1}') would be 00, 01, 10, 11 with equal probability $\frac{1}{4}$. Thus (y_i', y_{i-1}') would be 00, 01, 10, 11 with probability $\frac{19}{64}, \frac{13}{64}, \frac{13}{64}, \frac{19}{64}$ respectively.

In the following we compute how much information of R_1 could be recovered if $(n+1)$ bits of the key stream Y are known. Denote this $(n+1)$-bit key stream as Y_n. Randomly set the initial value of R_1 as a 29-bit non-zero z and generate an $(n+1)$-bit output $Y_{n,z}''$ which is related to Y_n. Let

$$Y_{n,z}' = Y_n \oplus Y_{n,z}''$$

Let n_{00}, n_{01}, n_{10} and n_{11} represent the number of 00, 01, 10 and 11 in $Y_{n,z}'$ respectively. If z is the correct R_1, 00, 01, 10 and 11 would appear in $Y_{n,z}'$ with probability $\frac{19}{64}, \frac{13}{64}, \frac{13}{64}, \frac{19}{64}$ respectively. Let

$$G_{n,x} = \{(n_{00}, n_{01}, n_{10}, n_{11}) \mid n_{00}, n_{11} \geq n \cdot (\frac{19}{64} - x), n_{01}, n_{10} \leq n \cdot (\frac{13}{64} + x)$$
$$\text{and } n_{00} + n_{01} + n_{10} + n_{11} = n\}$$

x is chosen such that if z is the correct R_1, $(n_{00}, n_{01}, n_{10}, n_{11}) \in G_{n,x}$ with probability P_1 close to 1. For the wrong z, $(n_{00}, n_{01}, n_{10}, n_{11}) \in G_{n,x}$ with probability P_2. These two probabilities are given as:

$$P_1 = \sum_{(n_{00},n_{01},n_{10},n_{11}) \in G_{n,x}} C(n; n_{00}, n_{01}, n_{10}, n_{11}) \left(\frac{19}{64}\right)^{n_{00}+n_{11}} \left(\frac{13}{64}\right)^{n_{01}+n_{10}} \quad (1)$$

$$P_2 = \sum_{(n_{00}, n_{01}, n_{10}, n_{11}) \in G_{n,x}} C(n; n_{00}, n_{01}, n_{10}, n_{11}) \left(\frac{1}{4}\right)^n \tag{2}$$

where $C(n; n_{00}, n_{01}, n_{10}, n_{11})$ is the multinomial coefficient $n!/(n_{00}! n_{01}! n_{10}! n_{11}!)$. The information leakage Δs of R_1 is given as

$$\Delta s = 29 - \left(-\sum_{i=1}^{|A|} \frac{P_1}{|A|} \cdot \log_2 \frac{P_1}{|A|} - \sum_{i=1}^{|B|} \frac{1 - P_1}{|B|} \cdot \log_2 \frac{1 - P_1}{|B|}\right) \tag{3}$$

where

$$A = \{z \mid \text{For } Y'_{n,z}, \ (n_{00}, n_{01}, n_{10}, n_{11}) \in G_{n,x}\}$$
$$B = \{z \mid \text{For } Y'_{n,z}, \ (n_{00}, n_{01}, n_{10}, n_{11}) \notin G_{n,x}\}$$

Let $|A| \approx 2^{29} \cdot P_2 + 1$ and $|B| = 2^{29} - |A|$, (3) is approximated as

$$\Delta s \approx P_1 \cdot \log_2 \frac{P_1}{P_2 + 2^{-29}} + (1 - P_1) \cdot \log_2 \frac{1 - P_1}{1 - P_2 - 2^{-29}} \tag{4}$$

It is difficult to compute P_1 and P_2 directly for n with large value. We approximate (1) and (2) with the multivariate normal distribution:

$$P_1 = \int_{n \cdot \left(\frac{19}{64} - x\right) - \frac{1}{2}}^{n} \int_{n \cdot \left(\frac{19}{64} - x\right) - \frac{1}{2}}^{n} \int_{0}^{n \cdot \left(\frac{13}{64} + x\right) + \frac{1}{2}} f(z_1, z_2, z_3) \, dz_1 \, dz_2 \, dz_3 \tag{5}$$

where

$$f(z_1, z_2, z_3) = \frac{1}{\sqrt{(2\pi)^3 (\det V)}} e^{-(z-u)^T V^{-1}(z-u)/2}$$

$$z = \begin{pmatrix} z_1 \\ z_2 \\ z_3 \end{pmatrix} \qquad u = \begin{pmatrix} \frac{13}{64} n \\ \frac{19}{64} n \\ \frac{19}{64} n \end{pmatrix}$$

$$V = \begin{pmatrix} \frac{13}{64} \times \frac{51}{64} n & -\frac{13}{64} \times \frac{19}{64} n & -\frac{13}{64} \times \frac{19}{64} n \\ -\frac{19}{64} \times \frac{13}{64} n & \frac{19}{64} \times \frac{45}{64} n & -\frac{19}{64} \times \frac{19}{64} n \\ -\frac{19}{64} \times \frac{13}{64} n & -\frac{19}{64} \times \frac{19}{64} n & \frac{19}{64} \times \frac{45}{64} n \end{pmatrix}$$

P_2 is approximated in a similar way as P_1 except that

$$u = \begin{pmatrix} \frac{n}{4} \\ \frac{n}{4} \\ \frac{n}{4} \end{pmatrix} \qquad V = \begin{pmatrix} \frac{3}{16} n & -\frac{1}{16} n & -\frac{1}{16} n \\ -\frac{1}{16} n & \frac{3}{16} n & -\frac{1}{16} n \\ -\frac{1}{16} n & -\frac{1}{16} n & \frac{3}{16} n \end{pmatrix} \tag{6}$$

From (4), (5) and (6), we compute the information leakage Δs of R_1 for different values of n. The numerical integration function in MATHEMATICA is used in the computation. Different values of x are tested for each n so that the maximum value of Δs could be obtained. The results are given in Table 4.

Table 4. $\Delta s_{\max}$ vs n

n	x	P_1	P_2	$\Delta s_{\max}$
512	$\frac{10}{512}$	0.645	$2^{-9.953}$	5.477
768	$\frac{14}{768}$	0.706	$2^{-13.41}$	8.588
1024	$\frac{17}{1024}$	0.728	$2^{-17.47}$	11.88
1280	$\frac{20}{1280}$	0.752	$2^{-21.44}$	15.32
1536	$\frac{24}{1536}$	0.796	$2^{-24.58}$	18.79
1792	$\frac{29}{1792}$	0.847	$2^{-26.92}$	21.94
2048	$\frac{35}{2048}$	0.897	$2^{-28.53}$	24.39
2304	$\frac{42}{2304}$	0.937	$2^{-29.45}$	26.09
2560	$\frac{49}{2560}$	0.962	$2^{-30.42}$	27.21
2816	$\frac{56}{2304}$	0.977	$2^{-31.44}$	27.93
3072	$\frac{64}{3072}$	0.987	$2^{-31.84}$	28.35

From Table 4 about 28 bits of R_1 could be recovered with about 3000 known plaintext bits. We implemented the attack for $n = 3072$, $x = \frac{64}{3072}$. The attack is repeated for 100 times for different initial values of R_1, R_2, R_3 and R_4. Each experiment takes about 3.6 hours on Pentium IV 1.7GHz. These 100 experiments give 90 correct R_1 and 11 wrong R_1 (80 experiments give only the correct R_1; 11 experiments give one correct R_1 and one wrong R_1; 9 experiments give no value for R_1). The experiment results are close to the estimated results given in Table 4.

4   Message Recovery in the Broadcast Applications

In Section 3, we recovered R_1 with known plaintext attack. With the knowledge of R_1 each bit of the ciphertext leaks $2^{-5.3}$-bit information since 00, 01, 10 and 11 appear in the output of R_2, R_3 and R_4 with probabilities $\frac{19}{64}$, $\frac{13}{64}$, $\frac{13}{64}$ and $\frac{19}{64}$ respectively. In some broadcast applications, one message is encrypted with different keys and sent to different users. For 31, 63, 127 and 255 different keys, the information leakage for each plaintext bit is 0.405, 0.650, 0.880 and 0.986 bit respectively.

If the message is longer than $(2^{29} - 1)$ bits, even the ciphertext only attack could be applied to recover a lot of information if the message is encrypted with sufficiently large number of different keys. Assume that the message is $(2^{30} - 2)$ bits long, denote the plaintext and ciphertext as $m_1 \parallel m_2$ and $c_1 \parallel c_2$ respectively, where m_1, m_2, c_1 and c_2 are $(2^{29} - 1)$-bit long and $\parallel$ denotes concatenation. The output of R_2, R_3 and R_4 is denoted as $Y_1' \parallel Y_2'$. Since the output of R_1 is with period $2^{29} - 1$, we obtain $c_1 \oplus c_2 = (Y_1' \oplus Y_2') \oplus (m_1 \oplus m_2)$. The 00, 01, 10 and 11 appear in $Y_1' \oplus Y_2'$ with probabilities $\frac{265}{1024}$, $\frac{247}{1024}$, $\frac{247}{1024}$ and $\frac{265}{1024}$ respectively. The information leakage is $2^{-10.1}$ for each bit of $m_1 \oplus m_2$. For 255, 511, 1023 and 2047 different keys, the information leakage for each bit of $m_1 \oplus m_2$ is 0.135, 0.252, 0.442 and 0.690 bit respectively.

5 Conclusions

The attack given in this paper recovers the 29-bit register R_1 from around 3000-bit known plaintext. The rest of the message could be recovered in the broadcast applications. It is an open problem whether R_2, R_3 and R_4 could be recovered by analyzing their non-uniformly distributed output.

References

1. R. Anderson, and M. Roe, A5, http://jya.com/crack-a5.htm, 1994.
2. S. Babbage, *A Space/Time Tradeoff in Exhaustive Search Attacks on Stream Ciphers*, European Convention on Security and Detection, IEE Conference publication, No. 408, May 1995.
3. M. Briceno, I. Goldberg, D. Wagner, "A pedagogical implementation of A5/1", http://www.scard.org, May 1999.
4. A. Biryukov, A. Shamir, D. Wagner, "Real Time Cryptanalysis of A5/1 on a PC", in *Fast Software Encryption*, LNCS 1978, pp. 1-18, Springer-Verlag 2000.
5. J. Golic, "Cryptanalysis of Alleged A5 Stream Cipher", in *Advances in Cryptology – Eurocrypt'97*, LNCS 1233, pp. 239 - 255, Springer-Verlag 1997.
6. N. Komninos, B. Honary, and M. Darnell, "An Efficient Stream Cipher Alpha1 for Mobile and Wireless Devices", in *Proceedings of the 8th IMA Conference on Cryptography and Coding*, LNCS 2260, pp. 294-300.

A Linear Algebraic Attack on the AAFG1 Braid Group Cryptosystem

James Hughes

Storage Technology Corporation, 7600 Boone Avenue North
Minneapolis, MN 55428, USA
http://www.network.com/hughes
Jim@network.com

Abstract. Our purpose is to describe a promising linear algebraic attack on the AAFG1 braid group cryptosystem proposed in [2] employing parameters suggested by the authors. Our method employs the well known Burau matrix representation of the braid group and techniques from computational linear algebra and provide evidence which shows that at least a certain class of keys are weak. We argue that if AAFG1 is to be viable the parameters must be fashioned to defend against this attack.

1 Introduction

Recently, a novel approach to public key encryption based on the algorithmic difficulty of solving the word and conjugacy problems for finitely presented groups has been proposed in [1]. The method is based on having a canonical minimal length form for words in a given finitely presented group, which can be computed rather rapidly, and in which there is no corresponding fast solution for the conjugacy problem.

This has led to some work on Braid group cryptography by a number of researchers including [22] (which has also been described as AAFG2 by [2]). Braid cryptography has brought the use of combinatorial group theory into play for the first time in public key cryptography.

The AAG authors have also introduced a "Braid Diffie Hellman" protocol BDH [3]. The present paper does not address this algorithm, but only focuses on the security of the AAFG1 algorithm.

The claims for the security of these systems are that the conjugacy problem in the Braid group is known to be hard. The Conjugacy problem in the Braid group was initially described by E. Artin in [4]. Given words a and b is there any c that satisfies $b = cac^{-1}$? Given that the braid group is an infinite group, there *might* be an infinite number of words that meet this condition. Work by [16,17] has shown how to enumerate the set of all possible minimal length conjugates of a and of b. These sets are called the Super Summit Sets (SSS) of a and of b. The Conjugacy problem can be reformulated as asking whether or not $SSS[a]$ intersects $SSS[b]$. Based on the size of these sets for the parameters provided, an attack by enumeration of the entire sets would fail.

In the definition of their cryptosystem [22] the term Conjugacy Search Problem was introduced in which it is assumed that to search for a group element that conjugates two words *that are known a priori to be conjugates* is as hard as the conjugacy problem. This assumption misrepresents the conjugacy problem.

L. Batten and J. Seberry (Eds.): ACISP 2002, LNCS 2384, pp. 176–189, 2002.

The hard part of the conjugacy problem is that, in order to prove that some words are *not* conjugates, one must completely enumerate the entire $SSS[a]$ or $SSS[b]$ before one has proven that these words are not conjugates. In the case of these cryptosystems, the words are known to be conjugates, and $SSS[a] = SSS[b]$. Clearly, if one begins enumerating both sets, the first intersecting word will provide a trace between the original words. Even if it is only easier because of a Birthday surprise, it is still certainly easier than fully enumerating the set.

It has recently been proven that the Braid group is linear[7], and that the Lawrence-Krammer representation is faithful. This allows linear algebraic methods to be used now in studying the word and conjugacy problems, and possibly could lead to an attack on Braid Cryptosystems. This paper does not use this fact because it is beyond the authors' computer resources, and because there seem to be easier methods.

Much earlier (1936) W. Burau [14] considered an image of the Braid Group in the general linear group, but that representation is not faithful (in the sense that it has a non-trivial kernel) and it has been discarded as a solution to the conjugacy problem because it does not work in all cases. Several papers have described specific structures that a word has to have before it is in this kernel [24,9].

This paper first attempts to determine what percentage of the AAFG1 keys are affected by the kernel of the Burau representation, and, for the keys that are not affected, assess whether or not this fact be used to mount a linear algebra attack on the AAFG1 Cryptosystem. The specification of the algorithm and the recommendations in the paper [2] represent a concrete implementation, and as such, addressing the probabilities of feasible computational bounds is a valuable effort, which is not incompatible with formal methods [27].

Rivest states that a successful attack "should be defined in the most generous manner, so that a proof of security rules out even the weakest form of success" [26]. This paper describes an relatively weak form of success, we use empirical evidence to provide an existence that there are keys that have been generated according to the AAFG1 cryptosystem suggestions that can be recovered. Actual challenges were not used because the AAFG1 authors have chosen not to publish any.

This has been accomplished without even appearing to weaken the underlying hard problem nor requiring detailed proofs that this is possible. Here we will present the heuristic for the method.

History has shown that even if a problem is known to be hard, it may still not be suitable for a cryptosystem. Several Knapsack and Groebner Bases Cryptosystems have been proposed, each using a proven hard problem which turned out not to be difficult enough, enough of the time [30,25,6]. Even after these cryptosystems failed, the hard problems on which they were based are still hard.

For the braid group itself, little work has been accomplished on the lower and average bounds of the conjugacy search problem for a system of known conjugates. There are no proofs that the conjugacy problem is hard all the time. The motivation to do this work has only occurred recently because these cryptosystems have been proposed. Some of this work includes an attack on long or complicated words using a Length Attack [20], a brief look at the probabilities of colored Burau representation [19], and other work attempting to demonstrate the Average Complexity of the Conjugacy problem [28] using a set measurement techniques for infinite groups [13]. Recent work has begun on calculating the Normalizer Set to solve the conjugacy problem [29] (but this does not help solve the problem because it assumes a known conjugator exists.)

This paper will show that, for some AAFG1 keys, the the Burau representation *is faithful enough* that the Conjugacy Search Problem for a system of known conjugates will be successful using linear algebra in polynomial time.

The paper does not include an introduction to Braid Group and suggests an excellent reference in [11]. This paper will discuss a brief introduction to the AAG cryptosystem with emphasis on the AAFG1 method for private key creation, an estimate on how faithful the Burau representation is for these keys, an estimate of the work and probabilities of using linear algebra to recover the key, and finally a conclusion that puts it all together.

The result of this paper is that the key generation suggestions for AAFG1 as defined in [2] are not secure.

2   AAG Cryptosystem

The AAG cryptosystem is based on determining a canonical form for the the commutator of two words.

$$K_{A,B} = f(A^{-1}B^{-1}AB)$$

The AAFG1 cryptosystem uses the colored Burau as the final canonical form for the key.

2.1   AAFG1 Key Generation

The process of key generation involves the creation of two independent subgroups which are exchanged and then returned conjugated by a secret word of the other's group. The results are combined to create the commutator of both secret words.

Alice creates a subgroup

$$S_A \in \langle a_1, a_2, a_3 \ldots a_m \rangle$$

according to the suggested parameters of the cryptosystem. Alice's subgroup S_A contains $m = 20$ elements in $\mathbb{B}_{80}$ where each subgroup element contains 5 generators from the set of all positive and negative Artin generators [18], and this is further restricted so that S_A involves all Artin generators. Alice then creates her secret word $A \in S_A$ as the product of $n = 100$ elements from the set of all random positive and negative words of S_A.

Alice does this by creating an index of the generators $\langle j_1, j_2, j_3, \cdots, j_n \rangle$ and calculating

$$A = a_{j_1} a_{j_2} a_{j_3} \cdots a_{j_n}$$

Bob creates and shares his S_B and creates his secret B using the index of the generators $\langle k_1, k_2, k_3 \cdots k_n \rangle$

$$B = b_{k_1} b_{k_2} b_{k_3} \cdots b_{k_n}$$

Alice then sends Bob back his generators X where each element $x_i = A^{-1} b_i A$, Bob does the same, $y_i = B^{-1} a_i B$

Bob calculates the commutator using the inner automorphism of the returned conjugates by retaining B and applying the index that was used to create B in the returned X.

$$A^{-1}B^{-1}AB = (B^{-1}x_{k_1}x_{k_2}x_{k_3} \cdots x_{k_n})^{-1}$$
$$= (B^{-1}A^{-1}b_{k_1}A\,A^{-1}b_{k_2}A\,A^{-1}b_{k_3}A \cdots A^{-1}b_{k_n}A)^{-1}$$
$$= (B^{-1}A^{-1}b_{k_1}b_{k_2}b_{k_3} \cdots b_{k_n}A)^{-1}$$
$$= (B^{-1}A^{-1}BA)^{-1}$$
$$= A^{-1}B^{-1}AB$$

Similarly, Alice does the same with one less step using the retained A and applying the index that was used to create A on Y.

$$A^{-1}B^{-1}AB = A^{-1}y_{j_1}y_{j_2}y_{j_3} \cdots y_{j_n}$$
$$= A^{-1}B^{-1}a_{j_1}B\,B^{-1}a_{j_2}B\,B^{-1}a_{j_3}B \cdots B^{-1}a_{j_n}B$$
$$= A^{-1}B^{-1}a_{j_1}a_{j_2}a_{j_3} \cdots a_{j_n}B$$
$$= A^{-1}B^{-1}AB$$

Both Alice and Bob have independently computed $K_{A,B}$ and, in theory, the eavesdropper can not. Clearly, if the eavesdropper can recover A and B, they can just as easily compute $K_{A,B}$

The AAFG1 specification of the algorithm puts significant emphasis on the use of the Colored Burau in the final step. In the specifications, the steps of exchanging subgroups and conjugated subgroups are accomplished in the Artin form, and A, B and the commutator $A^{-1}B^{-1}AB$ can all be calculated in the Artin form until the last step where it is mapped to the colored Burau representation.

There have been hints of problems problems with the choice of the Colored Burau[19], but this is not the subject of this paper. This paper attacks the public key when it is still in the Artin form.

In this paper we will demonstrate heuristically that the attacker can calculate A and B most of the time by mapping the Artin representation of the subgroups and the conjugated subgroups to the Burau representation, calculating the conjugators using linear algebra, and then lifting the result back to the Artin form. This allows the attacker to calculate the agreed key $K_{A,B}$.

3   Faithfulness of the Burau Representation for AAFG1 Keys

The previous section was explicit in the creation of a class of private words used to conjugate the other's subgroup and to use to create the agreed key. This section discusses the faithfulness of this specific class of words when taken through the Burau representation.

Figure 1 graphically describes the experiment. A new subgroup and a new word using the method described is created and private word G was mapped to the Burau representation G'. We then try to lift this back to the Artin representation H. This H will not look like G, but they may be a rewrite of the same word. To determine if the words G and H are indeed identical words, we calculate the canonical form of each using [12]. This canonical form is proven to solve the word problem in the Artin group. If the canonical form J of each are identical, then the words are equal. In this experiment, of the original 50 words, 48 when taken through the Burau representation recovered to identical words showing that for the class of AAFG1 keys, the Burau representation and these methods the result are faithful 96% of the time.

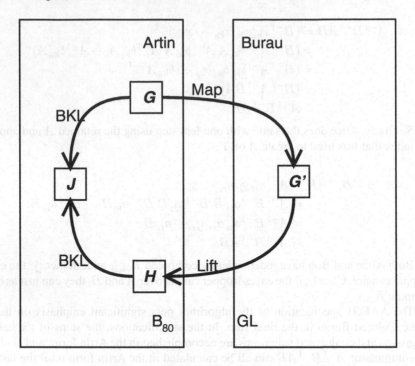

Fig. 1. Path from Artin through Burau back to Artin

3.1   Lift Back to the Artin Form

The lift back from the Burau representation to the Artin form is a heuristic based on detecting the highest power in the expressions in the first columns and using that information to "guess" which Artin Generator is best to take off.

The generators of the Burau representation of the Artin generators have the form

$$
\begin{pmatrix}
1 & & & & & \\
 & \ddots & & & & \\
 & & 1-t & t & & \\
 & & 1 & 0 & & \\
 & & & & \ddots & \\
 & & & & & 1
\end{pmatrix}
$$

for σ_i where $1 - t$ occurs in row and column i of the matrix. Note that

1. The entries are in $\mathbb{Z}[t]$
2. The det is $-t$ so that images of the braid group under the Burau representation are in the Laurent polynomials $\mathbb{Z}[t, t^{-1}]$ (polynomials in t and t^{-1} with integer coefficients).

In an set of examples in $\mathbb{B}_6$, one can see that the order of the generators is visible in the Burau representation.

Consider the word $\sigma_1\sigma_2\sigma_3$ which has Burau form of

$$\begin{pmatrix} 1-t & t-t^2 & t^2-t^3 & t^3 & 0 & 0 \\ 1 & 0 & 0 & 0 & 0 & 0 \\ 0 & 1 & 0 & 0 & 0 & 0 \\ 0 & 0 & 1 & 0 & 0 & 0 \\ 0 & 0 & 0 & 0 & 1 & 0 \\ 0 & 0 & 0 & 0 & 0 & 1 \end{pmatrix}$$

one notes that the first highest power t^3 occurs in column 3 which is the same as the last term of the word. The other generators are not as simply removed, and in this sense are not "free". That is, the other generators can not be directly manipulated from the right end of the word.

Conversely, for the word $\sigma_3\sigma_2\sigma_1$ the Burau representation is

$$\begin{pmatrix} 1-t & t & 0 & 0 & 0 & 0 \\ 1-t & 0 & t & 0 & 0 & 0 \\ 1-t & 0 & 0 & t & 0 & 0 \\ 1 & 0 & 0 & 0 & 0 & 0 \\ 0 & 0 & 0 & 0 & 1 & 0 \\ 0 & 0 & 0 & 0 & 0 & 1 \end{pmatrix}$$

where the column with the first highest power is column 1 indicating that σ_1 is "free" on the right and can be removed by multiplying on the right by σ_1^{-1}.

The last example provides some indication of *far commutativity*. In the example, $\sigma_1\sigma_2\sigma_4\sigma_5$, the maximum power occurs at index 2 and 5, but since both of these commute across the others to the end, then either σ_2 or σ_5 are possible to remove. This gives

$$\begin{pmatrix} 1-t & t-t^2 & t^2 & 0 & 0 & 0 \\ 1 & 0 & 0 & 0 & 0 & 0 \\ 0 & 1 & 0 & 0 & 0 & 0 \\ 0 & 0 & 0 & 1-t & t-t^2 & t^2 \\ 0 & 0 & 0 & 1 & 0 & 0 \\ 0 & 0 & 0 & 0 & 1 & 0 \end{pmatrix}$$

and the heuristic to remove the generator indicated by the first highest power is sufficient.

This process can be used repeatedly until there are no more positive powers. The process can be restarted by inverting the matrix (as is described next) or multiplying on the right by the generator indicated by the last most negative power minus 1.

It appears that unless one is "unlucky", the increase in the *negative* powers of t is significantly less that the decrease in *positive* powers in this process. As a result, Inverting the matrix yields a matrix with a smaller positive power and *no* negative powers, that is entries in $\mathbb{Z}[t]$. It appears that this reduce-and-invert process eventually yields the identity matrix in a significant number of cases.

Algorithm. The algorithm to lift the the word back to the Artin form involves a ordered removal of potential Artin generators. The goal is to simply remove Artin potential generators until either the remaining Burau word is the identity or the algorithm fails. This is not intended to prove that a word is in the Artin form, but attempts to recover an Artin representation for a suspected Artin word. Clearly, if the algorithm does result in a description of the matrix in terms of Artin generators, then that matrix is in the Braid group, but the converse is not true. If this algorithm fails, then this is not proof that the matrix is not in the braid group.

The method involves the following steps.

1. Find the first column i with the largest positive exponent.
2. If $i = n$, fail
3. Multiply on the right by σ_i^{-1}.
4. repeat steps 1-3 until there are no positive exponents.
5. If the matrix is the identity, success.
6. If the list of possible elements is too long, fail
7. Invert the matrix and list of removed generators and repeat steps 1-6.

The procedure has 2 failure modes. First, it can fail at step 2, if an "invalid" generator is removed. In $\mathbb{B}_n$ the generators are $\langle \sigma_1, \sigma_2 \cdots \sigma_{n-1} \rangle$ and the algorithm has failed if ever the algorithm suggests removing σ_n which is not a part of $\mathbb{B}_n$. (In experiments, this has not occurred). The second failure mode, it can fail at step 6, if after removing more than the expected number of generators, the algorithm has not yield the identity (this occurred 4% of the time).

The reason for the failure in line 6 results from a loop where the procedure creates a matrix that has been seen before. This is an issue for further investigation, as there may be a way to break out of this loop and still recover potential Artin words. Regardless of why this loop occurs, in 96% of the cases, this does not occur, and thus represents a significant threat to the algorithm.

If the algorithm yields the identity, the list of removed generators (Artin word) is guaranteed to create the same Burau matrix.

The goal of this procedure is to lift back the words that are shortest. Because the Burau is not faithful, any given word in the Burau representation may have infinitely many distinct Artin words that represent the same Burau matrix. From [7] the non-trivial kernel is due to a specific structure of both positive and negative generators aliasing to (collapsing to) a simpler structure. We conjecture that the probability of random AAG keys generating this specific structure is effectively small, and that the simplest word will have a highest probability of being the correct word. By alternately taking off all positive Artin Generators, then all negative generators, we are hoping to produce the simplest word, and thus reduce aliasing through the Burau kernel.

4   Recovering an AAG Key Using Linear Algebra

Figure 2 that graphically shows the path to the conjugacy search solution. A version of this path was suggested by S.J. Lee to the author at Crypto 2001.

In this diagram we take a subgroup D into the Burau D'. We then take the conjugated subgroup E into the Burau E' and then use linear algebra to determine a potential F' representing the secret word. We then lift the suggested F' back as F using the procedure in the previous section.

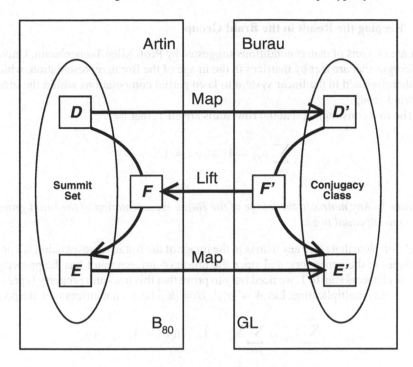

Fig. 2. Solving the conjugacy search problem through the Burau representation

This process is turned into a set of equations by

$$D'F' = F'E'$$

where $F' = [f_{ij}]$ is a matrix of unknowns. The exact procedure for creating the equations to solve use

$$R = [r_{ij}] = D'F'$$

and

$$S = [s_{ij}] = F'E'$$

and the resulting list of equations to solve are

$$r_{ij} - s_{ij} = 0 \quad (\text{for } i = 1, \ldots, n, \text{ and } j = 1, \ldots, n)$$

Since this is a system of simultaneous conjugates, we repeat this step for all conjugates to over-constrain the system.

There are two sets of constraints that we have used to aid in the recovery of the correct word. First we attempt to keep the linear algebra result in the Braid group and, second, to try to recover the minimal word (to try to eliminate as much freedom as possible) by assuming the banding of the unknown word.

4.1   Keeping the Result in the Braid Group

First are two sets of matrix conditions suggested by Prof. Allen Tannenbaum, University of Georgia, that are met by matrices in the image of the Burau representation, which we can therefore add to the linear system to keep partial computations within the image of the braid group.

The first constraint is that the row-sums are all 1, that is,

$$\sum_{j=1}^{n} a_{ij} = 1 \quad (\text{for } i = 1, \ldots, n)$$

Lemma 1. *Any matrix in the image of the Burau representation of the braid group has row sums all equal to 1.*

Proof: Note that since any matrix in the image of the Burau representation is a product of images of the generators, and since the image of any generator has the property that the row elements sum to 1, we need only to prove that this row-sum property is preserved under matrix multiplication. Let $A = [a_{ij}]$, $B = [b_{ij}]$ be $n \times n$ matrices with the property that

$$\sum_{j=1}^{n} a_{ij} = \sum_{j=1}^{n} b_{ij} = 1, \quad (\text{for } i = 1, \ldots, n)$$

Then for the product $C = [c_{ij}] = AB$ we have

$$c_{ij} = \sum_{k=1}^{n} a_{ik} b_{kj}.$$

and then

$$\sum_{j=1}^{n} c_{ij} = \sum_{j=1}^{n} \sum_{k=1}^{n} a_{ik} b_{kj}$$

$$= \sum_{k=1}^{n} \sum_{j=1}^{n} a_{ik} b_{kj}$$

$$= \left(\sum_{k=1}^{n} a_{ik} \right) \left(\sum_{j=1}^{n} b_{kj} \right)$$

$$= 1$$

QED

The second constraint is on certain weighted column sums. Consider the condition

$$\sum_{i=1}^{n} a_{ij} t^{i} = t^{j} \quad (\text{for } j = 1, \ldots, n)$$

Lemma 2. *Any matrix $[a_{ij}]$ in the image of the Burau representation of the braid group satisfies the preceding column-sum condition.*

Proof: Again, since any matrix in the image of the Burau representation is a product of images of generators, and since the image of any generator already has the asserted column-sum property, we need only prove that this property is preserved under matrix multiplication. Let $A = [a_{ij}], B = [b_{ij}]$ be $n \times n$ matrices with the properties that

$$\sum_{j=1}^{n} b_{ij} = 1, \quad (\text{for } i = 1, \ldots, n)$$

and

$$\sum_{i=1}^{n} a_{ij} t^i = t^j, \quad (\text{for } j = 1, \ldots, n)$$

Then in the product

$$C = [c_{ij}] = AB$$

we have

$$c_{ij} = \sum_{k=1}^{n} a_{ik} b_{kj}$$

and thus

$$\sum_{i=1}^{n} c_{ij} t^i = \sum_{i=1}^{n} \sum_{k=1}^{n} a_{ik} b_{kj} t^i$$

$$= \sum_{k=1}^{n} \sum_{i=1}^{n} a_{ik} b_{kj} t^i$$

$$= \left(\sum_{k=1}^{n} b_{kj} \right) \left(\sum_{i=1}^{n} a_{ik} t^i \right)$$

$$= t^j$$

QED

We then add these equations to the linear algebra step.

4.2   Banding of the Solution

There are linear algebra solvers that are significantly faster if all the variables are a short distance from the diagonal. These are called banded solvers [5]. In our case, the formulas span the entire matrix, but the unknowns are a small distance from the diagonal. This fact can be used to significantly reduce the number of variables and freedom of the solution.

Note that the maximum distance off the diagonal for an individual generator is 1, and when two generators $(\sigma_i \sigma_j)$ are multiplied together the offset increases only when $|i - j| = 1$. Only if they generators are adjacent does the offset increase. This is true regardless of if either generator is positive or negative.

Resorting to empirical evidence, a run of 500 AAFG1 keys show a distribution of the offset farthest left of diagonal to farthest right from the diagonal as shown in figure 3. In this figure, the diamonds are the probability distribution and the stars are the cumulative distribution to the 500 samples taken.

The actual left and right offset do not need to be the same, and are more typically are not the same. Further analysis can be accomplished to determine the 2 dimensional distribution of the left and right offsets.

Assuming that the non-zero entries on the left of the diagonal are within l of the diagonal and the entries on the right are within r of the diagonal, then we can add

$$f_{ij} = 0, \quad (\text{for} - l > j - i \mid j - i > r)$$

to the linear equations to solve.

The workload and the freedom can both be reduced through the assumption of banding by adding additional constraints to the linear algebra step.

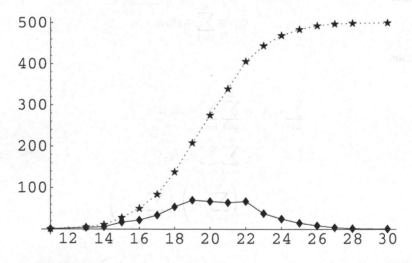

Fig. 3. Distribution and Cumulative Distribution of banding of 500 trials

4.3   Solving

The procedure for solving involves guessing the banding of the solution and then solving. Since the band size is not large ($l + r < 30$), the process can be either by exhaustion and testing the result, or iteratively looking for the solution with the minimal band size by increasing the band if it does not solve and decreasing the band if it solves with remaining freedom.

For this demonstration we assumed the former, that is, we assumed trying all band sizes. We simulated this (while also reducing run time) by providing a hint to the solution step of the actual left and right offsets with the worst case expectation that all incorrect band sizes would fail. Another optimization to aid in controlling the run time was that each independent trial created 5 private keys, and the key with the smallest band size was selected. A single run with the correct band size takes about 5 hours on a laptop. This program is written in Mathematica. While the Gaussian elimination step was customized to solve this problem, the language is not at all optimal if speed is the concern. Once could expect 1 to 3 orders of magnitude reduction in run time if the code were rewritten in a more machine-specific way.

Assuming that all offsets are tested, we will require at most a factor 155 more to achieve a 50% success rate and a factor of 410 to get more than 99%. The majority of the worlds top supercomputers have more than 410 processors, so a job like this can be trivially parallelized with the first correct solution stopping the job. Another factor is that the smaller band sizes have significantly lower run time than the larger ones.

There are three potential results; the solution may be correct, may contain some remaining freedom, or there may be a solution that is correct, but is not the same word. Of the 43 tests, 40 have been correct, 1 showed remaining freedom, and 3 incorrect solutions. At this time, no attempt was made to recover the keys that failed. It seems possible that additional work could be used to attempt to recover the keys from the solutions exhibiting freedom.

4.4 Complexity

The hardest step is the solution step. This results in a set of linear equations where the number of variables $v < (l + r)n$, The number of equations $e < vm$ where m is the number of generators in the subgroup ($m = 20$ in AAFG1). A table of samples includes

Bandsize (l+r)	Variables	Equations
18	1359	16710
18	1359	16557
19	1430	15915
20	1500	20486
19	1429	17018
18	1359	15918

Even a naive estimation of Gaussian Elimination complexity will require $O(ve)$ operations. In the samples, it is $O(3 \times 10^8)$ operations.

5   Conclusions

We have provided evidence which shows that at least a certain class of keys are vulnerable to a computational linear algebraic attack using the Burau representation. We argue that if AAFG1 is to be viable the suggested parameters must be changed to defend against this attack.

6   Other Braid Group Cryptosystems

The author has a conjecture that other Braid Group Cryptosystem [22], which is also described in §5.2 of [2], which has different word sizes and methods, may be similarly threatened by a Burau and linear algebra attack. By using cycling and decycling [11] of the public word of terms that are only in the private key's half, one can significantly reduce the word size that has to be put through this system [21]. Once this has been accomplished, the attack described in this paper is relevant. As of writing this paper, the actual result has not been completed.

Acknowledgments. I wish to thank Professor Allen Tannenbaum whose help and encouragement made this possible, Storage Technology Corporation for paying for my time, S.J. Lee for his objective comments, Don Coppersmith for suggesting that I not be intimidated by the hard nature of the Conjugacy problem, Paul Garrett for tightening up the mathematical language and the principals of Arithmetica Inc., Mike and Iris Anshel and Dorian Goldfeld who introduced me to the Braid Group, invented this interesting cryptosystem and whose claims motivate this work.

References

1. I. Anshel, M. Anshel, and D. Goldfeld. "An algebraic method for public-key cryptography". Mathematical Research Letters **6** (1999), 1–5
2. I. Anshel, M. Anshel, B. Fisher, and D. Goldfeld. "New Key Agreement Protocol in Braid Group Cryptography". *Topics in Cryptology - CT-RSA2001*. Lecture Notes in Computer Science, Vol. 2020. (Springer-Verlag, 2001), 13–27
3. I. Anshel, M. Anshel, and D. Goldfeld. "A Linear Time Matrix Key Agreement Protocol". *Contemporary Methods in Cryptography*. Institute for Pure and Applied Mathematics (IPAM), Winter 2002. From URL
   http://www.ipam.ucla.edu/programs/cry2002/abstracts/cry2002_dgoldfeld_abstract.html
4. E. Artin. "Theorie der Zopfe". *Hamburg Abh* **4** (1925), 47–72
5. A. Cleary, and J. Dongarra. "Implementation in ScaLAPACK of Divide-and-Conquer Algorithms for Banded and Tridiagonal Systems". Technical Report CS-97-358, University of Tennessee, Knoxville, TN, April 1997. Available as LAPACK Working Note #125 from URL
   http://www.netlib.org/lapack/lawns/
6. BOO BARKEE, DEH CAC CAN, JULIA ECKS, THEO MORIARITY, R. F. REE. "Why You Cannot Even Hope to use Gröbner Bases in Public Key Cryptography: An Open Letter to Those Who Have Not Yet Failed". *J. Symbolic Computation* **18** (1994), 497–501
7. S. Bigelow. "Homological representation of Braid groups". Ph.D. Thesis, Dept. of Mathematics, Berkeley Univ., 2000
8. S. Bigelow. "Braid Groups Are Linear". From URL
   http://citeseer.nj.nec.com/465605.html
9. S. Bigelow. "The Burau representation is not faithful for n = 5". *Geometry and Topology*. **3** (1999), 397–404
10. E. Brieskorn, and K. Saito. "Artin Gruppen und Coxeter Gruppen". *Invent. Math.* **17** (1972), 245–271
11. J. Birman. "Braids, Links, and Mapping Class Groups". *Annals of Mathematics Studies*. Princeton University Press, Princeton, New Jersey, 1975
12. J. Birman, K. Ko, and S. Lee. "A new approach to the word and conjugacy problems in the braid groups". *Advances in Math.* **139** (1998), 322–353

13. A.V. Borovik, A.G. Myasnikov, and V. Shpilrain. "Measuring sets in infinite groups", From URL http://www.ma.umist.ac.uk/avb/pdf/measurePrep.pdf
14. W. Burau. "Über Zopfgruppen und gleichsinning verdrillte Verkettungen". *Abh. Math. Sem. Ham. II* (1936), 171–178
15. P. Dehornoy. "A fast method for comparing braids". *Advances in Math.* **127** (1997), 200–235
16. E. A. Elrifai and H. R. Morton. "Algorithms for positive braids". *Quart. J. Math. Oxford.* **45** (1994), 479–497
17. H. Garside. "The braid group and other groups". *Quart. J. Math. Oxford.* **20** (1969), 235–254
18. D. Goldfeld, Private Correspondence, November 17, 2001, Message-ID: < 3BF6E636.40195953@veriomail.com >
19. S.G. Hahn, E.K. Lee, J.H. Park. "The Generalized Conjugacy Search Problem and the Burau Representation". Preprint, February, 2001, From URL http://crypt.kaist.ac.kr/pre_papers/hlp_revised1.ps
20. J. Hughes, and A. Tannenbaum. "Length-based attacks for certain group based encryption rewriting systems". *Institute for Mathematics and Its Applications*, April, 2000, Minneapolis, MN, Preprint number 1696
21. J. Hughes. "The LeftSSS attack on Ko-Lee-Cheon-Han-Kang-Park Key Agreement Protocol in B45", Rump Session Crypto 2000, Santa Barbara, CA, May, 2000. From URL http://www.network.com/hughes/Crypt2000.pdf
22. K. Ko, S. Lee, J. Cheon, J. Han, J. Kang, and C. Park. "New public-key cryptosystem using braid groups". Technical Report, Korea Advance Institute of Science and Technology, Taejon, Korea, February 2000
23. R.J. Lawrence. "Homological representations of the Hecke algebra". *Comm. Math. Phys.* **135** (1990), pp. 141-191.
24. D. Long and M. Paton. "The Burau representation is not faithful for n=6". *Topology* **32** (1993), 439–447.
25. A. Odlyzko. "Cryptanalytic attacks on the multiplicative knapsack cryptosystem and on Shamir's fast signature scheme". *IEEE Trans. Inform. Theory.* **30** (1984), 594–601.
26. R.L. Rivest. "Cryptography", Chapter 13 of *Handbook of Theoretical Computer Science*, (ed. J. Van Leeuwen). **1** (Elsevier, 1990), 717–755. http://theory.lcs.mit.edu/ rivest/Rivest-Cryptography.pdf
27. M. Abadi, and P. Rogaway. "Reconciling Two Views of Cryptography (The Computational Soundness of Formal Encryption)". *Journal of Cryptology.* **15** (2002), 103–127
28. V. Shpilrain. "Average Case Complexity of the Word and Conjugacy Problems in the Braid Groups". From URL http://zebra.sci.ccny.cuny.edu/web/shpil/complexity.ps
29. N. Franco, and J. Gonzalez-Meneses. "Computation of Normalizers in Braid groups and Garside Groups". From URL http://xxx.lanl.gov/abs/math.GT/0201243
30. A. Joux and J. Stern. "Cryptanalysis of another knapsack cryptosystem". *Advances in Cryptology: Proceedings of AsiaCrypt'91*, Volume 739 Lecture Notes in Computer Science, (Springer Verlag, 1991), 470–476

Isomorphism Classes of Hyperelliptic Curves of Genus 2 over $\mathbb{F}_q$*

Y. Choie and D. Yun

Department of Mathematics
Pohang University of Science and Technology
Pohang, 790–784, Korea
yjc@postech.ac.kr
manji@postech.ac.kr

Abstract. We present a simple and direct method of counting the number of the isomorphism classes of hyperelliptic curves of genus 2 over finite fields with characteristic different from 5. In this case it turns out that the number of isomorphism classes of genus-2 hyperelliptic curve over a given field $\mathbb{F}_q$ is on the order of q^3. These results have applications to hyperelliptic curve cryptography.

1   Introduction

Though discrete logarithm problems on the finite fields have advantages of computational efficiency of operations, there is well-known subexponential algorithm [1]. For security, larger group size should be used. Hence we need to find new type of finite abelian groups in some constrained computational environments; for example, smart cards, cellular telephones and pagers.

So, elliptic curve cryptosystems were proposed in 1985 independently by Victor Miller [12] and by Neal Koblitz [8]. Two advantages were the greater flexibility in choosing the group over a given field and especially the absence of subexponential time algorithms to break the system if E is suitably chosen.

Again, in 1989 Koblitz generalized the concept of elliptic curve cryptosystems to hyperelliptic curves [9]. Using the Jacobian of a hyperelliptic curve defined over a finite field instead of finite fields or elliptic curves, we can reduce the key size while maintaining the same level of security. One can use a hyperelliptic curve of genus 2 over a finite field $\mathbb{F}_q$, where $q \approx 2^{80}$, and achieve the same level of security as when an elliptic curve group $E(\mathbb{F}_q)$ is used, where $q \approx 2^{160}$ or a group $\mathbb{F}_q^*$ is used with $q \approx 2^{1024}$.

To select hyperelliptic curves, we need some security requirements. Let H be a hyperelliptic curve over the field $\mathbb{F}_q$ of genus g such that Jacobian order of $J_H(\mathbb{F}_q)$ over $\mathbb{F}_\parallel$ is of order $N = 2^l p$, where p is a prime. At first, p should be greater than 2^{160} to protect against Pollard-rho and Baby-Step/Giant-Step attacks. And if $q = 2^r$, then r should be a prime to protect against using Weil descent on $J_H(\mathbb{F}_q)$. To protect against the Tate-pairing attack, the smallest $s \geq 1$

---

* This work was partially supported by MSRC

L. Batten and J. Seberry (Eds.): ACISP 2002, LNCS 2384, pp. 190–202, 2002.

such that $q^s \equiv 1 \pmod{p}$ should be greater than twenty [5]. At last, g must be smaller than 4 to protect against the attack by Gaudry [6]. So we need only consider the hyperelliptic curves of genus 2 or 3.

It may be useful to classify the isomorphism classes of hyperelliptic curves of genus 2 and 3 over finite fields, in order to know how many essentially different choices of curves there are. And this classification is used to produce nonisomorphic hyperelliptic curves.

In this paper we count the number of isomorphism classes of hyperelliptic curves of genus 2 over a finite field $\mathbb{F}_{\shortmid\shortmid}$ with $char(\mathbb{F}_{\shortmid\shortmid}) \neq 5$. For practical purpose considering fields of characteristic 5 is not important as usually either binary fields $\mathbb{F}_{2^m}$, prime fields $\mathbb{F}_p$ of large characteristic p, or composite fields with medium characteristic are used.

This paper is organized as follows. In Section 2 we take hyperelliptic curve to mean a Weierstrass equation and define the notion of isomorphism between hyperelliptic curves. In Section 3 we classify the isomorphism classes of hyperelliptic curves of genus 2 over a finite field with characteristic 2. In Section 4 we modify the result of Hernández Encinas, Alered J. Menezes, and J. Muñoz, i.e. we classify the isomorphism classes of hyperelliptic curves of genus 2 over a finite field with characteristic different from 2 and 5.

2 Hyperelliptic Curves

In this section, we recall the basic definitions and theories. We follow notations given in [7].

A hyperelliptic curve over a field $\mathbb{F}$ of genus g is a nonsingular projective curve C over $\mathbb{F}$ of genus g for which there exists a map $C \longrightarrow \mathbb{P}^1(\mathbb{F})$ of degree two. We denote the set of all hyperelliptic curves over $\mathbb{F}$ of genus g by H_g.

A divisor on the curve C is a finite formal sum of points of the curve. For a divisor D, let $L(D)$ denote a vector space of rational functions f over C which satisfy $(f) + D \geq 0$ and $l(D) = dim L(D)$. For $C \in H_g$, $P \in C$ is called a Weierstrass point of C if $l(2P) > 1$. When $g = 1$, every point is a Weierstrass point. However, when $g > 1$, there are at least $2g + 2$ Weierstrass points (see [2], page 43). As in [10], we assume that $C \in H_g$ has an Weierstrass point.

Two curves in H_g are said to be isomorphic over $\mathbb{F}$ if they are isomorphic as projective varieties over $\mathbb{F}$. The relation of isomorphism over $\mathbb{F}$ is an equivalence relation on H_g.

It is known that if $C_1, C_2 \in H_g$ are isomorphic over $\mathbb{F}$, then their jacobian $J_{C_1}(\mathbb{F})$ and $J_{C_2}(\mathbb{F})$ are isomorphic ([13], Chapter III, Remark 2.6.1). But note that the converse is not true.

A Weierstrass equation E over $\mathbb{F}$ of genus g is

$$E/\mathbb{F} : y^2 + h(x)y = f(x),$$

where $h, f \in \mathbb{F}[x]$, $deg(h) \leq g$, $deg(f) = 2g + 1$, f is monic, and there are no singular points; a singular point on $E(x, y) = y^2 + h(x)y - f(x)$ is a solution

$(x, y) \in \bar{\mathbb{F}} \times \bar{\mathbb{F}}$ which satisfies $E(x, y), E_x(x, y)$ and $E_y(x, y)$. We denote the set of all Weierstrass equations of genus g over $\mathbb{F}$ by W_g.

For every hyperelliptic curve $C \in H_g$, there exists a Weierstrass equation $E \in W_g$ and a birational morphism $C \longrightarrow E$ (Proposition 1.2 in [10]). In fact, the following is true [10].

Proposition 2.1 *[10] There is a 1-1 correspondence between isomorphism classes of curves in H_g and equivalence classes of Weierstrass equations in W_g, where $E, \bar{E} \in W_g$ are said to be equivalent over $\mathbb{F}$ if there exist $\alpha, \beta \in \mathbb{F}$ with $\alpha \neq 0$ and $t \in \mathbb{F}[x]$ with $deg(t) \leq g$, such that the change of coordinates*

$$(x, y) \longrightarrow (\alpha^2 x + \beta, \alpha^{2g+1} y + t)$$

transforms equation E to equation $\bar{E}$

Thus, it is enough to count the number of equivalence classes in W_g in order to count the number of isomorphism classes in H_g. In the remainder we call $E \in W_g$ a hyperelliptic curve and let isomorphism denote a change of coordinates of the above type.

Next, we distinguish singular equations from nonsingular equations using the resultant.

Theorem 2.2 *[10] A curve $C : y^2 + h(x)y = f(x)$ is singular in a finite field $\mathbb{F}$ if and only if $Resultant(P, Q) = 0$, where*

$$P(x) = 4f(x) + h(x)^2$$
$$Q(x) = f'(x)^2 - f(x)h'(x)^2 + f'(x)h'(x)h(x)$$

Remark 2.3 *(i) Using Theorem 2.2, we can check whether or not a given Weierstrass equation is nonsingular. In particular, if $char(\mathbb{F}) = 2$, then a curve is singular if and only if h and $f'^2 - fh'^2$ have a common root.*
(ii) If $char\mathbb{F} \neq 2$, then $Resultant(P, Q) = 2^{8g}Resultant(P/4, P'/4)$.
(iii) Let $C : y^2 + h(x)y = f(x)$ and $\bar{C} : y^2 + \bar{h}(x)y = \bar{f}(x)$ be isomorphic curves. Then C is nonsingular if and only if $\bar{C}$ is nonsingular.

3   Isomorphism Classes of Genus-2 Hyperelliptic Curves over $\mathbb{F}_{2^m}$

In this section, we first classify the number of isomorphism classes of genus-2 hyperelliptic curves over $\mathbb{F}_{2^m}$.

Let E_1, E_2 be isomorphic hyperelliptic curves of genus 2 defined over $\mathbb{F}_{2^m}$ given by the equations;

$$E_1 : y^2 + (a_1x^2 + a_3x + a_5)y = x^5 + a_2x^4 + a_4x^3 + a_6x^2 + a_8x + a_{10}$$
$$E_2 : y^2 + (\bar{a}_1x^2 + \bar{a}_3x + \bar{a}_5)y = x^5 + \bar{a}_2x^4 + \bar{a}_4x^3 + \bar{a}_6x^2 + \bar{a}_8x + \bar{a}_{10}.$$

Since an isomorphism is given by a change of variables

$$\begin{cases} x \longmapsto \alpha^2 x + \beta \\ y \longmapsto \alpha^5 y + \alpha^4 \gamma x^2 + \alpha^2 \delta x + \epsilon, \end{cases}$$

for some $\alpha \in \mathbb{F}_{2^m}^*$, $\beta, \gamma, \delta, \epsilon \in \mathbb{F}_{2^m}$, this yields the following set of relations among the coefficients(also, see [7]) ;

$$(3.1) \quad \begin{cases} \alpha \bar{a}_1 = a_1 \\ \alpha^3 \bar{a}_3 = a_3 \\ \alpha^5 \bar{a}_5 = \beta^2 a_1 + \beta a_3 + a_5 \\ \alpha^2 \bar{a}_2 = \beta + \gamma^2 + \gamma a_1 + a_2 \\ \alpha^4 \bar{a}_4 = \delta a_1 + \gamma a_3 + a_4 \\ \alpha^6 \bar{a}_6 = \delta^2 + \beta^2 \gamma a_1 + \epsilon a_1 + \beta \gamma a_3 + \delta a_3 + \beta a_4 + \gamma a_5 + a_6 \\ \alpha^8 \bar{a}_8 = \beta^4 + \beta^2 \delta a_1 + \beta \delta a_3 + \epsilon a_3 + \beta^2 a_4 + \delta a_5 + a_8 \\ \alpha^{10} \bar{a}_{10} = \beta^5 + \epsilon^2 + \beta^2 \epsilon a_1 + \beta^4 a_2 + \beta \epsilon a_3 + \beta^3 a_4 + \epsilon a_5 \\ \qquad\qquad + \beta^2 a_6 + \beta a_8 + a_{10} \end{cases}$$

Lemma 3.1 *Let $E : y^2 + h(x)y = f(x)$ be a hyperelliptic curve over $\mathbb{F}$ of genus 2. Then if $h(x) = a_1 x^2 + a_3 x + a_5 = 0$, then $char(\mathbb{F}) \neq 2$.*

Proof Suppose that $h(x) = 0$ and $char(\mathbb{F}) = 2$. Then the partial derivative equations reduce to $f'(x) = 0$. Let $u \in \bar{\mathbb{F}}$ be a root of the equation $f'(x) = 0$, and let $v \in \bar{\mathbb{F}}$ be a root of the equation $y^2 = f(x)$. Then the point (u, v) is a singular point on E. $\square$

Now, we will consider the three types of hyperelliptic curves of genus 2 over $\mathbb{F}_{2^m}$;

Type I $a_1 \neq 0$ (also $\bar{a}_1 \neq 0$),
Type II $a_1 = 0$, $a_3 \neq 0$ (also $\bar{a}_1 = 0$, $\bar{a}_3 \neq 0$),
Type III $a_1 = a_3 = 0$, $a_5 \neq 0$ (also $\bar{a}_1 = \bar{a}_3 = 0$, $\bar{a}_5 \neq 0$).

We note that, from the relations in (3.1), the above three different types of the curves should belong to different isomorphism classes.

The following elementary results from finite field $\mathbb{F}_{2^m}$ will be needed to derive main results([11], page37).

Lemma 3.2 *Every element in $\mathbb{F}_{2^m}$ is quadratic residue.*

Proof For $a \in \mathbb{F}_{2^m}$, $a^{2^m} = a$. Then $x^2 = a$ has always a solution $x = a^{2^{m-1}}$.

Lemma 3.3 *For $a \in \mathbb{F}_{2^m}$, the equation $x^2 + x = a$ has a solution in $\mathbb{F}_{2^m}$ if and only if $Tr(a) = 0$. Here, $Tr(\alpha) = \sum_{i=1}^{m} \alpha^{i-1}$ is a trace function.*

The following is an immediate consequence of Lemma 3.3.

Corollary 3.4 *For $a, b \in \mathbb{F}_{2^m}$, $a \neq 0$, the equation $x^2 + ax + b = 0$ has a solution in $\mathbb{F}_{2^m}$ if and only if $Tr(a^{-2}b) = 0$. If x_1 is one solution, then the other solution is $x_1 + a$.*

3.1   Type I Curve

Let $E/\mathbb{F}_{2^m}$ be a hyperelliptic curve of Type I;

$$E : y^2 + (a_1 x^2 + a_3 x + a_5)y = x^5 + a_2 x^4 + a_4 x^3 + a_6 x^2 + a_8 x + a_{10}, \quad a_1 \neq 0$$

By changing variables,

$$\begin{cases} x \longmapsto a_1{}^2 x \\ y \longmapsto a_1{}^5 y, \end{cases}$$

E is transformed to the following form;
$\bar{E} : y^2 + (x^2 + a_3 x + a_5)y = x^5 + a_2 x^4 + a_4 x^3 + a_6 x^2 + a_8 x + a_{10}$.

Again, changing variables,

$$\begin{cases} x \longmapsto \alpha^2 x + \beta \\ y \longmapsto \alpha^5 y + \alpha^4 \gamma x^2 + \alpha^2 \delta x + \epsilon, \end{cases}$$

with , for $\gamma \in \mathbb{F}_{2^m}$,

$$\alpha = 1$$
$$\beta = \gamma^2 + \gamma + a_2,$$
$$\delta = \gamma + a_4$$
$$\epsilon = \delta^2 + \beta^2 \gamma + \beta \gamma a_3 + \delta a_3 \beta a_4 + \gamma a_5 + a_6,$$

$\bar{E}$ can be transformed to the form;
$E_1 : y^2 + (x^2 + a_3 x + a_5)y = x^5 + a_8 x + a_{10}$. So, we can assume that a hyperelliptic curve of Type I is of the form of E_1.

Lemma 3.5 *The number of hyperelliptic curve of Type I over $\mathbb{F}_{2^m}$ is $q^3(q-1)$ with $q = 2^m$.*

Proof Consider all the curves defined by $E/\mathbb{F}_{2^m} : y^2 + (x^2 + a_3 x + a_5)y + x^5 + a_8 x + a_{10}$.
We first count the number of singular curves.
Let $V = \{E : y^2 + (x^2 + a_3 x + a_5)y = x^5 + a_8 x + a_{10} \mid E \text{ is singular}\}$.
For $E \in V$, there is a solution $(\alpha, \beta) \in \bar{\mathbb{F}}_{2^m} \times \bar{\mathbb{F}}_{2^m}$ which satisfies

$$(i) \quad y^2 + (x^2 + a_3 x + a_5)y = x^5 + a_8 x + a_{10}$$
$$(ii) \quad a_3 y + x^4 + a_8 = 0$$
$$(iii) \quad x^2 + a_3 x + a_5 = 0$$

Let $V = V_1 \cup V_2 \cup V_3$ (disjoint union), where
$V_1 = \{E \in V \mid a_3 = 0\}$,
$V_2 = \{E \in V \mid a_3 \neq 0 \text{ and } \alpha \in \mathbb{F}_{2^m}\}$,
$V_3 = \{E(x,y) \in V \mid a_3 \neq 0 \text{ and } \alpha \in \bar{\mathbb{F}}_{2^m} \backslash \mathbb{F}_{2^m}\}$.
Case I : Suppose that $a_3 = 0$;
From (ii) and (iii), $a_8 = a_5^2$. And there is a solution $(\alpha, \beta) \in \bar{\mathbb{F}}_{2^m} \times \bar{\mathbb{F}}_{2^m}$ for every a_{10}. Therefore $|V_1| = q^2$, $q = 2^m$.

Case II : Suppose that $a_3 \neq 0$ and $\alpha \in \mathbb{F}_{2^m}$;
By Corollary 3.4, (iii) implies that $Tr(a_3^{-2}a_5) = 0$; for each $a_3 \in \mathbb{F}_{2^m}^*$, there are $\frac{2^m}{2}$ many choices of a_5. And $\alpha + a_3$ is also a solution of $x^2 + a_3 x + a_5 = 0$. From (i) and (ii), $a_{10} = \alpha^8/a_3^2 + \alpha^5 + a_8\alpha + a_8^2/a_3^2$, or $a_{10} = (\alpha + a_3)^8/a_3^2 + (\alpha + a_3)^5 + a_8(\alpha + a_3) + a_8^2/a_3^2$. Two of them are the same if and only if $a_8 = a_3^5 + \alpha^4 + a_3^4\alpha + a_3^4$. If $a_8 = a_3^5 + \alpha^4 + a_3^4\alpha + a_3^4$, then there is just one a_{10}. Otherwise, there are two distinct choices of a_{10}. In any case, there is a solution $(\alpha, \beta) \in \bar{\mathbb{F}}_{2^m} \times \bar{\mathbb{F}}_{2^m}$ satisfying (i),(ii),(iii). Therefore $|V_2| = (q-1)\frac{q}{2} + (q-1)\frac{q}{2}2(q-1)$, $q = 2^m$.

Case III : Suppose that $a_3 \neq 0$ and $\alpha \in \mathbb{F}_{2^m} \backslash \mathbb{F}_{2^m}$;
By Corollary 3.4, (iii) implies that $Tr(a_3^{-2}a_5) \neq 0$; for each $a_3 \in \mathbb{F}_{2^m}^*$, there are $\frac{2^m}{2}$ many choices of a_5. From (i), (ii) and (iii), $x^2 + a_3 x + a_5$ and $x^8 + a_3^2 x^5 + a_3^2 a_8 x + a_8^2 + a_3^2 a_{10}$ have a common root $\alpha \in \mathbb{F}_{2^m} \backslash \mathbb{F}_{2^m}$. The remainder is $(a_3^7 + a_3^6 + a_3^4 a_5 + a_3^2 a_5^2 + a_3^2 a_8)x + (a_8^2 + a_3^2 a_{10} + a_3^6 a_5 + a_3^4 a_5^2 + a_5^4 + a_3^5 a_5)$ when $x^8 + a_3^2 x^5 + a_3^2 a_8 x + a_8^2 + a^2 a_{10}$ divided by $x^2 + a_3 x + a_5$. Since $\alpha \in \mathbb{F}_{2^m} \backslash \mathbb{F}_{2^m}$, $a_3^7 + a_3^6 + a_3^4 a_5 + a_3^2 a_5^2 + a_3^2 a_8 = 0$, $a_8^2 + a_3^2 a_{10} + a_3^6 a_5 + a_3^4 a_5^2 + a_5^4 + a_3^5 a_5 6 = 0$. We have $a_8 = a_3^5 + a_3^4 + a_3^2 a_5 + a_5^2$ and $a_{10} = (a_8^2 + a_3^6 a_5 + a_3^4 a_5^2 + a_5^4 + a_3^5 a_5)/a_3^2$. This means that a_8 and a_{10} are determined from a_3, a_5. And there is a solution $(\alpha, \beta) \in \bar{\mathbb{F}}_{2^m} \times \bar{\mathbb{F}}_{2^m}$ satisfying (i),(ii),(iii). This concludes that $|V_3| = (q-1)\frac{q}{2}$, $q = 2^m$.

The number of hyperelliptic curve of Type I over $\mathbb{F}_{2^m}$ is $q^4 - |V| = q^4 - |V_1| - |V_2| - |V_3| = q^4 - q^2 - (q-1)\frac{q}{2} - (q-1)\frac{q}{2}2(q-1) - (q-1)\frac{q}{2} = q^3(q-1)$, $q = 2^m$. $\square$

Now, assume that E_1 and E_2 are isomorphic over $\mathbb{F}_{2^m}$, where

$$E_1 : y^2 + (x^2 + a_3 x + a_5)y = x^5 + a_8 x + a_{10},$$
$$E_2 : y^2 + (x^2 + \bar{a}_3 x + \bar{a}_5)y = x^5 + \bar{a}_8 x + \bar{a}_{10}.$$

Then, from (3.1), there exist $\beta, \gamma, \delta, \epsilon \in \mathbb{F}_{2^m}$, satisfying the following relations;

$$\beta = \gamma^2 + \gamma, \tag{1}$$
$$\delta = \gamma a_3, \tag{2}$$
$$\epsilon = \delta^2 + \beta^2\gamma + \beta\gamma a_3 + \delta a_3 + \gamma a_5, \tag{3}$$
$$\bar{a}_3 = a_3, \tag{4}$$
$$\bar{a}_5 = \beta^2 + \beta a_3 + a_5, \tag{5}$$
$$\bar{a}_8 = \beta^4 + \beta^2\delta + \beta\delta a_3 + \epsilon a_3 + \delta a_5 + a_8, \tag{6}$$
$$\bar{a}_{10} = \beta^5 + \epsilon^2 + \beta^2\epsilon + \beta\epsilon a_3 + \epsilon a_5 + \beta a_8 + a_{10}. \tag{7}$$

Note that the above relation in (5) gives polynomials in γ of degree 4 and the other relations in (6),(7) give polynomials in γ of degree 8 at least. There are at most 4 solutions for γ from (1) to (7). If γ is a solution, then $\gamma + 1$ is also a solution. Thus there are 2 or 4 solutions from (1) to (7). Since there are q-many distinct choices of γ and γ determines all β, δ, ϵ, the number of curves isomorphic to E_1 is from $q/2$ to $q/4$, $q = 2^m$. Thus the number of isomorphism classes of genus-2 hyperelliptic curves of Type I over $\mathbb{F}_q$ is from $q^3(q-1)/(q/2) = 2(q-1)q^2$ to $q^3(q-1)/(q/4) = 4(q-1)q^2$, $q = 2^m$.

We now summarize the results of this section.

Theorem 3.6 *(i) Every genus-2 hyperelliptic curve of Type I over $\mathbb{F}_{2^m}$ can be represented by an equation of the form*

$$E/\mathbb{F}_{2^m} : y^2 + (x^2 + a_3 x + a_5)y = x^5 + a_8 x + a_{10}.$$

(ii) Any isomorphism of curves of the above form is given by the equation (i) is of the form

$$(x, y) \longmapsto (x + \beta, y + \gamma x^2 + \delta x + \epsilon), where$$
$$\beta = \gamma^2 + \gamma,$$
$$\delta = a_3 \gamma,$$
$$\epsilon = \gamma^5 + (1 + a_3)\gamma^3 + (a_3 + a_3^2)\gamma^2 + (a_3^2 + a_5)\gamma, \ \gamma \in \mathbb{F}_{2^m}.$$

(iii) Let N_1 be the number of isomorphism classes of genus-2 hyperelliptic curves of Type I over $\mathbb{F}_{2^m}$. Then $2q^3(1 - \frac{1}{q}) \leq N_1 \leq 4q^3(1 - \frac{1}{q})$, $q = 2^m$.

Example 3.7 *we classify isomorphism classes of genus-2 hyperelliptic curves over $\mathbb{F}_2$ with Type I in Table 1.*

Table 1. Genus-2 hyperelliptic curves over $\mathbb{F}_2$ with Type I

No	Representative curve $E/\mathbb{F}_2$	Isomorphic curves $E/\mathbb{F}_2$
1	$y^2 + x^2 y = x^5 + x$	$y^2 + x^2 y = x^5 + x$
2	$y^2 + x^2 y = x^5 + x + 1$	$y^2 + x^2 y = x^5 + x + 1$
3	$y^2 + (x^2 + 1)y = x^5$	$y^2 + (x^2 + 1)y = x^5$
4	$y^2 + (x^2 + 1)y = x^5 + 1$	$y^2 + (x^2 + 1)y = x^5 + 1$
5	$y^2 + (x^2 + x)y = x^5 + 1$	$y^2 + (x^2 + x)y = x^5 + 1$
6	$y^2 + (x^2 + x + 1)y = x^5 + 1$	$y^2 + (x^2 + x + 1)y = x^5 + 1$
7	$y^2 + (x^2 + x + 1)y = x^5 + x$	$y^2 + (x^2 + x + 1)y = x^5 + x$
8	$y^2 + (x^2 + x + 1)y = x^5 + x + 1$	$y^2 + (x^2 + x + 1)y = x^5 + x + 1$

3.2   Type II Curve

Let E be a hyperelliptic curve of Type II over $\mathbb{F}_{2^m}$ with the defining equation;

$$E : y^2 + (a_3 x + a_5)y = x^5 + a_2 x^4 + a_4 x^3 + a_6 x^2 + a_8 x + a_{10}, \quad a_3 \neq 0.$$

By changing of variables

$$\begin{cases} x \longmapsto \alpha^2 x + \beta, \\ y \longmapsto \alpha^5 y + \alpha^4 \gamma x^2 + \alpha^2 \delta x + \epsilon, \end{cases}$$

where

$$\alpha \in \mathbb{F}_{2^{m*}},$$
$$\beta = a_5/a_3,$$
$$\gamma^2 = \beta + a_2,$$
$$\epsilon = (\beta^4 + \beta\delta a_3 + \beta^2 a_4 + \delta a_5 + a_8)/a_3,$$

E can be transformed to the form of

$$\bar{E} : y^2 + a_3 xy = x^5 + a_4 x^3 + a_6 x^2 + a_{10}, a_3 \neq 0.$$

Let $h(x) = a_3 x$ and $f(x) = x^5 + a_4 x^3 + a_6 x^2 + a_{10}$. From Remark 2.3, $h(x)$ and $f'(x)^2 - f(x)h'(x)^2$ have a common root if and only if $\bar{E}$ is singular. Since $(f'^2 - fh'^2)(0) = -a_3^2 a_{10}$ and $a_3 \neq 0$, then $a_{10} \neq 0$ if and only if $\bar{E}$ is nonsingular. So the total number of nonsingular curves of Type II is $(q-1)^2 q^2, q = 2^m$.

Now, suppose that E_1 and E_2 are isomorphic over $\mathbb{F}_{2^m}$;

$$E_1 : y^2 + a_3 xy = x^5 + a_4 x^3 + a_6 x^2 + a_{10},$$
$$E_2 : y^2 + \bar{a}_3 xy = x^5 + \bar{a}_4 x^3 + \bar{a}_6 x^2 + \bar{a}_{10}.$$

Then, from (3.1), there exists $\alpha, \delta \in \mathbb{F}_{2^m}, \alpha \neq 0$, satisfying the following relations ;

$$\alpha^3 \bar{a}_3 = a_3, \tag{8}$$
$$\alpha^4 \bar{a}_4 = a_4, \tag{9}$$
$$\alpha^6 \bar{a}_6 = \delta^2 + \delta a_3 + a_6, \tag{10}$$
$$\alpha^{10} \bar{a}_{10} = a_{10}. \tag{11}$$

(10) has exactly two solutions in $\mathbb{F}_q$, namely δ_1 and $\delta_1 + a_3$.
Since there are $(q-1)q$ choices of $\alpha, \delta \in \mathbb{F}_q$ for $q = 2^m$, we conclude that there are $(q-1)q/2$ curve isomorphic to E_1. Hence there are $(q-1)^2 q^2 / ((q-1)q/2) = 2(q-1)q$ isomorphism classes of hyperelliptic curves of Type II, $q = 2^m$.
We summarize the results of this section below.

Theorem 3.8 *(i) Every genus-2 hyperelliptic curve of Type II over $\mathbb{F}_{2^m}$ can be represented by an equation of the form*

$$E : y^2 + a_3 xy = x^5 + a_4 x^3 + a_6 x^2 + a_{10}, \ a_3 \neq 0.$$

(ii) Any isomorphism of E given by the equation (i) is of the form

$$(x, y) \longmapsto (\alpha^2 x, \alpha^5 y + \delta x), \ \alpha \in \mathbb{F}_{2^m}^* \ and \ \delta \in \mathbb{F}_{2^m}.$$

(iii) Let N_2 be the number of isomorphism classes of genus-2 hyperelliptic curves of Type II over $\mathbb{F}_{2^m}$. Then $N_2 = 2q^2(1 - \frac{1}{q}), q = 2^m$.

Example 3.9 *We classify isomorphism classes of genus-2 hyperelliptic curves over $\mathbb{F}_2$ with Type II in Table 2.*

Table 2. Genus-2 hyperelliptic curves over $\mathbb{F}_2$ with Type II

No	Representative curve $E/\mathbb{F}_2$	Isomorphic curves $E/\mathbb{F}$
1	$y^2 + xy = x^5 + 1$	$y^2 + xy = x^5 + 1$
2	$y^2 + xy = x^5 + x^2 + 1$	$y^2 + xy = x^5 + x^2 + 1$
3	$y^2 + xy = x^5 + x^3 + 1$	$y^2 + xy = x^5 + x^3 + 1$
4	$y^2 + xy = x^5 + x^3 + x^2 + 1$	$y^2 + xy = x^5 + x^3 + x^2 + 1$

3.3   Type III Curve

Let E be a hyperelliptic curve of Type III over $\mathbb{F}_{2^m}$ with defining equation;

$$E : y^2 + a_5 y = x^5 + a_2 x^4 + a_4 x^3 + a_6 x^2 + a_8 x + a_{10}, \quad a_5 \neq 0.$$

By changing variables

$$\begin{cases} x \longmapsto \alpha^2 x + \beta \\ y \longmapsto \alpha^5 y + \alpha^4 \gamma x^2 + \alpha^2 \delta x + \epsilon, \end{cases}$$

where

$$\alpha \in \mathbb{F}_{2^m}^*, \ \beta, \delta \in \mathbb{F}_{2^m} \ such \ that$$
$$\beta = \gamma^2 + a_2,$$
$$\delta^2 = \beta a_4 + \gamma a_5 + a_6,$$

we can transform E to the form of

$$\bar{E} : y^2 + a_5 y = x^5 + a_4 x^3 + a_8 x + a_{10}.$$

Remark 2.3 implies that $a_5 \neq 0$ if and only if $\bar{E}$ is nonsingular. So the total number of nonsingular Type III curve is $(q-1)q^3$, $q = 2^m$.

Let E_1, E_2 be isomorphic hyperelliptic curves of Type III over $\mathbb{F}_{2^m}$ with the following defining equations;

$$E_1 : y^2 + a_5 y = x^5 + a_4 x^3 + a_8 x + a_{10},$$
$$E_2 : y^2 + \bar{a_5} y = x^5 + \bar{a_4} x^3 + \bar{a_8} x + \bar{a_{10}}.$$

Then, there exists $\alpha \in \mathbb{F}_{2^m}^*, \gamma, \delta, \epsilon \in \mathbb{F}_{2^m}$ satisfying the following relations;

$$(3.2) \quad \begin{cases} \alpha^5 \bar{a_5} = a_5 \\ 0 = \beta + \gamma^2 \\ \alpha^4 \bar{a_4} = a_4 \\ 0 = \delta^2 + \beta a_4 + \gamma a_5 \\ \alpha^8 \bar{a_8} = \beta^4 + \beta^2 a_4 + \delta a_5 + a_8 \\ \alpha^{10} \bar{a_{10}} = \beta^5 + \epsilon^2 + \beta^3 a_4 + \epsilon a_5 + \beta a_8 + a_{10}. \end{cases}$$

Furthermore, (3.2) can be reduced to the following equations;

$$\alpha^5 \bar{a}_5 = a_5 \tag{12}$$

$$\alpha^4 \bar{a}_4 = a_4 \tag{13}$$

$$\alpha^{16} \bar{a}_8{}^2 = \gamma^{16} + \gamma^8 a_4^2 + a_8^2 + \gamma^2 a_4 a_5^2 + \gamma a_5^3 \tag{14}$$

$$\alpha^{10} a_{10}^- = \gamma^{10} + \epsilon^2 + \gamma^6 a_4 + \epsilon a_5 + \gamma^2 a_8 + a_{10} \tag{15}$$

There are at least 2 and at most 32 solutions for γ in $\mathbb{F}_{2^m}$ satisfying (12) to (15). Since there are $(q-1)q^2$ choices of $\alpha, \gamma \in \mathbb{F}_q$, $q = 2^m$, the number of curves isomorphic to E_1 is at least $\lceil (q-1)q^2/32 \rceil$ and at most $(q-1)q^2/2$. Therefore the number of isomorphism classes of genus-2 hyperelliptic curves of Type III over $\mathbb{F}_{2^m}$ is at least $2q$ and at most $32q$, $q = 2^m$.

We summarize the results of this section below.

Theorem 3.10 *(i) Every genus-2 hyperelliptic curve of Type III over $\mathbb{F}_{2^m}$ can be represented by an equation of the form*

$$E : y^2 + a_5 y = x^5 + a_4 x^3 + a_8 x + a_{10}, \ a_5 \neq 0.$$

(ii) Any isomorphism of E given by the equation (i) is of the form

$$(x, y) \longmapsto (\alpha^2 x + \beta, \alpha^5 y + \gamma x^2 + \delta x + \epsilon), where$$
$$\beta = \gamma^2,$$
$$\delta = \sqrt{a_4 \gamma^2 + \gamma a_5}, \ \alpha \in \mathbb{F}_{2^m}^* \ and \ \gamma, \epsilon \in \mathbb{F}_{2^m}.$$

(iii) Let N_3 be the number of isomorphism classes of genus-2 hyperelliptic curves of Type III over $\mathbb{F}_{2^m}$. Then $2q \leq N_3 \leq 32q$, $q = 2^m$.

Example 3.11 *We classify isomorphism classes of genus-2 hyperelliptic curves over $\mathbb{F}_2$ with Type III in Table 3.*

Table 3. Genus-2 hyperelliptic curves over $\mathbb{F}_2$ with Type III

No	Representative curve $E/\mathbb{F}_2$	Isomorphic curves $E/\mathbb{F}_2$
1	$y^2 + y = x^5$	$y^2 + y = x^5$, $y^2 + y = x^5 + 1$
2	$y^2 + y = x^5 + x$	$y^2 + y = x^5 + x$
3	$y^2 + y = x^5 + x + 1$	$y^2 + y = x^5 + x + 1$
4	$y^2 + y = x^5 + x^3$	$y^2 + y = x^5 + x^3$
5	$y^2 + y = x^5 + x^3 + 1$	$y^2 + y = x^5 + x^3 + 1$
6	$y^2 + y = x^5 + x^3 + x$	$y^2 + y = x^5 + x^3 + x$,
		$y^2 + y = x^5 + x^3 + x + 1$

4   Isomorphism Classes of Genus-2 Hyperelliptic Curves over Finite Fields with Characteristic Different from 2 and 5

In [7], the number of isomorphism classes of genus-2 hyperelliptic curves over $\mathbb{F}_q$, $char(\mathbb{F}_q) \neq 2, 5$, has been studied. However, there was a single error of counting process. In this section, we make a correction to the main Theorem given in [7]. We follow a idea given in [7].

Proposition 4.1 *[7] Let $\mathbb{F}_q$ be a finite field of $q = p^n$ elements for some prime p. Assume that $char(\mathbb{F}) \neq 2, 5$.*

i) Every hyperelliptic curve of genus 2 over $\mathbb{F}_q$ can be represented by an equation of the form

$$y^2 = x^5 + a_4 x^3 + a_6 x^2 + a_8 x + a_{10}.$$

ii) Let $H, \bar{H}$ be hyperelliptic curves of genus 2 given by

$$H : y^2 = x^5 + a_4 x^3 + a_6 x^2 + a_8 x + a_{10}, \quad \bar{H} : y^2 = x^5 + \bar{a}_4 x^3 + \bar{a}_6 x^2 + \bar{a}_8 x + \bar{a}_{10}.$$

Then the only change of coordinates transforming H to $\bar{H}$ is the form

$$(x, y) \longmapsto (\alpha^2 x, \alpha^5 y), \quad \alpha \in \mathbb{F}_q^*.$$

And their coefficients satisfy the following ;

$$\alpha^4 \bar{a}_4 = a_4, \quad \alpha^6 \bar{a}_6 = a_6, \quad \alpha^8 \bar{a}_8 = a_8, \quad \alpha^{10} \bar{a}_{10} = a_{10}.$$

Next theorem counts the number of singular Weierstrass equations.

Theorem 4.2 *[7] Let $V = \{g(x) \in \mathbb{F}_q[x] : g(x) = x^5 + a_4 x^3 + a_6 x^2 + a_8 x + a_{10}, \; Res(g(x), g'(x)) = 0\}$. Then $|V| = q^3$. Here $|V|$ denotes the cardinality of V.*

Theorem 4.3 *Let $\mathbb{F}_q, q = p^n$ with $p \neq 2, 5$. Let $\mathcal{H} = \{y^2 = g(x) : g(x) = x^5 + a_4 x^3 + a_6 x^2 + a_8 x + a_{10} \in \mathbb{F}_q[x], Res(g(x), g'(x)) \neq 0\}$. Let $\mathcal{G}$ be the group of transformations of the form $(x, y) \longmapsto (\alpha^2 x, \alpha^5 y), \alpha \in \mathbb{F}^*$. The number of isomorphism classes of genus-2 hyperelliptic curves over $\mathbb{F}_q$ is $|\mathcal{H}/\mathcal{G}| = 2q^3 + r(q)$.*

$r(q)$	$q \equiv 1 (mod\ 8)$	$q \equiv 5 (mod\ 8)$	$q \not\equiv 1 (mod\ 4)$
$q \equiv 1 (mod\ 5)$	$2q + 10$	$2q + 6$	8
$q \not\equiv 1 (mod\ 5)$	$2q + 2$	$2q - 2$	0

Remark 4.4 *In 2001, L.Hernández Encinas, Alered J. Menezes, and J. Muñoz proposed the classification of genus-2 hyperelliptic curve over finite fields $\mathbb{F}_q$ with $char(\mathbb{F}_q) \neq 2, 5$. They omited the subset $\mathcal{H}_3$ of $\mathcal{H}$ in their proof.*

Proof We follow the same procedure as suggested in [7].

Let $\mathcal{H}_1$, $\mathcal{H}_2$, $\mathcal{H}_3$, $\mathcal{H}_4$ be the subsets in $\mathcal{H}$ defined as follows:

$\mathcal{H}_1 = \{H \in \mathcal{H} : a_4 = a_6 = a_8 = 0, a_{10} \neq 0\}$,

$\mathcal{H}_2 = \{H \in \mathcal{H} : a_4 = a_6 = a_{10} = 0, a_8 \neq 0\}$,

$\mathcal{H}_3 = \{H \in \mathcal{H} : a_6 = a_{10} = 0, a_4 \neq 0, a_8 \neq 0\}$,

$\mathcal{H}_4 = \mathcal{H} \backslash (\mathcal{H}_1 \cup \mathcal{H}_2 \cup \mathcal{H}_3)$

$\mathcal{H} = \mathcal{H}_1 \cup \mathcal{H}_2 \cup \mathcal{H}_3 \cup \mathcal{H}_4$ (disjoint union). From Theorem (4.2), we have $|\mathcal{H}| = q^4 - q^3$. Since $y^2 = x^5 + a_{10}$, $y^2 = x^5 + a_8 x$ are nonsingular, $|\mathcal{H}_1| = |\mathcal{H}_2| = q - 1$. One can check, using Resultant, that $y^2 = x^5 + a_4 x^3 + a_8 x$ is singular if and only if $a_8 = \frac{a_4^2}{4}$. So $|\mathcal{H}_3| = (q - 1)(q - 2)$. Therefore, $|\mathcal{H}_4| = |\mathcal{H}| - |\mathcal{H}_1 \cup \mathcal{H}_2 \cup \mathcal{H}_3| = q(q - 1)^2(q + 1)$.

Since $\mathcal{G} \cong \mathbb{F}^*$, $|\mathcal{G}| = q - 1$. Moreover, the curves in each subset $\mathcal{H}_i$ have the same isotropy group $\mathcal{G}_i$ in $\mathcal{G}$ for $i = 1, 2, 3, 4$. By simple calculation,

$$\mathcal{G}_1 = \{\alpha \in \mathbb{F}_q^* : \alpha^{10} = 1\}, \ \mathcal{G}_2 = \{\alpha \in \mathbb{F}_q^* : \alpha^8 = 1\}$$

$$\mathcal{G}_3 = \{\alpha \in \mathbb{F}_q^* : \alpha^4 = 1\}, \ \mathcal{G}_4 = \{\alpha \in \mathbb{F}_q^* : \alpha^2 = 1\}$$

$$|\mathcal{H}/\mathcal{G}| = \frac{|\mathcal{H}_1|}{(\mathcal{G} : \mathcal{G}_1)} + \frac{|\mathcal{H}_2|}{(\mathcal{G} : \mathcal{G}_2)} + \frac{|\mathcal{H}_3|}{(\mathcal{G} : \mathcal{G}_3)} + \frac{|\mathcal{H}_4|}{(\mathcal{G} : \mathcal{G}_4)}$$

$$= \frac{|\mathcal{H}_1||\mathcal{G}_1|}{|\mathcal{G}|} + \frac{|\mathcal{H}_2||\mathcal{G}_2|}{|\mathcal{G}|} + \frac{|\mathcal{H}_3||\mathcal{G}_3|}{|\mathcal{G}|} + \frac{|\mathcal{H}_4||\mathcal{G}_4|}{|\mathcal{G}|}$$

$$= |\mathcal{G}_1| + |\mathcal{G}_2| + (q - 2)|\mathcal{G}_3| + q(q - 1)(q + 1)|\mathcal{G}_4|.$$

$$|\mathcal{G}_1| = \begin{pmatrix} 10 & \text{if } q \equiv 1 \pmod 5 \\ 2 & \text{if } q \not\equiv 1 \pmod 5 \end{pmatrix}$$

$$|\mathcal{G}_2| = \begin{pmatrix} 8 & \text{if } q \equiv 1 \pmod 8 \\ 4 & \text{if } q \not\equiv 1 \pmod 8 \text{ and } q \equiv 1 \pmod 4 \\ 2 & \text{if } q \not\equiv 1 \pmod 4 \end{pmatrix}$$

$$|\mathcal{G}_3| = \begin{pmatrix} 4 & \text{if } q \equiv 1 \pmod 4 \\ 2 & \text{if } q \not\equiv 1 \pmod 4 \end{pmatrix}$$

$$|\mathcal{G}_4| = 2.$$

$\square$

5 Conclusion

In 2001, L.Hernández Encinas, A. J. Menezes, and J. Muñoz proposed the classification of isomorphism classes of genus-2 hyperelliptic curve over finite fields $\mathbb{F}_q$ with characteristic different from 2 and 5. In this paper, using an direct counting method, we extend their result to char($\mathbb{F}_{ll}$) = 2 case. Moreover, we made a correction for the original formula in [7], which has an error. As a conclusion for the cryptographic purpose, the number of isomorphism classes of genus-2 hyperelliptic curve over $\mathbb{F}_q$ with $char(F_q) \neq 5$ is on the order of q^3. In practical purpose, it is not crucial to see a field with characteristic 5, instead, using a finite field $\mathbb{F}_{2^m}$ or $\mathbb{F}_p$, p large prime, is more efficient in many purpose.

Acknowledgement. We would like to thank to referee whose comments made our exposition better.

References

[1] L. M. Adleman, *A subexponential Algorithm for the discrete logarithm problem with applications to cryptography,* Proc. 20th IEEE Found. Comp. Sci. Symp., 55-60, 1979.

[2] E. Arabello, et al., *Geometry of algebraic curves,* Grundlehren Math. Wiss. 267, Springer-Verlag, New York, 1985.

[3] W. Diffie and M. E. Hellman, *New directions in cryptography,* IEEE Trans. Information Theory, vol 22, 644-654, 1976.

[4] T. ElGamal, *A public key cryptosystem and a signature scheme based on discrete logarithms,* IEEE Trans. Information Theory, vol 31, 469-472, 1985.

[5] G. Frey and H.-G. Rück, *A remark concerning m-divisibility and the discrete logarithm problem in the divisor class group of curves,* Math. Comp., 62, 865-874, 1994.

[6] P. Gaudry, *A variant of the Adleman-DeMarrais-Huang algorithm and its application to small genera,* In Advances in Cryptology, EUROCRYPT 2000, Springer-Verlag LNCS 1807, 19-34, 2000.

[7] L. Hernández Encinas, A. J. Menezes, and J. Muñoz Masqué, *Isomorphism classes of genus-2 hyperelliptic curves over finite fields,* to appear in Applicable Algebra in Engineering, Communication and Computing.

[8] N. Koblitz, *Elliptic curve cryptosystems,* Math. of Comp. vol 48, 203-209, 1987.

[9] N. Koblitz, *Hyperelliptic cryptosystems,* J. Crypto., 1,139-150, 203-209, 1989.

[10] P. Lockhart, *On the discriminant of a hyperelliptic curve,* Trans. Amer. Math. Soc. 342, 2, 729-752, 1994.

[11] A. Menezes and N. Koblitz, *Elliptic curve public key cryptosystems,* Kluwer Academic Publishers, 1993.

[12] V. Miller, *Uses of elliptic curves in cryptography,* Advances in cryptology - Crypto '85, LNCS 218, 417-426, 1986.

[13] J. Silverman, *The Arithmetic of Elliptic Curves,* Springer-Verlag, New York, 1986.

[14] H. Stichtenoth, *Algebraic Function Fields and Codes,* Springer-Verlag, 1993.

Compact Representation of Domain Parameters of Hyperelliptic Curve Cryptosystems

Fangguo Zhang[1], Shengli Liu[2], and Kwangjo Kim[1]

[1] International Research center for Information Security (IRIS)
Information and Communications University(ICU),
58-4 Hwaam-dong Yusong-ku, Taejeon, 305-732 KOREA
{zhfg, kkj}@icu.ac.kr

[2] Dept. of Computer Science, Shanghai Jiaotong University,
Shanghai 200030, P.R.China
liu-sl@cs.sjtu.edu.cn

Abstract. To achieve the same level of security, hyperelliptic curve cryptosystems (HCC) use a smaller field than elliptic curve cryptosystems (ECC). HCC has a more potential application to the product that has limited memory and computing power, for instance Smart cards. We discussed how to represent the domain parameters of HCC in a compact way. The domain parameters include the field over which the curve is defined, the curve itself, the order of the Jocobian and the base point. In our method, the representation of HCC with genus $g=4$ over $F_{2^{41}}$ (It can provide the same level of security with 164 bits ECC) only uses 339 bits.

Keywords: Hyperelliptic curve cryptosystems(HCC), Jacobian, Domain parameters

1 Introduction

Elliptic Curve Cryptosystems (ECC) are receiving more attention. Elliptic curves have shown to be good resources to obtain Abelian groups. The discrete logarithm problem based on the Abelian group can be intractable, and no sub-exponential time algorithm is known to solve the problem, if the curve is properly chosen. Hyperelliptic Curve Cryptosystems (HCC) was proposed by N. Koblitz in [11] as a generalization of ECC, since an elliptic curve be a hyperelliptic curve of genus $g = 1$. The Jacobians of a hyperelliptic curve can serve as a source of finite Abelian groups, over which the discrete logarithm problems are defined. Every scheme based on ECC, such as DSA and ElGamal, has its variant based on HCC. Suppose that F_q is the field on which the Jacobian of a hyperelliptic curve of genus g is defined. Then, there are about q^g points on the Jacobian. The advantage of HCC over ECC is that a smaller ground field F_q can be used to achieve the same order of magnitude of the Abelian group. That means that HCC can be implemented with a smaller word length in computers than ECC. Therefore, HCC may avoid multiprecision integer arithmetic when implemented.

L. Batten and J. Seberry (Eds.): ACISP 2002, LNCS 2384, pp. 203–213, 2002.
© Springer-Verlag Berlin Heidelberg 2002

Let $\overline{F_q}$ be the algebraic closure of the field F_q. A hyperelliptic curve C of genus g over F_q with $g \geq 1$ is given by the following equation:

$$C : y^2 + h(x)y = f(x) \tag{1}$$

where $f(x)$ is a monic polynomial of degree $2g + 1$, $h(x)$ is a polynomial of degree at most g, and there is no solutions $(x, y) \in \overline{F_q} \times \overline{F_q}$ simultaneously satisfying the equation $y^2 + h(x)y = f(x)$ and the partial derivative equations $2y + h(x) = 0$ and $h'(x)y - f'(x) = 0$.

We denote the Jacobian group over the hyperelliptic curve C of genus g over F_q by $J(C; F_q)$. The order of the Jacobian group is denoted by $\#J(C; F_q)$.

Like with ECC, not every hyperelliptic curve can be used for HCC. To build a secure HCC, the curves have to be chosen to satisfy the following properties:

1. A large prime number n of at least 160 bits can divide $\#J(C; F_q)$. The reason is the following. The complexity of Pohlig-Hellman algorithm for Hypercurve Discrete Logarithm Problem (HCDLP) is proportional to the square root of the largest prime in the factors of $\#J(C; F_q)$.

2. The large prime number n should not divide $q^k - 1$ for all small k's for which the discrete logarithm problem in F_{q^k} is feasible. This is to avoid the reduction attack proposed by Frey and Rück in [4]. The reduction attack reduces the HCDLP over the $J(C; F_q)$ to the logarithm problem in an extended field F_{q^k}. It is efficient especially for supersingular curves, see [5].

3. When q is prime, there should be no subgroup of order q in $J(C; F_q)$. Because there is an attack on anomalous curves investigated by Semaev [19], Satoh and Araki [18],Smart [21] for elliptic and generalized by Rück for hyperelliptic curves in [16].

4. $2g + 1 \leq \log q$. When $2g + 1 > \log q$, Adleman, DeMarrais and Huang gave a sub-exponential time algorithm to solve HCDLP in [1]. Further study by Gaudry in [7] suggested that $g \leq 4$.

Therefore, We will consider hyperelliptic curves $C : y^2 + h(x)y = f(x)$ of genus $g \leq 4$ over F_q, and $2^{160} \leq q^g \leq 2^{300}$.

When q is prime, according to Lemma 2 in [13], Equation (1) can be transformed to the form

$$y^2 = f(x)$$

by replacing y by $y - h(x)/2$. Here $f(x)$ has a degree $2g + 1$.

When $q = 2^m$, the following propositions hold.

Proposition 1. [5] Let C be a genus 2 curve over F_{2^m} of the form $y^2 + by = f(x)$ where $f(x)$ is monic of degree 5 and $b \in F_{2^m}^*$. Then C is supersingular.

Proposition 2. [20] For every integer $h \geq 2$, there are no hyperelliptic supersingular curves over $\overline{F_2}$ of genus $2^n - 1$.

From the above two propositions, we know that HCC can employ hyperelliptic curves over F_{2^m} of genus 3 or 4 of form

$$y^2 + y = f(x).$$

When $g = 2$, we avoid supersingular curves, and use curves of form

$$y^2 + xy = f(x)$$

instead.

When a public cryptosystem is employed in practice, the corresponding parameters should be distributed and stored. It is attractive if the parameters can be represented in a compact way, especially for the case when the available memory is limited (for instance, smart cards). In [22], Smart studied how the ECC parameters are represented with a very small number of bits. In this paper, we will investigate how to compress the parameters of a HCC with a given genus g. To define a HCC, the following parameters are necessary:

1. The finite field F_q;
2. A hyperelliptic curve defined over F_q;
3. The order of the Jacobian over the hyperelliptic curve;
4. The base point of the Jacobian.

2   Compact Representation of the Domain Parameters of a HCC

2.1   The Finite Field F_q

The discussion is restricted to two kinds of fields, namely large prime fields (with $q = 2^m - 1$ as a Mersenne number) and fields of characteristic 2, i.e. $q = 2^m$.

Large prime fields:

There is a good reason to choose q as a Mersenne number. No integer division is required for modular reduction in modular multiplication modulo a Mersenne number $q = 2^m - 1$, see [23] [9]. Suppose $a, b, t, u \in F_q$, and $c = ab = 2^m t + u$, we have $c = (t + u) \bmod q$.

There is no Mersenne number between 2^{160} and 2^{300}. Therefore, ECC cannot take advantage of the shortcut for modular multiplication modulo a Mersenne number, when $2^{160} \leq q \leq 2^{300}$. However, things are different for HCC since $2^{160} \leq q^g \leq 2^{300}$ is required. When $g = 2$, Mersenne numbers $q = 2^m - 1$ with $m = 89, 107$ or 127 can be used. When $g = 3$, Mersenne numbers with $m = 61$ or 89 can be applied. It is easy to see that 7 bits are enough to represent these Mersenne numbers (hence the finite field F_q).

Fields of characteristic 2:

We restrict F_{2^m} to those fields with primitive trinomial bases as their generators. With primitive trinomial bases, modular reduction is efficient. In the mean time, only three terms are required to represent the field, namely, $x^m + x^c + 1$.

We can choose $80 < m < 128$ for $g = 2$, $53 \leq m < 90$ for $g = 3$ and $41 \leq m < 75$ for $g = 4$. That trinomial $x^m + x^c + 1$ is primitive implies that $x^m + x^{m-c} + 1$ is also primitive. For instance, both $x^{97} + x^6 + 1$ and $x^{97} + x^{91} + 1$ are primitive. Hence, we can always choose a primitive trinomial $x^m + x^c + 1$ with $c \leq m/2$ to represent the fields. To thwart the *Weil Descent* attack [6], m is usually chosen as a prime number. Therefore, 12 bits, 6 bits for m and the other 6 bits for c, are enough to represent the field.

Between 40 and 128, there are 11 prime numbers from which m can be chosen, namely, 41, 47, 71, 73, 79, 89, 97, 103, 113, 119, and 127.

2.2   The Hyperelliptic Curve Defined over F_q

As suggested in Section 1, the following hyperelliptic curves (HC) will be considered.

Table 1. Hyperelliptic curves over F_q of genus g when q is prime and $g = 2, 3, 4$

g	HC over F_q, where q is prime, $f_i \in F_q$
2	$y^2 = x^5 + f_4 x^4 + f_3 x^3 + f_2 x^2 + f_1 x + f_0$
3	$y^2 = x^7 + f_6 x^6 + f_5 x^5 + f_4 x^4 + f_3 x^3 + f_2 x^2 + f_1 x + f_0$
4	$y^2 = x^9 + f_8 x^8 + f_7 x^7 + f_6 x^6 + f_5 x^5 + f_4 x^4 + f_3 x^3 + f_2 x^2 + f_1 x + f_0$

Table 2. Hyperelliptic curves over F_q of genus g when $q = 2^m$ and $g = 2, 3, 4$

g	HC over F_q, where $q = 2^m$, $f_i \in F_q$
2	$y^2 + xy = x^5 + f_4 x^4 + f_3 x^3 + f_2 x^2 + f_1 x + f_0$
3	$y^2 + y = x^7 + f_6 x^6 + f_5 x^5 + f_4 x^4 + f_3 x^3 + f_2 x^2 + f_1 x + f_0$
4	$y^2 + y = x^9 + f_8 x^8 + f_7 x^7 + f_6 x^6 + f_5 x^5 + f_4 x^4 + f_3 x^3 + f_2 x^2 + f_1 x + f_0$

Now we are ready to show how to represent the curves in fewer bits.

To represent the hyperelliptic curves over F_q, where q is prime, we have the following theorems:

Theorem 1. *When q is prime, hyperelliptic curves of genus $g = 2$ over F_q can be transformed to the form*

$$y^2 = x^5 + a_3 x^3 + a_2 x^2 + a_1 x + a_0. \tag{2}$$

A hyperelliptic curve of genus 3 over F_q can be transformed to the form

$$y^2 = x^7 + a_5 x^5 + a_4 x^4 + a_3 x^3 + a_2 x^2 + a_1 x + a_0. \tag{3}$$

A hyperelliptic curve of genus 4 over F_q can be transformed to the form

$$y^2 = x^9 + a_7 x^7 + a_6 x^6 + a_5 x^5 + a_4 x^4 + a_3 x^3 + a_2 x^2 + a_1 x + a_0. \tag{4}$$

where $a_i \in F_q$.

Proof. When the characteristic of the field F_q is not 2, a hyperelliptic curve of genus 2 over F_q is given by the following equation

$$y^2 = x^5 + f_4 x^4 + f_3 x^3 + f_2 x^2 + f_1 x + f_0, \tag{5}$$

where $f_i \in F_q$.

Changing variables x by $u^2 x - f_4/5$ and y by $u^5 y$ in Equation (5) we get

$$u^{10} y^2 = u^{10} x^5 + \left(f_3 u^6 - \frac{2}{5} u^6 f_4^2 \right) x^3 + \left(f_2 u^4 + \frac{4}{25} u^4 f_4^3 - \frac{3}{5} f_3 f_4 u^4 \right) x^2$$

$$+ \left(-\frac{2}{5} f_2 u^2 f_4 - \frac{3}{125} u^2 f_4^4 + \frac{3}{25} f_3 u^2 f_4^2 + f_1 u^2 \right) x$$

$$- \frac{1}{5} f_1 f_4 + f_0 + \frac{1}{25} f_2 f_4^2 + \frac{4}{3125} f_4^5 - \frac{1}{125} f_3 f_4^3.$$

Let

$$a_3 = \left(f_3 u^6 - \frac{2}{5} u^6 f_4^2 \right) / u^{10},$$

$$a_2 = \left(f_2 u^4 + \frac{4}{25} u^4 f_4^3 - \frac{3}{5} f_3 f_4 u^4 \right) / u^{10},$$

$$a_1 = \left(-\frac{2}{5} f_2 u^2 f_4 - \frac{3}{125} u^2 f_4^4 + \frac{3}{25} f_3 u^2 f_4^2 + f_1 u^2 \right) / u^{10},$$

and

$$a_0 = \left(-\frac{1}{5} f_1 f_4 + f_0 + \frac{1}{25} f_2 f_4^2 + \frac{4}{3125} f_4^5 - \frac{1}{125} f_3 f_4^3 \right) / u^{10}.$$

Then Equation (2) follows.

A hyperelliptic curve of genus 3 over F_q (recall that q is prime) is given by

$$y^2 = x^7 + f_6 x^6 + f_5 x^5 + f_4 x^4 + f_3 x^3 + f_2 x^2 + f_1 x + f_0.$$

With the change of variables $x \to x - f_6/7$ and $y \to y$, we get Equation (3).

With the change of variables $x \to x - f_8/9$ and $y \to y$, Equation (4) is obtained from

$$y^2 = x^9 + f_8 x^8 + f_7 x^7 + f_6 x^6 + f_5 x^5 + f_4 x^4 + f_3 x^3 + f_2 x^2 + f_1 x + f_0.$$

In fact, when the characteristic of the field F_q is not 2 and $2g+1$, hyperelliptic curves of genus g over F_q have the form of

$$y^2 = x^{2g+1} + a_{2g-1} x^{2g-1} + a_{2g-2} x^{2g-2} + \ldots + a_1 x + a_0,$$

where $a_i \in F_q$ for $i = 1, 2, \ldots, 2g - 1, 2g + 1$.

The results is given in Table 3 as a comparison with Table 1.

For a field of characteristic 2, we have two facts as follows:

Fact 1. The map $\sigma : x \to x^2$ is an isomorphism, and its inversion is given by $\sigma^{-1} : y \to y^{1/2}$.

Fact 2. For $a \in F_{2^m}$, the equation $x^2 + x = a$ has a solution in F_{2^m} if and only if $Tr(a) = 0$. Here $Tr(a) = \sum_{i=1}^{m} a^{2^{i-1}}$ is the trace function of F_{2^m}.

Table 3. Hyperelliptic curves over F_q of genus g when q is prime and $g = 2, 3, 4$

g	HC over F_q, where q is prime, $a_i \in F_q$
2	$y^2 = x^5 + a_3x^3 + a_2x^2 + a_1x + a_0$
3	$y^2 = x^7 + a_5x^5 + a_4x^4 + a_3x^3 + a_2x^2 + a_1x + a_0$
4	$y^2 = x^9 + a_7x^7 + a_6x^6 + a_5x^5 + a_4x^4 + a_3x^3 + a_2x^2 + a_1x + a_0$

Theorem 2. *When a hyperelliptic curve of genus $g = 2$ over F_{2^m} has a form*

$$y^2 + xy = x^5 + f_4x^4 + f_3x^3 + f_2x^2 + f_1x + f_0, \tag{6}$$

it can be transformed to a form of

$$y^2 + xy = x^5 + a_3x^3 + \epsilon x^2 + a_1x; \ here \ \epsilon \in F_2, a_1 \neq 0 \tag{7}$$

When a hyperelliptic curve of genus $g = 3$ over F_{2^m} has a form

$$y^2 + y = x^7 + f_6x^6 + f_5x^5 + f_4x^4 + f_3x^3 + f_2x^2 + f_1x + f_0, \tag{8}$$

it can be transformed to a form of

$$y^2 + y = x^7 + a_5x^5 + a_3x^3 + a_2x^2 + \epsilon; \ here \ \epsilon \in F_2 \tag{9}$$

When a hyperelliptic curve of genus $g = 4$ over F_{2^m} has a form

$$y^2 + y = x^9 + f_8x^8 + f_7x^7 + f_6x^6 + f_5x^5 + f_4x^4 + f_3x^3 + f_2x^2 + f_1x + f_0, \tag{10}$$

it can be transformed to a form of

$$y^2 + y = x^9 + a_7x^7 + a_5x^5 + a_3x^3 + a_2x^2 + \epsilon; \ here \ \epsilon \in F_2 \tag{11}$$

where $a_i \in F_q$.

Proof. Changing variable y by $y + f_4^{1/2}x^2 + f_0^{1/2}$ in Equation (6) leads to

$$y^2 + xy = x^5 + a_3x^3 + a_2x^2 + a_1x, \tag{12}$$

when $Tr(a_2) = 0$, let β be a solution of the equation $x^2 + x = a_2$, with the change of variables $x \to x$ and $y \to y + \beta x$, then obtained equation

$$y^2 + xy = x^5 + a_3x^3 + a_1x; \tag{13}$$

when $Tr(a_2) = 1$, since m is odd, so $Tr(a_2 + 1) = 0$, let β be a solution of the equation $x^2 + x = a_2 + 1$, with the change of variables $x \to x$ and $y \to y + \beta x$, then the obtained equation is:

$$y^2 + xy = x^5 + a_3x^3 + x^2 + a_1x. \tag{14}$$

So Equation (7) can be obtained from $y^2 + xy = x^5 + f_4x^4 + f_3x^3 + f_2x^2 + f_1x + f_0$;
Changing variable y by $y + f_6^{1/2}x^3 + f_4^{1/2}x^2 + f_1x$ in Equation (8), we obtain

$$y^2 + y = x^7 + a_5x^5 + a_3x^3 + a_2x^2 + a_0, \tag{15}$$

and discuss the value of $Tr(a_0)$, changing variables $x \to x$ and $y \to y + \beta$, here β is a solution of the equation $x^2 + x = a_0$ or $x^2 + x = a_0 + 1$. Then this leads to Equation (9);

Changing variable y by $y + f_8^{1/2}x^4 + f_6^{1/2}x^3 + \left(f_8^{1/2} + f_4\right)^{1/2} x^2 + f_1 x$ in Equation (10), we obtain

$$y^2 + y = x^9 + a_7x^7 + a_5x^5 + a_3x^3 + a_2x^2 + a_0, \qquad (16)$$

and discuss the value of $Tr(a_0)$, changing variables $x \to x$ and $y \to y + \beta$, here β is a solution of the equation $x^2 + x = a_0$ or $x^2 + x = a_0 + 1$. Then this leads to Equation (11).

To compare with the representations of hyperelliptic curves in Table 2, we illustrate the results of Theorem 2 in Table 4.

Table 4. Hyperelliptic curves over F_q of genus g when $q = 2^m$ and $g = 2, 3, 4$

g	HC over F_q, where $q = 2^m$, $a_i \in F_q$
2	$y^2 + xy = x^5 + a_3x^3 + \epsilon x^2 + a_1x$, here $\epsilon \in F_2, a_1 \neq 0$
3	$y^2 + y = x^7 + a_5x^5 + a_3x^3 + a_2x^2 + \epsilon$, here $\epsilon \in F_2$
4	$y^2 + y = x^9 + a_7x^7 + a_5x^5 + a_3x^3 + a_2x^2 + \epsilon$, here $\epsilon \in F_2$

2.3 The Order of the Jacobian over the Hyperelliptic Curve

To insure the security of hyperelliptic curve cryptosystems, the order of the Jacobian of the curve C, denoted by $\#J(C, F_q)$, should be chosen such that $\#J(C, F_q)$ contains a large prime divisor. Suppose that $\#J(C, F_q) = vn$, where n is a prime. Then the best known algorithm up to now for the HCDLP is of complexity $O(\sqrt{n})$. In this sequel, we limit $v \le 2^6$.

According to Corollary 55 in [13], we have

$$(\sqrt{q} - 1)^{2g} \le \#J(C, F_q) \le (\sqrt{q} + 1)^{2g}.$$

Then we can use $\log\left(\sqrt{q} + 1\right)^{2g}$ bit to represent $\#J(C, F_q)$. Let $t = q^g + 1 - \#J(C, F_q)$. It is easy to see that

$$|t| \le -\sum_{j=1}^{2g-1} \binom{2g}{j} q^{g-j/2}(-1)^j \le 2gq^{g-1/2}.$$

Hence t has $1 + \log_2\left(2gq^{g-1/2}\right)$ bits. It is easy to see that $\#J(C, F_q)$ is uniquely determined by t when q and g are known. That means that $1 + \log_2\left(2gq^{g-1/2}\right)$ bits are enough to represent $\#J(C, F_q)$ (n as well). Consequently, the factorization of $\#J(C, F_q)$ can be represented by $7 + \log_2\left(2gq^{g-1/2}\right)$ bits, where $1 + \log_2\left(2gq^{g-1/2}\right)$ bits describing n and 6 bits describing v.

2.4   The Base Point of the Jacobian Group

We consider the hyperelliptic curve $C : y^2 + h(x)y = f(x)$ of genus $g \leq 4$ over F_q. The order of the Jocobian of the curve is given by $\#J(C, F_q) = vn$, where n is prime and $v \leq 64$. The divisor of order n over the Jocobian is called the base point. This divisor generates a cyclic subgroup of order n. Any divisor D of $J(C, F_q)$ can be described by a pair of polynomials, one monomial of degree g and the other polynomial of degree $g - 1$, namely $D = [a(x), b(x)] = [x^g + a_{g-1}x^{g-1} + \ldots + a_1 x + a_0, b_{g-1}x^{g-1} + \ldots + b_1 x + b_0]$, where $a_i, b_i \in F_q$. Therefore, every divisor D can be described as a $2g$-dimension vector $(a_{g-1}, \ldots, a_0, b_{g-1}, \ldots, b_0)$.

N. Kobliz gave algorithms to get random elements (divisors) of $J(C; F_q)$ in [11]. When an element from Kobliz's algorithms has an order that cannot divide v, then the element can be used as a base point.

The following two probabilistic algorithms show how to find a base point over F_q.

Algorithm 1. Algorithm of finding base point on $J(C, F_q)$ when q is a prime.

1. Repeat randomly choosing $\alpha \in F_q$ and calculating $f(\alpha)$ until $f(\alpha)$ is quadratic.
2. Determine the square root β of $f(\alpha)$.
3. Let $a(x) = x - \alpha$, $b(x) = \beta$. Then $[a(x), b(x)]$ is an element of the Jocobian $J(C, F_q)$.
4. Compute $D = v \cdot [a(x), b(x)]$. If $D = [1, 0]$ goto 1.
5. Output D.

Algorithm 2. Algorithm of finding base point on $J(C, F_q)$ where $q = 2^m$.

1. Randomly choose $\alpha \in F_q$ and calculate $h(\alpha)$ and $f(\alpha)$.
2. Let $c = f(\alpha)/h(\alpha)^2$. If the trace of c to F_2 is 1, i.e., $Tr(c) = 1$, goto 1. Otherwise, let $\beta = \sum_{i=0}^{(m-1)/2} c^{2^{2i}}$.
3. Let $a(x) = x - \alpha$, $b(x) = \beta$, then $[a(x), b(x)]$ is an element of $J(C; F_{2^m})$.
4. Compute $D = v \cdot [a(x), b(x)]$. If $D = [1, 0]$ goto 1.
5. Output D.

When α is randomly chosen from F_q, both the probability that $f(\alpha)$ in Step 1 of Algorithm 1 and the probability that $Tr(c) = 1$ in Step 2 of Algorithm 2 are given approximately 0.5.

Let ρ denote the probability that $D \neq [1, 0]$ in Step 4 when $f(\alpha)$ is a square in Algorithm 1 (or $Tr(c) = 1$ in Algorithm 2). Now we determine the value of ρ. Suppose that the number of divisors $[a(x), b(x)]$ in $J(C; F_q)$ such that $D = v \cdot [a(x), b(x)] = [1, 0]$ is given by N. Then each of the N divisors is an element of a subgroup of order w of $J(C; F_q)$, where w is a divisor of v, and denoted by $w|v$. Let $v = p_1^{e_1} p_2^{e_2} \ldots p_s^{e_s}$. The number of divisors of v is $(e_1 + 1)(e_2 + 1) \ldots (e_s + 1)$. The number of subgroups of order w for all w such that $w|v$ is $(e_1 + 1)(e_2 + 1) \ldots (e_s + 1)$ as well. The number of elements in such a subgroup is not more than v. Therefore, we have $N \leq v(e_1 + 1)(e_2 + 1) \ldots (e_s + 1)$. Recall that we limit $v \leq 2^6$, so $N \leq 7^3 v$, and $\rho \geq (nv - 7^3 v)/nv = 1 - 7^3/n$.

The probability that t different α's are tried in the above algorithm without obtaining a base point D $(D \neq [1,0])$ in Step 5 is $1 - (1 - 0.5\rho)^t$.

When the value of α is limited to $-2^7 < \alpha < 2^7$, the above algorithms fail with a probability about $1 - (1 - 0.5\rho)^{255} \approx 1.73 \times 10^{-77}$ (there are 255 choices for α). The approximation comes from the fact that n is a prime of 160 bits. It means that there is a big chance to get a base point that can be represented by α, which only needs 8 bits.

The above analysis shows that we can use 8 bits to represent the base point.

The following two examples give a comparison between the general representation and compact representation of a HCC.

Example 1. Let q is a prime of 89 bits. A hyperelliptic curve of genus $g = 2$ over F_q is chosen for HCC. Then the general and compact representations of the HCC parameters are given in the following table:

Table 5. Comparison of general representation and compact representation for HCC over F_q for q prime and $g = 2$

Parameters	*general(bits)*	*compact(bits)*
Field	89	7
Hyperelliptic curve	$5 \cdot 89$	$4 \cdot 89$
Order of the Jacobian	$2 \cdot 89$	143
Base point	$4 \cdot 89$	8
Total	1068	514

Example 2. Let $q = 2^{41}$. A hyperelliptic curve of genus $g = 4$ over $F_{2^{41}}$ is chosen for HCC. Then the general and compact representations of the HCC parameters are given in the following table:

Table 6. Comparison of general representation and compact representation for HCC over F_{2^m} and $g = 4$

Parameters	*general(bits)*	*compact(bits)*
Field	≥ 12	$6 + 6 = 12$
Hyperelliptic curve	$9 \cdot 41$	$4 \cdot 41 + 1$
Order of the Jacobian	$4 \cdot 41$	154
Base point	$8 \cdot 41$	8
Total	≥ 853	339

From above two examples, the number of bits of our compact representation is less than half of general representation.

Note that the security level of the HCC in the first example corresponds to that of ECC over a field of 178 bits. The security level of the HCC in the second example corresponds to that of ECC over a field of 164 bits. A similar strength set of parameters for DSA would require 1024 bits for p, 160 bits for q and 1024 bits for the generator g, making 2208 bits in all.

3 Conclusion

How to represent the parameters of HCC in a very small number of bits and an efficient way are given. The domain parameters include the finite field on which the HCC is based, the representation of a hyperelliptic curve, the order of the Jacobian of the hyperelliptic curve, and the base point on the Jacobian. We shorten the representation of the prime field by choosing Mersenne numbers, and that of the field of characteristic 2 by choosing primitive trinomial base. How to eradicate an parameter in the equation of an hyperelliptic curve is also discussed. We also give the number of bits to represent the order of the Jacobian. As to the base point, we show it can be chosen with 8 bits for representation with high probability.

References

1. L. Adleman, J. De Marrais, M.-D Huang, *A Subexponential Algorithm for Discrete Logarithms over the Rational Subgroup of the Jacobians of Large Genus Hyperelliptic Curves over Finite Fields*, in ANTS-1, Algorithmic Number Theory , Editors L.M. Adlemand and M-D. Huang, Springer-Verlag, LNCS 877, pp. 28-40, 1994.
2. L. Adleman, M.-D Huang, *Counting rational points on curves and abelian varieties over finite fields*, In ANTS-2:, LNCS 1122, Springer-Verlag, pp. 1-16, 1996.
3. D.G. Cantor, *Computing in the Jacobian of a hyperelliptic curve*, Mathematics of Computation, Volume 48, pp.95-101, 1987.
4. G. Frey and H.Rück, *A remark concerning m-divisibility and the discrete logarithm in the divisor class group of curves*, Mathematics of Computation, 62, pp.865-874, 1994.
5. S.D. Galbraith, *Supersingular curves in cryptography*. Available at http://www.cs.bris.ac.uk/ stenve
6. S.D. Galbraith, *Weil descent of Jacobians*. Presented at WCC 2001. Available at http://www.cs.bris.ac.uk/ stenve.
7. P. Gaudry, *An algorithm for solving the discrete log problem on hyperelliptic curves*, In B.Preneel(ed.), Eurocrypt 2000, LNCS 1807, Springer-Verlag, pp.19-34, 2000.
8. P. Gaudry and R. Harley, *Counting Points on Hyperelliptic Curves over finite fields*. Available at http://www.cs.bris.ac.uk/Tools/Reports/Abstract/2000-gaudry.htm
9. D.E. Knuth, and E. Donald E., *Seminumerical Algorithms*, Addison-Wesley, 1981.
10. N. Koblitz, *Elliptic Curve Cryptosystems*, Mathematics of Computation,48, pp.203-209, 1987.
11. N. Koblitz, *Hyperelliptic cryptography*, J.of Crypto., No.1, pp. 139-150, 1989.
12. P. Lockhart, *On the discriminant of a hyperelliptic curve*, Trans. Amer. Math. Soc. 342 No.2, pp. 729-752, 1994.

13. A. Menezes, Y. Wu, R. Zuccherato, *An Elementary Introduction to Hyperelliptic Curves*. In: Koblitz, N., Algebraic Aspects of Cryptography, Springer-Verlag Berlin Heidelberg 1998. Available at http://www.cacr.math.uwaterloo.ca/techreports/1997/tech_reports97.html

14. V.S. Miller, *Use of Elliptic Curve in Cryptography*, In Advances in Cryptology-CRYPTO'85(Santa Barbara,Calif.,1985), LNCS.218, Spring-Verlag, pp.417-426, 1986.

15. J. Pila, *Frobenius maps of abelian varieties and finding roots of unity in finite fields*. Math.Comp., 55, pp.745-763, 1996.

16. H.G.Rück, *On the discrete logarithms in the divisor class group of curves*, Math.Comp., 68, pp.805-806, 1999.

17. T. Satoh, *Canonical Lifting of Elliptic Curves and p-Adic Point Counting - Theoretical Background*, Workshop on Elliptic Curve Cryptography - ECC'00, 2000. Available at http://www.exp-math.uni-essen.de/ galbra/eccslides/eccslides.html

18. T. Satoh, and K. Araki, *Fermat quotients and the polynomial time discrete log algorithm for anomalous elliptic curves*, Commentari Math. Univ. St. Pauli 47 (1998), 81-92.

19. I.A. Semaev, *Evaluation of discrete logarithms in a group of p-torsion points of an elliptic curve in characteristic p*, Mathematics of Computation 67 (1998), 353-356.

20. J. Scholten, and Huijun Zhu, *Hyperelliptic Supersingular Curves over Fields of Characteristic 2*. Available at http://www.math.berkeley.edu/ zhu/preprints.html

21. N.P. Smart, *The discrete logarithms problem on elliptic curves of trace one*, Journal of Cryptology 12 (1999), 193-196.

22. N.P. Smart, *Compressed ECC Parameters*. Available at http://www.secg.org/collateral/compressed_ecc.pdf

23. J.A. Solinas, *Generalized Mersenne number*, Technical Reports, CACR, Waterloo, 1999. Available at: http://www.cacr.math.uwaterloo.ca/techreports/1999/tech_reports99.html

A New Elliptic Curve Scalar Multiplication Algorithm to Resist Simple Power Analysis

Yvonne Hitchcock[1] and Paul Montague[2]

[1] Information Security Research Centre,
Queensland University of Technology,
GPO Box 2434,Brisbane,
Queensland, 4001, Australia.
hitchcock@isrc.qut.edu.au
[2] Motorola Australia Software Centre,
2 Second Ave,
Mawson Lakes, SA 5095, Australia.
pmontagu@asc.corp.mot.com

Abstract. Elliptic curve cryptosystems (ECCs) are becoming more popular because of the reduced number of key bits required in comparison to other cryptosystems (e.g. a 160 bit ECC has roughly the same security as 1024 bit RSA). ECCs are especially suited to smart cards because of the limited memory and computational power available on these devices. However, the side-channel attacks which have recently been proposed can obtain information about the cryptosystem by measuring side-channel information such as power consumption and processing time. This information may be used to break implementations that have not incorporated defences against these attacks. This paper presents a new defence against Simple Power Analysis (SPA). This new defence is based on the NAF (non-adjacent form) representation of a scalar and requires 44% fewer additions and 11% extra doublings than the commonly recommended defence of performing a point addition in every loop of the binary scalar multiplication algorithm.

1 Introduction

Elliptic curves were first proposed as a basis for public key cryptography in the mid 1980's independently by Koblitz [5] and Miller [7]. Elliptic curves provide a discrete log based public key cryptosystem and can use a much shorter key length than other public key cryptosystems to provide an equivalent level of security. For example, 160 bit elliptic curve cryptosystems (ECCs) provide about the same level of security as 1024 bit RSA [2, p. 51]. Also, the rate at which key size increases in order to obtain increased security is much slower than the rate at which discrete log (DL) and RSA key sizes must be increased for the same increase in security. ECCs can also provide a faster implementation than RSA or DL systems, and use less bandwidth and power [4]. These issues can be crucial in lightweight applications such as smart cards.

L. Batten and J. Seberry (Eds.): ACISP 2002, LNCS 2384, pp. 214–225, 2002.

In the last few years, confidence in the security of ECCs has also risen, to the point where they have now been included or proposed for inclusion in internationally recognized standards (specifically IEEE P1363, WAP (Wireless Application Protocol), ANSI X9.62, ANSI X9.63 and ISO CD 14888-3). Thus elliptic curve cryptography is set to become an integral part of lightweight applications in the immediate future.

More recently, Kocher et. al. [6] have described side-channel attacks on smart-card implementations of cryptosystems. These attacks can obtain information about the cryptosystem by measuring side-channel information such as power consumption and processing time. This information can then be used to break implementations that have not incorporated defences against these attacks. In this paper, we are concerned with side-channel attacks that use simple power analysis (SPA). In order to perform a SPA attack, the power consumption of the device is measured for a single execution of a cryptographic operation [3]. Because different operations performed by the device require differing amounts of power, the power consumption can be used to determine which operations were performed in what order. In the case of elliptic curves, it may be possible to determine which parts of the power trace were generated by a point doubling, and which parts were generated by a point addition. From this information, the secret key used as the scalar in the elliptic curve scalar multiplication can be recovered.

In order to ensure the resistance of an implementation to SPA, a simple defence based on the binary scalar multiplication algorithm is often recommended [3,9]. The binary scalar multiplication algorithm and the defended version are given in Figs. 1 and 2. Instead of only performing a point addition when the next bit of the scalar k is 1, the defended algorithm performs an addition in each iteration of the loop and discards the results of those additions which are irrelevant. This prevents SPA because the pattern of additions and doublings is the same for all scalar multiplications and does not reveal the scalar used.

Another method of defence against SPA proposed by Bodo Möller [8] involves using a windowing method. The digit 0 is not allowed as a value for a window, and thus each iteration of the scalar multiplication algorithm requires a point addition. However, because of the amount of memory needed to store the precomputation that is required, windowing methods are not generally used in smart cards.

This paper presents a new defence against SPA. This new defence is based on the NAF (non-adjacent form) representation of a scalar and requires 44% fewer additions and 11% extra doublings than the algorithm given in Fig. 2. It also requires at most two points in a precomputation.

2 New Defence

The new defence against SPA given in this paper is based on the NAF (non-adjacent form) [1] representation of a scalar. The NAF is a binary signed-digit representation of the scalar, has a minimum number of non-zero digits and is at

Input: P (the point to multiply), k (the scalar) such that $k = \sum_{i=0}^{n-1} k_{n-i-1} 2^i$,
            n (length of k)
Output: Q such that $Q = kP$
Algorithm: $Q = \phi$
           For $i = 0$ to $(n - 1)$
           $\left\{ \begin{array}{l} Q = 2Q \\ \text{If } (k_i == 1) \\ \{ Q = Q + P \} \end{array} \right\}$
           Return Q

Fig. 1. Binary scalar multiplication algorithm

Input: P (the point to multiply), k (the scalar) such that $k = \sum_{i=0}^{n-1} k_{n-i-1} 2^i$,
            n (length of k)
Output: $Q[0]$ such that $Q[0] = kP$
Algorithm: $Q[0] = \phi$
           For $i = 0$ to $(n - 1)$
           $\left\{ \begin{array}{l} Q[0] = 2Q[0] \\ Q[1] = P + Q[0] \\ Q[0] = Q[k_i] \end{array} \right\}$
           Return $Q[0]$

Fig. 2. Binary scalar multiplication algorithm defended against SPA

most one digit longer than the unsigned representation. It also has the property that no two adjacent digits are non-zero.

In order to defeat the SPA attack, it is necessary that the order in which additions, subtractions and doublings are performed does not reveal any useful information about the secret key. Here, we assume that additions are indistinguishable from subtractions using SPA. This could be ensured in practice by precomputing the negative of the point P, and adding this point wherever a subtraction of P is required.

Because each non-zero digit of the NAF is followed by a zero, when using the signed binary algorithm, the pattern of additions and doublings is a repetition of the basic unit: (double, (optional doubles), double, (add or subtract)). We decided to insert dummy doubles and additions so that the pattern of operations carried out would always be a repetition of the basic unit: (double, double, (add or subtract)). Stated another way, we have changed the NAF (by inserting dummy additions and doublings) to have the format 0!0!0!0!...0! where ! may be either 1 or −1. Thus, the only information about the secret scalar that the attacker can obtain using SPA is the number of repetitions of the (double, double, (add or subtract)) unit that were performed. This knowledge of the length of the new format of the scalar can reveal some information about the scalar, and this issue is addressed in Sect. 3.

The algorithm to convert the scalar to the new format is shown in Fig. 3, and has been designed in such a way that the actual algorithm also resists SPA where possible. Note that such resistance for the conversion algorithm may not be necessary in practice, since typically the scalar may be converted to and stored in the new format when it is initialized, but it may be required in some circumstances. The output is in groups of two bits, where (00) means perform two doublings and one dummy addition, (01) means perform two doublings and one addition, (10) means perform one doubling and one dummy doubling and one dummy subtraction and (11) means perform two doublings and one subtraction. To begin, the algorithm checks whether there are any leading zeros in the scalar. If there are, it moves the counter on to the second digit of the NAF. Otherwise, the counter is set to the first digit of the NAF. The algorithm works in such a way that if the counter is on the ith digit of the NAF, then the $i - 1^{th}$ digit is a zero, and the ith and $i + 1^{th}$ digits are used to determine how to encode the $i - 1^{th}$ and i^{th} digits. Once the counter has been set, the algorithm reads the next two bits of the scalar and outputs a value according to the lookup table. Finally, the algorithm moves on either one or two bits along the scalar and returns to the beginning of the loop. The algorithm uses a lookup table and outputs a value after reading only one or two bits of the scalar in order to be resistant to SPA. However, the algorithm's output is best explained by behaviour according to the number of zeros in the next run of zeros. If this is the last run of zeros, and the last bit of the NAF is a zero, then an odd run of zeros is encoded as $(00)^{(n-1)/2}(10)$ and an even run of zeros is encoded as $(00)^{n/2}$, where n is the number of zeros in the run. Otherwise, this is not the last run of zeros or the last digit of the NAF is non-zero, and an odd run of zeros followed by a non-zero digit is encoded as $(00)^{(n-1)/2}$ followed by either (01) or (11) (depending on whether an add or subtract is required), and an even run of zeros followed by a non-zero digit is encoded as $(00)^{(n/2)-1}(10)$ followed by either (01) or (11). This process is then repeated until all of the bits in the NAF have been processed, and is equivalent to the algorithm in Fig. 3. The time required to perform the conversion to an SPA resistant scalar is negligible compared to the time required to complete the entire scalar multiplication algorithm. Figure 4 shows a variant of the left-to-right binary scalar multiplication algorithm that uses the new protected NAF format.

3   Stopping Information Leakage

As observed in Sect. 2, the only information about the secret scalar that the attacker can obtain using SPA is the number of repetitions of the (double, double, (add or subtract)) unit that were performed. This knowledge of the length of the new format of the scalar can reveal some information about the scalar. Indeed, by obtaining the length of the new representation, the attacker knows approximately how many runs of zeros of an even length there were in the NAF

Input: s (the scalar in NAF) such that $s = \sum_{i=0}^{m-1} s_{m-i-1} 2^i$,
           m (length of s)
Output: k and n such that k is the protected NAF representation
           of s and has n bits in its representation
Algorithm: $n = 0$
           If $(s_0 == 0)$ Then
                   $\{ i = 1 \}$
           Else
                   $\{ i = 0 \}$
           End If

$$array = \begin{bmatrix} U & 11 & U & 11 \\ 10 & 00 & 10 & 00 \\ U & 01 & U & 01 \\ 10 & 10 & 10 & 10 \end{bmatrix} \quad \text{where values are specified in binary and } U \text{ indicates the value is unused}$$

           While $((i - 1) < m)$
           $\left.\begin{array}{l} \text{If } (i \geq m) \\ \quad \{ digit2 = 3 \} \\ \text{Else} \\ \quad \{ digit2 = s_i + 1 \} \\ \text{If } ((i + 1) \geq m) \\ \quad \{ digit3 = 3 \} \\ \text{Else} \\ \quad \{ digit3 = s_{i+1} + 1 \} \\ k_n k_{n+1} = array_{digit2\ digit3} \\ n = n + 2 \\ i = i + (array_{digit2\ digit3} \neq 2) + 1 \quad (\text{Where } true = 1,\ false = 0) \end{array}\right\}$
           Return k and n

Fig. 3. Protected NAF formatting algorithm with algorithm also resistant to SPA

Input: $P[0]$ (the point to multiply), k (the scalar in protected NAF format),
           n (Number of bits in k)
Output: $Q[0]$ such that $Q[0] = kP$
Algorithm: $Q[0] = \phi$
           $P[1] = -P[0]$
           For $i = 0$ to $(n - 1)$ by 2
           $\left.\begin{array}{l} doubleTwice = 0 \text{ if } (k_i k_{i+1} == 10), \text{ and 1 otherwise} \\ Q[0] = 2Q[0] \\ Q[1] = 2Q[0] \\ Q[0] = Q[doubleTwice] \\ Q[1] = Q[1] + P[k_i] \\ Q[0] = Q[k_{i+1}] \end{array}\right\}$
           Return $Q[0]$

Fig. 4. New binary scalar multiplication algorithm for protected NAF scalar

format of the scalar. This is the case because in general, two NAF digits become one symbol in the protected NAF representation, but each run of an even number of zeros requires an extra half of a protected NAF symbol to be used. The figure is not exact because there may have been no leading zero (which has the effect of using an extra half of a symbol), or the scalar may have ended in zero, in which case an even number of zeros at the end requires the usual one symbol per two NAF digits, but an odd number of zeros at the end requires an extra half of a symbol. Also, if the length of the new format is at least $\lceil \frac{N+1}{2} \rceil$ symbols (where N is the original number of bits in the scalar), the attacker does not know whether the original NAF had a length of N or $N + 1$ bits. It can be seen that the attacker may gain some valuable information. We show below how this information may be non-trivial, and also propose a scheme for rendering insignificant such information leakage.

In order to stop this leakage of information, there are several options available. One is to add a new symbol to perform two dummy additions and a dummy add (or subtract), and to insert this symbol at random places throughout the protected NAF representation in order to pad the length out to the maximum of $2\lfloor \frac{(N+1)}{3} \rfloor + (N + 1 \pmod 3)$ symbols. The major problem with this option is that padding the length out to the maximum would have an adverse affect on performance. However, other problems also exist. Three instead of two bits would be required to represent each symbol. In order to avoid introducing an extra symbol, it would be possible to insert extra (00) and (10) symbols at the beginning of the protected NAF format to pad out the length. However, for this to be effective, additions and doublings involving the point at infinity must be indistinguishable from other additions and doublings. Because of the increase in time required for the scalar multiplication, these options are not considered further in this paper.

If we start with an N bit scalar, the minimum length of the protected NAF is $\delta = \lceil \frac{N}{2} \rceil$ symbols (this is attained when all runs of zeros contain an odd number of zeros, for example the NAF $0101\ldots0101$), and the maximum length is $\epsilon = 2\lfloor \frac{(N+1)}{3} \rfloor + (N + 1 \pmod 3)$ symbols (this is attained by having as many runs of an even number of zeros as possible, for example the NAF $100\text{-}100100100100\ldots10010010$). Thus there are $\alpha = \epsilon - \delta + 1$ different protected NAF lengths. For example, for $N = 160$, there would be 29 symbol lengths. The distribution of the 2^N scalars amongst these categories is not uniform. For example, the protected NAF of the maximum length ϵ corresponds to only of order $2^{\frac{N}{3}}$ scalars. Hence, if an attacker measures the length of the protected NAF using SPA and finds it to be of such a length, then, given that there is an obvious algorithm for enumerating the scalars which correspond to a given protected NAF length, then the attacker's task is restricted to a simple brute force search over this comparatively small set. This demonstrates that the information leakage in the new algorithm is potentially significant. However, the above analysis also provides for a solution. Our proposal is to restrict the allowed scalars to those which correspond to a particular protected NAF length, and further to choose this particular length to be that which corresponds to the maximal number of scalars. Clearly, this maximum is at least $\gamma = \frac{\eta}{\alpha}$, which is $\frac{2^{160}}{29}$ for $N = 160$.

There remains the question of what particular length must be chosen in order to correspond to the maximum proportion of scalars. Clearly, for any given bit length, this is a straightforward computation. Below, we give a computationally efficient way of computing these proportions. Elementary probabilistic arguments suggest though that in general the average length of the protected NAF is of order $\frac{5N}{9}$ symbols (see Sect. 4), while this can also be argued to correspond to the maximum proportion of scalars. The computations below for $N = 160$ back up such arguments.

It is possible to find the probability of each possible number of symbols in the protected NAF for a given value of N by using a Markov chain model. The initial state of the model is that no NAF digits have been chosen. The model takes into account that since we start with a 160 bit scalar, the first non-zero digit of the NAF must be positive, and the NAF may have 160 or 161 bits. The states used are given in Table 1.

Table 1. States of the Markov chain model

State	Description
Itl	Initial state, no digits have been chosen.
0_e^L	Only zeros have been chosen so far, and there is an even number of them.
1_o^L	Only zeros have been chosen so far, and there is an odd number of them.
i_e	The last digit chosen was 0, the ending run of zeros has an even number of zeros in it and i extra half-symbols have been added to the NAF (i.e. a NAF of length k has exactly $\frac{k+i}{2}$ symbols in it).
i_o	The last digit chosen was 0, the ending run of zeros has an odd number of zeros in it and i extra half-symbols have been added to the NAF.
i_1	The last digit chosen was 1 and i extra half-symbols have been added to the NAF.

Note: i takes values from 0 to 2α.

We can then find the transition matrix, A. Let a_{ji} be the probability of moving from state i to state j. As per [1] it is possible to model a NAF by a Markov chain, with transition probabilities $P(0|0) = P(!|0) = \frac{1}{2}$, $P(0|!) = 1$ and $P(!|!) = 0$, where $P(b|a)$ denotes the probability of symbol b immediately following symbol a. These probabilities are used in the construction of our transition matrix. Let the first digit chosen be the first bit of an N bit NAF or the second bit of an $N + 1$ bit NAF. Note that for an N bit scalar to become an $N + 1$ bit NAF, the first digit of the NAF must be 1, and the next non-zero digit must be -1. Now the first digit chosen can be 1 or 0, but not -1, since two non-zero digits must be separated with at least one zero, and the scalar we are forming must be positive. The probabilities for this digit are 2/3 for choosing a 0 and 1/3 for choosing a 1. If a 1 is chosen, the NAF must have N digits. Otherwise, a 0 has been chosen, and the length of the NAF depends on the first non-zero digit. If it is a 1, the NAF is N bits with leading zeros. Otherwise, it must be a $N + 1$ bit NAF, and the first digit (a one) must be inserted at the beginning of the NAF. The transition matrix is shown in Fig. 5. To complete the matrix, the same pattern should be followed. Note that the sum of entries in each column is 1, with the exception of the impossible state, 0_o.

	Itl	0_e^L	1_o^L	0_e	0_o	0_1	1_e	1_o	1_1	2_e	3_o	2_1	3_e	3_o	3_1	
Itl	0	0	0	0	0	0	0	0	0	0	0	0	0	0	0	…
0_e^L	0	0	1/2	0	0	0	0	0	0	0	0	0	0	0	0	…
1_o^L	2/3	1/2	0	0	0	0	0	0	0	0	0	0	0	0	0	…
0_e	0	0	0	0	0	0	0	1/2	0	0	0	0	0	0	0	…
0_o	0	0	0	0	0	0	0	0	0	0	0	0	0	0	0	…
0_1	0	0	1/4	0	0	0	0	1/2	0	0	0	0	0	0	0	…
1_e	0	0	0	0	0	0	0	0	0	0	1/2	0	0	0	0	…
1_o	0	0	0	1/2	0	1	0	0	0	0	0	0	0	0	0	…
1_1	1/3	1/4	0	1/2	0	0	0	0	0	0	1/2	0	0	0	0	…
2_e	0	0	0	0	0	0	0	0	0	0	0	0	0	1/2	0	…
2_o	0	0	0	0	0	0	1/2	0	1	0	0	0	0	0	0	…
2_1	0	0	1/4	0	0	0	1/2	0	0	0	0	0	0	1/2	0	…
3_e	0	0	0	0	0	0	0	0	0	0	0	0	0	0	0	…
3_o	0	0	0	0	0	0	0	0	0	1/2	0	1	0	0	0	…
3_1	0	1/4	0	0	0	0	0	0	0	1/2	0	0	0	0	0	…
⋮	⋮	⋮	⋮	⋮	⋮	⋮	⋮	⋮	⋮	⋮	⋮	⋮	⋮	⋮	⋮	⋱

Fig. 5. Transition matrix A

Once the transition matrix, A has been found, the probability of being in a certain category in the final state can be found by $A^N b$, where $b = [1\,0\,0\,0\,\ldots]^T$. For each i, we then add the probabilities for i_e, i_o and i_1 to find the total probability of adding i half-symbols to the NAF. For a 160 bit scalar, the maximum probability is 0.22718, when adding 9 symbols (18 half-symbols), or a total length of 89 symbols. The probabilities of all possible categories are given in Table 2.

A simulation was performed for $N = 160$ which supports these results. In the simulation, 1,000,000 scalars were generated using a pseudo-random number generator. The protected NAF length corresponding to the largest number of scalars was a length of 89 symbols, with 21.8% of scalars having this protected NAF length.

It should be noted that the above analysis assumes that SPA will not reveal how many leading zeros a scalar may have had. This in turn requires that additions and doublings involving the point at infinity are indistinguishable from other additions and doublings. If this is not the case, the protected NAF al-

Table 2. Probability of each protected NAF length for a 160 bit scalar

Protected NAF length	Probability	Protected NAF length	Probability
80	$4.49 * 10^{-11}$	95	0.00141
81	$2.32 * 10^{-8}$	96	0.000187
82	$1.82 * 10^{-6}$	97	$1.75 * 10^{-5}$
83	$5.19 * 10^{-5}$	98	$1.14 * 10^{-6}$
84	0.000715	99	$5.01 * 10^{-8}$
85	0.00552	100	$1.46 * 10^{-9}$
86	0.0260	101	$2.72 * 10^{-11}$
87	0.0791	102	$3.09 * 10^{-13}$
88	0.161	103	$2.00 * 10^{-15}$
89	0.227	104	$6.75 * 10^{-18}$
90	0.225	105	$1.03 * 10^{-20}$
91	0.158	106	$5.68 * 10^{-24}$
92	0.0796	107	$7.02 * 10^{-28}$
93	0.0289	108	$4.11 * 10^{-33}$
94	0.00752		

gorithm must be modified to skip leading zeros, which will slightly change the analysis. However, simulations indicate that the category containing the most scalars will still have about $\frac{5N}{9}$ symbols.

4   Efficiency Analysis

In this section we compare the efficiency of the new algorithm that we have proposed with the efficiency of other algorithms that exist. Firstly, we compare our algorithm with the unprotected NAF format of the scalar, and then compare it with the algorithms in Figs. 1 and 2. This section assumes that the method is used as presented in Sect. 2. That is, none of the restrictions proposed in Sect. 3 are used. However, if the fixed length of $5N/9$ symbols is used as suggested in Sect. 3, the results for the average will apply to this case. It should be noted that in this discussion, "boundary" effects are ignored (i.e. the effect of ending the NAF with a zero, or starting with a 1), since these conditions will not have much impact on the results for sufficiently large scalars.

It can easily be shown that the expected length of a run of zeros in the NAF of a scalar is 2. For the protected NAF, an extra half of a symbol (i.e. an extra double and subtract) is added for every run of zeros of even length. The expected number of doubles (real or dummy) in the protected NAF between a (double, add) or (double, subtract) pair (where the add or subtract is not a dummy operation) is $2\frac{1}{3}$. Thus, if the scalar was originally of length N, then the length of the protected NAF is $\frac{10N}{9 \cdot 2} = \frac{5N}{9}$ symbols. The expected number of additions and doublings for each of the four algorithms considered is shown in Table 3.

Table 3. Comparison of Expected Number of Additions and Doublings

Algorithm	Adds	Doubles	Time as number of Adds, Assuming: D = A	D = 0.7 A
Protected unsigned binary	N	N	$2N$	$1.7N$
Möller's method (min. window)	$\frac{1}{2}N$	N	$1.5N$	$1.2N$
Unprotected unsigned binary	$\frac{1}{2}N$	N	$1.5N$	$1.2N$
Unprotected NAF	$\frac{1}{3}N$	N	$1.333N$	$1.033N$
Protected NAF	$\frac{5}{9}N$	$\frac{10}{9}N$	$1.667N$	$1.333N$

In the best case, the protected NAF does not need to add any extra symbols
to the NAF of a scalar, and thus the scalar multiplication takes no extra time
when using the protected NAF. In the worst case, let l_i for $1 \leq i \leq r$ be the
length of a non-zero digit followed by the ith run of an even number of zeros,
and let m_j for $1 \leq j \leq s$ be the length of a non-zero digit followed by the jth run
of an odd number of zeros in the original NAF. Then the original NAF requires
$(r + s)$ additions and N doublings, where $\sum_{i=1}^{r} l_i + \sum_{j=1}^{s} m_i = N$, and the protected NAF requires $(N + r)$ doublings and $\frac{N+r}{2}$ additions. If we assume that
the addition time is equal to the doubling time then the number of operations
for the original NAF is $(r + s + N)$ and the number of operations for the protected NAF is $\frac{3}{2}(N + r)$. To find the upper bound of the ratio (protected NAF :
unprotected NAF), we set $s = 0$ and find that the upper bound is 1.5. Thus the
ratio (protected NAF : unprotected NAF) is bounded by the values 1 and 1.5,
and from Table 3, the expected value of the ratio is 1.25.

If we consider the binary algorithm for an unsigned scalar (letting the doubling and addition times be equal), and find the bounds on the ratio (protected
unsigned binary algorithm : unprotected unsigned binary algorithm), then in the
best case, the scalar does not contain any zeros so that the two algorithms are
identical, and the lower bound on the ratio is 1. In the worst case, the scalar
contains only one non-zero digit, and the upper bound on the ratio is $\frac{2N}{N+1} \approx 2$.
Thus the ratio (protected unsigned binary algorithm : unprotected unsigned binary algorithm) is bounded by the values 1 and 2, and from Table 3 the expected
value of the ratio is 1.333.

We can also examine the ratio (protected unsigned binary algorithm : unprotected NAF) to see how much efficiency would be lost if the algorithm in Fig. 2
was used instead of the unprotected NAF. In the best case, as many additions
as possible $(\frac{N}{2})$ are performed in the NAF scalar multiplication, and the best
case ratio is $\frac{2N}{1.5N} = 1.333$. In the worst case, only one addition is performed for
the NAF, and the ratio is $\frac{2N}{N+1} \approx 2$. Thus the ratio (protected unsigned binary
algorithm : unprotected NAF) is bounded by 1.333 and 2, and from Table 3,
the expected value of the ratio is 1.5. If these bounds are compared with the

bounds on the (protected NAF : unprotected NAF) of 1 and 1.5, it can be seen that the protected NAF has a much smaller efficiency impact than the protected unsigned binary algorithm. Also, the upper bound of the (protected NAF : unprotected NAF) ratio is significantly smaller than the upper bound of the (protected unsigned binary algorithm : unprotected unsigned binary algorithm) ratio, indicating that the extra cost of a protected NAF algorithm compared to the original NAF algorithm is much less than the cost of a protected unsigned binary algorithm compared to the original unsigned binary algorithm.

If the new protected algorithm is compared with Bodo Möller's algorithm [8], the new algorithm would be somewhat slower because Möller's algorithm uses a windowing method to reduce the number of additions required. How much slower it was would depend on the size of window used. If the smallest possible size of window was used, Table 3 shows that Möller's (protected) method would have the same speed as the unprotected unsigned binary method. However, the new method proposed has an advantage when used on devices with limited memory because it requires enough memory for at most four points (one or two points in a precomputation and two points to store outputs from the algorithm), whereas Möller's algorithm requires enough memory for a minimum of five points (at least four points in the precomputation and one point to store the output of the algorithm). Indeed, our method would require fewer points in the precomputation (and thus a smaller amount of memory) than any windowing method using dummy operations to resist SPA, giving an advantage over these methods on devices with limited memory.

5   Conclusion

We have presented a new algorithm to convert a scalar to a signed digit representation that is resistant to SPA. On average, the new method takes about 80% of the time of the existing defence of adding in every loop of the binary algorithm, and takes 25% more time than the signed binary algorithm using the original NAF. The ratio of the time taken by the new algorithm to the time taken by the unprotected unsigned binary algorithm using a NAF scalar (if we assume that additions and doublings take the same amount of time) is bounded by the values 1 and 1.5. Also, the extra cost of a protected NAF algorithm compared to the original NAF algorithm is much less than the cost of a protected unsigned binary algorithm compared to the original unsigned binary algorithm.

As stated at the start of Sect. 4, if the scalars allowed are restricted to those such that the protected NAF is of length $5N/9$ symbols (appropriately rounded to the nearest bit length), then the average performance figures quoted above are in fact always achieved. However, it is up to a specific implementor to decide on what restrictions to place on the allowed scalars. As we have shown, for a given bit length, it is easy to compute the proportion of scalars which lead to a given protected NAF length, along the lines we have indicated above using the analysis of the Markov process, and so the implementor can choose to trade off loss of available scalars against information leakage to SPA. We have shown that the extreme case of restricting the scalars to a fixed protected NAF length leads to zero information leakage at the expense of a loss of a fraction of at most $1 - \frac{1}{\alpha}$ of available scalars.

Although the new algorithm may place restrictions on which scalars may be used without leaking information in an SPA attack, and is slightly slower than the one proposed by Möller, it has an advantage when used on devices with limited memory because it requires a smaller number of points in the precomputation, and thus a smaller amount of memory.

Acknowledgements. This research is part of an ARC SPIRT project (C10024103) undertaken jointly by Queensland University of Technology and Motorola.

References

[1] Ian Blake, Gadiel Seroussi, and Nigel Smart. *Elliptic Curves in Cryptography*, volume 265 of *London Mathematical Society Lecture Note Series*. Cambridge University Press, Cambridge, 1999.

[2] Henri Cohen, Atsuko Miyaji, and Takatoshi Ono. Efficient elliptic curve exponentiation using mixed coordinates. In *Advances in Cryptology—ASIACRYPT '98, Proceedings*, volume 1514 of *Lecture Notes in Computer Science*, pages 51–65. Springer-Verlag, 1998.

[3] Jean Sébastien Coron. Resistance against differential power analysis for elliptic curve cryptosystems. In *Cryptographic Hardware and Embedded Systems—CHES '99*, volume 1717 of *Lecture Notes in Computer Science*, pages 292–302. Springer-Verlag, 1999.

[4] Toshio Hasegawa, Junko Nakajima, and Mitsuru Matsui. A practical implementation of elliptic curve cryptosystems over $GF(p)$ on a 16-bit microcomputer. In *Public Key Cryptography – PKC '98,Proceedings*, volume 1431 of *Lecture Notes in Computer Science*, pages 182–194. Springer-Verlag, 1998.

[5] Neil Koblitz. Elliptic curve cryptosystems. In *Mathematics of Computation*, volume 48, pages 203–209, 1987.

[6] Paul Kocher, Joshua Jaffe, and Benjamin Jun. Differential power analysis. In *Advances in Cryptology—CRYPTO '99*, volume 1666 of *Lecture Notes in Computer Science*, pages 388–397. Springer-Verlag, 1999.

[7] Victor S. Miller. Use of elliptic curves in cryptography. In *Advances in Cryptology—Proceedings of Crypto 85*, volume 218 of *Lecture Notes in Computer Science*, pages 417–426. Springer-Verlag, 1986.

[8] Bodo Möller. Securing elliptic curve point multiplication against side-channel attacks. In *Information Security: 4th International Conference, Proceedings—ISC 2001*, volume 2200 of *Lecture Notes in Computer Science*, pages 324–334. Springer-Verlag, 2001.

[9] Elisabeth Oswald and Manfred Aigner. Randomized addition-subtraction chains as a countermeasure against power attacks. In *Cryptographic Hardware and Embedded Systems—CHES '01*, pages 40–52, 2001.

Strengthening the Key Schedule of the AES

Lauren May[1], Matt Henricksen[1], William Millan[1],
Gary Carter[2], and Ed Dawson[1]

[1] Information Security Research Centre, Queensland University of Technology
GPO Box 2434, Brisbane Q 4001, Australia
{l.may, m.henricksen, e.dawson, b.millan}@qut.edu.au
[2] School of Mathematics, Queensland University of Technology
GPO Box 2434, Brisbane Q 4001, Australia
g.carter@qut.edu.au

Abstract. In this paper we present practical guidelines for designing
secure block cipher key schedules. In particular we analyse the AES key
schedule and discuss its security properties both from a theoretical view-
point, and in relation to published attacks exploiting weaknesses in its
key schedule. We then propose and analyse an efficient and more secure
key schedule.

1 Introduction

The Advanced Encryption Standard (AES) is the most significant standard for
block ciphers, so its security is of paramount importance. However, the key
schedule of AES has clear weaknesses that directly assist the execution of some
effective attacks (an example being the Square attack [1].) To combat these
weaknesses, we propose a different approach to the AES key schedule design that
sacrifices a little speed in order to achieve a much higher level of security. Our
new proposal for the AES key schedule is efficient to implement. We demonstrate
that it avoids the weaknesses of the existing key schedule.

In contrast to the serious effort applied to algorithm design, the aspect of
key schedules for block ciphers has received comparatively little attention. This
is despite the fact that published block ciphers are vulnerable to known attacks
that exploit the weaknesses of their key schedules [2], [3], [4]. Weak key schedules
also affect the security of ciphers used in hashing mode [5], [6].

The analysis of weak key schedules has led to guidelines for robust key schedule design that borrows from well-known and accepted design principles for block
cipher algorithms in the broader sense. Our design follows these key schedule
guidelines.

Acknowledging the existence of a basic and unavoidable trade-off between
speed and security, we believe that there is no pressing reason to choose the
fastest possible key schedule (that also possesses easily exploitable weaknesses)
whilst there exist reasonable compromise solutions that offer greatly increased
security robustness and yet are also efficient in implementation. In providing
security that is resistant to unknown future attacks, we can only speculate on

L. Batten and J. Seberry (Eds.): ACISP 2002, LNCS 2384, pp. 226–240, 2002.

requirements based on accumulated wisdom and expertise. There is no reason for not addressing currently identified security issues which are easily solvable today.

It should be noted that no attacks, including key-schedule attacks, on the full-round AES [7] algorithm have been found and published in the open literature; however, future analysis may reveal such an attack particularly extending to the complete cipher system as opposed to solely the encryption/decryption algorithm. The nature of block cipher attacks is one of exploiting the weakest parts of the cipher system. Most published attacks on other block cipher systems are based on finding round subkeys, often exploiting relationships between subkeys and/or the master key.

In this paper we review serious security weaknesses in the key schedule that assist published attacks on reduced-round versions of AES. In the case of future attack scenarios, these key schedule weaknesses are very likely to be used directly as attack points or to extend other attacks. A more secure key schedule for the AES cipher is presented and analysed. There is a slight speed decrease in the key schedule implementation, but this is not excessive, maintaining a significant advantage over the key schedule speed of the majority of other short-listed AES cipher candidates.

2   Block Cipher Key Schedules

The goal of a strong key schedule is to overcome any perceived weakness which may be used in attacking the block cipher system, either hypothetically or practically. In practice this goal is achievable, so there is no reason why a block cipher's key schedule should not be *strong* in the technical sense. Designers already use techniques to achieve Shannon's [8] bit confusion and bit diffusion properties in their cipher algorithms, so achieving similar properties in key schedules is a natural progression.

In 1993 Biham [2] showed that in certain cases, simple key schedules exhibit relationships between keys that may be exploited. In the same year Knudsen [9] listed four necessary but not sufficient properties for secure Feistel ciphers. Two of these, *no simple relations* and *all keys are equally good*, are achievable with strong key schedules. Table 1 translates the generic properties of a strong key schedule, as outlined by Knudsen, into properties which are readily measurable. These properties are simultaneously achievable.

Table 1. Desired key schedule properties

Property 1: collision-resistant one-way function (function is infeasible to invert)
Property 2: minimal mutual information (between all subkey bits and master key bits)
Property 3: efficient implementation

2.1 One-Way Function

A block cipher can be considered a one-way function when the encryption key is unknown. The practice of using a cipher algorithm in the generation of its subkeys is considered a satisfactory technique for providing the key schedule with the property of non-invertibility [10], [11], [12], [13]. Note that it is assumed that the cipher algorithm satisfies Shannon's bit confusion and bit diffusion properties (ie: it is a strong cipher algorithm). Property 3 is, in general, easier to satisfy if the one-way function is the cipher function itself.

2.2 Minimal Mutual Information

This property aims to eliminate bit leakage between subkeys and the master key, weaknesses that assist cryptanalysis by reducing the complexity of some attack scenarios on block ciphers. Examples range from differential and linear cryptanalysis of DES through to the AES attacks in [14] where the authors summarise that "*Some of our attacks make use of the relations between expanded key bytes and would have a higher complexity if these relations did not exist.*" Leakage of information from Subkey i to Subkey $i-1$ or Subkey $i+1$ is directly prevented by Property 1. Using master key bits directly in subkeys leads to the worst case of bit leakage; however this can be easily avoided.

2.3 Efficient Implementation

The cipher algorithm and the key schedule should complement each other in implementation aspects as well as security. It is advantageous that the execution time of a key schedule be of the same order of speed as the cipher itself, as for all of the short-listed AES candidates. By re-using already optimised components of the encryption algorithm and with some careful consideration during the key schedule design, a fast implementation is attainable, without the necessity for major additional cost in circuitry or code size due to design constraints.

3 The AES Key Schedule

The AES encryption algorithm is an iterative process where each of the n rounds ($n \in \{10, 12, 14\}$ for 128-, 192- and 256-bit master keys respectively) consists of a non-linear substitution, a linear transformation and a subkey addition. The key schedule generates the round subkeys from the master key. In this section the key schedule is analysed in detail. Possible weaknesses in the cipher introduced through this key schedule are highlighted.

3.1 Description of Key Schedule

The key schedule is required to produce eleven, thirteen or fifteen 128-bit round subkeys from master keys of size 128, 192 or 256 bits respectively. The schedule is based on 32-bit words. The initial words are set to equal the master key. The remainder of the words are generated by an iterative process. Consecutive groups of four 32-bit words are concatenated to produce the 128-bit subkeys.

Tables 2, 3 and 4 detail the AES key schedules for 128-bit, 192-bit and 256-bit keys respectively. In these tables: W[i] is a 32-bit word; SubByte(x), Rotl(x) and Rcon[y] are functions defined in [7]; SubByte(x) is the concatenation of the four S-box substitutions of the four eight-bit values making up the 32-bit word x; Rotl(x) is a byte-rotation of the 32-bit value x; and Rcon[y] is a defined constant.

Table 2. AES key schedule for 128-bit master key

```
for i = 0 to 3
  W[i] = MasterKey[i]
for j = 4 to 40 (in steps of 4)
  W[j] = W[j-4]⊕ SubByte(Rotl(W[j-1]))⊕ Rcon[j/4]
  for i = 1 to 3
    W[i+j] = W[i+j-4]⊕ W[i+j-1]
```

Table 3. AES key schedule for 192-bit master key

```
for i = 0 to 5
  W[i] = MasterKey[i]
for j = 6 to 48 (in steps of 6)
  W[j] = W[j-6]⊕ SubByte(Rotl(W[j-1]))⊕ Rcon[j/6]
  for i = 1 to 5 (and while i+j<52)
    W[i+j] = W[i+j-6]⊕ W[i+j-1]
```

Table 4. AES key schedule for 256-bit master key

```
for i = 0 to 7
  W[i] = MasterKey[i]
for j = 8 to 56 (in steps of 8)
  W[j] = W[j-8]⊕ SubByte(Rotl(W[j-1]))⊕ Rcon[j/8]
  for i = 1 to 3
    W[i+j] = W[i+j-8]⊕ W[i+j-1]
  W[j+4] = W[j-4]⊕ SubByte(W[j+1])
  for i = 5 to 7
    W[i+j] = W[i+j-8]⊕ W[i+j-1]
```

3.2   Previous Cryptanalysis

This section overviews AES analysis papers with the emphasis on relating attack scenarios to the AES key schedule properties.

The most prominent attack on reduced-round AES is the Square attack ([1], [7]), proposed by Daemen and Rijmen. AES inherits many properties from the Square cipher [1]. The basic attack on Square is a dedicated chosen-plaintext attack that exploits the byte-oriented structure of Square and ciphers built on Square such as AES to recover the last-round subkey of reduced-round versions. This attack is concerned with following the *balance* of certain data bytes as they progress through the cipher, where the term *balance* refers to the bitwise exclusive-or sum ($\oplus$) of the data bytes, with a zero sum indicating balance. At the fourth round the change in *balance* is exploited by this attack, enabling the entire fourth-round subkey to be determined from the output of a four-round encryption. The Square attack can be extended from a four-round attack up to an eight-round attack inclusive.

A second AES analysis paper is [14], in which the implementation of the Square attack was improved. Two key schedule properties were also discussed: *partial key guessing* and *key splitting*. Partial key guessing is analogous to bit leakage in the terms of this paper. Key splitting is the observation that the master key can be *split* into two halves, each half controlling half the subkeys. This property could not be exploited in an attack. The paper outlined a theoretical 9-round related-key attack which made extensive use of the key bit leakage property, also noting the very slow diffusion in the key schedule structure when compared to the cipher algorithm, and the relatively few non-linear elements in the key schedule.

3.3   Our Analysis

No attacks on full-round AES have been found and published; however, future analysis may reveal such an attack. In the previous section, [14] pointed out some very disturbing issues relating to the AES key schedule, especially in view of the fact that published attacks on other block ciphers are usually based on finding round subkeys. We also note that the Square attack, combined with the bit leakage property, recovers all the subkeys including the master key from knowledge of a single n-round subkey ($n \in \{4, 5, 6, 7, 8\}$).

The overriding security concern with the AES key schedule, therefore, is the fact that, given knowledge of a round-subkey (or part of a round-subkey), knowledge of other round-subkeys (or parts) is immediately derivable. (Properties 1 and 2 from Table 1 are not satisfied in the key schedule.)

We now explicitly define this key schedule bit leakage problem as a prelude to proposing a rectification. From the key schedule algorithms in Tables 2 to 4 it is noted that successive W[i] values (determined after the initialisation with the master key) are related to previous W[i] values. An example of this for the 128-bit key schedule is that knowledge of, say, W[41] and W[42] (64 bits of the Round 11 subkey) immediately give knowledge of W[38] (32 bits of the Round

10 subkey). This is achievable since $W[42] = W[38] \oplus W[41]$, and hence $W[38]$ is explicitly determined by evaluating $W[42] \oplus W[41]$. It is noted from Table 2 that every master key bit is not involved with the generation of the subkey bits until $W[6]$. The iterative nature of the key schedule is generally used to enhance implementation efficiency (Property 3 is satisfied); the problem, however, lies with the definition of the iteration itself being too simplistic which leads to the bit leakage problem.

Having defined the problem we wish to avoid in our new key schedule proposal, we now outline our approach to the new design. In general the cipher designer strives to obtain bit confusion (or mixing) and bit diffusion (each input bit affecting each output bit), concepts introduced by Shannon [8] in 1949. Much effort is spent in obtaining these properties in cipher algorithms; indeed, the AES cipher algorithm attains these properties very elegantly and succinctly by the fourth round. The key schedule, however, is somewhat less rigorous in obtaining these properties.

As a yardstick against which to measure the confusion and diffusion properties of the key schedule proposal against those of the original key schedule, we use two basic statistical tests readily available in software such as the CryptX [15] statistical package.

The frequency test was performed to measure the bit mixing property, a basic measure which is fundamental in achieving Shannon's *confusion* property and which is so apparently lacking in the key schedule (see Table 5). The result of this test is a single probability (p) value where a small p indicates a significant result. See [15] for more details. A p value greater than 0.01/0.001 indicates that bit mixing is satisfied at the 1%/0.1% critical level. The Strict Avalanche Criterion (SAC) test was performed as a measure of the bit diffusion property. This test checks that a one-bit change in the input block produces, on average, changes to half the bits in the output block, which is a good measure of Shannon's *diffusion* property. This property is also deficient in the key schedule (see Table 5).

Table 5. AES key schedule CryptX statistical test results

Round Subkey	Freq (p)	SAC (D*)
1	0.0000	125.053
2	0.0000	105.433
3	0.0000	72.563
4	0.0000	46.858
5	0.0593	31.840
6	0.0000	28.057
7	0.0000	28.153
8	0.0034	28.237
9	0.0000	28.161
10	0.0110	28.215

Table 6. AES cipher algorithm CryptX statistical test results

Round	Freq (p)	SAC (D^*)
2	0.0000	96.083
3	0.0048	20.687
4	0.7560	1.183

The resulting test statistic is the Kolmogorov-Smirnoff statistic denoted by D^*. See [15] for more details. A D^* value less than $1.628/1.949$ indicates that bit diffusion is satisfied at the $1\%/0.1\%$ critical level.

Test results for the AES encryption algorithm are detailed in Table 6, indicating that both the frequency and SAC tests are satisfied after four rounds.

In comparison to the AES cipher algorithm, the key schedule's test results, detailed in Table 5, are much less impressive. Row i, $1 \leq i \leq 10$, gives the test results after applying the frequency test and the SAC test to the Round i subkey. The majority of subkeys do not attain complete bit mixing. The process does not satisfy the SAC test for any of the subkeys. These test results on the key schedule support the findings in [14].

3.4 Implementation

The AES key schedule is very fast in implementation, both explicitly and when expressed as a ratio over a single block encryption. Table 7 lists timings for the five AES shortlisted block ciphers taken from two separate implementations [16], [17]. Note that these two implementations are also included in [18] in Tables A.1 and A.11 for single block encryption and key setup respectively for 128-bit data and 128-bit key C implementations on Pentium 32-bit processors. The third column under each reference is the ratio of key setup time to single block encryption time.

It is noted that the AES key setup time is the fastest. However, sections 3.2 and 3.3 indicate that this speed is attained at the cost of shortcomings in the key schedule's security properties. It is reasonable, therefore, to propose a modified key schedule which addresses the basic security concerns, even though the proposed schedule is slightly slower than the current schedule.

4   A New AES Key Schedule Proposal

The analysis in the previous section highlights the fact that the AES key schedule does not satisfy two of the three desirable properties outlined in Table 1, satisfying Property 3 only. The aim of this section is to define a suitable key schedule which satisfies the desired properties in Table 1.

Efficient bit mixing and bit diffusion techniques have already been developed for the AES cipher algorithm (as is evidenced by Table 6), so it seems a logical

Table 7. Timings in clock cycles on Intel Pentium for 128-bit key 32-bit processor C implementations

	Reference [16]			Reference [17]		
	Key	Encrypt	K:E	Key	Encrypt	K:E
MARS	6934	656	7.5	2118	364	5.8
RC6	2278	318	7.2	1697	269	6.3
Rijndael	1289	805	1.6	215	362	0.6
Serpent	6944	1261	5.5	1300	953	1.4
Twofish	9263	780	11.9	8520	366	23.3

progression to include these techniques in the production of a strong key schedule. Re-use of these already optimised operations also assists greatly in keeping the speed of the key schedule satisfactorily fast.

4.1   128-Bit Key Schedule Proposal

A proposed AES key schedule for 128-bit keys is detailed in Table 8, where NR=10 is the number of rounds, a, b are 128-bit values, $a = a_0|a_1|\cdots|a_{15}$ (the a_i are 8-bit values and | represents concatenation), r is the round number and KR_r is the 128-bit round subkey for Round r. It involves generating each round subkey independently of each other round subkey. Each round subkey is the 128-bit output after the execution of three rounds of the cipher algorithm, using the master key (with the addition of different round constants) as both data input and key input.

Table 8. Key schedule proposal for 128-bit keys

```
for r = 0 to NR
  for j = 0 to 15
    aj = bj = MKj ⊕ S[r * 16 + j]
  for i = 0 to 2
    ByteSub(a)
    ShiftRow(a)
    MixColumn(a)
    AddRoundKey(a,b)
  KRr = a
```

Table 9 gives CryptX test results for generating a single subkey where the number of AES encryption rounds used in the generation is given in the first column. These results indicate that, for each 128-bit round subkey generated using the proposed key schedule, complete bit mixing and bit diffusion is attained after three rounds; thus clarifying the decision to use three encryption rounds to generate each round subkey.

Table 9. Proposed 128-bit key schedule CryptX statistical test results

Round	Freq (p)	SAC (D*)
2	0.1557	15.775
3	0.8757	1.212
4	0.3498	1.689

Table 10. AES modified cipher algorithm CryptX statistical test results

Round	Freq (p)	SAC (D*)
2	0.0000	21.113
3	0.2663	1.282
4	0.3110	1.347

The reason that the SAC test is not satisfied until the fourth round of AES encryption (Table 6) is that the MixColumn operation is deleted from the final round. Table 10 gives CryptX test results where the encryption algorithm has been altered to include the MixColumn operation in the final round. The AES authors state that the MixColumn function was deleted from the final round *"in order to make the cipher and its inverse more similar in structure"*.

The most important achievement of the proposed key schedule is that the frequency and SAC tests are satisfied, thus ensuring complete bit confusion and diffusion is achieved for every subkey. This is in stark contrast to the AES key schedule which does not satisfy the frequency test in the majority of subkeys generated and does not satisfy the SAC test for any subkey.

Note that the master key itself is bitwise exclusive-ored into each of the three rounds (instead of three distinct round subkeys being bitwise exclusive-ored as in the case of encryption). The reason for this is so that a separate key schedule is not required. This bitwise exclusive-oring of the master key (in place of generated round subkeys) does not degrade the security of the schedule in any way. The addition of the constants at the start of each round subkey generation not only isolates each resulting subkey from the others, but also breaks up possible weak keys; for example, if all the master key bytes were identical. In the interests of openness and simplicity, the constants used are the S-box constants.

4.2   192-Bit and 256-Bit Key Schedule Proposals

Tables 11 and 12 are the proposals for the 192-bit and 256-bit key schedules where NR=12 and NR=14 respectively. The only difference from the 128-bit key schedule in Table 8 is in the initialisation of the a and b values.

As indicated in Table 13 (where $b = 0$) the value b in the proposed key schedule is not relevant to the statistical properties of the resulting subkeys. In the case of a 192-bit and 256-bit master key, however, the schedule needs some way to incorporate the remaining 64 and 128 bits respectively (after the first 128

Table 11. Key schedule proposal for 192-bit keys

for $r = 0$ to NR
for $j = 0$ to 15
$\quad a_j = MK_j \oplus S[r * 16 + j] \oplus S[MK_{j+8}]$
$\quad b_j = MK_{j+8} \oplus S[r * 16 + j] \oplus S[MK_j]$
for $i = 0$ to 2
$\quad$ ByteSub(a)
$\quad$ ShiftRow(a)
$\quad$ MixColumn(a)
$\quad$ AddRoundKey(a,b)
$KR_r = a$

Table 12. Key schedule proposal for 256-bit keys

for $r = 0$ to NR
for $j = 0$ to 15
$\quad a_j = MK_j \oplus S[r * 16 + j] \oplus S[MK_{j+16}]$
$\quad b_j = MK_{j+16} \oplus S[r * 16 + j] \oplus S[MK_j]$
for $i = 0$ to 2
$\quad$ ByteSub(a)
$\quad$ ShiftRow(a)
$\quad$ MixColumn(a)
$\quad$ AddRoundKey(a,b)
$KR_r = a$

Table 13. Modified proposed 128-bit key schedule CryptX statistical test results

Round	Freq (p)	SAC (D^*)
2	0.6683	22.218
3	0.9628	1.841
4	0.6827	1.226

bits have been assigned to the value a) in the algorithm. One simple method of doing this is to use these remaining bits as the value b.

Tables 14 and 15 give the test results for the algorithms in Tables 11 and 12 respectively. For this testing the 192-bit/256-bit test input data blocks are fed into the key schedule as the master key and the resulting 128-bit subkeys for a single round provide the test output data. The subkeys generated by these key schedules satisfy the frequency and SAC tests for bit confusion and diffusion after three rounds.

Note that an intrinsic feature of any key schedule that determines a 128-bit subkey from a 192- or 256-bit master key is that it will have key collisions (where a key collision is defined here as finding two 192-bit/256-bit master keys which produce identical 128-bit subkeys). This is unavoidable since the larger

Table 14. Proposed 192-bit key schedule CryptX statistical test results

Round	Freq (p)	SAC (D*)
2	0.5593	11.891
3	0.2002	1.268
4	0.2041	1.155

Table 15. Proposed 256-bit key schedule CryptX statistical test results

Round	Freq (p)	SAC (D*)
2	0.8900	21.158
3	0.6766	1.196
4	0.9029	1.189

number of bits in the master key is being reduced to a smaller number of bits in the subkey. What the key schedule should strive to avoid is large classes of master keys, which will allow a second master key to be generated such that a key collision occurs, which may then be used in an attack scenario. In the case of the proposed key schedule each subkey satisfies the SAC test. This means that, if even one bit of the master key is changed, then approximately half the bits of the subkey will change. This is the best diffusion that is attainable; therefore any key collisions which do occur are the one-off result of two randomly-chosen master keys, and will not form a class of weak keys.

4.3   Implementation Efficiency of the Proposed Key Schedule

For 128-bit keys the proposed key schedule requires thirty-three cipher encryption rounds (three per round for eleven rounds) to generate the eleven, round subkeys. Table 7 indicates timings, in clock cycles, for a complete encryption of a single block for 128-bit master key which is ten rounds. Note that the first subkey is used only for whitening. Thirty-three rounds, then, will have a key schedule to block encryption ratio of 3.3 for any implementation. (Ratios for 192-bit and 256-bit keys are $\frac{39}{12} = 3.25$ and $\frac{45}{14} \approx 3.21$ respectively.) These figures are summarised in Tables 16, 17 and 18. These are very respectable figures, especially bearing in mind that the proposed key schedule has substantially increased security over the original and is still faster than most of the other short-listed AES candidates.

4.4   Security Analysis of the Proposed Key Schedule

As each round subkey is generated independently in the proposal, there is no bit leakage between subkeys and other subkeys or the master key. The master key is not used directly as a subkey in the proposal. One-wayness is achieved by encrypting the master key both as the data block and the key block. High

Table 16. Comparison of speed (clock cycles) for 128-bit master key

128-bit key	Key setup	Encrypt one block	K:E
Reference [16]	1289	805	**1.60**
Reference [17]	215	362	**0.59**
Proposal	-	-	**3.30**

Table 17. Comparison of speed (clock cycles) for 192-bit master key

192-bit key	Key setup	Encrypt one block	K:E
Reference [16]	2000	981	**2.04**
Reference [17]	215	428	**0.50**
Proposal	-	-	**3.25**

Table 18. Comparison of speed (clock cycles) for 256-bit master key

256-bit key	Key setup	Encrypt one block	K:E
Reference [16]	2591	1155	**2.24**
Reference [17]	288	503	**0.57**
Proposal	-	-	**3.21**

bit diffusion of each master key bit across each subkey is attained. This is particularly useful in thwarting related-key attacks, as altering even one bit in the master key changes approximately half the bits in each subkey. Since this feature is easily included in the design of a strong key schedule, it is included for completeness.

In the case of specific methods of cryptanalysis, conventional techniques applied to three rounds of the AES cipher algorithm, such as differential cryptanalysis or the Square attack, do not hold for direct attacks upon the proposed key schedule. These attacks typically require collections of chosen- or known-plaintexts. The analogs of these texts, as keys, are not available under the conditions of related-key attacks.

The minimum assumption for a key-schedule attack is that, given a known difference between subkeys, there is a mapping to an exploitable feature within the cipher algorithm. We could find no such mapping, so it is hard to see how conventional differential or linear cryptanalysis could weaken the proposed key schedule.

Standard related-key attacks [2] do not work, due to the strong non-linearity present in the schedule, the addition of constants to each of the master key bytes and the fact that each subkey satisfies the Strict Avalanche Criterion test.

In a differential related-key attack based upon the Square attack, a single plaintext is repeatedly encrypted under a set of 256 master keys, a Λ-set [7], where a single byte of each differs such that the binary sum of the texts is zero. However, we could find no way to practically exploit this.

A generic attack solicits some round subkey bits by forceful means. In contrast to the current AES key schedule, even if an entire 128-bit round subkey is known, it is infeasible to invert the three-round function and retrieve the master key. It is not possible to obtain subkey bits from one round using material purely from another. A prime example of this is the Square attack on reduced-round AES cipher versions which, when combined with the bit leakage property of the key schedule, recovers all the subkeys including the master key. Since our proposed key schedule does not allow bit leakage, its adoption would prevent this extension of the Square attack.

We believe the proposed key schedule to be safe from conventional methods of cryptanalysis.

5   Conclusion

We described and analysed the AES key schedule in detail, and provided an overview of AES analysis papers. We presented and analysed a strengthened key schedule, based upon information principles introduced by Claude Shannon in his seminal 1949 paper [8]. These principles still permeate the broader area of cryptographic design. Block cipher key schedules have not received the same focus as cipher algorithm design in the past, but are none-the-less vital to the overall security of the cipher system. A weak schedule can provide a *back door* through which an otherwise secure cipher system is attacked. As it is a relatively simple process to achieve Shannon's bit confusion and diffusion properties in our key schedule designs, it is most prudent for designers to do so. Published attacks on AES have been curtailed (to varying degrees), simply by designing a key schedule which adheres to basic communication theory but still maintains the extremely high cipher speed.

It was shown that the current 128-bit key schedule does not satisfy the bit frequency mixing test for the majority of subkeys and does not satisfy the avalanche (bit diffusion) test for any of the round subkeys. This indicates poor pseudorandomness properties in the key schedule. There is also the problem of bit leakage between subkeys which is exploited in some attack scenarios increasing the potency of the attack.

In contrast, for the proposed key schedule, every round subkey is effectively independent from each other round subkey, hence there is no bit leakage between round subkeys. Each round subkey also satisfies both the frequency and SAC tests indicating good pseudorandomness properties, in particular bit confusion and diffusion which is the basis of secure communications.

Table 19 compares speed ratios of key setup to single block encryption times for two implementations of AES and extrapolated speeds for AES using the proposed key schedules in Tables 8, 11 and 12. The ratio of the implementation of the

Table 19. Speed ratios of key-setup time to single block encryption

	Master key size		
	128	192	256
Reference [16]	1.60	2.04	2.24
Reference [17]	0.59	0.50	0.57
Proposal	3.30	3.25	3.21

proposed key schedules is approximately three times a single block encryption. The proposed key schedule is faster than the published instances of key schedule implementation of four short-listed AES cipher candidates (the exceptions being AES and one implementation of Serpent). These times are acceptable for the proposed key schedules (Tables 8, 11 and 12) used in AES for the majority of applications, especially as the proposed schedules have substantially increased the security of the cipher.

The primary goal of a symmetric block cipher is to provide security, with its speed of implementation a very important secondary goal. This proposal achieves increased security by limiting the extent to which previously published attacks can exploit the key schedule, at a very modest increase in initial key setup times.

References

1. J.Daemen, L.Knudsen and V.Rijmen. *The Block Cipher SQUARE*, Fast Software Encryption, Fourth International Workshop, LNCS 1267, Springer-Verlag, 1997, pp 149-165.
2. E.Biham. *New Types of Cryptanalytic Attacks using Related Keys*, Advances in Cryptology–EUROCRYPT'93, LNCS 765, Springer-Verlag, 1993, pp 398-409.
3. J.Daemen, R.Govaerts and J.Vandewalle. *Weak Keys for IDEA*, Advances in Cryptology–CRYPTO'93, LNCS 773, Springer-Verlag, 1993, pp 224-231.
4. L.Knudsen. *New Potentially Weak Keys for DES and LOKI*, Advances in Cryptology–EUROCRYPT'94, LNCS 950, Springer-Verlag, 1994, pp 419-424.
5. L.Knudsen. *Cryptanalysis of LOKI91*, AUSCRYPT'92, LNCS 718, Springer-Verlag, 1992, pp 196-208.
6. L.Knudsen. *A Key-Schedule Weakness in SAFER K-64*, Advances in Cryptology–CRYPTO'95, LNCS 963, Springer-Verlag, 1995, pp 274-286.
7. J.Daemen and V.Rijmen. *Rijndael*, First Advanced Encryption Standard Conference, August, 1998. Available at http://csrc.nist.gov/encryption/aes/.
8. C.E.Shannon. *Communication Theory of Secrecy Systems*, Bell System Technical Journal, ol.28, October 1949, pp 656-715.
9. L.Knudsen. *Practically Secure Feistel Ciphers*, Fast Software Encryption, First International Workshop Proceedings, LNCS 809, Springer-Verlag, 1993, pp 211-221.
10. M.Leech. *A Feistel Cipher with Hardened Key Scheduling*, Workshop on Selected Areas in Cryptography (SAC'96), pp 15-29.
11. V.Rijmen, J.Daemen, B.Preneel, A.Bosselaers and E.DeWin. *The Cipher SHARK*, Fast Software Encryption, Third International Workshop, LNCS 1039, Springer-Verlag, 1996, pp 99-111.

12. B.Schneier. *Description of a New Variable-Length Key, 64-bit Block Cipher (Blowfish)*, Fast Software Encryption, First International Workshop, LNCS 809, Springer-Verlag, 1993, pp 191-204.

13. K.Aoki, T.Ichikawa, M.Kanda, M.Matsui, S. Moriai, J. Nakajima and T. Tokita. *Camellia: A 128-Bit Block Cipher Suitable for Multiple Platforms - Design and Analysis*, Workshop on Selected Areas in Cryptography (SAC 2000), LNCS 2012, pp 39-56.

14. N.Ferguson, J.Kelsey, S.Lucks, B.Schneier, M.Stay, D.Wagner and D.Whiting. *Improved Cryptanalysis of Rijndael*, Fast Software Encryption, Seventh International Workshop, LNCS 1978, Springer-Verlag, 2000, pp 213-230.

15. H.Gustafson, E.Dawson, L.Nielsen and W.Caelli. *A Computer Package for Measuring the Strength of Ciphers*, Journal of Computers and Security, Vol.13, No.8, pp 687-697.

16. L.Bassham. *Efficiency Testing of ANSI C Implementations of Round 2 Candidate Algorithms for the Advanced Encryption Standard*, Third Advanced Encryption Standard Conference, April 2000. Available at http://csrc.nist.gov/encryption/aes/

17. B.Gladman. *AES Second Round Implementation Experience*, Second Advanced Encryption Standard Conference, Available at http://www.nist.gov/aes.

18. National Institute of Standards and Technology (NIST) (Computer Security Division), *Report on the Development of the Advanced Encryption Standard (AES)*, Available at http://www.nist.gov/aes

On the Necessity of Strong Assumptions for the Security of a Class of Asymmetric Encryption Schemes

Ron Steinfeld[1], Joonsang Baek[1], and Yuliang Zheng[2]

[1] School of Network Computing, Monash University, McMahons Road, Frankston,
VIC 3199, Australia
{joonsang.baek,ron.steinfeld}@infotech.monash.edu.au
[2] Dept. Software and Info. Systems, UNC Charlotte, NC 28223, USA
yzheng@uncc.edu

Abstract. Recently various public key encryption.schemes such as
DHIES by Abdalla, Bellare and Rogaway and REACT by Okamoto and
Pointcheval, whose security against adaptive chosen ciphertext attack
(CCA) is based on the Gap problems, have been proposed. Although
the Gap problems were proved to be a sufficient assumption for those
schemes to be secure against adaptive chosen-cipertext attack, a necessary condition for CCA security of those schemes has not been explicitly
discussed.

In this paper we clarify the necessary condition for CCA security of those
schemes. Namely we prove (in the random oracle model) that the Gap
Diffie-Hellman is not only sufficient, but also a *necessary* assumption for
the CCA security of DHIES and Diffie-Hellman version of REACT. We
also show that our result applies to a wider class of public key encryption
schemes. Furthermore we show that our result implies the equivalence,
in the random oracle model, between 'Strong Diffie-Hellman' and 'Oracle
Diffie-Hellman' assumptions proposed by Abdalla, Bellare and Rogaway.
Our results may be used as criteria for distinguishing public key encryption schemes whose CCA security is based on strong assumptions (such
as Gap Diffie-Hellman) from those schemes based on weaker ones (such
as Computational Diffie-Hellman).

1 Introduction

The design of practical public-key encryption schemes which are secure against
powerful attacks, namely adaptive chosen ciphertext attacks, has been a very
active research topic since the early work of Zheng and Seberry [6]. Recently,
a simple and efficient public key encryption scheme called 'Diffie-Hellman In-
tegrated Encryption Scheme (DHIES)', was proposed and analysed by Abdalla
Bellare and Rogaway [4]. In [4], the authors state that due to technical problems, it seems hard to prove that the scheme DHIES is secure against adaptive
Chosen Ciphertext Attack (CCA) assuming only the standard 'Computational
Diffie-Hellman' (CDH) assumption holds in the underlying group, and the random oracle model [2] for the hash function used in the scheme. Instead, the

L. Batten and J. Seberry (Eds.): ACISP 2002, LNCS 2384, pp. 241–256, 2002.

authors proved that the DHIES scheme is secure against adaptive chosen ciphertext attack in the random oracle model with respect to a strong computational
assumption on the underlying group called 'Strong Diffie-Hellman' (SDH) and
even secure in the standard model (i.e., not assuming the underlying hash function behaves as a random oracle) if another strong assumption called 'Oracle
Diffie-Hellman (ODH)' is considered.

In this paper we clarify the technical problems in proving that DHIES is
secure against adaptive chosen-ciphertext attack in the random oracle model
assuming the CDH assumption. We present a simple chosen ciphertext attack
which efficiently breaks DHIES if the SDH assumption does not hold. That is,
we show that SDH is not only sufficient, but also a *necessary* assumption for
the CCA security of DHIES. Our attack shows that the technical difficulties
in proving DHIES is as secure as the CDH assumption cannot be overcome by
a more careful analysis of the scheme DHIES. Rather, the problem is purely
a computational one in the underlying group, namely to prove that SDH is
equivalent to CDH. As an application of our work we also clarify the relationship
between the two new assumptions introduced by the authors of [4], 'Oracle Diffie-
Hellman' (ODH) and 'Strong Diffie-Hellman' (SDH). We show that these two
assumptions are in fact equivalent in the random oracle model.

As an extension of our work we consider Okamoto and Pointcheval' recent scheme called 'Rapid Enhanced-Security Asymmetric Cryptosystem Transform' (REACT) [5]. This transformation converts any 'weakly secure' encryption scheme (namely a 'One-Way Plaintext Checking Attacker', or OW-PCA)
scheme) into an encryption scheme secure against adaptive chosen-cipertext attack in the random oracle model. We show that a variation of our attack breaks
REACT in the CCA sense if the OW-PCA assumption does not hold, i.e. OW-
PCA is necessary as well as sufficient for the CCA security of REACT.

To emphasize the generality of our attack we present it in the following way.
We consider a primitive called a 'Key Encapsulation Mechanism (KEM)' [7] in-
spired by the Diffie-Hellman function, and propose a corresponding 'OW-PCA'
notion for it. This primitive can be simpler than a 'weakly secure encryption
scheme', since it only needs to generate a uniformly distributed key and a ciphertext for it, rather than encrypting specified input messages. Then we describe
two variants 'CCAKEM1' and 'CCAKEM2' of a conversion from any KEM to an
encryption scheme secure against adaptive chosen-ciphertext attack in the random oracle model. The first variant CCAKEM1 uses one random oracle and one
Message Authentication Code (MAC) and includes DHIES as a special instance
in which the KEM is the Diffie-Hellman one. The second variant CCAKEM2
uses two random oracles and includes REACT as a subclass in which the KEM
is implemented using an encryption scheme. We present variations of our attack for both CCAKEM1 and CCAKEM2 if the 'OW-PCA' assumption on the
KEM does not hold. This implies as special cases the above-mentioned attacks
on DHIES and REACT.

2 Preliminaries

In this section we review the KEM, and define a security notion for it called 'One-Wayness under Plaintext Checking Attacks' (OW-PCA). This notion is analogous to the OW-PCA notion defined for encryption schemes by Okamoto and Pointcheval in [5]. Note that definitions of asymmetric encryption schemes, symmetric encryption schemes, and MAC and the standard security notions for them are given in the Appendix.

2.1 Notation

We use the notation $A(.,.)$ to denote an algorithm, with input arguments separated by commas (our underlying computational model is a probabilistic Turing Machine). If algorithm A makes calls to oracles, we list the oracles separated from the algorithm inputs by the symbol '|'. Given a set SP_{sk} we denote by $sk \xleftarrow{R} SP_{sk}$ the assignment of a uniformly and independently distributed random element from the set SP_{sk} to the variable sk. Given an element $h \in \{0,1\}^k$, we denote by $h[i, ..., j]$ the substring of h consisting of the bits at positions i to j (where bit 1 is by convention the rightmost bit). We use the notation $\Pr[\text{Event}]_{exp}$ to denote the probability of event Event in experiment exp.

2.2 Key Encapsulation Mechanism (KEM)

The KEM is defined as follows.

Definition 1. *A Key Encapsulation Mechanism (KEM) consists of 3 algorithms:*

1 *Key-Pair Generation Algorithm* $\mathsf{GK}(k)$ — *Takes a security parameter $k \in \mathbb{N}$ and generates a secret and public key pair (sk, pk).*
2 *Random Key Encryption Algorithm* $\mathsf{E}_{pk}^{\mathsf{KEM}}(r)$ — *Takes a recipient's public key pk and a random string $r \in SP_R$, and outputs a pair (K, c), where $K \in SP_K$ is a key and c is a ciphertext for K.*
3 *Random Key Decryption Algorithm* $\mathsf{D}_{sk}^{\mathsf{KEM}}(c)$ — *Takes a recipient's secret key sk and a ciphertext c and outputs a decrypted key K.*

We require that for every key pair (sk, pk) output by $\mathsf{GK}(k)$ and each $r \in SP_R$, it is the case that if $(K, c) = \mathsf{E}_{pk}^{\mathsf{KEM}}(r)$ then $\mathsf{D}_{sk}^{\mathsf{KEM}}(c) = K$.

Example. The Diffie-Hellman KEM (DHKEM) in a multiplicatively-written group G is described as follows.

1 Algorithm $\mathsf{GK}(k)$ outputs common parameters (d_G, g, q) consisting of description d_G of a finite cyclic group G, a generator $g \in G$ and the order q of G and chooses $x \xleftarrow{R} \mathbb{Z}_q$ and computes $y \leftarrow g^x$ in G. It outputs (sk, pk), where $sk = x$ and $pk = (d_G, g, q, y)$.

2 Algorithm $\mathsf{E}_{\mathsf{pk}}^{\mathsf{DHKEM}}(r)$ accepts $r \xleftarrow{R} \mathbb{Z}_q$, computes key $K \leftarrow y^r$ and ciphertext $c \leftarrow g^r$ and outputs (K, c).

3 Algorithm $\mathsf{D}_{\mathsf{sk}}^{\mathsf{DHKEM}}(c)$ computes $K \leftarrow c^x$ and outputs K.

Notice that the DHKEM is simpler than the Diffie-Hellman-based El-Gamal encryption scheme because in KEM there is no need to encrypt a specified input message, only to encrypt a key derived from the input random string. Of course, any public-key encryption scheme can also function as an KEM by setting $K = r$, where r is a random message, and c is the encryption of r.

Analogously to [5], we define the 'OW-PCA security notion for an KEM as follows. First a plaintext checking oracle is defined.

Definition 2. (Plaintext Checking Oracle) *Given a Key Encapsulation Mechanism* $\mathsf{KEM} = (\mathsf{GK}, \mathsf{E}^{\mathsf{KEM}}, \mathsf{D}^{\mathsf{KEM}})$ *and a key pair* (sk, pk) *output by* GK, *we define an associated* Plaintext Checking Oracle *(PCO) algorithm* $\mathsf{PCO}_{\mathsf{KEM},\mathsf{sk}}(\cdot,\cdot)$, *where given a key* $K \in SP_K$ *and a ciphertext* c, $\mathsf{PCO}_{\mathsf{KEM},\mathsf{sk}}(K, c)$ *returns 1 if* $\mathsf{D}_{\mathsf{sk}}^{\mathsf{KEM}}(c) = K$ *and else returns 0.*

Then the OW-PCA notion is defined in a quantitative way.

Definition 3. (OW-PCA) *Let* $\mathsf{KEM} = (\mathsf{GK}, \mathsf{E}^{\mathsf{KEM}}, \mathsf{D}^{\mathsf{KEM}})$ *be a KEM. Let* A *be an attack algorithm. Define the experiment*

Experiment **OWPCAExp**$(k, \mathsf{KEM}, \mathsf{A})$

   $(sk, pk) \leftarrow \mathsf{GK}(k)$

   $r \xleftarrow{R} SP_R; (K, c) \leftarrow \mathsf{E}_{\mathsf{pk}}^{\mathsf{KEM}}(r)$

   $K' \leftarrow \mathsf{A}(pk, c | \mathsf{PCO}_{\mathsf{KEM},\mathsf{sk}}(\cdot, \cdot))$

   If $K' = K$ then **Return** 1 else **Return** 0

We quantify A's *success in breaking the OW-PCA notion of* KEM *by the probability* $\mathbf{Succ}_{\mathsf{A},\mathsf{KEM}}^{\mathrm{OW-PCA}}(k) \overset{\text{def}}{=} \Pr[\mathbf{OWPCAExp}(k, \mathsf{KEM}, \mathsf{A}) = 1]$. *We define* A's *resource parameters as* $RP = (t, q_{PC})$ *if* A *has running time/program size at most* t *and makes at most* q_{PC} *queries to the PCO oracle.*

Note that the attacker A is allowed to query the part of challenge ciphertext c.

3   The Transforms 'CCAKEM1' and 'CCAKEM2'

In this section we define the two transformations schemes 'CCAKEM1' and 'CCAKEM2' which convert any OW-CPA key encapsulation mechanism into an asymmetric encryption scheme secure against adaptive chosen ciphertext attack in the random oracle model, and explain how REACT and DHIES are related to them.

3.1   Transform CCAKEM1

The transform 'CCAKEM1' takes (1) A key encapsulation mechanism $\mathsf{KEM} = (\mathsf{GK}^{\mathsf{KEM}}, \mathsf{E}^{\mathsf{KEM}}, \mathsf{D}^{\mathsf{KEM}})$, (2) A MAC $\mathsf{MAC} = (\mathsf{MACG}, \mathsf{MACV})$ with key space $\{0,1\}^{l_m}$, (3) An IND-CPA symmetric encryption scheme $\mathsf{SYM} = (\mathsf{E}^{\mathsf{SYM}}, \mathsf{D}^{\mathsf{SYM}})$ with key space $\{0,1\}^{l_e}$, and (4) A hash function $H : \{0,1\}^* \rightarrow \{0,1\}^{l_e+l_m}$, modelled as a random oracle [2], and constructs an asymmetric encryption scheme $\mathsf{CCAKEM1} = (\mathsf{GK}^{\mathsf{CCAKEM1}}, \mathsf{E}^{\mathsf{CCAKEM1}}, \mathsf{D}^{\mathsf{CCAKEM1}})$ as follows.

Transform CCAKEM1

$$\mathsf{GK}^{\mathsf{CCAKEM1}}(k)$$
$$(sk, pk) \leftarrow \mathsf{GK}^{\mathsf{KEM}}(k)$$
$$\mathbf{Return}\ (sk, pk)$$

$$\mathsf{E}_{pk}^{\mathsf{CCAKEM1}}(m)$$
$$r \xleftarrow{R} SP_R$$
$$(K, c) \leftarrow \mathsf{E}_{pk}^{\mathsf{KEM}}(r)$$
$$h \leftarrow H(K, c)$$
$$km \leftarrow h[1, ..., l_m]$$
$$ke \leftarrow h[l_m + 1, ..$$
$$..., l_m + l_e]$$
$$c_s \leftarrow \mathsf{E}_{ke}^{\mathsf{SYM}}(m)$$
$$\sigma_s \leftarrow \mathsf{MACG}_{km}(c_s)$$
$$\mathbf{Return}\ (c, c_s, \sigma_s)$$

$$\mathsf{D}_{sk}^{\mathsf{CCAKEM1}}((c, c_s, \sigma_s))$$
$$K \leftarrow \mathsf{D}_{sk}^{\mathsf{KEM}}(c)$$
$$h \leftarrow H(K, c)$$
$$km \leftarrow h[1, ..., l_m]$$
$$ke \leftarrow h[l_m + 1, ..., l_m + l_e]$$
$$m \leftarrow \mathsf{D}_{ke}^{\mathsf{SYM}}(c_s)$$
$$d \leftarrow \mathsf{MACV}_{km}(c_s, \sigma_s)$$
$$\text{If } d = Acc\ \mathbf{Return}\ m$$
$$\text{Else } \mathbf{Return}\ Rej$$

Observe that this scheme is a very natural one for performing 'hybrid encryption'. To encrypt a message m, one first uses the KEM to encapsulate a 'session key' K into a KEM ciphertext c. Then the session key (and ciphertext c) is hashed using $H(.)$ to derive two symmetric keys: one key ke is used encrypt m into a ciphertext c_s using the symmetric encryption scheme and another key km is used to generate a MAC tag σ_s on the symmetric ciphertext c_s using the MAC scheme. The decryption algorithm recovers the session key K and then the symmetric keys, checking the MAC tag for validity before decrypting c_s to recover m.

We remark that by setting the scheme KEM to be the Diffie-Hellman KEM described in the previous section, this transformation yields the DHIES scheme, and the OW-PCA assumption on the KEM becomes the 'Strong Diffie-Hellman' Assumption (SDH): given (g^a, g^b), compute g^{ab} given a fixed-input Decision Diffie-Hellman (DDH) oracle, which given a pair of group elements (y, z) decides whether $z = y^a$ or not.

3.2   Transform CCAKEM2

The transform 'CCAKEM2' takes (1) A key encapsulation mechanism KEM = $(\mathsf{GK}^{\mathsf{ARK}}, \mathsf{E}^{\mathsf{KEM}}, \mathsf{D}^{\mathsf{KEM}})$, (2) An IND-CPA-secure Symmetric encryption scheme SYM = $(\mathsf{E}^{\mathsf{SYM}}, \mathsf{D}^{\mathsf{SYM}})$ with key space $\{0,1\}^{l_e}$, and (3) Two hash functions $H_1 : \{0,1\}^* \rightarrow \{0,1\}^{l_e}$ and $H_2 : \{0,1\}^* \rightarrow \{0,1\}^{l_\sigma}$, both modeled as random oracles, and constructs an asymmetric encryption scheme CCAKEM2 = $(\mathsf{GK}^{\mathsf{CCAKEM2}}, \mathsf{E}^{\mathsf{CCAKEM2}}, \mathsf{D}^{\mathsf{CCAKEM2}})$ as follows.

Transform CCAKEM2

$$\mathsf{GK}^{\mathsf{CCAKEM2}}(k)$$
$$(sk, pk) \leftarrow \mathsf{GK}^{\mathsf{KEM}}(k)$$
$$\mathbf{Return}\ (sk, pk)$$

$$\mathsf{E}_{pk}^{\mathsf{CCAKEM2}}(m)$$
$$r \xleftarrow{R} SP_R; (K, c) \leftarrow \mathsf{E}_{pk}^{\mathsf{KEM}}(r)$$
$$ke \leftarrow H_1(K, c)$$
$$c_s \leftarrow \mathsf{E}_{ke}^{\mathsf{SYM}}(m)$$
$$\sigma_s \leftarrow H_2(K, m, c, c_s)$$
$$\mathbf{Return}\ (c, c_s, \sigma_s)$$

$$\mathsf{D}_{sk}^{\mathsf{CCAKEM2}}((c, c_s, \sigma_s))$$
$$K \leftarrow \mathsf{D}_{sk}^{\mathsf{KEM}}(c)$$
$$ke \leftarrow H_1(K, c)$$
$$m \leftarrow \mathsf{D}_{ke}^{\mathsf{SYM}}(c_s)$$
$$d \leftarrow H_2(K, m, c, c_s)$$
$$\text{If } d = \sigma_s\ \mathbf{Return}\ m$$
$$\text{Else } \mathbf{Return}\ Rej$$

This scheme uses a similar natural approach as the previous one but using a second hash function for tagging the ciphertext. To encrypt a message m, one first uses the KEM to encapsulate a 'session key' K into a KEM ciphertext c. Then the session key is hashed using $H_1(.)$ to derive a symmetric encryption key ke used encrypt m into a ciphertext c_s using the symmetric encryption scheme. Then a tag σ_s is also generated using hash function $H_2(.)$ by hashing all of K, m, c, c_s. The decryption algorithm recovers the session key K and then the symmetric key ke and the decrypted message m, checking hash tag σ_s for validity before returning m.

We observe that by implementing the scheme KEM using a public key encryption scheme, namely by choosing a random message element as the key K and encrypting it, we obtain the REACT transformation. The OW-PCA assumption on the KEM becomes the OW-PCA assumption on the encryption scheme. As observed in [5], the OW-PCA assumption is equivalent to just the one-wayness assumption in the case of a deterministic encryption scheme with a one-to-one decryption algorithm (such as RSA), since the PC oracle can be implemented by re-encryption.

4   The Attacks

Now we present our attacks on the above conversions, assuming that the underlying KEM is *not* OW-PCA.

4.1   Attack on CCAKEM1 If the Underlying KEM Is Not OW-PCA

Theorem 1. *Let* A^{PC} *be an attack algorithm with resource parameters* (t^{PC}, q_{PC}) *for breaking OW-PCA of the key encapsulation mechanism* KEM. *Then we can construct an attack algorithm* $\mathsf{A}^{\mathsf{CC}} = (\mathsf{A}^{\mathsf{CC}}_{\mathsf{find}}, \mathsf{A}^{\mathsf{CC}}_{\mathsf{guess}})$ *with resource parameters* (t^{CC}, q_D, q_H) *such that*

$$\mathbf{Succ}^{\mathsf{CCA}}_{\mathsf{A}^{\mathsf{CC}}, \mathsf{CCAKEM1}}(k) \geq \mathbf{Succ}^{\mathsf{OW-PCA}}_{\mathsf{A}, \mathsf{KEM}}(k) - 2(q_{PC}+2)\mathbf{InSec}^{\mathsf{MAC-UF}}_{\mathsf{MAC}}(t^{CC}, 0, q_{PC})$$

and $t^{CC} = t^{PC} + (q_{PC} + 1)(O(1) + t_{MAC})$, $q_D = q_{PC}$, $q_H = 2q_{PC} + 1$ *(here* t_{MAC} *denotes the time to evaluate* MACG *or* MACV*).*

Proof. We construct CCA attacker A^{CC}. The idea of the construction is simple — A^{CC} essentially runs A^{PC} on the OW-PCA instance of KEM corresponding to the challenge ciphertext given to A^{CC}, and simulates the $\mathsf{PCO}_{\mathsf{KEM},\mathsf{sk}}(.,.)$ oracle to which A^{PC} makes queries, using the decryption oracle $\mathsf{D}^{\mathsf{CCAKEM1}}_{\mathsf{sk}}(.)$. Although the PC oracle simulation is not perfect, we will bound its error probability using the assumed bound on the insecurity of the MAC scheme.

We first give a detailed definition of the two sub-attacker algorithms $\mathsf{A}^{\mathsf{CC}}_{\mathsf{find}}$ and $\mathsf{A}^{\mathsf{CC}}_{\mathsf{guess}}$ making up A, as well as the PCO simulator algorithm $\mathsf{PCOSim}(.,.)$ which is used to answer the PCO queries of A^{PC} when the latter is run by $\mathsf{A}^{\mathsf{CC}}_{\mathsf{guess}}$. Then we analyse the attack to prove the claims of the theorem.

CCA Attacker $\mathsf{A^{CC}}$ against Scheme **CCAKEM1**

$\mathsf{A^{CC}_{find}}(pk|\mathsf{D^{CCAKEM1}_{sk}}(.))$ (Find Stage)
 Let m_0 and m_1 denote distinct messages in SP_M^{SYM}.
 $s \leftarrow (m_0, m_1)$
 Return (m_0, m_1, s)
$\mathsf{A^{CC}_{guess}}(pk, m_0, m_1, s, (c, c_s, \sigma_s)|\mathsf{D^{CCAKEM1}_{sk}}(.))$ (Guess Stage)
 $K' \leftarrow \mathsf{A^{PC}}(pk, c|\mathsf{PCOSim}(.,.))$
 $h' \leftarrow H(K', c)$
 $km' \leftarrow h'[1, ..., l_m];\ ke' \leftarrow h'[l_m + 1, ..., l_m + l_e]$
 If $d' \stackrel{\mathrm{def}}{=} \mathsf{MACV}_{km'}(c_s, \sigma_s) = \text{`Rej'}$ then $b' \stackrel{R}{\leftarrow} \{0, 1\}$
 Else
  $m' \leftarrow \mathsf{D^{SYM}_{ke'}}(c_s)$
  If $m' = m_j$ for $j \in \{0, 1\}$ then $b' \leftarrow j$ Else $b' \stackrel{R}{\leftarrow} \{0, 1\}$
 Return b'
$\mathsf{PCOSim}(K[i], c[i]\|H(.), \mathsf{D^{CCAKEM1}_{sk}}(.))$ (PCO Simulator)
 $h[i] \leftarrow H(K[i], c[i])$
 $km[i] \leftarrow h[i][1, ..., l_m];\ ke[i] \leftarrow h[i][l_m + 1, ..., l_m + l_e]$
 Find $j \in \{0, 1\}$ such that $c_s[i] \stackrel{\mathrm{def}}{=} \mathsf{E^{SYM}_{ke[i]}}(m_j) \neq c_s$
 $\sigma_s[i] \leftarrow \mathsf{MACG}_{km[i]}(c_s[i])$
 $d[i] \leftarrow \mathsf{D^{CCAKEM1}_{sk}}(c[i], c_s[i], \sigma_s[i])$
 (note: we define $km'[i] = h'[i] \leftarrow H(\mathsf{D^{KEM}_{sk}}(c[i]), c[i])$)
 If $d[i] \neq Rej$ then **Return** 1
 Else **Return** 0

We have not shown above the actions of the 'CCAExp' experiment while running $\mathsf{A^{CC}}$, which are described in definition 4 . Namely, before running $\mathsf{A^{CC}}$, a KEM key pair (sk, pk) is generated and $\mathsf{A^{CC}_{find}}$ is given the public key pk, and access to the decryption oracle $\mathsf{D^{CCAKEM1}_{sk}}(.)$, which makes use of the secret key sk, and the random oracle $H(.)$. When $\mathsf{A^{CC}_{find}}$ outputs the pair of messages m_0 and m_1, an independent and uniform bit b is chosen and the challenge ciphertext $\mathsf{E^{CCAKEM1}_{pk}}(m_b) = (c, c_s, \sigma_s)$ is generated. We denote by $K \stackrel{\mathrm{def}}{=} \mathsf{D^{KEM}_{sk}}(c)$ the encapsulated key used to generate the challenge ciphertext, and hence the portion (c_s, σ_s) of the challenge ciphertext satisfies $m_b = \mathsf{D^{SYM}_{ke}}(c_s)$, and $\mathsf{MACV}_{km}(c_s, \sigma_s) = Acc$, where $km = h[1, ..., l_m]$ and $ke = h[l_m + 1, ..., l_m + l_e]$ and $h = H(K, c)$. The challenge (c, c_s, σ_s) is given to $\mathsf{A^{CC}_{guess}}$ and when $\mathsf{A^{CC}_{guess}}$ outputs the guess bit b', it is compared with b and 'CCAExp' returns 1 if and only if $b' = b$.

Now we show that $\mathsf{A^{CC}}$ satisfies the claims of the theorem. In the following, we use the notation $\Pr[\mathsf{Event}]_{exp}$ to denote the probability of event Event in experiment exp (if no subscript is given it refers to experiment sim defined below). We first define two experiments: (1) Experiment $real$ denotes the 'OWPCAExp' experiment in definition 3 running with attacker $\mathsf{A^{PC}}$ whose queries are answered by the real PC Oracle. (2) Experiment sim denotes the above 'CCAExp' experiment running with attacker $\mathsf{A^{CC}}$ which runs $\mathsf{A^{PC}}$ and answers its queries with the simulator PCOSim. We define in this experiment the event $\mathsf{SuccSim}$ that the 'CCA-Exp' experiment returns 1. Hence $\mathbf{Succ}^{CCA}_{\mathsf{A^{CC}},\mathsf{CCAKEM1}}(k) \stackrel{\mathrm{def}}{=} 2(\Pr[\mathsf{SuccSim}]_{sim} - \frac{1}{2})$.

Also we let $(K[j], c[j])$ denote the j'th query of A^{PC} to its PCO oracle, and we define $(K[0], c[0]) \overset{\text{def}}{=} (K, c)$ to be the challenge key-ciphertext pair.

Define the following events:

1 SuccA: $\mathsf{A}^{\mathsf{PC}}(pk, c|\mathsf{PCO}_{\mathsf{sk}}(.,.)) = \mathsf{D}^{\mathsf{KEM}}_{\mathsf{sk}}(c)$. Note that this event is defined over the inputs to A^{PC} in both experiments *real* and *sim*.
2 Lie: $\mathsf{PCOSim}(K[j], c[j]) \neq \mathsf{PCO}_{\mathsf{sk}}(K[j], c[j])$ for some $j \in \{1, ..., q_{PC}\}$. This event is defined in experiment *sim* only.
3 Bad: $K' \overset{\text{def}}{=} \mathsf{A}^{\mathsf{PC}}(pk, c|\mathsf{PCOSim}_{\mathsf{sk}}(.,.)) \neq \mathsf{D}^{\mathsf{KEM}}_{\mathsf{sk}}(c)$ and $d' = Acc$. This event is defined in experiment *sim* only.

We also define the event $\mathsf{Err} \overset{\text{def}}{=} \mathsf{Lie} \vee \mathsf{Bad}$. The three disjoint events Err, $\mathsf{SuccA} \wedge \neg\mathsf{Err}$ and $\neg\mathsf{SuccA} \wedge \neg\mathsf{Err}$ partition the outcome space of the *sim* experiment. Splitting event $\mathsf{SuccSim}$ we have $\Pr[\mathsf{SuccSim}] = \Pr[\mathsf{SuccSim}|\mathsf{Err}]\Pr[\mathsf{Err}] + \Pr[\mathsf{SuccSim}|\mathsf{SuccA} \wedge \neg\mathsf{Err}]\Pr[\mathsf{SuccA} \wedge \neg\mathsf{Err}] + \Pr[\mathsf{SuccSim}|\neg\mathsf{SuccA} \wedge \neg\mathsf{Err}]\Pr[\neg\mathsf{SuccA} \wedge \neg\mathsf{Err}]$. We lower bound this probability using the last two terms. If event $\mathsf{SuccA} \wedge \neg\mathsf{Err}$ occurs then A^{PC} succeeds to decrypt c, so $K' = \mathsf{D}^{\mathsf{KEM}}_{\mathsf{sk}}(c) = K$ so $b' = b$ and $\mathsf{SuccSim}$ occurs. Hence $\Pr[\mathsf{SuccSim}|\mathsf{SuccA} \wedge \neg\mathsf{Err}] = 1$. Also, since the inputs to A^{PC} are distributed in *sim* as in *real*, we have $\Pr[\mathsf{SuccA}] = \Pr[\mathsf{SuccA}]_{real} = \mathbf{Succ}^{\mathsf{OW-PCA}}_{\mathsf{A}^{PC}, \mathsf{KEM}}(k)$ so $\Pr[\mathsf{SuccA} \wedge \neg\mathsf{Err}] = \mathbf{Succ}^{\mathsf{OW-PCA}}_{\mathsf{A}^{PC}, \mathsf{KEM}}(k) - \Pr[\mathsf{SuccA} \wedge \mathsf{Err}]$. If event $\neg\mathsf{SuccA} \wedge \neg\mathsf{Err}$ occurs then $K' \neq K$ but $d' = Rej$ so b' is chosen uniformly in $\{0, 1\}$ and hence $\Pr[\mathsf{SuccSim}|\neg\mathsf{SuccA} \wedge \neg\mathsf{Err}] = \frac{1}{2}$. Also $\Pr[\neg\mathsf{SuccA} \wedge \neg\mathsf{Err}] = \Pr[\neg\mathsf{SuccA}] - \Pr[\neg\mathsf{SuccA} \wedge \mathsf{Err}] = 1 - \mathbf{Succ}^{\mathsf{OW-PCA}}_{\mathsf{A}^{PC}, \mathsf{KEM}}(k) - \Pr[\neg\mathsf{SuccA} \wedge \mathsf{Err}]$. By substituting the above results in the last two terms of the splitting expression for $\Pr[\mathsf{SuccSim}]$ we get the lower bound $\Pr[\mathsf{SuccSim}] \geq \frac{1}{2} + \frac{1}{2}\mathbf{Succ}^{\mathsf{OW-PCA}}_{\mathsf{A}^{PC}, \mathsf{KEM}}(k) - \Pr[\mathsf{Err}]$, and hence:

$$\mathbf{Succ}^{\mathsf{CCA}}_{\mathsf{A}^{CC}, \mathsf{CCAKEM1}}(k) \geq \mathbf{Succ}^{\mathsf{OW-PCA}}_{\mathsf{A}^{PC}, \mathsf{KEM}}(k) - 2\Pr[\mathsf{Err}]. \tag{1}$$

The running time and query counts of the attacker A^{CC} can be readily verified. Therefore to establish the theorem it remains to show that $\Pr[\mathsf{Err}] \leq (q_{PC} + 2)\mathbf{InSec}^{\mathsf{MAC-UF}}_{\mathsf{MAC}}(t^{CC}, 0, q_{PC})$. Since $\Pr[\mathsf{Err}] = \Pr[\mathsf{Bad} \wedge \neg\mathsf{Lie}] + \Pr[\mathsf{Lie}]$ it suffices to show that

$$\Pr[\mathsf{Bad} \wedge \neg\mathsf{Lie}] \leq \mathbf{InSec}^{\mathsf{MAC-UF}}_{\mathsf{MAC}}(t^{CC}, 0, q_{PC}) \tag{2}$$

and

$$\Pr[\mathsf{Lie}] \leq (q_{PC} + 1) \cdot \mathbf{InSec}^{\mathsf{MAC-UF}}_{\mathsf{MAC}}(t^{CC}, 0, q_{PC}). \tag{3}$$

To get (2), note that Bad means that $\mathsf{MACV}_{km'}(c_s, \sigma_s) = Acc$, where $km' = H(K', c)$ and $K' \neq \mathsf{D}^{\mathsf{KEM}}_{\mathsf{sk}}(c)$. Hence $(K', c) \neq (K, c)$ and the pair (K', c) has not been previously queried to $H(.)$ by $\mathsf{D}^{\mathsf{CCAKEM1}}_{\mathsf{sk}}$ (since all such queries have the form $(\mathsf{D}^{\mathsf{KEM}}_{\mathsf{sk}}(\bar{c}), \bar{c})$). Furthermore, $\mathsf{Bad}\neg\mathsf{Lie}$ means that also $(K', c) \neq (K[j], c[j])$ for all $j \in \{1, ..., q_{PC}\}$ since we can assume without loss of generality that A^{PC} never outputs a queried key $K[j]$ for which the query $(K[j], c)$ was answered '0' by the PCO oracle (this key is never correct). Hence when $\mathsf{Bad} \wedge \neg\mathsf{Lie}$ occurs the pair (K', c) has not been queried to $H(.)$ before $km' = H(K', c)$ is computed, so $\Pr[\text{Bad} \wedge \neg\text{Lie}]$ is at most the probability that $\text{MACV}_k(\sigma_s, c_s) = Acc$ when the key k is chosen uniformly in the MAC key space $\{0, 1\}^{l_m}$. This probability is at most $\text{InSec}_{\text{MAC}}^{\text{MAC-UF}}(t^{CC}, 0, 0)$ for any choice of (c_s, σ_s). Hence $\Pr[\text{Bad} \wedge \neg\text{Lie}] \leq \text{InSec}_{\text{MAC}}^{\text{MAC-UF}}(t^{CC}, 0, 0) \leq \text{InSec}_{\text{MAC}}^{\text{MAC-UF}}(t^{CC}, 0, q_{PC})$, which gives (2).

To get the second bound (3) we construct a MAC forging algorithm F as follows.

MAC Forging Attacker F against MAC Scheme MAC

> $F(.|\text{MACG}_{km^*}(.), \text{MACV}_{km^*}(.))$
> $\quad i^* \xleftarrow{R} \{0, ..., q_{PC} + 1\}$
> $\quad i \leftarrow 0$
> $\quad (sk, pk) \leftarrow \text{GK}(k, cp)$
> $\quad (m_0, m_1, s) \leftarrow A_{\text{find}}(pk|D_{sk}^{\text{CCAKEM1}}(.))$
> $\quad b \xleftarrow{R} \{0, 1\} \; ; \; r \xleftarrow{R} SP_R; \; (K, c) \leftarrow E_{pk}^{\text{KEM}}(r)$
> $\quad h[l_m + 1, \ldots, l_m + l_e] \leftarrow H(K, c)[l_m + 1, \ldots, l_m + l_e]$
> $\quad ke \leftarrow h[l_m + 1, \ldots, l_m + l_e]$
> $\quad$ (note: if $i^* = 0$ define $km = km^*$, else $km = H(K, c)[1, \ldots, l_m]$).
> $\quad c_s \leftarrow E_{ke}^{\text{SYM}}(m)$
> $\quad K' \leftarrow A^{PC}(pk, c|\text{PCOSim}(., .))$
> $\quad km \leftarrow H(K, c)[1, \ldots, l_m]; \; \sigma_s \leftarrow \text{MACG}_{km}(c_s)$
> $\quad$ (note: define $km' = km^*$)
> $\quad$ Return forgery (c_s, σ_s)

> $\text{PCOSim}(K[i], c[i]|H(.), D_{sk}^{\text{CCAKEM1}}(.))$ (PCO Simulator for forger F)
> $\quad i \leftarrow i + 1$
> $\quad h[i] \leftarrow H(K[i], c[i])$
> $\quad km[i] \leftarrow h[i][1, ..., l_m]; \; ke[i] \leftarrow h[l_m + 1, ..., l_m + l_e]$
> $\quad$ Find $j \in \{0, 1\}$ such that $c_s[i] \stackrel{\text{def}}{=} E_{ke[i]}^{\text{SYM}}(m_j) \neq c_s$
> $\quad \sigma_s[i] \leftarrow \text{MACG}_{km[i]}(c_s[i])$
> $\quad$ If $i \geq i^*$ and $c[i] = c[i^*]$ then
> $\quad\quad K'[i] \leftarrow D_{sk}^{\text{KEM}}(c[i])$
> $\quad\quad ke'[i] \leftarrow H(K'[i], c[i])[l_m + 1, \ldots, l_m + l_e]$
> $\quad\quad$ (Note: we define $km'[i] = km^*$)
> $\quad\quad d[i] \leftarrow \text{MACV}_{km^*}(c_s[i], \sigma_s[i])$
> $\quad\quad$ If $d[i] = Acc$ then Terminate and Return forgery $(c_s[i], \sigma_s[i])$
> $\quad$ Else
> $\quad\quad d[i] \leftarrow D_{sk}^{\text{CCAKEM1}}(c[i], c_s[i], \sigma_s[i])$
> $\quad$ If $d[i] \neq Rej$ then Return 1
> $\quad$ Else Return 0

We denote by $fsim$ the experiment of running the forger F in the 'MACUF-Exp' MAC forging experiment defined in the Appendix and we let SuccF denote the event that the experiment returns 1, that is F succeeds in its MAC forgery realtive to the MAC key km^*. First observe that in sim the PCO simulator PCOSim never lies on queries $(K[j], c[j])$ for which $\text{PCO}_{sk}(K[j], c[j]) = 1$. This is because $\text{PCO}_{sk}(K[j], c[j]) = 1$ means $K[j] = D_{sk}^{\text{KEM}}(c[j])$ and hence the ciphertext $(c[j], c_s[j], \sigma_s[j])$ computed by PCOSim is valid and not rejected by

$D_{sk}^{CCAKEM1}$ so $PCOSim(K[j], c[j]) = 1$. Hence Lie means $PCO_{sk}(K[j], c[j]) = 0$ but $PCOSim(K[j], c[j]) = 1$ for some j, or equivalently $K[j] \neq D_{sk}^{KEM}(c[j])$ and $MACV_{km'[j]}(c_s[j], \sigma_s[j]) = Acc$, where $km'[j] = H(D_{sk}^{KEM}(c[j]), c[j])[1, \ldots, l_m]$ is the MAC key used by $D_{sk}^{CCAKEM1}$ to check the ciphertext $(c[j], c_s[j], \sigma_s[j])$.

We now split Lie into a union of disjoint events $Lie_{j,\ell}$, where $Lie_{j,\ell}$ is then event that a lie first occurred at PC query j and $\ell \leq j$ is the smallest index such that $c[\ell] = c[j]$. Note that $Lie_{j,\ell}$ means that (L.1) $(K[k], c[k]) \neq (D_{sk}^{KEM}(c[j]), c[j])$ for all $k \leq j$ (otherwise A^{PC} already knows the decryption of $c[j]$ before query j) and hence $(D_{sk}^{KEM}(c[j]), c[j]) = (D_{sk}^{KEM}(c[\ell]), c[\ell])$ was first queried to $H(.)$ by $D_{sk}^{CCAKEM1}$ when decrypting $(c[\ell], c_s[\ell], \sigma_s[\ell])$ and (L.2) $km'[j] = km'[\ell]$ and $MACV_{km'[j]}(c_s[j], \sigma_s[j]) = Acc$. Therefore if we set $i^* = \ell$ in experiment *fsim*, then due to (L.1), for all outcomes in $Lie_{j,\ell}$ *fsim* will run with random MAC key $km'[j] = km'[\ell] = km^*$ in the same way as *sim* runs with $km'[j] = km'[\ell] = H(D_{sk}^{KEM}(c[\ell]), c[\ell])[1, \ldots, l_m]$. This means, for all ℓ, j that

$$\Pr[Lie_{j,\ell} | i^* = \ell]_{fsim} = \Pr[Lie_{j,\ell}]_{sim}, \tag{4}$$

and from (L.2) the event $Lie_{j,\ell} \wedge i^* = \ell$ means that $km'[j] = km'[\ell] = km'[i^*] = km^*$ so $MACV_{km^*}(c_s[j], \sigma_s[j]) = Acc$ and SuccF occurs with no MAC generation queries and up to q_{PC} verify queries. So the following also holds (over all $j \in \{1, \ldots, q_{PC}\}$ and $\ell \in \{0, \ldots, j\}$):

$$\Pr[SuccF]_{fsim} \geq \sum_{j,\ell} \Pr[Lie_{j,\ell} \wedge i^* = \ell]_{fsim}. \tag{5}$$

Now, $\Pr[Lie_{j,\ell} \wedge i^* = \ell]_{fsim} = \Pr[Lie_{j,\ell} | i^* = \ell]_{fsim} \Pr[i^* = \ell]_{fsim}$ so $\Pr[Lie_{j,\ell} \wedge i^* = \ell]_{fsim} = \frac{1}{q_{PC}+1} \Pr[Lie_{j,\ell}]_{sim}$ for each j, ℓ using (4) and that i^* is uniformly chosen in $\{0, \ldots, q_{PC}\}$. Plugging this in (5) we get $\Pr[SuccF]_{fsim} \geq \frac{1}{q_{PC}+1} \Pr[Lie]_{sim}$ using $\Pr[Lie]_{fsim} = \sum_{j,\ell} \Pr[Lie_{j,\ell}]_{fsim}$. But on the other hand $\Pr[SuccF]_{fsim} \leq \mathbf{InSec}_{MAC}^{MAC-UF}(t^{CC}, 0, q_{PC})$. Combining these upper and lower bounds on $\Pr[SuccF]_{fsim}$ we immediately obtain the desired result (3), which completes the proof.   □

As a special case of this result, when KEM is the Diffie-Hellman one in a group (see previous section), we conclude that the 'Strong Diffie-Hellman' (SDH) assumption is necessary (and sufficient, as shown in [4]) for the CCA security of the DHIES scheme.

4.2   Attack on CCAKEM2 If the Underlying KEM Is Not OW-PCA

Using a chosen-ciphertext attack analogous to the one used to prove Theorem 1, we obtain the following result, whose proof is omitted due to lack of space.

Theorem 2. *Let A^{PC} be an attack algorithm with resource parameters (t^{PC}, q_{PC}) for breaking OW-PCA of KEM. Then we can construct an attack algorithm $A^{CC} = (A_{find}^{CC}, A_{guess}^{CC})$ with resource parameters $(t^{CC}, q_D, q_{H_1}, q_{H_2})$ such that*

$$\mathbf{Succ}_{A^{CC},CCAKEM2}^{CCA}(k) \geq \mathbf{Succ}_{A,KEM}^{OW-PCA}(k) - \frac{2(q_{PC}+1)}{2^{l_\sigma}}$$

and $t^{CC} = t^{PC} + (q_{PC}+1)O(1)$, $q_D = q_{PC}$, $q_{H_1} = 2q_{PC}+1$, $q_{H_2} = 2q_{PC}+1$.

As a special case, when the KEM is the Diffie-Hellman one, the SDH assumption is necessary for the CCA security of REACT. As pointed out earlier, when the KEM is built from a deterministic encryption scheme, the OW-PCA assumption on the KEM is equivalent to the one-wayness assumption on the KEM so this result does not imply the necessity of stronger assumptions than one-wayness in this case (e.g. in the case of RSA).

5   Relations between ODH and SDH Assumptions

In this section, we clarify the relation between Strong Diffie-Hellman (SDH) and Oracle Diffie-Hellman (ODH) assumptions under the random oracle model. Formal definitions for SDH and ODH are given in the appendix (definitions 6 and 7). Note that the reduction from SDH to ODH, namely, breaking SDH using ODH attacker was already shown in [4].

However, the attack on CCAKEM1 presented in the previous section implies that there exists an opposite way of reduction, i.e., a reduction from ODH to SDH: Since OW-PCA for the Diffie-Hellman KEM is exactly the same as the SDH assumption, the theorem 2 implies that there exists a reduction from CCA security for CCAKEM1 to SDH. But, in [4], the reduction from ODH to CCA security was shown in the standard model (and hence in the random oracle model) and therefore there exists a reduction from ODH to SDH. Consequently, ODH and SDH are equivalent in the random oracle model.

Apart from the trivial deduction described above we provide an explicit and tight reduction from ODH to SDH in the random oracle model.

Theorem 3. *Let* A^{SDH} *be an attack algorithm with resource parameters* $(t^{SDH}, q_{\mathcal{O}_x})$ *for breaking SDH. Then we can construct an attack algorithm* A^{ODH} *for ODH with resource parameter* $(t^{ODH}, q_{\mathcal{H}_x})$ *such that*

$$\mathbf{Succ}_{A^{ODH}}^{ODH}(k) \geq \mathbf{Succ}_{A^{SDH}}^{SDH}(k) - \frac{q_{\mathcal{O}_x}+1}{2^{l_h}}$$

and $t^{ODH} = t^{SDH} + (q_{\mathcal{O}_x}+1)O(1)$ *and* $q_{\mathcal{H}_x} = q_{\mathcal{O}_x}$. *Here,* l_h *denotes the length of the outputs of a random oracle* H.

Proof. Let $H : \{0,1\}^* \to \{0,1\}^{l_h}$ be a random oracle. Let G be a multiplicatively-written group as defined in the definitions 6 and 7. We construct an attack algorithm A^{ODH} for breaking ODH using an attack algorithm A^{SDH} for SDH. Note that A^{SDH} can simulate the restricted DDH oracle $\mathcal{O}_x(.,.)$ using its oracles $H(.)$ and $\mathcal{H}_x(.)$. A complete specification for A^{ODH} is as follows.

Attacker $\mathsf{A}^{\mathsf{ODH}}$ against ODH Assumption

$\mathsf{A}^{\mathsf{ODH}}(g^r, g^x, \gamma | H(.), \mathcal{H}_x(.))$
 Run $\mathsf{A}^{\mathsf{SDH}}(g^r, g^x | \mathcal{O}_x\text{-Sim}(., .))$
 $K \leftarrow \mathsf{A}^{\mathsf{SDH}}(g^r, g^x | \mathcal{O}_x\text{-Sim}(., .))$
 If $\gamma = H(K)$ **Return** 1 Else **Return** 0

$\mathcal{O}_x\text{-Sim}(c[i], w[i] | H(.), \mathcal{H}_x(.))$
 If $c[i] \neq g^r$ and $H(w[i]) = \mathcal{H}_x(c[i])$
  Return 1 Else **Return** 0
 If $c[i] = g^r$ and $H(g^x w[i]) = \mathcal{H}_x(gc[i])$
  Return 1 Else **Return** 0

Now we show that $\mathsf{A}^{\mathsf{ODH}}$ satisfies the claim of the theorem. We use the notation $\Pr[\mathsf{Event}]_{exp}$ to denote the probability of event Event in experiment exp. Let $real$ denote the 'SDHExp' experiment in definition 6 running with attacker $\mathsf{A}^{\mathsf{SDH}}$ whose queries are answered by the real oracle $\mathcal{O}_x(., .)$. We define in this experiment the event $\mathsf{SuccReal}$ that the experiment returns 1. Hence $\Pr[\mathsf{SuccReal}]_{real} \overset{def}{=} \mathbf{Succ}^{SDH}_{\mathsf{A}^{\mathsf{SDH}}}(k)$. Let sim denote the 'ODHRealExp' and 'ODHRandExp' experiments in definition 7 running with attacker $\mathsf{A}^{\mathsf{ODH}}$ which runs $\mathsf{A}^{\mathsf{SDH}}$ and answers its queries with the simulator $\mathcal{O}_x\text{-Sim}$. Then by definition we have $\mathbf{Succ}^{ODH}_{\mathsf{A}^{\mathsf{ODH}}}(k) = \Pr[\mathbf{ODHExpReal}(k, \mathsf{A}^{\mathsf{ODH}}) = 1]_{sim} - \Pr[\mathbf{ODHExpRrand}(k, \mathsf{A}^{\mathsf{ODH}}) = 1]_{sim}$.

First, we lower bound $\Pr[\mathbf{ODHExpReal}(k, \mathsf{A}^{\mathsf{ODH}}) = 1]_{sim}$. Now we define the following events.

- Lie: $\mathcal{O}_x\text{-Sim}(c[j], w[j]) \neq \mathcal{O}_x(c[j], w[j])$ for some $j \in [1, ..., q_{\mathcal{O}_x}]$.

Note that if Lie does not happen in experiment sim $\mathsf{A}^{\mathsf{SDH}}$ cannot distinguish its environment in $real$ from sim. Hence we get $\Pr[\mathbf{ODHExpReal}(k, \mathsf{A}^{\mathsf{ODH}}) = 1]_{sim} \geq \Pr[\mathsf{SuccReal} | \neg \mathsf{Lie}]_{sim} = \Pr[\mathsf{SuccReal} | \neg \mathsf{Lie}]_{real} \geq \Pr[\mathsf{SuccReal} \wedge \neg \mathsf{Lie}]_{real} = \Pr[\mathsf{SuccReal}]_{real} - \Pr[\mathsf{Lie}]_{real} = \Pr[\mathsf{SuccReal}]_{real} - \Pr[\mathsf{Lie}]$.

Now we upper bound $\Pr[\mathsf{Lie}]$. Assume that Lie is true: We have the following two cases (events).

- Case (1): $\mathcal{O}_x\text{-Sim}(c[j], w[j]) = 1$ and $\mathcal{O}_x(c[j], w[j]) = 0$
- Case (2): $\mathcal{O}_x\text{-Sim}(c[j], w[j]) = 0$ and $\mathcal{O}_x(c[j], w[j]) = 1$

From case (1), we have $H(w[j]) = \mathcal{H}_x(c[j])(= H(c[j]^x))$ but $w[j] \neq c[j]^x$ when $c[j] \neq g^r$ by the definition of $\mathcal{O}_x\text{-Sim}(., .)$. When $c[j] = g^r$, we have $H(g^x w[j]) = \mathcal{H}_x(gc[j])(= H(g^x c[j]^x))$. In both cases (whether $c[j] = g^r$ or not), we have $\Pr[\text{Case (1)}] = \frac{1}{2^{l_h}}$ since $H(.)$ is assumed to be a random oracle. However $\Pr[\text{Case (2)}] = 0$ as long as H is a well-defined function. Therefore we get $\Pr[\mathsf{Lie}] = \frac{q_{\mathcal{O}_x}}{2^{l_h}}$. Then we obtain $\Pr[\mathbf{ODHExpReal}(k, \mathsf{A}^{\mathsf{ODH}}) = 1]_{sim} \geq \Pr[\mathsf{SuccReal}]_{real} - \Pr[\mathsf{Lie}] = \mathbf{Succ}^{SDH}_{\mathsf{A}^{\mathsf{SDH}}}(k) - \frac{q_{\mathcal{O}_x}}{2^{l_h}}$.

Now we upper bound $\Pr[\mathbf{ODHExpRand}(k, \mathsf{A}^{\mathsf{ODH}}) = 1]$ where γ is given to $\mathsf{A}^{\mathsf{ODH}}$ as a random string of the length l_h. Since γ is uniform and independent of g^r and g^x, we have $\Pr[\mathbf{ODHExpRand}(k, \mathsf{A}^{\mathsf{ODH}}) = 1] \leq \frac{1}{2^{l_h}}$.

Then subtracting the bounds on $\Pr[\mathbf{ODHExpReal}(k, \mathsf{A}^{\mathsf{ODH}}) = 1]_{sim}$ and $\Pr[\mathbf{ODHExpRand}(k, \mathsf{A}^{\mathsf{ODH}}) = 1]$, we obtain $\mathbf{Succ}^{ODH}_{\mathsf{A}^{\mathsf{ODH}}}(k) \geq \mathbf{Succ}^{SDH}_{\mathsf{A}^{\mathsf{SDH}}}(k) - \frac{q_{\mathcal{O}_x}}{2^{l_h}} - \frac{1}{2^{l_h}}$.

As a result we obtain the following:

$$\mathbf{Succ}_{A^{ODH}}^{ODH}(k) \geq \mathbf{Succ}_{A^{SDH}}^{SDH}(k) - \frac{q_{O_x} + 1}{2^{l_h}}. \tag{6}$$

The running time and query counts can be readily checked. □

We remark that the reduction from ODH to SDH still holds even if the random oracle H is replaced by a collision-resistant hash function, i.e., in the standard model. However, we were not able to find a reduction from SDH to ODH in the standard model, which implies that ODH (in the standard model) on which the CCA security of DHIES is based is a very *strong* assumption.

6   Conclusion

In this paper we clarified the necessary assumptions for the security of recently proposed schemes DHIES and REACT, and indeed for a wider class of natural asymmetric encryption schemes which include the latter two as special cases. We also clarified the relationship between ODH and SDH, two new Diffie-Hellman related assumptions. The results in this paper can be served as criteria for distinguishing the asymmetric encryption schemes whose CCA security is based on stronger assumptions such as GDH from the schemes based on weaker ones such as Computational Diffie-Hellman and Decisional Diffie-Hellman.

A   Appendix

In this appendix we review the definitions of standard primitives and their security notions. These definitions are referred to in the body of the paper.

A.1   Asymmetric Encryption Schemes

Here we review the standard indistnguishability-based notion 'CCA' for the chosen ciphertext attack security for asymmetric encryption schemes, sometimes known as IND-CCA2 (see, eg. [1]).

An asymmetric encryption scheme consists of 3 algorithms: (1) A key-pair generation algorithm $\mathsf{GK}(k)$ which generates a secret/public key pair (sk, pk); (2) A probabilistic encryption algorithm $\mathsf{E}_{pk}^{ASYM}(m)$, which takes a public key pk and a message m and returns a ciphertext c; (3) A decryption algorithm $\mathsf{D}_{sk}^{ASYM}(c)$, which takes a secret key and a ciphertext c and returns a message m.

The CCA security notion is then quantitatively defined as follows.

Definition 4. (CCA) *Let* $\mathsf{ASYM} = (\mathsf{GK}, \mathsf{E}^{ASYM}, \mathsf{D}^{ASYM})$ *be an asymmetric encryption scheme. Let* $\mathsf{A} = (\mathsf{A}_1, \mathsf{A}_2)$ *be an attack algorithm, consisting of two 'sub-attack' algorithms* A_{find} *and* A_{guess}. *Define the experiment*
Experiment $\mathbf{CCAExp}(k, \mathsf{ASYM}, \mathsf{A})$
$\quad (sk, pk) \leftarrow \mathsf{GK}(k)$
$\quad (m_0, m_1, s) \leftarrow \mathsf{A}_{find}(pk | \mathsf{D}_{sk}^{ASYM}(.))$
$\quad b \xleftarrow{R} \{0, 1\}; \ c \leftarrow \mathsf{E}_{pk}^{ASYM}(m_b)$
$\quad b' \leftarrow \mathsf{A}_{guess}(pk, s, c | \mathsf{D}_{sk}^{ASYM}(.))$
$\quad$ If $b' = b$ and A_{guess} did not query c to $\mathsf{D}_{sk}^{ASYM}(.)$ then
$\quad \quad$ **Return** 1 else **Return** 0

We quantify A*'s success in breaking the* CCA *security notion of scheme* ASYM *by the advantage* $\mathbf{Succ}^{CCA}_{A,ASYM}(k) \stackrel{\text{def}}{=} 2(\Pr[\mathbf{CCAExp}(k, ASYM, A) = 1] - \frac{1}{2})$. *We define* A*'s resource parameters as* $RP = (t, q_D, q_{RO_1}, ..., q_{RO_n})$ *if* A *has running time/program size at most* t *and makes at most* q_D *queries to the decryption oracle, and, if the scheme makes use of* n *random oracles, at most* q_{RO_i} *queries to the* i*'th random oracle* RO_i, *for* $i \in \{1, ..., n\}$.

A.2   Message Authentication Code (MAC) Schemes

We review the definition of a MAC and its unforgeability security notion 'MAC – UF'.

A MAC scheme consists of 2 algorithms: (1) A MAC generation algorithm $\mathsf{MACG}_{sk}(m)$, which takes a secret key $sk \in SP_K$ and a message m and returns a MAC tag σ; (2) A MAC verification algorithm $\mathsf{MACV}_{sk}(m, \sigma)$, which takes a secret key $sk \in SP_K$, a message m, and a MAC tag σ and returns a verification decision $d \in \{Acc, Rej\}$.

The MAC – UF unforgeability security notion for a MAC scheme is then quantitatively defined as follows.

Definition 5. (MAC-UF) *Let* MAC = (MACG, MACV) *be a MAC scheme with key space* SP_K. *Let* A *be an attack algorithm. Define the experiment*

Experiment **MACUFExp**(MAC, A)

$sk \stackrel{R}{\leftarrow} SP_K$

$(m^*, \sigma^*) \leftarrow A(|\mathsf{MACG}_{sk}(.), \mathsf{MACV}_{sk}(.))$

If $\mathsf{MACV}_{sk}(m^*, \sigma^*) = Acc$ and A did not query
   m^* to $\mathsf{MACG}_{sk}(.)$ then **Return** 1 Else **Return** 0

We quantify A*'s success in breaking the* MAC – UF *security notion of scheme* MAC *by the probability* $\mathbf{Succ}^{MAC-UF}_{A,MAC} \stackrel{\text{def}}{=} \Pr[\mathbf{MACUFExp}(MAC, A) = 1]$. *We quantify the insecurity of scheme* MAC *in the sense of* MAC – UF *against arbitrary attackers with resource parameters* $RP = (t, q_{MG}, q_{MV})$ *by the probability* $\mathbf{InSec}^{MAC-UF}_{MAC}(t, q_{MG}, q_{MV}) \stackrel{\text{def}}{=} \max_{A \in AS_{RP}} \mathbf{Succ}^{MAC-UF}_{A,MAC}$. *The attacker set* AS_{RP} *contains all attackers with resource parameters* RP, *meaning running time+program size at most* t, *and at most* q_{MG} *queries to the MAC generation oracle and* q_{MV} *queries to the MAC verification oracle.*

A.3   Symmetric Encryption Schemes

An symmetric encryption scheme consists of 2 algorithms: (1) A probabilistic encryption algorithm $\mathsf{E}^{SYM}_{sk}(m)$, which takes a secret key $sk \in SP_K$ and a message m and returns a ciphertext c; (2) A decryption algorithm $\mathsf{D}^{SYM}_{sk}(c)$, which takes a secret key $sk \in SP_K$ and a ciphertext c and returns a message m.

A.4   Oracle Diffie-Hellman and Strong Diffie-Hellman Assumptions

We review the definition of the SDH (Strong Diffie-Hellman) and ODH (Oracle Diffie-Hellman), which are computational and decisional assumptions, respectively, defined in [4].

Definition 6. (Strong Diffie-Hellman: SDH) *Let G be a multiplicatively-written group. Let* $\mathsf{GenGParm}(k)$ *be an algorithm that outputs common parameters* $cp = (d_G, g, q)$ *consisting of description d_G of a finite cyclic group G, a generator $g \in G$ and the order q of G. Let* $\mathsf{A}^{\mathsf{SDH}}$ *be an attack algorithm. Define the experiment*

Experiment **SDHExp**$(k, \mathsf{A}^{\mathsf{SDH}})$

    $cp \leftarrow \mathsf{GenGParm}(k)$

    $r, x \xleftarrow{\mathrm{R}} \{1, \ldots, q\};\ K \leftarrow g^{rx}$

    $K' \leftarrow \mathsf{A}^{\mathsf{SDH}}(g^r, g^x | \mathcal{O}_x(., .))$

    If $K' = K$ then **Return** 1 Else **Return** 0

Here, $\mathcal{O}_x(., .)$ *is a restricted DDH oracle. On input (c, w) it outputs 1 if $w = c^x$, otherwise, outputs 0. We quantify* $\mathsf{A}^{\mathsf{SDH}}$'s *success in computing the Diffie-Hellman key g^{rx} by the probability* $\mathbf{Succ}_{\mathsf{A}^{\mathsf{SDH}}}^{SDH}(k) \overset{\mathrm{def}}{=} \Pr[\mathbf{SDHExp}(k, \mathsf{A}^{\mathsf{SDH}}) = 1]$. *We define A's resource parameters as $RP = (t, q_{\mathcal{O}_x})$ if A has running time/program size at most t and makes at most $q_{\mathcal{O}_x}$ queries to the restricted DDH oracle.*

Definition 7. (Oracle Diffie-Hellman: ODH) *Let G be a multiplicatively-written group. Let* $\mathsf{GenGParm}(k)$ *be an algorithm that outputs common parameters* $cp = (d_G, g, q)$ *consisting of description d_G of a finite cyclic group G, a generator $g \in G$ and the order q of G. A hash function $H : \{0, 1\}^* \rightarrow \{0, 1\}^{l_h}$, modelled as a random oracle. Let* $\mathsf{A}^{\mathsf{ODH}}$ *be an attack algorithm and $b' \in \{0, 1\}$. Define two experiments*

Experiment **ODHExpReal**$(k, \mathsf{A}^{\mathsf{ODH}})$ Experiment **ODHExpRand**$(k, \mathsf{A}^{\mathsf{ODH}})$

    $cp \leftarrow \mathsf{GenGParm}(k)$ $cp \leftarrow \mathsf{GenGParm}(k)$

    $r, x \xleftarrow{\mathrm{R}} \{1, \ldots, q\}$ $r, x \xleftarrow{\mathrm{R}} \{1, \ldots, q\};\ h \leftarrow \{0, 1\}^{l_h}$

    $b' \leftarrow \mathsf{A}^{\mathsf{ODH}}(g^r, g^x, H(g^{rx}) | H(.), \mathcal{H}_x(.))$ $b' \leftarrow \mathsf{A}^{\mathsf{ODH}}(g^r, g^x, h | H(.), \mathcal{H}_x(.))$

    Return b' **Return** b'

Here, $\mathcal{H}_x(c) \overset{\mathrm{def}}{=} H(c^x)$ *and* $\mathsf{A}^{\mathsf{SDH}}$ *is not allowed to query g^r to $\mathcal{H}_x(.)$. We quantify* $\mathsf{A}^{\mathsf{ODH}}$'s *success in distinguishing the hash of Diffie-Hellman key g^{rx}, i.e, $H(g^{rx})$ from the random string h by the probability* $\mathbf{Succ}_{\mathsf{A}^{\mathsf{ODH}}}^{ODH}(k) \overset{\mathrm{def}}{=} \Pr[\mathbf{ODHExpReal}(k, \mathsf{A}^{\mathsf{ODH}}) = 1] - \Pr[\mathbf{ODHExpRand}(k, \mathsf{A}^{\mathsf{ODH}}) = 1]$. *We define A's resource parameters as $RP = (t, q_H, q_{\mathcal{H}_x})$ if A has running time/program size at most t and makes at most q_H and $q_{\mathcal{H}_x}$ queries to the oracles $H(.)$ and $\mathcal{H}_x(.)$, respectively.*

References

1. M. Bellare, A. Desai, D. Pointcheval, and P.Rogaway. Relations Among Notions of Security for Public-Key Encryption Schemes. In *Advances in Cryptology - Proceedings of CRYPTO '98*, volume 1462 of *LNCS*, pages 26–45, Berlin, 1998. Springer-Verlag.
2. M. Bellare and P. Rogaway. Random Oracles are Practical: A Paradigm for Designing Efficient Protocols. In *Proceedings of First ACM Conference on Computer and Communications Security*, pages 62–73. ACM, 1993.
3. M. Bellare and P. Rogaway. Minimizing the use of random oracles in authenticated encryption schemes. In *Information and Communications Security*, volume 1334 of *LNCS*, pages 1–16, Berlin, 1997. Springer-Verlag.
4. M. Bellare M. Abdalla and P. Rogaway. The Oracle Diffie-Hellman Assumptions and an Analysis of DHIES. In *Topics in Cryptology - CT-RSA 2001*, volume 2020 of *LNCS*, pages 143–158, Berlin, 2001. Springer-Verlag. See full paper available at www-cse.ucsd.edu/users/mihir.
5. T. Okamoto and D. Pointcheval. REACT: Rapid Enhanced-security Asymmetric Cryptosystem Transform. In *Topics in Cryptology - CT-RSA 2001*, volume 2020 of *LNCS*, pages 159–174, Berlin, 2001. Springer-Verlag.
6. Y. Zheng and J. Seberry. Immunizing public key cryptosystems against chosen ciphertext attacks. In the Special Issue on Secure Communications, IEEE Journal on Selected Areas in Communications, Vol. 11, No. 5, 1993, pages 715-724.
7. V. Shoup. A Proposal for an ISO Standard for Public Key Encryption (Cersion 1.1). *ISO/IEC JTC 1/SC 27*, 2001.

Security Management: An Information Systems Setting

M.J. Warren [1] and L.M. Batten [2]

School of Computing & Mathematics,
Deakin University, Victoria, Australia

[1]Waurn Ponds, Geelong, 3217 m.warren@deakin.edu.au
[2] 221 Burwood Highway, Burwood, 3125 lmbatten@deakin.edu.au

Abstract. Information Systems have been used for many years to analyze problems and compare options in a managed environment. The introduction of computer and information security systems into such an environment is a typical example of a situation to which an Information Systems approach can be applied. In this paper, we examine the issues peculiar to implementation of security in a healthcare environment, looking specifically at one such specially designed system, SIM-ETHICS, which takes a participational approach.

1 Introduction

The development of a new Information System (IS) can have an overwhelming impact on the individuals contained within the organization as well as on the organization itself [24].

An IS contains many different parts, including people and procedures, information, software and hardware [3]. Different approaches to the development of such a system tend to focus specifically on one or more of these parts. For example, Jackson Structured Development is oriented towards software requirements rather than organisational needs [2].

The use of participational techniques allows users to have some level of input into the system development life cycle. However, the user participant is often called upon after the major decisions have been taken, thus limiting user involvement within the system development [18].

In fact, it is virtually impossible to remove the participation and involvement of users and stake holders from the design of a system. At some point, users will have some degree of input into the system, whether it be deciding upon the budget, determining the key functionality of a system or reacting to the system once it is at the implementation stage. There are a number of methodologies used within IS that specifically encourage users to have a large say in how the impending system is designed and how

L. Batten and J. Seberry (Eds.): ACISP 2002, LNCS 2384, pp. 257-270, 2002.
© Springer-Verlag Berlin Heidelberg 2002

key areas of functionality are implemented. A primary example of this approach is ETHICS which stands for **E**ffective **T**echnical and **H**uman **I**mplementation of **C**omputer based **S**ystems). The work on ETHICS was undertaken by E. Mumford of the Manchester Business School, UK [8]. It incorporates a participational (also referred to as a socio-technical) approach that focuses upon people and procedures. The socio-technical approach is defined as "one which recognises the interaction of technology and people and produces work systems which are both technically efficient and have social characteristics which lead to high job satisfaction" [9].

The increasing importance of security issues in a computing environment raises the possibility of adapting the ETHICS method to deal with the implementation of security practices. Consequently, Security Implementation Method ETHICS, or SIM-ETHICS, was first introduced in 2000 [23] to address this situation.

We present the design and development of the SIM-ETHICS framework, which was used as part of a European Union IT security research project within a healthcare environment and represents an extension of Mumford's research into ETHICS. Case studies are used to demonstrate its effectiveness as an IS mechanism for managing security issues. We report on the outcomes as determined by an analysis of the feedback from various participants. SIM-ETHICS is the first system of its kind to focus on the security aspects of a soft systems management approach.

This work appeared in abbreviated form in a Deakin University technical report [20].

2 ETHICS

The original ETHICS methods were developed in the UK in the late 1960's to deal with the impending information revolution [16] of the 1970's. The early conceptual models of ETHICS were concerned with:

- ensuring users were satisfied with their jobs and trying to determine the impact that computers could have upon their jobs; and
- the perception that computers were perceived as agents of change within organizations.

These principles were used as the foundation of the formalized ETHICS method. Around this time Mumford [6] examined the impact of implementing computers within organizations, and determined that the successful introduction of technical changes required:

- the use of interdisciplinary planning teams, particularly when goals and objectives are being defined;
- awareness of the fact that technical changes have secondary as well as primary consequences; and
- planning does not take place in a static situation.

A continuation of the research saw development in the key area of participation and analyzed how different forms of participation could be used within the ETHICS method. In [14], the following levels of participation were defined:

- *Consultative* - This is when an existing body, e.g. steering committee, is used to implement the change process. This committee would then consult users on the effect that change will have upon them;
- *Representative* - This is when a cross selection of users affected by change, are brought together into a design group. This ensures that representatives effected by change have the same powers in the committee as those bringing about change; and
- *Consensus* - This is when all the staff impacted by the change are involved in the design process. Representatives of the staff are elected to form the design committee.

The ETHICS method was used in a wide variety of organizations to test its applicability and further develop the methodology. ETHICS has been used to develop unusual systems such as an expert system for Digital Equipment Corporation, the XSEL system was developed for their sales office to help configure DEC hardware system for customers [15]. The ETHICS principles were also used to determine the value system of large organizations [7].

A common criticism of the ETHICS method is that it is impractical [2]. The use of committees to make decisions means that unskilled workers could make decisions about very technical applications. The other argument against ETHICS is that it removes the rights of managers to manage, which could have dramatic impacts in the development of the system. To overcome some of these concerns of applicability of ETHICS a newer version of ETHICS was developed called QUICKETHICS (QUality Information from Considered Knowledge). It was developed to create and maintain manager interest [2] and it is broken down into four main areas:

- self-reflection;
- self-identification;
- group discussion; and
- group decision.

The QUICKETHICS method was also used to implement information systems within healthcare establishments [11], this research acted as a focal point for the research described later in this paper

The importance of ETHICS is in determining the system requirements. The requirements process is arguably the most important phase within system development as errors made in this phase have a potentially high impact on the eventual information systems [4]. This pioneering work by Mumford was important in establishing the role of users with the system design process.

3 The SIM-ETHICS Method

We now turn to the focus of the present paper, which is the analysis of the IS issues peculiar to implementation of security, looking specifically at one such specially designed system for a healthcare environment, SIM-ETHICS.

In overcoming the problems of implementing an IS for managing security related issues a new management methodology was developed called SIM-ETHICS (SIM stands for **S**ecurity **I**mplementation **M**ethod) which is a continuation of Mumford's ETHICS method, and which was introduced in [23]. The philosophy behind SIM-ETHICS is that computer security is not only a technical problem but also an organizational issue and hence a socio-technical approach is required.

This attitude is consistent with that of Schneier [19] who states that " ...every organization needs a security policy for its computer network. The policy should outline who is responsible for what (implementation, enforcement, audit, review), what the basic network security policies are, and why they are the way they are. The last one is important; arbitrary policies brought down from on high with no explanation are likely to be ignored. A clear, concise, coherent, and consistent policy is more likely to be followed." Thus, Schneier implicitly argues for a participational approach. He makes this more explicit: "Security measures that aren't understood and agreed to by everyone, don't work. Remember that the hardest security problems to solve are the ones that involve people; the easiest are the ones that involve bits."

Features of SIM-ETHICS not appearing in ETHICS are the development of an evaluation mechanism, a more detailed focus on technology, and a more effective manner of using user committees to develop user collective viewpoints. The main organizational issues are identified and described below [23]:

Technical and Organizational Impact
The introduction of new technology often has a technical impact within the organization. Computer systems should be phased in gradually in order to smooth out any incompatibility problems with existing technologies.

Additionally, the introduction of new types of technology could have a direct or indirect impact upon the culture of the organization. For example, new technology may be seen as a status symbol, as jobs are redesigned around it.

Costs
New technology is generally more expensive that existing technology. Costs of reduced production while the organization is in the transition phase must also be anticipated.

The introduction of new computer systems requires the training of users in order to use them effectively. Training considerations include the level of training required, the number of staff requiring training and the amount of time lost by staff because of training. Of particular concern is the need to make users aware of the limitations and advantages of new security features.

The implementation of the SIM-ETHICS method is based on a number of steps, which are identified and described in this section.

Initial Committee Consultation
The committee will be made up of a cross section of staff directly involved or affected by the implementation of the new security features. For example, representatives of staff from the different departments affected by the change, representatives of the IT department, and representatives of the other users who will be using the new security systems.

The SIM-ETHICS method uses the participational approach in order to allow user input into the process of change [8]. The levels of participation are Consultation, Representation and Consensus. The committee will decide initially what should be considered the major impacts, which may include:

- impact of introducing security systems;
- training of users;
- cost of new equipment; and
- compatibility with existing clinical and administrative computer systems.

Other areas that need to be addressed are job satisfaction, efficiency and effectiveness [8],[20]. Job satisfaction is defined as the attainment of a good "fit" between what employees are seeking from their work (their job needs, expectations and aspirations) and what they are required to do in their work; their organizational job requirement. Efficiency and effectiveness are essentially measures of performance and both aim to ensure that tasks already being carried out could be carried out in a more effective manner. Efficiency is a set of support services that help individuals to work in an organized way with all the necessary back-up facilities that they require. These will include information, materials, technical aids, specialist knowledge and supervisory help. Employees who do not receive support services which they regard as essential to their job performance, are likely to become frustrated and dissatisfied.

Managerial consultation
The intended security measures are evaluated against the SIM-ETHICS criteria to determine the level of impact implementation will have. The criteria relate to [20]:

- *Ease of Implementation* - How easily can new security features be added to a system and/or new security procedures added to an organization?
- *Training Issues* - What are the training requirements needed by the staff to use these new security features?

- *User Impact* - What is the impact that security could have upon users, e.g. how does it affect user satisfaction, efficiency or effectiveness?
- *Organizational Impact* - What affect will security features have upon the organization, e.g. changing of the organizational culture?
- *Human Issues* - What is the impact that security has upon a user from the human perspective, e.g. changes in jobs, creation of new management roles?

A representative of the committee would meet the following people, for example, system managers of existing clinical systems, and specialist IT managers, such as network managers, managers and staff involved in implementing the new security features. At these meetings, issues relating to the introduction of the security systems would be discussed (as determined in the Initial Committee Consultation stage) as well as any other possible problems that managers could foresee.

Committee stage
The views of the managers are discussed within the committee. It is now that initial problems are discussed. The committee decides on how to approach the user consultation stage by asking users how they feel about having to deal with a new system.

Users consultation
A representative of the committee then meets the users to explain the proposed security measures and asks them a series of pre-set questions. The security measures are then re-evaluated against the SIM-ETHICS criteria to take into account the newly raised user issues.

Committee stage
The views of the users are discussed. If problems are found concerning the system, ways would be discussed on how to overcome the problem. For instance an increase in the level of training might be suggested.

Post implementation review
This meeting takes place after the implementation to determine if any unforeseen problems have occurred and if so to discuss ways in which to rectify them.

4 Research Focus

SIM-ETHICS was used to determine the impact of two new security measures, a new computer information system and also a multimedia information system [22] within a major UK hospital. This major hospital was located in the South of England and was used as part of the European Union SEISMED (Secure Environment for Information Systems in Medicine) project and the ISHTAR Project Implementing Secure Health Telematics Applications in Europe [13,17]. The hospital was used as a reference centre for the implementation of new security systems. The lessons learned from the implementation were shared with other partners within the project consortium and are detailed below in case studies. The areas looked at were:

- *Passwords* - To determine user perception on the need and use of passwords as a form of access control for computer systems.
- *Multimedia Medical System* - To determine design issues in developing a new medical multimedia system [22].
- *Physical Access Control Cards* - The use of 'Swipe Cards' to control access of staff and visitors within the hospital. These cards were used to control access after working hours and in sensitive areas, e.g. maternity wards.
- *Information Message System* - A universal information message display system, the information on the system related to general administration and guidelines, and clinical practices, protocols and guidelines. Some of the information contained on the Information Message System was considered to be sensitive in nature, e.g. drug dosage levels for medicines. If this information were entered incorrectly into the system, patients could potentially be given overdoses.

SIM-ETHICS has also been used in Australia [1,5,10] to help determine the effectiveness of on-line medical information systems and determine associated security issues. The Australian state of New South Wales is planning to implement such an on-line system by the year 2003. Each patient would have a single Unique Patient Identifier and use this with a password to gain access to their medical records [25]. As the online medical system has not been developed yet, it was decided to evaluate the security requirements of a very similar style of on-line system, Web-CT. Web-CT is an online teaching system that is widely used by Universities to run courses. It allows students to remotely access the system and access their student records as well as post queries on discussion boards. The outcome of the evaluation was to find a range of security flaws that should be tested for in the intended on-line medical systems.

5 Case Study Examples

We will look at three case studies of the implementation of SIM-ETHICS within a healthcare environment.

Case Study 1 - Access Swipe Cards

Access swipe cards were used to enforce physical access control of selected areas and also as identification cards. Access control systems were being implemented in the following areas:

- Child Health;
- Maternity Units;
- Certain external doors to the main hospital.

The access control cards were controlled by a central computer system based in the security office. This system recorded details of which areas staff have access to and where staff are presently.

Each staff member was given an introductory session on how to use the access system. General talks on the basic operation of the system were also given to groups of users.

System managers were told that standardized cards across the system would make implementation more efficient. They were also informed that it was important to keep the user information current, adding new users as they came into the system, and deleting old ones as they left.

Case Study 2: VTX

VTX (Video TeXt system) is an information message system that is used to display and share clinical information, e.g. hazard notices, medical images, ward procedures or urgent information. The aim of VTX is to ensure that users are given the information that is relevant to them.

The notices were sent out via a distribution list. Once a notice had been read a message was automatically returned to the system to signify this event.

Another aim of VTX is to use the system within clinical departments to circulate details relating to practice guidelines, surgical protocols, medical dosage levels, etc.

A simple written instruction guide was provided to users, and several 'open days' were run demonstrating system use.

Determining which people have rights to add what data to the system was critical. Moreover, ensuring the accuracy of the data added was a primary concern. (For instance, drug dosages to be given to patients might be the kind of data entered.)

Case Study 3: User Perception of Passwords

This case study was concerned with trying to determine what users thoughts of computer security passwords as a method of authentication. The example made use of focused interviews of users and questionnaires in order to determine user opinions.

This case study was different to the previous examples. The focus was not on an actual technology. The case study aim was to determine users perception on the need and use of passwords as a form of access control for computer systems, and to determine if there was a need to run security awareness programs within the organization.

6   Post-installation Evaluation

Evaluation of the installation of the three systems was done in two ways. A set of consultation questions was discussed with sixteen members of the staff and the results analyzed by the group as a whole. In addition, a questionnaire containing thirteen questions was distributed to all systems managers.

Results of SIM-ETHICS assessment of Access SwipeCcards

The following were the results of applying the SIM-ETHICS method to the access control case study.

Ease of implementation

The implementation of the access cards system would require an extensive amount of effort. This therefore means that certain areas of the hospital will have access control before others, this could cause problems, as, for instance, if the main external entrances were fitted with access control, all staff would have to carry these cards, while they may not be usable at other access points.

Training issues

Training a large number of people could be expensive. In order to keep costs down, it was suggested that training could be implemented by a mixture of:

- demonstration of cards to certain staff, e.g. system managers within the department. Then these staff can train the rest of the department; and

- circulation of leaflets explaining how to use the cards and what to do in unusual circumstances, e.g. loss of the card

User impact

The introduction of the access control system had limited impact upon users actual jobs. The implementation of the system did reassure users about the security of the environment in which they operate.

Organizational impact

It helped to enforce the 'Security Culture' concept to staff.

Human issues

The introduction of the access control system would not have a huge impact apart from giving the security manager and departmental managers some extra responsibilities.

Overall

Access cards were accepted as being needed, and there was overall support for their implementation. It was agreed that they would help in raising levels of security awareness amongst staff.

A cost-effective method of training from 1000 to 4000 users would have to be found.

Results of SIM-ETHICS assessment of VTX

The following were the results of applying the SIM-ETHICS method to the VTX information system.

Ease of implementation

Implementation was based upon user types and areas, e.g. system managers, business managers and the main clinical areas impacting all users. A great deal of effort was needed to guarantee satisfactory implementation.

Training issues

The system was designed to be user friendly, and so it was assumed that most staff would not have difficulty with it. This was indeed the case. Those users who did have problems were able to contact their system managers.

User impact

Users wanted a check built into the system to verify data.

Organizational impact

The use of VTX dramatically changed the way notices and guidelines were distributed within the organization.

It was anticipated that the culture of the organization might change in one of the following ways:
- the organization moves towards a greater acceptance of IT;
- the organization accepts IT in ways that were not planned for, e.g. VTX expands to cover new areas such as community healthcare;
- the system 'snowballs' and similar systems are developed, e.g notice boards;
- the development continues until it is out of control and problems occur, e.g. inaccurate information being entered and distributed on the systems.

Human issues

Certain jobs may need to be restructured, e.g. the person who photocopies the notices may find their job function reorganized.

Overall

Accuracy of the data on the system needs to be a primary concern.
The introduction of VTX is likely to have an impact on the culture of the organization.

Results of SIM-ETHICS assessment of Passwords

User impact

Users were unhappy about having one password for each system, especially when they use three or four systems. Because of this issue some users had a written record of their passwords. Many users would prefer one password that would give them access to all the information systems that they use.

Users were also unhappy with a system which forced them to change their password every three months.

Organizational impact

Changes to the password mechanisms on the hospital information systems helped to reinforce a security culture within the hospital.

Human issues

There was no direct impact because passwords were already used as the authentication mechanism of the hospital information systems.

Ease of implementation

The changes to the password (authentication) mechanism of the hospital systems had an impact upon all users.

Overall

A good solution to multiple passwords and frequent password changing was not found.

Subsequent Action:

Based upon the above SIM-ETHICS analysis, the management of the hospital under-took the following actions:

Access Swipe Cards

Altered the staff training program by training key trainers from the separate departments. These key trainers would then train the rest of the staff in their department.

A general promotion campaign was organized within the hospital to raise awareness of the new system and answer many of the commonly asked questions.

VTX Information System

Staff whose jobs would be affected by the introduction of the VTX system were to be given new tasks, e.g. the receptionist who photocopied the notices was re-assigned to cross-checking data to ensure matching.

Mechanisms were implemented to slow the introduction of certain parts of the system to ensure that the system did not "snowball" but was able to still meet user requirements.

Passwords

Management would introduce a hospital wide computer security awareness program focusing upon the use of passwords.

The results of the SIM-ETHICS evaluation allowed management to make decisions relating to the change management aspect of implementing new information systems. The SIM-ETHICS method as stated before, is based around committees which allows a consensus approach to be taken for the implementation of security measures [20]. In the healthcare scenario where SIM-ETHICS was applied it proved to be a highly successful method to assist in the implementation of security systems.

7 Other Uses of SIM-ETHICS

SIM-ETHICS has also been used as part of a computer security risk analysis methodology called ODESSA (Organizational DEScriptive Security Analysis) and is used to determine the security requirements of healthcare organizations. Any security countermeasures that are being implemented will effect the healthcare organization as a whole. The SIM-ETHICS method is used to give management feedback on how security measures will impact an organization [21].

8 Conclusions

Participational IS systems are particularly necessary for the implementation of security systems, and can work well, as exhibited by the success of the SIM-ETHICS method. One of the positive outcomes of such a system is a 'buy-in' on the part of the users to a security culture. In addition, the level of understanding of security issues and practices is raised across the company with the participational process.

The use of SIM-ETHICS enables management to collect the consensus view of users relating to new security systems and gives them the chance to implement solutions to future problems, before they occur. This method also allows users to raise issues and concerns about implementing new security features. The use of SIM-ETHICS was a success because it allowed users to determine how information systems and security systems could be implemented within their organizations. It also allowed management to anticipate problems before they arose, and take precautionary measures, e.g. developing training strategies for several hundred staff.

The SIM-ETHICS system was successfully used within a healthcare environment in the UK and also within Australia. The research did identify a number of weaknesses of the method. One of the major problems was the cost involved in setting up and running a project using the SIM-ETHICS method. Staff are required to attend committees on a regular basis and complete questionnaires. There was criticism by management of the time taken by staff to partake in the method. Another major problem was the fact that the methodology only provided qualitative data for management to make decisions, some managers felt that a quantitative aspect of the SIM-ETHICS method might have been beneficial. Future work will focus on supplying both types of information to the client.

References

1. Warren, M.J. and Hutchinson.: W. A Security Method for Healthcare Organisations, 8th IFIP Annual Working Conference on Information Security Management, pp 157-167, Las Vegas, USA, September (2001).
2. Avison, D.E. & Fitzgerald, G.: Information Systems Development: Methodologies, Techniques and Tools. McGraw-Hill, UK (1995).
3. Flynn, D.: Information Systems Requirements: Determination and Analysis. McGraw-Hill, UK (1998).
4. Flynn D. and Jazi M. D.: Constructing user requirements: a social process for a social context. Information Systems Journal, Vo: 8, No1 53-83. Blackwell Science, UK (1998).
5. Leitch S., Hutchinson W. and Warren M.J: Healthcare IT Security: Can the European Union experiences assist Australia, ACIS (Australasian Conference on Information Systems) 00, pp 101-107, Brisbane, Australia, December (2000).
6. Mumford, E.: Computers, Planning and Personnel Management, Institute of Personnel Management, UK (1969).
7. Mumford, E.: Values, Technology and Work. Martinus Nijhoff Publishers, The Netherlands, (1981).
8. Mumford, E.: Designing Participatively, Technical Report, Manchester Business School, UK (1983).
9. Mumford, E.: Designing Human Systems, Technical Report, Manchester Business School, Manchester, UK (1983).
10. Warren,M.J. and Warren S.: The Role of Participation in Systems, International Conference on Systems Thinking in Management, (Incorporating the First Australasian Conference on System Dynamics and Sixth Australia and New Zealand Systems Conference), pp 638-642, Geelong, Australia, November, (2000).
11. Mumford, E.: Designing Human Systems For Health Care, The ETHICS Method, 4C Corporation, Netherlands, (1993).
12. Mumford, E.: Effective Requirement Analysis and Systems Design: The Ethics Method, Macmillan, UK (1995).
13. Furnell, S.M. Warren M.J and Evans M.P.: The ISHTAR World Wide Web Dissemination and Advisory Service for Healthcare Information Security, Published in "Implementing Secure Healthcare Telematics Applications in Europe", pp 249-289, IOS Press, The Netherlands, ISBN 90-5199-489-3, (2001).
14. Mumford, E. and Henshall, D.: A participative approach to computer systems design, Associated Business Press, UK (1979).
15. Mumford, E. and MacDonald, W.: XSEL'S Progress: The Continuing Journey of an Expert System, John Wiley & Sons Ltd, UK (1989).
16. Mumford, E and Ward, T.B.: Computers: Planning for People, Batsford Limited, UK (1968).

17. Furnell S.M, Gritzalis D., Katsikas S., Mavroudakis K., Sanders P. and Warren M.J.: Methods of responding to healthcare security incidents, CD Proceedings, Medinfo 98, Seoul, South Korea, August (1998).
18. Nurminen, N.: People of Computers: Three ways of Looking at Information Systems, Chartwell-Bratt, Sweden (1988).
19. Schneier, B.: Secrets and Lies, Wiley Computer Publishing (2000).
20. Warren, M.J.: A Practical Soft System Management Approach to Implementing Security, Deakin University Technical Report CC99/05, Deakin University, Australia. (1999).
21. Warren, M.J.: A Risk Analysis Model to reduce computer security risks among healthcare organisations, Risk Management: An International Journal, Perpetuity Press, Vol 3: No 1, pp 27-37, UK. (2000).
22. Warren, M.J. Sanders, P.W & Gaunt, P.N.: Participational Management and the Implementation of Multimedia Systems, In Proceedings MEDIACOMM 95 - International Conference on Multimedia Communications, Southampton, pp 131-155, UK (1995).
23. Warren, M.J., Warren, S. and Love, P.E.D: Using Participation Effectively to Implement and Evaluate Information Security within an Organisation, In Proceedings of Americas Conference on Information Systems 2000 (AMCIS 2000). pp 310-316, Long Beach, California, USA, (2000).
24. Zuboff, S.: In the Age of the Smart Machine, Basic Books, New York, USA (1988).
25. New South Wales Government (NSW). Report of the NSW Health Council – A Better Health System for NSW, ISBN 0-7347-3138-8, Australia. (2000).

Resolving Conflicts in Authorization Delegations

Chun Ruan and Vijay Varadharajan

School of Computing and Information Technology
University of W.Sydney
Kingswood, NSW 2747, Australia
{chun,vijay}@cit.uws.edu.au

Abstract. In this paper, we first discuss some drawbacks of the existing conflict authorization resolution methods when access rights are delegated, and then propose a flexible authorization model to deal with the conflict resolution problem with delegation. In our model, conflicts are classified into comparable and incomparable ones. With comparable conflicts, the conflicts come from the grantors that have grant connectivity relationship with each other, and the predecessor's authorizations will always take precedence over the successor's. In this way, the access rights can be delegated but the delegation can still be controlled. With incomparable conflicts, the conflicts come from the grantors that do not have grant connectivity relationship with each other. Multiple resolution policies are provided so that users can select the specific one that best suits their requirements. In addition, the overridden authorizations are still preserved in the system and they can be reactivated when other related authorizations are revoked or the policy for resolving conflicts is changed. We give a formal description of our model and describe in detail the algorithms to implement the model. Our model is represented using labelled digraphs, which provides a formal basis for proving the semantic correctness of our model.

1 Introduction

In an access model with both positive and negative authorizations, conflicting situations can arise. If a subject (user) is granted both positive and negative authorizations on the same object, then we say that these two authorizations *conflict* with each other with respect to this subject. For instance, when a subject s is granted both "read" and "not read" rights on a file F from different subjects (grantors), then these two authorizations are in conflict with each other. Solving authorization conflicts in security policy specification is an important design issue in an access control model. Several previous research work have looked at this issue of conflict resolution policy, though in practice the realisation of such schemes has lagged behind the need.

Currently the proposed conflict resolution policies can be summarised as follows(see references [2,3,5,6,7,8]):

Negative (Positive)-takes-precedence: If a conflict occurs on some subject, the negative (positive) authorizations will take precedence over positive (negative) ones.

L. Batten and J. Seberry (Eds.): ACISP 2002, LNCS 2384, pp. 271–285, 2002.
© Springer-Verlag Berlin Heidelberg 2002

Strong-and-Weak: Authorizations are classified into two types, strong and weak. The strong authorizations will always override the weak ones when conflict occurs. Conflicts between strong authorizations are not permitted. When conflict occurs between weak authorizations, the negative ones will take precedence.

More specific-take-precedence: The authorization granted to a subject will take precedence over the authorizations granted to a group to which the subject belongs when conflict occurs.

Time-take-precedence: The new authorization will take precedence over the old one.

In a flexible access control model, it is necessary to have delegation of access rights between subjects especially in a large distributed system. Furthermore, there could be multiple administrators in such a distributed authorization model. Most of the conflict resolution policies are limited when delegation requirements are taken into consideration. For instance, they suffer from the following common problem: when a subject s_1 delegates some privilege to another subject s_2, s_1 can lose control of the delegated privilege with respect to further delegations. This situation can lead to unexpected situations; for instance, s_2 may then give back to s_1 a negative authorization for the same access privilege. For example, in a company, suppose the chairman creates a file and then delegates its "read" right to each member of the executive committee. Let us assume that each member of the executive committee further delegates this "read" right to his (her) subordinate managers so that they can grant the "read" right to the members in their project teams. In this circumstance, this file's "read" right has multiple administrators, i.e. the chairman, executive committee members and managers. If the policies mentioned above are used to resolve the conflicts, it may not be possible to prevent the following situation: a manager can grant a "not read" right for the file to the member of the executive committee (his/her) grantor) or even to the chairman (his/her) grantor's grantor); furthermore, this negative authorization can dominate the previous positive one the member already has. As a result, the member of the executive committee or the chairman can be denied to read the file. This is certainly not reasonable in practice. We claim that the problem comes from delegation without any control. This can lead to users not exercising the delegation of access rights since this means that they can lose control of the object and therefore risk sacrificing their privileges. We believe that delegation of rights should be supported in a large-scale decentralized access control system for flexibility, but at the same time, the delegation must be controlled. A promising approach to exercising this control is to adopt an appropriate conflict resolution policy.

In this paper, we propose a conflict resolution policy to achieve this controlled delegation. In our policy, if s_1 delegates or transtively delegates to s_2 some privilege, then for this privilege, s_1's granted privilege will have higher priority than s_2's granted privilege whenever they conflict over some other subject. Moreover s_2 is not allowed to grant s_1 any further authorizations. In other words, the priority of the subject decreases as the privilege delegation moves from one subject to another, and the subject with lower priority cannot grant authorizations to the subject with higher priority. Assuming all the rights on an object are first delegated from the owner of this object, the owner will always have the highest priority for this object and his/her authorizations can never be overridden. Thus users do not need to worry about losing control of the objects by using delegation of rights. The priority information comes from the grant connectivity relationship, which is dynamic and is usually different from object to object. In this way we can support controlled delegation of access rights, and take advantage of both distributed and centralised administrations of rights. As for the above example, since the priorities of subjects for "read" right on the file decreases from the chairman to committee members to managers, the unexpected situation discussed above will not occur. Furthermore, if some member of a team gets both "read" right on the file from his manager and "not read" right from the chairman, the chairman's granted privilege will dominate the other.

The remainder of this paper is organized as follows. In section 2, we propose a formal model of authorization conflict resolution. In section 3, we present the relevant algorithms that implement our model. In section 4, we briefly consider authorization state transformations based on our model. Finally, in section 5 we summarize the major contributions of this paper and outline some future work.

2   The Authorization Conflict Resolution Model

In this section, we outline the basic idea and provide a formal description of our authorization conflict resolution model.

2.1   The Basic Idea

In our authorization model, we allow both positive and negative authorizations, and permit access rights to be delegated from one subject to another. So, for any access right on any object, it may have multiple administrators that can grant authorizations. Different to the previously proposed conflict resolution policies, we classify conflict authorizations into two categories namely *comparable* and *incomparable* conflicts. Consider the situation where a subject s_3 is granted two conflicting authorizations with respect to an access right r on an object o from subjects s_1 and s_2 respectively. We say that these two conflicting authorizations are comparable if s_2's administrative privilege for r on o is granted (or transitively granted) by s_1, or vice versa. In the first case we assign a higher priority to s_1's grant than s_2's grant to solve the conflict occurring over the subject s_3. On the other hand, if there is no grant connectivity relationship between s_1 and s_2, then this conflicting authorization is said to be incomparable. In our model, we support multiple policies to solve incomparable conflicts to meet different users' requirements. For example, we may use the positive authorization to override the negative authorization or vice versa. We require that all the rights of an object be originally delegated from the owner of the object, so that the owner's authorization will take precedence over any other conflicting authorizations.

In addition, although some authorizations may be overridden by other authorizations, they are not eliminated from the authorization state. We preserve all the authorizations; they are either revoked explicitly or by recursive revocation. So conflicting authorizations can be present simultaneously in our model. The main advantages of this approach include the ability of re-activating the overridden authorizations after the other related authorizations are revoked, and the ability of changing the policy of incomparable conflicts resolution.

2.2   Notation and Definitions

Let S be a finite set of subjects (users), O be a finite set of objects (files, relations), R be a finite set of access rights (e.g. read, write, select, etc.), and T be a finite set of grant types. Then we have the following definition for authorization.

Definition 1. (**Authorization**) *An* authorization *is a 5-ary tuple* (s, o, t, r, g), *where* $s \in S, o \in O, t \in T, r \in R, g \in S$.

Intuitively, an authorization (s, o, t, r, g) states that a grantor g has granted subject s the access right r on object o with grant type t. In this paper, we will consider three grant types: $T = \{*, +, -\}$, where

* $*$: delegatable, which means the subject has been granted the access right r on o as well as the privilege for administration of r on o.
* $+$: positive, which means the subject has been granted the access right r on o.
* $-$: negative, which means the subject has been denied the access right r on o.

For example, $(user_1, file_1, +/-, read, user_2)$ states that $user_1$ is granted / denied to "read" $file_1$ by $user_2$, and $(user_1, file_1, *, read, user_2)$ states that $user_1$ is granted by $user_2$ not only the privilege to "read" $file_1$, but also the privilege to grant authorizations with respect to the "read" right on $file_1$ to other subjects.

Note that $*$ means $+$ together with administrative privilege on an access. The administrative privilege is related to a specific access right on an object. That is a subject may have the administrative privilege for "read" but not for "write".

Definition 2. (**Authorization State**) *An* authorization state *is the set of all authorizations at a given time.*

In this paper, we will usually use $\mathcal{A}$ and a (possibly with subscripts) to denote an authorization set and a single authorization respectively, and use $a.s$, $a.o$, $a.t$, $a.r$, $a.g$ to denote the corresponding components of subject, object, type, right and grantor of a respectively.

In order to formalize our approach, we use a *labelled digraph* to represent an authorization state as follows. For every object o, G_o is used to represent all the authorizations with respect to the object o. Let $G_o = (V, E, t, l)$ be a labelled digraph, where V is a finite set of vertices representing the subjects that hold some authorizations on o, E is a finite set of arcs such that if there exists an authorization (s, o, t, r, g) in authorization state $\mathcal{A}$, then (g, s) is in E, t is a type function from E to T, which maps every arc in E to a specific type in T. We will use different types of arcs, denoted as $t(e)$, to represent different grant types, as shown in Figure 1.

Fig. 1. Different Arc Types for Different Grant Types.

Suppose E_*, E_+, E_- denote the sets of $*$ arcs, $+$ arcs, and $-$ arcs respectively. Then $E = E_* \cup E_+ \cup E_-$. l is a label function from E to the power set of R, which maps every arc (g, s) of type t in E to a set of rights on o

that g grants to s and the grant type is t. For instance, if $t((g, s)) = *$, then $l((g, s)) = \{r \mid \exists(s, o, *, r, g) \in \mathcal{A}\}$. In G_o, every arc e is labelled with $l(e)$. In the rest of this paper, we will sometimes omit t and l and simply write $G = (V, E)$, whenever there is no confusion in the context. Following this, an authorization state $\mathcal{A}$ can be represented by a digraph G, which is a set of G_o for all objects o in the system. That is, $G = \{G_o \mid o \in O\}$. Figure 2 is an example of G_o.

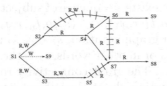

Fig. 2. G_o: an example of graph representation of authorizations on an object o, where $S1, ..., S9$ are subjects, R and W are access rights.

In addition, we will use $G_{o,r}$ to denote all the authorizations with respect to a specific access right r on o. That is, $G_{o,r}$ is a subgraph of $G_o = (V, E, t, l)$ that contains all arcs with the label containing r and the corresponding vertices. More formally, $G_{o,r} = (V', E', t')$, where $E' = \{(s_1, s_2) \mid (s_1, s_2) \in E$ and $r \in l((s_1, s_2))\}$, $V' = \{v \mid \exists v'(v, v') \in E'$ or $(v', v) \in E'\}$, and for any $e' \in E'$, $t'(e') = t(e')$. Note that there is no need for arc labels in $G_{o,r}$ anymore. For example, with reference to the G_o denoted in Figure 2, $G_{o,R}$ and $G_{o,W}$ can be illustrated in Figure 3 and Figure 4 respectively.

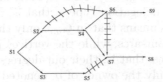

Fig. 3. $G_{o,R}$ of Figure 2.

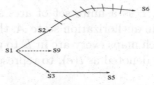

Fig. 4. $G_{o,W}$ of Figure 2.

In the rest of this paper, we will use the following graph terminologies. For an arc (a, b) in a digraph, a is called the *initial vertex* of (a, b), and b is called the *terminal vertex* of (a, b). *In-arc* of a vertex v is the arc with v as its terminal vertex and *in-degree* of a vertex v is the number of its *in-arcs*. *Out-arc* of a vertex v is the arc with v as its initial vertex and *out-degree* of a vertex v, is the number of its out-arcs. A *path* of *length* n from a to b is a sequence of one or more arcs (a, x_1) $(x_1, x_2), ..., (x_{n-1}, b)$, denoted by $a, x_1, \cdots, x_{n-1}, b$, and a is called the *predecessor* of b, while b is called the *successor* of a.

Now we define a binary relation on the set of subjects.

Definition 3. *(Grant Connectivity Relation $<_{o,r}$ on Subjects) Given an authorization state $\mathcal{A}$, for any subjects $s_1, s_2 \in S$, object $o \in O$, and access right $r \in R$, we say that s_1 is grant-connected to s_2 with respect to r and o in $\mathcal{A}$, denoted by $s_1 <_{o,r} s_2$, if there exists an authorization (s_2, o, t, r, s_1) for some t in $\mathcal{A}$, or there exists some subject s_3 satisfying $s_1 <_{o,r} s_3$, and $s_3 <_{o,r} s_2$.*

$s_1 <_{o,r} s_2$ means there exists a sequence of subjects $s_1, x_1, x_2, \cdots, x_n, s_2$ such that $(x_1, o, t_0, r, s_1), (x_2, o, t_1, r, x_1), \cdots, (s_2, o, t_n, r, x_n)$ are all in the authorization state. In terms of our graph notation, $s_1 <_{o,r} s_2$ if and only if there exists a path from s_1 to s_2 in $G_{o,r}$, or in other words, s_1 is the predecessor of s_2 and s_2 is the successor of s_1 in $G_{o,r}$. The grant connectivity relation provides us with an important priority information about the subjects, which will be used later to solve the conflict problem. When the object and right are clear in the context, we sometimes simply write $s_1 < s_2$. For example, in the digraph $G_{o,R}$ of Figure 3, we have:

$$S_1 < S_2 < S_4 < S_6 < S_7 < S_8,$$
$$S_1 < S_2 < S_4 < S_6 < S_9, \text{ and}$$
$$S_1 < S_3 < S_5 < S_7 < S_8.$$

2.3   Formal Description of the Model

We say that an authorization state $\mathcal{A}$ is **delegation correct**, if for any subject s, object o and right r, s can grant r on o to other subjects if and only if s has been granted r on o with delegation type $*$, that is, $\exists g, (s, o, *, r, g) \in \mathcal{A}$. In our graph representation, this means that in $G_{o,r}$, only the vertices pointed to by at least one $*$ arc can have out-arcs, while the vertices pointed to only by $+$ or $-$ arcs must be terminal ones, that is, their out-degrees must be zero. We assume that for every object o, only the owner of o, denoted by s_o, has been implicitly granted all the rights on o with delegation type by the system when the object is created. So if a state is delegation correct, then there will be a path from s_o to any other vertex in $G_{o,r}$.

We say that an authorization a_1 **contradicts** an authorization a_2 if $a_1.s = a_2.s$, $a_1.o = a_2.o, a_1.g = a_2.g, a_1.r = a_2.r$, but $a_1.t \neq a_2.t$. The contradictory authorizations state that a grantor gives the same subject two different types of authorizations over the same object with the same access right. For example, authorizations $(s_2, F_1, *, R, s_1), (s_2, F_1, +, R, s_1)$ and $(s_2, F_1, -, R, s_1)$ contradict each other. Figure 5 gives the corresponding graph representation. An authorization state $\mathcal{A}$ is **not contradictory** if for any a and a' in $\mathcal{A}$, a does not contradict a'. In our graph representation, this means that in any $G_{o,r}$ there is only one arc from each vertex to another.

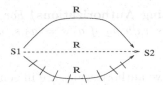

Fig. 5. Contradictory grants on object F_1.

Definition 4. *(Consistent Authorization State) An authorization state is consistent if it satisfies the following three conditions: 1. It is delegation correct, 2. It is not contradictory, and 3. For any object o and access right r, $<_{o,r}$ is a strict partial order.*

Recall that a strict partial order is transitive and anti-symmetric. In our graph notation, requiring relation $<_{o,r}$ to be a strict partial order means that the corresponding $G_{o,r}$ is acyclic.

In fact, by considering the properties of delegation correctness and not contradictory together, we have the following theorem:

Theorem 1. *Let $\mathcal{A}$ be a consistent state, then for any object o and access right r, $G_{o,r}$ in $\mathcal{A}$ is a simple rooted acyclic digraph, with the owner of the object as the root.*

Remember that in a simple graph there are no multiple arcs between each pair of vertices, and in the rooted acyclic graph, from the root one can reach any vertex in the graph. This theorem is easy to prove using the definition of consistent authorization state; so we omit the proof here. Figure 6 shows three examples of inconsistent authorization state, where $G1_{o,r}$ is not delegation correct because of the arc (s_2, s_3); $G2_{o,r}$ is contradictory because there are two arcs from s_5 to s_6; and $G3_{o,r}$ is cyclic because of the cycle s_8, s_9, s_8.

By requiring that $G_{o,r}$ acyclic, we have the following: if a subject s receives an authorization directly or indirectly from another subject s' on some object o and access right r, then s cannot grant s' any further authorization on o and r later on. In this way, we can solve the problem that exists in most conflict resolution methods discussed in section 1.

For a consistent authorization state $\mathcal{A}$ and a single authorization a, if $\mathcal{A} \cup \{a\}$ is still consistent, then we call a is *consistent* with $\mathcal{A}$. In our model, we require that the authorization state should always be consistent.

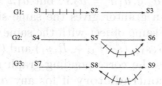

Fig. 6. Examples of Inconsistent Authorization State.

Definition 5. *(Conflicting Authorizations) For any two authorizations a_1 and a_2 in $\mathcal{A}$, a_1 conflicts with a_2 if $a_1.s = a_2.s$, $a_1.o = a_2.o$, $a_1.r = a_2.r$, $a_1.t \neq a_2.t$ and $a_1.g \neq a_2.g$.*

From the definition, two authorizations are in conflict if they have the same subject, object and access right, but have different grant types and grantors. In our graph $G_{o,r}$, this means that the conflicting arcs have the same terminal vertex but different initial vertices and arc types. Since there are three grant types in our model, three kinds of conflicts may arise, as illustrated in Figure 7.

Note that type $*$ and $+$ are considered conflicting in the sense that $*$ holds the administrative privilege on an access right while $+$ does not. Conflicts are additionally classified into comparable conflicts and incomparable conflicts as follows.

Definition 6. *(Comparable Conflicts) Suppose a_1 and a_2 are any two conflicting authorizations on object o and access right r. Then a_1 and a_2 are comparable if $a_1.g <_{o,r} a_2.g$ or $a_2.g <_{o,r} a_1.g$. Otherwise they are incomparable.*

In other words, two conflicting authorizations are comparable if their grantors are grant-connected to each other. In our graph $G_{o,r}$, two conflicting arcs are comparable if there is a path between their initial vertices. For example, in Figure 3, (s_2, s_6) and (s_4, s_6), (s_4, s_7) and (s_6, s_7) are two pairs of comparable conflicts, while (s_4, s_7) and (s_5, s_7) are pairs of incomparable conflicts.

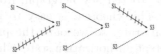

Fig. 7. Three Kinds of Conflicting Grants.

In fact, the grantors are comparable in comparable conflicts. In the grant relation path, we have higher priorities for the predecessors than the successors. So, when authorizations conflict with each other, the predecessor's grant will take precedence over the successor's. This idea can be formalized by the following overriding rule.

Definition 7. *(Overriding Rule) For any two authorizations a_1 and a_2 in $\mathcal{A}$, a_1 overrides a_2 if $a_1.s = a_2.s$, $a_1.o = a_2.o$, $a_1.r = a_2.r$, and $a_1.g <_{o,r} a_2.g$. An authorization is* inactive *if there exists some authorization that overrides it. Otherwise it is* active. *We use $Act(\mathcal{A})$ to denote the set of all active authorizations in an authorization state $\mathcal{A}$.*

The overriding rule tells us that if two authorizations are about the same subjects, objects and rights, and their grantors are grant-connected to each other, then the authorization from the predecessor will override the one from the successor. Note that this definition does not require the grant types of the two authorizations to be different. Hence the predecessor's authorization will override the successor's even though they are not in conflict. This is reasonable since this means that the two authorizations are identical except for the grantor.

Correspondingly in the graph $G_{o,r}$ for some o and r, if two arcs point to the same vertex, and there is a path between their initial vertices, then the arc from the predecessor will override the arc from the successor. Let G be the graph corresponding to an authorization state $\mathcal{A}$; then active graph of G, denoted by $Act(G)$, is the subgraph of G that contains only active arcs. It is easy to show that for any $G_{o,r}$, $Act(G_{o,r})$ is still a rooted acyclic graph, since by using the overriding rule, the in-degrees of some vertices may be reduced but not to zero. But $Act(G_{o,r})$ may become inconsistent. For example, in Figure 3, (s_2, s_6) overrides (s_4, s_6) because s_2 is s_4's predecessor. For the same reason (s_4, s_7) overrides (s_6, s_7). Figure 8 gives the active graph of Figure 3. Note that it is inconsistent because the arc (s_6, s_9) is not delegation correct.

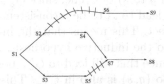

Fig. 8. Active Graph of Figure 3.

Definition 8. *(Effective State) If an authorization state $\mathcal{A}$ is consistent, then the maximal consistent subset of $Act(\mathcal{A})$ forms the* effective state *of $\mathcal{A}$, denoted by $Eff(\mathcal{A})$.*

Let G be the graph corresponding to an authorization state $\mathcal{A}$, then the effective graph of G, denoted by $Eff(G)$, corresponds to $Eff(\mathcal{A})$. $Eff(G)$ is in fact a set of $Eff(G_{o,r})$ for all objects o and access rights r of the system. Note that in the effective state, we have already eliminated all the comparable conflicts, that is, the conflicts in which their grantors are grant-connected to each other. Hence only the incomparable conflicts exist. Figure 9 gives effective graph of Figure 3.

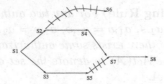

Fig. 9. Effective Graph of Figure 3.

Theorem 2. *A consistent authorization state A has a unique effective state $Eff(A)$.*

Proof. Obviously $Act(A)$ is unique. So we only need to prove that the maximal consistent subset of $Act(A)$ is unique.

Let A_1 and A_2 be two maximal consistent subsets of $Act(A)$, and $a = (s, o, t, r, g)$ be any authorization in A_1. Then there should be a corresponding arc (g, s) in $G'_{o,r}$ of A_1. We need to prove (g, s) is also in $G''_{o,r}$ of A_2. Since A_1 and A_2 are both consistent, $G'_{o,r}$ and $G''_{o,r}$ are both rooted acyclic graph with root s_o. Let $maxlen(g)$ denote the length of the largest paths from the root s_o to g in $G'_{o,r}$. We will prove by induction of the $maxlen(g)$.

When $maxlen(g) = 0$, g is the root of $G'_{o,r}$, and is the owner of object o, and hence the result is certainly true. Suppose that the result is true when $maxlen(g) \leq k$. Consider the case when $maxlen(g) = k+1$. Suppose (g, s) is not in $G''_{o,r}$, then since A_2 is a maximal consistent subset of $Act(A)$, (g, s) must be not consistent with $G''_{o,r}$. But (g, s) can not make $G''_{o,r}$ contradictory (i.e. there is more than one arc from g to s) or cyclic, since $G''_{o,r} \cup (g, s)$ is still a subgraph of $G_{o,r}$ of A and this will lead to A to be inconsistent. So (g, s) must make $G''_{o,r}$ to be not delegation correct. This means that the in-arcs of g does not have $*$ type in $G''_{o,r}$. According to the inductive hypothesis, all the in-arcs of g in $G'_{o,r}$ will be in $G''_{o,r}$ too and hence this will lead to $G'_{o,r}$ being not delegation correct. This is a contradiction. So (g, s) is also in $G''_{o,r}$. This concludes that $A_1 \subseteq A_2$. For the same reason $A_2 \subseteq A_1$. Thus $A_1 = A_2$.

Now let us consider the incomparable conflicts. We call an authorization state A is *conflict-free* if for any $a_1 \in A$ and $a_2 \in A$, a_1 is not in conflict with a_2.

Definition 9. *(Stable State) If an authorization state A is consistent, then the maximal consistent and conflict-free subset of $Eff(A)$ forms a stable state of A, denoted as $stable(A)$.*

Note that an authorization state may have more than one stable state. In theory, one stable state presents one resolution to incomparable conflicts. Let G be the graph corresponding to an authorization state A, then the stable graph of G, denoted by $stable(G)$, corresponds to $stable(A)$. $stable(G)$ is in fact a set of $stable(G_{o,r})$ for all objects o and access rights r in the system. Figure 10 and Figure 11 are two stable graphs of Figure 3.

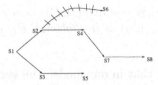

Fig. 10. One Stable Graph of Figure 3.

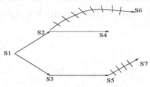

Fig. 11. Another Stable Graph of Figure 3.

For incomparable conflicts, we cannot resolve them using their grantor's priorities, since their priorities are not comparable. In our model we can support different strategies for resolving incomparable conflicts by evaluating different stable states. For example, we can support the following three strategies according to the grant types of authorizations:

(1) Pessimistic: the priority sequence is $- > + > *$;
(2) Optimistic: the priority sequence is $* > + > -$;
(3) Any : the priority sequence is $* = + = -$.

Hence a user can select the appropriate strategy that best suits the needs of his/her application. Even in one application, the strategy can vary from object to object. For example, for some objects that are very confidential, one can select the pessimistic strategy; for other objects that are not that sensitive, one can select the optimistic strategy. One can tell the system which strategy to apply to an object when the object is created, and one can change the strategy later when the sensitivity of the object is changed.

Another possible strategy for resolving incomparable conflicts is to grant an additional authorization to the subject over whom the conflicts occur by a common predecessor of the grantors of these conflicting authorizations, in particular, by the owner of the object. In this way we can change the incomparable conflicts to comparable conflicts and then can resolve them. In fact, the common predecessor here works like a judge in the sense that his/her decision has higher priority and hence can solve the dispute.

Now we can define our access control policy. We use 3-ary tuple (s, o, r) to denote an *access request* to the system, where $s \in S$, $o \in O$, $r \in R$. It states that a subject s requests to exercise access right r on object o. Then we have following access control policy.

Definition 10. (Access Control Policy) *Let $\mathcal{A}$ be an authorization state, (s, o, r) be an access request, P be a policy to resolve the incomparable conflict authorizations on o, and stable($\mathcal{A}, P$) be a stable state of $\mathcal{A}$ when applying P to o. We say that (s, o, r) is permitted if there exists some grantor g such that*

$(s, o, *, r, g)$ or $(s, o, +, r, g)$ is in stable$(\mathcal{A}, P)$; (s, o, r) is denied if there is some grantor g such that $(s, o, -, r, g)$ is in stable$(\mathcal{A}, P)$; otherwise, (s, o, r) is undecided.

It is worth mentioning that in our model, the system is the implicit grantor of any object's owner for all access rights on this object with delegatable grant type. In practice, the answer undecided may be treated as denial too. We prefer to distinguish them here to make the semantics more clear.

3   Algorithms

According to our access control policy, to determine an access request (s, o, r), we need to compute stable$(G_{o,r})$, which then need to compute $Eff(G_{o,r})$, and then compute $G_{o,r}$ from G_o. $G_{o,r}$ can be easily obtained by selecting all the arcs with r in their label and corresponding vertices from G_o. For $Eff(G_{o,r})$ and stable$(G_{o,r})$, we give the detailed algorithms in this section. We will also give the theorems about correctness and computational complexity of the algorithms, but will omit their proofs because of space limit.

Algorithm 3.1 is used to evaluate the effective graph of a $G_{o,r}$ for some object o and right r. The output is a graph G', and G'' is a temporary working graph used to construct a topological sorting of $<_{o,r}$.

Algorithm 3.1: $Evaluate\_Eff\_Graph(G_{o,r}, s_o)$
Input: $G_{o,r} = (V, E, t)$ for some object o and access right r, with root s_o
                    and arc type function t
Output: $Eff(G_{o,r}) = G' = (V', E', t')$
begin
1      $E' = \{(s_o, x)|(s_o, x) \in E\}$;
2      $V' = \{s_o\} \cup \{x|(s_o, x) \in E'\}$;
3   **for all** $e' \in E'$ **do** $t'(e') = t(e')$;
4      $E'' = E - E'$;
5      $V'' = V - \{s_o\}$; (* copy the root and out-arcs of root from $G_{o,r}$ to G' and then copy
                    the remaining part of $G_{o,r}$ to G''*)
6   **for each** $v \in V''$ with 0 in-degree **do begin**
7   **if** the in-arcs of v in E' include $*$ type **then begin**
8              $P = \{x|(x, v) \in E\}$;
9   **for each** $p \in P$ **do** $P = P \cup \{x|(x, p) \in E\}$;
                    (* compute all predecessors of v in $G_{o,r}$*)
10   **for each** arc (v, x) that goes out from v in E **do begin**
11   **if for each** $p \in P$, $(p, x) \notin E$ **then begin**
12                      $E' = E' \cup \{(v, x)\}$;
13                      $V' = V' \cup \{x\}$;
14                      $t'(e') = t(e')$;
15   **end**

```
16        end
17      end
18      E'' = E'' - {(v,x)|(v,x) ∈ E''};
19      V'' = V'' - {v};
20    end
end
```

Theorem 3. *Algorithm Evaluate_Eff_Graph is correct, and $Eff(G_{o,r})$ can be computed by $Evaluate\_Eff\_Graph(G_{o,r}, s)$ in $\mathcal{O}(N^3)$ time, where N is the number of vertices in $G_{o,r}$.*

Algorithm 3.2 evaluates a stable graph according to the policy for incomparable conflicts. Its input includes an effective graph G of $G_{o,r}$ for some object o and right r, the root s_o, and the policy P to be used. Its output is G', the stable graph of $G_{o,r}$ corresponding to P. G'' is a temporary working graph used to construct a topological sorting of $<_{o,r}$.

Algorithm 3.2: *Evaluate_Stable_Graph(G, P, s_o)*
Input: $G = (V, E, t)$ – G is a effective graph of $G_{o,r}$ for some object o and access right r,
          with root s_o and arc type function t,
      P – the policy of solving incomparable conflicts over o
Output: $stable(G_{o,r}, P) = G' = (V', E', t')$
begin
```
1      E' = {(s,x)|(s,x) ∈ E};
2      V' = {s} ∪ {x|(s,x) ∈ E'};
3      for all e' ∈ E' do t'(e') = t(e');
4      E'' = E - E';
5      V'' = V - {s}; (* copy the root and out-arcs of root in G to G' and
                        then copy the remaining part in G to G'' *)
6      for each v ∈ V'' with 0 in-degree do begin
7        if the in-degree of v is greater than 1 in G'
8        then select any in-arc that has the highest priority according
                  to policy P for incomparable conflicts and delete other in-arcs
from G'
9        if v's in-arc in E' is type * then begin
10          E' = E' ∪ {(v,x) | (v,x) ∈ E} ;
11          V' = V' ∪ {x | (v,x) ∈ E'};
12          t'((v,x)) = t((v,x)) for all (v,x) ∈ E';
13        end
14        E'' = E'' - {(v,x)|(v,x) ∈ E''};
15        V'' = V'' - {v};
16      end
end
```

Theorem 4. *Algorithm Evaluate_Stable_Graph is correct, and stable$(G_{o,r})$ can be computed by Evaluate_Stable_Graph(G, P, s) in $\mathcal{O}(N^2)$ time, where N is the number of vertices in G.*

4   Authorization State Transformation

In a dynamic environment, an authorization state is not static since users may need to add, update, or revoke certain authorizations. In this section, we consider how our proposed authorization state can be changed. Since an update can be implemented by revoking and adding, here we only consider the addition and revocation of authorizations in our model. Note that adding and revoking authorizations will update both the effective and stable state.

In the case of addition, an authorization $a = (s, o, t, r, g)$ can be added to the authorization state $\mathcal{A}$ if and only if it is consistent with the current state $\mathcal{A}$. This means that in $\mathcal{A}$, g must get the delegatable right for r on o, a can not contradict with any other authorization in $\mathcal{A}$ and $<_{o,r}$ must still be a partial order after the addition.

For revocation, on the other hand, we adopt a cascading revocation approach to implement this operation. An authorization $a = (s, o, t, r, g)$ can be revoked from the system if the requester is g, and the authorization state must remain consistent after the revocation. Users are also allowed to change the policy of resolving incomparable conflicts for an object. This would lead to an update of the stable state.

For example, for the $G_{o,R}$ shown in Figure 3, $(s_3, o, R, -, s_7)$ or $(s_8, o, R, -, s_7)$ cannot be added to $G_{o,R}$ because adding $(s_3, o, R, -, s_7)$ will result in a cyclic graph while adding $(s_8, o, R, -, s_7)$ generates a graph which represents a contradictory authorization state. But adding $(s_5, o, R, +, s_1)$ is allowed. On the other hand, consider the situation where s_2 requests to revoke $(s_4, o, R, *, s_2)$. This will lead to the deletion of arc (s_2, s_4) and cascading deletion of arcs (s_4, s_6), (s_6, s_9), (s_6, s_7) (s_4, s_7), and (s_7, s_8) from the graph. The resulting $G_{o,R}$ after the addition and revocation is shown in Figure 12.

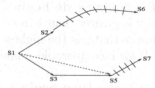

Fig. 12. $G_{o,R}$ after update.

5   Conclusions and Future Work

In this paper, we have proposed a conflict resolution model to resolve conflicts that can occur when access rights are delegated. A major feature of our approach is that we classified conflicts into comparable and incomparable ones and this classification is useful not only in the control of access right delegation but also for supporting multiple policies to resolve conflicts. Our model also provides a flexible framework to preserve conflict authorizations so that it is possible to re-activate some early overridden access rights if proper authorizations are revoked or the policy of conflict resolution is changed.

With respect to the incomparable conflict resolution, our current model provides four different policies. In fact, this can be further extended. For example, under some situations, we may expect to have a logical mechanism to deal with incomparable conflicts. In this case, we can re-formalize the notion of stable state by associating proper logical relationships among those incomparable conflicts. The other issue we have not discussed in this paper is concerned with inheritance in conflict resolution. If we consider the inheritance relationship between subjects, objects, and access rights respectively, then the conflict resolution can become complex because many conflicts may be *implicit* and solving these implicit conflicts will require some reasoning procedure to deal with inheritance in the access control model. These issues will be investigated in our future work.

References

1. E. Bertino, F.Buccafurri, E.Ferrari, P.Rullo, A logical framework for reasoning on data access control policies. *proceedings of the 12th IEEE Computer Society Foundations Workshop*, IEEE Computer Society Press, Los Alamitos, 1999, pp.175-189.
2. E. Bertino, S. Jajodia, P. Samarati, Supporting multiple access control policies in database systems. *Proc.of the IEEE Symposium on Research in Security and Privacy*, Oakland(CA), 1996.
3. R. Fagin, On an authorization mechanism. *ACM Transaction on Database Systems*, Vol. 3, 1978, pp 310-319.
4. M.Harrison, W.Ruzzo and J.Ullman, Protection in operating systems. *Communications of ACM 19(8)*,pp 461-471, 1976.
5. N.Gal-Oz, E. Gudes, and E.B. Fernandez, A model of methods access authorization in object-oriented databases. *Proceedings of International Conference on Very Large Data Bases*, pp 52-61, 1993.
6. T.F. Lunt et al, *Secure Distributed Data Views*, Vol. 1-4, SRI International, 1989.
7. F. Rabitti, E. Bertino, W. Kim, and D. Woelk, A model of authorization for next generation database systems. *ACM Transaction on Database Systems*, Vol 16, pp 88-131, 1991.
8. M. Satyanarayanan, Integrating security in a large distributed system. *ACM-TOCS*, vol.7, no.3, pp 247-280, Aug. 1989.
9. T. Woo and S. Lam, Designing a distributed authorization service. *Proceedings of IEEE INFOCOM'98*, 1998.

Policy Administration Domains

M. Hitchens[1], Vijay Varadharajan[1], and G. Saunders[2]

[1]Distributed System and Network Security Research Group
Department of Computing
Macquarie University
{michaelh,vijay}@ics.mq.edu.au
[2]Department of Computer Science
University of Sydney
gsaunder@cs.usyd.edu.au

Abstract. We present a model for policy administration structures. The model consists of a mathematical notation that captures the relationship between policies and objects and the entities that manage policies for those objects. In the model a system is viewed as consisting of a number of policy administration domains. The domains are arranged in a hierarchy, representing descending levels of authority. The presence of an object in a domain represents the ability of the manager of that domain to write policy for that object. A number of important issues for policy administration are identified and addressed within the model. These include meta-policy questions, such as who has control over the placement of an object in a policy administration domain and where it can be moved within the hierarchy. A number of possible approaches to each of these questions is identified and expressed in the notation presented. The model is capable of expressing policy administration in DAC, MAC and combined systems.

1. Introduction

The majority of computing today takes place in distributed systems. Networks have taken the place of centralised systems with the result that data and services can be located throughout the distributed computing environment. With the increasing importance of distributed systems the question of access to those systems and their data acquires a corresponding significance. Access control involves specifying the activities that authenticated users can carry out on the resources of the system.

There is a variety of existing access control mechanisms, such as access control lists, capabilities [3], role based access control [5] and lattice based access control [12]. These mechanisms are all vehicles for expressing the access control policies that govern a system. The policies that can be expressed using these mechanisms can be very simple, such as with Unix access control lists, or very complicated, depending on the facilities provided [2,7,16]. Regardless of the mechanism employed the access control policies must be specified and managed.

As with the policies themselves their administration can vary in complexity. Much work has been done in the area of policy specification, in terms of both mechanisms, for example [2,6,7,8,16], and potential policy settings, for example [4,10]. Comparatively little attention has been given to the topic of policy administration,

L. Batten and J. Seberry (Eds.): ACISP 2002, LNCS 2384, pp. 286–302, 2002.

especially in terms of the administration structure. Some work, such as [15], considers the administration of policy solely as an extension of a given mechanism or propose a new mechanism [1,11] but do not consider the possible forms the administrative structures may take. Even work, such as [17], which has considered some of the issues of decentralised and context-sensitive policy management, does not address the structures such management may take. Many access control proposals [6,9] consider policy administration to be centralised, with all decisions being made by a security administrator or equivalent. This allows good control and regulation of what polices exist in the system, but does constrict users. Even Unix-like systems, which do not have a centralised policy manager, have a very simple model of policy administration, where each user administers the polices for objects they own, with any super user being able to override these settings. This presents a simple, two level, hierarchy of administration. With the increasing complexity of systems it appears worthwhile to examine a more extensive range of options, beyond the limits of commonly used models. In the first instance this should be done in a mechanism independent manner, as this will simplify the analysis, while recognising that in practice the policy mechanism chosen will affect the policy administration. The results of such analysis should be a better understanding of the options available for policy management.

In this paper we examine possible structures for the administration of access control policies. We start by identifying some central issues that distinguish policy administration models. The majority of these issues do not submit to single answers. From these issues a number of options are identified that could realistically be employed. We then use a mathematical notation to express the range of policy management options identified. This should allow comparisons to be made between various systems and proposals. The framework developed should further allow other practical arrangements for the administration of access control policy to be identified.

In section 2 we present our basic definition of a policy and policy administration domains. Section 3 discusses the issues of policy management and presents our mathematical expression of the options, in a mechanism independent manner. This section concludes with a simple extension to our model, to handle some differentiation in the power of managers, in order to demonstrate the flexibility of the model. The model presented in section 3 is presented in a mechanism independent manner. As with any abstraction this can lead to a loss of detail. In section 4 we present an extension of our model to Role Based Access Control, the loss of generality being countered by a corresponding improvement in the representation. Section 5 presents our conclusions and discusses future work.

2. Policy

A policy is an expression of the allowable access to an object. The exact expression of this depends on the mechanism employed. In Unix it takes the form of an access control list, such as

```
-rwx------
```

In a more complex system, such as [2,7,16], a policy may be expressed using programming language based constructs, for example:

```
create_privilege := privilege
    {create}
    condition if time>=09.00 and time <=17.00
end_privilege
```

Regardless of the means of expression, for a policy to actually allow access it must be related to one or more objects. This defines the *scope* of the policy. The linkage between policy and object may be explicit, to one or more objects, or implicit. Unix, for example, explicitly links a policy to a single object, by having a separate access control list for each file and directory. Other systems allow a single policy to apply to a number of explicitly named objects. Still further proposals allow the use of policy domains, where policies within the domain apply to all objects also within the domain, making the linkage more implicit than explicit. For the purposes of this paper we will confine ourselves to systems where the linkage between policy and object is explicit. While the use of policy domains is obviously an important issue in the administration of policy, we leave its consideration to future, both in the interests of space and to avoid confusion here between policy domains and the orthogonal policy administration domains.

2.1 Policy Administration Domains

In a given system there will be a set of policies that a user has expressed and objects to which those policies can be made to apply. We call such a set a *policy administration domain* as it consists of the entities under the policy control of that user. Obviously, in certain systems and for some users, this set will be empty.

In many systems we can identify a single user (or group of users) who can, potentially at least, write policies that apply to all objects within the system. While it is unlikely, except in MAC (Mandatory Access Control) [12] systems, that any given policy will be so broad in actual scope, the potential exists and defines a notional limit. The objects within such a limit (and the policies applying to them) form a single administration domain. This domain can be considered the root administration domain for the system. In some systems it is the only administration domain, such tasks being limited to a single policy administrator. While tempting to those that favour centralised control, the task may be beyond the abilities of single individual (or even a small group), or this approach may simply be deemed undesirable from an organisational point of view.

As an alternative to centralised management, some policy administration functions may be devolved to other users. If the administration of certain policies and objects is entirely removed from the ambit of the chief administrator then, for our purposes, those entities so separated can be considered to constitute a separate system and we need not consider this for the moment. Instead, we need to consider the case where policy administration duties are given to other users, but without lessening the abilities of the grantor. As an example, Unix can be considered to act in this way, with policy administration domains forming a two level hierarchy, the super user domain at the top level, general users at the bottom.

More generally, the structure of the policy administration domains can be viewed as a hierarchical tree (or possibly directed graph). The depth, conceptually at least, is unlimited. Once such a structure is in place, we need to consider how it is to be managed. More specifically, how is the domain structure managed and altered and how is the placement of policies and objects handled. There will be a need for defined answers to these questions. For example, in Unix, the placement of objects is altered by use of the *chown* operation and the target user of a *chown* operation can be any user in the system. This, it must be admitted, is a very unrestrictive rule. The two cases of a single entity controlling all policy administration decisions (centralised) or all users having an independent area of authority (fully distributed) should not be viewed in terms of an either/or choice, but rather as two ends of a spectrum. Some limits may be desired on the administration choices available to users. For example, more restrictive rules might be

- The target user of a *chown* operation issued by a member of workgroup1 must be another member of workgroup1
- The target user of a *chown* operation issued by a member of workgroup2 must be a member of workgroup2 or workgroup3 or workgroup4

It may appear that the above two rules should not appear in the same hierarchy. If the of arrangement of policy administration domains into a hierarchy is to have any meaning, then it appears sensible to have uniform rules governing its management (Unix for one certainly follows this guideline). However, it should be obvious that the division of policy administration into a number of domains lends itself to uniform policies. For example, the two rules above need not imply a one-to-one mapping between workgroups and policy administration domains. If the second rule also applies to members of workgroups 3 and 4 then we could have two domains, one consisting of the objects of workgroups1, the other consisting of the objects of workgroups 2, 3 and 4. Alternatively, if there is a one-to-one mapping between workgroups and domains in our hypothetical organisation, then the domain of workgroup2 may be the parent of those of workgroups 3 and 4. Either way, we can postulate the single rule that

- The target user of a chown operation issued by a member of a domain must be another member of that domain or one of its descendant domains

Implicitly in the above rule is the idea of multiple managers for a policy administration domain. For simplicity, from this point, we consider each policy administration domain to have a single, unique, manager. It should be noted that a policy administration domain includes the objects and policies of its descendant domains. That is the manager of a policy administration domain can exercise policy administration authority over the objects and policies in their domain and in the descendant domains of that domain.

Some authority needs to decide upon the rules to be applied throughout the hierarchy. The obvious candidate is the manager of the root domain. We note that this model does not reflect all possible situations, specifically those where no central management entity is desired, or where it is possible to limit the rights of a central management entity. However we believe that the situation we have described is general enough to merit discussion. A policy administration domain hierarchy may or may not correspond to a single network or intranet. However, as it embodies a single management approach, a single intranet (or other organisational network) would consist of one or more, identifiable, policy administration domain hierarchies.

We recognise that the rules that govern the policy administration domains can be regarded as policies themselves (or, more properly, meta-policies). It may even be possible, in some systems, to implement them using the mechanism for expressing policy on general objects. While this may be so, for purposes of analysis it is worthwhile considering them separately.

What we have described so far is independent of a particular mechanism for expressing the access control policy. This allows us, potentially, to compare the administration structures of hierarchies regardless of the actual policy expression mechanism.

2.2 Root Policy Manager

Within a single policy administration hierarchy ultimate authority resides with a single management entity, the manager of the root domain. It is not important whether this management entity corresponds to one or a number of real world system users. However, the number of managers is considered to be much smaller than the total number of users of the system. We shall refer to a single root domain manager, while realising that this could correspond to a number of actual users.

The root domain manager has total control over the rules that govern the hierarchy. This also gives the root domain manager control over all policy decisions, as control over the hierarchy allows them to take control of any or all policy decisions.

While it may appear from our definition of a root domain manager that we are advocating a centralised approach, two points must be remembered. First is that the root domain manager may not be a single real world entity. Second, a 'system' (i.e. an intranet, LAN, etc) may consist of a number of policy administration hierarchies. Each hierarchy could have its own root domain manager and rules, allowing for any desired level of decentralisation.

This may be desirable for some organisations, which do not wish a single entity to have the authority over all decisions. It could also be provided for by removing automatic authority over descendant domains. However, we will not discuss these options for two reasons. Firstly, it complicates the discussion beyond what can comfortably be discussed in the space allowed here. Secondly, the notion of a root policy administration manager that cannot administer all policies seems rather contradictory. Especially when one considers that such a manager would still be able to assign which users can manage these policies (and so include themselves at any time). It would be better to consider these as separate policy administration hierarchies, and provide mechanisms for agreeing on meta-policies across multiple domains. Some of the issues involved in such a structure are discussed below.

2.3 Delegation

The hierarchical arrangement of policy administration described above can be looked at as a question of delegation. Consider an initial state of a system, where all policy decision authority ultimately rests with a single, root, management entity. Over time that entity decides to delegate some of this authority to particular users. That is, the root authority creates new domains, moves objects to those domains and appoints managers for the domains. These entities can, if they wish, delegate the authority further, in the same way. Viewed in this way the relation to delegation is clear. Even Unix can be viewed in this manner, as the system manager (super user) can change the policy settings for any object, but usually delegates most of this to the users, by way of the ownership property.

In our model, we will provide a single method to handle delegation, including both static (long term) and dynamic (short term) delegation. This is the ability to move objects between domains and will be further discussed below. As a domain manager can add objects to a descendant domain (i.e. delegate) and remove them from such domains (i.e. revoke) the ability to delegate is straightforward. We acknowledge that this is a fairly simple approach to delegation, but it is sufficient for our purposes. A more thorough discussion would at least require consideration of possible limitations being placed on the authority delegated (for example, restrictions being placed on the recipient of the delegated object moving it to another domain) but space prohibits such considerations.

3. Policy Domains

We shall restrict our discussion to a single policy administration hierarchy. That is, we are considering a system or organisation that can be regarded as having a single management structure for the administration of access control policies. The policies for this organisation are organised in a hierarchy of policy administration domains. After this we shall discuss some issues related to multiple hierarchies.

Each domain is under the control of a management entity. It would be possible to call each node of the tree a sub-domain and the entire hierarchy a policy administration domain, but the meaning of the term domain in the following should be clear from the context. The identity and nature of the management entities is not further specified at the moment, but left for later discussion. All that we will assume for now is that each management entity manages no more than one domain (node) within the hierarchy. Note that one domain being the child (or descendant) of another in the hierarchy means that the child domain is a part of the parent domain, at least in the sense that a manager has the same authority over the contents of a descendant domain as over the domain managed. An alternative view of the situation is domains residing inside their parent. The hierarchy is still apparent.

A hierarchy of policy objects can also be found in other work, such as [17]. However, such work does not address the issues involved in the management of the hierarchy itself.

Every object in the system resides in a domain. We consider policies to be a subset of the objects that exist within a system. Our initial system description is as follows:

Definition 1: System Description

1. A set O of objects
2. A set P of policies where P is a subset of O
3. A set D of policy domains
4. A set M of management entities
5. A set U of users
6. $OD: O$->D a function mapping each object o_i to a single domain d_i, $OD(o_i)$
7. $DH \subseteq D \times D$, a partial order on D called the domain hierarchy, also written as $\leq$ and $\geq$
8. $MD: M$<->D a function mapping each manager mi to a single domain d_i, $MD(m_i)$

There is a maxima for the partial order DH, $max(DH)$ which is the root domain, and $max(DH) \geq D_i$ for all D_i in D.

The manager of the root domain is called the *root domain manager*. We can consider a newly initialised system to simply consist of the root domain, some objects within that domain, and the domain's manager. Note that we have not required that M (the set of management entities) be a subset of U. While this may seem an unusual distinction, and in some following examples we will consider $M \subseteq U$, separating them out allows us to consider systems where the policies are not under control of the users. This is particularly useful for MAC systems.

What meaning follows from the location of an object within a domain? That is, what can the manager of that domain do with (and to) the object? These questions are simplistic statements of the questions of formulating policy and meta-policy for an object.

In terms of policy, the obvious answer to the question is that if an object resides within a domain then the manager of that domain may express policy for that object. It is worth noting that this means the entities that can express policy for an object are then the manager of the domain in which it directly resides and the managers of all the ancestors of that domain.

There are two basic issues to consider in the realm of meta-policy:

1. By who is it decided in which domain an object resides (and how is the location changed)?
2. By who is the shape of the tree itself decided?

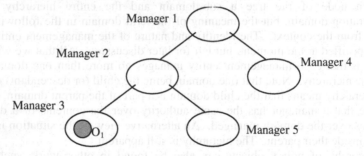

Fig. 1. Example Domain Hierarchy

3.1 Domain Location

Consider the example in figure 1. Object O_1 resides in the domain managed by Manager 3.

Who has the authority to move an object to another domain? For example, which manager or managers can move object O_1 to the domain managed by manager 5? We can immediately rule out managers 4 and 5. Manager 4 has no authority over O_1 at all. Manager 5 has no current authority over O_1 (even if the point of the exercise is to give it the authority) and managers should not be able to arbitrarily assume authority over another domain's objects.

Can manager 3 make the transfer? This operation is obviously related to the Unix *chown* operation and other equivalent mechanisms. In many popular variants of Unix there are no restrictions on the target user of a *chown* operation. Indeed, ownership of an object in these systems can be transferred to a user without consulting that user, in fact without their knowledge. So, if we are considering a Unix-like system, manager 3's ability to make the transfer is a viable option.

Managers 1 and 2 may also be able to make this change. Object O_1 resides in their domains, so it could be argued that they should be able to carry out the operation. In fact, it could well be argued that only they could be do it, as once a manager is given responsibility for an object they can not divest themselves of it (ie, manager 3 should **not** be able to make the transfer). Alternatively, it may be desired to restrict the authority to make all such changes to only a single entity (in this case, manager 1).

So we have possible three options, each reflecting different organisational approaches:

1. The managers of the ancestor domains of the domain in which the object resides.
2. Both the manager of the immediate domain in which the object resides and the managers of the ancestor domains of the domain in which the object resides.
3. The manager of the root domain

As an example, we can state for option 2

Rule 1.   A manager m_i can change the mapping OD for object o_i from d_i to d_j only
if $MD(d_i) = m_i$ or $MD(m_i) > d_i$ (alternately, $MD(m_i) \geq d_i$)

For space reasons we will only give the mathematical expression for selected options. It is left as an exercise for the interested reader to complete the formulations.

It could be argued that a fourth option exists, that only the manager of the immediate domain can change the mapping, but as the meaning of the hierarchy is that an object resides in both its immediate domain and in the ancestor domains of that domains, this seems counter-intuitive. For our example, if only manager 3 was to have authority, then it should not be placed subordinate to the other managers. Note that option 1 presents a problem in the case of objects in the domain of manager 1 (the root domain). This can be solved either by not allowing any objects to actually reside in that domain or by making an exception for that domain (effectively combining options 1 and 3). In some sense the manager of the root domain is a super user. Some organisations may not wish such a user to exist, but for our purposes this could be handled by multiple separate hierarchies, each representing the responsibilities given to each user. Some of the issues relating to this are discusses in section 3.5.

The next question is, are there any limits on the destination of the object? Again, considering Unix, it is obvious that one viable answer is that an object can be moved to any other domain. While this offers great flexibility, it also offers little control. Other alternatives are available. The most restrictive is to allow a manager to move an object only to a domain that the manager controls (i.e. the immediate domain managed and any descendants of that domain). Less restrictive options are to allow an object to be passed to the parent domain or any ancestral domains. Organisationally, this relates to a manager passing an issue up the chain of control.

The target domain when an object is moved in the tree may be:

1. Any domain in the tree
2. The domain of the manager making the move or any descendant domains
3. As in 2 plus the immediate parent domain
4. As in 2 plus any ancestor domains

As an example, we can state for option 4

Rule 2.   A manager m_i can change the mapping OD for object o_i from d_i to d_j only
if $MD(m_i) \geq d_j$ or $d_j \geq MD(m_i)$.

Combining this with the example above, we would have the rule that a manager can relocate any object which resides in their domain or any descendant domain and that the target domain can be the domain managed, any descendant domain or any ancestor domain. This can be expressed as

Rule 3. A manager m_i can change the mapping OD for object o_i from d_i to d_j if and only if $MD(m_i) \geq d_i$ and $(MD(m_i) \geq d_j$ or $d_j \geq MD(m_i))$

Note that this also gives us a rule for in which domain a new object could be placed when created by a user.

Let us again consider our example, from figure 1, of moving O_1 from domain 3 to domain 5. Under rule 3 above only managers 1 or 2 could perform the operation. Only under option 2 for which manager can make the move and option 1 for destination could manager 3 move the object. Even with option 2 for who can make the move, any other choice but 1 for destination control prevents manager 3 making the change. Other examples can easily be found which illustrate the differences between the various combinations. We leave construction of such examples to the reader.

Another possible option might be that objects could be transferred to sibling domains. This would, in our example, allow manager 3 to move object O_1 to the domain of manager 5. We find it likely that some organisations would not allow such transfers of responsibility without the involvement of more senior authority. However it would allow structures to be created where objects could be transferred between the domains of a specified group of managers without allowing unrestricted transfers to any point in the tree. This could be combined with any of options 2,3 and 4 above.

3.2 Writing Policy

Membership of an object in a policy administration domain means that the manager of that domain can write policy for that object. As we have described policy above (section 2) a policy contains no indication of the objects it governs. This link must be made separately.

We assume that a new policy (like a new object) can be placed in any administration domain to which a user could move an object. It could be argued that only the root domain manager be allowed to create new polices or that an organisation could wish for something between these two extremes, i.e. policies can only be created by some nominated subset of managers. While the former can easily be expressed using the notation presented here the later would require more sophisticated techniques, which are beyond the scope of the current paper.

As policies do not, in themselves, specify objects and therefore, independently, grant no access, there appears to be no need to restrict the writing of policies. It is the association of policies with actual objects that is important. As discussed above we only consider explicit linkage of policies and objects, not policy domains. We do allow the mapping between policies and objects to be many-to-many. We recognise that this may require some conflict resolution mechanism, but the issue of conflicting policies can be considered separately to who is actually allowed to set policies. We further add to our system description

9. $PO \subseteq P \times O$ a many-to-many policy to object assignment relation

The act of making a policy apply to an object can be regarded as the basic function of policy administration. It seems obvious that, for a user to do this, both the policy and the object should be under their control (that is, present in the user's policy administration domain. This can be expressed as

Rule 4.   A manager m_i can add (p_j, o_k) to PO, where $p_j \in P$ and $o_k \in O$ if and only if $MD(m_i) \geq OD(p_j)$ and $MD(m_i) \geq OD(o_k)$

That is, the policy and the object must reside in the domain managed by the user or one of that domain's descendants (but they do not have to reside in the same domain). A similar rule can be written for a removing an object from the scope of a rule.

It may seem counter-intuitive to consider policy objects that do not exist separately from objects. However, making this separation allows for a greater choice of policy administration structures. Making the mapping PO a many-to-one (or even one-to-one) relation can simply represent a structure where policies are directly related to objects. Access control list systems, such as Unix, can easily be viewed in this way. Separating the policy expression from the assignment of that policy to objects allows PO to be many-to-many and enables our model to encompass systems which abstract over objects and are hence easier to manager due to the smaller number of actual policy objects (or expressions of policy).

This limit that the mapping can only be made by a manager in whose domain both the policy and the object exist may appear overly restrictive. Some organisations may find this overly burdensome on their higher-level policy administrators. For example, referring to figure 1, the organisation may wish there to be a mechanism for mapping an object in the domain of manager 3 to a policy in the domain of manager 5 without having to consult either manager 1 or manager 2.

A number of possibilities exist. We could remove the restriction on the policy having to be within the domain, but as the manager then has no obvious policy authority over the policy object (it is not in the manager's domain) this appears undesirable. It would be possible to allow two managers to jointly make the decision by some means of consensus (the means of implementing this may not be trivial but is irrelevant to our discussion). However, this would require a degree of elaboration beyond the space available and we leave topics of negotiation and consensus for future work.

A more promising option is to alter our tree structure for domains to that of a directed graph. A new domain could be created, subordinate to the domains of managers 3 and 5 (from our example) and the policy and object placed therein. While feasible it raises a number of issues, such as who is allowed to create such a domain (as it effects the domains of the ancestor managers) and who manages the domain. Again, space is insufficient to pursue this notion further. However, we note that a graph would solve other problems, such as allowing all managers to attach objects to a given policy by having a domain containing all such policies at the bottom of the graph.

3.3 Domain Management

The discussion in the previous sub-sections implicitly assumed a static tree of domains. We will now consider the creation and deletion of domains (and the appointment of managers for newly created domains).

A manager should only be able to create and delete descendants of the domain that they manage. Manipulating domains for which the manager has no responsibility is obviously undesirable.

Rule 5.   A manager m_i can create $D_j \in D$ and add $D_j < D_k$ to DH, if and only if $MD(m_i) \geq D_k$

Organisations may wish to restrict the manipulation of the shape of the domain tree to the root manager.

Rule 6. A manager m_i can create $D_j \in D$ and add $D_j < D_k$ to DH, if and only if
$MD(m_i) = max(DH)$

Similar rules can be written for deleting domains. Note that a variant of rule 6, as follows, describes the standard Unix situation

Rule 6' A manager m_i can create $D_j \in D$ and add $D_j < D_k$ to DH, if and only if
$MD(m_i) = max(DH)$ and $D_k = max(DH)$

Once a domain has been created, a manager for it needs to be appointed. One simple answer is that a manager is simply appointed, with no restrictions (beyond our implicit assumption that each management entity manages only one domain). If we assume that managers are (some subset of) the users of the system and that an object, for management purposes, represents the users then a more sophisticated approach is possible. This is that the creator of a new domain can only appoint a manager from amongst those users that they manager. As managing a user means setting policy for that user, this appears natural enough. As a real world analogy, consider a team leader. The team leader is given management responsibility over the team members, which can include defining domain over which each member has policy management authority.

Rule 7. A manager m_i can add m_j to M and (m_j, D_k) to MD, if and only if m_j is represented by $o_k \in O$ and $MD(m_i) \geq OD(o_k)$ and $MD(m_i) > D_k$

Transfer of management of a domain from one entity to another can be considered as a process of creating a new domain, transferring all objects from the old domain to the new domain and the deletion of the old domain. As such, we do not need to discuss it further.

3.4. Limits on Child Managers

In the discussion above each manager has, within the sub-tree rooted at the domain which they manage, the same power as any other manager in an equivalent scope. In particular all managers can alter the structure of the policy administration domain hierarchy rooted at their domain. If it is required that not all managers be able to alter the hierarchy, it can be modelled as follows:

Add to definition 1

10. A set D' of policy domains where $D' \subset D$

Replace Rule 5 above with

Rule 5'a A manager m_i can create $D_j \in D$ where $D_j \in D'$ and add $D_j < D_k$ to DH, if and only if $MD(m_i) \geq D_k$ and $MD(m_i) \notin D'$

Rule 5'b A manager m_i can create $D_j \in D$ where $D_j \notin D'$ and add $D_j < D_k$ to DH, if and only if $MD(m_i) \geq D_k$ and $MD(m_i) \notin D'$

Note that Rule 5b allows D_j to not be element of D' without checking whether D_k is or not. If this is not desired than an interested reader should be able to formulate a suitable rule.

3.5. Relationship to MAC and DAC

At a superficial level it may appear that the model outlined above is directly related to DAC (Discretionary Access Control). The concept of authority to write policy is a central part of the DAC approach, often encapsulated by a notion of *ownership* (as in Unix). The model abstracts the notion of ownership into the authority to write policy for an object, captured by the presence of an object in a domain.

The model can also encompass MAC systems. A simple MAC system, where a uniform set of access control policies is enforced on all objects, can be modelled by a single domain. The model can also handle combined MAC/DAC systems. As a simple example, the MAC policies could be located in the root domain, and be mapped to all objects. The DAC policies could be appear in the lower level domains. The model thereby captures the essence of the policy administration (as opposed to policy enforcement) distinction between MAC and DAC. In both system types policy must be set and administered. Unlike others, eg., [14], we do not see the mechanism used to express policy as essential to distinguishing between MAC and DAC. The essential feature of MAC is that certain policy decisions cannot be amended or rescinded by users, regardless of mechanism. The domain hierarchy can easily represent this notion. Our model is not an alternative to MAC or DAC, as these are fundamental perspectives on access control. Rather it is simply away to view the rules that are being applied.

4. Role Based Access Control

The description in the preceding sections applies to policy administration frameworks in general. Once a particular mechanism for expressing policy is to be considered, some elaboration is required. We have used a Unix like system, which is representative of simple access control list systems, in a number of examples above. As a further example, we will consider Role Based Access Control. The essential elements of RBAC are the mappings between users and roles and permissions and roles. In section 3 we were able to consider setting a policy to be a unitary action, requiring only authority over an object (ie, the object to reside within the domain of the manager who wishes to express the policy) and a policy. While in RBAC systems this is equivalent to creating (or changing) a permission, in itself this is insufficient. For a policy (permission) in an RBAC system to be useful, the permission must be mapped to at least one role. There must also be a mapping between that role and at least one user. We now must consider the management of these mappings. However, it will become evident that the fundamental property of these mappings is very similar to that between object and policy, indicating a useful generality of our approach.

Definition 2: RBAC System Description

1., 3. – 8. from definition 1

2. A set P of permissions where P is a subset of O (note this replaces the policy set)

9. $PO \subseteq P \times O$ a many-to-many permission to object assignment relation

10. A set R of roles where R is a subset of O

11. $PR \subseteq P \times R$ a many-to-many permission to role assignment relation

12. $RU \subseteq P \times O$ a many-to-many role to user assignment relation

4.1 Permissions and Roles

The most flexible approach to the creation of roles and permissions is to allow any manager to create a new (empty) role or permission. A role expresses meaningful policy when it has users and permissions mapped to it, a permission when it actually applies to some objects, so this flexibility does not allow arbitrary policy decisions. The placement of a new role or permission should depend on the organisational decision as to where object can be moved within the domain hierarchy, as with policies and objects above. The same argument can be made about restricting this ability to certain users.

Domain membership for an object means that the manager of that domain can write policy about that object. In an RBAC system this means having a permission, which includes that object in its scope. Obviously a manager should only be able to add objects to the scope of a permission they manage (i.e. is within their domain) Therefore, in our terms, being able to write policy for an object in an RBAC system means that a manager can add it to (or subtract it from) the scope of a permission, as long as that permission is also within the manager's domain. This mirrors the discussion of policy and objects above and can be expressed as follows:

Rule 8. A manager m_i can add (p_j, o_k) to PO, where $p_j \in P$ and $o_k \in O$ if and only if $MD(m_i) \geq OD(p_j)$ and $MD(m_i) \geq OD(o_k)$

We can now consider the mapping between roles and permissions. If the role and permission exist in the same domain the manager of that domain should be able to make the mapping. Given our definition of domain it seems sensible that this should also be open to the ancestors of this domain. More generally, the mapping can be made if both role and permission exist somewhere within the domain of the manager. This means that domain membership for a permission means that a manager can add objects to its scope and map it to a role, as long as the object and role are also within the domain. Similarly for subtracting objects and removing the permissions from a role. The meaning of a role being in a domain should now be clear.

Rule 9. A manager m_i can add (p_j, r_k) to PR, where $p_j \in P$ and $r_k \in R$ if and only if $MD(m_i) \geq OD(p_j)$ and $MD(m_i) \geq OD(r_k)$

Note the similarity of this rule to rules 7 and 8. This may seem straightforward, but consider the situation in figure 2.

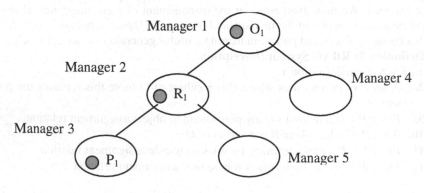

Fig. 2. Role Mapping Example

Manager 1 could map object o_l to permission p_l. Manager 2 could, at a later point, map permission p_l to role r_l. The result of this is that object o_l is now accessible to any member of role r_l and, most importantly, a manager whose domain did not include o_l made this decision. This appears to be a violation of our basic rule that policy decisions can only be made about an object if that object lies within the domain of the manager making the decision. We could prevent this from happening by replacing rule 9 with

Rule 9' A manager m_i can add (p_j, r_k) to PR, where $p_j \in P$ and $r_k \in R$ if and only if $MD(m_i) \geq OD(p_j)$ and $MD(m_i) \geq OD(r_k)$ and $\forall\ o_l : (p_j, o_l) \in PO\ MD(m_i) \geq OD(o_l)$

This variant requires all objects indirectly linked to a role by a role-permission mapping to fall within the domain of the manager making the mapping. It could be argue that this is overly restrictive and that, by mapping the object to the permission in this example, manager 1 has delegated to lower level managers the ability to map the object (indirectly) to roles. Such an approach would retain rule 9. This is another case of two different, but both potentially valid, approaches. Adoption of one or the other would depend upon organisational requirements.

Similar rules to 9 and 9' could be written for the RU mapping if we treat users as objects (or at least represent the ability to set policy for a user by having an object which represents a user). However, it should be apparent by this stage that we have a fundamental principle, that where we have two policy relevant objects (such as a policy (permission) and object or permission and role or role and user) then a direct mapping between the two can only be made by a manager whose domain includes both objects. We add to our system description for RBAC

13. A set MA of mappings where $MA = \{OD, PO, PR, RU\}$

And the following rule as a generalisation of the less restrictive approach

Rule 10. A manager m_i can add (x_j, y_k) to XY, where $XY \in MA$ and $x_j\ X$ and $y_k \in Y$ if and only if $MD(m_i) \geq OD(x_j)$ and $MD(m_i) \geq OD(y_k)$

The general principle represented by rule 10 may appear obvious, but does neatly encapsulate policy management. Writing an equivalent of this rule for the more restrictive approach represented by rule 9' is more difficult, due to the possibly recursive nature of the relationship (for example from user to role to permission to object). We introduce the predicate $related(x,y)$

$related(x,y)$, where $x \in O$ and $y \in O$, is $true$ if $\exists\ m \in MA$ and $(x,y) \in m$ or $\exists\ o : o \in O$ and $related(x,o)$ and $related(y,o)$

This allows us to formulate the general case of rule 9'

Rule 10': A manager m_i can add (x_j, y_k) to XY, where $XY \in MA$ and $x_j \in X$ and $y_k \in Y$ if and only if $MD(m_i) \geq OD(x_j)$ and $MD(m_i) \geq OD(y_k)$ and $\forall\ o_l : related(x_j, o_l)$ or $related(y_k, o_l)$ then $MD(m_i) \geq OD(o_l)$

For example, this rule would only allow a manager to assign a user to a role if all permissions mapped to the role, objects mapped to those permissions and all roles, etc to which the user is mapped, are under the authority of the manager making the new mapping. Requiring other roles to which the user is already mapped also be in the manager's domain is possible overly restrictive. However a general rule does not allow us to distinguish between the related objects of one side of the new mapping and the related objects of the other side of the mapping, so we would have to rely on a specific rule, such as

Rule 10'': A manager m_i can add (r_j, u_k) to RU where $r_j \in R$ and $u_k \in U$ if and only if $MD(m_i) \geq OD(r_j)$ and $MD(m_i) \geq OD(u_k)$ and $\forall\, p_l, o_m : (r_j, p_l) \in PR$ and $(o_m, p_l) \in PO$ then $MD(m_i) \geq OD(p_l)$ and $MD(m_i) \geq OD(o_m)$

4.2 Role Hierarchies

In section 4.1, in our discussion of creating a role, we did not consider the effect of the role hierarchy, as described in RBAC1[13]. The effect of a role hierarchy is to make permissions available to the users of a role without the permissions being directly mapped to that role. Establishing an inheritance relationship between two roles obviously relates to the management of policy. For the purpose of examples below, call the role that will be inheriting R_1 and the role that will be inherited from R_2.

We need to consider which managers can make such a relationship. Obviously if both roles and the all permissions of the role to be inherited are in the domain of a manager than that manager can assign one role to inherit from the other. As the manager controls the permissions the manager could directly assign them to R_1, so assigning them via inheritance seems sensible. If the permissions are not within the domain of the manager then we have similar arguments to those discussed at the end of the previous section.

The role hierarchy can be represented by

14. $RH \subseteq R \times R$, a partial order on R called the role hierarchy, also written as $\leq$ and $\geq$

and adding RH to MA. Rule 10 would then cover the simple case of only requiring the two roles to be within the manager's domain. More restrictive meta-policies, such as considering what preventing the mapping if R_2 inherits from other roles that are outside the manager's domain, can be handled as discussed in the previous section and so we omit the details for reasons of space.

5. Conclusions and Future Work

This paper presents a coherent model of policy administration structures. The model is able to capture the relationship between managers and the policy objects they manage and the arrangement of those objects into separate policy administration domains. The model is flexible, in that it does not prescribe fixed answers to fundamental questions of policy administration, such as who is able to change the domain structure and which managers can change the placement of an object within the structure. The identification of the meta-policy choices allows a greater understanding of policy administration.

The wide scope of the model allows many varied policy administration structures to be compared. The model can capture MAC, DAC and combined MAC/DAC approaches. It an also be used as a framework in which to design a policy administration structure, by choice amongst the alternative rule formulations and hierarchical structures. This allows other practical structures for policy administration, beyond those in current use, to be designed and implemented. As well as mechanism independent comparisons of policy administration in different systems, the model can also be used to examine policy administration for particular mechanisms, as shown by the example of RBAC.

The model encapsulates the intuitive basic principle that explicit relationships between policy significant objects can only be made by an entity with policy authority over both objects. It is sufficiently flexible to allow for indirect relationships to be handled this way or in a less restrictive manner.

Despite its advantages this model represents only an initial step in capturing the possible arrangements of policy administration. A number of other important issues, such as co-operative managements, relationships between multiple hierarchies and a graph rather than tree based structure, have been identified. Space considerations meant these must be left for future work.

References

1. Barkley, J. & Cincotta, A., 'Managing role/permission relationships using object access types', Proceedings of the 3rd ACM workshop on Role-based access control, Fairfax, USA, 1998, pp. 73-80.
2. Damianou, N., Dulay, N., Lupu, E. & Sloman, M., 'The Ponder Policy Specification Language', Proceedings of International workshop on Policies for Distributed Systems and Networks, Bristol, UK, January, 2001, pp.18-38.
3. Fabry, R., 'Capability-Based Addressing', Communications of the ACM, 17(7), July, 1974, pp. 403-412.
4. Faden. G., 'RBAC in UNIX administration', Proceedings of the 4th ACM workshop on role-based access control, Fairfax, USA, 1999, pp. 95-101.
5. Ferraiolo, D., and Kuhn, R.: 'Role based access controls', Proceedings of the 15th NIST-NCSC National Computer Security Conference, Baltimore MD, USA, 1992, pp. 554-563.
6. Gavrila, S. & Barkley, J., 'Formal specification for role based access control user/role and role/role relationship management', Proceedings of the 3rd ACM workshop on Role-based access control, Fairfax, USA, 1998, pp. 81-90.
7. Hitchens, M. & Varadharajan, V., 'Tower: A Language for Role Based Access Control', Proceedings of International workshop on Policies for Distributed Systems and Networks, Bristol, UK, January, 2001, pp.88-106.
8. Kanada, Y., 'Taxonomy and Description of Policy Combination Methods', Proceedings of International workshop on Policies for Distributed Systems and Networks, Bristol, UK, January, 2001, pp.171-184.
9. Marshall, I. & McKee, P., 'A Policy Based Management Architecture for Large Scale Active Communication Systems', Proceedings of International workshop on Policies for Distributed Systems and Networks, Bristol, UK, January, 2001, pp.202-213.
10. Mönkeberg, A. & Rakete, R., 'Three for one: role-based access-control management in rapidly changing heterogeneous environments', Proceedings of the 5th ACM workshop on role-based access control, Berlin, Germany, 2000, pp. 83-88.
11. Osborn, S, & Guo, Y., 'Modeling users in role-based access control', Proceedings of the 5th ACM workshop on role-based access control, Berlin, Germany, 2000, pp. 31-37.
12. Sandhu, R. 'Lattice based access control models', Computer, 26(11), November, 1993, pp.9-19.
13. Sandhu, R., Coyne, E.J., and Feinstein, H.L., 'Role based access control models', IEEE Computer, 1996, 29, (2), pp. 38-47.
14. Sandhu, R. & Munawer, Q., 'How to do discretionary access control using roles', Proceedings of the 3rd ACM workshop on Role-based access control, Fairfax, USA, 1998, pp. 47-52.

15. Sandhu, R. & Munawer, Q., 'The ARBAC99 Model for Administration of Roles', Proceedings of 15th Annual Computer Security Applications Conference, Phoenix, USA, 1999,

16. Zurko, M., Simon, R., and Sanfilippo, T.: 'A user-centered, modular authorization service built on an RBAC foundation', Proceedings of the IEEE Symposium on Security and Privacy, Oakland, USA, 1999. pp. 57-71.

17. Perwaiz, N. & Sommerville, I. 'Structured management of role-permission relationships', Proceedings of the 6th ACM workshop on role-based access control, Chantilly, USA, 2000, pp. 163-169.

Maintaining the Validity of Digital Signatures in B2B Applications

Jianying Zhou

Labs for Information Technology
21 Heng Mui Keng Terrace
Singapore 119613
jyzhou@lit.org.sg

Abstract. Electronic transactions with commercial values between two business parties may want to be legally bound. Digital signature is an important security mechanism to provide evidence regarding the status of a transaction. However, evidence solely based on digital signatures may not enforce strong non-repudiation. Additional mechanisms are required to make digital signatures as valid non-repudiation evidence in the settlement of possible disputes. The conventional approach is to invoke a time-stamping service from a trusted third party. But it may become hard to deploy B2B applications in which no on-line third party is involved. In this paper, we present an efficient mechanism for maintaining the validity of digital signatures in direct B2B applications without the involvement of a trusted third party.

1 Introduction

The Internet has created a tremendous opportunity to conduct business electronically and a large number of companies are now participating in the global electronic marketplace for high efficiency and low cost. However, the security concerns of open computer networks become a major barrier to the success of electronic commerce. The fundamental security services needed in electronic commerce include authentication, data confidentiality, data integrity, and non-repudiation [Ford97]. Non-repudiation is a security service that protects parties involved in electronic transactions against a participating party denying that a particular event or action took place [ISO13888-1]. Customers supported with the non-repudiation and other security services will be more confident in doing business on-line.

To protect customers involved in electronic transactions with commercial values, evidence with legal effect may need to be created, collected, and stored for the settlement of possible disputes [Zhou01]. Digital signature is an important security mechanism to provide evidence regarding the status of a transaction [ISO13888-3]. When a signature is attached to a message being transferred in a transaction, the receiver of such a message could use the digital signature as evidence to prove to a third party, e.g. an adjudicator, that the signer is involved in the transaction. The binding between the signer's identity and the public key for signature verification could be achieved with a public-key certificate issued by a trusted party called the certification authority (CA) [X509, Housley99]. The non-repudiability is based on the assumption that only

L. Batten and J. Seberry (Eds.): ACISP 2002, LNCS 2384, pp. 303-315, 2002.

the signer holds the private key for generating the corresponding digital signatures. Without knowing such a key, it is computationally infeasible for others to forge the signatures. Secure digital signature schemes such as DSS [DSS] and ISO/IEC 9796 [ISO9796] have already been deployed in many commercial products.

In practice, however, a private key might be compromised, and a party holding the compromised key could forge the signatures. Hence, the compromised key needs to be revoked so that all signatures generated after revocation of the compromised key will be deemed invalid. On the other hand, digital signatures generated before revocation of the compromised key should remain valid. Otherwise, the signer who wants to repudiate signatures that he has generated may deliberately compromise his signature key and falsely claim those signatures as forged by somebody else.

Therefore, additional mechanisms are required to distinguish the signatures generated before and after key revocation [Zhou00]. The conventional approach to ensuring digital signatures as valid non-repudiation evidence in the settlement of possible disputes is to invoke a time-stamping service from a trusted third party for each newly generated signature [Adams01, Schneier96]. Other optimized approaches based on a trusted time-stamping service, such as using temporary certificates [Zhou99], also exist. But it may become hard to deploy B2B applications in which no on-line third party is involved. Forward-secure digital signature schemes [Bellare99, Krawczyk00], which update the private signing key at regular intervals while the public key is fixed throughout the lifetime of the certificate, could preserve the validity of past signatures without using a trusted time-stamping service even if the current private key has been compromised. However, a certificate revocation service should be provided by the CA or other third parties, thus an attacker cannot use the compromised current signing key (and the subsequent signing keys derived from the current one) to forge current (and future) signatures. Even so, all signatures generated with the current signing key are still in question without the time-stamping service. In this paper, we present an efficient mechanism for maintaining the validity of digital signatures in direct B2B applications without the involvement of a trusted third party.

The rest of the paper is organized as follows. In Section 2, we identify two typical B2B transaction models and point out the factors that will influence the solutions for maintaining the validity of digital signatures. In Section 3, we outline the conventional solution of invoking the time-stamping service from the service provider in indirect B2B applications. In Section 4, we present a new solution based on the one-way sequential link to make the validity of digital signatures undeniable in direct B2B applications. In Section 5, we discuss the issues related to the correct and efficient implementation of the new solution. We conclude the paper in Section 6.

2 B2B Transaction Models

We consider two typical B2B transaction models here (see Figure 1).
- Two transacting parties do business directly.
- Two transacting parties do business through a disinterested third party, e.g. electronic marketplace.

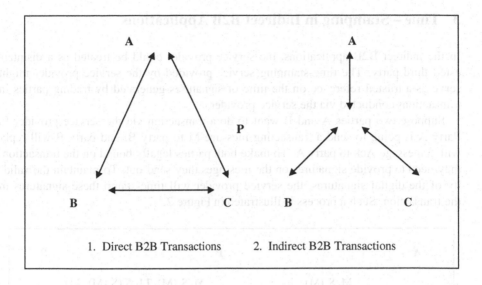

1. Direct B2B Transactions   2. Indirect B2B Transactions

Fig. 1. B2B Transaction Models

In the first transaction model, two transacting parties will do business directly without the involvement of third parties. For example, the workflow of a direct B2B transaction for ordering product might be as follows.

1. The customer requests for purchasing a product.
2. The supplier provides the quotation.
3. The customer sends out the purchase order.
4. The supplier confirms the transaction.
5. The customer makes the payment.
6. The supplier ships the product.

In the second transaction model, global trading partners come together to conduct business at an on-line marketplace. Oracle Exchange is an example of such a service provider, which supports a full range of purchasing including buyer auctions, seller auctions, catalog and spot purchases, and contract-based purchases. Only the members who have made a registration with the service provider can do business in the marketplace. All transactions are managed by the service provider, which could be regarded as indirect B2B transactions.

It becomes quite straightforward to support the non-repudiation service with digital signature and time-stamping mechanisms in the indirect B2B transaction model. The service provider could act as a disinterested third party to provide a trusted time-stamping service for trading parties.

Such a third party does not exist in the direct B2B transaction model. Obviously it will completely change the framework in the deployment of direct B2B applications if an extra third party is introduced to support the non-repudiation service. Therefore, a new solution is needed to maintain the validity of digital signatures in the direct B2B transaction model without changing its framework.

3   Time – Stamping in Indirect B2B Applications

In the indirect B2B applications, the service provider could be treated as a disinterested third party. The time-stamping service provided by the service provider might serve as a trusted reference on the time of signatures generated by trading parties in transactions conducted via the service provider.

Suppose two parties A and B want to do a transaction via the service provider P. Party A is going to send a transacting message M to party B, and party B will reply with a message Ack to party A. To make both parties legally bound on the transaction, they need to provide signatures on the messages they send out. To maintain the validity of the digital signatures, the service provider will time-stamp these signatures in the transaction. Such a process is illustrated in Figure 2.

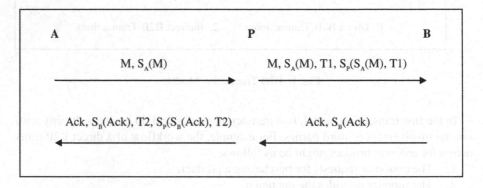

Fig. 2. Time-stamping Digital Signatures

In the above figure, $S_A(\ )$, $S_B(\ )$, and $S_P(\ )$ are digital signatures generated by A, B and P, respectively. T1 and T2 are time-stamps generated by P. When the service provider P receives a transacting message from A, in addition to the routine process related to the transaction, P will attach a time-stamp T1 to A's digital signature $S_A(M)$ and generate a counter-signature $S_P(S_A(M), T1)$ before forwarding the transacting message to B. It could be used to testify that A's digital signature $S_A(M)$ has existed before the time T1. Similarly, when P receives a transacting message from B, P will attach a time-stamp T2 to B's digital signature $S_B(Ack)$ and generate a counter-signature $S_P(S_B(Ack), T2)$. It could be used to testify that B's digital signature $S_B(Ack)$ has existed before the time T2.

As a disinterested third party, the service provider P needs to take extra precaution to protect its signature key for time-stamping. In addition, P should maintain a reliable log of time-stamping messages. Thus, in case P's signature key is compromised, P can check the log to tell whether a time-stamping message was signed by itself or forged by others.

If party B wants to check the validity of party A's digital signature $S_A(M)$, B needs to go through the following steps.

1. B verifies P's signature $S_P(S_A(M), T1)$.
2. B checks the expiry date T_e of A's public-key certificate C_A. If $T_e < T1$, A's signature was generated after A's public key had expired thus is invalid.
3. B checks the revocation information, e.g., the CRL. If C_A was revoked at the time of T_r and $T_r < T1$, A's signature was generated after A's public key had been revoked thus is invalid.
4. B verifies A's signature $S_A(M)$ with A's public-key certificate C_A.

Only if all of the above verifications are successful, will B accept A's signature as valid non-repudiation evidence. B needs to store M, $S_A(M)$, T1, $S_P(S_A(M), T1)$, as well as C_A and the revocation information safely. Then, B can use the same process to prove to a third party about the validity of A's signature at any time later.

4 New Solution to Direct B2B Applications

It is undesirable to introduce an extra trusted third party to provide the time-stamping service in direct B2B applications. This will significantly increase the burden on the deployment of such applications. The new solution proposed here could maintain the validity of digital signatures generated in transactions between two trading parties without any involvement of a third party.

4.1 One-Way Sequential Link

The idea behind this new solution is to link all digital signatures generated by a transacting party in a way that any change to the linked signatures, including changing the link order, inserting a new signature, removing or replacing an existing signature, will be detected. The digital signatures appeared in such a one-way sequential link will be regarded as valid. The transacting party can revoke his signature key by sending the first and the latest digital signatures in the link to the trading partner for countersigning. With the trading partner's approval, the transacting party can deny digital signatures that are generated with his revoked signature key but are not in the countersigned link.

Suppose two parties A and B are going to do a series of transactions, and A needs to generate signatures on messages X_1, X_2, ..., X_i. A can establish a one-way sequential link of his digital signatures σ_A_1, σ_A_2, ..., σ_A_i (see Figure 3).

In Figure 3, H is a collision-resistant one-way hash function. n_1,..., n_i are incremental sequential numbers or local time-stamps serving as an index of the one-way sequential link, which could be used to facilitate dispute resolution. The link established in such a way has the following properties [Zhou00].

 - σ_A_1, σ_A_2, ..., σ_A_i are *sequential*. That means, for $1 < p <= i$, σ_A_p is generated later than σ_A_{p-1}.

- $\sigma\_A_1, \sigma\_A_2, ..., \sigma\_A_i$ are *one-way linked*. That means, for $1 <= p <= i$, it is computationally infeasible to insert a new signature $\sigma\_A'_p$ before σ_A_p, or replace σ_A_p with $\sigma\_A'_p$ or remove σ_A_p from the link without being detected.

$$\sigma\_A_1 = S_A(X_1, n_1)$$
$$\sigma\_A_2 = S_A(X_2, H(\sigma\_A_1), n_2)$$
$$......$$
$$\sigma\_A_i = S_A(X_i, H(\sigma\_A_{i-1}), n_i)$$

Fig. 3. Definition of One-way Sequential Link

4.2 Generation and Termination of Links

Now we discuss how parties A and B will generate and terminate their one-way sequential links in a series of transactions conducted between them (see Figure 4).

- **T_1 – A starts a one-way sequential link**

Suppose party A starts his one-way sequential link at point T_1 by generating $\sigma\_A_1 = S_A(X_1, n\_A_1)$ for a transacting message X_1. A sends the signed message, optionally with his public-key certificate C_A, to B. After receiving this message, B needs to make the following checks before accepting and saving it.

1. B verifies A's signature σ_A_1.
2. B checks that C_A has not expired and is not marked as revoked in B's transaction log.
3. B checks that σ_A_1 is the first signature in the one-way sequential link associated with A's public-key certificate C_A.

- **T_2 – B starts a one-way sequential link**

Suppose party B starts his one-way sequential at point T_2 by generating $\sigma\_B_1 = S_B(Y_1, n\_B_1)$ for a transacting message Y_1. B sends the signed message, optionally with his public-key certificate C_B, to A. A needs to make the same checks as B did at point T_1 before accepting and saving it.

- **T_3 – B continues his one-way sequential link**

At point T_3, B generates $\sigma\_B_2 = S_B(Y_2, H(\sigma\_B_1), n\_B_2)$ for a transacting message Y_2. After receiving B's signed message, A should make similar checks as at point T_2. The only difference is that A should check whether σ_B_2 is linked to σ_B_1 properly.

Both A and B may continue to exchange signed transacting messages, where digital signatures are linked in a way as defined in Section 4.1.

- **T_i – A terminates his one-way sequential link**

Suppose party A wants to revoke his public-key certificate C_A at point T_i. A needs to get the approval of revocation from B. A generates a signed revocation request as follows, which includes the first signature (σ_A_1) and the latest signature (σ_A_{i-1}) of the link.

$$\sigma\_A_i = S_A(\text{revoke}, \sigma\_A_1, \sigma\_A_{i-1}, H(\sigma\_A_{i-1}), n\_A_i)$$

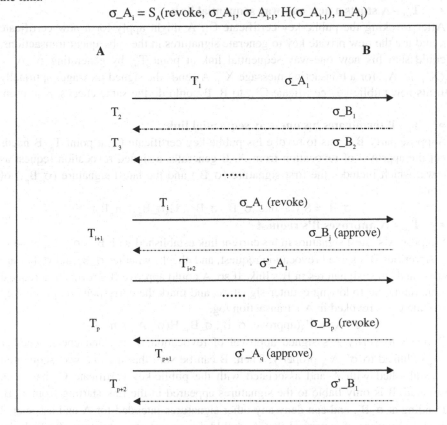

Fig. 4. Generation and Termination of Links

- **T_{i+1} – B approves A's request**

Suppose B's latest signature in his link established with A is σ_B_{j-1} at point T_{i+1}. B verifies A's signed revocation request, and checks whether σ_A_1 and σ_A_{i-1} are the first and latest signatures in A's link. If so, B could approve A's revocation request by generating the following counter-signature, and mark the corresponding public-key certificate C_A as revoked in B's transaction log.

$$\sigma\_B_j = S_B(\text{approve}, \sigma\_A_1, \sigma\_A_i, H(\sigma\_B_{j-1}), n\_B_j)$$

A needs to verify B's signed approval of revocation σ_B_j, and check whether σ_B_j is linked to σ_B_{j-1} properly. Then, A can be sure that the one-way sequential link established with B and associated with the public-key certificate C_A has been terminated. A is only liable to the signatures appeared in the link starting from σ_A_1 and ending at σ_A_i, and can deny any other signatures intended for B and associated with C_A. Therefore, it is critical that B should not accept any signature of which the associated public-key certificate C_A has been marked as revoked.

- **T_{i+2} – A starts a new one-way sequential link**

After revoking the public-key certificate C_A, A might apply for a new certificate C'_A, and use the new private key to generate signatures in the subsequent transactions. A could start his new one-way sequential link at point T_{i+2} by generating $\sigma'\_A_1 = S'_A(X'_1, n'\_A_1)$ for a transacting message X'_1. A sends the signed message, optionally with his new public-key certificate C'_A, to B. B could do the same checks as at point T_1.

- **T_p – B terminates his one-way sequential link**

Suppose party B wants to revoke his public-key certificate C_B at point T_p. B needs to get the approval of revocation from A. B generates a signed revocation request as follows, which includes the first signature (σ_B_1) and the latest signature (σ_B_{p-1}) of the link.

$$\sigma\_B_p = S_B(\text{revoke}, \sigma\_B_1, \sigma\_B_{p-1}, H(\sigma\_B_{p-1}), n\_B_p)$$

- **T_{p+1} – A approves B's request**

Suppose A's latest signature in his current link established with B is σ'_A_{q-1} at point T_{p+1}. A verifies B's signed revocation request, and checks whether σ_B_1 and σ_B_{p-1} are the first and latest signatures in B's link. If so, A could approve B's revocation request by generating the following counter-signature, and mark the corresponding public-key certificate C_B as revoked in A's transaction log.

$$\sigma'\_A_q = S'_A(\text{approve}, \sigma\_B_1, \sigma\_B_p, H(\sigma'\_A_{q-1}), n'\_A_q)$$

B needs to verify A's signed approval of revocation σ'_A_q, and check whether σ'_A_q is linked to σ'_A_{q-1} properly. Then, B can be sure that the one-way sequential link established with A and associated with the public-key certificate C_B has been terminated. B is only liable to the signatures appeared in the link starting from σ_B_1 and ending at σ_B_p, and can deny any other signatures intended for A and associated with C_B. Therefore, it is critical that A should not accept any signature of which the associated public-key certificate C_B has been marked as revoked.

- **T_{p+2} – B starts a new one-way sequential link**

After revoking the public-key certificate C_B, B might apply for a new certificate C'_B, and use the new private key to generate signatures in the subsequent transactions. B could start his new one-way sequential link at point T_{p+2} by generating $\sigma'\_B_1 = S'_B(Y'_1, n'\_B_1)$ for a transacting message Y'_1. B sends the signed message, optionally with his new public-key certificate C'_B, to A. A could do the same checks as at point T_2.

4.3 Dispute Resolution

In the above illustrative scenario, A created two one-way sequential links.

- Terminated link associated with C_A, starting from $\sigma\_A_1 = S_A(X_1, n\_A_1)$ and ending at $\sigma\_A_i = S_A(\text{revoke}, \sigma\_A_1, \sigma\_A_{i-1}, H(\sigma\_A_{i-1}), n\_A_i)$
- Open link associated with C'_A, starting from $\sigma'\_A_1 = S'_A(X'_1, n'\_A_1)$

B also created two one-way sequential links.
- Terminated link associated with C_B, starting from $\sigma\_B_1 = S_B(Y_1, n\_B_1)$ and ending at $\sigma\_B_p = S_B(\text{revoke}, \sigma\_B_1, \sigma\_B_{p-1}, H(\sigma\_B_{p-1}), n\_B_p)$
- Open link associated with C'_B, starting from $\sigma'\_B_1 = S'_B(Y'_1, n'\_B_1)$

Suppose the validity of A's signature $\sigma\_A_k = S_A(X_k, H(\sigma\_A_{k-1}), n\_A_k)$ is in dispute. As σ_A_k is associated with A's public-key certificate C_A, and the one-way sequential link associated with C_A has already been terminated, we only need to verify whether σ_A_k is a signature located within the link. The evidence requested for dispute resolution is listed in Figure 5.

Evidence from A	Evidence from B
1. A's signed message in dispute: $\quad \sigma\_A_k, X_k, H(\sigma\_A_{k-1}), n\_A_k$ 2. B's approval of revocation: $\quad \sigma\_B_j, \text{approve},$ $\quad \sigma\_A_1, \sigma\_A_i, H(\sigma\_B_{j-1}), n\_B_j$ 3. B's public-key certificate: $\quad C_B$	1. A's signed messages in the link: $\quad \sigma\_A_1, X_1, n\_A_1$ $\quad \sigma\_A_2, X_2, n\_A_2$ $\quad \cdots\cdots$ $\quad \sigma\_A_i, \text{revoke}, n\_A_i$ 2. A's public-key certificate: $\quad C_A$

Fig. 5. Evidence Requested for Dispute Resolution

The adjudicator can take the following steps to verify the evidence.
1. The adjudicator first uses C_A to check whether σ_A_1 and σ_A_i are A's signatures on (X_1, n_A_1) and $(\text{revoke}, \sigma\_A_1, \sigma\_A_{i-1}, H(\sigma\_A_{i-1}), n\_A_i)$, respectively.
2. The adjudicator also uses C_B to check whether σ_B_j is B's signature on (approve, $\sigma\_A_1, \sigma\_A_i, H(\sigma\_B_{j-1}), n\_B_j)$. If so, the adjudicator believes that B approved A's revocation request, and the one-way sequential link starting from σ_A_1 has been terminated at σ_A_i.
3. Then, the adjudicator uses C_A to check whether σ_A_k is A's signatures on $(X_k, H(\sigma\_A_{k-1}), n\_A_k)$. If so, the adjudicator uses the index n_A_k to decide the location of σ_A_k. If $n\_A_k < n\_A_1$ or $n\_A_k > n\_A_i$, the adjudicator believes that σ_A_k is not in the terminated one-way sequential link and thus is invalid.
4. Finally, the adjudicator checks whether σ_A_k is linked properly in the one-way sequential link by verifying the signatures from σ_A_1 to σ_A_i. If so, σ_A_k is a valid signature.

If B further denies the approval of A's revocation and claims that σ_A_k is A's valid signature properly linked beyond σ_A_i, a similar process could be taken to check the validity of B's approval of revocation σ_B_j. Obviously, even if B has revoked his public-key certificate C_B, σ_B_j remains valid as long as σ_B_j is properly linked in B's terminated one-way sequential link.

Suppose a signature in an open link, e.g., $\sigma'\_A_k = S'\_A(X'_k, H(\sigma'\_A_{k-1}), n'\_A_k)$ is in dispute. As A has not requested for revoking his public-key certificate C'_A, the validity of σ'_A_k can be decided by simply verifying σ'_A_k with C'_A.

5 Implementation Issues

The following issues may need to be taken into consideration in the implementation of one-way sequential link mechanism.

5.1 Loss of Order in Receiving Signatures

It is possible that messages transferred in the asynchronized mode may not reach the destination in the same order as being dispatched. For example, when A sends the transacting messages $X_1, X_2, X_3, X_4, \ldots, X_i$, B may receive them in the order of $X_2, X_3, X_1, X_4, \ldots, X_i$. Then, when B first receives X_2 and the corresponding signature $\sigma\_A_2 = S_A(X_2, H(\sigma\_A_1), n\_A_2)$, B is unable to verify σ_A_2 without σ_A_1. Therefore, it is necessary that $H(\sigma\_A_1)$ is also sent with σ_A_2. Thus, if B has not received σ_A_1, B can use $H(\sigma\_A_1)$ to verify σ_A_2. In this case, B needs to store $H(\sigma\_A_1)$ until receiving σ_A_1. When σ_A_1 arrives, B could calculate the hash of σ_A_1 and compare it with the stored $H(\sigma\_A_1)$. If they match, σ_A_2 is linked to σ_A_1 properly.

It is important to note that before C_A is revoked, all signatures associated with C_A are regarded as valid. Once C_A is revoked, only signatures appeared in the terminated link are regarded as valid. Therefore, when B receives a revocation request from A, B should make sure that B has received all of the linked signatures and has verified that they are properly linked from the start to the end of the link before B approves the revocation request. Otherwise, B must reject the revocation request.

5.2 Use of Check Points

The one-way sequential links established by trading parties may become very long if they do not intend to revoke their public-key certificates. As we can see in Section 4.3, to settle a possible dispute over the validity of a digital signature, all signatures in the link has to be verified whether they are linked properly. Obviously, a long link will make the dispute resolution inefficient.

This problem could be tackled by generating a set of checkpoints along the one-way sequential link. For example, B can regularly create check points for A's one-way sequential link in the following way (see Figure 6), and pass them to A.

B can control the interval of two check points by selecting an appropriate parameter t. Each check point is linked to the starting point σ_A_1. Note that the one-way sequential link is not terminated at any of the check points; that is, $\sigma\_A_{mt+1} = S_A(X_{mt+1}, H(\sigma\_A_{mt}), n\_A_{mt+1})$ will be linked to σ_A_{mt} when a check point P_m is created.

Suppose the validity of A's signature $\sigma\_A_k = S_A(X_k, H(\sigma\_A_{k-1}), n\_A_k)$ in dispute is located between check points $P_m = S_B(\text{checkpoint}, \sigma\_A_1, \sigma\_A_{mt}, H(\sigma\_B_{jm-1}), n\_B_{jm})$ and $P_{m+1} = S_B(\text{checkpoint}, \sigma\_A_1, \sigma\_A_{(m+1)t}, H(\sigma\_B_{j(m+1)-1}), n\_B_{j(m+1)})$ based on its index. Then, A needs to provide P_m and P_{m+1} in addition to the evidence listed in Figure 5, and the process of dispute resolution described in Section 4.3 will be changed as follows after Step 3.

4. The adjudicator checks whether P_m and P_{m+1} are B's signatures. If so, the adjudicator believes that P_m and P_{m+1} are check points located before and after σ_A_k.

5. Finally, the adjudicator checks whether σ_A_k is linked properly in the one-way sequential link by verifying the signatures between P_m and P_{m+1}, i.e., from σ_A_{mt} to $\sigma\_A_{(m+1)t}$. If so, σ_A_k is a valid signature.

$$P_1 = S_B(\text{checkpoint}, \sigma\_A_1, \sigma\_A_t, H(\sigma\_B_{j1-1}), n\_B_{j1})$$
$$P_2 = S_B(\text{checkpoint}, \sigma\_A_1, \sigma\_A_{2t}, H(\sigma\_B_{j2-1}), n\_B_{j2})$$
......
$$P_m = S_B(\text{checkpoint}, \sigma\_A_1, \sigma\_A_{mt}, H(\sigma\_B_{jm-1}), n\_B_{jm})$$

Fig. 6. Definition of Check Points

In addition to mitigating the overheads of signature verification at the stage of dispute resolution, the check points could also be used to reduce the storage of digital signatures in the one-way sequential link. Suppose a check point is created at the end of each month. It can be specified in the non-repudiation policy that signatures generated earlier than two current check points are expired. Then all those expired signatures except the starting one of the link (σ_A_1 in the above example) need not be stored for dispute resolution.

5.3 Restrictions on Certificates

In the one-way sequential link mechanism, a trading party's public-key certificate is revoked not through the certification authority as usual. Instead, the certificate is revoked with the approval of the other party who accepts the signatures in the transactions. Suppose party A has got the approval of revocation of his certificate C_A from party B. Then A is only liable for the signatures appeared in the terminated one-way sequential link established with B. However, if a party D gets A's compromised signing key, he will be able to forge A's signatures. A cannot deny the validity of those signatures as A did not get the approval of revocation from D, even though A has never intended to do transactions with D. Obviously, it is impossible for A to revoke C_A by obtaining the approval from unlimited number of parties. Thus, a restriction needs to be set in C_A, which enumerates the parties who are eligible to accept the signatures associated with C_A. In other words, such a certificate will be used only for transactions with the parties specified in the certificate. If the certificate owner wants to revoke the certificate, he should get the approval of revocation from each of these legitimate parties.

In the one-way sequential link mechanism, the signer can only deny the validity of signatures outside the terminated one-way sequential link. As long as the private key is not compromised, it is safe to leave the one-way sequential link open even after the associated public-key certificate has expired. A more prudent way is to terminate the one-way sequential link once the associated public-key certificate has expired. Then, the signer is only liable for a fixed number of signatures in the terminated one-way sequential link.

6   Conclusion

The purpose of the non-repudiation service is to support the dispute resolution by providing the cryptographic evidence such as digital signatures. As disputes may arise well after the end of a transaction, it is critical to ensure that the signatures generated before the corresponding public-key certificate expires or is revoked remain valid.

We presented an efficient mechanism for maintaining the validity of digital signatures in B2B applications without the involvement of a trusted third party. It should be noted that this mechanism is not suitable for B2C applications because of the following difference in these two types of applications.

- In B2B applications, the transacting parties usually have a regular business relationship, and both sides maintain a long-term transaction log.
- In B2C applications, the transacting parties may only have a casual business relationship, and customers may not maintain a long-term transaction history.

That means it is hard to establish a one-way sequential link at the customer side in B2C applications, which is an important requirement to maintain the validity of digital signatures in our mechanism. Further research might be desirable on efficient approaches for maintaining the validity of digital signatures in B2C applications without the involvement of a trusted third party.

It should be further noted that our mechanism only provides the technical support for the non-repudiation service. The legal framework is needed to support this new service in the digital world.

Acknowledgements. Part of the research was done when I was working in Oracle Corporation. Thanks to Ramu Sunkara for his encouragement and to Supreet Oberoi for valuable discussions.

References

[Admas01]   C. Admas, P. Cain, D. Pinkas, and R. Zuccherato. *"Internet X.509 public key infrastructure time-stamp protocol (TSP)"*. RFC 3161, August, 2001.

[Bellare99]   M. Bellare and S. Miner. *"A forward-secure digital signature scheme"*. Lecture Notes in Computer Science 1666, Advances in Cryptology: Proceedings of Crypto'99, pages 431--438, Santa Barbara, California, August 1999.

[Ford97]   W. Ford and M. Baum. *"Secure electronic commerce -- Building the infrastructure for digital signatures and encryption"*. New Jersey: Prentice Hall, 1997.

[Housley99]   R. Housley, W. Ford, W. Polk, and D. Solo. *"Internet X.509 public key infrastructure certificate and CRL profile"*. RFC 2459, January 1999.

[ISO13888-1]   ISO/IEC 13888-1. *"Information technology - Security techniques - Non-repudiation - Part 1: General"*. ISO/IEC, 1997.

[ISO13888-3]   ISO/IEC 13888-3. *"Information technology - Security techniques - Non-repudiation - Part 3: Mechanisms using asymmetric techniques"*. ISO/IEC, 1997.

[ISO9796]   ISO/IEC 9796. *"Information technology – Security techniques - Digital signature scheme giving message recovery"*. ISO/IEC, 1991.

[X509]   ITU-T. *"Information technology - Open systems interconnection - The directory: Public-key and attribute certificate frameworks"*. ITU-T Recommendation X.509(V4), 2000.

[Krawczyk00]   H. Krawczyk. *"Simple forward-secure signatures from any signature scheme"*. Proceedings of 7th ACM Conference on Computer and Communications Security, pages 108--115, Athens, Greece, November 2000.

[DSS]   NIST FIPS PUB 186. *"Digital signature standard"*. National Institute of Standards and Technology, May 1994.

[Schneier96]   B. Schneier. *"Applied cryptography -- Protocols, algorithms, and source code in C"*. New York: John Wiley & Sons, 1996 (second edition).

[Zhou99]   J. Zhou and K. Y. Lam. *"Securing digital signatures for non-repudiation"*. Computer Communications, 22(8):710--716, Elsevier, May 1999.

[Zhou00]   J. Zhou and R. H. Deng. *"On the validity of digital signatures"*. Computer Communication Review, 30(2):29--34, ACM Press, April 2000.

[Zhou01]   J. Zhou. *"Non-repudiation in electronic commerce"*. Computer Security Series, Artech House, August 2001.

Short 3-Secure Fingerprinting Codes for Copyright Protection*

Francesc Sebé and Josep Domingo-Ferrer

Universitat Rovira i Virgili, Dept. of Computer Engineering and Mathematics,
Av. Països Catalans 26, E-43007 Tarragona, Catalonia, Spain
{fsebe,jdomingo}@etse.urv.es

Abstract. A construction is presented to obtain 3-secure fingerprinting codes for copyright protection. Resistance against collusions of up to three buyers is achieved with a codeword length dramatically shorter than the one required by the general Boneh-Shaw construction. Thus the proposed fingerprints require much less embedding capacity. Due to their very clandestine nature, collusions tend to involve a small number of buyers, so that there is plenty of use for codes providing cost-effective protection against collusions of size up to 3.

Keywords: Electronic copyright protection, Fingerprinting, Watermarking, Buyer collusion.

1 Introduction

Successive failure of copy prevention systems has caused copy detection systems to become the most promising option to protect the intellectual property of multimedia content. In copy detection, the merchant embeds an imperceptible mark into the content before selling it. There are two kinds of mark: watermarks and fingerprints. A watermark is a message that allows ownership of the marked content to be proven, whereas a fingerprint allows buyer identification.

Collusion attacks are not an issue for watermarking (all marked copies being identical), but should be considered in the case of fingerprinting. In a collusion attack, a set of dishonest buyers compare their copies in order to locate differences between them and try to fabricate a new content whose mark is either no longer recoverable or does not allow identification of any of the colluders.
In [1,2], the concept of fingerprinting secure against buyer collusions is introduced. A general construction is given to obtain fingerprinting codes secure against collusions of up to c buyers (c-secure codes). For N possible buyers and given $\epsilon > 0$, $L = 2c \log(2N/\epsilon)$ and $d = 8c^2 \log(8cL/\epsilon)$ a code with N codewords of length

$$l = 2Ldc = 32c^4 \log(2N/\epsilon) \log(8cL/\epsilon) \tag{1}$$

* This work has been partly supported by the European Commission under project IST-2001-32012 "Co-Orthogonal Codes" and by the Spanish Ministry of Science and Technology and the European FEDER fund through project no. TIC2001-0633-C03-01 "STREAMOBILE".

L. Batten and J. Seberry (Eds.): ACISP 2002, LNCS 2384, pp. 316–327, 2002.
© Springer-Verlag Berlin Heidelberg 2002

is constructed which allows one of the colluders to be identified with probability $1 - \epsilon$. The authors also show that, for $c \geq 2$ and $N \geq 3$, it is not possible to obtain c-secure codes where colluders are identified with probability 1.

In [3] it is shown that, for $c = 2$, collusion security can be obtained using the error-correcting capacity of dual Hamming codes. In this way, 2-secure fingerprinting codes are obtained which are much shorter than 2-secure codes obtained via the general construction [1,2].

We show in this paper that, for $c = 3$, it is also possible to come up with collusion-secure fingerprinting codes much shorter than 3-secure codes obtained from the general construction [1,2]. The basic idea is to compose a new kind of code, which we call *scattering code*, with a dual Hamming code.

Section 2 presents some results on dual Hamming codes. Section 3 presents a set of lemmas on the probability of successful collusion as a function of the strategy of colluders. The construction and decoding of scattering codes are introduced in Section 4. Finally, Section 5 explains how to generate fingerprinting codes secure against collusions of up to three buyers by composing a dual Hamming code with a scattering code. Section 6 compares the length of our proposal codewords and those of [1,2]. Section 7 is a conclusion. *The Appendix contains proofs for all presented results.*

2   Dual Binary Hamming Codes

The dual code of a binary Hamming code (denoted by $DH(n)$) is a binary code with 2^n codewords of length $N = 2^n - 1$ such that the distance between any two codewords is 2^{n-1} (see [4] for an introduction). A few definitions and properties related to such codes are presented next.

Definition 1. Let a^1, a^2, a^3 be three codewords of a $DH(n)$ code, *i.e.* $a^i = a^i_1 a^i_2 \cdots a^i_N$. Define $inv(a^1, a^2, a^3)$ as the set of invariant positions between all three codewords, that is, those bit positions in which all three codewords have the same bit value. Formally speaking,

$$inv(a^1, a^2, a^3) = \{i,\ 1 \leq i \leq N,\ a^1_i = a^2_i = a^3_i\}$$

Definition 2. Let a^1, a^2, a^3 be three codewords of a $DH(n)$ code. Define $minor(a^1; a^2, a^3)$ as the set of bit positions in which a^1 has a value different from the values in a^2 and a^3 (for such positions, $a^2_i = a^3_i$). Formally speaking,

$$minor(a^1; a^2, a^3) = \{i,\ 1 \leq i \leq N,\ a^1_i \neq a^2_i,\ a^1_i \neq a^3_i\}$$

Lemma 3. *Let a^1, a^2, a^3 be three codewords of a $DH(n)$ code. Then it holds that $|inv(a^1, a^2, a^3)| = 2^{n-2} - 1$, $|minor(a^1; a^2, a^3)| = 2^{n-2}$, $|minor(a^2; a^1, a^3)| = 2^{n-2}$ and $|minor(a^3; a^1, a^2)| = 2^{n-2}$.*

Lemma 4. *Let a^1, a^2, a^3 be three codewords of a $DH(n)$ code. Then it holds that:*

- *There exists one and only one codeword $a^z \in DH(n) \backslash \{a^1, a^2, a^3\}$ such that $a_i^z = a_i^1 = a_i^2 = a_i^3, \forall i \in inv(a^1, a^2, a^3)$. Furthermore, $a_i^z = a_i^1, \forall i \in minor(a^1; a^2, a^3)$, $a_i^z = a_i^2, \forall i \in minor(a^2; a^1, a^3)$ and $a_i^z = a_i^3, \forall i \in minor(a^3; a^1, a^2)$.*
- *The remaining codewords satisfy that $\forall a^j \in DH(n) \backslash \{a^1, a^2, a^3, a^z\}$, $d_{inv(a^1, a^2, a^3)}(a^j, a^1) = d_{minor(a^1; a^2, a^3)}(a^j, a^1) = d_{minor(a^2; a^1, a^3)}(a^j, a^1) = d_{minor(a^3; a^1, a^2)}(a^j, a^1) = 2^{n-3}$, where $d_P(x, y)$ denotes Hamming distance between codewords x and y restricted to bit positions in P. The same distances hold with respect to a^2 and a^3.*

3   3-Collusions over $DH(n)$

Let us assume that three dishonest buyers c^1, c^2, c^3 compare their copies of the same multimedia content. According to the marking assumption [1,2], they can only modify the embedded marks in those *detectable* positions where not all three marks take the same bit value. In those positions, the colluders can set the corresponding bit to 0, 1 or "unreadable". In this way, we conclude that, if three different buyers are assigned codewords a^1, a^2 and a^3 of a $DH(n)$ code, the result of their collusion will be a codeword a^{coll} where no bit has been modified in the $2^{n-2} - 1$ positions in $inv(a^1, a^2, a^3)$. On the other hand, colluders will be able to identify positions in $minor(a^1; a^2, a^3)$ as the bit positions of those content fragments which are identical between the copies of c^2 and c^3 and different from the copy of c^1. In a similar way, $minor(a^2; a^1, a^3)$ and $minor(a^3; a^1, a^2)$ can be identified as well.

In order for a collusion to be successful, colluders must generate, by mixing fragments in their copies, a codeword such that the closest codeword in the fingerprinting code is not in $\{a^1, a^2, a^3\}$. In this way, another buyer will be accused in lieu of the colluders. Intuitively, it can be realized that a reasonable strategy to come up with a codeword as distant as possible from the colluders' codewords is to build that codeword in such a way that each colluder contributes the same number of bits.

Definition 5. *A p-majority collusion strategy is one in which colluders choose with probability p the majority bit value in positions $minor(a^i; a^j, a^k)$ (that is, the bit values in a^j or a^k).*

Lemma 6. *Let a^{coll} be a codeword that has been generated using a p-majority collusion strategy between three codewords $a^1, a^2, a^3 \in DH(n)$. It holds that $d_1 = d(a^{coll}, a^i) = K_1, \forall i = 1, 2, 3$ with*

$$p_1(k) = p(K_1 = k) = \sum_{t=\max(0, k-2^{n-1})}^{\min(k, 2^{n-2})} b(t; 2^{n-2}, p) b(k - t; 2^{n-1}, 1 - p)$$

where $b(x_1; x_2, x_3) = \binom{x_2}{x_1} x_3^{x_1}(1-x_3)^{x_2-x_1}$ is the binomial probability function
(x_2 is the number of trials, x_3 the success probability per trial and x_1 is the number of successful trials).

Lemma 7. *Let a^{coll} be a codeword generated using a p-majority collusion strategy between three codewords $a^1, a^2, a^3 \in DH(n)$. It holds that $d_2 = \min_{i=1,2,3} d(a^{coll}, a^i) = K_2$ with*

$$p_2 = p(K_2 = k) = \sum_{i=1}^{3} \binom{3}{i} p_1(k)^i \left[\sum_{k'>k} p_1(k') \right]^{3-i}$$

Lemma 8. *Let a^{coll} be a codeword generated using a p-majority strategy between three codewords $a^1, a^2, a^3 \in DH(n)$ and let a^z be the only codeword in $DH(n) \backslash \{a^1, a^2, a^3\}$ with $a_i^z = a_i^1 = a_i^2 = a_i^3$, $\forall i \in inv(a^1, a^2, a^3)$ (existence and uniqueness of a^z are guaranteed by Lemma 4). Then, $d_3 = d(a^z, a^{coll}) = K_3$ with*

$$p_3(k) = p(K_3 = k) = b(k; 3 \cdot 2^{n-2}, p)$$

Lemma 9. *Let a^{coll} be a codeword generated using a p-majority strategy between three codewords $a^1, a^2, a^3 \in DH(n)$ and let a^z be the only codeword in $DH(n) \backslash \{a^1, a^2, a^3\}$ with $a_i^z = a_i^1 = a_i^2 = a_i^3$, $\forall i \in inv(a^1, a^2, a^3)$. Then, for any codeword $a \in DH(n) \backslash \{a^1, a^2, a^3, a^z\}$, it holds that $d_4 = d(a, a^{coll}) = 2^{n-3} + K_4$ with*

$$p_4(k) = p(K_4 = k) = \sum_{t=\max(0, k-3 \cdot 2^{n-3})}^{\min\{k, 3 \cdot 2^{n-3}\}} b(t; 3 \cdot 2^{n-3}, 1-p) b(k-t; 3 \cdot 2^{n-3}, p)$$

For the sake of simplicity, let us assume in what follows that d_3 is distributed like d_4. Since for $p > 0.\hat{6}$ the number of different bits expected for d_3 is greater than the number of different bits expected for d_4, such a distributional assumption will cause actual security to be even slightly higher than computed in what follows.

Lemma 10. *Let a^{coll} be a codeword generated using a p-majority strategy between three codewords $a^1, a^2, a^3 \in DH(n)$. It holds that $d_5 = \min_{i \notin \{1,2,3\}} \{d(a^{coll}, a^i)\} = 2^{n-3} + K_5$, with*

$$p_5(k) = p(K_5 = k) = \sum_{i=1}^{2^n-3} \binom{2^n-3}{i} p_4(k)^i \left[\sum_{k'>k} p_4(k') \right]^{2^n-3-i}$$

Lemma 11. *Let a^{coll} be a codeword generated using a p-majority strategy between three codewords $a^1, a^2, a^3 \in DH(n)$. The probability that the codeword in $DH(n)$ closest to a^{coll} is not in $\{a^1, a^2, a^3\}$ is expressed by*

$$\epsilon = \sum_{k=0}^{2^n - 1} p(d_2 = k)p(d_5 \leq k)$$

ϵ is the probability that decoding a^{coll} yields as a result a codeword different from any of the colluders' codewords, that is, the probability of an honest buyer being unjustly accused instead of the colluders.

Table 1. Probability ϵ of success of a 3-collusion in $DH(7)$ and $DH(8)$ for several values of p

				p		
	0.0	0.6	0.7	0.8	0.9	1.0
$DH(7)$	1.0	$0.59 \cdot 10^{-3}$	$0.14 \cdot 10^{-3}$	$0.14 \cdot 10^{-6}$	$0.77 \cdot 10^{-14}$	0.0
$DH(8)$	1.0	$0.17 \cdot 10^{-7}$	$0.10 \cdot 10^{-7}$	$0.15 \cdot 10^{-13}$	$0.70 \cdot 10^{-28}$	0.0

It can be observed from Table 1 that, as n increases and p approaches 1, the probability $1 - \epsilon$ of correctly identifying one of the colluders can be made arbitrarily close to 1. *The problem is that the parameter p defining the collusion strategy is chosen by the colluders, which implies they can take $p = 0$ to make sure they are not identified!* In Section 4, we present a technique to prevent colluders from avoiding identification in this way.

4   Scattering Codes

4.1   Construction

We define a *scattering code* $SC(d, t)$ with parameters (d, t) as a binary code consisting of $2t$ codewords of length $(2t + 1)d$ constructed as follows:

1. Start generating the codewords of $SC(1, t)$ as:
   a) The i-th codeword for $1 \leq i \leq t$ is constructed by setting the first and the $(i + 1)$-th bits of the codeword to '1'. The remaining bits are set to '0'.
   b) The i-th codeword for $t + 1 \leq i \leq 2t$ is constructed by setting the $(i + 1)$-th bit of the codeword to '1'. The remaining bits are set to '0'.
2. The code $SC(d, t)$ is generated by replicating d times every bit in the codewords of $SC(1, t)$. Define a *block* to be a group of d replicated bits.
3. By convention, the first t codewords of $SC(d, t)$ are defined to encode a '1' and the last t codewords are defined to encode a '0'. The first block of the code is called 'Zone-A', the next t blocks are called 'Zone-B' and the last t blocks are called 'Zone-C'. See an example in Table 2.

Table 2. Codewords of a scattering code $SC(4,3)$

Encodes	Zone-A	Zone-B	Zone-C
	1111	1111 0000 0000	0000 0000 0000
'1'	1111	0000 1111 0000	0000 0000 0000
	1111	0000 0000 1111	0000 0000 0000
	0000	0000 0000 0000	1111 0000 0000
'0'	0000	0000 0000 0000	0000 1111 0000
	0000	0000 0000 0000	0000 0000 1111

Using scattering codes, a '1' is encoded by randomly choosing one of the first t codewords and a '0' is encoded by randomly choosing one of the last t codewords.

4.2 Decoding

A scattering code is decoded by using the first applicable rule among the following ordered list:

1. If all bits in 'Zone-A' are '1' and all bits in 'Zone-C' are '0', decode as '1'.
2. If all bits in 'Zone-A' are '0' and all bits in 'Zone-B' are '0', decode as '0'.
3. If in two blocks of 'Zone-B' there is at least one bit with value '1' in each one, decode as '1'.
4. If in two blocks of 'Zone-C' there is at least one bit with value '1' in each one, decode as '0'.
5. If there are more '1' bits than '0' bits in 'Zone-A', decode as '1'.
6. If there are more '0' bits than '1' bits in 'Zone-A', decode as '0'.
7. Decode as 'Unreadable'

Lemma 12. *Let b^{coll} be a codeword generated by using a p-majority strategy between three codewords $b^1, b^2, b^3 \in SC(d,t)$ encoding the same bit value v. Then, b^{coll} decodes as v with probability 1.*

Lemma 13. *Let b^{coll} be a codeword generated using a p-majority strategy between three codewords $b^1, b^2, b^3 \in SC(d,t)$, with two of them ($b^1$ and b^2) encoding a value v and the other (b^3) a value $\bar{v}$. Then, the probability that b^{coll} decodes as v is given by*

$$p(v) = (1 - \frac{1}{t})p_{diff}(v) + \frac{1}{t}p_{same}(v)$$

where $p_{diff}(v)$ is the probability of decoding as v when $b^1 \neq b^2$ and can be computed as $p_{diff}(v) = 1 - p_{diff}(\bar{v})$ and

$$p_{diff}(\bar{v}) = (1-p)^d p^{2d} +$$
$$+ 2 \cdot p^d(1-p^d) \sum_{k=0}^{\lfloor \frac{d-1}{2} \rfloor} b(k; d, p) +$$
$$+ p^{2d} \sum_{k=1}^{\lfloor \frac{d-1}{2} \rfloor} b(k; d, p)$$

and $p_{same}(v)$ *is the probability of decoding as v when $b^1 = b^2$ and can be computed as*

$$p_{same}(v) = p^{2d} +$$
$$+ (1 - p^d) \sum_{k=\lfloor \frac{d+2}{2} \rfloor}^{d} b(k; d, p) +$$
$$+ p^d \sum_{k=\lfloor \frac{d+2}{2} \rfloor}^{d-1} b(k; d, p) +$$

Table 3 shows, for several codes $SC(d, t)$, the least probability $p(v)$ of decoding as the majority bit in a collusion of three codewords (two encoding v and one $\bar{v}$).

Table 3. Probability $p(v)$ of decoding as the majority bit v in a collusion of three buyers, for several parameter choices (d, t).

d	t	$\min p(v)$
3	4	0.68
5	5	0.8
7	9	0.89
31	100	0.99

5   Construction of 3-Secure Code

If there are $N = 2^n - 1$ buyers, each buyer c^i is assigned a different codeword $a^i \in DH(n)$. Rather than directly embedding a^i in the content to be sold, the merchant generates a codeword A^i by composing a scattering code $SC(d, t)$ with a^i. Such a composition is performed by replacing each bit of a^i with a codeword in $SC(d, t)$ that encodes the value of the bit of a^i. In this way, the codeword A^i will have bitlength

$$l = (N - 1)(2t + 1)d \tag{2}$$

The merchant then permutes the bits in A^i using a pseudo-random permutation seeded by a secret key known only to the merchant. Finally, the merchant embeds the permuted version of A^i in the content being sold.

What is achieved with the above composition is that, regardless of the p'-majority strategy used by colluders to generate codewords A^{coll}, the $p(v)$-majority strategy resulting from decoding A^{coll} as a^{coll} has a value $p(v)$ that can be controlled by the merchant by choosing appropriate values for parameters d and t (see Table 3). It can be seen from Table 1 that controlling $p(v)$ is necessary to the keep low the probability ϵ of successful collusion. If A^i has some bits with value 'Unreadable', those bits are randomly set to '0' or '1'.

6   Numerical Results

Once parameters d and t have been chosen, the number of buyers can be increased by increasing n. Table 4 shows, for $d = 5$ and $t = 5$, the size of the code (number of buyers), the length of codewords in our proposal, the probability ϵ of a successful collusion and the length of codewords in the Boneh-Shaw proposal for the same parameters. It can be seen that the Boneh-Shaw construction requires much longer codewords than our proposal. Furthermore, as n increases, their codeword length increases faster than ours.

Table 4. Codeword length comparison between our proposal and Boneh-Shaw's for the same number of users n and security level ϵ (parameter choice $d = 5$, $t = 5$)

n	buyers	ϵ	Our length	Boneh-Shaw's length
7	128	$0.14 \cdot 10^{-6}$	6,985	2,788,320
8	256	$0.15 \cdot 10^{-13}$	14,025	8,393,220
9	512	$0.19 \cdot 10^{-27}$	28,105	28,340,928

In our proposal, once d and t have been fixed, the value ϵ decreases exponentially as n increases, so that the security level reached may be unnecessarily high. A better comparison is to use a fixed ϵ assuming that, for our security requirements, any $\epsilon' < \epsilon$ can be regarded as negligible. Table 5 presents a codeword length comparison for $\epsilon = 10^{-10}$. It can be observed that, for $\epsilon = 10^{-10}$, our proposal is shorter up to $n = 16$ (number of buyers below $65,536$). For values of $n > 16$, Boneh-Shaw's proposal has a shorter codeword length. This is due to the fact that our codeword length increases as $O(N)$ while Boneh-Shaw's increases as $O(\log N)$. Nonetheless, the Boneh-Shaw proposal would only be *substantially* shorter than ours if the number of buyers were *really huge*; for usual figures, our proposal is the one substantially shorter.

Table 5. Codeword length comparison between our proposal and Boneh-Shaw's assuming $\epsilon = 10^{-10}$

buyers	Our length	Boneh-Shaw's length
512	28,105	5,148,000
1,024	56,265	5,269,992
...	...	...
32,768	1,802,185	5,883,888
65,536	3,604,425	6,006,780
131,072	7,208,905	6,129,816

7   Conclusion

Codes for fingerprinting have been presented which, for collusions of up to three buyers and not too large a number of possible buyers, require a codeword length much shorter than the one required by the Boneh-Shaw construction. Thus, the proposed scheme is especially useful when the capacity of the embedding scheme is low, as it may happen when protecting precision-critical content (medical images, etc.). On the other hand, collusions tend to be small due to their clandestine nature (joining a large group of colluders is risky for a buyer); therefore, there is plenty of use for codes that, like the ones presented here, provide efficient protection against small collusions.

References

1. D. Boneh and J. Shaw, "Collusion-secure fingerprinting for digital data", in *Advances in Cryptology-CRYPTO'95*, LNCS 963, pp. 452-465, 1995.
2. D. Boneh and J. Shaw, "Collusion-secure fingerprinting for digital data", *IEEE Trans. Inf. Theory*, vol **IT-44**, no. (5), pp. 1897-1905, 1998.
3. J. Domingo-Ferrer and J. Herrera-Joancomartí, "Short collusion-secure fingerprints based on dual binary Hamming codes", *Electronics Letters*, vol. 36, no. 20, pp. 1697-1699, 2000.
4. F. J. MacWilliams and N. J. A. Sloane, *The Theory of Error-Correcting Codes*. Amsterdam: North-Holland, 1977.

Appendix

Proof (Lemma 3): Let a^1, a^2, a^3 be three codewords of a $DH(n)$ code. Since $d(a^i, a^j)_{i \neq j} = 2^{n-1}$, then $|inv(a^1, a^2)| = 2^{n-1} - 1$. Let $x = |inv(a^1, a^2, a^3)|$; then $|minor(a^3; a^1, a^2)| = 2^{n-1} - 1 - x$. Let $y = |minor(a^2; a^1, a^3)|$; then $|minor(a^1; a^3, a^2)| = 2^{n-1} - y$. On the other hand, $|inv(a^1, a^3)| = x + y = 2^{n-1} - 1$ and $|inv(a^2, a^3)| = 2^{n-1} - 1 = x + 2^{n-1} - y$. By solving the following equation system,

$$\begin{cases} x + y = 2^{n-1} - 1 \\ 2^{n-1} - 1 = x + 2^{n-1} - y \end{cases}$$

we get $x = 2^{n-2} - 1$ and $y = 2^{n-2}$ and thus $|inv(a^1, a^2, a^3)| = 2^{n-2} - 1$, $|minor(a^1; a^3, a^2)| = 2^{n-2}$, $|minor(a^2; a^1, a^3)| = 2^{n-2}$ and $|minor(a^3; a^1, a^2)| = 2^{n-2}$.

Proof (Lemma 4): First of all, we prove the existence and properties of a^z. As a $DH(n)$ code is a linear code, any linear combination of codewords results in another codeword. Then, we get $a^z = a^1 \oplus a^2 \oplus a^3$, where $\oplus$ denotes the component-wise modulo 2 addition.

We prove that $a_i^z = a_i^1 = a_i^2 = a_i^3$, $\forall i \in inv(a^1, a^2, a^3)$. This is true because if $a_i^1 = a_i^2 = a_i^3 = 1$, then $a_i^1 \oplus a_i^2 \oplus a_i^3 = 1$, and if $a_i^1 = a_i^2 = a_i^3 = 0$, then $a_i^1 \oplus a_i^2 \oplus a_i^3 = 0$.

Then, we prove $a_i^z = a_i^1$, $\forall i \in minor(a^1; a^2, a^3)$. This is true because $a_i^z = a_i^1 \oplus a_i^2 \oplus a_i^3$ and as $a_i^2 = a_i^3$, then $a_i^z = a_i^1$.

Using the same procedure we can prove $a_i^z = a_i^2$, $\forall i \in minor(a^2; a^1, a^3)$ and $a_i^z = a_i^3$, $\forall i \in minor(a^3; a^1, a^2)$.

Next we prove the second part of the Lemma. Let $a^j \in DH(n) \backslash \{a^1, a^2, a^3, a^z\}$
Call x the number of positions in $inv(a^1, a^2, a^3)$ where $a_i^j = a_i^1$. Then the number of positions in $inv(a^1, a^2, a^3)$ where $a_i^j \neq a_i^1$ is $2^{n-2} - 1 - x$ (see Lemma 3).
Call y the number of positions in $minor(a^1; a^2, a^3)$ where $a_i^j = a_i^1$. Then the number of positions in $minor(a^1; a^2, a^3)$ where $a_i^j \neq a_i^1$ is $2^{n-2} - y$.
Call z the number of positions in $minor(a^2; a^1, a^3)$ where $a_i^j = a_i^1$. Then the number of positions in $minor(a^2; a^1, a^3)$ where $a_i^j \neq a_i^1$ is $2^{n-2} - z$.
Call t the number of positions in $minor(a^3; a^1, a^2)$ where $a_i^j = a_i^1$. Then the number of positions in $minor(a^3; a^1, a^2)$ where $a_i^j \neq a_i^1$ is $2^{n-2} - t$.
As $d(a^j, a^1) = d_{inv(a^1,a^2,a^3)}(a^j, a^1) + d_{minor(a^1;a^2,a^3)}(a^j, a^1) + d_{minor(a^2;a^1,a^3)}(a^j, a^1) + d_{minor(a^3,a^1,a^2)}(a^j, a^1) = 2^{n-1}$, then

$$(2^{n-2} - 1 - x) + (2^{n-2} - y) + (2^{n-2} - z) + (2^{n-2} - t) = 2^{n-1}$$

As $d(a^j, a^2) = d_{inv(a^1,a^2,a^3)}(a^j, a^2) + d_{minor(a^1;a^2,a^3)}(a^j, a^2) + d_{minor(a^2;a^1,a^3)}(a^j, a^2) + d_{minor(a^3,a^1,a^2)}(a^j, a^2) = 2^{n-1}$, then

$$(2^{n-2} - 1 - x) + (2^{n-2} - y) + z + t = 2^{n-1}$$

As $d(a^j, a^3) = d_{inv(a^1,a^2,a^3)}(a^j, a^3) + d_{minor(a^1;a^2,a^3)}(a^j, a^3) + d_{minor(a^2;a^1,a^3)}(a^j, a^3) + d_{minor(a^3,a^1,a^2)}(a^j, a^3) = 2^{n-1}$, then

$$(2^{n-2} - 1 - x) + y + (2^{n-2} - z) + t = 2^{n-1}$$

As $d(a^j, a^z) = d_{inv(a^1,a^2,a^3)}(a^j, a^z) + d_{minor(a^1;a^2,a^3)}(a^j, a^z) + d_{minor(a^2;a^1,a^3)}(a^j, a^z) + d_{minor(a^3,a^1,a^2)}(a^j, a^z) = 2^{n-1}$, then

$$(2^{n-2} - 1 - x) + y + z + (2^{n-2} - t) = 2^{n-1}$$

From the expressions above we build the following equation system:

$$\begin{cases} x + y + z + t = 2^{n-1} - 1 \\ -x - y + z + t = 1 \\ -x + y - z + t = 1 \\ -x + y + z - t = 1 \end{cases}$$

By solving it, we get $x = 2^{n-3} - 1$ and $y = z = t = 2^{n-3}$.
Finally, we conclude,
$d_{inv(a^1,a^2,a^3)}(a^j, a^1) = 2^{n-2} - 1 - x = 2^{n-3}$
$d_{minor(a^1;a^2,a^3)}(a^j, a^1) = 2^{n-2} - y = 2^{n-3}$
$d_{minor(a^2;a^1,a^3)}(a^j, a^1) = 2^{n-2} - z = 2^{n-3}$
$d_{minor(a^3;a^1,a^2)}(a^j, a^1) = 2^{n-2} - t = 2^{n-3}$

In the same way, we can prove that these distances hold between a^j and a^2, a^3.

Proof (Lemma 6): Without loss of generality, take $i = 1$. We have that, for bit positions in $inv(a^1, a^2, a^3)$, there is no difference between a^1 and a^{coll} since bits in those positions are undetectable. Also, each of the 2^{n-2} bits in $minor(a^1; a^2, a^3)$ differs between a^1 and a^{coll} with probability p; therefore, the probability of there being t differing bits in those positions is given by a binomial probability function $b(t; 2^{n-2}, p)$. Also, each of the $2 \cdot 2^{n-2}$ bits in $minor(a^2; a^1, a^3)$ and $minor(a^3; a^1, a^2)$ differs between a^1 and a^{coll} with probability $(1 - p)$; therefore, the probability of there being $k - t$ differing bits in those positions is given by a binomial probability function $b(k - t; 2^{n-1}, 1 - p)$. In this way, the expression in the Lemma corresponds to the probability of there being a total of $t + (k - t) = k$ differing bits between a^1 and a^{coll}.

Proof (Lemma 7): The expression in the Lemma corresponds to the probability of one, two or three codewords in $\{a^1, a^2, a^3\}$ being at distance k from a^{coll} and the remaining codewords being at a greater distance.

Proof (Lemma 8): Lemma 4 says that bits of a^z are identical to bits of a^i in the positions in $minor(a^i; a^j, a^k)$ for $(i, j, k) \in \{(1, 2, 3), (2, 1, 3), (3, 1, 2)\}$. Therefore, the probability of there being k different bits in those $3 \cdot 2^{n-2}$ positions is given by a binomial probability function $b(k; 3 \cdot 2^{n-2}, p)$.

Proof (Lemma 9): According to Lemma 4, a^{coll} and a have 2^{n-3} differing bits in positions in $inv(a^1, a^2, a^3)$. In each $minor(a^i; a^j, a^k)$, for $(i, j, k) \in \{(1, 2, 3), (2, 1, 3), (3, 1, 2)\}$, a^{coll} has all 2^{n-3} bits each of which is different with probability p and 2^{n-3} bits each of which is different with probability $(1 - p)$. Therefore, we have $3 \cdot 2^{n-3}$ bits with probability p of being different, and thus the probability that t of such bits are different is $b(t; 3 \cdot 2^{n-3}, p)$. On the other hand, we have $3 \cdot 2^{n-3}$ bits with probability $1 - p$ of being different, and thus the probability that $k - t$ of such bits are different is $b(k - t; 3 \cdot 2^{n-3}, 1 - p)$. In this way, the expression in the Lemma computes the probability of there being $t + (k - t) = k$ different bits between a and a^{coll}.

Proof (Lemma 10): The expression in the Lemma computes the probability that at least one out of the $2^n - 3$ codewords in $DH(n) \backslash \{a^1, a^2, a^3\}$ is at distance k of a^{coll}, with the remaining codewords at a greater distance.

Proof (Lemma 12): It can be seen that, if $v = 1$, bits in 'Zone-A' and in 'Zone-C' stay undetectable and thus decoding will use Rule 1 and return a value 1.

If $v = 0$, bits in 'Zone-A' and in 'Zone-B' stay undetectable. Thus, decoding will use Rule 2 and return a value 0.

Proof (Lemma 13): In a collision between three codewords $b^1, b^2, b^3 \in$ $SC(d,t)$ with two of them (b^1 and b^2) encoding a value v (without loss of generality, assume $v = 1$ and $\overline{v} = 0$), we have $b^1 = b^2$ with probability $\frac{1}{t}$ and $b^1 \neq b^2$ with probability $1 - \frac{1}{t}$.

In the case $b^1 \neq b^2$, we compute $p_{\text{diff}}(v) = 1 - p_{\text{diff}}(\overline{v})$ (it can be shown that for odd values of d Rule 7 is never reached), where $p_{\text{diff}}(\overline{v})$ corresponds to the probability of decoding $\overline{v}$ after a collusion based on a p-majority strategy. $p_{\text{diff}}(\overline{v})$ is actually the probability of decoding using Rules 2 or 6 (Rule 4 is never used when $b^1 \neq b^2$).

In the case $b^1 = b^2$, we compute $p_{\text{same}}(v)$ as the probability of decoding v after a collusion based on a p-majority strategy. $p_{\text{same}}(v)$ is actually the probability of decoding using Rules 1 or 5 (Rule 3 is never used when $b^1 = b^2$).

An Order-Specified Multisignature Scheme Secure against Active Insider Attacks

Mitsuru Tada

Institute of Media and Information Technology,
Chiba University, JAPAN.
mt@math.s.chiba-u.ac.jp

Abstract. In *an order-specified multisignature scheme*, one can verify not only a set of signers who have signed the message but also its signing order. Though we have seen several scheme with such properties proposed, none of them is given the security proof against active adversaries. In the scheme by [6], no polynomial-time active adversary can forge a signature for a new message, but it is possible for active adversaries to forge a signature changing its signing order. Furthermore, that scheme has the restriction that the possible signing orders are only ones of the type of serial signing. In this paper, we propose an order-specified multisignature scheme, which is shown to be secure against adaptive chosen-message insider attacks for bath a message and a signing order, and which allows the signing orders to form like any series-parallel graphs unlike the scheme [6]. The security is shown by using ID-reduction technique, which reduces the security of multisignature schemes to those of multi-round identification schemes. Furthermore, we discuss the efficiency of the proposed scheme and the upper bound of the possible number of participating signers.

1 Introduction

In *a multisignature scheme*, which, in general, is obtained by extending (or modifying) a (single) signature scheme, plural signers (say, n signers) jointly generate a signature for an identical message. Such a situation can also be realized by applying a (single) signature scheme n times. Hence a multisignature scheme is required to provide the property that the total signature size is smaller than n times of that in the corresponding single signature scheme. Actually, we can see several multisignature schemes proposed in [6,10] etc.

In *an order-specified multisignature scheme*, a signature can guarantee not only the set of signers who have signed the message, but also its signing order. For example, in a company, a document should be signed by members in a project, and after that, should be signed by the boss of those members. In case those entities collude, a signing order can easily be forged even if the document, actually, is not signed in that order, but a recipient (a verifier) may pay attention and want to verify its signing order, or at least that the signers are conscious to their signing order. For general example, suppose that a signer P may want to

L. Batten and J. Seberry (Eds.): ACISP 2002, LNCS 2384, pp. 328–345, 2002.

sign after a certain signer P', and that she actually did so. But in most (non-order-specified) multisignature schemes, even if a multisignature is generated by P and P' in the signing order P after P', from a multisignature by P and P', the signature only by P can be calculated with P''s assistance. Even if P insists that she has signed after P' did, no one can verify it. For a critical case, consider the generating a contract requiring a guarantor for the contractor. Then the guarantor G does want to sign after her intending contractor C (a person she intends to guarantee). If G has signed before her intending contractor, then C may maliciously use the intermediate multisignature by the guarantor. For example, the malicious contractor gives another contractor C', and C' can make a contract with the guarantor G, even if G does not intend guarantee the contractor C'. For a critical case again, election returns should be signed by the committee members $\mathcal{M}$ ($:= \{M_1, \ldots, M_n\}$) and the witnesses $\mathcal{W}$ ($:= \{W_1, \ldots, W_k\}$), and $\mathcal{W}$ shall sign after all of $\mathcal{M}$ have signed. No attention is paid for the order among $\mathcal{M}$ (or $\mathcal{W}$).

Up to present, we can see several order-specified multisignature schemes proposed in [3,4,5]. The scheme in [3] is based on modified ElGamal signature scheme, and one in [4] is based on RSA scheme. In [5], two schemes are proposed. One is based on DSA scheme, and the other is based on RSA. In the schemes [3,4], the public-keys corresponding signing orders have to be registered in advance, but in the scheme [5], such a task is not necessary. The signing orders in [5] are restricted to be serial signing orders such as the signing order that P_2 signs after P_1, P_3 signs after P_2, and similarly P_n signs after P_{n-1}, whereas ones in [3,4] are allowed to form like *series-parallel graphs*. (For the definition, see Section 2.) The scheme [5] has the flexibility for a message to be signed and its signing order, whereas the scheme [3] provides neither of them. The scheme [4] has the order-flexibility, but it is necessary to register as many public-keys as the number of the signing orders to be verified as well as in the scheme [3].

Unfortunately, none of the schemes given above is shown to be secure against active adversaries. To be sure that the security proofs are given in those papers, but those are only against passive adversaries. The scheme [6] can be regarded as an order-specified multisignature scheme, even if it is not mentioned in the paper, because a signature generated by P_1 and P_2 in the signing order P_2 after P_1, cannot be accepted by the verification algorithm for the signing order P_1 after P_2. The security proof in [6] states that no polynomial-time (adaptive chosen-message insider) adversary can forge a multisignature for a new message with a non-negligible probability. (For the definition of 'negligible (probability)', see later in this section.) But such an adversary can forge a multisignature changing the signing order. Fortunately, we can easily modify the scheme [6] to be secure also for signing orders by adding the signing order into the arguments of hash functions. (Hereafter, we call such a scheme the Modified Ohta-Okamoto (MOO) scheme.) The security proof given in Section 4 can be applied to the MOO scheme, and we can say that the MOO scheme is an order-specified multisignature scheme which is secure against active attacks. The signing order, however, is restricted to be serial signing. That means the scheme cannot be applied for the first or the third example given above.

In this paper, we propose an order-specified multisignature scheme which is secure against *adaptive chosen-message insider attacks*. The proposed scheme is an extension of so-called *a generic signature scheme* [8] which is obtained by translating a three-pass identification scheme using an appropriate hash function. All the signing orders represented by *series-parallel graphs* are allowed. Furthermore, the proposed scheme has the order-flexibility as well as the schemes [6, 4,5]. The security of the proposed scheme is shown by using *ID-reduction technique* introduced by [6]. As seen in the attack model (MS-adversary) given in Section 4.1, an adversary can query, to the signing oracles, not only a message but also its signing order. The output of the adversary is a set of a message m, a signing order φ and a multisignature Σ for m in the signing order φ, with the condition that the adversary has never queried, to the signing oracles, the very pair (m, φ). Then a pair (m, φ') with $\varphi' \neq \varphi$ can appear in the queries to the signing oracles, and so can (m', φ) with $m \neq m'$.

This paper is organized as follows: At the end of this section, we will provide our notations. In Section 2, we will review the definition of series-parallel graphs, and will see some fundamental properties on series-parallel graphs. The proofs of Lemmas 1 and 2 will be given in Appendix. In Section 3, we will present the proposed order-specified multisignature scheme. In Section 4, we will give the security proof for the proposed scheme. The security of the proposed can be reduced to those of the corresponding *multi-round identification schemes*. Here two multi-round identification schemes are introduced, and those are slightly different from each other. In Section 5, we will discuss the efficiency of the proposed scheme, and will give the upper bound for the possible number of participating signers to prevent some kind of attacks we name Attack-0. Finally Section 6 will conclude this paper.

Notations and Preliminaries

Throughout this paper, we denote, by n, the number of the participating signer. Then for denoting an n-tuple $(a_1, \dots, a_n)$, we simply write as $\boldsymbol{a}$. For a k-tuple $(a_1, \dots, a_k)$ and an ℓ-tuple $(b_1, \dots, b_\ell)$, we define $(a_1, \dots, a_k) \oplus (b_1, \dots, b_\ell)$ to be the $(k + \ell)$-tuple $(a_1, \dots, a_k, b_1, \dots, b_\ell)$.

For events $E_1, \dots, E_k$ and a proposition $\wp$, the probability that $\wp$ is true after the execution of $E_1, \dots, E_k$, is, due to [1], denoted by $\Pr[E_1; \cdots; E_k : \wp]$. A (positive) function $f(sp) : \mathbb{N} \to \mathbb{R}$ is said to be *negligible (with respect to the security parameter sp)*, if for any constant $c > 0$, it holds $f(sp) = o(sp^{-c})$. A probability $p(sp)$ is said to be *overwhelming*, if $1 - p(sp)$ is negligible with respect to sp. Hereafter we omit the words "with respect to the security parameter sp" in case the omission can cause no confusion.

2 Series-Parallel Graphs

Among n signers, we have various signing orders. To represent signing orders, we, as well as [3], use *series-parallel graphs* defined by [2] etc., which are directed graphs with some characteristic properties. In this paper, we deal with graphs with labeled (directed) edges. An edge with label $i \in \mathbb{N}$ indicates that the signer P_i signs a message. For two graphs, even if both those structure and the sets of those labels are of the same, those graphs are regarded as different ones if those labels are placed at different positions. Hence, we use the following representation for a directed graph, not usual representation like such as one in [2].

In this paper, we suppose that one signer signs a message at most once during generating a multisignature. Then in a graph, the number of edges labeled i is at most one. For an edge labeled i, the initial vertex of the edge is denoted by I_i, and the terminal vertex is denoted by T_i. A directed graph φ can be denoted by a pair of the set of the labels in it and the relation among the vertices. Such a relation is a conjunction of the equalities among those vertices. Thus a directed graph φ can be denoted as $Gr[\![\{i_1, \ldots, i_k\}; E_1 \wedge \cdots \wedge E_\ell]\!]$, where each i_j is a label of an edge included in the graph φ, and where each E_j is an equality among the vertices in the graph. Such a definition seems to be somewhat complicated, but is convenient to define the composition of graphs, as seen in Section 2.2. For a graph $\varphi = Gr[\![\{i_1, \ldots, i_k\}; E_1 \wedge \cdots \wedge E_\ell]\!]$, we denotes the set $\{i_1, \ldots, i_k\}$ and the conjunction $E_1 \wedge \cdots \wedge E_\ell$ by $L(\varphi)$ and $E(\varphi)$, respectively. For two graphs φ_1 and φ_2, if φ_1 is a subgraph of φ_2, then we write as $\varphi_1 \sqsubset \varphi_2$. For a graph φ and a label i, if φ has an edge whose label is i, then we simply write as $i \in \varphi$, which is equivalent to $i \in L(\varphi)$. For a graph φ, the number of the edges in φ is simply denoted by $\#\varphi$, which is equal to $\#L(\varphi)$. For a graph φ and x_i's ($i \in \varphi$), we denote the $\#\varphi$-tuple $\bigoplus_{i \in \varphi}(x_i)$ by $\boldsymbol{x}^{(\varphi)}$.

2.1 Definitions

In the following, we inductively define *series-parallel graphs*. Though we use different notations, that definition is almost the same with one in [2] except for that every edge has a distinct label.

(i) A graph of the form $Gr[\![\{i\}; \top]\!]$ is a series-parallel graph, where $\top$ means the tautology for the vertices I_i and T_i. We call such kind of a graph *an atomic graph*, and denote such a graph by the label i. For an atomic graph $\varphi = Gr[\![\{i\}; \top]\!]$ $(= i)$, the initial vertex of φ is defined to be I_i, and the terminal vertex of φ is defined to be T_i.

(ii) Suppose that two graphs ψ_1 and ψ_2 satisfy $L(\psi_1) \cap L(\psi_2) = \emptyset$. Then the graph φ defined to be $Gr[\![L(\psi_1) \cup L(\psi_2); E(\psi_1) \wedge E(\psi_2) \wedge (I_{\psi_2} = T_{\psi_1})]\!]$ is a series-parallel graph, and denoted by $\psi_1 \wedge \psi_2$. The initial vertex of φ is defined to be I_{ψ_1}, and the terminal vertex of φ is defined to be T_{ψ_2}. In other words, if $L(\psi_1) \cap L(\psi_2) = \emptyset$, then the graph φ obtained by identifying the vertex I_{ψ_2} with the vertex T_{ψ_1}, is a series-parallel graph.

(iii) Suppose that two graphs ψ_1 and ψ_2 satisfy $L(\psi_1) \cap L(\psi_2) = \emptyset$. Then the graph φ defined to be $Gr[\![L(\psi_1) \cup L(\psi_2); E(\psi_1) \wedge E(\psi_2) \wedge (I_{\psi_1} = I_{\psi_2}) \wedge (T_{\psi_1} = T_{\psi_2})]\!]$ is a series-parallel graph, and denoted by $\psi_1 \vee \psi_2$. The initial vertex of φ is defined to be I_{ψ_1} $(= I_{\psi_2})$, and the terminal vertex of φ is defined to be T_{ψ_1} $(= T_{\psi_2})$. In other words, if $L(\psi_1) \cap L(\psi_2) = \emptyset$, then the graph φ obtained by identifying I_{ψ_1} with I_{ψ_2} and T_{ψ_1} with T_{ψ_2}, is a series-parallel graph.

(iv) Only the graphs obtained by the rules (i), (ii) and (iii), are series-parallel graphs.

Hereafter we deal with series-parallel graphs with labels in $\mathbb{N}$, and mean such kind of graphs by the term *graph*. The set of all graphs is denoted by $\mathcal{G}$.

From the definition, we can see that the operations $\wedge$ and $\vee$ are associative. Then for example, we simply write as $\varphi_1 \wedge \varphi_2 \wedge \varphi_3$ or $\wedge(\varphi_1 \; \varphi_2 \; \varphi_3)$ instead of $(\varphi_1 \wedge \varphi_2) \wedge \varphi_3$ and $\varphi_1 \wedge (\varphi_2 \wedge \varphi_3)$. Also we often write as $\bigwedge_{j=1}^{k} \varphi_j$ instead of $\varphi_1 \wedge \cdots \wedge \varphi_k$.

2.2   Composition of Graphs

Here for two graphs $\varphi_1, \varphi_2 \in \mathcal{G}$, we define those composition, which is analogous to the operation $\vee$. The difference is that the composition can be defined even if $L(\varphi_1) \cap L(\varphi_2) \neq \emptyset$. For $\varphi_1, \varphi_2 \in \mathcal{G}$, we define those composition written as $\varphi_1 \sqcup \varphi_2$ to be $Gr[\![L(\varphi_1) \cup L(\varphi_2); E(\varphi_1) \wedge E(\varphi_2) \wedge (I_{\varphi_1} = I_{\varphi_2}) \wedge (T_{\varphi_1} = T_{\varphi_2})]\!]$. The operation $\sqcup$ is associative and commutative. Note that even if φ_1 and φ_2 are in $\mathcal{G}$, the composition $\varphi_1 \sqcup \varphi_2$ is not always in $\mathcal{G}$. For example, in case $\varphi_1 = (1 \vee 2) \wedge 3$ and $\varphi_2 = (1 \vee 2) \wedge 4$, the composition $(1 \vee 2) \wedge (3 \vee 4)$ is in $\mathcal{G}$. On the other hand, in case $\varphi_1 = (1 \vee 2) \wedge 3$ and $\varphi_2 = 1 \wedge 2$, the composition is not in $\mathcal{G}$. In case $L(\varphi_1) \cap L(\varphi_2) = \emptyset$, the graph $\varphi_1 \sqcup \varphi_2$ is always in $\mathcal{G}$ and is exactly the same with $\varphi_1 \vee \varphi_2$ from those definitions.

2.3   GFP and GBP

For a graph $\varphi \in \mathcal{G}$ and an edge $i \in \varphi$, we define *the greatest forward part (GFP)* for (the edge) i in φ to be the graph $i \wedge \xi$, where ξ is the greatest subgraph of φ (with respect to the relation $\sqsubseteq$) such that $I_\xi = T_i$ and $T_\xi = T_\varphi$. The GFP for i in φ is denoted by $\varphi_{\mathcal{F}}^{(i)}$, and the graph ξ is denoted by $\varphi_{\mathcal{F}}^{(i)-}$. Similarly, we define *the greatest backward part (GBP)* for (the edge) i (in φ) to be the graph $\psi \wedge i$, where ψ is the greatest subgraph of φ such that $I_\psi = I_\varphi$ and $T_\psi = I_i$. The GBP for i in φ is denoted by $\varphi_{\mathcal{B}}^{(i)}$, and the graph ψ is denoted by $\varphi_{\mathcal{B}}^{(i)-}$.

Let $\varphi = \psi_1 \wedge \psi_2$. Then from the definition, it holds $\varphi_{\mathcal{F}}^{(i)} = \psi_1{}_{\mathcal{F}}^{(i)} \wedge \psi_2$ for $i \in \psi_1$, and it holds $\varphi_{\mathcal{F}}^{(i)} = \psi_2{}_{\mathcal{F}}^{(i)}$ for $i \in \psi_2$. For a graph $\varphi = \psi_1 \vee \psi_2$, it holds $\varphi_{\mathcal{F}}^{(i)} = \psi_b{}_{\mathcal{F}}^{(i)}$ for $i \in \psi_b$ and $b \in \{1, 2\}$.

2.4   Representation of Signing Orders

By using graphs, we can represent various signing orders. For example, the signing order that first P_1 and P_2 sign parallel, and P_3 signs after them, can be represented by a graph $(1 \vee 2) \wedge 3$ as seen in Figure 1. The signing order discussed in

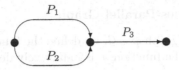

Fig. 1. The signing order $(1 \vee 2) \wedge 3$

[5] is the order that P_1 signs first, P_2 signs after P_1, and similarly P_n signs after P_{n-1}. Such an order can be represented as the graph $\bigwedge_{i=1}^{n} i \ (:= 1 \wedge 2 \wedge \cdots \wedge n)$.

In a signing order φ, a signer P_i with $I_i = I_\varphi$, is called *an initial signer*, and a signer P_i with $T_i = T_\varphi$, is called *a terminal signer*.

2.5   Graph Numbers

A graph can be coded as a bit string (natural number), and such a number can be individual for each graph. Hereafter we call such a number *a graph number*. Let $\langle * \rangle : \mathcal{G} \to \mathbb{N}$ be a function which computes the graph number for a given graph. There are many examples for $\langle * \rangle$. It does not matter which of them we adopt as the function $\langle * \rangle$, under the condition that it holds $\langle \varphi \rangle \neq \langle \varphi' \rangle$ for distinct $\varphi, \varphi' \in \mathcal{G}$ and that it is feasible to compute $\langle * \rangle$ and $\langle * \rangle^{-1}$. In general, such computational cost depends only upon $\#\varphi$, the number of the edges in the graph φ. In this paper, $\#\varphi$ is bounded by the number of participating signers, which is considered as a constant. Hence we can say that the functions $\langle * \rangle$ and $\langle * \rangle^{-1}$ are indeed computable.

2.6   Consistency for Signing Orders

In an order-specified multisignature scheme, each signer should be convinced that there is no contradiction for given signing orders. For example, suppose that P_1 receives partial multisignatures and former signing orders ψ_2 and ψ_3 from P_2 and P_3, respectively. In case $\psi_2 = 4 \wedge 2$ and $\psi_3 = 5 \wedge 4 \wedge 3$, the signer P_1 must not go on the signature generation, since ψ_2 and ψ_3 yield the contradiction that ψ_2 says P_4 is (one of) the initial signer(s) whereas ψ_3 says P_5 had signed before P_4 did. Then in this subsection, we define *consistency* among signing orders. Before the definition of consistency, we define *the history* of a signing order.

Definition 1. For a graph $\varphi \in \mathcal{G}$, *the history of φ* is defined to be the set $\left\{ \varphi_{\mathcal{B}}^{(i)} \right\}_{i \in \varphi}$, and is denoted by $\mathsf{H}(\varphi)$.

Definition 2. For graphs $\varphi_1, \ldots, \varphi_k \in \mathcal{G}$, we say $\varphi_1, \ldots, \varphi_k$ are *consistent*, if $\bigsqcup_{j=1}^{k} \varphi_j$ is in $\mathcal{G}$ and if it holds $\bigcup_{j=1}^{k} \mathsf{H}(\varphi_j) = \mathsf{H}(\bigsqcup_{j=1}^{k} \varphi_j)$.

2.7 Weight of a Series-Parallel Graph

In this subsection, for a graph $\varphi \in \mathcal{G}$, we define the function $w : \mathcal{G} \to \mathbb{N}$, and call $w(\varphi)$ *the weight* of φ. The function w is inductively defined as follows:

(i)   For an atomic graph $\alpha \in \mathcal{G}$, we define $w(\alpha) := 1$;
(ii) For a graph $\varphi = \psi_1 \wedge \psi_2$, we define $w(\varphi) := w(\psi_1) \cdot w(\psi_2)$;
(iii) For a graph $\varphi = \psi_1 \vee \psi_2$, we define $w(\varphi) := w(\psi_1) + w(\psi_2)$.

The following lemma shows the upper bound of the weights of the graphs with some fixed number of edges.

Lemma 1. For any $\varphi \in \mathcal{G}$, it holds $w(\varphi) \leqq 3^{\#\varphi/3}$.

Proof.   The proof is given in Appendix.   ∎

Now we consider the following series of operations for a graph $\varphi \in \mathcal{G}$, $x \in \mathbb{N}$ and $\#\varphi$-tuple $\boldsymbol{a}^{(\varphi)} \in \mathbb{N}^{\#\varphi}$:

(i) Assign x to the initial vertex I_φ, and assign a_i to the edge labeled i in φ;
(ii) Suppose that the edges $i_1, \ldots, i_k$ satisfy $T_{i_1} = \cdots = T_{i_k} (=: T)$, and that $x_{i_1}, \ldots, x_{i_k}$ are assigned to $I_{i_1}, \ldots, I_{i_k}$, respectively. Then T is assigned $\sum_{j=1}^{k}(x_{i_j} + a_{i_j})$.

Let y be the natural number assigned to the terminal vertex T_φ of φ. Then y is a function on $(x, \boldsymbol{a}^{(\varphi)})$, and we denote that function by $W_\varphi(x, \boldsymbol{a}^{(\varphi)})$. For example, let $\varphi = 1 \wedge ((2 \wedge (3 \vee 4)) \vee 5)$, and suppose that x is assigned to I_φ and that a_i is assigned to the edge i for each $i \in \{1, 2, 3, 4, 5\}$.

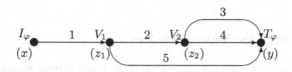

Fig. 2. The graph $1 \wedge ((2 \wedge (3 \vee 4)) \vee 5)$

See Figure 2. Here we name the two vertices between I_φ and T_φ V_1 and V_2, respectively. Let z_1 and z_2 be the numbers assigned to V_1 and V_2, respectively. Then from the definition given above, we can have $z_1 = x + a_1$, $z_2 = z_1 + a_2 = x + a_1 + a_2$. Eventually, we can get that the number y assigned to the terminal vertex T_φ, is $y = (z_2 + a_3) + (z_2 + a_4) + (z_1 + a_5) = 3x + 3a_1 + 2a_2 + a_3 + a_4 + a_5$. For a general case, we can have the following lemma.

Lemma 2. For any $\varphi \in \mathcal{G}$, $x \in \mathbb{N}$ and $\boldsymbol{a}^{(\varphi)} \in \mathbb{N}^{\#\varphi}$, it holds $W_\varphi(x, \boldsymbol{a}^{(\varphi)}) = w(\varphi)x + \sum_{i \in \varphi} w(\varphi_{\mathcal{F}}^{(i)})a_i$.

Proof. The proof is given in Appendix. ∎

3 Proposed Scheme

In this section, we present the proposed order-specified multisignature scheme. This scheme can be obtained by modifying the Type III scheme [6] which can be seen as a variant of Schnorr scheme [9]. Hence as well as those schemes, the proposed scheme can be implemented not only on a finite field $\mathbb{Z}_p$ but also by using elliptic curves.

3.1 The Scheme

In the following, we describe the scheme constructed on a finite field $\mathbb{Z}_p$ with p prime. The set of signers is denoted by $\mathcal{P}$ $(:= \{P_1, \ldots, P_n\})$, and the verifier is denoted by V. Each P_i has (public) random oracle functions [1] f_i and h_i both of which maps $\mathbb{N}$ to $\mathbb{Z}_q$ with q being a part of the system parameter.

The system parameter: Let p and q be primes with $q|(p-1)$, and let g be an order-q element in $\mathbb{Z}_p^*$. Then the system parameter is the set (p, q, g).

Key-generation step: Each signer P_i provides a pair of a secret-key $s_i \in \mathbb{Z}_q$ and the corresponding public-key $v_i := g^{s_i} \pmod{p}$.

Signature generation step: Suppose that P_i receives a message to be signed, partial multisignatures and former signing orders from N signers. Concrete to say, suppose that P_i receives $m \in \mathbb{N}$, $(\boldsymbol{x}^{(\psi_{i_j})}, y_{\psi_{i_j}}) \in \mathbb{Z}_p^{*\#\psi_{i_j}} \times \mathbb{Z}_q$ and $\psi_{i_j} \in \mathcal{G}$ from P_{i_j} $(j \in [1, N])$. Then P_i shall check whether $\psi_{i_1}, \ldots, \psi_{i_N}$ are consistent, or not. If not, then P_i must not go on the signature generation, since those signing orders yield the contradiction. If those are consistent, then P_i figures out the graphs $\psi_i^- := \bigsqcup_{j=1}^N \psi_{i_j}$ and $\psi_i := \psi_i^- \wedge i$, and computes $y_{\psi_i^-} := \sum_{j=1}^N y_{\psi_{i_j}} \pmod{q}$. In case P_i is one of the initial signers, the process given above is omitted.

The signer P_i picks up a random $r_i \in \mathbb{Z}_q$ to compute $x_i := g^{r_i} \pmod{p}$. Also P_i computes $y_{\psi_i} := y_{\psi_i^-} + \sigma_i \pmod{q}$, where $\sigma_i := e_i r_i + d_i s_i \pmod{q}$, $e_i := f_i(\boldsymbol{x}^{(\psi_i)}, m, \langle \psi_i \rangle)$ and $d_i := h_i(\boldsymbol{x}^{(\psi_i)}, m, \langle \psi_i \rangle)$. The signer P_i sends m, $(\boldsymbol{x}^{(\psi_i)}, y_{\psi_i})$ and ψ_i to the successive signer(s).

Note that letting φ be the whole signing order in signature generation, it holds that $\psi_i = \varphi_{\mathcal{B}}^{(i)}$ and $\psi_i^- = \varphi_{\mathcal{B}}^{(i)-}$.

Suppose that there are N terminal signers $P_{i_1}, \ldots, P_{i_N}$. Then the whole signing order φ is $\bigsqcup_{j=1}^N \psi_{i_j}$, and the total multisignature is defined to be $(\boldsymbol{x}^{(\varphi)}, y_\varphi)$, where $y_\varphi := \sum_{j=1}^N y_{\psi_{i_j}} \pmod{q}$.

Verification step: Suppose that the verifier V receives the message $m \in \mathbb{N}$, the total multisignature $(\boldsymbol{x}^{(\varphi)}, y_\varphi) \in \mathbb{Z}_p^{*\#\varphi} \times \mathbb{Z}_q$ and the whole signing order $\varphi \in \mathcal{G}$. Then V figures out each $\psi_i := \varphi_\mathcal{B}^{(i)}$, $\xi_i := \varphi_\mathcal{F}^{(i)}$, and computes each $e_i := f_i(\boldsymbol{x}^{(\psi_i)}, m, \langle \psi_i \rangle)$ and $d_i := h_i(\boldsymbol{x}^{(\psi_i)}, m, \langle \psi_i \rangle)$. Then V accepts the multisignature, if and only if the following holds:

$$g^{y_\varphi} \equiv \prod_{i \in \varphi} \left(x_i^{e_i} v_i^{d_i} \right)^{w(\xi_i)} \pmod{p}.$$

This verification comes from $y_\varphi = W_\varphi(0, \boldsymbol{\sigma}^{(\varphi)}) \pmod{p}$.

The MOO scheme from [6] is the special case of $\varphi = \bigwedge_{i=1}^{n} i$. Then we have $w(\xi_i) = 1$ for each $i \in [1, n]$.

4   Security of the Proposed Scheme

In this section, we show that the proposed scheme is secure against *adaptive chosen-message insider attacks* with respect to both forgery for messages and that for signing orders. First, we present an attack model for order-specified multisignature schemes, and define the security of order-specified multisignature schemes. As seen later, the security of our scheme is reduced to that of some kinds of identification schemes. In Section 4.3, we present two multi-round identification schemes and an attack model for such schemes, and define the security of multi-round identification schemes. Finally, we show the security of our proposed scheme.

4.1   Attack Model for Order-Specified Multisignature Schemes

In the following, we present an attack model which involves adaptive chosen-message insider attacks.

MS-adversary: Given the system parameter (p, q, g) and the public-keys $\boldsymbol{v}$, an MS-adversary $\mathcal{M}$ which can access to the random oracle functions f_i and h_i ($i \in [1, N]$), executes the following series of the steps (S1), (S2), (S3) and (S4), for each $j \in [1, Q]$ with a given Q which can be a function on the security parameter:

(S1) $\mathcal{M}$ determines a message $m_j \in \mathbb{N}$, a signer $P_{i_j} \in \mathcal{P}$ and a signing order $\varphi_j \in \mathcal{G}$ with $i_j \in \varphi_j$;

(S2) By colluding with $\mathcal{P} \backslash \{P_{i_j}\}$, $\mathcal{M}$ generates a valid partial multisignature Σ_j for m_j in the signing order $\varphi_{j\mathcal{B}}^{(i_j)-}$, where Σ_j denotes the tuple $(\boldsymbol{x}^{(\varphi_{j\mathcal{B}}^{(i_j)-})}, \boldsymbol{e}^{(\varphi_{j\mathcal{B}}^{(i_j)-})}, \boldsymbol{d}^{(\varphi_{j\mathcal{B}}^{(i_j)-})}, y_{\varphi_{j\mathcal{B}}^{(i_j)-}})$;

(S3) $\mathcal{M}$ sends m_j, Σ_j and $\varphi_{j\mathcal{B}}^{(i_j)-}$ to P_{i_j}, and ask P_{i_j} to sign m_j in the order $\varphi_{j\mathcal{B}}^{(i_j)}$;

(S4) Then $\mathcal{M}$ gets a valid multisignature $(x^{(\varphi_{j_B}^{(i_j)})}, e^{(\varphi_{j_B}^{(i_j)})}, d^{(\varphi_{j_B}^{(i_j)})}, y_{\varphi_{j_B}^{(i_j)}})$

and the order $\varphi_{j_B}^{(i_j)}$ from P_{i_j}.

After Q iterations of this series, the MS-adversary $\mathcal{M}$ computes a multisignature for $m \in \mathbb{N}$ in the signing order $\varphi \in \mathcal{G}$, where for every $j \in [1, Q]$, it has to hold at least one of $m \neq m_j$ and $\varphi_B^{(i_j)} \neq \varphi_{j_B}^{(i_j)}$.

Here note that in [7], *the key generation phase attack* is introduced, but we do not have to consider such an attack since our scheme has *the sensitive reduction* defined in [7].

4.2   Definition of the Security

As well as in many papers, also in this paper, the security is evaluated using the parameters t, Q, F, H and ε, where t denotes the running time of the adversary, where Q denotes the times the adversary can ask a valid partial multisignature of a legitimate signer, where for each $i \in [1, n]$, F_i (and H_i) denotes the times the adversary can query to the random oracle function f_i (and h_i, respectively), and where ε denotes the success probability of the adversary. In the following, we give formal definitions for the security of order-specified multisignature schemes.

Definition 3. Suppose an MS-adversary $\mathcal{M}$ can ask F_i-time queries to f_i and H_i-time queries to h_i for each $i \in [1, n]$, and is allowed to execute the series from (S1) to (S4) Q times. If such an $\mathcal{M}$ can forge a multisignature (x, e, d, y) for a message m in the signing order φ in time of at most t with success probability of at least ε, then we say that $\mathcal{M}$ can $(t, Q, F, H, \varepsilon)$-*break the (order-specified multisignature) scheme.*

Definition 4. An order-specified multisignature scheme is said to be $(t, Q, F, H, \varepsilon)$-*secure*, if there is no MS-adversary which can $(t, Q, F, H, \varepsilon)$-break the scheme, and if for a message m, a multisignature (x, y) generated in the order φ, is invalid for another signing order $\varphi' \in \mathcal{G}$ with overwhelming probability.

4.3   Multi-round Identification Schemes

As mentioned before, the security of our scheme is reduced to those of some kinds of multi-round identification schemes. In the following, we present two identification schemes, which are slightly different from each other.

Scheme-A

The participating entities are the prover P and the verifier V.

System parameter: The system parameter in Scheme-A is the same with that in the proposed multisignature scheme.

Key-generation step: The prover P provides n pair of a secret key $s_i \in \mathbb{Z}_q$ and the corresponding public-key $v_i := g^{s_i} \pmod{p}$ $(i \in [1, n])$.

Identification step: The prover P choose a graph $\varphi \in \mathcal{G}$ with $\#\varphi = n$. Then P and V execute the following step (I) for $i \in [1, n]$:

(I) P figures out $\psi_i := \varphi_{\mathcal{B}}^{(i)}$, and picks up random numbers $\boldsymbol{r}^{(\psi_i)}$ where each r_i is in $\mathbb{Z}_q$ $(i \in \psi_i)$. For $j \in \psi_i$ with $j \in \psi_{i'}$ for $i' < i$, P uses the same r_j. Then P computes $x_i := g^{r_i} \pmod{p}$ $(i \in \psi_i)$, and sends $\boldsymbol{x}^{(\psi_i)}$ and ψ_i to the verifier V. Receiving $(\boldsymbol{x}^{(\psi_i)}, \psi_i)$, V randomly picks up $e_i \in \mathbb{Z}_q$ and $d_i \in \mathbb{Z}_q$, and sends e_i and d_i to P.

After this iteration, P computes $y := \sum_{i=1}^{n} w(\xi_i)(e_i r_i + d_i s_i) \pmod{q}$, and sends y and φ to V, where $\xi_i := \varphi_{\mathcal{F}}^{(i)}$ for each $i \in \varphi$.

Receiving (y, φ), the verifier V accepts the proof, if and only if $\{\psi_1, \ldots, \psi_n\} = \mathsf{H}(\varphi)$ and the following holds:

$$g^y \equiv \prod_{i=1}^{n} \left(x_i^{e_i} v_i^{d_i} \right)^{w(\xi_i)} \pmod{p}.$$

Scheme-B

As well as the previous one, the participating entities are the prover P and the verifier V.

System parameter: The system parameter in Scheme-B is also the same with that in the proposed multisignature scheme.

Key-generation step: This step is the same with that in Scheme-A.

Signing order declaration step: The prover P chooses a signing order $\varphi \in \mathcal{G}$ with $\#\varphi = n$, and publishes φ, in advance.

Identification step: Then P and V execute the same step (I) in Scheme-A for $i \in [1, n]$. For the rest, the process is the same with that in Scheme-A.

ID-Adversary

Here we give an attack model for Scheme-A as follows: An ID-adversary $\mathcal{M}$ is a machine, which, on input $\boldsymbol{v}$, executes Scheme-A with an honest verifier V, and tries to pass the verification for some graph $\varphi \in \mathcal{G}$. An ID-adversary we consider here, is so-called a passive attacker which cannot accomplish *the attack in the middle*.

Definition of the Security for Multi-round Identification Schemes

In the following, we define the security for Scheme-A and Scheme-B.

Definition 5. Suppose that an ID-adversary $\mathcal{M}$ which does not know $\boldsymbol{s}$, can pass the verification for some $\varphi \in \mathcal{G}$ with $\#\varphi = n$ in time of at most t with probability of at least ε. Then we say that $\mathcal{M}$ *can (t, ε)-break Scheme-A*.

Definition 6. We say that *Scheme-A is* (t, ε)-*secure*, if there is no ID-adversary which can (t, ε)-break Scheme-A, and if (x, e, d, y) which is generated by a legitimate P and V for $\varphi \in \mathcal{G}$, is rejected for another $\varphi' \in \mathcal{G}$ with overwhelming probability.

In the following, we define *the zero-knowledge property* for Scheme-B.

Definition 7. We say that Scheme-B has *the perfect zero-knowledge property*, if there is a polynomial-time simulator $\mathcal{S}$ with input (v, φ), which satisfy the following:

$$\Delta := \sum_{\alpha, \beta, \gamma, \delta} \left| \begin{array}{l} \Pr\left[(x, e, d, y) \leftarrow [P(s, \varphi), V(v, \varphi)] : (x, e, d, y) = (\alpha, \beta, \gamma, \delta) \right] \\ -\Pr\left[(x', e', d', y') \leftarrow \mathcal{S}(v, \varphi) : (x', e', d', y') = (\alpha, \beta, \gamma, \delta) \right] \end{array} \right| = 0,$$

where $(x, e, d, y) \leftarrow [P(s, \varphi), V(v, \varphi)]$ means that (x, e, d, y) is obtained by the execution of Scheme-B between $P(s, \varphi)$ and $V(v, \varphi)$.

Then Scheme-B is shown to have the perfect zero-knowledge property, by constructing a simulator $\mathcal{S}$ as follows:

– First $\mathcal{S}$ randomly picks up $e \in \mathbb{Z}_q^n$, $d \in \mathbb{Z}_q^n$ and $y \in \mathbb{Z}_q$, and finds $\kappa \in \mathbb{Z}_q^n$ such that $y := \sum_{i=1}^n \kappa_i w(\varphi_{\mathcal{F}}^{(i)}) e_i \pmod{q}$ and $\boldsymbol{\lambda} \in \mathbb{Z}_q^n$ such that $\lambda_i e_i + d_i \equiv 0 \pmod{q}$ for each $i \in [1, n]$. Then $\mathcal{S}$ sets each x_i to be $g^{\kappa_i} v_i^{\lambda_i} \pmod{p}$.

Such a tuple (x, e, d, y) indeed passes the verification since $\prod_{i=1}^n \left(x_i^{e_i} v_i^{d_i} \right)^{w(\varphi_{\mathcal{F}}^{(i)})}$
$\equiv g^y \pmod{p}$. Furthermore, we can say that Scheme-B provides the perfect zero-knowledge property, since for any $(\alpha, \beta, \gamma, \delta)$ which passes the verification, that is, which satisfies $g^\delta \equiv \prod_{i=1}^n \left(\alpha^{\beta_i} v_i^{\gamma_i} \right)^{w(\varphi_{\mathcal{F}}^{(i)})} \pmod{q}$, both of the followings hold:

$$\Pr\left[(x, e, d, y) \leftarrow [P(s, \varphi), V(v, \varphi)] : (x, e, d, y) = (\alpha, \beta, \gamma, \delta) \right] = \frac{1}{q^{3n}}$$

and

$$\Pr\left[(x', e', d', y') \leftarrow \mathcal{S}(v, \varphi) : (x', e', d', y') = (\alpha, \beta, \gamma, \delta) \right] = \frac{1}{q^{3n}},$$

which imply the difference Δ of the two distributions is exactly zero.

4.4   ID-Reduction Lemma

Since Scheme-B has the (perfect) zero-knowledge property, we can obtain the following ID-reduction lemma, as well as in [6].

Lemma 3. Suppose that it holds the following:

$$\varepsilon \geq \frac{1}{q} \left(\left(\cdots \left(\left(\left(\frac{2^{n+2}}{q^{2n-1}} + Q \right) H_n + 1 \right) F_n + 1 \right) H_{n-1} + 1 \right) \cdots \right) F_1 + 1 \right).$$

Then we can obtain the followings:

(i) If there exists an MS-adversary $\mathcal{A}_a$ which can $(t,Q,\boldsymbol{F},\boldsymbol{H},\varepsilon)$-break the scheme, then there also exists an MS-adversary $\mathcal{A}_1$ which can $(t, Q, \boldsymbol{1}, \boldsymbol{1}, \varepsilon_1)$-break the scheme, where $\boldsymbol{1}$ is the n-tuple $(1,\ldots,1)$, and where ε_1 is defined to be a_n with $a_0 := \varepsilon$, and with for each $i \in [1,n]$, $b_i := \left(a_{i-1} - \frac{1}{q}\right)/F_i$ and $a_i := \left(b_i - \frac{1}{q}\right)/H_i$.

(ii) If there exists an MS-adversary $\mathcal{A}_1$ which can $(t, Q, \boldsymbol{1}, \boldsymbol{1}, \varepsilon_1)$-break the scheme, then there also exists an MS-adversary $\mathcal{A}_p$ which can $(t^+, 0, \boldsymbol{1}, \boldsymbol{1}, \varepsilon_p)$-break the scheme. Here the parameter t^+ is defined to be $t + \Phi_S$ where Φ_S is the required time for Q-time simulation of partial multisignatures, and the parameter ε_p is def ined to be $\varepsilon_1 - \frac{Q}{q}$.

(iii) If there exists an MS-adversary $\mathcal{A}_p$ which can $(t^+, 0, \boldsymbol{1}, \boldsymbol{1}, \varepsilon_p)$-break the scheme, then there also exists an ID-adversary $\mathcal{A}_{id}$ which can (t^+, ε_p)-break the scheme.

Proof.(Sketch) For (i) and (ii), the proof is exactly the same with that of Lemma 9 in [6]. To show (iii), we, using $\mathcal{A}_p$, construct a machine $\mathcal{A}_{id}$ as follows: Given $\boldsymbol{v}$, a machine $\mathcal{M}$ which can access $\mathcal{A}_p$, tries to pass the verification of Scheme-A. First $\mathcal{M}$ sends $\boldsymbol{v}$ to $\mathcal{A}_p$, and receives a query $\mathcal{Q}_1$ $(= (\boldsymbol{x}^{(\psi_1)}, m, \langle\psi_1\rangle))$ for e_1 and d_1. Then $\mathcal{M}$ sends $\mathcal{Q}_1$ (without m) to the verifier to get random challenges e_1 and d_1, and sends e_1 and d_1 to $\mathcal{A}_p$. Because of the randomness, $\mathcal{A}_p$ cannot distinguish (e_1, d_1) from the outputs of f_1 and h_1. This is similar for each $i \in [2, n]$. After these transmission, $\mathcal{A}_p$ outputs a multisignature Σ for a message m in the signing order φ. Receiving those, $\mathcal{M}$ sends the y-component of Σ and φ to the verifier. This proof is accepted with success probability of ε_p from the assumption for $\mathcal{A}_p$'s success probability. Let $\mathcal{A}_{id}$ be $\mathcal{M}$ plus $\mathcal{A}_p$. ∎

The following lemma shows the relationship between the difficulty of breaking Scheme-A and that of finding $\boldsymbol{s}$ from $\boldsymbol{v}$.

Lemma 4. Suppose $\varepsilon_p \geq \frac{2^{n+2}}{q^{2n}}$. If there exists an ID-adversary $\mathcal{A}_{id}$ which can (t^+, ε_p)-break the scheme, then there also exists a machine $\mathcal{M}$ which, on input $\boldsymbol{v}$, can compute $\boldsymbol{s}$ in time at most t' with success probability at least ε'. Here the parameters t' and ε' are defined as follows:

$$t' := \frac{t^{++}}{\varepsilon_p}\left(2^{2n+1} + 3 \cdot 2^{n+1}(n-1) + 1\right) + \Phi_E;$$
$$\varepsilon' := \left(\tfrac{1}{2}\right)^{2^n + n - 2} \theta_0(\varepsilon_p)\left(\prod_{i=1}^n \theta_i(\varepsilon_p)^{2^{i-1}}\right)\theta_{n+1}(\varepsilon_p)^{n-1},$$

where t^{++} is $t^+ + \Phi_V$ with Φ_V being the required time for verification in Scheme-A, where Φ_E is the required time for the computation to find $\boldsymbol{s}$ from $2^n + n - 1$ simultaneous equations, and where the function $\theta_i(x)$ is defined to be $1 - \left(1 - \frac{x}{2^i}\right)^{2^i/x}$, for each $i \in [0, n]$ and $x \in \mathbb{R}\backslash\{0\}$.

Proof.(Sketch) The proof is the same with that Lemma 19 in [6]. Here note that the distribution of $w(\varphi_{\mathcal{F}}^{(i)})$ is not uniform over $\mathbb{Z}_q$ and that its value cannot be zero. But fortunately, the distribution of $w(\varphi_{\mathcal{F}}^{(i)})e_i$ (and $w(\varphi_{\mathcal{F}}^{(i)})d_i$) is uniform over $\mathbb{Z}_q$, from the following fact:

- For two stochastic variables X and Y in $\mathbb{Z}_q$, providing that X can be take an arbitrary distribution but cannot be zero, and that Y is uniform over $\mathbb{Z}_q$, the stochastic variable Z $(:= XY)$ is uniform over $\mathbb{Z}_q$, since for any $z \in \mathbb{Z}_q$, the probability for $Z = z$ is given as follows:

$$\Pr[Z = z] = \sum_{\alpha \in \mathbb{Z}_q^*} \Pr\left[(X = \alpha) \& (Y = \alpha^{-1}z)\right] = \frac{1}{q} \sum_{\alpha \in \mathbb{Z}_q^*} \Pr[X = \alpha] = \frac{1}{q}.$$

Thus in the simultaneous equations on s and r's which are obtained by Heavy Low Lemma [6], every coefficient shall be uniform over $\mathbb{Z}_q$. Therefore the same result with one in [6] can be obtained.   ∎

Here we show a lemma which is necessary because of the latter half of the conditions in Definition 4.

Lemma 5. Suppose that Σ $(= (x, y))$ is a valid multisignature for a message m in the signing order $\varphi \in \mathcal{G}$ generated by legitimate signers. Then the very Σ is rejected for another signing order $\varphi' \in \mathcal{G}$ with overwhelming probability.

Proof.   It comes from the following:

$$\Pr\left[m \leftarrow \mathbb{N}; \varphi, \varphi' \leftarrow \mathcal{G}; \Sigma \leftarrow \mathcal{P}(s, m, \varphi) : \wp(v, \Sigma, m, \varphi') \,\middle|\, \varphi \neq \varphi'\right] \leqq \frac{1}{q},$$

where $\wp(v, \Sigma, m, \varphi)$ is the predicate that is true if and only if a multisignature Σ is, by using the public-keys v, verified to be valid for the message m and the signing order φ. The probability for rejection is at least $1 - \frac{1}{q}$ which is overwhelming.   ∎

Combining Lemmas 3, 4 and 5, we can obtain the following theorem.

Theorem 1. Let t' and ε' be the parameters defined as the statements in the previous lemmas. If there is no machine which, on input v, can compute s in time of t' with success probability of ε', then the proposed order-specified multisignature scheme is $(t, Q, F, H, \varepsilon)$-secure.

5   Discussion

In this section, we first estimate the efficiency of the proposed order-specified multisignature scheme, then discuss some attack using the system parameter, and give the condition of n for preventing such an attack.

5.1   Efficiency of the Proposed Scheme

There are a few order-specified multisignature schemes proposed. Unfortunately, the existing order-specified multisignature scheme are not shown to be secure against active attacks. Hence we compare the efficiency of the proposed scheme with that of the MOO scheme (Type III) from [6] and that of the scheme which is, in the trivial way, constructed using the Type III variant of [9]. (For detail, see [6].) In the latter scheme, a signature of the signer P_i for a message m is Σ_i ($:= (x_i, y_i)$), where $x_i := g^{r_i} \pmod{p}$ with a random $r_i \in \mathbb{Z}_q$, and where $y := e_i r_i + d_i s_i \pmod{q}$, $e_i := f_i(x_i, m, \langle \varphi_B^{(i)} \rangle, \Sigma^{(\varphi_B^{(i)})})$, and $d_i := h_i(x_i, m, \langle \varphi_B^{(i)} \rangle, \Sigma^{(\varphi_B^{(i)})})$[1]. Here we call this scheme the trivial scheme.

In the comparison, we estimate the computational cost for verification and the size of a multisignature. The computational cost is evaluated by counting the number of modulo-p multiplication. In the cost evaluation, we adopt the simple binary method, and use the fact that, then, the number of the required number of modulo-p multiplication for computing $g_1^{a_1} \cdots g_N^{a_N} \pmod{p}$ with $g_i \in \mathbb{Z}_p^*$ and $a_i \in \mathbb{Z}_q$ for each $i \in [1, N]$, is $E(N) := \left(\frac{N}{2} + 1\right)|q| - 1$. The computational cost of modulo-q multiplication is denoted M. Under the condition that the computational cost of modulo multiplication is proportional to the square of the size of the modulo, we can see $M = \frac{|q|^2}{|p|^2}$.

Suppose that n signers participate the scheme. Then in the proposed scheme, the verification cost is $E(2n + 1) + 2nM$, whereas in the trivial scheme, that is $E(3)n$, and that is $E(3n) + 3nM$ in case Batch verification is applied. In Table 1, we can see the comparison.

Table 1. Performance evaluation

Scheme	The required number of multiplication (mod p)	The total signature size
The trivial scheme	$E(3n) + 3nM$ $(= (\frac{3}{2}|q| + 3M)n + |q| - 1)$	$(|p| + |q|)n$
The MOO scheme from [6]	$E(2n + 1)$ $(= |q|n + \frac{3}{2}|q| - 1)$	$|p|n + |q|$
The proposed scheme	$E(2n + 1) + 2nM$ $(= (|q| + 2M)n + \frac{3}{2}|q| - 1)$	$|p|n + |q|$

The MOO scheme from [6] is shown to be secure against adaptive chosen-message insider attacks, by the same proof with Theorem 1. In that scheme, the possible signing order is, however, restricted to the graphs of the form $\bigwedge_{i=1}^n \alpha_i$ where each α_i is an atomic graph. The difference between the cost in [6] and that in the proposed one, is $2nM$, which can be said to be quite smaller comparing with the cost for one modular-p multiplication.

---

[1] The reason why $\Sigma^{(\varphi_B^{(i)})}$ is into the argument of f_i (and h_i), is because P_i has to show that she indeed knows (at least, a part of) the signatures which has already generated by the previous signers.

5.2   Attack Using a Weight-Zero Graph

Though we have given a formal proof of the proposed scheme in Section 4, we here present another type of attacks named Attack-0. Here we use the same symbols with those in Section 3.

Attack-0: Note that y-component of the signature for a message m in the signing order φ, turns out to be $\sum_{i \in \varphi} w(\xi_i)\sigma_i \pmod{q}$. Hence a subset $\mathcal{C} \subset \mathcal{P}$ of colluding members may be able to construct a graph $\varphi_0 \in \mathcal{G}$ such that $w(\varphi_0)$ is a multiple of q. The weight of such a graph is zero under the modulo q.

Then for any subset $\mathcal{A} \subset \mathcal{P} \backslash L(\varphi_0)$, for any message m, and for any signing order $\varphi_{\mathcal{A}} \in \mathcal{G}$ with $L(\varphi_{\mathcal{A}}) = \mathcal{A}$, the colluding members $\mathcal{C}$ can generate a multisignature for m in the signing order φ $(:= \varphi_{\mathcal{A}} \wedge \varphi_0)$ without $\mathcal{A}$'s assistance, since for any $i \in \varphi_{\mathcal{A}}$, it holds $w(\xi_i) = w(\varphi_{\mathcal{A}\mathcal{F}}^{(i)})w(\varphi_0) \equiv 0 \pmod{q}$. Concrete to say, the multisignature is $(\boldsymbol{x}^{(\varphi)}, y_\varphi)$ where for $i \in \mathcal{A}$, x_i is a random number in $\mathbb{Z}_p^*$ and $y_\varphi = \sum_{i \in \mathcal{C}} w(\xi_i)\sigma_i \pmod{q}$.

To avoid such an attack, it must hold $w(\varphi) < q$ for any $\varphi \in \mathcal{G}$ with at most n edges. From Lemma 1, the weight of a graph consisting of n edges, is at most $3^{n/3}$, and hence it is sufficient that $n < \frac{3}{\log 3} \log q$ holds, in order to prevent Attack-0. In case q is a 160-bit prime, it is possible that at most 300 signers participate the scheme.

6   Conclusion

In this paper, we have proposed an order-specified multisignature scheme, which is secure even against adaptive chosen-message insider attacks. A signing order is represented by a series-parallel graph. First we have reviewed the definition of series-parallel graphs, and have defined the weight of a graph φ, $w(\varphi)$, which is inductively defined as well as a series-parallel graph. Then we have given the upper bound of the weight of a graph consisting of at most n edges (Lemma 1). From the upper bound, we can obtain the condition to prevent Attack-0 given in Section 5.2, and the condition gives the upper bound of the possible number of the participating signers in the scheme. From the lemma on the function W_φ (Lemma 2), we can find the verification in the scheme. The security of the proposed scheme is shown by using ID-reduction technique introduced in [6], and is reduced to the soundness of Scheme-A and the zero-knowledge property of Scheme-B. After showing the security, we have discussed the efficiency of the proposed scheme.

References

1. M. Bellare and P. Rogaway: *"Random oracles are practical: a paradigm for designing efficient protocols"*, Proceedings of the 1st ACM Conference on Computer and Communications Security (CCS), 1993.

2. H. L. Bodlaender and B. de Fluiter: *"Parallel algorithm for series parallel graphs"*, Europian Symposium on Algorithms, pp.277-289, 1996.

3. M. Burmester, Y. Desmedt, H. Doi, M. Mambo, E. Okamoto, M. Tada and Y. Yoshifuji: *"A structured ElGamal-type multisignature scheme"*, Proceedings of PKC2000, Lecture Notes in Computer Science 1751, pp.466-483, Springer-Verlag, 2000.

4. H. Doi, M. Mambo and E. Okamoto: *"On the security of the RSA-based multisignature scheme for various group structure"*, Proceedings of ACISP2000, Lecture Notes in Computer Science 1841, pp.352-367, Springer-Verlag, 2000.

5. S. Mitomi and A. Miyaji: *"A multisignature scheme with message flexibility, order flexibility and order verifiability"*, Proceedings of ACISP2000, Lecture Notes in Computer Science 1841, pp.298-312, Springer-Verlag, 2000.

6. K. Ohta and T. Okamoto: *"Multi-signature schemes secure against active insider attacks"*, IEICE transactions of fundamentals, vol.82-A, no.1, pp.22-31, 1999.

7. K. Ohta and T. Okamoto: *"Generic construction methods of multi-signature schemes"*, Proceedings of The 2001 Symposium on Cryptography and Information Security (SCIS2001), vol.I, pp.31-36, 2001.

8. D. Pointcheval and J. Stern: *"Security arguments for digital signatures and blind signatures"*, Journal of cryptology, vol.13, no.3, pp.361-396, Springer-Verlag, 2000.

9. C. P. Schnorr: *"Efficient signature generation by smart cards"*, Journal of cryptology, vol.4, pp.161-174, Springer-Verlag, 1991.

10. A. Shimbo: *"Design of a modified ElGamal signature scheme"*, Workshop on Design and Evaluation of Cryptographic Algorithms, pp.37-44, 1996.

Appendix – The Proofs of Lemmas 1 and 2

Here we give the proofs of Lemmas 1 and 2.

Lemma 1. For any $\varphi \in \mathcal{G}$, it holds $w(\varphi) \leqq 3^{\#\varphi/3}$.

Proof. We show this lemma by induction on the construction of φ.

(i) In case φ is an atomic graph, we can easily see $w(\varphi) = 1 \leqq 3^{1/3} = 3^{\#\varphi/3}$.

(ii) Suppose that for $\psi_1, \psi_2 \in \mathcal{G}$ with $L(\psi_1) \cap L(\psi_2) = \emptyset$, it holds that $w(\psi_1) \leqq 3^{\#\psi_1/3}$ and $w(\psi_2) \leqq 3^{\#\psi_2/3}$. Let $\varphi = \psi_1 \wedge \psi_2$. Then we have $w(\varphi) = w(\psi_1) \cdot w(\psi_2) \leqq 3^{\#\psi_1/3} \cdot 3^{\#\psi_2/3} = 3^{(\#\psi_1 + \#\psi_2)/3} = 3^{\#\varphi/3}$.

(iii) Suppose that for $\psi_1, \psi_2 \in \mathcal{G}$ with $L(\psi_1) \cap L(\psi_2) = \emptyset$, it holds that $w(\psi_1) \leqq 3^{\#\psi_1/3}$ and $w(\psi_2) \leqq 3^{\#\psi_2/3}$. Let $\varphi = \psi_1 \vee \psi_2$.

In case both $\#\psi_1$ and $\#\psi_2$ are greater or equal to 2, we have $w(\varphi) = w(\psi_1) + w(\psi_2) \leqq 3^{\#\psi_1/3} + 3^{\#\psi_2/3} \leqq 3^{\#\psi_1/3} \cdot 3^{\#\psi_2/3} = 3^{\#\varphi/3}$, since for any $x \geqq 2$ and $y \geqq 2$, it holds $x + y \leqq xy$, and since $3^{\#\psi_b/3} \geqq 3^{2/3} > 2$ for $b \in \{1, 2\}$.

In case $\#\psi_1 = \#\psi_2 = 1$, we can easily have $w(\varphi) = 2 < 3^{2/3} = 3^{\#\varphi/3}$.

In case either $\#\psi_1$ or $\#\psi_2$ is 1, without loss of generality, we may suppose $\#\psi_1 = 1$ and $\#\psi_2 \geqq 2$. Suppose $\#\psi_2 \geqq 4$. Then we have $w(\varphi) \leqq 3^{1/3} + 3^{\#\psi_2/3} \leqq 3^{1/3} \cdot 3^{\#\psi_2/3} = 3^{\#\varphi/3}$, since $3^{\#\psi_2/3} \geqq 3^{4/3} > 4$ and $3^{1/3} + 4 < 3^{1/3} \cdot 4$. Suppose $\#\psi_2 = 3$ (or 2). Then we can easily see $w(\psi_2) \leqq 3$ (or 2, respectively), by exhaustive investigation of graphs with 3 (or 2, respectively) edges. Hence we can get $w(\varphi) \leqq 4 < 3^{4/3} = 3^{\#\varphi/3}$ (or $w(\varphi) \leqq 3 = 3^{3/3} = 3^{\#\varphi/3}$, respectively).

The statements (i), (ii) and (iii) complete the proof. ∎

Lemma 2. For any $\varphi \in \mathcal{G}$, $x \in \mathbb{N}$ and $\boldsymbol{a}^{(\varphi)} \in \mathbb{N}^{\#\varphi}$, it holds $W_\varphi(x, \boldsymbol{a}^{(\varphi)}) = w(\varphi)x + \sum_{i \in \varphi} w(\varphi_{\mathcal{F}}^{(i)})a_i$.

Proof. This lemma is also shown by induction on the construction of φ.

(i) In case φ is an atomic graph i, we have $W_i(x, a_i) = x + a_i = w(\varphi)x + w(\varphi_{\mathcal{F}}^{(i)})a_i$.

(ii) Suppose that for $\psi_1, \psi_2 \in \mathcal{G}$ with $L(\psi_1) \cap L(\psi_2) = \emptyset$, the statement of this lemma holds. That means $W_{\psi_b}(x, \boldsymbol{a}^{(\psi_b)}) = w(\psi_b)x + \sum_{i \in \psi_b} w(\psi_{b\mathcal{F}}^{(i)})a_i$, for $b \in \{1, 2\}$, any $x \in \mathbb{N}$ and any $\boldsymbol{a}^{(\psi_b)} \in \mathbb{N}^{\#\psi_b}$. Let $\varphi = \psi_1 \wedge \psi_2$. Then from the definitions of weight, $\varphi_{\mathcal{F}}^{(i)}$ and W_φ, we have the following:

$$
\begin{aligned}
W_\varphi(x, \boldsymbol{a}^{(\varphi)}) &= W_{\psi_2}(W_{\psi_1}(x, \boldsymbol{a}^{(\psi_1)}), \boldsymbol{a}^{(\psi_2)}) \\
&= w(\psi_2)\left(w(\psi_1)x + \sum_{i \in \psi_1} w(\psi_{1\mathcal{F}}^{(i)})a_i\right) + \sum_{i \in \psi_2} w(\psi_{2\mathcal{F}}^{(i)})a_i \\
&= w(\psi_1 \wedge \psi_2)x + \sum_{i \in \psi_1} w(\psi_{1\mathcal{F}}^{(i)} \wedge \psi_2)a_i + \sum_{i \in \psi_2} w(\psi_{2\mathcal{F}}^{(i)})a_i \\
&= w(\varphi)x + \sum_{i \in \psi_1} w(\varphi_{\mathcal{F}}^{(i)})a_i + \sum_{i \in \psi_2} w(\varphi_{\mathcal{F}}^{(i)})a_i \\
&= w(\varphi)x + \sum_{i \in \varphi} w(\varphi_{\mathcal{F}}^{(i)})a_i.
\end{aligned}
$$

(iii) Suppose that for $\psi_1, \psi_2 \in \mathcal{G}$ with $L(\psi_1) \cap L(\psi_2) = \emptyset$, the statement of this lemma holds. Let $\varphi = \psi_1 \vee \psi_2$. Then we have the following:

$$
\begin{aligned}
W_\varphi(x, \boldsymbol{a}^{(\varphi)}) &= W_{\psi_1}(x, \boldsymbol{a}^{(\psi_1)}) + W_{\psi_2}(x, \boldsymbol{a}^{(\psi_2)}) \\
&= w(\psi_1)x + \sum_{i \in \psi_1} w(\psi_{1\mathcal{F}}^{(i)})a_i + w(\psi_2)x + \sum_{i \in \psi_2} w(\psi_{2\mathcal{F}}^{(i)})a_i \\
&= w(\psi_1 \vee \psi_2)x + \sum_{i \in \psi_1} w(\varphi_{\mathcal{F}}^{(i)})a_i + \sum_{i \in \psi_2} w(\varphi_{\mathcal{F}}^{(i)})a_i \\
&= w(\varphi)x + \sum_{i \in \varphi} w(\varphi_{\mathcal{F}}^{(i)})a_i
\end{aligned}
$$

Thus the proof is completed. ∎

Authenticated Operation of Open Computing Devices

Paul England and Marcus Peinado

Microsoft
Redmond, WA 98052, USA
(pengland,marcuspe)@microsoft.com

Abstract. We describe how an open computing device can be extended
to allow individual programs and operating systems to have exclusive access to cryptographic keys. This problem is of fundamental importance in
areas such as virus protection, protection of servers from network attacks,
network administration and copy protection. We seek a system that can
be unconditionally robust against software attacks. This requires measures in hardware and in software. Our analysis allows us to minimize
the amount of additional hardware needed to support the system.

1 Introduction

Consider a computing platform that allows arbitrary software to be executed.
This paper investigates how individual operating-systems and programs can be
given exclusive access to platform resources, even in the presence of adversarial
software. We focus particularly on one type of resource: cryptographic keys.
In this context, our goal is to allow individual programs to use or gain access
to cryptographic keys, such that no other program can use or gain access to
these keys. We call this mode of operation of a computing device *authenticated
operation.*

Authenticated operation is of fundamental importance for a large range of
applications of computer security, such as protecting personal data from viruses,
protecting confidential server data from network attacks, network administration, copy protection, and trustworthy distributed computing. Authenticated
operation allows different programs, which execute on the same computer without being in a particular trust relationship, to preserve their cryptographic resources irrespective of the actions of other software. This allows software to be
compartmentalized and the size of the trusted computing base [1] to be reduced.

We work with the access control model [5]. In this model guards control
access to resources. Guards can be implemented in hardware or software, and
receive resource-access requests from principals. The guard can grant or deny
access. Typically, the guard is a server, which is contacted by requesting clients
over a network. In this case, the guard decides whether the request should be
granted based on credentials (e.g. certificates, passwords) sent by the requesting
principal over the network. Typical resources include files, printers etc.

L. Batten and J. Seberry (Eds.): ACISP 2002, LNCS 2384, pp. 346–361, 2002.

Authenticated operation leads us to analyze the case in which the resource, the guard and the requesting principals are located in a single computing device. In our analysis, the requesting principals are programs, and the guard gates access to the resources (keys) based on the identity of the requesting program. It ascertains this identity by directly inspecting and controlling the program. While our descriptions apply to arbitrary resources, we focus on cryptographic keys. We can represent the different layers present in modern computers (e.g. hardware, bios, kernel, application software) by composing several instances of the components of the access control model. That is, a principal requesting access to resources in lower layers can also act as a guard to higher layers. In concrete terms, a (hardware) platform guard can control access to cryptographic resources based on the identity of the running operating system. Similarly, the operating system can grant selective cryptographic services to the application programs that it runs. Authenticated operation also allows program and operating-system authentication to be extended across networks. We will show how a network guard can authenticate software on hosts that may not be under its direct control.

The first part of this paper describes an architecture that enables authenticated operation. In general, programs that implement guards and the corresponding resources have to be isolated from other – potentially adversarial – programs executing on the same device. Furthermore, guards have to be able to authenticate requesting programs. Such authentication cannot be based on cryptographic protocols which require the requesting program to access cryptographic keys since passing the authentication step is a prerequisite to being granted access to the keys. We will describe methods for isolation, authentication and initialization of programs that work within this restriction.

The second part of the paper introduces several primitives, by means of which guards can expose restricted resources. We define the concepts of a *gating function*, *sealed storage* and *remote authentication* as general abstractions for cryptographic resource control. We show that the different gating functions we consider can be reduced to a set of three functions.

The third part of the paper describes the hardware extensions necessary to support authenticated operation. It was the goal of our analysis to identify a minimal set of hardware changes. This has the benefit of minimizing the cost of implementing these changes, in addition to identifying the true hardware primitives needed to enable authenticated operation.

Our attack model includes arbitrary software attacks. That is, given correct hardware and correct guard software, no program should be able to gain unauthorized access to resources – even in the presence of arbitrary adversarial software.

The definitions in this paper are abstract, so that they can apply to a broad class of computing devices. At the same time, it was our goal to show that our descriptions apply directly to real-world computers.

1.1   Related Work

This paper builds on several concepts of [10] and [7]. However, while [10] develops a general theory for authentication in distributed system, we focus on authenticated operation in a single stand-alone device.

Several authors describe systems that implement secure boot [3,8] or secure coprocessors [15,13,12,14]. While there are similarities between some of the techniques used there and authenticated operation, these works do not describe systems for authenticated operation. Secure boot focuses on the CPU as the only resource and achieves security by restricting the software that can execute on the device. Similarly, a secure coprocessor is an isolated processing environment, into which only authorized software is admitted. In contrast, authenticated operation imposes no restriction on admissible software. Instead, it allows each program exclusive access to a unique resource.

Secure booting approaches are typically based on a layered model, in which every layer i is isolated from all higher layers. Execution begins in a well-defined initial state of the bottom layer (hardware reset). Control is transferred successively from layer i to layer $i + 1$ for $i \geq 1$. Before layer i transfers control to layer $i + 1$, it authenticates the software in layer $i + 1$. Secure boot implements an access control policy, which is typially PKI based. That is, code is expected to be accompanied by credentials in the form of public key certificates. In the simplest case, a file containing executable code can be loaded and executed in layer $i + 1$ if and only if it is accompanied by a valid certificate chain, whose signatures are rooted in a public key known to the access control logic in layer i. This key constitutes the access control policy. If the credentials of a given binary file are in accordance with the access policy, the file is loaded and control is transferred to a well-defined entry point in the loaded image for layer $i + 1$. Otherwise, layer i retains control and reports an error or tries to obtain software that is authorized to run in layer $i + 1$ [3].

The specification of the Trusted Computing Platform Alliance (TCPA) [2] describes a hardware device that exposes several functions, which are related to authenticated operation. However, the overall description falls short of providing unconditional security against software attacks on a general purpose computing device. Furthermore, the hardware capabilities prescribed by TCPA are clearly not minimal.

The problem of allowing programs to maintain exclusive access to secrets is being studied in connection with software tamper-resistance or code obfuscation techniques (e.g. [4]). However, these software-only techniques are subject to attacks by software. In the absence of provable lower bounds for the robustness of software tamper resistance techniques and in light of complexity theoretic evidence against strong software tamper resistance [5], the true strength of these techniques is unclear. In contrast, this paper studies a minimal set of hardware measures, which allow the overall system to be unconditionally secure against attacks by software.

The rest of this paper is structured as follows. Section 2 describes how the access control model applies to authenticated operation and how isolation, authentication and initialization of guard components can be implemented. Section 3 defines several functions that can be used by guard components to expose access to resources and analyzes their relationship. Section 4 describes how existing computer hardware can be extended to enable authenticated operation. Finally, Sect. 5 concludes the paper.

2 System Architecture

This section identifies a small set of system capabilities, which are necessary to enable authenticated operation, and describes how these capabilities can be implemented. As these capabilities and implementations are quite general in nature, we describe them in a machine model which contains only those properties of real-world computers that are relevant to our discussion. This approach has the benefit of making the level of generality of our results obvious and of not burdening the discussion with unnecessary detail. However, we stress that our results are directly applicable to concrete real-world computers. This applicability is demonstrated in Sect. 4.

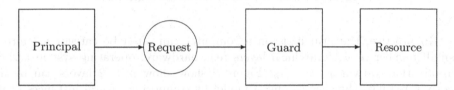

Fig. 1. Components of the access control model [9,10].

2.1 System Model

Figure 1 displays the components of the access control model [9]. *Principals* make *requests* to access-protected *resources*. Each request is received by a *guard* – a component, which controls access to a resource. A guard examines requests and decides whether to grant each request based on an access policy for the resource and information, such as the identity of the principal that issued the request.

This paper focuses on the case in which the protected resources are cryptographic keys. In this context, we distinguish between *disclosure guards* and *service guards*. Service guards perform certain operations (encryption, signing etc.) with the resource (key) at the request of principals without disclosing the key. In contrast, disclosure guards reveal the protected key to authorized requestors.

As described in the introduction, we are interested in the case in which all principals and guards are programs executing on a single computing device. We assume that the computing device is a programmable, state-based computer with a central processing unit (CPU) and memory. The memory is used to store state information (data) and transition rules (programs). The CPU executes instructions stored at a memory location, which is identified by an internal register (instruction pointer IP). Finally, at least one protectable resource is embedded in the device. In the rest of the paper, we will refer to this semi-formal definition as a *computing device* or our *machine model*.

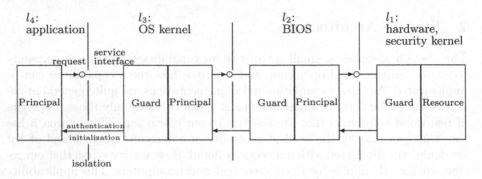

Fig. 2. A layered system in the access control model.

In practice, the principals on a computer can often be categorized into a small number n of hierarchical layers (e.g. hardware, operating system kernel, application software) $l_1, \ldots, l_n$. Figure 2 shows how $n > 2$ layers can by incorporated into the access control model by composing several instances of its components. In our model, the lowest layer guards a root resource. Programs in the intermediate layers act as principals that request access from the next lower layer. At the same time, they act as guards towards principals in the next layer. The significance of the intermediate layers in our model is twofold: (a) They correspond to properties of real-world computers. (b) The intermediate layers can add functionality for principals in higher layers. This is relevant if the guard in the lowest layer is simple (e.g. a cheap hardware implementation).

2.2 System Capabilities

We say that a program has *protected access* to a cryptographic resource K if no other program can gain the same access to K, with the exception of the guard of the resource. Clearly, the exception is necessary in the access control model, since the guard of a resource has at least as much access to the resource as a principal that requests access from the guard. Note that, in the layered model, the exception does not only apply to the guard g from which the principal is directly requesting access, but also to all guards, on which the access depends indirectly (Fig. 3).

Definition 1. *A computing device enables* authenticated operation *of software if it is possible to let every program obtain protected access (from a disclosure guard or from a service guard) to at least one cryptographic resource.*

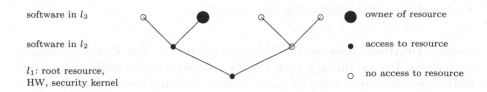

software in l_3 owner of resource

software in l_2 access to resource

l_1: root resource,   no access to resource
HW, security kernel

Fig. 3. Protected access in the access control model: Only the programs (guards) on the path from program A to the root can access the resource.

The rest of this section describes an architecture that enables authenticated operation.

Definition 2. *We say that a program C is* isolated *from another program D if (a) there is memory that can be accessed by C but not by D and (b) D cannot initiate execution of C, except, possibly, at a well-defined entry point (determined by C).*

A program is given by its transition rules (executable code) and by its initial state (entry point - or initial value of the instruction pointer IP). The first condition of Def. 1 guarantees integrity of the program code and the state information of C, even in the presence of adversarial behavior by D, since these data can be stored in the memory that cannot be accessed by D. This condition also allows C to protect confidential data (e.g. cryptographic secrets) from observation by D. The second condition guarantees that D cannot subvert the behavior of C by choosing the initial state adversarially.

Definition 3. *Given a computing device, we say that a program C can* authenticate *a program D if C is able to identify the transition rules (program code) and the initial state of D.*

We require the computing device to enable isolation for any program C from any other program D, with the exception of a single program E_j for each layer $j < i$, where i is the layer of C (cf. Fig 3). Furthermore, for any layer i, the computing device has to enable a program executing in layer i to authenticate at least some programs in layer $i + 1$.

The first requirement protects programs from observation and interference by any program, except for the sequence $E_1, E_2, \ldots, E_{i-1}$ of guards through which C request access to its resources. As explained above, protection of C from these programs is not meaningful, since they have the same access to C's resources as C itself. The second requirement allows a program to act as a guard for requests from principals in the next layer. These two observations give rise to an inductive argument that programs in any layer can act as guards for resources by requesting access to a resource from their predecessor, protecting their integrity and the resource through isolation and authenticating requests from principals in the next layer. We summarize these observations in the following

Fact 1 *A computing device that enables authentication and isolation as described above, enables authenticated execution.*

Implementation: Isolation can be implemented by means of physical memory protections. We call this approach *isolation in space*. For example, the ring and virtual memory protections found in modern microprocessors are sufficient to implement isolation. An operating system kernel (layer i) running in privileged mode can set up page tables for applications (layer $i + 1$), such that any application can only access those parts of physical memory that the operating system kernel chooses to map into the application's virtual address space. Furthermore, the kernel restricts applications' privileges so that they cannot change the memory mapping, and ensures that applications can initiate execution of kernel code only at well defined entry points (e.g. system calls).

A second approach to implementing isolation between two layers is to separate their execution in time. A program in a first layer i executes to completion, makes certain resources unavailable and terminates. Subsequently, control is transferred to the next layer $i + 1$. We call this approach *isolation in time*.

Authentication occurs between subsequent layers ($j = i + 1$). C has to authenticate the program (transition rules) and the initial state of the configuration of j. The former can be achieved by letting C inspect the program in layer j. That is, typically C reads the memory, which contains the program for layer j and computes a cryptographic digest over this memory range.[1]

The second task for C is to identify the initial state of D. In general, it is not possible to determine the initial state of a program from its state at an arbitrary execution stage. More precisely, given a program P and two states σ_1 and σ_2, the question whether a computation of P could evolve σ_1 into σ_2 is undecidable. Thus, C has to control the initial state of D. In practical terms, this means that C can only ascertain the initial state σ_1 of D if C initiates the execution of D at σ_1.

In summary, in order to authenticate D, C inspects the memory contents it deems relevant (program and, possibly, data) and computes a cryptographic digest. After that, C transfers execution to a well-defined entry point of D.

3   Access Primitives

This section considers the case in which the resources are cryptographic keys. In this case, authenticated operation allows each operating system and application program to have exclusive access to a secret. The isolation requirement of the previous section protects each secret from attacks by adversarial code. The authentication requirement allows the system to identify programs, such that each secret is disclosed only to the program that owns it.

---

[1] The goal at this point is only to ascertain the identity of the code, but not to evaluate statements made by other principals about the code. Thus, certificates are not necessary at this point.

We focus on two types of uses for secrets, which are bound to a program. The program can store long lived confidential and integrity protected information, such as banking records. Secondly, access to a secret allows a program to participate in cryptographic authentication protocols (for example with a remote server). We call these functions *sealed storage* and *remote authentication*. This section introduces several abstractions for the functions and investigates their relationship.

3.1   Gating Functions

Many of the abstractions we introduce in this section follow the same pattern. Given a request from a program, a guard establishes the identity of the program (i.e. authenticates it). If the program is not authorized to access or use the requested secret, the guard rejects the request. Otherwise, the guard computes some function of the secret and, possibly, further information provided by the program and returns the result. As an alternative to explicitly accepting or rejecting requests, the guard may always service the request, but bind the identity of the caller into the result. The latter approach is appropriate if the result returned by the guard does not contain confidential information (e.g. requests to use a secret to produce a digital signature). We use the term *gating functions* to refer to both types of functions. In either case, the guard has to authenticate the caller. In the rest of this section, we will model this step by a call to a function ID(), which returns a digest of the calling program.

3.2   Sealed Storage

The first class of gating functions we consider in this paper implements sealed storage. The purpose of sealed storage is to allow programs to store long lived secrets, such that only a well-defined set of programs (defined by the program that stores the secret) can retrieve them. In the simplest case, only the programs that originally stored (sealed) the secret can retrieve (unseal) it. Typically, the life time of these secrets will exceed the time of individual executions of the program. Isolation and a random number generator allows a configuration to maintain secrets during a single execution. Sealed storage allows a configuration to maintain secrets across different executions, which may not overlap in time. A layer l_i exposes sealed storage to the next layer l_{i+1} by means of the following interface.

Seal
Input: a secret s, the digest of a target program t
Output: c – an identifier for s
Description:
$d =$ID()
$c =$ store (s, t, d)
return c

UnSeal
Input: c – an identifier for secrets
Output: a number s, the digest of a program t
Description:
$(s, t, d) = \text{retrieve}(c)$
if $t = \text{ID}()$ then return (s, d)
else fail

The Seal() operation stores its inputs (the secret and an indentifier for the configuration which may retrieve the secret) together with an identifier for the caller and returns an identifier, which allows the stored data to be referenced in subsequent UnSeal() operations. The function UnSeal() retrieves the data associated with its input, tests if the caller is authorized to read the secret ($t = \text{ID}()$) and returns the secret s and information that identifies its source (d). We note that Seal() and UnSeal() as well as the functions described later in this section can be easily extended to include more sophisticated access policies than the simple $t = \text{ID}()$ equality check described here.

There are two approaches to implementing sealed storage. It is possible to implement store() and retrieve() by means of physically protected non-volatile memory – an expensive and limited resource. We prefer an implementation based on cryptography.

Cryptographic Implementations of Sealed Storage: This section describes an implementation, in which the required resource is a cryptographic key K, rather than physically protected memory. Store() will not physically store its inputs. Instead, it will produce a cryptographically protected output c, which contains its inputs in encrypted and integrity protected form. The former property results from applying a symmetric cipher to the input. The latter property results from applying a message authentication code MAC (e.g. the HMAC of [6]). This leads to the following implementation of Store() and Retrieve().

Store
Input: a bit string b
Output: a bit string c
Description:
$m = \text{MAC}_{K_1}(b)$
$c = (m, \text{Encrypt}_{K_2}(b))$
return c

Retrieve
Input: a bit string c
Output: a bit string b
Description:
Let $(m, d) = c$
$b = \text{Decrypt}_{K_2}(c))$

if $m = \text{MAC}_{K_1}(b)$ then return b
else fail

For technical reasons, we have partitioned K into two independent keys K_1 and K_2, in order to avoid using the same key for the MAC and the cipher. A number of alternatives for combining the MAC and the cipher exist. This type of implementation has the benefit of not imposing a limit on the number of secrets that can be stored – as is the case for physically protected memory. However, it should be observed that the purely cryptographic implementation has slightly weaker semantics. It guarantees only that corruption of c can be detected and that b cannot be retrieved from c without access to K_2. However, it it does not prevent corruption or the complete disappearance of c. This results in certain denial of service attacks, which are not possible for implementations based on physically protected memory.

3.3   Remote Authentication

The authentication mechanism described in Sect 2.2 allows a program to be authenticated to a closely coupled guard (a program on the same computing device). In particular, the authenticator must have direct read access to the memory containing the authenticated program code.

In this section, we introduce gating functions that allow programs to be authenticated even in the absence of a strong physical coupling to the authenticator (e.g. servers, smart cards). In this situation, authentication has to be based on cryptography. That is, both entities go through a cryptographic authentication protocol (cf. [11] for a summary of common protocols). This requires the authenticated configuration to have access to a secret, which, depending on the protocol, is typically a private key or a symmetric key. Going beyond pure cryptography, the computing device must tie the use of these authentication secrets to the identity of the configuration that requests their use – relying on the local authentication mechanism of Sect 2.2. Thus, the authenticator can not only establish the indentity of the computing device, but, more importantly, of the software stack executing on it.

The following two functions are the respective gating functions for public key signing and public key decryption. We assume that the guard implementing these functions has access to a private signing key K_s and a private decryption key K_d.

Quote
Input: an arbitrary data block a
Output: a signature s
Description:
$d = \text{ID}()$
return $\text{Signature}_{K_s}(d, a)$

PKUnseal
Input: a ciphertext block c

Output: a number s
Description:
$(d, s) = \text{Decrypt}_{K_d}(c)$
if $d =\text{ID}()$ then return s
else fail

The Quote operation returns a public key signature over the concatenation of its input and an identifier d for the calling program. The only assertion inherent in the signature is that it was performed at the request of d. Quote works in conjunction with a Verify() operation, which typically executes on a remote device, and which performs a standard public key signature verification and retrieves and evaluates d.

The PKUnseal operation is a version of public key decryption, which is gated on the identity of the caller. The result of the public key decryption of the input c is interpreted as a pair (d, s), where s is a secret and d identifies a configuration to which s may be revealed. If the caller of PKUnseal is not d then the operation fails. The input c is generated by a second operation *PKSeal*, which is typically executed on a remote device, and which performs a public key encryption of a pair (d, s).

Quote and PKUnseal are intended to be used in connection with public key authentication protocols [11]. Most protocols can be straightforwardly adapted, by replacing any call to public key decryption, public key encryption, signing, signature verification by a call to PKUnseal, PKSeal, Quote, Verify, respectively. Given appropriate management of program digests in PKSeal and Verify, the adapted protocols will prove to an authenticator which software is executing on a remote computing device.

3.4   Random Number Generation

The gating functions described so far are concerned with the restricted use of secrets that already exist on the computing device. It remains to address how these secrets can be initially obtained or generated. So far, our machine model is fully deterministic. Clearly, we have to provide a source of randomness. Typically, this source will be internal – implemented as a cryptographically strong random number generator in the machine hardware. We call the function through which the source of randomness is exposed *GetRandom()*. Let each call to GetRandom() return a fixed number of random bits.

Typically, calls to GetRandom() will be followed by calls to Seal(), in order to store the newly generated secret securely. We introduce the function GenSeal(), which combines both calls.

GenSeal
Input: the digests t_1, t_2 of two target programs
Output: c – an identifier for s
Description:
$d =\text{ID}()$

s =GenRandom()

c = store (s, t_1, t_2, d)

return c

GenSeal() is an optimization for certain restricted situations, which will be explained in Sect. 4.

3.5   Implementation of System Calls

The functions defined so far have the character of system calls. Given two subsequent layers i and $i + 1$ of the computing device, software or hardware in layer i exposes system calls for sealed storage and remote authentication, which can be used from layer $i + 1$. In general, the implementation of a system call mechanism depends strongly on the isolation mechanism between the two layers.

Isolation in space: In practice, the memory protections that enable isolation in space typically include provisions for system calls. The software in the calling layer $(i + 1)$ issues a special instruction, which blocks its execution and passes control to a well-defined entry point of layer i. The software (or hardware) in layer i uses its secret to service the system call and returns control to the caller in layer $i + 1$. In practice, the performance overhead is typically small.

Isolation in time: System calls across layers, which are isolated in time are more complicated and costly due to the fact that, by the time the system call is made from layer $i + 1$, layer i is no longer active. In particular, its secrets have been made inaccessible. Servicing a system call which depends on these secrets requires reinitialization of layer i and, possibly, the layers below it. In the most extreme – and probably typical – case, servicing the system call requires a full reset of the device.

In light of the high cost of system calls under isolation in time, the following optimization is intended to improve system performance by replacing most system calls by library calls. Conceptually, any service guard functionality in layer i is moved into layer $i + 1$ and converted into library code. Layer i acts only as a disclosure guard. After an initial GenSeal() or UnSeal() operation by the disclosure guard in layer i for the library code in layer $i + 1$, the latter can cache the returned secret and expose sealed storage and remote authentication in a self contained way. That is, after the initial GenSeal() or UnSeal() operation by layer i, which can be executed during boot, all calls by code in layer $i + 1$ to the functions defined in this section can be executed with minimal overhead as library calls within layer $i + 1$ and without any further system calls into layer i.

We note, however, that this optimization results in somewhat weaker semantics for certain operations in the presence of security failures. For example, in any system that exposes Quote() by means of a service guard in layer i, security bugs in layer $i + 1$ may allow an adversary to obtain false signatures by making system calls into Quote() *only until* the bug is repaired. In contrast, under the optimization, the signing key used by Quote() is available in layer $i + 1$. Thus, a security bug in layer $i + 1$ may allow an adversary to extract the signing key and to produce signatures even after the error has been corrected.

One consequence of the optimization described above is that the remote authentication functions (Quote(), PKUnseal()) can be implemented given only sealed storage and appropriate initialization. During initialization (e.g. manufacture of the device), a public key pair is generated, the private key is sealed to an appropriate software configuration, and the public key is certified. This observation has practical significance, as it allows devices without hardware or microcode support for public key cryptography to support remote authentication.

We conclude that a device with the following hardware primitives can implement sealed storage and remote authentication: (a) GenSeal(), (b) Unseal(), (c) an isolation mechanism, and (d) a means for correctly initializing the device. The next section will outline hardware implementations of these primitives.

4   Hardware Implementation

In this section we describe a family of hardware implementations that will enable platforms to support authenticated operation. As with higher layers in the system, the characteristics of the lowest layer (l_1) are a) secret key resources, b) privileged code that has access to these keys, and c) controlled initialization of the layer.

4.1   Layer 1: Initialization and Resources

Authenticated operation provides a strong binding between programs and secret keys. At higher layers, we have assumed that guards in lower layers guarantee this binding. At the lowest layer we do not have an underlying software guard that can gate access to the platform secrets; hence we need another mechanism to support the strong association of the l_1-keys to the l_1-program. The most straightforward way of accomplishing this binding is to require l_1 software be platform microcode or firmware that is not changeable following manufacture, and give the l_1 software unrestricted access to the l_1 keys. In the remainder of this paper we will call the platform-microcode the security kernel, and the l_1 keys the platform keys.

This mechanism is a simple form of secure boot. The platform will only pass control to a predetermined security kernel. The hardware behavior can also be explained as a simple resource guard that discloses the platform keys to the predefined security kernel.

We have no specific requirements regarding whether the platform keys and security-kernel firmware are part of the processor or in other platform components. In general, keys and code that are embedded into the microprocessor chip will be harder to subvert, but other manufacturing considerations can make off-chip solutions attractive.

Authenticated operation requires that programs are started in a controlled initial state. At higher levels, the software running at lower-levels can be entrusted to start execution at the correct entry point. At l_1 we need hardware to perform this function. Fortunately, on power-up or following reset, all processors already begin execution by following some well-defined deterministic sequence. In the simplest case the processor starts fetching and executing code from an architecturally-defined memory location. In this case (and with minor variations for the more complicated startup sequences), it is sufficient for hardware to ensure that the security kernel is the code that executes on startup.

Another requirement is that no other platform state can subvert execution of the security kernel. Reset and power-up provide a robust and a well-debugged state-clear for the processor. We will call the platform state change that is used to start or invoke the security kernel a security reset.

Finally, a device manufacturer must arrange for the generation or installation of the platform keys used by the l_1 implementation of Seal and Unseal. If the device is to be recognized as part of a PKI, the manufacturer must also certify a public key for the platform. This can be a platform-key used directly be l_1, or a key used by a higher layer (cf. Sect. 3.5).

Key generation and certification can be the responsibility of the CPU manufacturer, the responsibility of the OEM that assembles the CPU into a device, or both parties.

4.2   Layer 1: Isolation and Guard

Once the security kernel is executing it can use the isolation mechanisms we have described to protect itself from code executing at higher layers.

No additional platform support is needed to implement space isolation on most processors: an exiting privilege mode or level will suffice (as long as the hardware resource that allows access to the platform key can be protected from higher layers). However, to support time-isolation, we need hardware assistance to allow the security kernel to conceal the platform key before passing control to higher layers [10].

The simplest way to provide platform-key security in the time-isolation model is to employ a stateful guard circuit that we call a reset latch. A reset latch is a hardware circuit that has the property that it is "open" following reset or power-up, but any software at any time can programmatically "close" the latch [14]. Once closed, the latch remains closed unto the next reset or power-up. A platform that implements a time-isolated security-kernel should gate platform-key access on the state of a reset-latch, and the security-kernel should close the latch before passing control to higher layers. As we have already described, the security kernel will have to take additional actions like clearing memory and registers before passing control, but these steps are identical to those required at higher levels.

4.3 Layer 1: Service Invocation

If the platform employs space-isolation the security kernel must use privilege modes to protect itself and its platform keys from programs (e.g. operating systems) that it hosts. Furthermore, the security kernel must establish a system call interface for invocation of the authentication operations.

If the platform employs time-isolation, then the platform must also contain storage that survives a security-reset to pass parameters to service routines. To invoke a service, an operating system must prepare a command and parameter block in a memory location known to the security kernel and perform a security-reset. If the OS wishes to continue execution following the service call (as opposed to a simple restart) then it and the security kernel must take extra measures to ensure that this can be done reliably and safely.

To conclude, a security kernel that implements time isolation with a reset-latch can be built with existing processors with a very small amount of external or internal logic. Furthermore, if the primitives exposed are Unseal and GenSeal then the security kernel is very small.

5 Conclusions

We have defined authenticated operation and identified properties, which allow a computing device to enable authenticated operation. In particular, we have identified isolation and local authentication as critical capabilities and outlined implementation options for them. A critical component in the implementation is a booting procedure, which successively tranfers control from layer to layer through well-defined entry points.

The main goal of authenticated operation is to enable mutually distrustful software components on a computer to have exclusive access to cryptographic keys. We have discussed abstractions for the main uses of these keys (sealed storage and remote authentication), and we have tried to identify a minimal set of primitives, which enable these uses. Finally, we have outlined the hardware measures necessary to implement these primitives.

References

1. DOD 5200.28-STD. Department of defense trusted computer system evaluation criteria. December 1985.
2. Trusted Computing Platform Alliance. TCPA main specification version 1.1. http://www.trustedpc.org, 2001.
3. W. A. Arbaugh, D. J. Faber, and J. M. Smith. A secure and reliable bootstrap architecture. In *Proceedings of the 1997 IEEE Symposium on Security and Privacy*, pages 65–71, 1997.
4. D. Aucsmith. Tamper-resistant software: An implementation. In Ross Anderson, editor, *Information hiding: first international workshop, Cambridge, U.K.*, volume 1174 of *Lecture Notes in Computer Science*, pages 317–333. Springer-Verlag, 1996.

5. B. Barak, O. Goldreich, R. Impagliazzo, S. Rudich, A. Sahai, S. Vadhan, and K. Yang. On the (im)possibility of obfuscating programs. In *Advances in Cryptology – CRYPTO 2001*, pages 1–18. Springer-Verlag, 2001.
6. M. Bellare, R. Canetti, and H. Krawczyk. Keying hash functions for message authentication. In *Advances in Cryptology – Crypto'96*, number 1109 in Lecture Notes in CS, 1996.
7. P. England, J. DeTreville, and B. Lampson. A trusted open platform. Unpublished.
8. N. Itoi, W. A. Arbaugh, S. J. Pollack, and D. M. Reeves. Personal secure booting. In V. Varadharajan and Y. Mu, editors, *Information Security and Privacy – 6th Australasian Conference, ACISP 2001*. Springer-Verlag, 2001.
9. B. Lampson. Protection. *ACM Operating Systems Review*, 8(1):18–24, 1974.
10. B. Lampson, M. Abadi, and M. Burrows. Authentication in distributed systems: Theory and practice. *ACM Transactions on Computer Systems*, 10:265–310, November 1992.
11. A. Menezes, P. van Oorschot, and S. Vanstone. *Handbook of Applied Cryptography*. CRC Press, 1997.
12. S. W. Smith and V. Austel. Trusting trusted hardware: Towards a formal model for programmable secure coprocessors. In *Proceedings of the Third USENIX Workshop on Electronic Commerce*, pages 83–98, 1998.
13. S. W. Smith, E. R. Palmer, and S. Weingart. Using a high-performance, programmable secure coprocessor. In *Proceedings of the Second International Conference on Financial Cryptography*. Springer-Verlag, 1998.
14. S. W. Smith and S. Weingart. Building a high-performance, programmable secure coprocessor. *Computer Networks*, 31(8):831–860, April 1999.
15. B. Yee. *Using Secure Coprocessors*. PhD thesis, Carnegie Mellon University, 1994.

A New Identification Scheme Based on the Bilinear Diffie-Hellman Problem

Myungsun Kim and Kwangjo Kim

International Research center for Information Security (IRIS)
Information and Communications Univ. (ICU)
58-4 Hwaamdong, Yuseong-gu, Daejon, 305-732, Korea.
{ms.kim, kkj}@icu.ac.kr

Abstract. We construct an interactive identification scheme based on the bilinear Diffie-Hellman problem and analyze its security. This scheme is practical in terms of key size, communication complexity, and availability of identity-variance provided that an algorithm of computing the Weil-pairing is feasible. We prove that this scheme is secure against active attacks as well as passive attacks if the bilinear Diffie-Hellman problem is intractable. Our proof is based on the fact that the computational Diffie-Hellman problem is hard in the additive group of points of an elliptic curve over a finite field, on the other hand, the decisional Diffie-Hellman problem is easy in the multiplicative group of the finite field mapped by a bilinear map. Finally, this scheme is compared with other identification schemes.

Keywords: Gap-problems, Identification scheme, Bilinear Diffie-Hellman problem, Weil-pairing

1 Introduction

It is well known that an *identification scheme* is a very important and useful cryptographic tool. The identification scheme is an interactive protocol where a prover, $\mathcal{P}$, tries to convince a verifier, $\mathcal{V}$, of his identity. Only $\mathcal{P}$ knows the secret value corresponding to his public one, and the secret value allows to convince $\mathcal{V}$ of his identity. If we replace "identity" by "authenticity" of messages, identification schemes are nearly equivalent to *signature schemes*. As mentioned by Fiat and Shamir [7] and Shoup [21], the distinction between identification and signature schemes is very subtle. Therefore, two types of schemes can be used interchangeably [7,10,17,15].

Since Okamoto and Pointcheval [16] initiated the concept of the Gap-problems and proposed that a Gap Diffie-Hellman problem offers a signature scheme, several cryptographic schemes based on such variants of Diffie-Hellman assumption have been studied. Using the bilinear Diffie-Hellman problem as an instance of the Gap Diffie-Hellman problem, Boneh and Franklin [2] and Boneh et al. [3] suggested an efficient ID-based encryption scheme and a short signature scheme, respectively. These imply that the bilinear Diffie-Hellman problem

L. Batten and J. Seberry (Eds.): ACISP 2002, LNCS 2384, pp. 362–378, 2002.

provides identification schemes. To the best of our knowledge, there is no identification scheme based on the bilinear Diffie-Hellman problem published in the open literature.

In this paper, we construct a new identification scheme based on the Bilinear Diffie-Hellman problem, which is a typical instance of the Gap Diffie-Hellman problem and prove that this scheme is secure against passive and even active attacks if the bilinear Diffie-Hellman problem is intractable, which are the main contribution of this paper.

The rest of this paper is organized as follows: After describing several identification schemes in this section, we formally state our definition of security as well as basic tools used in our scheme in Section 2. Our basic identification scheme is presented based on the Bilinear Diffie-Hellman problem in Section 3. In Section 4 we give a proof of security for our scheme. In Section 5 we present a generalized model of our basic identification scheme. In what follows, we compare with other schemes in the light of performance, and finally, we end with concluding remarks.

1.1   Previous Works

Types of attacks.
In general, an identification scheme is said to be broken if an adversary succeeds in an impersonation attempt (making the verifier accept with non-negligible probability). We can classify the type of attacks according to the interaction allowed to the adversary before an impersonation attempt [21].

The weakest form of attack is a *passive attack*, where the adversary is not allowed to interact with the system at all before attempting an impersonation; the only available information to the adversary is the public key of the prover. Other attacks of intermediate level such as *eavesdropping attack* or *honest-verifier attack* are essentially equivalent to the passive attack.

The strongest form of attack is an *active attack*, in which the adversary is allowed to interact with $\mathcal{P}$ several times, posing as $\mathcal{V}$. We may consider active attacks as adaptive chosen ciphertext attacks. We should note that active attacks are quite feasible in practice.

Fiat-Shamir (FS) scheme. Fiat and Shamir [7] proposed the identification scheme based on the factorization problem. A key generation algorithm constructs a modulus n by multiplying two distinct random primes, chooses randomly an element $a \in \mathbb{Z}_n^*$, and sets $b = a^2$. The public key is $\langle b, n \rangle$, and the secret key is a.

The protocol repeats the following steps t times:

1. $\mathcal{P}$ chooses $r \in \mathbb{Z}_n^*$ at random, computes $x = r^2$, and sends x to $\mathcal{V}$.
2. $\mathcal{V}$ chooses $\epsilon \in \{0, 1\}$ at random, and sends ϵ to $\mathcal{P}$.
3. $\mathcal{P}$ computes $y = r \cdot a^\epsilon$ and sends y to $\mathcal{V}$; $\mathcal{V}$ accepts if $y^2 = x \cdot b^\epsilon$, and rejects otherwise.

The FS scheme is secure against active attacks if factorization is hard.

Feige-Fiat-Shamir (FFS) scheme. This scheme is also based on the factorization problem. A key generation algorithm chooses a modulus n as in the FS scheme. A secret key consists of a list $a_1, \ldots, a_l \in \mathbb{Z}_n^*$ chosen randomly, where l is a given constant, and the corresponding public key consists of $b_1, \ldots, b_l \in \mathbb{Z}_n^*$, where $b_i = a_i^2$ for $1 \leq i \leq l$.

The protocol executes the followings t times in parallel:

1. $\mathcal{P}$ chooses $r \in \mathbb{Z}_n^*$ at random, computes $x = r^2$, and sends x to $\mathcal{V}$.
2. $\mathcal{V}$ randomly chooses $\epsilon_1, \ldots, \epsilon_l \in \{0, 1\}$, sends $\epsilon_1, \ldots, \epsilon_l$ to $\mathcal{P}$.
3. $\mathcal{P}$ computes $y = r \prod_{j=1}^{l} a_j^{\epsilon_j}$ and sends y to $\mathcal{V}$; $\mathcal{V}$ accepts if $x = y^2 \prod_{j=1}^{l} b_j^{\epsilon_j}$, and rejects otherwise.

This scheme is also secure against active attacks if factorization is hard [6].

Other schemes. The Guillou-Quisquater (GQ) scheme is based on the RSA-inversion problem. Guillou [10] shows that this scheme is secure against passive attacks provided that factorization is hard. Ohta and Okamoto (OO) [17] present a modification of the FS scheme on the basis of the difficulty of extracting the L-th roots, and they prove that their scheme is as secure as the FS scheme. Okamoto [15] proposes three identification schemes. The first one is based on the discrete logarithm problem (DLP), the second on the RSA-problem, and the last one on the factorization problem. All of these schemes are proved to be secure against active attacks. Schnorr [20] also proposes identification schemes that are based on the factorization problem or DLP.

2   Definitions

A general approach of proving that an identification scheme is secure is to show that it exhibits a zero-knowledge proof of knowledge. However, the results of Goldreich and Krawczyk [8], together with the argument of Shoup [21] say that any efficient black box simulator for a three round, public coin system can be turned into a prover that succeeds with non-negligible probability.

In this paper, we make use of a computational reduction from solving a well-established problem to break the cryptosystem rather than zero-knowledge proof techniques. That is to say, the proving method is to use an adversary that breaks the cryptosystem to solve the computational Diffie-Hellman problem.

2.1   Notions of Security

We formally define a secure identification scheme, using the same notations as in [19] and [21].

If $A(\cdot)$ is a probabilistic algorithm, then for any input x, the notation A_x refers to the probability space that assigns to the string σ the probability space that A, on input x, outputs σ.

If S is a probability space, then $[S]$ denotes the set of elements in this space that occur with non-zero probability, and $\Pr_S[e]$ denotes the probability that S

associates with the element e. If S is any probability space, then $x \leftarrow S$ denotes the algorithm which assigns to x an element randomly selected according to S.

The notation $\Pr[p(x_1, x_2 \ldots) | x_1 \leftarrow S_1; x_2 \leftarrow S_2; \ldots]$ denotes the probability that the predicate $p(x_1, x_2, \ldots)$ will be true after the ordered execution of the algorithms $x_1 \leftarrow S_1, x_2 \leftarrow S_2, \ldots$.

In addition, we use the same conventions in [6]:

1. $\bar{\mathcal{P}}$ represents an honest prover who follows its designated protocol, $\tilde{\mathcal{P}}$ does a polynomial-time cheater, and $\mathcal{P}$ acts as $\bar{\mathcal{P}}$ or $\tilde{\mathcal{P}}$.
2. $\bar{\mathcal{V}}$ represents a valid verifier who follows the designated protocol, $\tilde{\mathcal{P}}$ does an arbitrary polynomial-time algorithm which may try to extract additional information from $\mathcal{P}$, and $\mathcal{V}$ acts as $\bar{\mathcal{V}}$ or $\tilde{\mathcal{V}}$.
3. $(\mathcal{P}, \mathcal{V})$ represents the execution of the two party protocol where $\mathcal{P}$ is the prover and $\mathcal{V}$ is the verifier.

In general, an identification scheme $(\mathcal{G}, \mathcal{P}, \mathcal{V})$ consists of a probabilistic polynomial-time algorithm $\mathcal{G}$, and two probabilistic polynomial-time interactive algorithms $\mathcal{P}$ and $\mathcal{V}$ with the following properties [6,21]:

1. The algorithm $\mathcal{G}$ is a *key generation algorithm*. It takes a string of the form 1^k as input, and outputs a pair of string (I, S). k is called a security parameter, I is called a *public key*, and S is called a *secret key*.
2. As input, $\mathcal{P}$ receives the pair (I, S) and $\mathcal{V}$ does I. After an interactive execution of $\mathcal{P}$ and $\mathcal{V}$, $\mathcal{V}$ outputs either 1 (indicating "accept") or 0 (indicating "reject"). For given I and S, the output of $\mathcal{V}$ at the end of this interaction is a probability space which is denoted by $\langle \mathcal{P}(I, S), \mathcal{V}(I) \rangle$.
3. A valid prover should always be able to succeed in convincing the verifier. Formally speaking, for all k and for all $(I, S) \in [\mathcal{G}(1^k)]$, $\langle \mathcal{P}(I, S), \mathcal{V}(I) \rangle = 1$ with probability 1.

An *adversary* $(\tilde{\mathcal{P}}, \tilde{\mathcal{V}})$ is a pair of probabilistic polynomial-time interactive algorithms. For given key pair (I, S), we denote by $\langle \bar{\mathcal{P}}(I, S), \tilde{\mathcal{V}}(I) \rangle$ the string h output by $\tilde{\mathcal{V}}$ after interacting with $\bar{\mathcal{P}}$ several times. For given I and S, yet again $\langle \bar{\mathcal{P}}(I, S), \tilde{\mathcal{V}}(I) \rangle$ is a probability space. The string h (called a "help string") is used as input to $\tilde{\mathcal{P}}$ who attempts to convince $\bar{\mathcal{V}}$. We denote by $\langle \tilde{\mathcal{P}}(h), \bar{\mathcal{V}}(I) \rangle$ the output of $\tilde{\mathcal{V}}$ after interacting with $\tilde{\mathcal{P}}(h)$.

We adopt the definition of security against active attacks with respect to such adversaries from [21] as follows:

Definition 1. *An identification scheme* $(\mathcal{G}, \mathcal{P}, \mathcal{V})$ *is secure against active attacks if for all adversaries* $(\tilde{\mathcal{P}}, \tilde{\mathcal{V}})$, *for all constants* $c > 0$, *and for all sufficiently large* k,

$$\Pr\left[\sigma = 1 \,\middle|\, \begin{array}{l} (I, S) \leftarrow \mathcal{G}(1^k); \\ h \leftarrow \langle \bar{\mathcal{P}}(I, S), \tilde{\mathcal{V}}(I) \rangle; \\ \sigma \leftarrow \langle \tilde{\mathcal{P}}(h), \bar{\mathcal{V}}(I) \rangle \end{array}\right] < k^{-c}.$$

2.2 Bilinear Diffie-Hellman Problem

The computational assumptions when constructing cryptographic schemes can mainly be classified into two types. One is the intractability of an inverting problem such as inverting the RSA function, and computing the Diffie-Hellman (DH) problem. The other is the intractability of a decision problem such as the decisional Diffie-Hellman problem.

In addition to these problems, Okamoto and Pointcheval [16] define a new class of problems, called the Gap-problem. Let $f : \{0,1\}^* \times \{0,1\}^* \to \{0,1\}$ and $R : \{0,1\}^* \times \{0,1\}^* \times \{0,1\}^* \to \{0,1\}$ be any relation.

- The *inverting problem* of f is, given x, to compute any y such as $f(x,y) = 1$ if it exists, or to answer Fail.
- The *R-decision problem* of f is, given (x,y), to decide whether $R(f,x,y) = 1$ or not. Here y may be the null string, $\perp$.

Usually, it is accepted that there exists the gap of difficulty between two problems. Using this property, the Gap-problem can be defined as follows:

Definition 2. *The R-gap problem of f is to solve the inverting problem of f with the help of the oracle of the R-decision problem of f.*

Okamoto and Pointcheval [16] claim that the DH problems are the typical instance of the Gap problem. Since the inverting problem can be viewed as the computational problem, the computational Diffie-Hellman (C-DH) problem corresponds to the inverting one, and the decisional Diffie-Hellman (D-DH) problem does to the R-decision one. Here, we describe the Gap Diffie-Hellman (G-DH) problem. Let $\mathbb{G}$ be any group of prime order m.

- The C-DH problem: given a triple of $\mathbb{G}$ elements (g, g^a, g^b), find the element $C = g^{ab}$.
- The D-DH problem: given a quadruple of $\mathbb{G}$ elements (g, g^a, g^b, g^c), decide whether $c = ab \pmod{q}$ or not.
- The G-DH problem: given a triple of $\mathbb{G}$ elements (g, g^a, g^b), find the element $C = g^{ab}$ with the help of a D-DH oracle (which answers whether a given quadruple is a DH quadruple or not).

The Tate-pairing is given as a specific example that satisfies the property of the G-DH problem [16].

We focus on the bilinear Diffie-Hellman (B-DH) problem that is a variant of the C-DH problem, which is the underlying problem of our new design. Now we describe the B-DH problem and the security defined over this problem.

Let $\mathbb{G}_1$ and $\mathbb{G}_2$ be two cyclic groups of prime order m and let P be a generator of $\mathbb{G}_1$. Let $\hat{e} : \mathbb{G}_1 \times \mathbb{G}_1 \to \mathbb{G}_2$ be a bilinear map which will be discussed in Section 2.3.

Definition 3. *The B-DH problem in $(\mathbb{G}_1, \mathbb{G}_2, \hat{e})$ is the following: given (P, aP, bP, cP) for some $a, b, c \in \mathbb{Z}_m^*$, compute $v \in \mathbb{G}_2$ such that $v = \hat{e}(P, P)^{abc}$.*

In practice, we make use of the Weil-pairing as the bilinear map. The security over groups in which the B-DH problem is defined is as follows.

Definition 4. *Let $\mathbb{G}$ be a cyclic group of a prime order with an arbitrary generator. For any polynomial-time probabilistic algorithm $\mathcal{A}$:*

- $\mathbb{G}$ *is said to be a τ-breakable D-DH group if the D-DH problem can be computed on $\mathbb{G}$ by $\mathcal{A}$ whose running time is bounded by τ.*
- $\mathcal{A}$ *is said to (t, ϵ)-break C-DH problem in $\mathbb{G}$ if the C-DH problem can be solved by $\mathcal{A}$ whose running time is bounded by t, the success probability $\mathrm{Succ}^{\mathbb{G}}(\mathcal{A}) \geq \epsilon$.*
- $\mathbb{G}$ *is said to be a (τ, t, ϵ)-B-DH group if it is a τ-breakable D-DH group and no algorithm (t, ϵ)-breaks C-DH on it.*

2.3 Weil-Pairing

We can make use of any bilinear map on an elliptic curve to construct a group $\mathbb{G}$ in which the C-DH problem is intractable, but the D-DH problem is tractable [11,2,3]. In particular, we make use of the Weil-pairing among bilinear maps.

Let E be a elliptic curve over a base field K and let $\mathbb{G}_1$ and $\mathbb{G}_2$ be two cyclic groups of order m for some large prime m. The *Weil pairing* [22,12,4,2,3] is defined by a bilinear map e,

$$e : \mathbb{G}_1 \times \mathbb{G}_1 \longrightarrow \mathbb{G}_2,$$

where $\mathbb{G}_1$ corresponds to the additive group of points of E/K, and $\mathbb{G}_2$ corresponds to the multiplicative group of an extension field $\overline{K}$ of K.

Let $P, Q \in \mathbb{G}_1$. The Weil pairing e has the following properties:

1. *Identity:* For all $P \in \mathbb{G}_1$, $e(P, P) = 1$.
2. *Alternation:* For all $P, Q \in \mathbb{G}_1$, $e(P, Q) = e(Q, P)^{-1}$.
3. *Bilinearity:* For all $P, Q, R \in \mathbb{G}_1$, $e(P+Q, R) = e(P, R) \cdot e(Q, R)$ and $e(P, Q + R) = e(P, Q) \cdot e(P, R)$.
4. *Non-degeneracy:* If $e(P, Q) = 1$ for all $Q \in \mathbb{G}_1$, then $P = \mathcal{O}$, where $\mathcal{O}$ is a point at infinity.

In addition to these properties, we have an efficient algorithm to compute $e(P, Q)$ for all $P, Q \in \mathbb{G}_1$ by [14]. In practice, in our basic scheme, we employ the *modified* Weil-pairing $\hat{e}(P, Q) = e(P, \phi(Q))$, where ϕ is an automorphism on the group of points of E [2,3]. For more details, we can refer to [4], [2], and [12].

As noted in [2], the existence of the bilinear map e implies (1) DLP in $\mathbb{G}_1$ can be reduced to DLP in $\mathbb{G}_2$, (2) C-DH problem in $\mathbb{G}_1$ is still hard even though D-DH in $\mathbb{G}_1$ is easy [11].

3 Basic Identification Scheme

For a security parameter k, a pair of secret and public parameters is generated as follows:

Key generation.
On input k, the key generation algorithm $\mathcal{G}$ works as follows:

1. Generate two cyclic groups $\mathbb{G}_1$ and $\mathbb{G}_2$ of order m for some large prime m and a bilinear map $\hat{e} : \mathbb{G}_1 \times \mathbb{G}_1 \to \mathbb{G}_2$.
2. Generate an arbitrary generator $P \in \mathbb{G}_1$.
3. Choose randomly $a, b, c \in \mathbb{Z}_m^*$ and compute $v = \hat{e}(P, P)^{abc}$.
4. The public parameter is $\mathsf{Pub} = \langle \mathbb{G}_1, \mathbb{G}_2, P, aP, bP, cP, \hat{e}, v \rangle$, and the secret parameter is $\mathsf{Sec} = \langle a, b, c \rangle$. And then publish them.

Protocol actions between $\mathcal{P}$ and $\mathcal{V}$.
As is the case for other identification schemes, this scheme consists of several rounds. The protocol executes just once the following:

1. $\mathcal{P}$ chooses $r_1, r_2, r_3 \in \mathbb{Z}_m^*$ at random, computes $x = \hat{e}(P, P)^{r_1 r_2 r_3}$, $Q = r_1 r_2 r_3 P$, and sends $\langle x, Q \rangle$ to $\mathcal{V}$.
2. $\mathcal{V}$ picks $\omega \in \mathbb{Z}_m^*$ at random, and sends $R = \omega P$ to $\mathcal{P}$.
3. On receiving R, $\mathcal{P}$ sets $S = r_1 r_2 r_3 R$, computes $Y \in \mathbb{G}_1$ such that

$$Y = abcP + (a + b + c)S,$$

and sends it to $\mathcal{V}$; $\mathcal{V}$ accepts $\mathcal{P}$'s proof of identity if both $x = \hat{e}(P, Q)$ and $\hat{e}(Y, P) = v \cdot \hat{e}(aP + bP + cP, Q)^\omega$, and rejects otherwise.

4   Proof of Security

Our proof of security is based on the intractability of the B-DH problem. First, we formally describe this assumption as follows, called as it the bilinear Diffie-Hellman Intractability Assumption (B-DHIA):

Definition 5. *Let Z be a probability space consisting uniform distribution over all integers in $\mathbb{Z}_m^*$. Let G_1 be a probability space consisting the uniform distribution over all elements of the form $nP \neq \mathcal{O} \in \mathbb{G}_1$, where $n \in_{\mathcal{U}} Z$ and let G_2 be a probability space consisting of uniform distribution over all elements in $\mathbb{G}_2$. B-DHIA is defined as the following: Given $C = \hat{e}(P, P)^{abc} \in \mathbb{G}_2$, for all polynomial-time probabilistic algorithm $\mathcal{A}$, for all constant $c > 0$, and for all sufficiently large k,*

$$\Pr_{G_2} \left[C = C' \left| \begin{array}{l} x \leftarrow Z, xP \in G_1; \\ y \leftarrow Z, yP \in G_1; \\ z \leftarrow Z, zP \in G_1; \\ C' \leftarrow \mathcal{A}(\hat{e}, xP, yP, zP) \end{array} \right. \right] < k^{-c}.$$

Now we are ready to prove:

Theorem 1. *Under B-DHIA, the basic identification scheme on (τ, t, ϵ)-B-DH groups is secure against active attacks.*

Proof. As mentioned before, the basic way of proving this theorem is just to show that any adversary $\mathcal{I}$ who succeeds in impersonating with non-negligible probability can be reduced into a polynomial-time probabilistic algorithm $\mathcal{A}$

that (τ, t, ϵ)-breaks C-DH problem with non-negligible probability. This will be proved in Lemma 2.

First to construct such an adversary $\mathcal{I} = (\tilde{\mathcal{P}}, \tilde{\mathcal{V}})$, we consider the adversary with the following polynomials [21]:

- $T_{\mathcal{V}}(k)$: a time bound required for $\tilde{\mathcal{V}}$ to run the protocol once with $\bar{\mathcal{P}}$ including $\bar{\mathcal{P}}$'s computing time.
- $N_{\mathcal{V}}(k)$: an iteration bound for $\tilde{\mathcal{V}}$ to run the protocol with $\bar{\mathcal{P}}$.
- $T_{\text{off}}(k)$: an off-line time bound for $\tilde{\mathcal{V}}$ to spend other than running the protocol with $\bar{\mathcal{P}}$.
- $T_{\mathcal{P}}(k)$: a time bound for $\tilde{\mathcal{P}}$ to run the protocol with $\bar{\mathcal{V}}$.

Then for a given public parameter Pub and "help string" h, let

$$\Pr[(\tilde{\mathcal{P}}(h), \tilde{\mathcal{V}}(\text{Pub}) = 1] = \varepsilon(h, \text{Pub}),$$

where the probability is taken over the coin tosses of $\tilde{\mathcal{P}}$ and $\tilde{\mathcal{V}}$. Since we assume that the adversary succeeds in breaking the protocol, there must exist polynomial $\Pi_1(k)$ and $\Pi_2(k)$ such that, for sufficiently large k,

$$\Pr\left[\varepsilon(h, \text{Pub}) \geq \tfrac{1}{\Pi_2(k)} \;\middle|\; \begin{matrix} (\text{Sec}, \text{Pub}) \leftarrow \mathcal{G}(1^k); \\ h \leftarrow (\bar{\mathcal{P}}(\text{Sec}, \text{Pub}), \tilde{\mathcal{V}}(\text{Pub})) \end{matrix} \right] \geq \frac{1}{\Pi_1(k)}.$$

Lemma 1. *Let $\hat{e}$ be the modified Weil-pairing as defined in Section 2.3. The sample space is the set of all triples $\mathcal{S} = \{(P, Q) | P, Q \in E(K)\}$, where E is an elliptic curve over K, and the distribution on the sample points is uniform, i.e., $P, Q \in_{\mathcal{U}} \mathcal{S}$. Let a, b, and c be indeterminates and consider the polynomial*

$$e_{a,b,c}(P, Q) = \hat{e}(P, Q)^{abc}.$$

For all $a, b, c \in \mathbb{Z}_m^*$, define random variable

$$X_i(a, b, c) = e_{a_i, b_i, c_i}(P, Q).$$

Then $\langle X_0, \ldots, X_{\ell(m)-1} \rangle$, where $\ell(m)$ is the order of the extension field $\overline{K}$ of K, are uniformly distributed in $\overline{K}$ and pairwise independent.

Proof. For any pair i, j in positive integers, $i \neq j$, and for any pair of points $P, Q \in E(K)$, there is a unique solution $a, b, c \in \mathbb{Z}_m^*$ to the pair of equations:

$$e_{a_i, b_i, c_i}(P, Q) = \alpha,$$
$$e_{a_j, b_j, c_j}(P, Q) = \beta.$$

Thus, $\Pr\left[(X_i(P, Q) = \alpha) \wedge (X_j(P, Q) = \beta)\right] = \Pr[X_i(P, Q) = \alpha] \cdot \Pr[X_j(P, Q) = \beta] = 1/\ell(m)^2$. ∎

Lemma 2. *Assume that there exists an adversary $\mathcal{I}$ as above. Then there exists a polynomial-time probabilistic algorithm $\mathcal{A}$ that (t, ϵ)-breaks* C-DH *problem, whose running time τ is defined by*

$$O((N_{\mathcal{V}}(k)T_{\mathcal{V}}(k) + T_{\mathcal{P}}(k))\Pi_2(k) + T_{\mathsf{off}}(k))$$

and for a valid C-DH *value C, the success probability ϵ is bounded by*

$$\Pr_{G_2}\left[C = C' \left| \begin{array}{l} x \leftarrow Z, xP \in G_1; \\ y \leftarrow Z, yP \in G_1; \\ z \leftarrow Z, zP \in G_1; \\ C' \leftarrow \mathcal{A}(\hat{e}, xP, yP, zP) \end{array} \right. \right] \geq \frac{\Pi_1(k)^{-1}}{16}.$$

Proof. First let E denote an elliptic curve over a field K, with $E[m]$ its group of m-torsion points. From the definition of the Weil pairing, we know that if $p = 0$ or p does not divides m then $E[m] \cong (\mathbb{Z}/m\mathbb{Z}) \times (\mathbb{Z}/m\mathbb{Z})$, where p is the characteristic of the field. Let Φ be a natural map in the modified Weil pairing. Note that, for random $P \in E(K)$, revealing $\hat{e}(P, P)$ gives no information on $\Phi(P)$; *i.e.* the distribution of $\hat{e}(P, P)$ and $\Phi(P)$ are independent from Lemma 1.

Throughout this paper, the underlying probability space consists of the random choice of input $x, y, z \in \mathbb{Z}_m^*$ and $P \in_R E(K)$ including the coin tosses of the algorithm.

As a proving method, rather than constructing the algorithm $\mathcal{A}$ *in toto*, we will increasingly construct $\mathcal{A}$ in series of "phases". The algorithm runs in five phases. In the first phase, we generate a public parameter $\mathsf{Pub} = \langle P, aP, bP \rangle$ with the corresponding secret parameter $\mathsf{Sec} = \langle a, b \rangle$.

In this phase we simulate the view that the adversary $\mathcal{I}$ would have if it interacted with a proving holding a "real" witness. In the second phase we make the adversary try to convince a honest verifier. In the third phase we use the approximate witness to solve the C-DH problem, $\hat{e}(P, P)^{ab}$. In the fourth phase, we rerun the adversary $\mathcal{I}$ with the public parameter $\mathsf{Pub} = \langle P, aP, bP, cP \rangle$ with additional value cP and its corresponding secret parameter $\mathsf{Sec} = \langle a, b, c \rangle$. In practice, this phase simply executes the above three phases repeatedly. In the last phase, the final algorithm $\mathcal{A}$ is constructed, which solves the C-DH problem, $\hat{e}(P, P)^{abc}$.

Phase 1. This phase takes as input P, aP, bP, runs in the expected time

$$O(N_{\mathcal{V}}(k)T_{\mathcal{V}}(k)\Pi_2(k) + T_{\mathsf{off}}(k)),$$

and outputs $(\tilde{a}, \gamma_i^f, v, h)$, where $v = \hat{e}(P, P)^{\tilde{a}\gamma_i^f}$, and h is a `"help string"`. In addition, we know that

i. $\Pr[\varepsilon(h, \mathsf{Pub}) \geq \Pi_2(k)^{-1}] \geq \Pi_1(k)^{-1}$,
ii. The distribution of $\Phi(\tilde{c})$ is uniform and independent of that of (h, Pub).

This stage runs as follows: We choose $\tilde{a}, \gamma_i^f \in \mathbb{Z}_m^*$, at random and compute $v = \hat{e}(P, P)^{\tilde{a}\gamma_i^f}$ and $\hat{X}_i \equiv \tilde{a}\gamma_i^f \pmod{m}$, where $f \not\equiv (m-1) \pmod{m}$. With the help of D-DH oracle, we can easily verify that $(P, \tilde{a}P, \gamma_i{}^f P, abP)$ is a valid DH value. We then simulate the interaction $(\bar{\mathcal{P}}(\cdot, \mathsf{Pub}), \tilde{\mathcal{V}}(\mathsf{Pub}))$.

To simulate the interaction, we employ a zero-knowledge simulation technique [9,21]. We then modify the identification protocol as the following:

I. $\bar{\mathcal{P}}$ chooses $\omega_0', r_1, r_2 \in \mathbb{Z}_m^*$ at random, computes $x = \hat{e}(P, P)^{\omega_0' r_1 r_2}$, $Q = \omega_0' r_1 r_2 P$, and sends $\langle x, Q \rangle$ to $\tilde{\mathcal{V}}$.

II. $\tilde{\mathcal{V}}$ chooses $\omega \in \mathbb{Z}_m^*$ at random, sets $R = \omega P$, and sends R to $\bar{\mathcal{P}}$.

III. On receiving R, $\bar{\mathcal{P}}$ checks $\hat{e}(R, P) = \hat{e}\left(\frac{\tilde{a}+\gamma_i{}^f - \omega_1}{(\tilde{a}+\gamma_i{}^f)\omega_0} P, P\right)$. If $\omega_0' \neq \omega_0$, we go back to step I. Otherwise, $\bar{\mathcal{P}}$ sets $S = r_1 r_2 P$, computes $Y = \tilde{a}\gamma_i{}^f P + (\tilde{a} + \gamma_i{}^f - \omega_1) S$, and sends it to $\tilde{\mathcal{V}}$.

When the adversary completes the protocol, we outputs the **"help string"** h that $\tilde{\mathcal{V}}$ outputs, along with $\hat{X}_i$.

In this step, the distribution of C is uniformly distributed in $\mathbb{G}_2$, and its distribution is independent of every variable other than in the adversary's view up to that point, and is also independent of the hidden variable ω'. Therefore, up to this point, this simulation is perfectly correct, and furthermore, the probability that $\omega_0 = \omega_0'$ is $1/|\mathbb{Z}_m^*|$. If $\omega_0 = \omega_0'$, then

$$v \cdot \hat{e}(\tilde{a}P + \tilde{b}P, Q)^\omega = v \cdot \hat{e}(\tilde{a}P + \gamma_i{}^f P, \omega_0' r_1 r_2 P)^\omega$$
$$= \hat{e}(P, P)^{\tilde{a}\gamma_i{}^f} \cdot \hat{e}(P, P)^{(\tilde{a}+\gamma_i{}^f)\omega_0' r_1 r_2 \omega}$$
$$= \hat{e}(P, P)^{\tilde{a}\gamma_i{}^f + (\tilde{a}+\gamma_i{}^f)\omega_0' r_1 r_2 \omega},$$

and

$$\hat{e}(Y, P) = \hat{e}(\tilde{a}\gamma_i{}^f P + (\tilde{a} + \gamma_i{}^f - \omega_1) r_1 r_2 P, P)$$
$$= \hat{e}(P, P)^{\tilde{a}\gamma_i{}^f + (\tilde{a}+\gamma_i{}^f - \omega_1) r_1 r_2}.$$

Since $\omega_0 = \omega_0'$ and

$$\tilde{a}\gamma_i{}^f + (\tilde{a} + \gamma_i{}^f)\omega_0' r_1 r_2 \omega \equiv \tilde{a}\gamma_i{}^f + (\tilde{a} + \gamma_i{}^f)\omega_0' r_1 r_2 \frac{\tilde{a} + \gamma_i{}^f - \omega_1}{(\tilde{a} + \gamma_i{}^f)\omega_0}$$
$$\equiv \tilde{a}\gamma_i{}^f + (\tilde{a} + \gamma_i{}^f - \omega_1) r_1 r_2,$$

we have $\hat{e}(Y, P) = v \cdot \hat{e}(\tilde{a}P + \tilde{b}P, Q)^\omega$.

Moreover, C reveals no information of $\Phi(Q_1), \Phi(Q_2)$, and $\Phi(\mathsf{Sec})$, and the distribution of $\Phi(Y)$ is uniform and independent of $\Phi(\mathsf{Sec})$. From the above result, the expected value of the total number of iteration rounds is $(|\mathbb{Z}_m^*| \cdot N_{\mathcal{V}}(k))$. This completes *Phase 1*.

Phase 2. This phase takes as input h, Pub, and output from *Phase 1*, and runs in time $O(T_{\mathcal{P}}(k)\Pi_2(k))$. It outputs Fail or Success according to success outputs u such that $u \equiv \tilde{a}\gamma_i{}^f \equiv ab \pmod{m}$, since $\hat{e}(P, P)^u = \hat{e}(P, P)^{\tilde{a}\gamma_i{}^f} = \hat{e}(P, P)^{ab}$. The probability of success, given that $\varepsilon(h, \mathsf{Pub}) \geq \Pi_2(k)^{-1}$, is at least $1/2$.

For the sake of convenience, let $\varepsilon = \varepsilon(h, \mathsf{Pub})$, and assume $\varepsilon \geq \Pi_2(k)^{-1}$.

This stage runs as follows: First run $(\tilde{\mathcal{P}}(h), \bar{\mathcal{V}}(\mathsf{Pub}))$ up to $\lceil \Pi_2(k) \rceil$ times, or until $\bar{\mathcal{V}}$ accepts. If $\bar{\mathcal{V}}$ accepts, let

$$\hat{e}(Y, P) = \hat{e}(\tilde{a}\tilde{b}P + (\tilde{a} + \gamma_i{}^f - \omega_1)S$$
$$= \hat{e}(\omega P, P)^{\tilde{a}\tilde{b} + (\tilde{a} + \gamma_i{}^f - \omega_1)r_1 r_2}$$
$$= v \cdot \hat{e}(\tilde{a}P + \gamma_i{}^f P, Q)^\omega$$

be the accepting conversation. Fixing the coin tosses of $\tilde{\mathcal{P}}$, run the interaction again up to $\lceil 4\Pi_2(k) \rceil$, or until $\bar{\mathcal{V}}$ accepts again with a challenge $\omega'' \not\equiv \omega \pmod{m}$. In this case, let $\hat{X}_j \equiv \tilde{a}\gamma_j{}^f \pmod{m}$. If $\bar{\mathcal{V}}$ accepts this challenge, then we have another accepting conversation

$$\hat{e}(Y', P) = \hat{e}(\tilde{a}\gamma_j{}^f P + (\tilde{a} + \gamma_j{}^f - \omega_1')S$$
$$= \hat{e}(\omega P, P)^{\tilde{a}\gamma_j{}^f + (\tilde{a} + \gamma_j{}^f - \omega_1')r_1 r_2}$$
$$= v \cdot \hat{e}(\tilde{a}P + \gamma_j{}^f P, Q)^{\omega''}$$

where $u \equiv a\gamma_i{}^f \pmod{m}$, $u \equiv a\gamma_j{}^f \pmod{m}$, and $\omega a\gamma_i{}^f \equiv \omega'' a\gamma_j{}^f \pmod{m}$. Therefore, we can easily calculate $f = \log_{\frac{\gamma_j}{\gamma_i}} \omega - \log_{\frac{\gamma_j}{\gamma_i}} \omega''$.

To show that there is another solution with non-negligible probability, we make use of the same method as employed in [6,17,21]. Let M be a Boolean matrix of which rows are indexed by the coin tosses ω' of $\tilde{\mathcal{P}}$ and of which columns are indexed by the challenge ω of $\bar{\mathcal{V}}$. Let $M(\omega', \omega) = 1$ if and only if the pair of (ω', ω) makes $\bar{\mathcal{V}}$ be convinced by $\tilde{\mathcal{P}}$.

Just the same as in [6,17,21], we call a row ω' in M "heavy" if the fraction of 1's in this row is at least $3\varepsilon/4$. Then the fraction of 1's in M that lies in heavy rows is at least $1/4$. The reason comes from the following equations: let r be the number of rows in M and c be the number of columns in M, and $\bar{r}$ be the number of non-heavy rows, then the total number of 1's in M is $rc\varepsilon$. Then the total number of 1's that lies in non-heavy rows is $\bar{r}c\frac{3\varepsilon}{4} \leq \left(\frac{3}{4}\right)rc\varepsilon$. Therefore, the fraction of 1's in heavy rows is induced by

$$rc\varepsilon - \bar{r}c\frac{3\varepsilon}{4} \geq rc\varepsilon - rc\frac{3\varepsilon}{4}$$
$$= \frac{1}{4}(rc\varepsilon).$$

Now consider an accepting conversations by (ω', ω) such that $M(\omega', \omega) = 1$. Since we have another accepting conversation by (ω'', ω) satisfying that $M(\omega'', \omega) = 1$. Then the fraction of ω'' which satisfies

$$M(\omega'', \omega) = 1 \qquad \omega'' \not\equiv \omega \pmod{m}$$

is at least

$$\left| \frac{3\varepsilon}{4} - \frac{1}{|\mathbb{Z}_m^*| - 2} \right| \geq \left| \frac{3(\Pi_2(k)^{-1})}{4} - \frac{1}{\Pi_2(k)} \right|$$
$$= \frac{1}{4}\frac{1}{\Pi_2(k)} = \frac{\Pi_2(k)^{-1}}{4}.$$

To complete the construction of this phase, we use the simple fact that if ε is a small real number, then $(1 - \varepsilon) \leq e^{-\varepsilon}$ [23]. Let ε be a success probability. When an experiment is repeated at least t times, the probability that all of experiments fail is at most $(1 - \varepsilon)^t \leq e^{-t\varepsilon}$. Thus, if $t \geq 1/\varepsilon$, the probability that at least one experiment succeeds is at least $1 - e^{-1}$. Therefore, for two accepting conversations, the probability that the above procedure succeeds is at least

$$(1 - e^{-1}) \cdot \frac{1}{4} \cdot (1 - e^{-1}) = \frac{\left(1 - e^{-1}\right)^2}{4}.$$

Thus, by a simple calculation, we can obtain the fact that one of fourteen experiments must succeed, thus the probability that one of seven experiments succeeds is at least $1/2$.

Phase 3. This phase takes as input, the output $\hat{X}_i$ from *Phase 1*, and the value u from *Phase 2*. Its running time is $O(\Pi_2(k) \cdot \log(\Pi_2)^2)$. When *Phase 2* succeeds, the probability that it solves the C-DH problem is $1/2$.

Recall that $\omega \equiv \frac{\tilde{a} + \gamma_i{}^f - \omega_1}{(\tilde{a} + \gamma_i{}^f)\omega_0} \pmod{m}$, if $\omega' = \omega_0$ then

$$\tilde{a}\gamma_i{}^f \equiv \hat{X}_i \pmod{m}, \tag{1}$$

$$f \not\equiv (m - 1) \pmod{m} \quad \text{and} \quad f = \log_{\frac{\gamma_j}{\gamma_i}} \omega - \log_{\frac{\gamma_j}{\gamma_i}} \omega'', \tag{2}$$

$$u \equiv \tilde{a}\gamma_i{}^f \pmod{m} \quad \text{or} \quad u \equiv \tilde{a}\gamma_j{}^f \pmod{m}, \tag{3}$$

and

$$u \equiv \tilde{a}\tilde{b} \equiv ab \pmod{m}.$$

Now consider only the case where *Phase 2* succeeds at least with the probability $1/2$. First from Eq. (1), we have $\hat{e}(aP, \gamma_i P) = \hat{e}(P, P)^{a\gamma_i}$, and from Eqs. (2) and (3), we have

$$\begin{aligned}
\hat{e}(P, P)^u &= \hat{e}(P, P)^{\tilde{a}\gamma_i{}^f} \\
&= \hat{e}(\tilde{a}P, \gamma_i{}^f P) \\
&= \hat{e}(\tilde{a}P, \tilde{b}P) \\
&= \hat{e}(P, P)^{\tilde{a}\tilde{b}} = \hat{e}(P, P)^{ab}.
\end{aligned}$$

Then with the probability $1/2$, we can solve the C-DH problem from the following equations: This completes *Phase 3*.

It follows that, for sufficiently large k, the overall success probability of the algorithm $\mathcal{A}$ is at least

$$\varepsilon(h, \mathsf{Pub}) \times \frac{1}{2} \times \frac{1}{2} = \Pi_1(k)^{-1} \times \frac{1}{2} \times \frac{1}{2} = \frac{\Pi_1(k)^{-1}}{4}.$$

Phase 4. This phase repeatedly executes *Phase 1* to *Phase 3* to solve the C-DH problem, $\hat{e}(P, P)^{xc}$, where $x \equiv ab \pmod{m}$. If phases from 1 to 3 succeed, it is straightforward that this phase must succeed with the above probability.

Phase 5. If *Phase 4* succeeds with given probability, it is equivalent to solving the C-DH problem

$$\hat{e}(P, P)^{xc} = \hat{e}(P, P)^{abc}$$

with probability

$$\Pr_{G_2}[C = C'] = \frac{\Pi_1(k)^{-1}}{16}.$$

This completes the proof of Lemma 2.   ∎

Therefore, we can conclude that the basic scheme satisfies the requirement of Definition 1. This completes the proof of Theorem 1.   ∎

5   Generalized Scheme

We now describe a generalized model of the basic identification scheme. The generalized identification scheme extends the basic scheme in Section 3 using k random numbers. The key generation algorithm $\mathcal{G}$ is similar to that of the basic scheme except generating k random numbers.

Key generation.
On input k, the key generation algorithm $\mathcal{G}$ works as follows:

1. Generates two cyclic groups $\mathbb{G}_1$ and $\mathbb{G}_2$ of order m for some large prime m and a bilinear map $\hat{e} : \mathbb{G}_1 \times \mathbb{G}_1 \to \mathbb{G}_2$.
2. Generates an arbitrary generator $P \in \mathbb{G}_1$.
3. Chooses randomly $a_1, \dots, a_{3k} \in \mathbb{Z}_m^*$ and computes $v_1 = \hat{e}(P, P)^{a_1 a_2 a_3}, \cdots,$ $v_k = \hat{e}(P, P)^{a_{3k-2} a_{3k-1} a_{3k}}$.
4. The public parameter is $\mathsf{Pub} = \langle \mathbb{G}_1, \mathbb{G}_2, P, a_1 P, \dots, a_{3k} P, \hat{e}, v_1, \cdots, v_k \rangle$, and the secret parameter is $\mathsf{Sec} = \langle a_1, \dots, a_{3k} \rangle$. And then publishes them.

Protocol actions between $\mathcal{P}$ and $\mathcal{V}$.
The generalized scheme is similar to the basic scheme, however, each round is performed in parallel as follows:

1. $\mathcal{P}$ chooses $r_1, r_2, r_3 \in \mathbb{Z}_m^*$ at random, computes $x = \hat{e}(P, P)^{r_1 r_2 r_3}$, $Q_1 = r_1 r_2 r_3 P$, and sends $\langle x, Q \rangle$ to B.
2. $\mathcal{V}$ picks $\omega_1, \dots, \omega_k \in \mathbb{Z}_m^*$ at random, and sends $R_1 = \omega_1 P, \dots, R_k = \omega_k P$ to $\mathcal{P}$.

3. On receiving k random values, $\mathcal{P}$ sets

$$S_1 = r_1 r_2 r_3 R_1, S_2 = r_1 r_2 r_3 R_2, \ldots, S_k = r_1 r_2 r_3 R_k,$$

computes Y such that

$$Y = \sum_{i=1}^{k} a_{3i-2} a_{3i-1} a_{3i} P + \sum_{i=1}^{k} (a_{3i-2} + a_{3i-1} + a_{3i}) S_i$$

and sends it to $\mathcal{V}$; $\mathcal{V}$ accepts if both $x = \hat{e}(P, Q)$ and $\hat{e}(Y, P) = \prod_{i=1}^{k} v_i \cdot \hat{e}(a_{3i-2} P + a_{3i-1} P + a_{3i} P, Q)^{\omega_i}$, and rejects otherwise.

Theorem 2. *Under B-DHIA, the generalized identification scheme in this section on (τ', t', ϵ')-B-DH groups is secure against active attacks.*

Proof(sketch) At first we assume that there exists an (t', ϵ')-breakable adversary $\mathcal{A}$ who can break this identification scheme. Then from the proof of Theorem 1, we can prove Theorem 2.

6 Comparison

In this section, we compare our basic scheme with the prior schemes in terms of not only the computation overhead in the light of key size, communication overhead, processing complexity but also their security.

We assume that an elliptic curve E over a base field K is chosen in the same manner as [2]. That is, let E be the elliptic curve defined by the equation $y^2 = x^3 + 1$ over $\mathbb{F}_p$, where p is a prime satisfying $p \equiv 2 \pmod 3$ and $p = 6q - 1$ for some prime $q > 3$. Note that for the sake of the convenience m is replaced by q. As pointed out in [2], from the practical point of view, we can assume that p and q is a 512-bit prime and a 140-bit prime respectively, since the MOV reduction [13] then leads to a DLP in a finite field of size approximately 2^{1024}.

In addition, we assume that system parameters p and q for our basic scheme, Schnorr, and Okamoto are 512-bit and 140-bit respectively, and the modulus n for FFS, GQ scheme is 512-bit. We assume that the standard binary method is employed for the modular exponentiation as well as for the point multiplication in polynomial basis form. We also assume that the parameters for FFS are $l = 20$ and $t = 1$. Here, we only consider Okamoto scheme as an *Identification scheme 1* proposed in [15]. Note that for the purpose of comparison with arithmetic operations of each scheme, we denote M the cost of modular multiplication over a given finite field and A the cost of point addition over a given elliptic curve. Table 1 shows the comparison of identification schemes. If the Weierstraß equation over the affine coordinates in fields of characteristic two is given by $y^2 + xy = x^3 + a_2 x^2 + a_6$, then our scheme has $a_2 = 0$. Furthermore, since a generator P of the group $\mathbb{G}_1$ is initially known all parties, we can enable the point multiplication in elliptic curves to be more faster. In fact, the point multiplication consists of point doublings and point additions. The binary

Table 1. Comparison of identification schemes

	Our scheme	Schnorr	Okamoto	FFS	GQ
Security proof	Yes	Yes	Yes	Yes	Yes
Secure against active attacks	Yes	No	Yes	Yes	No
Underlying problem	B-DH	DLP	DLP	RSA	RSA
ID-based variant	Possible	Possible	Possible	Possible	Possible
Public key size (bits)	512	512	512	10,240	1,024
Private key size (bits)	420	140	280	10,240	512
Communication overhead (bits)	932	672	812	1,044	1,044
Preprocessing (Prover) (# of field multiplications or point additions)	140A	210M	245M	1M	30M
On-line processing (Prover) (# of field multiplications over a given finite field)	2M	Almost 0M	Almost 0M	10M	31M
On-line processing (Verifier) (# of field multiplications over a given finite field)	141M	210M	248M	11M	35M

method requires $(\ell-1)$ point doublings and $(W-1)$ point additions, where ℓ is the bit length and W the Hamming weight of the binary expansion, in general, $W = \ell/2$. Therefore, if the point doublings are pre-computed, the point multiplication requires $\frac{\ell}{2}$A-point addition in average and ℓA-point addition in the worst case [4]. The pre-computation is possible because P is initially given. In these cases, we can estimate that A costs less than or equal to two times M, i.e., $A \le 2M$.

From Table 1, we can state the properties of our scheme as follows: (1) Our scheme is more efficient than Schnorr and Okamoto with respect to preprocessing of prover and on-line processing overhead of both parties (prover and verifier). (2) However, our scheme requires memory for secret key about two times that of Schnorr and Okamoto. Moreover, its communication overhead increases around four times more than those two schemes.

7 Concluding Remarks

In this paper we present a practical construction of a new identification scheme based on the B-DH problem using the Weil pairing. Then we prove that our identification scheme is secure against active attacks. Our proposal can be extended to a signature scheme using the Weil pairing. Also similar to IBE (Identity-Based Encryption) scheme proposed by Boneh et al., our scheme can be associated with the public identity such as e-mail. It remains as an open problem to implement an algorithm to efficiently compute the Weil pairing as suggested in [24].

Acknowledgement. The authors are grateful to Fangguo Zhang for his useful comments to improve the 1st version of this paper.

References

1. M. Bellare and P. Rogaway, "Random Oracles are Practical: A Paradigm for Designing Efficient Protocols", *ACM Conference on Computer and Communications Security*, pp. 62–73, 1993.
2. D. Boneh and M. Franklin, "ID-based encryption from the Weil-pairing", *Advances in Cryptology – Crypto '2001*, LNCS 2139, Springer-Verlag, pp. 213–229, 2001.
3. D. Boneh, H. Shacham, and B. Lynn, "Short signatures from the Weil-pairing", *Advances in Cryptology – Asiacrypt '2001*, LNCS 2248, Springer-Verlag, pp. 514–532, 2001.
4. I. Blake, G. Seroussi and N. Smart, "Elliptic curves in cryptography", Cambridge University Prress, LNS 265, 1999.
5. J.-S. Coron, "On the security of full domain hash", *Advances in Cryptology – Crypto '2000*, LNCS 1880, Springer-Verlag, pp. 229–235, 2000.
6. U. Feige, A. Fiat, and A. Shamir, "Zero-knowledge proofs of identity", *J. Cryptology*, 1: 77–94, 1988.
7. A. Fiat and A. Shamir, "How to prove yourself: pratical solutions to identification and signature problems", *Advances in Cryptology – Crypto '86*, LNCS 263, Springer-Verlag, pp. 186-194, 1987.
8. O. Goldreich and H. Krawczyk, "On the composition of zero-knowledge proof systems", In *Proceedings of the 17th ICALP*, LNCS 443, Springer-Verlag, pp. 268–282, 1990.
9. S. Goldwasser, S. Micali, and C. Rackoff, "The knowledge complexity of interactive proof systems", *SIAM J. Comput.*, 18: 186–208, 1989.
10. L. Guillou and J. Quisquater, "A practical zero-knowledge protocol fitted to security microprocessors minimizing both transmission and memory", *Advances in Cryptology – Eurocrypt '88*, LNCS 330, Springer-Verlag, pp. 123–128, 1989.
11. A. Joux and K. Nguyen, "Seperating decision Diffie-Hellman from Diffie-Hellman in cryptographic groups", available from `eprint.iacr.org`.
12. A. J. Menezes, "Elliptic curve public key cryptosystems", Kluwer Academic Publishers, 1993.
13. A. J. Menezes, T. Okamoto, and S. A. Vanstone, "Reducing elliptic curve logarithms to logarithms in a finite field", *IEEE Trans. Inform. Theory*, 39(1993), pp. 1639–1646.
14. V. Miller, "Short programs for functions on curves", unpublished manuscript, 1986.
15. T. Okamoto, "Provably secure and practical identification schemes and corresponding signature schemes", *Advances in Cryptology – Crypto '92*, LNCS 740, Springer-Verlag, pp. 31–53, 1993.
16. T. Okamoto and D. Pointcheval, "The gap-problem: a new class of problems for the security of cryptographic schemes", *PKC 2001*, LNCS 1992, Springer-Verlag, pp. 104–118, 2001.
17. K. Ohta and T. Okamoto, "A modification of the Fiat-Shamir scheme", *Advances in Cryptology – Crypto '88*, LNCS 403, Springer-Verlag, pp. 232–243, 1990.
18. C. Popescu, "An identification scheme based on the elliptic curve discrete logarithm problem", *IEEE High Performance Computing in the Asia-Pacific Region*, Volume: 2, pp. 624–625, 2000.
19. A.D. Santis, S. Micali, and G. Persiano, "Non-interactive zero-knowledge proof systems", *Advances in Cryptology – Crypto '87*, LNCS 293, pp. 52–72, 1988.
20. C. Schnorr, "Security of 2^t-root identification and signatures", *Advances in Cryptology – Crypto '96*, LNCS 1109, Springer-Verlag, pp. 143–156, 1996.

21. V. Shoup, "On the security of a practical identification scheme", *J. Cryptology* 12: 247–260, 1999.
22. J. H. Silverman, "The arithmetic of elliptic curves", Springer-Verlag, GTM 106, 1986.
23. D.R. Stinson, "Cryptography: Theory and Practice", CRC Press, Boca Raton, Florida, pp. 236, 1995.
24. T. Yamanaka, R. Sakai, and M. Kasahara, "Fast computation of pairings over elliptic curves", *Proc. of SCIS 2002*, pp. 709–714, Jan. 29 – Feb. 1, 2002, Shirahama, Japan.

A Brief Outline of Research on Correlation Immune Functions

Bimal Roy*

Applied Statistics Unit,
Indian Statistical Institute,
203, B.T. Road, Calcutta 700 108, INDIA
bimal@isical.ac.in

Abstract. The correlation immune functions have a rich history of research. Balanced correlation immune Boolean functions with high nonlinearity and algebraic degree are important in the design of stream cipher systems. In this paper we mainly outline the development in the field of constructing such functions. We also briefly survey related issues in this area.

Keywords: Algebraic Degree, Autocorrelation, Boolean Function, Balancedness, Correlation Immunity, Enumeration, Multiple Output Function, Nonlinearity, Stream Cipher, Symmetry.

1   Introduction

One standard model of stream cipher combines the outputs of several independent Linear Feedback Shift Registers using a nonlinear Boolean function. To be cryptographically robust, the Boolean function used in this model must be correlation immune [51,52]. Moreover, such functions should be balanced and should have high nonlinearity and algebraic degree [15]. See Section 2 for definitions.

Construction procedures for correlation immune (CI) functions were first described by Siegenthaler in [51]. One of the methods described in [51] is recursive, where a function of $(n + 1)$ variables is built from a function of n variables. The order of correlation immunity of the derived function also increases by one. Further attempts towards these constructions were made by Camion, Carlet, Charpin and Sendrier in [3], where construction procedure for a certain subset of correlation immune functions were described using orthogonal arrays. Seberry, Zhang and Zheng [49], also provided a method of constructing the same subset of correlation immune functions as in [3]. Importantly, they also considered the algebraic degree, nonlinearity and propagation characteristics of their construction method [49]. The construction proposed in [49] has been interpreted as concatenation of small affine functions in [26].

It was proved in [51] that for an n-variable Boolean function with order of correlation immunity m and algebraic degree d, $m + d \leq n$. Moreover, if

---

* This draft for the invited lecture has been prepared in collaboration with Dr. Subhamoy Maitra of Indian Statistical Institute.

L. Batten and J. Seberry (Eds.): ACISP 2002, LNCS 2384, pp. 379–394, 2002.
© Springer-Verlag Berlin Heidelberg 2002

the function is balanced, then $m + d \leq n - 1$. This is referred as Siegenthaler's inequality in the literature. The functions attaining the upper bound on algebraic degree are called optimized with respect to Siegenthaler's inequality.

In [26], some existing constructions were analyzed in details and functions with better nonlinearity were achieved by modification of some existing constructions [51,3,49]. The technique proposed in [49] has also been considered in [9]. It shows how concatenation of affine functions can provide good nonlinearity. However, the optimization of algebraic degree was not considered in [49,9].

The balanced correlation immune functions are also known as resilient functions. Construction of resilient functions by concatenating small affine functions was advanced in [43]. It has been shown in [43] that it is possible to construct balanced correlation immune functions with nonlinearity strictly greater than $2^{n-1} - 2^{\lceil \frac{n-1}{2} \rceil}$.

Apart from the deterministic construction techniques, search methods has also been applied for construction of such functions. Genetic algorithm was applied in [33] to design first order balanced correlation immune functions with high nonlinearity. Filiol and Fontaine [18, Section 5] describe a method to construct correlation immune functions using good initial functions achieved by searching over idempotents. Heuristic methods have also been applied in [37] in construction of correlation immune functions. These methods found to work well for Boolean functions upto 12 variables, though they could not actually generate any function which could not be achieved by deterministic construction techniques.

Upto 1999, the motivation was only towards construction of resilient functions with nonlinearity as high as possible. The question unattended upto 1999 was what could be the maximum nonlinearity of correlation immune and resilient Boolean functions? This problem has been taken care of in the year 2000 and almost at the same time three independent works were presented in this direction [44,55,60]. The work of Sarkar and Maitra [44] described the weight divisibility results of correlation immune and resilient Boolean functions and translated those results to provide nontrivial upper bounds on correlation immune and resilient Boolean functions. The work of Tarannikov [55] talked about the upper bound on nonlinearity without using the weight divisibility results. It identified that the functions achieving upper bound on nonlinearity must have the maximum possible algebraic degree. The work of Zheng and Zhang [60] presented detailed weight divisibility results on correlation immune Boolean functions. Thereafter, the weight divisibility results including the algebraic degree was settled by Carlet in [7] and subsequently in more details in [8].

Let us now concentrate on the exact upper bounds on nonlinearity of resilient Boolean functions from the weight divisibility results. We use the term $nlmax(n)$ to denote the maximum nonlinearity of any n-variable Boolean function. It is known that for even n, $nlmax(n) = 2^{n-1} - 2^{\frac{n}{2}-1}$ [42]. However, the problem remains open for odd n [40,41,36]. It is clear that the bent functions [42] cannot be correlation immune. To derive the upper bound on nonlinearity in case of odd n, we assume that the functions attaining the maximum possible nonlinearity $nlmax(n)$ may have correlation immunity property. We first consider the case of n-variable, m-resilient (balanced mth order correlation immune) functions of degree d and nonlinearity x.

1. If n is even, and $m + \lfloor \frac{n-m-2}{d} \rfloor > \frac{n}{2} - 2$, then $x \leq 2^{n-1} - 2^{m+1+\lfloor \frac{n-m-2}{d} \rfloor}$.
2. If n is even, and $m + \lfloor \frac{n-m-2}{d} \rfloor \leq \frac{n}{2} - 2$, then $x \leq 2^{n-1} - 2^{\frac{n}{2}-1} - 2^{m+1+\lfloor \frac{n-m-2}{d} \rfloor}$.
3. If n is odd, and $nlmax(n) \geq 2^{n-1} - 2^{m+1+\lfloor \frac{n-m-2}{d} \rfloor}$, then $x \leq 2^{n-1} - 2^{m+1+\lfloor \frac{n-m-2}{d} \rfloor}$.
4. If n is odd, and $nlmax(n) < 2^{n-1} - 2^{m+1+\lfloor \frac{n-m-2}{d} \rfloor}$, then x is the highest multiple of $2^{m+1+\lfloor \frac{n-m-2}{d} \rfloor}$ which is $\leq nlmax(n)$.

It is already explained that the maximum value of $d = n - m - 1$ and also the best possible nonlinearity is achievable in this case [55,7,8]. In this context, let us now explain the upper bound on nonlinearity for degree $n - m - 1$ functions.

1. If n is even, and $m > \frac{n}{2} - 2$, then $x \leq 2^{n-1} - 2^{m+1}$.
2. If n is even, and $m \leq \frac{n}{2} - 2$, then $x \leq 2^{n-1} - 2^{\frac{n}{2}-1} - 2^{m+1}$.
3. If n is odd, and $nlmax(n) \geq 2^{n-1} - 2^{m+1}$, then $x \leq 2^{n-1} - 2^{m+1}$.
4. If n is odd, and $nlmax(n) < 2^{n-1} - 2^{m+1}$, then x is the highest multiple of 2^{m+1} which is $\leq nlmax(n)$.

Given these upper bound results, the motivation clearly directs towards getting n-variable, m-resilient, degree $n-m-1$ functions achieving the upper bound on nonlinearity. Let us refer these functions as *optimized* functions. Tarannikov provided a recursive construction, which when properly used, can generate such functions [55] for certain ranges of order of correlation immunity. This construction was further analyzed in [56,17]. The construction of [55] was also modified in [38]. However, the deterministic constructions provided in [55,56,17,38] can not achieve some functions on low number of variables. Classical computer search has taken a major role in this direction and some important functions on 5 to 10 variables were identified in [38,32] by interlinking combinatorial results and computer search. Very recently simulated annealing techniques has also been applied to get such functions [13].

Enumeration of correlation immune functions has also been an interesting area of research as evident from [50,34,16,58,35,25,27]. All the works in this direction are mainly motivated towards finding out necessary and sufficient conditions in construction of such functions which in turn provides upper and lower bound on the number of correlation immune functions.

The paper is organized as follows. In the next section we present the basic definitions. In Section 3, we discuss the existing recursive constructions. The construction using small affine function concatenation is presented in Section 4. Search methods in this direction has been considered in Section 5. Other related issues are considered in the Section 6. In this section apart from the enumeration issues, we also discuss the autocorrelation properties of correlation immune functions. Moreover, nonlinearity issues of multiple output resilient functions have been mentioned.

2 Preliminaries

An n-variable Boolean function may be viewed as a mapping from $\{0,1\}^n$ into $\{0,1\}$. By Ω_n we mean the set of all Boolean functions of n variables. We interpret a Boolean function $f(X_1,\dots,X_n)$ as the output column of its *truth table* f, i.e., a binary string of length 2^n,

$$f = [f(0,0,\cdots,0), f(1,0,\cdots,0), f(0,1,\cdots,0),\dots,f(1,1,\cdots,1)].$$

For binary strings S_1, S_2 of the same length λ, we denote by $\#(S_1 = S_2)$ (respectively $\#(S_1 \neq S_2)$), the number of places where S_1 and S_2 are equal (respectively unequal). The *Hamming distance* between S_1, S_2 is denoted by $d(S_1, S_2)$, i.e.,

$$d(S_1, S_2) = \#(S_1 \neq S_2).$$

We also define

$$wd(S_1, S_2) = \#(S_1 = S_2) - \#(S_1 \neq S_2).$$

Note that, $wd(S_1, S_2) = \lambda - 2\, d(S_1, S_2)$. Also the *Hamming weight* or simply the *weight* of a binary string S is the number of ones in S. This is denoted by $wt(S)$. An n-variable function f is said to be *balanced* if its output column in the truth table contains equal number of 0's and 1's (i.e., $wt(f) = 2^{n-1}$).

Addition operator over $GF(2)$ is denoted by $+$. An n-variable Boolean function $f(X_1,\dots,X_n)$ can be considered to be a multivariate polynomial over $GF(2)$. This polynomial can be expressed as a sum of products representation of all distinct k-th order products $(0 \leq k \leq n)$ of the variables. More precisely, $f(X_1,\dots,X_n)$ can be written as

$$a_0 + \sum_{i=1}^{i=n} a_i X_i + \sum_{1 \leq i < j \leq n} a_{ij} X_i X_j + \dots + a_{12\dots n} X_1 X_2 \dots X_n,$$

where the coefficients $a_0, a_{ij},\dots,a_{12\dots n} \in \{0,1\}$. This representation of f is called the *algebraic normal form* (ANF) of f. The number of variables in the highest order product term with nonzero coefficient is called the *algebraic degree*, or simply the *degree* of f.

Consider $f_1, f_2 \in \Omega_{n-1}$ and $f \in \Omega_n$. Then by concatenation of f_1 and f_2, we mean that the output columns of truth table of f_1, f_2 will be concatenated to obtain the output column of the truth table of an n-variable function. We denote the concatenation of f_1, f_2 by $f_1 \| f_2$. Thus, $f = f_1 \| f_2$ means that in algebraic normal form, $f(X_1,\dots,X_n) = (1 + X_n) f_1(X_1,\dots,X_{n-1}) + X_n f_2(X_1,\dots,X_{n-1})$. Also, for the complement function of f we use the notation $\overline{f}$, i.e., $\overline{f} = 1 + f$.

Functions of degree at most one are called *affine* functions. An affine function with constant term equal to zero is called a *linear* function. The set of all n-variable affine (respectively linear) functions is denoted by $A(n)$ (respectively $L(n)$). The nonlinearity of an n-variable function f is

$$nl(f) = min_{g \in A(n)}(d(f, g)),$$

i.e., the distance from the set of all n-variable affine functions.

Let $X = (X_1, \ldots, X_n)$ and $\omega = (\omega_1, \ldots, \omega_n)$ both belong to $\{0,1\}^n$ and

$$X \cdot \omega = X_1\omega_1 + \ldots + X_n\omega_n.$$

Let $f(X)$ be a Boolean function on n variables. Then the *Walsh transform* of $f(X)$ is a real valued function over $\{0,1\}^n$ that can be defined as

$$W_f(\omega) = \sum_{X \in \{0,1\}^n} (-1)^{f(X) + X \cdot \omega}.$$

Note that $W_f(\omega) = wd(f, l_\omega)$, where l_ω denotes the linear function on n variables given by $l_\omega(X) = \omega \cdot X$. For a Boolean function f, we define

$$NZ(f) = \{\omega \mid W_f(\omega) \neq 0\},$$

where W_f is the Walsh transform of f.

Let us now consider the following characterization that has been presented in [22]. A function $f(X_1, \ldots, X_n)$ is m-th order *correlation immune* (CI) iff its Walsh transform satisfies $W_f(\omega) = 0$, for $1 \leq wt(\omega) \leq m$. Note that f is balanced iff $W_f(0) = 0$. Balanced m-th order correlation immune functions are called m-*resilient* functions. Thus, a function $f(X_1, \ldots, X_n)$ is m-resilient iff its Walsh transform satisfies $W_f(\omega) = 0$, for $0 \leq wt(\omega) \leq m$. Recently the characterization of correlation immune Boolean functions has been revisited in [45].

By an (n, m, d, x) function we denote an n-variable, m-resilient function with algebraic degree d and nonlinearity x. An $(n, 0, d, x)$ function denotes a balanced n-variable function with degree d and nonlinearity x, which is not correlation immune. By $[n, m, d, x]$ function we denote an n-variable unbalanced correlation immune function of order m, nonlinearity x and degree d. In the above notation a component is replaced by a '$-$', if it is not specified, e.g., $(n, m, -, x)$, when the degree is not specified.

3   Recursive Constructions

Let us consider a construction of (n, m, d, x) function f. The basic idea was proposed in [51, Section VI]. To start with, one can consider an unbalanced function g on $n - m - 1$ variables. Next note that the $(n - m)$-variable function $h = X_{n-m} + g(X_1, \ldots, X_{n-m-1})$ is balanced. Now consider the function f on n variables as $X_n + \ldots + X_{n-m+1} + h(X_1, \ldots, X_{n-m})$. This is an (n, m, d, x) function. We will talk about the values of d, x little later. That is after getting the balanced function h, addition of each new variable increases the order of correlation immunity by 1.

Extension of this kind of construction has been discussed in [3, Corollary 4.1]. Let $h_{k,i}$ be a k-variable resilient function of order i. Just as notation we consider the unbalanced functions as resilient functions of order -1 and balanced non correlation immune functions as resilient functions of order 0. It is now clear that $X_{k+1} + h_{k,i}$ is always a $(k + 1)$-variable, $(i + 1)$-resilient function [51]. Let us call this c (complement) operation, since the truth table of $h_{k,i}$ and its complement are concatenated to get the $(k + 1)$-variable function.

Now note the following two constructions also.

1. If i is even, then $(1+X_{k+1})h_{k,i}(X_1,\ldots,X_k)+X_{k+1}h_{k,i}(1+X_1,\ldots,1+X_k)$ is $(k+1)$-variable, $(i+1)$-resilient function. We call this as r (reverse) operation, since the truth table of $h_{k,i}$ and its reverse string are concatenated to get the $(k+1)$-variable function.

2. If i is odd, then $(1+X_{k+1})h_{k,i}(X_1,\ldots,X_k)+X_{k+1}(1+h_{k,i}(1+X_1,\ldots,1+X_k))$ is $(k+1)$-variable, $(i+1)$-resilient function. We call this as rc (reverse and complement) operation, since the truth table of $h_{k,i}$ and its reverse and then complemented string are concatenated to get the $(k+1)$-variable function.

The above two constructions were first described in [3, Corollary 4.1] and then revisited in [26]. The total construction idea is as follows. Depending on the requirement, start with a k-variable, i-resilient function h. Then construct an $(k+l)$-variable $(i+l)$-resilient function f, where for $(i+j)$ even, choose either r or c operation and for $(i+j)$ odd, choose either rc or c operation for $0 \le j \le l-1$.

Now what are the values of d, x? Considering the algebraic normal form of f, it becomes clear that the algebraic degree of f is equal to the algebraic degree of h. Moreover, the nonlinearity gets exactly doubled in each step. Thus, if the function h has the nonlinearity y, then $x = 2^l y$.

An important point in this direction is if the initial function is optimized in terms of balancedness, order of correlation immunity, algebraic degree and nonlinearity. Then after applying these set of operations either once or more always generate a series of functions which are once again optimized. The constraint here is, given the order of correlation immunity of order i of the k-variable function, i must be greater than $\frac{k}{2} - 2$. In such a case the Walsh spectra of these functions are three valued [44]. The sequences of such functions are referred as *saturated sequences* in [44].

Note that for the case $i \le \frac{k}{2} - 2$, even if we start with a function which has best possible combination of parameters, the construction may not generate functions with optimized parameters [32]. In fact, such sequences of functions with suboptimal parameters having five valued Walsh spectra has been discussed in [31].

Another important recursive construction was described in [55]. Given an (n, m, d, x) function h, by the recursive construction of [55] an $(n+3, m+2, d+1, 2^{n+1}+4x)$ function could be constructed. To use this construction successfully, the function h should be of some desired form. This construction has been slightly modified in [38]. This is as follows. An $(n, m, d, -)$ function f is in *desired* form if it is of the form $f = (1 + X_n)f_1 + X_nf_2$, where f_1, f_2 are $(n-1, m, d-1, -)$ functions.

Let f be an (n, m, d, x) function in *desired* form, where f_1, f_2 are both $(n-1, m, d-1, -)$ functions. Let

$$F = f||\overline{f}||\overline{f}||f,$$

or written in ANF,

$$F = X_{n+2} + X_{n+1} + f.$$

Let

$$G = g||h||\overline{h}||\overline{g} \text{ where } g = f_1||\overline{f}_1 \text{ and } h = f_2||\overline{f}_2.$$

In ANF the function G is given by,

$$G = (1 + X_{n+2} + X_{n+1})f_1 + (X_{n+2} + X_{n+1})f_2 + X_{n+2} + X_n.$$

In the language of [55], the function G above is said to depend quasilinearly on the pair of variables (X_{n+2}, X_{n+1}). We construct a function H in $n+3$ variables in the following way,

$$H = (1 + X_{n+3})F + X_{n+3}G.$$

Then the function H constructed from f is an $(n + 3, m + 2, d + 1, 2^{n+1} + 4x)$ function in the *desired* form.

Once again, this construction generates a series of optimized functions for $m > \frac{n}{2} - 2$, once we start with an optimized function itself. In this case the Walsh spectra of the functions are three valued. However, this is not guaranteed for functions with $m \leq \frac{n}{2} - 2$ and the Walsh spectra is not three valued. This construction [55,38] can provide construction of optimized $(n, m, n - m - 1, 2^{n-1} - 2^{m+1})$ functions for all n having $m \geq \frac{2n-7}{3}$. Further advancement in this direction has been carried out in [56,17] and it has been shown that it is possible to construct $(n, m, n - m - 1, 2^{n-1} - 2^{m+1})$ functions for all n having $m \geq 0.59n$ approximately. It should be noted that the recursive constructions are successful for high order of correlation immunity. On the other hand, the constructions using small affine functions and other search methods prove to be successful for lower order of correlation immunity.

4   Concatenation of Small Affine Functions

Highly nonlinear resilient functions can also be constructed using concatenation of small affine functions. The basic construction has been proposed in [3,49]. This is as follows.

An n-variable function f is seen as concatenation of 2^{n-k} affine functions of k-variables. Moreover, each affine function is nondegenerate on $m + 1$ variables, which guarantees that the function is m-resilient. Consider t is the maximum number of times an affine function (i. e., a linear function and its complement) is repeated. Then the nonlinearity of f is at least $2^{n-1} - t2^{k-1}$. It has been shown [26] that in some cases the recursive constructions of [51,3] with proper initial function provide better nonlinearity than the above construction [3,49]. This construction has later been considered in [9]. For given n and m, $n > m+2$, it is possible to construct a nonlinear $(n, m, d, 2^{n-1} - 2^{k-1})$ function f, where $k = \min k_p$, is the minimum integer satisfying $\binom{k_p}{m+1} + \binom{k_p}{m+2} + \cdots + \binom{k_p}{k_p} \geq 2^{n-k_p}$. This provides a subset of the construction proposed in [49] which attains good nonlinearity. Here each affine function is used exactly once. The limitation in this construction is the algebraic degree may not reach the maximum value $n - m - 1$. In [32], it has been shown that the (n, m, d, x) functions provided in [9] can be modified to degree optimized $(n, m, n - m - 1, y)$ functions, where $y \in \{x, x \pm 2^{m+1}\}$.

Advanced techniques in construction of resilient functions have been considered in [43]. The points considered for the construction of (n, m, d, x) functions are as follows.

1. In [49,9] the affine functions nondegenerate on at least $m+1$ variables have been considered. In [43], all the affine functions (may be nondegenerate on less than $m+1$ variables) have been considered in concatenation. Moreover, small nonlinear resilient functions are also used in the construction.
2. Each affine functions were concatenated more than once and each one is used same or different number of times. Moreover, the same linear function can be repeated as composition with highly nonlinear functions such as bent functions. The concept of fractional nonlinearity has been introduced in [43].
3. The construction of $(n, 1, n-2, 2^{n-1} - 2^{\frac{n-1}{2}})$ functions has been proposed for odd n.
4. It has been shown, that given some m, it is always possible to get some n, such that there exists n-variable, m-resilient functions with nonlinearity strictly greater than $2^{n-1} - 2^{\lceil \frac{n-1}{2} \rceil}$.

Let us now provide some ideas of affine concatenation based constructions presented in [43]. Given a bit b and a string $s = s_0 \ldots s_{n-1}$, the string b AND $s = s'_0 \ldots s'_{n-1}$, where $s'_i = b$ AND s_i. The Kronecker product of two strings $x = x_0 \ldots x_{n-1}$ and $y = y_0 \ldots y_{m-1}$ is a string of length nm, denoted by $x \otimes y = (x_0 \text{ AND } y) \ldots (x_{n-1} \text{ AND } y)$. The direct sum of two strings x and y, denoted by $x\$y$ is given by $x\$y = (x \otimes y^c) + (x^c \otimes y)$. As an example, if $f = 01$, and $g = 0110$, then $f\$g = 01101001$.

Let us now describe the construction of $(2p + 1, 1, 2p - 1, 2^{2p} - 2^p)$ functions for $p \geq 2$. Let $\lambda_1, \lambda_2, \lambda_3, \lambda_4$ be the affine functions of 3 variables which are nodegenerate on at least two variables. Also μ_1, μ_2, μ_3 be the affine functions on three variables which are nondegenerate on a single variable. For $p = 2$, let $f = \lambda_1||\lambda_2||\lambda_3||\lambda_4$. For $p = 3$, let f be the concatenation of the following sequence of functions : $h_1\$\lambda_1, h_2\$\lambda_2, \mu_1\mu_1^c, \mu_2\mu_2^c, \mu_3\mu_3^c, \lambda_3, \lambda_4$, where h_1 and h_2 are 2-variable bent functions. For $p \geq 4$, we have the following construction. Let $g_i = \mu_i\mu_i^c$, for $1 \leq i \leq 3$. Let h_1, h_2 be bent functions of $2p - 4$ variables, h_3, h_4, h_5 be bent functions of $2p - 6$ variables and h_6, h_7 be two strings of lengths $2^{2p-6} + 1$ and $2^{2p-6} - 1$ and (fractional) nonlinearity $nlmax(2p - 6)$ and $nlmax(2p - 6) - 1$ respectively. Let f be a concatenation of the following sequence of functions : $h_1\$\lambda_1, h_2\$\lambda_2, h_3\$g_1, h_4\$g_2, h_5\$g_3, h_6\$\lambda_3, h_7\$\lambda_4$. It can be shown that f is a $(2p + 1, 1, 2p - 1, 2^{2p} - 2^p)$ function.

5 Search Methods

Search methods have been used to construct resilient functions on small number of variables. In [33], genetic algorithm has been used to construct the functions $(8, 1, -, 112), (9, 1, -, 232), (10, 1, -, 476), (11, 1, -, 976), (12, 1, -, 1972)$ where the algebraic degrees were not mentioned. In [18], $(7, 0, 6, 56)$ function has been formed by search on idempotents and this has been used to get $(8, 1, 6, 112),$ $(9, 2, 6, 224)$ functions using recursive constructions. Heuristic search techniques has been exploited in [37] to construct $(8, 1, 6, 112), (9, 1, 7, 236), (10, 1, 8, 480),$ $(11, 1, 9, 976)$ functions. In this paper [37], non correlation immune Boolean functions are transformed into correlation immune functions using linear transformation. However, these results were suboptimal and could be improved further using the deterministic technique proposed in [43].

Another approach used in search technique is to first find out a small subset of Boolean functions using combinatorial techniques and then to perform exhaustive search over that reduced domain. The $(8, 3, 4, 112)$ function has been achieved in this manner in [44]. However, the method proposed in [55] could present a recursive construction at the same time using a $(5, 1, 3, 12)$ function as the initial function. The major success in this direction was achieved in [38,32]. In [38], the $(7, 2, 4, 56)$ function has been generated using search method by concatenating two $(6, 2, 3, 24)$ functions. This function, using the recursive method provided in [55,38], could generate a series of optimized resilient functions which were not known earlier. The unbalanced correlation immune function $[6, 1, 5, 26]$ has also been found in [38] using search technique. Using these $[6, 1, 5, 26]$ functions, construction of $[8, 1, 5, 116]$ functions has been proposed in [28]. These functions were suitably modified to get $(8, 1, 6, 116)$ function in [32] using classical search method. This function has also been used to generate a few more functions which were not known earlier. Very recently $(7, 2, 4, 56)$ and $(8, 1, 6, 116)$ functions with very good autocorrelation properties have been found using simulated annealing technique [13].

6 Other Issues

6.1 Enumeration

For enumeration, we consider the properties (C1) Balancedness, (C2) Nonaffinity, (C3) Nondegeneracy, (C4) Correlation Immunity of first order, (C5) Symmetry. Also we denote the set of n-variable Boolean functions which have the properties $Ci_1, \ldots, Ci_t$ by $A_n(i_1, \ldots, i_t)$. *The set of all correlation immune (CI) Boolean functions of n variables is denoted by A_n, i.e., $A_n = A_n(4)$.*

We now briefly review the works related to lower bounds on number of correlation immune functions. This is done by construction of some subsets of correlation immune Boolean functions. A subset of A_n with cardinality $2^{2^{n-1}}$ was presented by Mitchell in [34]. This is basically the set of correlation immune Boolean functions whose truth tables are palindromic (i. e., the truth table string and its reverse are same). The other known subsets of A_n have the following cardinalities.

1. A subset of cardinality $2^{2^{n-1}} + 2^n - 2n + 2^{2^{n-4}} - 2^{n-3}$ was identified by Yang et al in [58].
2. Another subset of size $\mid A_{n-1} \mid^2$ was proposed by Park et al in [35]. This has been done by recursive construction.
3. An improved lower bound by finding different disjoint subsets has been presented in [25], which gives, $\mid A_n \mid \; > \; \mid A_{n-1} \mid^2 + 2^{2^{n-2}} - \mid A_{n-2} \mid + $
$$4 \sum_{r=1}^{2^{n-3}-1} C_{n-2}^2(2r) \, N_{n-2}(2r), \; n \geq 4.$$ Here, $C_n(a)$ is the number of n-variable, weight a correlation immune functions and $N_n(a)$ is the number of n-variable, weight a non correlation immune functions.

The recent results on the supersets of A_n using necessary conditions are as follows.

1. Yang and Guo [58] provided a superset of size $\sum_{k=0}^{2^{n-1}} \sum_{r=0}^{k} \binom{2^{n-2}}{r}^2 \binom{2^{n-2}}{k-r}^2$.

2. A superset of size $\sum_{j=0}^{2^{n-2}} \binom{2^{n-2}}{j}^4$ was obtained by Park et al [35].

3. An improved upper bound on $|A_n|$ has also been presented in [43]. This gives, $|A_n| \leq \sum_{j=0}^{2^{n-2}} \binom{2^{n-2}}{j}^4 - \sum_{k=0}^{7} \binom{8}{k} \sum_{a=0}^{2^{n-3}} C_{n-3}^k(a) N_{n-3}(a)$.

Related results are also presented in [48,14].

It is important to mention the work of Denisov [16] at this point. In [16] the asymptotic formula $\dfrac{2^{2^n}}{2^k \exp\{\sum_{i=1}^{k} (\ln \sqrt{\frac{\pi}{2}} + (\frac{n}{2}-i) \ln 2) \binom{n}{i}\}}$ for the number of n-variable, k-th order correlation immune function has been obtained. For first order correlation immune functions, we get $A_n \sim \dfrac{2^{2^n}}{2 \exp\{(\ln \sqrt{\frac{\pi}{2}} + (\frac{n}{2} - 1) \ln 2)n\}}$, putting $k = 1$. The result in Denisov's paper is a probabilistic estimate which provides an asymptotic formula of $N(n, k)$. This result, when considered as an upper bound, presents the best known result in terms of enumeration.

In [27], weight distribution of correlation immune Boolean functions has been discussed. It has been proved in [27] that the number of CI functions of weight $2a$ is strictly lesser than the number of CI functions of weight $2a + 2$ where $2a < 2^{n-1}$. Moreover, it has been shown [30] that, $|A_n| = \sum_{i=0}^{2^{n-2}} 2^{2i} C_{n,4i}(2^{n-1} - 2i)$, where $C_{n,x}(2a)$ is the number of n-variable correlation immune functions of weight $2a$, where the function truth table and its reverse string matches at x number of places.

Construction and enumeration of symmetric correlation immune function has been considered in [34,58]. In [20], it has been shown that it is possible to construct balanced, correlation immune, nonlinear symmetric Boolean functions, i.e., $A_n(1, 2, 3, 4, 5) \neq \emptyset$ for some values of n. Further constructions and enumerations of symmetric correlation immune Boolean functions has been mentioned in [30,47].

6.2   Autocorrelation

Very recently autocorrelation property of correlation immune functions have received a lot of attention as evident from [5,61,62,57,29]. In [61], it has been noted that the autocorrelation property goes against correlation immunity. Let $X \in \{0,1\}^n$ be an n-tuple $X_n, \ldots, X_1$ and $\alpha \in \{0,1\}^n$ be an n-tuple $\alpha_n, \ldots, \alpha_1$. Let $f \in \Omega_n$ and $\Delta_f(\alpha) = wd(f(X), f(X \oplus \alpha))$, the autocorrelation value of f with respect to the vector α. Two important parameters in this connection are the sum-of-square indicator

$$\sigma_f = \sum_{\alpha \in \{0,1\}^n} \Delta_f^2(\alpha), \text{ and the absolute indicator } \Delta_f = \max_{\alpha \in \{0,1\}^n, \alpha \neq 0} | \Delta_f(\alpha) |.$$

The autocorrelation property of higher order correlation immune functions has been considered in [57]. It has been shown in [57] that for an n-variable, m-resilient function $\Delta_f \geq 2^n \frac{2m-n+3}{n+1}$. However, the result is not applicable for low order of correlation immunity.

In [62], it has been shown that $\Delta_f \geq 2^{m-1} \sum_{i=0}^{+\infty} 2^{i(m-1-n)}$ for an unbalanced n-variable m-th order correlation immune function for the range $2 \leq m \leq n$. Also $\Delta_f \geq 2^m \sum_{i=0}^{+\infty} 2^{i(m-n)}$ for an n-variable m-resilient function for the range $1 \leq m \leq n-1$. In [29], improved results have been shown. For an n-variable m-th order correlation immune function f, $\Delta_f > 2^{\frac{n}{2}} \sqrt{\frac{\sum_{i=1}^m \binom{n}{i}}{2^n - \sum_{i=1}^m \binom{n}{i}}}$. Similarly,

$\Delta_f > 2^{\frac{n}{2}} \sqrt{\frac{\sum_{i=0}^m \binom{n}{i}}{2^n - \sum_{i=0}^m \binom{n}{i}}}$ for an n-variable m-resilient function f.

Let $f \in \Omega_n$ be an m-th order correlation immune function. Then, in [29] it has been shown that, $\sigma_f > 2^{2n} + 2^{n+\log_2 \sum_{i=1}^m \binom{n}{i}}$. Similarly, if f is m-resilient, then $\sigma_f > 2^{2n} + 2^{n+\log_2 \sum_{i=0}^m \binom{n}{i}}$. Current results [55,7,8] clearly identify that the nonlinearity and algebraic degree of the correlation immune and resilient functions get optimized simultaneously. The algebraic degree is also maximized in this case [55,7,8]. At this situation, the sum-of-square indicator attains its minimum value too [29]. For an n-variable, m-resilient function ($m > \frac{m}{2} - 2$) with maximum possible algebraic degree and maximum possible nonlinearity, the sum-of-square indicator value is minimized at 2^{n+2m+4}. This gives that for an n-variable, m-resilient function, the nonlinearity, algebraic degree and sum-of-square indicator of autocorrelation values are optimized simultaneously.

Though, the sum-of-square indicator is minimized automatically, the absolute value may differ for the optimized functions. In fact, in [13], it has been shown that for $(7, 2, 4, 56)$ functions, it is possible to get functions with different Δ_f values 24, 32, and 40 using search methods. In [13] also an $(8, 1, 6, 116)$ function with Δ_f value 24 has been demonstrated. However, in [29,46], it has been noted that the existing recursive construction techniques [55,38,31] are not good enough in terms of the Δ_f values. Getting a generalized construction technique with good correlation immunity and autocorrelation is an important research direction.

6.3 Multiple Output

Research on multiple output binary resilient functions has received attention from mid eighties [12,1,19,53,2,21,59,24,23,10,11]. The initial works on multiple output binary resilient functions were directed towards linear resilient functions. The concept of multiple output resilient functions had been introduced independently by Chor et al [12] and Bennett et al [1]. The similar concept was introduced at the same time for single output Boolean functions by Siegenthaler [51].

Besides its importance in random sequence generation for stream cipher systems, these resilient functions have applications in quantum cryptographic key distribution, fault tolerant distributed computing, etc.

Given the definitions related to single output Boolean functions, we now introduce the concepts with respect to the multiple output Boolean functions $\mathbb{F}_2^n \mapsto \mathbb{F}_2^m$. In this case, the truth table contains m different output columns, each of length 2^n. Let us consider the function $F(x) : \mathbb{F}_2^n \mapsto \mathbb{F}_2^m$ such that $F(x) = (f_1(x), \ldots, f_m(x))$. Then the nonlinearity of F is defined as,

$$nl(F) = \min_{\tau \in \mathbb{F}_2^{m*}} nl(\bigoplus_{j=1}^m \tau_j f_j(x)).$$

Here, $\mathbb{F}_2^{m*} = \mathbb{F}_2^m \backslash 0$ and $\tau = (\tau_1, \ldots, \tau_m)$. Similarly the algebraic degree of F is defined as,

$$deg(F) = \min_{\tau \in \mathbb{F}_2^{m*}} deg(\bigoplus_{j=1}^m \tau_j f_j(x)).$$

Now we define an n-variable, m-output, t-resilient function, denoted by (n, m, t), as follows. A function F is an (n, m, t) resilient function, iff $\bigoplus_{j=1}^m \tau_j f_j(x)$ is an $(n, 1, t)$ function (n-variable, t-resilient Boolean function) for any choice of $\tau \in \mathbb{F}_2^{m*}$. By $\mathbb{F}_2^n$ we denote the vector space corresponding to the finite field $\mathbb{F}_{2^n}$.

Nonlinearity issue for such multiple output resilient functions was first discussed in [54]. After that, serious attempts were made towards construction of nonlinear resilient functions [59,24,23,11]. Given the number of input variables n, the number of output variables m, and the order of resiliency t, the research concentrates on construction of functions $F : \mathbb{F}_2^n \mapsto \mathbb{F}_2^m$ that achieve higher nonlinearity values than existing constructions for different choices of n, m, t.

The currently best known results on nonlinearity are available in [39]. The result is as follows. Given a linear $[u, m, t+1]$ code, it is possible to construct n-variable, m-output, t-resilient function $F = (f_1, \ldots, f_m)$, where the nonlinearity values $nl(F) =$

$$
\begin{array}{ll}
2^{n-1} - 2^{u-1}, & u \le n < u + m, \\
2^{n-1} - 2^{n-m}, & u + m \le n < u + m + 2, \\
2^{n-1} - 2^{n-m} + 2^u \nu(n - u - m + 1, m), & u + m + 2 \le n < u + 2m - 1, \\
2^{n-1} - 2^{\frac{n+u-m+1}{2}}, & u + 2m - 1 \le n < u + 3m - 3, \ \pi \text{ even}, \\
2^{n-1} - 2^{\frac{n+u-m+2}{2}}, & u + 2m \le n < u + 3m - 3, \ \pi \text{ odd}, \\
2^{n-1} - 2^{u+m-1}, & u + 3m - 3 \le n < u + 3m, \\
2^{n-1} - 2^{\frac{n+u-m-1}{2}}, & n \ge u + 3m - 1, \ \pi \text{ even}, \\
2^{n-1} - 2^{\frac{n+u-m}{2}}, & n \ge u + 3m, \ \pi \text{ odd}.
\end{array}
$$

Here $\pi = n - u - m + 1$. Also $\nu(p, r)$ is the maximum possible nonlinearity of a p-input r-output function with $3 \le p < r$.

The work in [59, Corollary 6] provides better result than [39] for a small range when $n < u + \frac{m}{2} - 1$, which gives the nonlinearity $2^{n-1} - 2^{n-\frac{m}{2}}$. There are also a few cases for low values of n, when the exhaustive search based results of [23] are better than that of [39]. On the other hand, the construction of [11] provides very good algebraic degree for such functions, though the nonlinearity is not very high.

Correlation immune functions on Galois fields and Galois rings have been considered in [6], and such functions on finite alphabet has been considered in [4].

7 Conclusion

In this initiative we provide a brief outline of research on correlation immune functions. We mostly talk about the basic results without proof and tried to provide references to most of the existing works. This area still contains a lot of open questions which are available in these references.

Acknowledgment. Mr. Sandeepan Chowdhury has read earlier versions of this draft carefully and provided important suggestions to improve it.

References

1. C. H. Bennet, G. Brassard, and J. M. Robert. Privacy amplification by by public discussion. *SIAM Journal on Computing*, 17:210–229, 1988.
2. J. Bierbrauer, K. Gopalakrishnan, and D. R. Stinson. Bounds on resilient functions and orthogonal arrays. In *Advances in Cryptology - CRYPTO'94*, number 839 in Lecture Notes in Computer Science, pages 247–256. Springer Verlag, 1994.
3. P. Camion, C. Carlet, P. Charpin, and N. Sendrier. On correlation immune functions. In *Advances in Cryptology - CRYPTO'91*, number 576 in Lecture Notes in Computer Science, pages 86–100. Springer-Verlag, 1992.
4. P. Camion and A. Canteaut. Correlation-Immune and Resilient Functions Over a Finite Alphabet and Their Applications in Cryptography. *Designs, Codes and Cryptography*, 16(2): 121–149, 1999.
5. A. Canteaut, C. Carlet, P. Charpin and C. Fontaine. Propagation characteristics and correlation immunity of highly nonlinear Boolean functions. In *Advances in Cryptology - EUROCRYPT'00*, pages 507–522. Springer-Verlag, LNCS 1807, 2000.
6. C. Carlet. More Correlation-Immune and Resilient Functions over Galois Fields and Galois Rings. In *Advances in Cryptology - Eurocrypt '97*, number 1233 in Lecture Notes in Computer Science, pages 422–433. Springer-Verlag, 1997.
7. C. Carlet. On the coset weight divisibility and nonlinearity of resilient and correlation immune functions. In *Sequences and Their Applications - SETA 2001*, Discrete Mathematics and Theoretical Computer Science, pages 131–144. Springer Verlag, 2001.
8. C. Carlet and P. Sarkar. Spectral domain analysis of correlation immune and resilient Boolean functions. Accepted in *Finite Fields and Its Applications*, 2001.
9. S. Chee, S. Lee, D. Lee, and S. H. Sung. On the correlation immune functions and their nonlinearity. In *Advances in Cryptology - ASIACRYPT '96*, number 1163 in Lecture Notes in Computer Science, pages 232–243. Springer-Verlag, 1996.
10. J. H. Cheon and S. Chee. Elliptic Curves and Resilient Functions. In *ICISC 2000*, number 2015 in Lecture Notes in Computer Science, pages 64–72. Springer Verlag, 2000.

11. J. H. Cheon. Nonlinear Vector Resilient Functions. In *Advances in Cryptology - CRYPTO 2001*, Lecture Notes in Computer Science. Springer Verlag, 2001.
12. B. Chor, O. Goldreich, J. Hastad, J. Friedman, S. Rudich, and R. Smolensky. The bit extraction problem or t-resilient functions. In *26th IEEE Symposium on Foundations of Computer Science*, pages 396–407, 1985.
13. J. Clark, J. Jacob, W. Millan, and S. Maitra. Evolution of Boolean Functions Satisfying Multiple Criteria with Simulated Annealing. Preprint, 2002.
14. E. Dawson and C. K. Wu. Construction of correlation immune Boolean functions. In *Information and Communications Security*, Lecture Notes in Computer Science, pages 170–180. Springer-Verlag, 1997.
15. C. Ding, G. Xiao, and W. Shan. *The Stability Theory of Stream Ciphers*. Number 561 in Lecture Notes in Computer Science. Springer-Verlag, 1991.
16. O. V. Denisov. An asymptotic formula for the number of correlation-immune of order k Boolean functions. *Discrete Mathematics and Applications*, 2(4):407–426, 1992.
17. M. Fedorova and Y. V. Tarannikov. On the constructing of highly nonlinear resilient Boolean functions by means of special matrices. In *Progress in Cryptology - INDOCRYPT 2001*, number 2247 in Lecture Notes in Computer Science, pages 254–266. Springer Verlag, 2001.
18. E. Filiol and C. Fontaine. Highly nonlinear balanced Boolean functions with a good correlation-immunity. In *Advances in Cryptology - EUROCRYPT'98*, number 1403 in Lecture Notes in Computer Science, pages 475–488. Springer-Verlag, 1998.
19. J. Friedman. On the bit extraction problem. In *33rd IEEE Symposium on Foundations of Computer Science*, pages 314–319, 1982.
20. K. Gopalakrisnan, D. G. Hoffman, and D. R. Stinson. A note on a conjecture concerning symmetric resilient functions. *Information Processing Letters*, 47(3):139–143, 1993.
21. K. Gopalakrishnan. A study of Correlation-immune, resilient and related cryptographic functions. *PhD thesis, University of Nebraska*, 1994.
22. X. Guo-Zhen and J. Massey. A spectral characterization of correlation immune combining functions. *IEEE Transactions on Information Theory*, 34(3):569–571, May 1988.
23. T. Johansson and E. Pasalic, A construction of resilient functions with high nonlinearity, In *IEEE International Symposium on Information Theory*, ISIT, June 2000, full version available at *Cryptology ePrint Archive, eprint.iacr.org, No.2000/053*.
24. K. Kurosawa, T. Satoh, and K. Yamamoto Highly nonlinear t-Resilient functions. *Journal of Universal Computer Science*, vol. 3, no. 6, pp. 721–729, Springer Publishing Company, 1997.
25. S. Maitra and P. Sarkar. Enumeration of correlation immune Boolean functions. In *4th Australasian Conference on Information, Security and Privacy*, number 1587 in Lecture Notes in Computer Science, pages 12–25. Springer Verlag, April 1999.
26. S. Maitra and P. Sarkar. Highly nonlinear resilient functions optimizing Siegenthaler's inequality. In *Advances in Cryptology - CRYPTO'99*, number 1666 in Lecture Notes in Computer Science, pages 198–215. Springer Verlag, August 1999.
27. S. Maitra and P. Sarkar. Hamming weights of correlation immune Boolean functions. *Information Processing Letters*, 71(3-4):149–153, 1999.
28. S. Maitra. Correlation immune Boolean functions with very high nonlinearity. *Cryptology ePrint Archive, eprint.iacr.org, No. 2000/054*, October 27, 2000.
29. S. Maitra. Autocorrelation Properties of correlation immune Boolean functions. INDOCRYPT 2001, number 2247 Lecture Notes in Computer Science. Pages 242–253. Springer Verlag, December 2001.

30. S. Maitra. Boolean Functions with Important Cryptographic Properties. PhD Thesis, Indian Statistical Institute, 2001.
31. S. Maitra and P. Sarkar. Cryptographically significant Boolean functions with five valued Walsh spectra. *Theoretical Computer Science*, To be published in 2002.
32. S. Maitra and E. Pasalic. Further constructions of resilient Boolean functions with very high nonlinearity. *IEEE Transactions on Information Theory*, To be published in July 2002.
33. W. Millan, A. Clark, and E. Dawson. Heuristic design of cryptographically strong balanced Boolean functions. In *Advances in Cryptology - EUROCRYPT'98*. Springer-Verlag, 1998.
34. C. J. Mitchell. Enumerating Boolean functions of cryptographic significance. *Journal of Cryptology*, 2(3):155–170, 1990.
35. P. Sung Mo, L. Sangjin, S. Soo Hak, and K. Kwangjo. Improving bounds for the number of correlation immune Boolean functions. *Information Processing Letters*, 61(4):209–212, 1997.
36. J. J. Mykkeltveit. The covering radius of the $(128, 8)$ Reed-Muller code is 56. *IEEE Transactions on Information Theory*, IT-26(3):358–362, 1983.
37. E. Pasalic and T. Johansson. Further results on the relation between nonlinearity and resiliency of Boolean functions. In *IMA Conference on Cryptography and Coding*, number 1746 in Lecture Notes in Computer Science, pages 35–45. Springer-Verlag, 1999.
38. E. Pasalic, S. Maitra, T. Johansson and P. Sarkar. New constructions of resilient and correlation immune Boolean functions achieving upper bounds on nonlinearity. In *Workshop on Coding and Cryptography - WCC 2001*, Paris, January 8–12, 2001. Electronic Notes in Discrete Mathematics, Volume 6, Elsevier Science, 2001.
39. E. Pasalic and S. Maitra. Linear codes in constructing resilient functions with high nonlinearity. In *Selected Areas in Cryptography - SAC 2001*, number 2259 in Lecture Notes in Computer Science. Pages 60–74, Springer Verlag, August 2001. (An extended version of this paper contains further improved results.)
40. N. J. Patterson and D. H. Wiedemann. The covering radius of the $(2^{15}, 16)$ Reed-Muller code is at least 16276. *IEEE Transactions on Information Theory*, IT-29(3):354–356, 1983.
41. N. J. Patterson and D. H. Wiedemann. Correction to - the covering radius of the $(2^{15}, 16)$ Reed-Muller code is at least 16276. *IEEE Transactions on Information Theory*, IT-36(2):443, 1990.
42. O. S. Rothaus. On bent functions. *Journal of Combinatorial Theory, Series A*, 20:300–305, 1976.
43. P. Sarkar and S. Maitra. Construction of nonlinear Boolean functions with important cryptographic properties. In *Advances in Cryptology - EUROCRYPT 2000*, number 1807 in Lecture Notes in Computer Science, pages 485–506. Springer Verlag, 2000.
44. P. Sarkar and S. Maitra. Nonlinearity bounds and constructions of resilient Boolean functions. In *Advances in Cryptology - CRYPTO 2000*, number 1880 in Lecture Notes in Computer Science, pages 515–532. Springer Verlag, 2000.
45. P. Sarkar. A note on the spectral characterization of correlation immune Boolean functions. *Information Processing Letters*, 74(5-6):191–195, 2000.
46. P. Sarkar and S. Maitra. Cross-correlation analysis of cryptographically useful Boolean functions and S-boxes. *Theory of Computing Systems*, to be published in 2002.
47. P. Sarkar and S. Maitra. Balancedness and Correlation Immunity of Symmetric Boolean Functions. Preprint, 2000.

48. M. Schneider. On the construction and upper bounds of balanced and correlation immune functions. In *SAC'97*, January 1997.

49. J. Seberry, X. M. Zhang, and Y. Zheng. On constructions and nonlinearity of correlation immune Boolean functions. In *Advances in Cryptology - EUROCRYPT'93*, number 765 in Lecture Notes in Computer Science, pages 181–199. Springer-Verlag, 1994.

50. W. Shan. The structure and the construction of correlation immune functions. *MS Thesis, NTE Institute, Xian*, 1987.

51. T. Siegenthaler. Correlation-immunity of nonlinear combining functions for cryptographic applications. *IEEE Transactions on Information Theory*, IT-30(5):776–780, September 1984.

52. T. Siegenthaler. Decrypting a class of stream ciphers using ciphertext only. *IEEE Transactions on Computers*, C-34(1):81–85, January 1985.

53. D. R. Stinson. Resilient functions and large sets of orthogonal arrays. *Congressus Numerantium*, 92:105–110, 1993.

54. D. R. Stinson and J. L. Massey. An infinite class of counterexamples to a conjecture concerning non-linear resilient functions. *Journal of Cryptology*, 8(3):167–173, 1995.

55. Y. V. Tarannikov. On resilient Boolean functions with maximum possible nonlinearity. In *Progress in Cryptology - INDOCRYPT 2000*, number 1977 in Lecture Notes in Computer Science, pages 19–30. Springer Verlag, 2000.

56. Y. V. Tarannikov. New constructions of resilient Boolean functions with maximal nonlinearity. In *Fast Software Encryption - FSE 2001*, pages 70–81 in preproceedings, 2001.

57. Y. V. Tarannikov, P. Korolev and A. Botev. Autocorrelation coefficients and correlation immunity of Boolean functions. In *ASIACRYPT 2001*, Lecture Notes in Computer Science. Springer Verlag, 2001.

58. Y. X. Yang and B. Guo. Further enumerating Boolean functions of cryptographic significance. *Journal of Cryptology*, 8(3):115–122, 1995.

59. X. M. Zhang and Y. Zheng. Cryptographically resilient functions. *IEEE Transactions on Information Theory*, 43(5):1740–1747, 1997.

60. Y. Zheng and X. M. Zhang. Improved upper bound on the nonlinearity of high order correlation immune functions. In *Selected Areas in Cryptography - SAC 2000*, number 2012 in Lecture Notes in Computer Science, pages 264–274. Springer Verlag, 2000.

61. Y. Zheng and X. M. Zhang. On relationships among propagation degree, nonlinearity and correlation immunity. In *Advances in Cryptology - ASIACRYPT'00*, Lecture Notes in Computer Science. Springer Verlag, 2000.

62. Y. Zheng and X. M. Zhang. New results on correlation immune functions. In *International Conference on Information Security and Cryptology - ICISC 2000*, number 2015 in Lecture Notes in Computer Science, pages 49–63. Springer Verlag, 2001.

m out of n Oblivious Transfer

Yi Mu, Junqi Zhang, and Vijay Varadharajan

Department of Computing
Macquarie University, Sydney, Australia
{ymu, janson, vijay}@ics.mq.edu.au

Abstract. We present three novel constructions of m out of n oblivious transfer, which demonstrate significant improvement over the existing schemes in terms of completeness, robustness and flexibility. We also show how to construct a non-interactive m out of n oblivious transfer, based on discrete logarithm. These constructions have potential applicability in electronic commerce.

1 Introduction

The concept of Oblivious Transfer(OT) was introduced by Rabin[1]. Rabin's OT can be considered as a game between two polynomial time parties, Alice and Bob. Alice sends a bit to Bob in such a way that with $1/2$ probability Bob will receive the same bit and with $1/2$ probability Bob will receive nothing. Alice does not know which event has happened. Rabin's initiative has attracted a lot of attentions. Various OT methods have been subsequently proposed (e.g., [2,3, 4,5,6,7]), where most notable ones are one out of two OT and chosen one out of two OT. In a one out of two OT ($\binom{2}{1}$-OT), Alice sends two bits to Bob who receives one of these bits with equal probability and knows which bit he has received, while Alice does not know which bit Bob received. A chosen one out of two OT is similar to a normal one out of two OT; the different between them is that, in the former, Bob can choose an index c and receives bit b_c. Alice does not learn c.

One direct extension to $\binom{2}{1}$-OT is 1 out of n oblivious transfer[8,9]. However, there has been little study in m out of n oblivious transfer, $\binom{n}{m}$-OT. The closest scheme is the $n-1$ out of n OT proposed by Bellare and Micali[10]. Roughly speaking, in an m out of n oblivious transfer, Bob can receive only m messages out of n messages ($n > m$) sent by Alice; and Alice has no idea about which ones have been received. The OT proposed by Bellare and Micali[10] is non-interactive. By non-interactive we mean that Bob does not need to communicate with Alice during an OT process. Santis and Persiano[8] also proposed a non-interactive OT protocol. Their scheme falls within the case of 1 out of n.

In this paper, we go one step further by giving some new OT schemes (either interactive or non-interactive) that cover the complete OT spectrum. We called them m out of n OT, $\binom{n}{m}$-OT. Here, m is an arbitrary number in $1 \leq m < n$. The original OT scheme by Rabin can be considered as one of cases in our schemes. One important feature in our schemes is that the sender and the recipient can

L. Batten and J. Seberry (Eds.): ACISP 2002, LNCS 2384, pp. 395–405, 2002.

securely implement an OT process without the involvement of a trusted third party, because the security can be proved by both the sender and the recipient. To the best of our knowledge, our methods have not been considered previously in the literature.

The paper is organised as follows. Section 2 describes a new interactive $\binom{n}{m}$-OT. Section 3 gives a new setting. Based on this setting, we propose a computationally efficient interactive $\binom{n}{m}$-OT scheme and an non-interactive $\binom{n}{m}$-OT scheme. The final section discusses potential applicability of proposed schemes and gives our concluding remarks.

2 m out of n Oblivious Transfer

m of n oblivious transfer is defined as follows. Alice knows n messages and wants to send m of them to Bob. Bob gets m of them with probability $m!(n-m)!/n!$ and knows which ones he has got, but Alice has no idea about which m messages Bob has received.

In this section, we describe a simple interactive $\binom{n}{m}$-OT, which is hybrid, using both symmetric-key and asymmetric-key algorithms. As the sender, Alice generates n pairs of private-public keys based on the key generator $\mathcal{G}(1^\ell)$ for security parameter ℓ. All public keys are then published. Bob generates m ($m < n$) secret symmetric keys, encrypts these keys using m of Alice's public keys, and then sends these encrypted keys to Alice. Alice has no idea which public keys have been used and therefore decrypts each encrypted key using all n private keys. Obviously, one of those decryptions is correct, but Alice does not know which one. Alice has to repeat the process for all encrypted symmetric keys sent to her by Bob. Alice in turn encrypts n messages using all these encrypted "keys" in order. Upon receiving all encrypted messages, Bob can decrypt m of them, since he knows which ones have been correctly encrypted by Alice.

The detailed protocol of our first m out of n OT scheme is given as follows. Suppose that Alice has n messages $M_i, i = 1, \cdots, n$. Bob can get only m of them. Since this scheme can be implemented under any symmetric and asymmetric key algorithms, we can in general denote by $E_k(.)$ and $D_k(.)$ the symmetric encryption and decryption with respect to k respectively, and denote by $\langle.\rangle_e$ and $\langle.\rangle_d$ the asymmetric encryption and decryption for public key e and private key d respectively. The OT protocol is given below (see also Figure 1).

0: Alice and Bob agree on a public key algorithm such as RSA and a symmetric key algorithm such as AES.
1: Alice chooses n private/public key pairs (d_i, e_i). All public keys should be certified by a trusted authority. For simplicity of the presentation, we omit the details and public key certificates. Bob sends the public keys to Bob.
2: Bob chooses m symmetric keys $k_j, j = 1, \cdots, m$, and then encrypts k_j using m public keys (e_s) selected from n public keys, where the indices (s) of those used public keys are known to Bob only. The encrypted public keys, $\langle k_j \rangle_{e_s}$, are then sent to Alice.

$$
\begin{array}{lll}
\text{Alice} & & \text{Bob} \\
(d_i, e_i),\ i = 1, \cdots, n & & k_j,\ (m \text{ of them},\ j = 1, \cdots, m) \\[4pt]
& \xrightarrow{\quad e_i \quad} & \\[4pt]
& & k'_j = \langle k_j \rangle_{e_s},\ (m \text{ of them}) \\[4pt]
& \xleftarrow{\quad k'_j \quad} & \\[4pt]
k_{ij} = \langle k'_j \rangle_{d_i},\ C_{ij} = E_{k_{ij}}(M_i) & & \\
j = 1, \cdots, m,\ i = 1, \cdots, n & & \\[4pt]
& \xrightarrow{\quad C_{ij} \quad} & \\[4pt]
& & M_j = D_{k_j}(C_{ij})
\end{array}
$$

Fig. 1. The interactive *m* out of *n* oblivious transfer protocol.

3: Alice decrypts each of $k'_j = \langle k_j \rangle_{e_s}$ using all n private keys, d_i, to form $k_{ij} = \langle k'_j \rangle_{d_i}$, and encrypts all messages using k_{ij}, $i = 1, \cdots, n$, respectively. The encrypted messages are $C_{ij} = E_{k_{ij}}(M_i)$, $j = 1, \cdots, m$, $i = 1, \cdots, n$. Alice could shuffle messages prior to the encryption, otherwise it is a chosen *m* out of *n* OT. C_{ij} are then sent to Bob.

5: Bob decrypts *m* messages using k_j, based on the indices of the public key known to him only.

Claim 1: (*Completeness*) *If Alice correctly follows the process, Bob will receive exactly m of n messages sent by Alice.*

Bob encrypts $k_j, j = 1, \cdots, m$, using *m* out of *n* Alice's public keys and keeps the chosen public keys' indices secret. Although Alice does not know the chosen public keys, she simply decrypts each encrypted k_j using all *n* her private keys in order, $k_{ij} = \langle k'_j \rangle_{d_i}$, $i = 1, \cdots, n$. Obviously, one of them has been correctly decrypted. Although all *n* decrypted keys (both correct and incorrect) are used for encrypting *n* messages, Bob knows which one has been correctly done and then uses the associated k_j to decrypt it. Therefore, Bob can receive *m* messages out of *n* sent messages.

Claim 2: (*Soundness*) *Bob cannot get more than m messages.*

As explained in Claim 1, Bob sends to Alice *m* encrypted symmetric keys and Alice blindly encrypts them and uses them in encryption. Alice does not know which messages Bob has got, because she does not know which encryption keys are correct (used by Bob). However, Alice knows for sure that she uses exactly *m* correct encryption keys, k_j.

Alice has to do $n \times m$ encryptions. If *m* and *n* are large, this scheme will not be efficient. We will later introduce another $\binom{n}{m}$-OT scheme, which requires only *n* encryptions.

3   Better m out of m Oblivious Transfers

We now present a novel OT system that can be used to construct either interactive or non-interactive OT's.

3.1   System Setup

Assume that Alice intends to send n messages, $M_1, \cdots, M_n \in \mathbb{Z}_p$, to Bob and
knows for sure that Bob can receive m of them. Which ones will be received
by Bob is unknown to Alice. We now describe the Bob's public key generation
algorithm that will be used to our $\binom{n}{m}$-OT's.

Let p be a large prime number, $\mathbb{Z}_p^*$ be a multiplicative group, $g \in \mathbb{Z}_p^*$ be the
generator of order $q = p - 1$, and $x_i \in \mathbb{Z}_p$, $i = 1, \cdots, n$, be a set of integers. All
these data are pre-agreed and made public. For simplicity, we omit modulus p
in the rest of the presentation.

The public key setup is done by Bob who selects m private keys $s_i \in \mathbb{Z}_q$ and
then computes $y_i = g^{s_i}$, $i = 1, \cdots, m$ $(m < n)$. Given x_i, the n public keys are
constructed by using a set of m linear equations with respect to $a_1, \cdots, a_m$,

$$a_1 x_i + a_2 x_i^2 + \cdots + a_m x_i^m = y_i, \ i = 1, \cdots, m. \tag{1}$$

The corresponding linear equations in a matrix form are as follows:

$$\begin{pmatrix} 1 & x_1 & x_1^2 & \cdots & x_1^{m-1} \\ 1 & x_2 & x_2^2 & \cdots & x_2^{m-1} \\ \vdots & \vdots & \vdots & & \vdots \\ 1 & x_m & x_m^2 & \cdots & x_m^{m-1} \end{pmatrix} \begin{pmatrix} a_1' \\ a_2' \\ \vdots \\ a_m' \end{pmatrix} = \begin{pmatrix} y_1 \\ y_2 \\ \vdots \\ y_m \end{pmatrix}. \tag{2}$$

Here $a_i' = a_i x_i$. The coefficient matrix A is a so-called Vandermonde matrix or
a non-singular matrix. The determinant of a Vandermonde matrix is not equal
to zero:

$$det\ A = \prod_{1 \leq i < k \leq m} (x_i - x_k) \neq 0.$$

This is because x_i Bob chose are distinct and no element $(x_i - x_k)$ in this
product equals zero. Since the determinant of the coefficient matrix is non-zero,
the equations have a unique solution over the field $\mathbb{Z}_p$.

After Bob has got the unique solution $a_1, \cdots, a_m$, he can calculate other $n - m$
"public keys" (their discrete logs are unknown), using the following formula:

$$y_j = a_1 x_j + \cdots + a_m x_j^m, \ m < j \leq n$$

As a result, he has n public keys $\{x_i, y_i\}_{i=1}^n$.

Bob shuffles his public keys such that the order is known to himself only.
The shuffled public keys are then made public. For convenience, we denote by
$\mathbb{U}$ the subset of public key indices whose associated public key discrete logs are
unknown to Bob and by $\mathbb{K}$ those known. Since the pubic keys will always come
with a shuffled form, we still denote by $\{x_i, y_i\}_{i=1}^n$ the shuffled public key set.

The public keys can be easily verified without knowing the corresponding private keys. Given the public key set $(x_i, y_i)_{i=1}^n$, we can choose **any** m of public keys from the public key set, and then calculate $\hat{a}_i$ for $i = 1, \cdots, m$ with respect to the m public keys, where $\hat{a}_i \subset \{a_i\}_{i=1}^n$. With the resultant $\hat{a}_i$, we can verify the rest of $(n - m)$ public keys,

$$\hat{y}_j = \hat{a}_1 x_j + \cdots + \hat{a}_m x_j^m, \quad m < j \le n.$$

Here, $\hat{y}_j \subset \{y_i\}_{i=1}^n$ have not been used in computation of $\hat{a}_i$.

Claim 3: *Given x_i, Bob cannot cheat by pre-selecting y_i.*

The explanation is as follows. After Bob found the unique coefficient set $\{a'_i\}_{i=1}^m$, he can compute y_i for $i \in \mathbb{U}$ in terms of the given $\{x_i\}_{i=m+1}^n$. However, it is infeasible for him to compute the discrete logs of these values in poly-time. Bob should not be able to cheat by pre-selecting $\{y_i\}_{i=m+1}^n$ and then trying to find $\{a'_i\}_{i=1}^m$ that satisfies all n equations. To fix this potential problem, we give the following lemma.

Lemma 1. *To prevent Bob from cheating by pre-selecting all $\{y_i\}_{i=m+1}^n$, the rank of matrix A' must be $m + 1$, where*

$$A' = \begin{pmatrix} 1 & x_1 & x_1^2 & \cdots & x_1^{m-1} & y_1 \\ 1 & x_2 & x_2^2 & \cdots & x_2^{m-1} & y_2 \\ \vdots & \vdots & \vdots & & \vdots & \vdots \\ 1 & x_n & x_n^2 & \cdots & x_n^{m-1} & y_n \end{pmatrix},$$

which is an $n \times (m + 1)$ matrix.

Proof: Rewrite Equations (2) as

$$A' \begin{pmatrix} a_1 \\ a_2 \\ \vdots \\ a_m \\ -1 \end{pmatrix} = \begin{pmatrix} 0 \\ 0 \\ \vdots \\ 0 \end{pmatrix}.$$

Because the rank of A' is $m + 1$, it can be rewritten as

$$A' = \begin{pmatrix} & & B \\ & 0 & \\ 0 & & \end{pmatrix}$$

The triangle matrix is an $(m + 1) \times (m + 1)$ non-singular matrix, where B represents the non-zero part. Assuming that the triangle matrix is T, we have

$$
\begin{pmatrix} a_1 \\ a_2 \\ \vdots \\ a_m \\ -1 \end{pmatrix} = T^{-1} \begin{pmatrix} 0 \\ 0 \\ \vdots \\ 0 \\ 0 \end{pmatrix}
$$

Because T^{-1} is non-zero, it implies that the equations with respect to a_i have no solution at all. In other words, Bob cannot find a solution if he wants to cheat by precomputing y_i. □

Therefore, in the verification of public keys, we also need to check if or not the rank of A' is equal to $m + 1$.

Claim 4: *The setup is correct for $1 \leq m < n$.*

We have clearly described how to set up the public keys. The correctness for $m > 1$ is obvious. However, let us look at the special case when $m = 1$. In this case, Equation (1) is reduced into one equation, $a_1 x_1 = y_1$, where Bob has one private key s_1 and associated public key y_1. Actually, we can see that the setup process works in the same way. Given x_1 and y_1, a_1 can be determined. Using a_1 and $\{x_i\}_{i=2}^n$ we can form $y_i = a_1 x_i$ for $i = 2, \cdots, n$.

3.2   Efficient Interactive m out of n OT Schemes

An interactive $\binom{n}{m}$-OT scheme can be easily converted into a chosen $\binom{n}{m}$-OT version, therefore it is worth for us to extend our presentation in Section 2 in order to describe a more efficient interactive $\binom{n}{m}$-OT. Based on the setup given in the preceding subsection, the new scheme requires Alice to implement only n encryptions.

The setup phase has been given the preceding subsection, but we need to assume that the public keys $\{x_i, y_i\}_{i=1}^n$ are shared by Alice and Bob only. The correctness of these public keys can be verified by both parties.

The $\binom{n}{m}$-OT protocol is described as follows:

1: Bob:
  - Chooses m session keys, k_j.
  - Encrypts k_j:
    * Selects a random number $w_j \in_R \mathbb{Z}_q$, $j \in \mathbb{K}$.
    * Computes $r_j = k_j g^{w_j}$ and $k_j' = s_j r_j + w_j \bmod q$. The ciphertext is the doublet (r_j, k_j'), which can be decrypted with y_j, $j \in \mathbb{K}$. Note that we are actually using the Nyberg-Rueppel digital signature scheme[11]. Here, we treat the signature as encryption since the public keys are shared by Alice and Bob only. The reason we choose this scheme is that the verification of a Nyberg-Rueppel signature reveals the message.

Alice	Bob
$y_i, i = 1, \cdots, n$	$y_i, s_i, k_j, i = 1, \cdots, n, j \in \mathbb{K}$
	$w_j \in_R \mathbb{Z}_q, r_j = k_j g^{w_j}$
	$k'_j = s_j r_j + w_j \bmod q$
	$k'_j \to k''_i, r_j \to r'_i$
$\xleftarrow{\quad k''_i, r'_i \quad}$	
$k_i = g^{-k''_i} y_i^{r'_i} r'_i$	
$C_i = E_{k_i}(M_i)$	
$\xrightarrow{\quad C_i \quad}$	
	$M_j = D_{k_j}(C_j), j \in \mathbb{K}$

Fig. 2. The efficient interactive *m* out of *n* oblivious transfer protocol.

- Extends the k'_j set by adding $n - m$ random numbers (as dummies) to those positions whose indices are in $\mathbb{U}$ to form k''_i, $i = 1, \cdots, n$, which are placed in order. Similarly, extends r_j to r'_i.
- Sends k''_i and r'_i to Alice.

2: Alice:
  - Decrypts k''_i using all y_i in order, $k_i = g^{-k''_i} y_i^{r'_i} r'_i$, to get n "keys". Only *m* of them are correct.
  - Encrypts *n* messages using k_i in order, $C_i = E_{k_i}(M_i)$.
  - Sends C_i to Bob.

3: Bob decrypts *m* of C_i, $M_j = D_{k_j}(C_j), j \in \mathbb{K}$.

The obvious save is that Alice needs to compute only *n* encryptions but not $m \times n$ encryptions as in the first $\binom{n}{m}$-OT protocol.

Claim 5: *(Completeness) The completeness of the protocol is twofold: Alice can correctly decrypt m out of n keys in Step 2, if Bob has encrypted the m keys using his correct private keys. Bob can then correctly decrypt m messages in Step 3, if Alice correctly follows the process.*

The second one is obvious. The first one is due to the correctness of the Nyberg-Rueppel digital signature scheme. The decryptions are in fact the verification of the signatures.

Claim 6: *(Soundness) Bob can obtain at most m correct messages.*

Bob can at most select *m* symmetric keys, since he has only *m* private keys, s_j. If these session keys are properly encrypted, then in decryption Alice can obtain *m* of them only. Of course, Alice should have carefully checked the correctness of the public keys prior to the OT. Although Bob's encryption of k_j is the variant of Nyberg-Rueppel Digital Signature Scheme, the security is not compromised. This is because the "public keys", y_i, are actually known to Alice and Bob only; none else except Alice and Bob can decrypt the "signatures". Bob cannot cheat by using a his private key more than once, since his public keys on Alice side are placed in order and are used once only.

3.3   Non-interactive m out of n OT

The OT scheme given in preceding subsection is interactive, because it requires Alice and Bob interact each other during a transfer. In this section, we describe a new noninteractive OT scheme, where Bob does not need to communicate to Alice during a transfer.

Using the setup phase given in Section 3.1, Bob obtains his private keys s_i for $i = 1, \cdots, m$ and his public keys $\{x_i, y_i\}_{i=1}^n$ where the discrete logs of y_i for $i \in \mathbb{U}$ are not known. The protocol is described as follows.

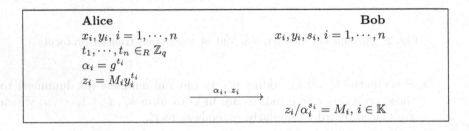

Fig. 3. Non-interactive m out of n OT protocol.

- Alice:
    - randomly chooses $t_1, \cdots, t_n \in_R \mathbb{Z}_q$,
    - calculates $\alpha_i = g^{t_i}$, $i = 1, \cdots, n$,
    - generates the order of messages at random,
    - based on the order, calculates $z_i = M_i y_i^{t_i}$ for $i = 1, \cdots, n$, and
    - then sends to Bob $\alpha_1, \cdots, \alpha_n$ and $z_1, \cdots, z_n$.
- Bob: decrypts z_i to recover m messages, $z_i / \alpha_i^{s_i} = M_i$, $i \in \mathbb{K}$.

Claim 7: *(Completeness) If Alice correctly follows the procedure, Bob can recover m out of n messages, $1 \le m < n$.*

This is obvious. Note the facts that the order of the public keys are not changed and Bob knows their indices. Bob has m private decryption keys s_i, $i \in \mathbb{K}$, and knows which ones to decrypt. The encryptions done by Alice are based on the standard ElGamal encryption scheme.[12]

Claim 8: *(Soundness) Both Alice and Bob cannot cheat.*

Alice does not know which public keys are associated with Bob's m private keys, so she cannot know which messages Bob can decrypt and has no control over which messages Bob will receive. Bob cannot cheat by manipulating his public keys. This is because Alice can check the correctness of Bob's public key using the method described earlier in this paper. The security is, however, based on the assumption that our system is poly-time-bounded. Bob cannot solve the discrete log problem in poly-time.

3.4   Non-malleable Encryption

In the schemes presented in this section, Alice was assumed to be honest in that she always uses Bob's public keys in encryption. The assumption is reasonable, since Alice wants Bob to receive m out of n messages she sent. However, if the order of the public keys or the order of the ciphertext is changed by accident (or by an adversary) during the transmission, Bob will not be able to find the fraud in the case that the messages consist of unrecognised strings. This kind of fraud could be fixed by also sending hashed messages when Alice is absolutely honest. However, since hash functions are computed by Alice, Bob cannot find out the potential fraud if Alice attempts to manipulate the process. We now modify the scheme so that he can check if or not the encrypted messages sent by Alice are correctly constructed. The obvious method is to make non-malleable encryption by using double encryptions. The protocol is then modified as

1: Alice randomly chooses $t_1, \cdots, t_n \in_R \mathbb{Z}_q$ and $t'_1, \cdots, t'_n \in_R \mathbb{Z}_q$, calculates
   - $\alpha_i = g^{t_i}$ and $\alpha'_i = g^{t'_i}$, $i = 1, \cdots, n$,
   - $z_i = M_i y_i^{t_i}$ and $z'_i = M_i y_i^{t'_i}$ for $i = 1, \cdots, n$,
   and then sends to Bob $\alpha_1, \cdots, \alpha_n$, $\alpha_1, \cdots, \alpha_n$, $z_1, \cdots, z_n$, and $z'_1, \cdots, z'_n$.
2: Bob decrypts: $z_i/\alpha_i^{s_i} = M_i$ and $z'_i/\alpha_i'^{s_i} = M_i$, $i \in \mathbb{K}$ to recover m messages and checks the messages obtained from two separate encryptions are equal.

The completeness of the protocol is obvious: if Alice has used Bob's public keys in encryption, Bob can find the messages from two different encryptions are equal. Let us then take a look at the soundness. If a substituted/different public key $y'_l = g^{s_l}$ is used in the encryption of message M_l, the messages from two different decryptions will not be equal because $t \neq t'$.

The drawback of this scheme is the compromise of the computational efficiency. We now construct a non-malleable encryption by reconstructing the private keys: select private keys, $s_i \in \mathbb{Z}_q$, and some integers, $s'_i \in \mathbb{Z}_q$, such that they satisfy $s_i s'_i \bmod q = s_i$. It is not hard to find that we can select any s_i and s'_i that satisfy $s_i(s'_i - 1) = q$ and $s'_i \neq 1$. Bob needs to keep s_i and s'_i secret. His public keys are still the same. The correctness of the encryptions can then be verified during the decryption. Bob now decrypts the obliviously transferred messages using two different methods: for message M_i,

Method 1: Compute $z_i^{s'_i}/\alpha_i^{s_i} = M_i^{s'_i}$ and then remove s'_i.
Method 2: Compute $z_i/\alpha_i^{s_i} = M_i$.

Bob then checks the equality of two messages. The completeness is straightforward. To prove the soundness, we assume that Alice has not correctly used Bob's public keys in her encryptions, but uses g^{σ_i}. Bob can immediately find the fraud.

Method 1: Compute $(M_i g^{t_i \sigma_i})^{s'_i}/\alpha_i^{s_i} = M_i^{s'_i} g^{t_i(s'_i \sigma_i - s_i)}$. Remove s'_i from the message, Bob then gets $M_i g^{t_i(\sigma_i - s_i s'^{-1}_i)}$.
Method 2: Compute $M_i g^{t_i \sigma_i}/\alpha_i^{s_i} = M_i g^{t_i(\sigma_i - s_i)}$.

Obviously, they are not equal.

4 Concluding Remarks

We have proposed several novel $\binom{n}{m}$-OT schemes that have been proved secure. Our schemes cover all possible types of OT, i.e., n can be an arbitrary number that is greater than one and $0 < m < n$. Actually, these schemes also cover the Rabin's original scheme, where Alice sends only one message to Bob, while she does not know if or not Bob receives the message. Let us take our first m out of n OT protocol as an example. Let $m = 1$ and $n = 2$. To convert the protocol to the Rabin's type, Alice, in Step 4, picks only one decrypted key at random and encrypts a message using the key. Alice then sends the encrypted message to Bob and tells him which "key" (the first one or the second one) was used in the encryption. Upon receiving the encrypted message, Bob in turn decrypts it. The decryption is correct, only if Alice has picked the sole correct key (with probability $1/2$); otherwise Bob gets nothing.

There are numerous applications of OT.[9,13,14,15,16] A straightforward application of the proposed $\binom{n}{m}$-OT's is in electronic commerce. Take the protocol in Section 2 as an example. Using the protocol, we can construct an online video shop. What we should do is to convert the protocol into a chosen $\binom{n}{m}$-OT by assuming that messages (videos) to be sent to Bob are placed in order and the order will not be changed by Alice. Alice is now the Internet merchant who wants to sell videos over the Internet, while her clients can get what they want without revealing which ones they have selected (assume all prices are equal).

Acknowledgements. The authors thank the anonymous referees for useful comments on the previous version of this paper.

References

1. M. O. Rabin, "How exchange secrets by oblivious transfer," tech. rep., TR-81, Computer Science Laboratory, Harvard, 1981.
2. S. Even, O. Goldreich, and A. Lempel, "A randomized protocol for signing contracts," in *Advances in cryptology - CRYPTO'82, Lecture Notes in Computer Science*, pp. 205–210, Springer Verlag, Berlin, 1982.
3. C. Crepeau, "Equivalence between two flavours of oblivious transfers," in *Advances in cryptology - CRYPTO'87, Lecture Notes in Computer Science 1403*, pp. 350–354, Springer-Verlag, Berlin, 1987.
4. C. Crepeau and J. Kilian, "Weakening security assumptions and oblivious tranfer," in *Advances in cryptology - CRYPTO'88, Lecture Notes in Computer Science 1403*, pp. 2–7, Springer-Verlag, Berlin, 1988.
5. G. Brassard, C. Crepeau, and J.-M. Robert, "Information theoretic reductions among disclose problem," in *Symp. of Found of computer science*, pp. 168–173, IEEE, 1986.
6. B. den Boer, "Oblivious transfer protecting secrecy," in *Advances in cryptology - EUROCRYPT'90, Lecture Notes in Computer Science 1403*, pp. 31–46, Springer-Verlag, Berlin, 1990.
7. G. Brassard and C. Crepeau, "All or nothing disclosure of secrets," in *Advances in cryptology - CRYPTO'86, Lecture Notes in Computer Science 1403*, Springer-Verlag, Berlin, 1987.

8. A. D. Santis and G. Persiano, "Public-randomness in public-key cryptography," in *Advances in cryptology - EUROCRYPTO'90, Lecture Notes in Computer Science 1403*, pp. 46–61, Springer-Verlag, Berlin, 1990.
9. B. Aiello, Y. Ishai, and O. Reingold, "Priced oblivious transfer: how to sell digital goods," in *Advances in cryptology - EUROCRYPTO 2001, Lecture Notes in Computer Science 2045*, pp. 119–135, Springer-Verlag, Berlin, 2001.
10. M. Bellare and S. Micali, "Non-interactive oblivious transfer and application," in *Advances in cryptology - CRYPTO'89, Lecture Notes in Computer Science 1403*, pp. 547–557, Springer-Verlag, Berlin, 1989.
11. K. Nyberg and R. A. Rueppel, "Message recovery for signature schemes based on the discrete logarithm problem," pp. 182–193, Springer-Verlag, 1994.
12. T. ElGamal, "A public-key cryptosystem and a signature scheme based on discrete logarithms," pp. 10–18, Springer-Verlag, Berlin, 1985.
13. M. Stadler and J.-M. Piveteau, "Fair blind signature," in *Advances in cryptology - CRYPTO'95, Lecture Notes in Computer Science 1403*, pp. 209–219, Springer-Verlag, Berlin, 1995.
14. J. Kilian, "Basing cryptography on oblivious transfer," in *Proc. of STOC*, 1988.
15. O. Goldreich, S. Micali, and A. Wigderson, "How to play any mental game," in *Proc. of STOC*, 1987.
16. A. C. Yao, "How to generate and exchange secrets," in *Proc. of STOC*, 1986.

On the Security of Reduced Versions of 3-Pass HAVAL

Sangwoo Park[1], Soo Hak Sung[2], Seongtaek Chee[1], and Jongin Lim[3]

[1] National Security Research Institute, Korea,
{psw,chee}@etri.re.kr
[2] Department of Applied Mathematics, Pai Chai University, Korea
sungsh@woonam.paichai.ac.kr
[3] Center for Information Security Technologies(CIST), Korea University, Korea
jilim@cist.korea.ac.kr

Abstract. HAVAL is a dedicated hash function of the MD family which was proposed by Zheng *et al.* In this paper, we study the security of reduced versions of 3-pass HAVAL. We find a 256-bit collision of the first two passes of 3-pass HAVAL and of the last two passes of 3-pass HAVAL.

1 Introduction

Hash functions are used for many cryptographic applications, such as message authentication and digital signature. A hash function is a computationally efficient function which maps binary strings of arbitrary length to binary strings of some fixed length. A compression, an easy computing, and a collision resistance are criteria for cryptographic hash functions. The collision resistance of a hash function means that it is computationally infeasible to find any two distinct messages with the same hash value. Since the hash function MD4 [11] was introduced by R. Rivest, many dedicated hash functions based on design principles of MD4 have been proposed. MD5 [12], HAVAL [14], RIPEMD [10], RIPEMD-160 [7], SHA-1 [9] are dedicated hash functions of the MD family.

The dedicated hash functions of the MD family have been cryptanalyzed during the past years. An attack on the last two rounds of the MD4 was proposed by den Boer and Bosselaers [3], and an attack on the first two rounds of the MD4 was proposed by Vaudenay [13]. Dobbertin established a collision attack on the full rounds of the MD4 [6]. Furthermore, Dobbertin found collisions for both the first and the last two rounds of the compression function of RIPEMD [5]. Debaert and Gilbert presented a method for finding collisions in each of the parallel lines of RIPEMD [2]. The pseudo collisions on the whole MD5 compression function were found by den Boer and Bosselaers [4]. Chabaud and Jaux discovered an attack that allowed them to find collisions for SHA-0 in approximately 2^{61} SHA-0 computations. Finally, Kasselman and Penzhorn found collisions for the last two passes of 3-pass HAVAL [8].

HAVAL is a dedicated hash function of the MD family which was proposed by Zheng *et al.* [14]. HAVAL compresses a message of arbitrary length into a hash

L. Batten and J. Seberry (Eds.): ACISP 2002, LNCS 2384, pp. 406–419, 2002.
© Springer-Verlag Berlin Heidelberg 2002

value of 128, 160, 192, 224, or 256 bits. HAVAL has a parameter that controls the number of passes a message block of 1024 bits is processed. A message block can be processed in 3,4, or 5 passes. When a message block is processed in three passes, we call such a case 3-pass HAVAL. So, there are three kinds of HAVAL: 3-pass HAVAL, 4-pass HAVAL, and 5-pass HAVAL.

In this paper, we study the security of reduced versions of 3-pass HAVAL. We propose a method for finding the collisions for the first two passes of 3-pass HAVAL and for the last two passes of 3-pass HAVAL. This approach of reducing the number of passes is similar to the initial attacks on MD4 [3,13]. We represent the first two passes of 3-pass HAVAL as HAVAL[12] and the last two passes of 3-pass HAVAL as HAVAL[23].

2   Description of the HAVAL Compression Function

Throughout this paper, the $+$ symbol represents a modulo 2^{32} addition. $X \oplus Y$, XY and $X \vee Y$ represent the bitwise exclusive OR, bitwise AND, and the bitwise OR of X and Y, respectively. The symbol $\sim X$ represents the bitwise complement of X. The symbol $X^{\gg s}$ denotes the right cyclic shift of X by s bit positions to the right.

The HAVAL compression function transforms a 8-word(256 bits) initial value $(A_0, B_0, C_0, D_0, E_0, F_0, G_0, H_0)$ and a 32-word message block $X = (X_0, X_1, \ldots, X_{31})$ into a 256-bit output value $(AA, BB, CC, DD, EE, FF, GG, HH)$. The 8-word initial value is as followings:

$$A_0 = 0xec4e6c89, \ B_0 = 0x082efa98, \ C_0 = 0x299f31d0, \ D_0 = 0xa4093822$$
$$E_0 = 0x03707344, \ F_0 = 0x13198a2e, \ G_0 = 0x85a308d3, \ H_0 = 0x243f6a88.$$

Each of the passes of the HAVAL compression function consists of 32 steps and each step processes a different word. The orders in which the words are processed differ from pass to pass. Word processing orders are presented in Table 1.

Table 1. Word Processing Orders

pass 1	0	1	2	3	4	5	6	7	8	9	10	11	12	13	14	15
	16	17	18	19	20	21	22	23	24	25	26	27	28	29	30	31
pass 2	5	14	26	18	11	28	7	16	0	23	20	22	1	10	4	8
	30	3	21	9	17	24	29	6	19	12	15	13	2	25	31	27
pass 3	19	9	4	20	28	17	8	22	29	14	25	12	24	30	16	26
	31	15	7	3	1	0	18	27	13	6	21	10	23	11	5	2
pass 4	24	4	0	14	2	7	28	23	26	6	30	20	18	25	19	3
	22	11	31	21	8	27	12	9	1	29	5	15	17	10	16	13
pass 5	27	3	21	26	17	11	20	29	19	0	12	7	13	8	31	10
	5	9	14	30	18	6	28	24	2	23	16	22	4	1	25	15

In addition, each pass employs a different Boolean function to perform bit-wise operations on words. The Boolean function $f_i(i = 1, 2, 3, 4, 5)$ is employed by the i-th pass.

$$f_1(x_6, x_5, x_4, x_3, x_2, x_1, x_0) = x_1x_4 \oplus x_2x_5 \oplus x_3x_6 \oplus x_0x_1 \oplus x_0$$

$$f_2(x_6, x_5, x_4, x_3, x_2, x_1, x_0) = x_1x_2x_3 \oplus x_2x_4x_5 \oplus x_1x_2 \oplus x_1x_4 \oplus x_2x_6 \oplus x_3x_5 \oplus$$
$$x_4x_5 \oplus x_0x_2 \oplus x_0$$

$$f_3(x_6, x_5, x_4, x_3, x_2, x_1, x_0) = x_1x_2x_3 \oplus x_1x_4 \oplus x_2x_5 \oplus x_3x_6 \oplus x_0x_3 \oplus x_0$$

$$f_4(x_6, x_5, x_4, x_3, x_2, x_1, x_0) = x_1x_2x_3 \oplus x_2x_4x_5 \oplus x_3x_4x_6 \oplus x_1x_4 \oplus x_2x_6 \oplus x_3x_4$$
$$\oplus x_3x_5 \oplus x_3x_6 \oplus x_4x_5 \oplus x_4x_6 \oplus x_0x_4 \oplus x_0$$

$$f_5(x_6, x_5, x_4, x_3, x_2, x_1, x_0) = x_1x_4 \oplus x_2x_5 \oplus x_3x_6 \oplus x_0x_1x_2x_3 \oplus x_0x_5 \oplus x_0$$

Now, we describe the step function of the HAVAL. Let $T_{i,j}(j = 0, 1, \ldots, 7)$ be the input of the step function at step i. Then, the step function of the HAVAL has a transformation of the form

$$Q = \begin{cases} f_r(P_{3,r}(T_{i,6}, T_{i,5}, T_{i,4}, T_{i,3}, T_{i,2}, T_{i,1}, T_{i,0})), & \text{for 3-pass HAVAL} \\ f_r(P_{4,r}(T_{i,6}, T_{i,5}, T_{i,4}, T_{i,3}, T_{i,2}, T_{i,1}, T_{i,0})), & \text{for 4-pass HAVAL} \\ f_r(P_{5,r}(T_{i,6}, T_{i,5}, T_{i,4}, T_{i,3}, T_{i,2}, T_{i,1}, T_{i,0})), & \text{for 5-pass HAVAL} \end{cases}$$
$$R = Q^{\gg 7} + T_{i,7}^{\gg 11} + X_{ord_r(i)} + K_i;$$
$$T_{i+1,7} = T_{i,6}; T_{i+1,6} = T_{i,5}; T_{i+1,5} = T_{i,4}; T_{i+1,4} = T_{i,3};$$
$$T_{i+1,3} = T_{i,2}; T_{i+1,2} = T_{i,1}; T_{i+1,1} = T_{i,0}; T_{i+1,0} = R,$$

where r denotes the pass number, $ord_r(i)$ denotes the word processing order in Table 1, and K_i denotes the 32-bit constant word. All constant words used in HAVAL are taken from the fraction part of π. In pass 1, the constant words $K_i(i = 0, \ldots, 31)$ are omitted and, from pass 2 to pass 5, the constant words are different from step to step. Note that the input to step i ($T_{i,6}$, $T_{i,5}$, $T_{i,4}$, $T_{i,3}$, $T_{i,2}$, $T_{i,1}$, $T_{i,0}$) is permuted according to $P_{3,r}$ for 3-pass HAVAL, $P_{4,r}$ for 4-pass HAVAL, and $P_{5,r}$ for 5-pass HAVAL before being passed to f_r. Here $P_{3,r}$, $P_{4,r}$ and $P_{5,r}$ are permutations on coordinates specified in Table 2.

3   Attack on HAVAL[12]

In this section, we propose an attack allowing us to find collisions for HAVAL[12]. For two 32-bit vectors X and $\tilde{X}$, we will define the difference of X and $\tilde{X}$ as follows:

$$\Delta X = X - \tilde{X} \quad (\text{mod } 2^{32}).$$

$A_i, B_i, C_i, D_i, E_i, F_i, G_i, H_i$ represent the chaining variables after step i for a message block $X = (X_0, \ldots, X_{31})$, and $\tilde{A}_i, \tilde{B}_i, \tilde{C}_i, \tilde{D}_i, \tilde{E}_i, \tilde{F}_i, \tilde{G}_i, \tilde{H}_i$ represent the chaining variables after step i for a message block $\tilde{X} = (\tilde{X}_0, \ldots, \tilde{X}_{31})$.

To find collisions for HAVAL[12], we should find two distinct message blocks X and $\tilde{X}$ which have the same chaining variables after step 64, i.e. $A_{64} = \tilde{A}_{64}$,

Table 2. Permutations on Coordinates

Permutation	x_6 x_5 x_4 x_3 x_2 x_1 x_0
$P_{3,1}$	x_1 x_0 x_3 x_5 x_6 x_2 x_4
$P_{3,2}$	x_4 x_2 x_1 x_0 x_5 x_3 x_6
$P_{3,3}$	x_6 x_1 x_2 x_3 x_4 x_5 x_0
$P_{4,1}$	x_2 x_6 x_1 x_4 x_5 x_3 x_0
$P_{4,2}$	x_3 x_5 x_2 x_0 x_1 x_6 x_4
$P_{4,3}$	x_1 x_4 x_3 x_6 x_0 x_2 x_5
$P_{4,4}$	x_6 x_4 x_0 x_5 x_2 x_1 x_3
$P_{5,1}$	x_3 x_4 x_1 x_0 x_5 x_2 x_6
$P_{5,2}$	x_6 x_2 x_1 x_0 x_3 x_4 x_5
$P_{5,3}$	x_2 x_6 x_0 x_4 x_3 x_1 x_5
$P_{5,4}$	x_1 x_5 x_3 x_2 x_0 x_4 x_6
$P_{5,5}$	x_2 x_5 x_0 x_6 x_4 x_3 x_1

$B_{64} = \tilde{B}_{64}$, $C_{64} = \tilde{C}_{64}$, $D_{64} = \tilde{D}_{64}$, $E_{64} = \tilde{E}_{64}$, $F_{64} = \tilde{F}_{64}$, $G_{64} = \tilde{G}_{64}$, $H_{64} = \tilde{H}_{64}$.

The HAVAL compression function has eight chaining variables and only one chaining variable is updated at each step. If non-zero difference happens between some chaining variable updated by X and that of $\tilde{X}$ at step i, we do not have any chance to eliminate the difference till $i + 8$ step.

The underlying observation is that the message word X_{28} is used at step 29 and at step 38 of HAVAL[12] and the difference between those steps is 9. Therefore, we consider two distinct message blocks X and $\tilde{X}$ such that

$$X_{28} \neq \tilde{X}_{28}, \quad X_i = \tilde{X}_i (i \neq 28).$$

Table 3 shows the chaining variables and message words that are employed from step 29 to step 38. The boxed variable represents the chaining variable which is updated at each step.

To make $(X,\tilde{X})$ a collision of HAVAL[12], we should have that $A_{38} = \tilde{A}_{38}$, $B_{38} = \tilde{B}_{38}$, $C_{38} = \tilde{C}_{38}$, $D_{38} = \tilde{D}_{38}$, $E_{38} = \tilde{E}_{38}$, $F_{38} = \tilde{F}_{38}$, $G_{38} = \tilde{G}_{38}$, and $H_{38} = \tilde{H}_{38}$. Since we know that $\Delta A_{38} = \Delta A_{32}$, $\Delta B_{38} = \Delta B_{31}$, $\Delta D_{38} = \Delta D_{37}$, $\Delta E_{38} = \Delta E_{36}$, $\Delta F_{38} = \Delta F_{35}$, $\Delta G_{38} = \Delta G_{34}$, and $\Delta H_{38} = \Delta H_{33}$, we can establish the following conditions under which $(X,\tilde{X})$ can be a collision for HAVAL[12]:

$$\Delta A_{32} = 0, \Delta B_{31} = 0, \Delta C_{38} = 0, \Delta D_{37} = 0,$$
$$\Delta E_{36} = 0, \Delta F_{35} = 0, \Delta G_{34} = 0, \Delta H_{33} = 0.$$

Now, we analyze each step from step 29 to step 38 and establish the set of equations satisfying the conditions under which $(X, \tilde{X})$ can be a collision. D_{29} and $\tilde{D}_{29}$ are updated at step 29 as follows:

Table 3. Chaining variables updated from step 29 to step 38

step	chaining variables								message word
29	A_{29}	B_{29}	C_{29}	D_{29}	E_{29}	F_{29}	G_{29}	H_{29}	X_{28}
30	A_{30}	B_{30}	C_{30}	D_{30}	E_{30}	F_{30}	G_{30}	H_{30}	X_{29}
31	A_{31}	B_{31}	C_{31}	D_{31}	E_{31}	F_{31}	G_{31}	H_{31}	X_{30}
32	A_{32}	B_{32}	C_{32}	D_{32}	E_{32}	F_{32}	G_{32}	H_{32}	X_{31}
33	A_{33}	B_{33}	C_{33}	D_{33}	E_{33}	F_{33}	G_{33}	H_{33}	X_{5}
34	A_{34}	B_{34}	C_{34}	D_{34}	E_{34}	F_{34}	G_{34}	H_{34}	X_{14}
35	A_{35}	B_{35}	C_{35}	D_{35}	E_{35}	F_{35}	G_{35}	H_{35}	X_{26}
36	A_{36}	B_{36}	C_{36}	D_{36}	E_{36}	F_{36}	G_{36}	H_{36}	X_{18}
37	A_{37}	B_{37}	C_{37}	D_{37}	E_{37}	F_{37}	G_{37}	H_{37}	X_{11}
38	A_{38}	B_{38}	C_{38}	D_{38}	E_{38}	F_{38}	G_{38}	H_{38}	X_{28}

$$D_{29} = (G_{28}H_{28} \oplus C_{28}E_{28} \oplus B_{28}F_{28} \oplus A_{28}G_{28} \oplus A_{28})^{\ggg 7} + D_{28}^{\ggg 11} + X_{28}$$
$$\tilde{D}_{29} = (\tilde{G}_{28}\tilde{H}_{28} \oplus \tilde{C}_{28}\tilde{E}_{28} \oplus \tilde{B}_{28}\tilde{F}_{28} \oplus \tilde{A}_{28}\tilde{G}_{28} \oplus \tilde{A}_{28})^{\ggg 7} + \tilde{D}_{28}^{\ggg 11} + \tilde{X}_{28}.$$

Since $A_{28} = \tilde{A}_{28}$, $B_{28} = \tilde{B}_{28}$, $C_{28} = \tilde{C}_{28}$, $D_{28} = \tilde{D}_{28}$, $E_{28} = \tilde{E}_{28}$, $F_{28} = \tilde{F}_{28}$, $G_{28} = \tilde{G}_{28}$, and $H_{28} = \tilde{H}_{28}$, we arrive at the following equation:

$$\Delta D_{29} = \Delta X_{28} \neq 0.$$

At step 30, C_{30} and $\tilde{C}_{30}$ are updated as follows:

$$C_{30} = (F_{29}G_{29} \oplus B_{29}D_{29} \oplus A_{29}E_{29} \oplus H_{29}F_{29} \oplus H_{29})^{\ggg 7} + C_{29}^{\ggg 11} + X_{29}$$
$$\tilde{C}_{30} = (\tilde{F}_{29}\tilde{G}_{29} \oplus \tilde{B}_{29}\tilde{D}_{29} \oplus \tilde{A}_{29}\tilde{E}_{29} \oplus \tilde{H}_{29}\tilde{F}_{29} \oplus \tilde{H}_{29})^{\ggg 7} + \tilde{C}_{29}^{\ggg 11} + \tilde{X}_{29}.$$

Since $\Delta A_{29} = \Delta B_{29} = \Delta C_{29} = \Delta E_{29} = \Delta F_{29} = \Delta G_{29} = \Delta H_{29} = 0$ and $\Delta X_{29} = 0$, we can establish the following equation:

$$C_{30} - \tilde{C}_{30} = (F_{29}G_{29} \oplus B_{29}D_{29} \oplus A_{29}E_{29} \oplus H_{29}F_{29} \oplus H_{29})^{\ggg 7}$$
$$- (F_{29}G_{29} \oplus B_{29}\tilde{D}_{29} \oplus A_{29}E_{29} \oplus H_{29}F_{29} \oplus H_{29})^{\ggg 7}.$$

At the next step, B_{31} and $\tilde{B}_{31}$ are updated as follows:

$$B_{31} = (E_{30}F_{30} \oplus A_{30}C_{30} \oplus H_{30}D_{30} \oplus G_{30}E_{30} \oplus G_{30})^{\ggg 7} + B_{30}^{\ggg 11} + X_{30}$$
$$\tilde{B}_{31} - (\tilde{E}_{30}\tilde{F}_{30} \oplus \tilde{A}_{30}\tilde{C}_{30} \oplus \tilde{H}_{30}\tilde{D}_{30} \oplus \tilde{G}_{30}\tilde{E}_{30} \oplus \tilde{G}_{30})^{\ggg 7} + \tilde{B}_{30}^{\ggg 11} + \tilde{X}_{30}.$$

Since we know that $\Delta A_{30} = \Delta B_{30} = \Delta E_{30} = \Delta F_{30} = \Delta G_{30} = \Delta H_{30} = 0$ and $\Delta X_{30} = 0$, we arrive at the following equation:

$$\Delta B_{31} = 0$$
$$\Longleftrightarrow E_{30}F_{30} \oplus A_{30}C_{30} \oplus H_{30}D_{30} \oplus G_{30}E_{30} \oplus G_{30}$$
$$= E_{30}F_{30} \oplus A_{30}\tilde{C}_{30} \oplus H_{30}\tilde{D}_{30} \oplus G_{30}E_{30} \oplus G_{30}$$
$$\Longleftrightarrow A_{30}C_{30} \oplus H_{30}D_{30} = A_{30}\tilde{C}_{30} \oplus H_{30}\tilde{D}_{30}$$
$$\Longleftrightarrow H_{30} \cdot (D_{30} \oplus \tilde{D}_{30}) = A_{30} \cdot (C_{30} \oplus \tilde{C}_{30}).$$

Using a similar method, we analyze each step from step 32 to step 38 and establish the following ten equations:

$$D_{29} - \tilde{D}_{29} = X_{28} - \tilde{X}_{28} \tag{1}$$
$$C_{30} - \tilde{C}_{30} = (F_{27}G_{26} \oplus B_{23}D_{29} \oplus A_{24}E_{28} \oplus H_{25})^{\gg 7}$$
$$-(F_{27}G_{26} \oplus B_{23}\tilde{D}_{29} \oplus A_{24}E_{28} \oplus H_{25})^{\gg 7} \tag{2}$$
$$(C_{30} \oplus \tilde{C}_{30})A_{24} = (D_{29} \oplus \tilde{D}_{29})H_{25} \tag{3}$$
$$(D_{29} \oplus \tilde{D}_{29})(E_{28} \oplus F_{27}) = (C_{30} \oplus \tilde{C}_{30})G_{26} \tag{4}$$
$$(C_{30} \oplus \tilde{C}_{30})(F_{27}B_{31} \oplus A_{32} \oplus B_{31}) = (D_{29} \oplus \tilde{D}_{29})(F_{27}A_{32} \oplus F_{27} \oplus B_{31}) \tag{5}$$
$$(C_{30} \oplus \tilde{C}_{30})(E_{28}H_{33} \oplus E_{28} \oplus A_{32}) = (D_{29} \oplus \tilde{D}_{29})E_{28} \tag{6}$$
$$(D_{29} \oplus \tilde{D}_{29})(B_{31}G_{34} \oplus H_{33}A_{32} \oplus B_{31} \oplus E_{28}) = D_{29}C_{30} \oplus \tilde{D}_{29}\tilde{C}_{30} \tag{7}$$
$$(C_{30} \oplus \tilde{C}_{30})(A_{32}F_{35} \oplus G_{34}H_{33} \oplus A_{32} \oplus B_{31})$$
$$= D_{29}C_{30} \oplus \tilde{D}_{29}\tilde{D}_{30} \oplus D_{29} \oplus \tilde{D}_{29} \tag{8}$$
$$(H_{33}B_{31}E_{36} \oplus B_{31}F_{35}G_{34} \oplus H_{33}B_{31} \oplus H_{33}F_{35} \oplus B_{31}A_{32} \oplus E_{36}G_{34}$$
$$\oplus F_{35}G_{34} \oplus C_{30}B_{31} \oplus C_{30})^{\gg 7} + D_{29}^{\gg 11} = (H_{33}B_{31}E_{36} \oplus B_{31}F_{35}G_{34}$$
$$\oplus H_{33}B_{31} \oplus H_{33}F_{35} \oplus B_{31}A_{32} \oplus E_{36}G_{34} \oplus F_{35}G_{34} \oplus C_{30}B_{31} \oplus C_{30})^{\gg 7}$$
$$+\tilde{D}_{29}^{\gg 11} \tag{9}$$
$$C_{30}^{\gg 11} + X_{28} = \tilde{C}_{30}^{\gg 11} + \tilde{X}_{28} \tag{10}$$

Note that for $i = 1, 2, \ldots, 7$, $A_{24} = A_{24+i}$, $A_{32} = A_{32+i}$, $B_{23} = B_{23+i}$, $B_{31} = B_{31+i}$, $C_{30} = C_{30+i}$, $D_{29} = D_{29+i}$, $E_{28} = E_{28+i}$, $E_{36} = E_{36+i}$, $F_{27} = F_{27+i}$, $F_{35} = F_{35+i}$, $G_{26} = G_{26+i}$, $G_{34} = G_{34+i}$, $H_{25} = H_{25+i}$, and $H_{33} = H_{33+i}$.

Now, we find the solutions for the above set of equations and decide the values of chaining variables which provide that $(X, \tilde{X})$ can be a collision. At first, we specify the following:

$$A_{24} = H_{25} = G_{26} = F_{27} = E_{28} = B_{31} = A_{32} = 0.$$

Then, the equation (3), (4), (5), and (6) are satisfied. By equation (1) and equation (10), we obtain the following equation:

$$C_{30}^{\gg 11} - \tilde{C}_{30}^{\gg 11} + D_{29} - \tilde{D}_{29} = 0.$$

As a result, we should find the solutions for the following five equations:

$$C_{30} - \tilde{C}_{30} = (B_{23}D_{29})^{\gg 7} - (B_{23}\tilde{D}_{29})^{\gg 7} \tag{11}$$

$$D_{29}C_{30} \oplus \tilde{D}_{29}\tilde{C}_{30} = 0 \tag{12}$$

$$(C_{30} \oplus \tilde{C}_{30})G_{34}F_{35} = D_{29}C_{30} \oplus \tilde{D}_{29}\tilde{C}_{30} \oplus D_{29} \oplus \tilde{D}_{29} \tag{13}$$

$$(H_{33}F_{35} \oplus E_{36}G_{34} \oplus F_{35}G_{34} \oplus C_{30})^{\gg 7} + D_{29}^{\gg 11}$$
$$= (H_{33}F_{35} \oplus E_{36}G_{34} \oplus F_{35}G_{34} \oplus \tilde{C}_{30})^{\gg 7} + \tilde{D}_{29}^{\gg 11} \tag{14}$$

$$C_{30}^{\gg 11} - \tilde{C}_{30}^{\gg 11} + D_{29} - \tilde{D}_{29} = 0 \tag{15}$$

The following are solutions for equations (11), (12), (13), (14), and (15).

$$B_{23} = 2^7 = 0x80$$
$$D_{29} = -1 = 0xffffffff, \quad \tilde{D}_{29} = 0$$
$$C_{30} = 0, \quad \tilde{C}_{30} = -1 = 0xffffffff$$
$$H_{33} = G_{34} = -1 = 0xffffffff$$
$$E_{36} = 0$$

Note that we can not specify the value of F_{35}, because F_{27} and F_{35} are updated by X_{26} at step 27 and at step 35, respectively, and we already let $F_{27} = 0$ to find the solutions.

Table 4. The solutions for the set of equations from equation (1) to equation (10)

B_{23}	0x80		
A_{24}	0		
H_{25}	0		
G_{26}	0		
F_{27}	0		
E_{28}	0		
D_{29}	0xffffffff	$\tilde{D}_{29}$	0
C_{30}	0	$\tilde{C}_{30}$	0xffffffff
B_{31}	0		
A_{32}	0		
H_{33}	0xffffffff		
G_{34}	0xffffffff		
F_{35}	arbitrary		
E_{36}	0		

Now, we decide a collision $(X, \tilde{X})$. It is easy to compute the values of $X_i(22 \le i \le 25, 27 \le i \le 31)$. The operation at step 33 is $H_{33} = (D_{32}F_{32}A_{32} \oplus F_{32}B_{32}C_{32} \oplus D_{32}F_{32} \oplus D_{32}B_{32} \oplus F_{32}E_{32} \oplus A_{32}C_{32} \oplus B_{32}C_{32} \oplus G_{32}F_{32} \oplus G_{32})^{\gg 7} + H_{32}^{\gg 11} + X_5 + 0x452821e6$. By using the solutions in Table 4, we can compute

$$X_5 = 0xffffffff - 0x452821e6.$$

Similarly, from step 34, we can have

$$X_{14} = 0xffffffff - 0x38d01377.$$

Next, we will explain how to decide the values of X_{18} and X_{26}. Since F_{35} can have an arbitrary value at step 35, we can use the value of X_{26} which we obtain from step 27. At step 35, since $F_{35} = (B_{34}D_{34}G_{34} \oplus D_{34}H_{34}A_{34} \oplus B_{34}D_{34} \oplus B_{34}H_{34} \oplus D_{34}C_{34} \oplus G_{34}A_{34} \oplus H_{34}A_{34} \oplus E_{34}D_{34} \oplus E_{34})^{\gg 7} + F_{34}^{\gg 11} + X_{26} + 0xbe5466cf$, we can know that

$$F_{35} = X_{26} + 0xbe5466cf.$$

Furthermore, at step 36, since $E_{36} = (A_{35}C_{35}F_{35} \oplus C_{35}G_{35}H_{35} \oplus A_{35}C_{35} \oplus A_{35}G_{35} \oplus C_{35}B_{35} \oplus F_{35}H_{35} \oplus G_{35}H_{35} \oplus D_{35}C_{35} \oplus D_{35})^{\gg 7} + E_{35}^{\gg 11} + X_{18} + 0x34e90c6c$, we can have that

$$X_{18} = -(F_{35}^{\gg 7} + 0x34e90c6c).$$

So, we can have the following equation:

$$X_{26} = -0xbe5466cf + (-0x34e90c6c - X_{18})^{\gg 25}.$$

Since, from step 27, $X_{26} = -(C_{22}^{\gg 7} + F_{19}^{\gg 11})$, we can establish the condition for X_{18} as follows:

$$-(C_{22}^{\gg 7} + F_{19}^{\gg 11}) = -0xbe5466cf + (-0x34e90c6c - X_{18})^{\gg 25}.$$

To solve the above equation, we let X_{18} be an arbitrary value and compute C_{22}.

$$C_{22} = (F_{19}^{\gg 11} + 0xbe5466cf - (-0x34e90c6c - X_{18})^{\gg 25})^{\gg 25}.$$

Since, from step 22, $C_{22} = (F_{21}G_{21} \oplus B_{21}D_{21} \oplus A_{21}E_{21} \oplus H_{21}F_{21} \oplus H_{21})^{\gg 7} + C_{21}^{\gg 11} + X_{21}$, we can have the following equation for X_{21}:

$$X_{21} = (F_{19}^{\gg 11} + 0xbe5466cf - (-0x34e90c6c - X_{18})^{\gg 25})^{\gg 25}$$
$$- (F_{21}G_{21} \oplus B_{21}D_{21} \oplus A_{21}E_{21} \oplus H_{21}F_{21} \oplus H_{21})^{\gg 7} + C_{21}^{\gg 11}.$$

We can list the conditions under which $(X, \tilde{X})$ is a collision as follows:

$$X_5 = 0xffffffff - 0x452821e6$$
$$X_{14} = 0xffffffff - 0x38d01377$$
$$X_{21} = (F_{19}^{\gg 11} + 0xbe5466cf - (-0x34e90c6c - X_{18})^{\gg 25})^{\gg 25}$$
$$- (F_{21}G_{21} \oplus B_{21}D_{21} \oplus A_{21}E_{21} \oplus H_{21}F_{21} \oplus H_{21})^{\gg 7} + C_{21}^{\gg 11}.$$

Note that $X_i(22 \leq i \leq 31)$ can be decided from the step function, and $X_j(j \neq 5, 14, 21 \leq i \leq 31)$ can have an arbitrary value. Therefore, there are many collisions for HAVAL[12].

We give a collision for HAVAL[12] in Table 5 which has the following hash value:

$$0xa273fd7f, \ 0x483d4aa4, \ 0xab5eafc5, \ 0x2e8b8ef9,$$
$$0xe1d63dc2, \ 0xa2c51648, \ 0xdbf75650, \ 0x13548df.$$

Table 5. A collision for HAVAL[12]

$X_i(\tilde{X}_i)$	the values of $X_i(\tilde{X}_i)$	$X_i(\tilde{X}_i)$	the values of $X_i(\tilde{X}_i)$
$X_0(\tilde{X}_0)$	0	$X_{16}(\tilde{X}_{16})$	0
$X_1(\tilde{X}_1)$	0	$X_{17}(\tilde{X}_{17})$	0
$X_2(\tilde{X}_2)$	0	$X_{18}(\tilde{X}_{18})$	0
$X_3(\tilde{X}_3)$	0	$X_{18}(\tilde{X}_{19})$	0
$X_4(\tilde{X}_4)$	0	$X_{20}(\tilde{X}_{20})$	0
$X_5(\tilde{X}_5)$	0xbad7de19	$X_{21}(\tilde{X}_{21})$	0xeccfd659
$X_6(\tilde{X}_6)$	0	$X_{22}(\tilde{X}_{22})$	0xb593ece4
$X_7(\tilde{X}_7)$	0	$X_{23}(\tilde{X}_{23})$	0x2d8e2ef4
$X_8(\tilde{X}_8)$	0	$X_{24}(\tilde{X}_{24})$	0xcd6f4a4a
$X_9(\tilde{X}_9)$	0	$X_{25}(\tilde{X}_{25})$	0x4a45d2f3
$X_{10}(\tilde{X}_{10})$	0	$X_{26}(\tilde{X}_{26})$	0xcd256396
$X_{11}(\tilde{X}_{11})$	0	$X_{27}(\tilde{X}_{27})$	0xb9107999
$X_{12}(\tilde{X}_{12})$	0	$X_{28}(\tilde{X}_{28})$	0x260791c2(0x260791c3)
$X_{13}(\tilde{X}_{13})$	0	$X_{29}(\tilde{X}_{29})$	0x92102afd
$X_{14}(\tilde{X}_{14})$	0xc72fec88	$X_{30}(\tilde{X}_{30})$	0xf0000000
$X_{15}(\tilde{X}_{15})$	0	$X_{31}(\tilde{X}_{31})$	0

4   Attack on HAVAL[23]

Kasselman and Penzhorn already found a collision for the last two passes of 3-pass HAVAL, HAVAL[23] [8]. In this section, we find a collision of HAVAL[23] by a similar method which was proposed by Kasselman and Penzhorn. To find collisions of HAVAL[23], we should find two distinct message blocks X and $\tilde{X}$ which have the same chaining variables after step 96, i.e. $A_{96} = \tilde{A}_{96}$, $B_{96} = \tilde{B}_{96}$, $C_{96} = \tilde{C}_{96}$, $D_{96} = \tilde{D}_{96}$, $E_{96} = \tilde{E}_{96}$, $F_{96} = \tilde{F}_{96}$, $G_{96} = \tilde{G}_{96}$, $H_{96} = \tilde{H}_{96}$.

We consider two distinct message blocks X and $\tilde{X}$ as follows:

$$X_{19} \neq \tilde{X}_{19}, \quad X_i = \tilde{X}_i (i \neq 19).$$

Note that since the message word X_{19} is used at step 57 and at step 65 in HAVAL[23], the difference of those steps is 8. Table 6 shows the chaining variables and message blocks are employed from step 29 to step 38. The boxed variable represents the chaining variable which is updated at each step.

To make $(X, \tilde{X})$ a collision of HAVAL[23], we should have that $A_{65} = \tilde{A}_{65}$, $B_{65} = \tilde{B}_{65}$, $C_{65} = \tilde{C}_{65}$, $D_{65} = \tilde{D}_{65}$, $E_{65} = \tilde{E}_{65}$, $F_{65} = \tilde{F}_{65}$, $G_{65} = \tilde{G}_{65}$, and $H_{65} = \tilde{H}_{65}$. Since we know that $\Delta A_{65} = \Delta A_{64}$, $\Delta B_{65} = \Delta B_{63}$, $\Delta C_{65} = \Delta C_{62}$, $\Delta D_{65} = \Delta D_{61}$, $\Delta E_{65} = \Delta E_{60}$, $\Delta F_{65} = \Delta F_{59}$, $\Delta G_{65} = \Delta G_{58}$, we can establish the following conditions under which $(X, \tilde{X})$ can be a collision of HAVAL[23].

$$\Delta A_{64} = 0, \Delta B_{63} = 0, \Delta C_{62} = 0, \Delta D_{61} = 0,$$
$$\Delta E_{60} = 0, \Delta F_{59} = 0, \Delta G_{58} = 0, \Delta H_{65} = 0.$$

Table 6. Chaining variables updated from step 57 to step 65

step	chaining variables								message word
57	A_{57}	B_{57}	C_{57}	D_{57}	E_{57}	F_{57}	G_{57}	$\boxed{H_{57}}$	X_{19}
58	A_{58}	B_{58}	C_{58}	D_{58}	E_{58}	F_{58}	$\boxed{G_{58}}$	H_{58}	X_{12}
59	A_{59}	B_{59}	C_{59}	D_{59}	E_{59}	$\boxed{F_{59}}$	G_{59}	H_{59}	X_{15}
60	A_{60}	B_{60}	C_{60}	D_{60}	$\boxed{E_{60}}$	F_{60}	G_{60}	H_{60}	X_{13}
61	A_{61}	B_{61}	C_{61}	$\boxed{D_{61}}$	E_{61}	F_{61}	G_{61}	H_{61}	X_{2}
62	A_{62}	B_{62}	$\boxed{C_{62}}$	D_{62}	E_{62}	F_{62}	G_{62}	H_{62}	X_{25}
63	A_{63}	$\boxed{B_{63}}$	C_{63}	D_{63}	E_{63}	F_{63}	G_{63}	H_{63}	X_{31}
64	$\boxed{A_{64}}$	B_{64}	C_{64}	D_{64}	E_{64}	F_{64}	G_{64}	H_{64}	X_{27}
65	A_{65}	B_{65}	C_{65}	D_{65}	E_{65}	F_{65}	G_{65}	$\boxed{H_{65}}$	X_{19}

We analyze each step from step 57 to step 65 and establish the following nine equations:

$$H_{57} - \tilde{H}_{57} = X_{19} - \tilde{X}_{19} \tag{16}$$

$$(H_{57} \oplus \tilde{H}_{57})(C_{54}E_{52} \oplus B_{55}) = 0 \tag{17}$$

$$(H_{57} \oplus \tilde{H}_{57})(D_{53}A_{56} \oplus B_{55} \oplus A_{56}) = 0 \tag{18}$$

$$(H_{57} \oplus \tilde{H}_{57})(C_{54}G_{58} \oplus F_{59} \oplus G_{58}) = 0 \tag{19}$$

$$(H_{57} \oplus \tilde{H}_{57})(B_{55}E_{60} \oplus B_{55} \oplus F_{59}) = 0 \tag{20}$$

$$(H_{57} \oplus \tilde{H}_{57})A_{56} = 0 \tag{21}$$

$$(H_{57} \oplus \tilde{H}_{57})(F_{59}C_{62} \oplus D_{61}E_{60} \oplus F_{59} \oplus G_{38} \oplus A_{56}) = 0 \tag{22}$$

$$(H_{57} \oplus \tilde{H}_{57})(G_{58} \oplus 0xffffffff) = 0 \tag{23}$$

$$H_{57}^{\ggg 11} - \tilde{H}_{57}^{\ggg 11} = -(X_{19} - \tilde{X}_{19}) \tag{24}$$

At first, we find the values of H_{57} and $\tilde{H}_{57}$. ¿From equation (16) and equation (24), we arrive at the following equation:

$$H_{57}^{\ggg 11} - \tilde{H}_{57}^{\ggg 11} + H_{57} - \tilde{H}_{57} = 0. \tag{25}$$

At Eurocrypt'92, Berson proved that given n-bit X and Y, the value of $(X - Y)^{\ggg k} - (X^{\ggg k} - Y^{\ggg k})$ is the one of 0, $2^{n-k}-1$, 2^{n-k}, and $2^n - 1$ [1]. Therefore, we can find the solutions for equation (25) by finding the solutions for the following equations:

$$(H_{57} - \tilde{H}_{57})^{\ggg 11} + (H_{57} - \tilde{H}_{57}) = 0 \tag{26}$$

$$(H_{57} - \tilde{H}_{57})^{\ggg 11} + (H_{57} - \tilde{H}_{57}) = 2^{21} - 1 \tag{27}$$

$$(H_{57} - \tilde{H}_{57})^{\ggg 11} + (H_{57} - \tilde{H}_{57}) = 2^{21} \tag{28}$$

$$(H_{57} - \tilde{H}_{57})^{\ggg 11} + (H_{57} - \tilde{H}_{57}) = 2^{32} - 1. \tag{29}$$

Let $t = H_{57} - \tilde{H}_{57}$. Then, $t = 0$ for equation (26), $t = 0x5555555b$ and $t = 0xaaaaaaab$ for equation (28), and $t = 0x55555555$ and $t = 0xaaaaaaaa$ for equation (29). There is no solution for equation (27). Therefore, to decide the values of H_{57} and $\tilde{H}_{57}$, we find H_{57} and $\tilde{H}_{57}$ such that $H_{57} - \tilde{H}_{57} = 0x55555555, 0x5555555b, 0xaaaaaaaa$ or $0xaaaaaaab$, and confirm that such H_{57} and $\tilde{H}_{57}$ are the solutions of the equation (25).

Let $(H_{57} \oplus \tilde{H}_{57})(k)$ be the k-th bit of $H_{57} \oplus \tilde{H}_{57}$. If $(H_{57} \oplus \tilde{H}_{57})(k)$ is equal to 1, then we know the following from equation (17) to equation (23):

$$C_{54}(k)E_{52}(k) \oplus B_{55}(k) = 0$$
$$D_{53}(k)A_{56}(k) \oplus B_{55}(k) \oplus A_{56}(k) = 0$$
$$C_{54}(k)G_{58}(k) \oplus F_{59}(k) \oplus G_{58}(k) = 0$$
$$B_{55}(k)E_{60}(k) \oplus B_{55}(k) \oplus F_{59}(k) = 0$$
$$A_{56}(k) = 0$$
$$F_{59}(k)C_{62}(k) \oplus D_{61}(k)E_{60}(k) \oplus F_{59}(k) \oplus G_{38}(k) \oplus A_{56}(k) = 0$$
$$G_{58}(k) \oplus 1 = 0$$

The solutions for the set of the above equations are

$$E_{52}(k) = 0, C_{54}(k) = 1, B_{55}(k) = 0, A_{56}(k) = 0,$$
$$G_{58}(k) = 1, F_{59}(k) = 0, E_{60}(k) = 1, D_{61}(k) = 1,$$

and, $D_{53}(k)$ and $C_{62}(k)$ can be arbitrary values. The solutions for the set of equations from equation (16) to equation (24) are listed in Table 7. In Table 7, $S = H_{57} \oplus \tilde{H}_{57}$ and R denotes the 32-bit random value.

Table 7. The solutions for the set of equations from equation 16 to equation 24

E_{52}	$(\sim S)R$	G_{58}	$S \vee R$
D_{53}	arbitrary value	F_{59}	$(\sim S)R$
C_{54}	$S \vee R$	E_{60}	$S \vee R$
B_{55}	$(\sim S)R$	D_{61}	$S \vee R$
A_{56}	$(\sim S)R$	C_{62}	arbitrary value

Now, we decide a collision $(X, \tilde{X})$ of HAVAL[23] by the following order:

Step 1. Specify the values of X_i as arbitrary values for $i \neq$ 2,6,9,12,13, 15,19,24,29

Step 2. Compute X_9:

$$X_9 = E_{52} - (A_{51}C_{51}F_{51} \oplus C_{51}G_{51}H_{51} \oplus A_{51}C_{51} \oplus A_{51}G_{51} \oplus C_{51}B_{51}$$
$$\oplus F_{51}H_{51} \oplus G_{51}H_{51} \oplus D_{51}C_{51} \oplus D_{51})^{\gg 7} - E_{51}^{\gg 11} - 0xb3916cf7$$

Step 3. Let D_{53} be as follows:

$$D_{53} = (H_{52}B_{52}E_{52} \oplus B_{52}F_{52}G_{52} \oplus H_{52}B_{52} \oplus H_{52}F_{52} \oplus B_{52}A_{52} \oplus E_{52}G_{52}$$
$$\oplus F_{52}G_{52} \oplus C_{52}B_{52} \oplus C_{52})^{\ggg 7} + D_{52}^{\ggg 11} + X_{17} + 0x0801f2e2$$

Step 4. Compute X_{24}, X_{29} and X_6:

$$X_{24} = C_{54} - (G_{53}A_{53}D_{53} \oplus A_{53}E_{53}F_{53} \oplus G_{53}A_{53} \oplus G_{53}E_{53} \oplus A_{53}H_{53}$$
$$\oplus D_{53}F_{53} \oplus E_{53}F_{53} \oplus B_{53}A_{53} \oplus B_{53})^{\ggg 7} - C_{53}^{\ggg 11} - 0x858efc16$$

$$X_{29} = B_{55} - (F_{54}H_{54}C_{54} \oplus H_{54}D_{54}E_{54} \oplus F_{54}H_{54} \oplus F_{54}D_{54} \oplus H_{54}G_{54}$$
$$\oplus C_{54}E_{54} \oplus D_{54}E_{54} \oplus A_{54}H_{54} \oplus A_{54})^{\ggg 7} - B_{54}^{\ggg 11} - 0x636920d8$$

$$X_6 = A_{56} - (E_{55}G_{55}B_{55} \oplus G_{55}C_{55}D_{55} \oplus E_{55}G_{55} \oplus E_{55}C_{55} \oplus G_{55}F_{55}$$
$$\oplus B_{55}D_{55} \oplus C_{55}D_{55} \oplus H_{55}G_{55} \oplus H_{55})^{\ggg 7} - A_{55}^{\ggg 11} - 0x71574e69$$

Step 5. Compute X_{19} and $\tilde{X}_{19}$:

$$X_{19} = H_{57} - (D_{56}F_{56}A_{56} \oplus F_{56}B_{56}C_{56} \oplus D_{56}F_{56} \oplus D_{56}B_{56} \oplus F_{56}E_{56}$$
$$\oplus A_{56}C_{56} \oplus B_{56}C_{56} \oplus G_{56}F_{56} \oplus G_{56})^{\ggg 7} - H_{56}^{\ggg 11} - 0xa458fea3$$

$$\tilde{X}_{19} = \tilde{H}_{57} - (D_{56}F_{56}A_{56} \oplus F_{56}B_{56}C_{56} \oplus D_{56}F_{56} \oplus D_{56}B_{56} \oplus F_{56}E_{56}$$
$$\oplus A_{56}C_{56} \oplus B_{56}C_{56} \oplus G_{56}F_{56} \oplus G_{56})^{\ggg 7} - H_{56}^{\ggg 11} - 0xa458fea3$$

Step 6. Similarly, compute X_{12}, X_{15}, X_{13} and X_2

Let $H_{57} = 0xaaaab004$, $\tilde{H}_{57} = 0x0000055a$, and $S = H_{57} \oplus \tilde{H}_{57} = 0xaaaab55e$. In Table 8, we give a collision for HAVAL[23] which has the following hash value:

$$0xd3ad3176, 0x40e4b13c, 0x374e6bde, 0xcda35c41,$$
$$0x83b2496d, 0xb4931a23, 0xa08a1d28, 0x5b8ef68c.$$

5   Conclusion

In this paper, we have analyzed the security of reduced versions of 3-pass HAVAL. We consider the security of HAVAL[12], the first two passes of 3-pass HAVAL and the security of HAVAL[23], the last two passes of 3-pass HAVAL. We have established the conditions under which there exist collisions and have found a collision for HAVAL[12] and HAVAL[23]. Although our methods for finding the collisions for HAVAL[12] and HAVAL[23] have not led yet to a successful attack on the full 3-pass HAVAL, with the results in [8], our results indicate that 3-pass HAVAL has some weaknesses.

Table 8. A collision for HAVAL[23]

$X_i(\tilde{X}_i)$	the values of $X_i(\tilde{X}_i)$	$X_i(\tilde{X}_i)$	the values of $X_i(\tilde{X}_i)$
$X_0(\tilde{X}_0)$	0	$X_{16}(\tilde{X}_{16})$	0
$X_1(\tilde{X}_1)$	0	$X_{17}(\tilde{X}_{17})$	0
$X_2(\tilde{X}_2)$	0xd58a764	$X_{18}(\tilde{X}_{18})$	0
$X_3(\tilde{X}_3)$	0	$X_{19}(\tilde{X}_{19})$	0xe65c265f(0x3bb17bb5)
$X_4(\tilde{X}_4)$	0	$X_{20}(\tilde{X}_{20})$	0
$X_5(\tilde{X}_5)$	0	$X_{21}(\tilde{X}_{21})$	0
$X_6(\tilde{X}_6)$	0xa7891c3e	$X_{22}(\tilde{X}_{22})$	0
$X_7(\tilde{X}_7)$	0	$X_{23}(\tilde{X}_{23})$	0
$X_8(\tilde{X}_8)$	0	$X_{24}(\tilde{X}_{24})$	0x73e6fac2
$X_9(\tilde{X}_9)$	0xbe38682c	$X_{25}(\tilde{X}_{25})$	0
$X_{10}(\tilde{X}_{10})$	0	$X_{26}(\tilde{X}_{26})$	0
$X_{11}(\tilde{X}_{11})$	0	$X_{27}(\tilde{X}_{27})$	0
$X_{12}(\tilde{X}_{12})$	0x4dcf6368	$X_{28}(\tilde{X}_{28})$	0
$X_{13}(\tilde{X}_{13})$	0xe34933c9	$X_{29}(\tilde{X}_{29})$	0x6ea73074
$X_{14}(\tilde{X}_{14})$	0	$X_{30}(\tilde{X}_{30})$	0
$X_{15}(\tilde{X}_{15})$	0x9a31cbb	$X_{31}(\tilde{X}_{31})$	0

References

1. Thomas A. Berson. Differential cryptanalysis mod 2^{32} with applications to MD5. In Rainer A. Rueppel, editor, *Advances in Cryptology - Eurocrypt'92*, volume 658 of *Lecture Notes in Computer Science*, pages 71–80. Springer-Verlag, Berlin, 1992.
2. Christophe Debaert and Henri Gilbert. The RIPEMD^L and RIPEMD^R improved variants of MD4 are not collision free. In *Preproceegins of FSE 2001, 8th Fast Software Encryption Workshop*, pages 54–69, Yokohama, Japan, April 2001.
3. Bert den Boer and Antoon Bosselaers. An attack on the last two rounds of MD4. In Joan Feigenbaum, editor, *Advances in Cryptology - Crypto'91*, volume 576 of *Lecture Notes in Computer Science*, pages 194–203. Springer-Verlag, Berlin, 1992.
4. Bert den Boer and Antoon Bosselaers. Collisions for the compression function of MD5. In Tor Helleseth, editor, *Advances in Cryptology - Eurocrypt'93*, volume 765 of *Lecture Notes in Computer Science*, pages 293–304. Springer-Verlag, Berlin, 1993.
5. Hans Dobbertin. RIPEMD with two rounds compress function is not collision-free. *Journal of Cryptology*, 10(1):51–69, 1997.
6. Hans Dobbertin. Cryptanalysis of MD4. *Journal of Cryptology*, 11(4):253–271, 1998.
7. Hans Dobbertin, Antoon Bosselaers, and Bart Prencel. RIPEMD-160: A strengthened version of RIPEMD. *ftp.esat.kuleuven.ac.be/pub/COSIC/bossselae/ripemd*, April 1996.
8. P.R. Kasselman and W.T. Penzhorn. Cryptanalysis of reduced version of HAVAL. *Electronics Letters*, 36(1):30–31, January 2001.
9. National Institute of Standards and Technology. FIPS PUB 180-1 : Secure Hash Standard, April 1995.

10. Research and Development in Advanced Communications Technologies in Europe. RIPE: Integrity primitives for secure information systems. Final Report of RACE Integrity Primitives Evaluation(R1040),RACE, 1995.
11. Ronald L. Rivest. The MD4 message digest algorithm. In Alfred J. Menezes and Scott A. Vanstone, editors, *Advances in Cryptology - Crypto'90*, volume 537 of *Lecture Notes in Computer Science*, pages 303–311. Springer-Verlag, 1991.
12. Ronald L. Rivest. The MD5 message digest algorithm. In *Request for Comments(RFC) 1321*, April. Internet Activities Board, Internet Privacy Task Force, 1992.
13. Serge Vaudenay. On the need for multipermutations: Cryptanalysis of MD4 and SAFER. In Bart Preneel, editor, *Fast Software Encryption, Second International Workshop*, volume 1008 of *Lecture Notes in Computer Science*, pages 286–297, Leuven, Belgium, December 1995. Springer-Verlag, Berlin.
14. Yuliang Zheng, Josef Pieprzyk, and Jennifer Seberry. HAVAL-A One-Way Hashing Algorithm with Variable Length of Output. In Jennifer Seberry and Yuliang Zheng, editors, *Advances in Cryptology - Auscrypt'92*, volume 718 of *Lecture Notes in Computer Science*, pages 83–104. Springer, 1992.

On Insecurity of the Side Channel Attack Countermeasure Using Addition-Subtraction Chains under Distinguishability between Addition and Doubling

Katsuyuki Okeya[1] and Kouichi Sakurai[2]

[1] Hitachi, Ltd., Systems Development Laboratory,
292, Yoshida-cho, Totsuka-ku, Yokohama, 244-0817, Japan
ka-okeya@sdl.hitachi.co.jp
[2] Kyushu University,
Graduate School of Information Science and Electrical Engineering,
6-10-1, Hakozaki, Higashi-ku, Fukuoka, 812-8581, Japan
sakurai@csce.kyushu-u.ac.jp

Abstract. We show that a randomized addition-subtraction chains countermeasure against side channel attacks is vulnerable to SPA attack, a kind of side channel attack, under distinguishability between addition and doubling. A side channel attack is an attack that takes advantage of information leaked during execution of a cryptographic procedure. The randomized addition-subtraction chains countermeasure has been proposed by Oswald-Aigner, and is a random decision inserted into computations. However, its immunity to side channel attacks is still controversial. As for timing attack, a kind of side channel attack, the randomized addition-subtraction chains countermeasure is also vulnerable. Moreover, compared with other countermeasures against side channel attacks, the randomized addition-subtraction chains countermeasure, after being improved to prevent side channel attacks, is much slower.

Keywords: *Elliptic Curve Cryptosystems, Side Channel Attacks, Randomized Addition-Subtraction Chains Countermeasure, SPA Attack, Timing Attack*

1 Introduction

A *randomized addition-subtraction chains countermeasure* has been considered to be effective in preventing *side channel attacks*. However, its immunity to side channel attacks is still controversial. In this paper, we will show that the randomized addition-subtraction chains countermeasure is vulnerable to SPA attack, which is a kind of side channel attack.

L. Batten and J. Seberry (Eds.): ACISP 2002, LNCS 2384, pp. 420–435, 2002.

1.1 Side Channel Attacks

Kocher *et al.* were first to propose the side channel attack [Koc,Koc96,KJJ98, KJJ99] in which an attacker infers secret information using leaked data from a cryptographic device while it executes cryptographic procedures. Later, Coron extended the side channel attacks to elliptic curve cryptosystems [Cor99].

Proposed countermeasures against such an attack are varied up to the present. Coron proposed three countermeasures [Cor99]: randomization of the private exponent, blinding the point P and randomized projective coordinates. Countermeasures on a Koblitz curve by Hasan [Has00], those on a Montgomery-form elliptic curve by Okeya-Sakurai [OS00], those on a Jacobi-form elliptic curve by Liardet-Smart [LS01], those on a Hessian-form elliptic curve by Joye-Quisquater [JQ01], those using random isomorphic elliptic curves by Joye-Tymen [JT01], those using window method by Möller [Möl01], and those on a Weierstrass-form elliptic curve by Brier-Joye [BJ02], Fischer *et al.* [FGKS02] and Izu-Takagi [IT02] have also been proposed.

1.2 Randomized Addition-Subtraction Chains Countermeasure

Oswald-Aigner proposed the randomized addition-subtraction chains counter-measure [OA01] as a side channel attack prevention method of an elliptic scalar multiplication. Here a speed-up scalar multiplication method using addition-subtraction chains, which had been proposed by Morain-Olivos [MO90], was modified to insert a random decision into the computation. According to Oswald-Aigner [OA01], side channel attack is ineffective against it because of the randomization. In a recent presentation [Osw01], analysis using the probabilities of addition and doubling was proposed. However, keys could not be detected in the most cases, although the analysis was effective for some weak keys. Thus, analysis of this method's immunity to side channel attacks is not complete.

1.3 Our Contributions

We will show that the randomized addition-subtraction chains countermeasure is vulnerable to SPA attack.

Assume that an attacker can distinguish addition and doubling by one-time measurement of power consumption. Then, the randomized addition-subtraction chains countermeasure is vulnerable to SPA attack. Concretely speaking, the attacker can detect the secret information d with $O(\ln d)$-time measurements of power consumption for scalar multiplications and with $O(\ln^3 d)$ bit operations. The success probability is more than $1 - |d| \cdot (\frac{1}{2})^{|d|}$.

In addition, according to our considerations, the randomized addition-subtraction chains countermeasure is vulnerable to the timing attack also. Specifically, an attacker can detect the secret scalar by using the statistical data of computational timings and by using a computational attack.

The computational cost of an improved randomized addition-subtraction chains countermeasure to side channel attacks is 3852 multiplications for a 160-bit scalar. Compared with a countermeasure on a Montgomery form and that on a Weierstrass form, the randomized addition-subtraction chains countermeasure is much slower, as the computational cost of the countermeasure on a Montgomery form is 1468.4 multiplications and that on a Weierstrass form is 2641.8 multiplications.

2   Side Channel Attacks

In cryptographic devices such as smart cards, data other than input data and output data may 'leak out' during cryptographic procedures. The computation timing of cryptographic procedures is one such kind of data. So is power consumption because the smart card uses an external power source. Kocher *et al.* developed the side channel attack in which an attacker infers stored secret information in a cryptographic device by using such leaked data [Koc,Koc96,KJJ98, KJJ99]. This type of attack, which includes timing attack [Koc,Koc96], SPA attack [Koc,Koc96], and differential power analysis (DPA) attack [KJJ98,KJJ99], render smart cards particularly vulnerable.

A timing attack [Koc,Koc96] is a side channel attack in which an attacker infers the secret information by using computation time as leaked data. Some methods of timing attack use to statistical analysis to reveal the secret information, others infer it from a one-time computation. An SPA attack [Koc,Koc96] is a side channel attack in which an attacker infers the secret information by using power consumption as leaked data. SPA attack reveals the secret information by direct observation of a device's power consumption without the need for statistical analysis. A DPA attack [KJJ98,KJJ99] is a side channel attack in which an attacker infers the secret information by using statistical analysis of power consumption. This attack is the most powerful side channel attack.

Okeya and Sakurai proposed the following two requirements for preventing side channel attacks [OS00]:

1. Independency of secret information and computation procedures.
2. Randomization of computing objects.

Requirement 1 is equivalent to preventing an SPA attack. Coron's SPA prevention scalar multiplication method using dummy operations [Cor99], a countermeasure on a Montgomery-form elliptic curve [OS00,OMS01], a countermeasure on a Weierstrass-form elliptic curve [BJ02,FGKS02,IT02], and a countermeasure using the window method [Möl01] satisfy Requirement 1. These countermeasure compute with identical procedures independently on the secret scalars. Randomized projective coordinates [Cor99,OS00,OMS01] and random isomorphic elliptic curves [JT01,IT02] satisfy Requirement 2.

3   Randomized Addition-Subtraction Chains Countermeasure

Oswald-Aigner proposed a side channel attack prevention method of an elliptic scalar multiplication type, namely the randomized addition-subtraction chains countermeasure [OA01].

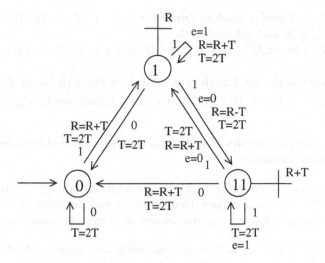

Fig. 1. The randomized addition-subtraction chains countermeasure

3.1   Algorithm

A point P on an elliptic curve and a scalar value d is inputted to the randomized addition-subtraction chains countermeasure [OA01], which then computes and outputs a scalar-multiplied point dP as follows[1]:

- (Initialization) Set $R \leftarrow \mathcal{O}$, $T \leftarrow P$ and $j \leftarrow 0$, and set $state = 0$, where $\mathcal{O}$ is the identity element of addition, namely the point at infinity.

(0) $state = 0$
   - If $d_j = 1$; set $R \leftarrow R + T$, $T \leftarrow 2T$ and $j \leftarrow j + 1$; and set $state = 1$.
   - If $d_j = 0$; set $T \leftarrow 2T$ and $j \leftarrow j + 1$; and set $state = 0$.

(1) $state = 1$
   - If $j = |d|$; output R as dP.
   - If $d_j = 1$ and a random number $e = 1$; set $R \leftarrow R + T$, $T \leftarrow 2T$ and $j \leftarrow j + 1$; and set $state = 1$.
   - If $d_j = 1$ and a random number $e = 0$; set $R \leftarrow R - T$, $T \leftarrow 2T$ and $j \leftarrow j + 1$; and set $state = 11$.
   - If $d_j = 0$; set $T \leftarrow 2T$ and $j \leftarrow j + 1$; and set $state = 0$.

(11) $state = 11$
   - If $j = |d|$; output $R + T$ as dP.
   - If $d_j = 1$ and a random number $e = 1$; set $T \leftarrow 2T$ and $j \leftarrow j + 1$; and set $state = 11$.

---

[1] The randomized addition-subtraction chains method proposed by Oswald-Aigner [OA01] has two versions. The algorithm described in this paper is the simple version.

- If $d_j = 1$ and a random number $e = 0$; set $T \leftarrow 2T$, $R \leftarrow R + T$ and $j \leftarrow j + 1$; and set $state = 1$.
- If $d_j = 0$; set $R \leftarrow R + T$, $T \leftarrow 2T$ and $j \leftarrow j + 1$; and set $state = 0$.

Here, $|d|$ denotes the bit length of d, and d_j is the j-th bit of d. That is, $d = \sum_{j=0}^{|d|-1} d_j 2^j$, $d_j \in \{0, 1\}$. In addition, the most significant bit $d_{|d|-1}$ is alway 1.

3.2 SPA Attack versus Randomized Addition-Subtraction Chains Countermeasure

In general, since the computational cost of addition is larger than that of doubling [CMO98], it is quite likely that addition and doubling in scalar multiplication are distinguishable by measurement of power consumption.

Distinguishability 1 *Addition and doubling are distinguishable by one-time measurement of power consumption, whereas addition and subtraction are indistinguishable.*

An attacker who has the capability of Distinguishability 1 obtains a sequence of addition and doubling (AD sequence) when he feeds a message to a cryptographic device.

Proposition 1. *Assume that the attacker has Distinguishability 1. Then, the randomized addition-subtraction chains countermeasure is vulnerable to SPA attack[2]. That is, the attacker can detect the scalar value d with N measurements of power consumption for scalar multiplications and with $O(N \ln^2 d)$ bit operations. The success probability is more than $1 - |d| \cdot (\frac{1}{2})^{N-1}$.*

Remark 1. Actually, $(|d| + 100)$ measurements are enough for detection. In this case, the attacker can detect the scalar value d with $O(\ln d)$ measurements of power consumption for scalar multiplications and with $O(\ln^3 d)$ bit operations. The success probability is more than $1 - |d| \cdot (\frac{1}{2})^{|d|}$.

Remark 2. Proposition 1 shows that the randomized addition-subtraction chains countermeasure of Oswald-Aigner [OA01] does not satisfy Requirement 1 for preventing side channel attacks. As for Requirement 2, althogh computations are complicated and objects seem to be randomized, this is not the case. In other words, the attacker can predict the values of the objects. For example, in the j-th step, $R = d^{j-1}P$, $T = 2^j P$ if $state = 0$; $R = d^{j-1}P$, $T = 2^j P$ if $state = 1$; $R = (d^{j-2} - 2^{j-1})P$, $T = 2^j P$ if $state = 11$, where $d^k = \sum_{i=0}^{k} d_i 2^i$.

---

[2] According to Joye and Quisquater [JQ01], "When only a single measurement is performed the attack is referred to as *simple side-channel attack*." But, in this paper, an attack which uses Distinguishability 1 is referred to as SPA attack.

Table 1. AD sequence if $state = 0, 1$

state(before)	d_j	AD sequence	state(after)	e
0	1	AD	1	-
	0	D	0	-
1	1	AD	1	1
		AD	11	0
	0	D	0	-

Remark 3. In naive implementations of elliptic operations, it is quite likely that an attacker has Distinguishability 1. However, we can deprive the attacker of Distinguishability 1 by using the Hessian form [JQ01] or the Jacobi form [LS01] because addition and doubling formulae are identical in such elliptic curves.

Remark 4. The proposed attack is not directly adapted to the complex version of the randomized addition-subtraction chains method, because $d_j = 0$ does not imply $state = 0$ in the complex version. Construction of an SPA attack to the complex version is an open question.

Notations and Preliminaries. Let S be an AD sequence, *i.e.*, it is a sequence consisting of only additions A and doublings D. $S[k]$ denotes the k-th value of S, where $S[0]$ denotes the leading value. $S[k, n]$ denotes the AD sequence which is the consecutive n values from the k-th value of S. $\#S$ denotes the length of S.

Example 1. $S = ADDAADA$. Then $S[2] = D$, $S[3] = A$, $S[0] = A$, $S[2, 4] = DAAD$, and $\#S = 7$.

Table 1 shows that AD sequences and *states* after the computation for the bit d_j of the scalar value d in the cases of $state = 0, 1$. For example, in the case of $state = 0$ and $d_j = 0$, its AD sequence is D and *state* after the computation is 0. In the case of $state = 1$ and $d_j = 1$, there are two AD sequence combnations. One is AD and *state* after the computation is 1, if the random number e is 1. The other is also AD, but the *state* after the computation is 11, if the random number e is 0.

Table 2 shows that AD sequences and *states* after the computation for d_j, d_{j+1}, d_{j+2} in the case of $state = 1$ and $d_j = 1$. For example, in the case of d_j, d_{j+1}, d_{j+2} to be 111, and random numbers e to be 1, 1, 0 in order, the AD sequence is $ADADAD$ and *state* after the computation is 11. We see from Table 3 that the *state* after the computation which corresponds to d_j, d_{j+1} is 1.

Table 4 shows that AD sequences and *states* after the computation for d_j, d_{j+1} in the case of $state = 11, 1$ and $d_j = 1$. For example, in the case of *state* before the computation to be 11, d_j to be 11, and random numbers e to be 0, 1 in order, the AD sequence is $DAAD$ and *state* after the computation is

Table 2. AD sequence if $state = 1$, $d_j = 1$

state(before)	d_j, d_{j+1}, d_{j+2}	AD sequence	state(after)	e
1	111	ADADAD	1	1,1,1
		ADADAD	11	1,1,0
		ADADD	11	1,0,1
		ADADDA	1	1,0,0
		ADDD	11	0,1,1
		ADDDA	1	0,1,0
		ADDAAD	1	0,0,1
		ADDAAD	11	0,0,0
	110	ADADD	0	1,1
		ADADAD	0	1,0
		ADDAD	0	0,1
		ADDAD	0	0,0
	101	ADDAD	1	1
		ADADAD	1	0
	100	ADDD	0	1
		ADADD	0	0

Table 3. AD sequence if $state = 1$, $d_j = 1$, $d_{j+1} = 1$

state(before)	d_j, d_{j+1}	AD sequence	state(after)	e
1	11	ADAD	1	1,1
		ADAD	11	1,0
		ADD	11	0,1
		ADDA	1	0,0

1. We see from Table 5 that the *state* after the computation which corresponds to d_j is 1.

Attack Algorithm. Next, we describe an algorithm in order for an attacker to detect the scalar value d.

An attacker inputs an elliptic point into a cryptographic device with the randomized addition-subtraction chains countermeasure and obtains an AD sequence because of his Distinguishabilty 1. He repeats this procedure N times and gathers N AD sequences. Let S_i ($i = 1, \cdots, N$) be the AD sequences. He detects the secret information d under N AD sequences S_i as follows:

- (Initialization) $state_i$ at the beginning of a scalar multiplication computation is 0 for any i. Set $state_i = 0$, $k_i = 0$ for each i, and $j = 0$; then go to (a).
- (a) $state_i = 0$ for any i
  - If $S_{i_1}[k_{i_1}] = A$ for some i_1; set $\tilde{d}_j = 1$, $j \leftarrow j + 1$, $k_i \leftarrow k_i + 2$ for all i; and set $state_i = 1$; then go to (b).

Table 4. AD sequence if $state = 1, 11, d_j = 1$

state(before)	d_j, d_{j+1}	AD sequence	state(after)	e
11	11	DD	11	1,1
		DDA	1	1,0
		DAAD	1	0,1
		DAAD	11	0,0
	10	DAD	0	1
		DAD	0	0
1	11	ADAD	1	1,1
		ADAD	11	1,0
		ADD	11	0,1
		ADDA	1	0,0
	10	ADD	0	1
		ADAD	0	0

Table 5. AD sequence if $state = 1, 11, d_j = 1$

state(before)	d_j	AD sequence	state(after)	e
11	1	D	11	1
		DA	1	0
1	1	AD	1	1
		AD	11	0

- If $S_{i_1}[k_{i_1}] = D$ for some i_1; set $\tilde{d}_j = 0$, $j \leftarrow j + 1$, $k_i \leftarrow k_i + 1$ for all i; and set $state_i = 0$; then go to (a).

(b) $state_i = 1$ for any i
  - If $j = |d|$, then go to (g).
  - If $S_{i_1}[k_{i_1}] = A$ for some i_1; set $(\tilde{d}_j = 1)$; and then go to (c).
  - If $S_{i_1}[k_{i_1}] = D$ for some i_1; set $\tilde{d}_j = 0$, $j \leftarrow j + 1$, $k_i \leftarrow k_i + 1$ for all i; and set $state_i = 0$; then go to (a).

(c) $state_i = 1$ for any i and $\tilde{d}_j = 1$
  - If $j \geq |d| - 2$, then go to (e).
  - If $S_{i_1}[k_{i_1}, 4] = ADDD$ for some i_1 and $S_{i_2}[k_{i_2}, 5] = ADADA$ or $ADDAA$ for some i_2; set $\tilde{d}_j = 1$, $\tilde{d}_{j+1} = 1$, $(\tilde{d}_{j+2} = 1)$, $j \leftarrow j+2$; and set $k_i \leftarrow k_i+3$ for i such that $S_i[k_i, 4] = ADDD$, and $k_i \leftarrow k_i + 4$ for the others; and set $state_i = 1$ for i such that $S_i[k_i, 5] = ADADA$ or $ADDAA$, and $state_i = 11$ for i such that $S_i[k_i, 4] = ADDD$ or $S_i[k_i, 5] = ADADD$; then go to (d).
  - If $S_{i_1}[k_{i_1}, 5] = ADDAD$ for some i_1 and $S_{i_2}[k_{i_2}, 5] = ADADD$ for some i_2; set $\tilde{d}_j = 1$, $\tilde{d}_{j+1} = 1$, $\tilde{d}_{j+2} = 0$, $j \leftarrow j + 3$; and set $k_i \leftarrow k_i + 6$ for i such that $S_i[k_i, 5] = ADADA$, and $k_i \leftarrow k_i + 5$ for the others; and set $state_i = 0$ for all i; then go to (a).

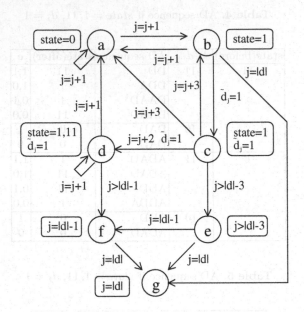

Fig. 2. An attack algorithm versus the randomized addition-subtraction chains countermeasure

- If $S_{i_1}[k_{i_1}, 4] = ADDD$ for some i_1 and $\forall i, S_i[k_i, 5] \neq ADADA$ or $ADDAA$; set $\tilde{d}_j = 1$, $\tilde{d}_{j+1} = 0$, $\tilde{d}_{j+2} = 0$, $j \leftarrow j + 3$; and set $k_i \leftarrow k_i + 4$ for i such that $S_i[k_i, 4] = ADDD$, and $k_i \leftarrow k_i + 5$ for the others; and set $state_i = 0$ for all i; then go to (a).
- If $S_{i_1}[k_{i_1}, 5] = ADDAD$ for some i_1 and $\forall i, S_i[k_i, 5] \neq ADADD$; set $\tilde{d}_j = 1$, $\tilde{d}_{j+1} = 0$, $\tilde{d}_{j+2} = 1$, $j \leftarrow j + 3$; and set $k_i \leftarrow k_i + 5$ for i such that $S_i[k_i, 5] = ADDAD$, and $k_i \leftarrow k_i + 6$ for the others; and set $state_i = 1$ for all i; then go to (b).

(d) $state_i = 11$ for some i and $\tilde{d}_j = 1$

- If $j = |d| - 1$, then go to (f).
- If $S_{i_1}[k_{i_1}, 2] = DD$ or $S_{i_1}[k_{i_1}, 3] = DAA$ for some i_1 such that $state_{i_1} = 11$; set $\tilde{d}_j = 1$, $(\tilde{d}_{j+1} = 1)$, $j \leftarrow j + 1$; and set $k_i \leftarrow k_i + 1$ for i such that $S_i[k_i, 2] = DD$, and $k_i \leftarrow k_i + 2$ for the others; and set $state_i = 11$ for i such that $S_i[k_i, 2] = DD$ or $S_i[k_i, 3] = ADD$, and $state_i = 1$ for the others; then go to (d).
- If $S_{i_1}[k_{i_1}, 3] = DAD$ for some i_1 such that $state_{i_1} = 11$; set $\tilde{d}_j = 1$, $\tilde{d}_{j+1} = 0$, $j \leftarrow j + 1$; and set $k_i \leftarrow k_i + 3$ for i such that $S_i[k_i, 3] = DAD$ or ADD, $k_i \leftarrow k_i + 4$ for the others; and set $state_i = 0$ for all i; then go to (a).

(e) $j \geq |d| - 2$

- If $j = |d| - 1$, then go to (f).

- If $S_{i_1}[k_{i_1}] = A$ for some i_1; set $\tilde{d}_{|d|-2} = 1$, $\tilde{d}_{|d|-1} = 1$, and $j \leftarrow |d|$; then go to (g).
- If $S_{i_1}[k_{i_1}] = D$ for some i_1; set $\tilde{d}_{|d|-2} = 0$, $\tilde{d}_{|d|-1} = 1$ and $j \leftarrow |d|$; then go to (g).

(f) $j = |d| - 1$
- Set $\tilde{d}_{|d|-1} = 1$ and $j \leftarrow |d|$; then go to (g).

(g) $j = |d|$
- Set $\tilde{d} = \sum_{j=0}^{|d|-1} \tilde{d}_j 2^j$; then $d = \tilde{d}$.

Validity of the Attack. We will show that $d_j = \tilde{d}_j$ for any j. To do so, we assume that $d_{j'} = \tilde{d}_{j'}$ for any $j' < j$ and show that for the next $j (>$ the current $j)$, $d_{j'} = \tilde{d}_{j'}$ for any $j' < j$.

- (Initialization) The $state_i$ at the beginning is 0 for any i. That is, the state is (a), and $state_i = 0$, $k_i = 0$, $j = 0$ for each i.

(a) $state_i = 0$ for any i
- If $state_{i_1} = 0$, $S_{i_1}[k_{i_1}] = A$; then $d_j = 1$ from Table 1. $d_j = \tilde{d}_j$ holds since $\tilde{d}_j = 1$. The corresponding AD sequence is AD since the $state_i$ of the j-th step is 0 for any i, and $d_j = 1$. The $state_i$ becomes 1, and the position of the AD sequence S_i is $k_i + 2$ at the $(j + 1)$-th step because of $\#AD = 2$.
- If $state_{i_1} = 0$, $S_{i_1}[k_{i_1}] = D$; then $d_j = 0$ from Table 1. $d_j = \tilde{d}_j$ holds since $\tilde{d}_j = 0$. The corresponding AD sequence is D since the $state_i$ of the j-th step is 0 for any i, and $d_j = 0$. The $state_i$ is still 0, and the position of the AD sequence S_i is $k_i + 1$ at the $(j + 1)$-th step because of $\#D = 1$.

(b) $state_i = 1$ for any i
- We do not need to consider $j = |d|$ because the flow goes to (g) as it is.
- Thus we only need to consider the case of $j < |d|$.
  - * If $state_{i_1} = 1$, $S_{i_1}[k_{i_1}] = A$; then $d_j = 1$ from Table 1, and $d_j = \tilde{d}_j$ holds. We do not need to consider this case because the flow goes to (c) with the same j.
  - * If $state_{i_1} = 1$, $S_{i_1}[k_{i_1}] = D$; then $d_j = 0$ from Table 1. $d_j = \tilde{d}_j$ holds since $\tilde{d}_j = 0$. The corresponding AD sequence is D since the $state_i$ of the j-th step is 0 for any i, and $d_j = 0$. The $state_i$ becomes 0, and the position of the AD sequence S_i is $k_i + 1$ at the $(j + 1)$-th step because of $\#D = 1$.

(c) $state_i = 1$ for any i and $\tilde{d}_j = 1$
- We do not need to consider $j = |d|$ because the flow goes to (e) as it is.
- We only need to consider the case of $j < |d| - 2$
  - * If $d_j = 1$, $state_{i_1} = 1$, $S_{i_1}[k_{i_1}, 4] = ADDD$, and $state_{i_2} = 1$, $S_{i_2}[k_{i_2}, 5] = ADADA$ or $ADDAA$; then $d_{j+1} = 1$, $d_{j+2} = 1$ from Table 2. $d_j = \tilde{d}_j$, $d_{j+1} = \tilde{d}_{j+1}$ hold since $\tilde{d}_j = 1$, $\tilde{d}_{j+1} = 1$. We see from Tables 2 and 3 that the $state_i$ of the $(j + 2)$-th step is still 1 for i such that $S_i[k_i, 5] = ADADA$ or $ADDAA$, and becomes 11 for

i such that $S_i[k_i, 4] = ADDD$ or $S_i[k_i, 5] = ADADD$. Moreover, we obtain the value of k_i from Tables 2 and 3.

Next, we consider that the attacker fails to detect d_j, $dj + 1$ and d_{j+2}. Because of $d_j = 1$, $d_{j+1} = 1$ and $d_{j+2} = 1$ in this case, we have only two cases in which the attacker can fails to detect such values: The first case is that we have neither $ADADA$ nor $ADDAA$. The second case is that we have $ADADA$ and $ADADD$ only. Both of the probabilities of mistakes are $(\frac{1}{2})^N$.

* In the other cases, we obtain the value of d_j from Tables 2 and 3 in the same way, and probabilities of failure as well.

(d) $state_i = 11$ for some i and $\tilde{d}_j = 1$

- We have only two possibilities to reach (d): $(c) \to (d)$ or $(d) \to (d)$. Thus, we have to reach (d) via (c). Hence, $j \neq |d|$.
- We do not need to consider $j = |d| - 1$ because the flow goes to (f) as it is.
- Thus we only need to consider the case of $j < |d| - 1$.

  * If $state_{i_1} = 11$, $S_{i_1}[k_{i_1}, 2] = DD$ or $S_{i_1}[k_{i_1}, 3] = DAA$; then $d_j = 1$, $d_{j+1} = 1$ from Table 4. $d_j = \tilde{d}_j$ holds since $\tilde{d}_j = 1$. We see from Tables 4 and 5 that the $state_i$ of the $(j+1)$-th step becomes 11 for i such that $S_i[k_i, 2] = DD$ or $S_i[k_i, 3] = ADD$, and becomes 1 for the others. Moreover, we obtain the value of k_i from Tables 4 and 5. Next, we consider that the attacker fails to detect d_j, d_{j+1} and d_{j+2}. Because of $d_j = 1$, $d_{j+1} = 1$ in this case, we have only one case in which the attacker can fail to detect such values, for which $state_i = 1$ for any i. The probability of the mistake is $(\frac{1}{2})^N$.
  * In the other cases, we obtain the value d_j from Tables 4 and 5 in the same way, and probabilities of mistakes as well.

(e) $j \geq |d| - 2$

- We have to reach (e) via (b) and (c) $((b) \to (c) \to (e))$. Hence, $j \neq |d|$. Moreover, $state_i = 1$ for any i.
- We do not need to consider $|d| - 1$ because the flow goes to (f) as it is.
- Thus we only need to consider the case of $j = |d| - 2$.

  * If $state_{i_1} = 11$ and $S_{i_1}[k_{i_1}] = A$; then $d_{|d|-2} = 1$ from Table 1, and $d_{|d|-2} = \tilde{d}_{|d|-2}$ holds. In addition, $d_{|d|-1} = \tilde{d}_{|d|-1}$ holds since the most significant bit $d_{|d|-1}$ of the scalar value d is always 1.
  * If $state_{i_1} = 1$ and $S_{i_1}[k_{i_1}] = D$; then $d_{|d|-2} = 0$ from Table 1, and $d_{|d|-2} = \tilde{d}_{|d|-2}$ holds. In addition, $d_{|d|-1} = \tilde{d}_{|d|-1}$ holds since the most significant bit $d_{|d|-1}$ of the scalar value d is always 1.

(f) $j = |d| - 1$

- $d_{|d|-1} = \tilde{d}_{|d|-1}$ holds, since the most significant bit $d_{|d|-1}$ of the scalar value d is always 1.

(g) $j = |d|$

- $d = \tilde{d}$ holds since $j = |d|$ and $d_{j'} = \tilde{d}_{j'}$ for any $j' < j$ by the assumption.

j is equal to 0 at the beginning, and monotonously increases except when the flow goes to (c) from (b). Since j increases whenever the flow returns to (b) from (c), j does not remain constant. Hence, j eventually becomes $|d|$, and the flow goes to (g). As a result, $d = \tilde{d}$ holds.

The computational cost of the attack algorithm is as follows. In the worst case of (c), we have $10N$ examinations for AD sequences of the length 5, $(N+1)$ additions for k_i and j, and $(N+3)$ substitutions of $\tilde{d}_j$ and $state_i$. Operations in states except for (c) are less than that in the worst case of (c). The number of intermediate states in order to reach (g) is at most $2|d|$. Hence, the number of bit operations is $(10N \cdot 5 + (N+1) \cdot |d| + (N+3) \cdot 2)(2|d|) = O(N \ln^2 d)$.

The success probability is computed as follows. The probability of mistakes in (c) or (d) is $(\frac{1}{2})^{N-1}$ in the worst case. The number of executions of (c) and (d) is less than or equal to $|d|$ since j increases by more than 1 in (c) and (d). Hence, the success probability is more than $(1 - (\frac{1}{2})^{N-1})^{|d|}$, which is slightly larger than $1 - |d| \cdot (\frac{1}{2})^{N-1}$.

3.3   Example

We will give an example to illustrate the above-mentioned attack against the randomized addition-subtraction chains countermeasure.

Assume that the attacker obtains the following AD sequences for a 10-bit scalar d:

$$S_1 = DADADDADADADDDAD$$
$$S_2 = DADADADADADADADDAD$$
$$S_3 = DADADADADADDADDAD$$
$$S_4 = DADADDADADDADDAD$$
$$S_5 = DADADADADADDADDAD$$

Then, the attacker detects the scalar d as follows:

0: (Initialization) Set $state_i = 0$, $k_i = 0$ for $i = 1, \cdots, 5$, and $j = 0$.

1: (a) Since $S_1[0] = D$; set $\tilde{d}_0 = 0$, $j = 1$, and $k_i = 1$ for $i = 1, \cdots, 5$; then go to (a).

2: (a) Since $S_1[1] = A$; set $\tilde{d}_1 = 1$, $j = 2$, and $k_i = 3$ for $i = 1, \cdots, 5$; then go to (b).

3: (b) Since $S_1[3] = A$; set $(\tilde{d}_2 = 1)$; then go to (c).

4: (c) Since $S_1[3,5] = ADDAD$ and $\forall i, S_i[3,5] \neq ADADD$; set $(\tilde{d}_2, \tilde{d}_3, \tilde{d}_4) = (1,0,1)$, $j = 5$, and $(k_1, k_2, k_3, k_4, k_5) = (8,9,9,8,9)$; then go to (b).

5: (b) Since $S_1[8] = A$; set $(\tilde{d}_5 = 1)$; then go to (c).

6: (c) Since $S_3[9,5] = ADDAD$ and $S_1[8,5] = ADADD$; set $(\tilde{d}_5, \tilde{d}_6, \tilde{d}_7) = (1,1,0)$, $j = 8$, and $(k_1, k_2, k_3, k_4, k_5) = (13, 15, 14, 13, 14)$; then go to (a).

7: (a) Since $S_1[13] = D$; set $\tilde{d}_8 = 0$, $j = 9$, and $(k_1, k_2, k_3, k_4, k_5) = (14, 16, 15, 14, 15)$; then go to (a).

Table 6. Statistical data of additions for consecutive 1 bit blocks

Block	Average	Deviation	Minimum	Maximum
0	0	0	0	0
10	1	0	1	1
110	2.5	0.25	2	3
1110	3.25	0.1875	3	4
11110	4	0.5	3	5
111110	4.75	0.8125	3	6
1111110	5.5	1.125	3	7

8: (a) Since $S_1[14] = A$; set $\tilde{d}_9 = 1$, $j = 10$, and $(k_1, k_2, k_3, k_4, k_5) = (16, 18, 17, 16, 17)$; then go to (b).

9: (b) Since $j = |d|$; go to (g).

10: (g) Set $\tilde{d} = (1001110110)_2$; then $d = \tilde{d}$.

3.4 Timing Attack

In the randomized addition-subtraction chains countermeasure, the number of elliptic additions and doublings is determined uniquely, depending on the scalar value and the random numbers chosen in the computations. The computation timing depends on the number of additions and doublings. Thus, the distribution of computation timings is determined for a secret scalar value. Hence, it is quite likely that an attacker can detect the scalar value using the distribution of computation timings.

To begin with, the number of doublings does not depend on the bit pattern of the scalar, although it depends on the bit length of the scalar. On the other hand, the number of additions depends on the bit pattern. To put it plainly, the number of additions depends on consecutive 1 bits blocks. Table 6 shows the average number of additions, the deviation, the minimum number and the maximum number for each consecutive 1 bits block. The attacker can infer the values[3] which are summed up the weighted length of the consecutive 1 bit blocks from the average and the deviation of computation timings for the scalar. In addition, the attacker can infer[4] the number and the entire length of consecutive 1 bit blocks from the shortest and the longest computation timings for the scalar, respectively. Consequently, the attacker can detect the number and the length of consecutive 1 bit blocks by using statistical data of the computation timings. Therefore, the randomized addition-subtraction chains countermeasure is vulnerable to the timing attack.

---

[3] That is, $\sum_i av_i$ and $\sum_i \sigma_i$, where av_i and σ_i are the average number of additions and deviation for the i-th block, respectively.

[4] It is likely that the probabilities to obtain the shortest or longest computation timings are small. However, the possibilities of the scalar are restricted by the current shortest or longest computation timings.

However, not all scalars can be detected completely by using only the computation timings. For hamming-weight-2 scalars whose second significant bit is 0, addition is executed for only the bit whose value is 1 except for the most significant bit. Since the attacker cannot detect the time when the addition is executed, the attacker cannot distinguish such scalars. Nevertheless, since such scalars are very restricted, the attacker attempts to validate such scalars, and can easily detect the secret scalar. Thus, we find the following:

Proposition 2. *The randomized addition-subtraction chains countermeasure is vulnerable to the timing attack. That is, an attacker can detect the scalar by using the statistical data of the computational timings and by using the computational attack.*

3.5 Countermeasures

In order to prevent the above-mentioned attacks, we deprive the attacker of Distinguishability 1. For example, if we use the Hessian form [JQ01] or the Jacobi form [LS01] as elliptic curves, the attacker cannot have Distinguishability 1, because the addition and doubling formulae are identical in such elliptic curves. Additionally, we interleave dummy operations with operations from some *state* to the next *state*, in order that the operations are identical. For example, we interleave a dummy addition with operations consisting of a doubling, that is, we always compute an addition and a doubling. This trick effectively prevents the timing attack.

However, even if we can prevent SPA and timing attacks, it is possible that the randomized addition-subtraction chains countermeasure is vulnerable to DPA attacks. To prevent DPA attacks, we need to use randomized projective coordinates [Cor99,OS00,OMS01] or random isomorphic elliptic curves [JT01].

We can improve the randomized addition-subtraction chains countermeasure using a Hessian-form elliptic curve, dummy operations and randomized projective coordinates, in order to prevent side channel attacks. The computational cost[5] is $3852M$ for a 160-bit scalar value, where M denotes the finite-field operation of multiplication. Compared with other countermeasures against side channel attacks such as a countermeasure on a Montgomery form [OMS01] and that on a Weierstrass form [IT02], the randomized addition-subtraction chains countermeasure is much slower, as the computational cost of the countermeasure on a Montgomery form is $1468.4M$ and that on a Weierstrass form is $2641.8M$.

References

[BJ02]   Brier, É., Joye, M., *Weierstrass Elliptic Curves and Side-Channel Attacks*, Public Key Cryptography (PKC2002), LNCS2274, (2002), 335-345.

---

[5] The computational costs per bit are $24M$, $9.2M$ and $16.2M$, for the randomized addition-subtraction chains countermeasure, the countermeasure on the Montgomery form and that on the Weierstrass form, respectively.

[CMO98]   Cohen, H., Miyaji, A., Ono, T., *Efficient Elliptic Curve Exponentiation Using Mixed Coordinates*, Advances in Cryptology - ASIACRYPT '98, LNCS1514, (1998), 51-65.

[Cor99]   Coron, J.S., *Resistance against Differential Power Analysis for Elliptic Curve Cryptosystems*, Cryptographic Hardware and Embedded Systems (CHES'99), LNCS1717, (1999), 292-302.

[FGKS02]   Fischer, W., Giraud, C., Knudsen, E.W., Seifert, J.P., *Parallel scalar multiplication on general elliptic curves over $\mathbf{F}_p$ hedged against Non-Differential Side-Channel Attacks*, International Association for Cryptologic Research (IACR), Cryptology ePrint Archive 2002/007, (2002). Available at http://eprint.iacr.org/

[Has00]   Hasan, M.A., *Power Analysis Attacks and Algorithmic Approaches to Their Countermeasures for Koblitz Curve Cryptosystems*, Cryptographic Hardware and Embedded Systems (CHES2000), LNCS1965, (2000), 93-108.

[IT02]   Izu, T., Takagi, T., *A Fast Parallel Elliptic Curve Multiplication Resistant against Side Channel Attacks*, Public Key Cryptography (PKC2002), LNCS2274, (2002), 280-296.

[JQ01]   Joye, M., Quisquater, J.J., *Hessian elliptic curves and side-channel attacks*, Cryptographic Hardware and Embedded Systems (CHES'01), LNCS2162, (2001), 402-410.

[JT01]   Joye, M., Tymen, C., *Protections against Differential Analysis for Elliptic Curve Cryptography - An Algebraic Approach -*, Cryptographic Hardware and Embedded Systems (CHES'01), LNCS2162, (2001), 377-390.

[Kob87]   Koblitz, N., *Elliptic curve cryptosystems*, Math. Comp. 48, (1987), 203-209.

[Koc]   Kocher, C., *Cryptanalysis of Diffie-Hellman, RSA, DSS, and Other Systems Using Timing Attacks*. Available at http://www.cryptography.com/

[Koc96]   Kocher, C., *Timing Attacks on Implementations of Diffie-Hellman, RSA,DSS, and Other Systems*, Advances in Cryptology - CRYPTO '96, LNCS1109, (1996), 104-113.

[KJJ98]   Kocher, C., Jaffe, J., Jun, B., *Introduction to Differential Power Analysis and Related Attacks*. Available at http://www.cryptography.com/dpa/technical /index.html

[KJJ99]   Kocher, C., Jaffe, J., Jun, B., *Differential Power Analysis*, Advances in Cryptology - CRYPTO '99, LNCS1666, (1999), 388-397.

[LS01]   Liardet, P.Y., Smart, N.P., *Preventing SPA/DPA in ECC systems using the Jacobi form*, Cryptographic Hardware and Embedded System (CHES'01), LNCS2162, (2001), 391-401.

[Mil86]   Miller, V.S., *Use of elliptic curves in cryptography*, Advances in Cryptology - CRYPTO '85, LNCS218,(1986),417-426.

[MO90]   Morain, F., Olivos, J., *Speeding up the computation on an elliptic curve using addition-subtraction chains*, Inform. Theory Appl. 24, (1990), 531-543.

[Möl01]   Möller, B., *Securing Elliptic Curve Point Multiplication against Side-Channel Attacks*, Information Security (ISC2001), LNCS2200, (2001), 324-334.

[OA01]   Oswald, E., Aigner, M., *Randomized Addition-Subtraction Chains as a Countermeasure against Power Attacks*, Cryptographic Hardware and Embedded Systems (CHES'01), LNCS2162, (2001), 39-50.

[OMS01]   Okeya, K., Miyazaki, K, Sakurai, K., *A Fast Scalar Multiplication Method with Randomized Projective Coordinates on a Montgomery-form Elliptic Curve Secure against Side Channel Attacks*, The 4th International Conference on Information Security and Cryptology (ICISC 2001), LNCS2288, (2002), 428-439.

[OS00]   Okeya, K., Sakurai, K., *Power Analysis Breaks Elliptic Curve Cryptosystems even Secure against the Timing Attack*, Progress in Cryptology - INDOCRYPT 2000, LNCS1977, (2000), 178-190.

[Osw01]   Oswald, E., *On Countermeasures against Power Analysis Attacks on Elliptic Curve Cryptosystem*, DPA-Workshop organized by the ECC-Brainpool, (2001). Available at http://www.iaik.tu-graz.ac.at/aboutus/people/oswald/index.php

On the Security of a Modified Paillier Public-Key Primitive

Kouichi Sakurai[1] and Tsuyoshi Takagi[2]

[1] Kyushu University
Department of Computer Science and Communication Engineering
Hakozaki, Fukuoka 812-81, Japan
sakurai@csce.kyushu-u.ac.jp
[2] Technische Universität Darmstadt, Fachbereich Informatik,
Alexanderstr.10, D-64283 Darmstadt, Germany
ttakagi@cdc.informatik.tu-darmstadt.de

Abstract. Choi et al. proposed the modified Paillier cryptosystem (M-Paillier cryptosystem). They use a special public-key $g \in \mathbb{Z}/n\mathbb{Z}$ such that $g^{\varphi(n)} = 1 + n \bmod n^2$, where n is the RSA modulus. The distribution of the public key g is different from that of the original one. In this paper, we study the security of the usage of the public key. Firstly, we prove that the one-wayness of the M-Paillier cryptosystem is as intractable as factoring the modulus n, if the public key g can be generated only by the public modulus n. Secondly, we prove that the oracle that can generate the public-key factors the modulus n. Thus the public keys cannot be generated without knowing the factoring of n. The Paillier cryptosystem can use the public key $g = 1 + n$, which is generated only from the public modulus n. Thirdly, we propose a chosen ciphertext attack against the M-Paillier cryptosystem. Our attack can factor the modulus n by only one query to the decryption oracle. This type of total breaking attack has not been reported for the original Paillier cryptosystem. Finally, we discuss the relationship between the M-Paillier cryptosystem and the Okamoto-Uchiyama scheme.

Keywords: One-wayness, Factoring, Chosen ciphertext attack, Key distribution, Composite residuosity problem, Paillier cryptosystem.

1 Introduction

Paillier proposed a probabilistic encryption scheme [Pai99]. The Paillier cryptosystem encrypts a message m by $E(m, r) = g^m h^n \bmod n^2$, where g, n is the public key and h is a random integer. The encryption function $E(m, r)$ has a homomorphic property: $E(m_1, r_1)E(m_2, r_2) = E(m_1 + m_2, r_1 r_2)$. Therefore, the Paillier cryptosystem has several attractive applications, for example, voting systems, threshold schemes, etc.

The security of the Paillier cryptosystem has been investigated [Pai99]. Its one-wayness is as intractable as breaking the computational composite residuosity problem (C-CRP). Its semantic security (IND-CPA) is as hard as breaking

L. Batten and J. Seberry (Eds.): ACISP 2002, LNCS 2384, pp. 436–448, 2002.

the decisional composite residuosity problem (D-CRP) in the standard model. Paillier and Pointcheval proposed a conversion technique to be semantically secure against the adaptive chosen ciphertext attack (IND-CCA2) in the random oracle model [PP99]. Catalano et al. proved that $n - b$ least significant bits of the message are simultaneously secure under the difficulty 2^b-hard C-CRP [CGH01].

The Paillier cryptosystem have been extended to various schemes. Damgård and Jurik proposed a scheme with moduli $n^i (i > 2)$ that is useful for voting systems [DJ01]. Galbraith extended the Paillier cryptosystem to a scheme over elliptic curves [Gal01]. Catalano et al. proposed an efficient variant scheme that encrypts a message by $r^e(1 + mn) \bmod n^2$, where e, n is the RSA public key and r is random integer in $(\mathbb{Z}/n\mathbb{Z})^\times$ [CGHN01]. Because the encryption key e can be chosen small, the encryption speed of their scheme is much faster than that of the original scheme. Sakurai and Takagi investigated the security of their scheme [ST02]. Galindo et al. constructed their scheme over elliptic curves [GMMV02].

The decryption algorithm of the Paillier cryptosystem involves a modular inversion $L(g^\lambda)^{-1} \bmod n$, where $n = pq$ and $\lambda = \text{lcm}(p - 1, q - 1)$. Choi et al. proposed how to eliminate the inverse by modifying the generation of the key g [CCW01]. They use a special public-key g that satisfies $g^\lambda = 1 + n \bmod n^2$. The distribution of their keys is not the same as that of the original one. The reduced number-theoretic problems are different from the original scheme. However, they did not prove the one-wayness/semantic security for the distribution. We call their scheme as the modified Paillier cryptosystem (M-Paillier cryptosystem).

Contribution of This Paper

In this paper, we investigate the security of the M-Paillier cryptosystem. Let $G_{M-Paillier}$ be the set of all keys g for the M-Paillier cryptosystem. The density of the set $G_{M-Paillier}$ is n, and the probability that a random $g \in (\mathbb{Z}/n^2\mathbb{Z})^\times$ is contained in the set $G_{M-Paillier}$ is at most $1/\varphi(n)$, which is negligible in the bit-length of the public modulus n. Firstly, we prove that the one-wayness of the M-Paillier cryptosystem is as intractable as factoring the modulus n if the public key g can be generated only by the public modulus n, i.e., g is samplable from $\mathbb{Z}/n^2\mathbb{Z}$ in the polynomial time of $\log n$. The semantic security of the M-Paillier cryptosystem is as hard as breaking the decisional composite residuosity problem for the key distribution $G_{M-Paillier}$. Secondly, we prove that the oracle that can generate the public-key factors the modulus n. Thus the public keys cannot be generated without knowing the factoring of n. The Paillier cryptosystem can use the public key $g = 1 + n$, which is generated only from the public modulus n. Thirdly, we propose a chosen ciphertext attack against the M-Paillier cryptosystem. Our attack can factor the modulus n by only one query to the decryption oracle. This type of total breaking attack has not been reported for the original Paillier cryptosystem. Finally, we discuss the relationship between the M-Paillier cryptosystem and the Okamoto-Uchiyama scheme, regarding the distribution of the public key g.

The proposed chosen ciphertext attack is similar to that for the Rabin cryptosystem [Rab79]. The public key of the Rabin cryptosystem is only the modulus

n, however for the M-Paillier cryptosystem not only the modulus n but also the key g compose the public key pair. If we can generate the public key g only by the public modulus n, the one-wayness of the M-Paillier cryptosystem can be proved as intractable as factoring n, like in the case of the Rabin cryptosystem. However, we prove that the public key g can not be generated without factoring n. There is a gap between the one-wayness of the M-Paillier and factoring. The Okamoto-Uchiyama scheme uses a similar public key, which is not only the modulus n but also a key $g \in \mathbb{Z}/n\mathbb{Z}$ such that the order of g in $\mathbb{Z}/p^2\mathbb{Z}$ is divisible by p [OU98]. The Okamoto-Uchiyama scheme can be proved as intractable as factoring n. Although the public key g is used, we can generate the public key g of the Okamoto-Uchiyama scheme from only the public modulus n in the polynomial time of $\log n$. It is an open problem to consider the security of the Okamoto-Uchiyama for the special public key g, e.g., $g^{p-1} = 1 + p \bmod p^2$ proposed by [CCW01].

Notation. In this paper we choose $\{0, 1, 2, .., m - 1\}$ as the residue class of modulo m, namely the elements of $\mathbb{Z}/m\mathbb{Z}$ are $\{0, 1, 2, .., m - 1\}$. We denote by $(\mathbb{Z}/m\mathbb{Z})^\times$ the reduced residue class of modulo m such that $\{a \in \mathbb{Z}/m\mathbb{Z}| \gcd(a, m) = 1\}$. The notation $ord_m(r)$ means the order of element r in $(\mathbb{Z}/m\mathbb{Z})^\times$, in the other words, the smallest positive integer x such that $r^x = 1 \bmod m$.

2 Paillier Cryptosystem

We review the Paillier cryptosystem [Pai99] in this section.

Key Generation
$n = pq$, the RSA modulus
$\lambda = \mathrm{lcm}\,(p - 1, q - 1)$
$g \in \mathbb{Z}/n^2\mathbb{Z}$ s.t. $n | ord_{n^2}(g)$
Public-key: (n, g), Secret key: λ
Encryption of m
$m \in \{0, 1, ..., n - 1\}$, a message
$h \in_R \mathbb{Z}/n\mathbb{Z}$
$c = g^m h^n \bmod n^2$, a ciphertext
Decryption of c
$m = L(c^\lambda \bmod n^2)L(g^\lambda \bmod n^2)^{-1} \bmod n$

Fig. 1. Paillier Cryptosystem

The public key of the Paillier cryptosystem is the RSA modulus n and an element $g \in (\mathbb{Z}/n^2\mathbb{Z})^\times$ whose order is divisible by n. The secret key is $\lambda = \mathrm{lcm}\,(p-1, q-1)$, where p, q are the primes of $n = pq$. A message $m \in \{0, 1, ..., n-1\}$ is encrypted by $c = g^m h^n \bmod n^2$ for a random integer $h \in \mathbb{Z}/n\mathbb{Z}$. Therefore the

Paillier cryptosystem is a probabilistic encryption and has a homomorphic property. The ciphertext c is decrypted by $m = L(c^\lambda \bmod n^2)L(g^\lambda \bmod n^2)^{-1} \bmod n$ using the secret key λ, where $L(a \bmod n^2) = (a-1)/n$ for an integer a such that $a = 1 \bmod n$.

The key g is the element of $(\mathbb{Z}/n^2\mathbb{Z})^\times$ s.t. $n | ord_{n^2}(g)$. In the group $(\mathbb{Z}/n^2\mathbb{Z})^\times$, there are $(n-1)\varphi(n)$ elements whose order is divisible by n. The order of the group $(\mathbb{Z}/n\mathbb{Z})^\times$ is $n\varphi(n)$. The probability that a random element satisfies the key condition is $1 - 1/n$, and it is an overwhelming probability in the bit-length of the public modulus n. Therefore we can use a random g of $\mathbb{Z}/n^2\mathbb{Z}$ as the public key.

2.1 Security of the Paillier Cryptosystem

In order to discuss the security of the Paillier cryptosystem, we define the following number theoretic problems. Denote by $RSA_{modulus}$ and $G_{Paillier}$ the set of the RSA modulus n and the public key g of the Paillier cryptosystem, respectively.

Let c be an integer of $(\mathbb{Z}/n^2\mathbb{Z})^\times$. The n-th residuosity class of c with respect to $g \in G_{Paillier}$ is the unique integer x which satisfies $c = g^x h^n \bmod n^2$ for an integer $h \in \mathbb{Z}/n\mathbb{Z}$. We denote by $[[c]]_g$ the n-th residuosity class of c with respect to g. The computational composite residuosity problem (C-CRP) is to compute the $[[c]]_g$ for given $c \in (\mathbb{Z}/n^2\mathbb{Z})^\times$, $g \in G_{Paillier}$, and $n \in RSA_{modulus}$. The decisional composite residuosity problem (D-CRP) is to decide whether $x = [[c]]_g$ holds for given $x \in \mathbb{Z}/n\mathbb{Z}$, $c \in (\mathbb{Z}/n^2\mathbb{Z})^\times$, $g \in G_{Paillier}$, and $n \in RSA_{modulus}$. An algorithm that factors the modulus n can solve the C-CRP, but the opposite direction is unknown. There is a possibility that the C-CRP is solved without factoring the modulus n.

The problem of breaking the one-wayness of the Paillier cryptosystem is to find the integer m for given $n \in RSA_{modulus}$, $g \in G_{Paillier}$, $h \in \mathbb{Z}/n\mathbb{Z}$, and $c = g^m h^n \bmod n^2$. The one-wayness assumption of the Paillier cryptosystem is that for any probabilistic polynomial time algorithm $A^{OW}_{Paillier}$ the probability

$$Pr_{m \in_R \mathbb{Z}/n\mathbb{Z}}[n \leftarrow RSA_{modulus}, h \leftarrow_R \mathbb{Z}/n\mathbb{Z},$$
$$g \leftarrow G_{Paillier}, c = g^m h^n \bmod n^2 : A^{OW}_{Paillier}(c) = m]$$

is negligible in $\log n$. It is known that the one-wayness of the Paillier cryptosystem is as intractable as breaking the computational composite residuosity problem (C-CRP) [Pai99].

A semantic security adversary $A^{SS}_{Paillier}$ against the Paillier cryptosystem consists of two stages: the find stage $A^{SS1}_{Paillier}$ and the guess stage $A^{SS2}_{Paillier}$. Algorithm $A^{SS1}_{Paillier}$ returns two messages m_0, m_1 and a state information st from a public-key n. Let c be a ciphertext of either m_0 or m_1. The $A^{SS1}_{Paillier}$ guesses whether the ciphertext c is the encryption of $m_b (b \in \{0, 1\})$ for given (c, m_0, m_1, st) and outputs b. The semantic security of the Paillier cryptosystem is that for any probabilistic polynomial time algorithm $A^{SS}_{Paillier}$ the probability

$$2Pr\left[n \leftarrow RSA_{modulus}, (m_0, m_1, st) \leftarrow A_{Paillier}^{SS1}(e, n), b \leftarrow \{0, 1\}, h \leftarrow_R \mathbb{Z}/n\mathbb{Z},\right.$$
$$\left. g \leftarrow_R G_{Paillier}, c = g^m h^n \bmod n^2 : A_{Paillier}^{SS2}(c, m_0, m_1, st) = b\right] - 1$$

is negligible in $\log n$. It is known that the semantic security of the Paillier cryptosystem is as intractable as breaking the decisional composite residuosity problem (D-CRP) [Pai99]. The semantic security is often called as the indistiguishability. If a semantic security adversary is allowed to access the decryption oracle, the attack model is called chosen ciphertext attack. A public cryptosystem that is semantically secure against the chosen ciphertext attack is called an IND-CCA2 scheme [BDPR98]. The IND-CCA2 security has become one of the criteria for a general purpose public-key cryptosystem.

3   The Modified Paillier Cryptosystem

We review the modified Paillier cryptosystem [CCW01], which we call the M-Paillier cryptosystem in the following.

The main differences of the M-Paillier cryptosystem from the original one are the choice of the key g and the decryption algorithm. The public key g is chosen from the set

$$G_{M\text{-}Paillier} = \{g \in (\mathbb{Z}/n^2\mathbb{Z})^{\times} \ s.t. \ g^{\lambda} = 1 + n \bmod n^2\}. \tag{1}$$

The set $G_{M\text{-}Paillier}$ is a subset of all public keys g of the original Paillier cryptosystem, i.e., $G_{M\text{-}Paillier} \subset G_{Paillier}$.

Then the computation $L(g^{\lambda} \bmod n^2)$ in the Paillier decryption is equal to 1, due to $g^{\lambda} \bmod n^2 = 1 + n$. We do not have to compute the inversion in the decryption process for any $g \in S_{M\text{-}Paillier}$. The encryption and the decryption of the M-Paillier cryptosystem is as follows:

Key Generation
$n = pq$, the RSA modulus
$\lambda = \text{lcm}\,(p - 1, q - 1)$
$g \in \mathbb{Z}/n^2\mathbb{Z}$ s.t. $g^{\lambda} = 1 + n \bmod n^2$
Public-key: (n, g), Secret key: λ

Encryption of m
$m \in \{0, 1, ..., n - 1\}$, a message
$h \in_R \mathbb{Z}/n\mathbb{Z}$
$c = g^m h^n \bmod n^2$, a ciphertext

Decryption of c
$m = L(c^{\lambda} \bmod n^2)$

Fig. 2. The Modified Paillier Cryptosystem

We can generate the public key g as follows: We write the public-key g as the n-adic representation such that $g = a + bn$, where $0 \leq a, b < n$ are unique. Because of $(a + bn)^{\lambda} = 1 + (L(a^{\lambda}) + \lambda a^{-1}b)n \bmod n^2$, the public key $g = a + bn$ has relationship:

$$L(a^{\lambda}) + \lambda a^{-1}b = 1 \bmod n, \tag{2}$$

where $L(r) = (r-1)/n$. Thus, b is computed by $b = (1 - L(a^{\lambda}))a\lambda^{-1} \bmod n$ for a given random $a \in \mathbb{Z}/n\mathbb{Z}$ and the secret key λ.

The density of the $G_{M\text{-}Paillier}$ is at most n. The probability that a random element of $(\mathbb{Z}/n^2\mathbb{Z})^{\times}$ is contained in the $G_{M\text{-}Paillier}$ is at most $1/\varphi(n)$, which is negligible in the bit-length of the public key n. This is an important observation for the security of the M-Paillier cryptosystem and we state it in the following lemma.

Lemma 1. *The probability that a random* $g \in (\mathbb{Z}/n^2\mathbb{Z})^{\times}$ *is contained in the set* $G_{M\text{-}Paillier}$ *is at most* $1/\varphi(n)$.

We have the other description of the $G_{M\text{-}Paillier}$. Because of $g^{\lambda} = 1 + n \bmod n^2$, we have the following relations $[[1+n]]_g = \lambda \bmod n$ and $[[g]]_{1+n} = \lambda^{-1} \bmod n$. Therefore, the element $g \in G_{M\text{-}Paillier}$ can be represented as

$$\{g \in (\mathbb{Z}/n^2\mathbb{Z})^{\times} \mid [[g]]_{1+n} = \lambda^{-1} \bmod n\}. \tag{3}$$

The n-th residuosity class of the key g with respect to $1 + n$ is $\lambda^{-1} \bmod n$.

The one-wayness assumption of the M-Paillier cryptosystem is that for any probabilistic polynomial time algorithm $A^{OW}_{M\text{-}Paillier}$ the probability

$$Pr_{m \in_R \mathbb{Z}/n\mathbb{Z}}[n \leftarrow RSA_{modulus}, h \leftarrow_R \mathbb{Z}/n\mathbb{Z},$$

$$g \leftarrow G_{M\text{-}Paillier}, c = g^m h^n \bmod n^2 : A^{OW}_{M\text{-}Paillier}(c) = m]$$

is negligible in $\log n$. The semantic security of the M-Paillier cryptosystem is that for any probabilistic polynomial time algorithm $A^{SS}_{M\text{-}Paillier}$ the probability

$$2Pr\,[n \leftarrow RSA_{modulus}, (m_0, m_1, st) \leftarrow A^{SS1}_{M\text{-}Paillier}(e, n),$$

$$b \leftarrow \{0,1\}, h \leftarrow_R \mathbb{Z}/n\mathbb{Z}, g \leftarrow_R G_{M\text{-}Paillier},$$

$$c = g^m h^n \bmod n^2 : A^{SS2}_{M\text{-}Paillier}(c, m_0, m_1, st) = b] - 1$$

is negligible in $\log n$. The distribution of the public key $g \in G_{M\text{-}Paillier}$ in the security assumption is different from that of the original one. The author asserted that the one-wayness or semantic security is as intractable as the C-CRP or D-CRP, respectively [CCW01]. However, there is no proof for their statements. We will investigate the security of the M-Paillier cryptosystem in the following.

4 Security of the M-Paillier Cryptosystem

We will redefine the number theoretic problems related to the M-Paillier cryptosystem. The only difference between the Paillier cryptosystem and the M-Paillier cryptosystem is the distribution of the public key g. We discuss the

C-CRP and D-CRP for the public key g from the M-Paillier cryptosystem. We can prove that the one-wayness of the M-Paillier cryptosystem is as intractable as factoring the modulus n, if the public key g can be generated only by the public information n, i.e., g is samplable from $\mathbb{Z}/n^2\mathbb{Z}$ in the polynomial time of $\log n$.

The computational composite residuosity problem for the $G_{M\text{-}Paillier}$ is to compute the $[[c]]_g$ for given $c \in (\mathbb{Z}/n^2\mathbb{Z})^\times$, $g \in G_{M\text{-}Paillier}$, and $n \in RSA_{modulus}$. Then we can prove the following theorem.

Theorem 1. *Breaking the C-CRP for the $G_{M\text{-}Paillier}$ is as intractable as factoring n, if the public key g can be generated only by the public modulus n.*

Proof. If the modulus n is factored, the C-CRP can be easily solved. We prove the different direction. Let A be the algorithm, which solves the C-CRP for the $G_{M\text{-}Paillier}$ in time t and with advantage ε. The algorithm A can compute the $[[c]]_g$ for given $c \in (\mathbb{Z}/n^2\mathbb{Z})^\times$, $g \in G_{M\text{-}Paillier}$, and $n \in RSA_{modulus}$. Note that if the key g is generated only by public key information, there is no information leakage about the secret keys from the $G_{M\text{-}Paillier}$. Here, let $c = (1+rn)h^n \bmod n^2$ for random integers $r \in \mathbb{Z}/n\mathbb{Z}$ and $h \in (\mathbb{Z}/n\mathbb{Z})^\times$, then the integer c is uniformly distributed in the ring $(\mathbb{Z}/n^2\mathbb{Z})^\times$. The distribution of c is equivalent to that of instances to C-CRP. Note that $L(c^\lambda \bmod n^2) = r\lambda \bmod n$ holds for the decryption of the M-Paillier cryptosystem, where the λ is the secret key. Thus the algorithm A outputs $t = r\lambda \bmod n$ for inputs c and the secret key λ is recovered by $\lambda = tr^{-1} \bmod n$. The probability that $gcd(r,n) > 1$ holds is negligible. The modulus n can be factored using λ. The time and advantage of the algorithm A is $t + \mathcal{O}((\log n)^2)$ and ε, respectively.

We can mount this result to the one-wayness of the M-Paillier cryptosystem.

Corollary 1. *The one-wayness of the M-Paillier cryptosystem is as intractable as factoring n, if the public key g can be generated by only the public modulus n.*

Proof. We prove that breaking the one-wayness of the M-Paillier cryptosystem is as hard as breaking the D-CRP for the $G_{M\text{-}Paillier}$. However, this is trivial from the definitions.

There are several general conversion techniques, which enhance the security of a public-key cryptosystem to make it an IND-CCA2 scheme [FO99a], [FO99b], [OP01b], [Poi00]. The conversion techniques [FO99b], [Poi00] can convert a one-way public-key scheme to be an IND-CCA2 scheme. Therefore the M-Paillier cryptosystem converted using these techniques can be proved as intractable as factoring the modulus n if the public key g can be generated by only the public modulus n.

The semantic security of the M-Paillier cryptosystem is also different from the original D-CRP. We have to redefine the D-CRP. The decisional composite residuosity problem (D-CRP) for the $G_{M\text{-}Paillier}$ is to decide whether $x = [[c]]_g$ holds for given $x \in \mathbb{Z}/n\mathbb{Z}$, $c \in (\mathbb{Z}/n^2\mathbb{Z})^\times$, $g \in G_{\text{-}Paillier}$, and $n \in RSA_{modulus}$. Then we can prove that the semantic security of the M-Paillier cryptosystem is as hard as breaking the D-CRP for the $G_{M\text{-}Paillier}$. We state that as a theorem:

Theorem 2. *The semantic security of the M-Paillier cryptosystem is as hard as breaking the decisional composite residuosity problem for the $G_{M\text{-}Paillier}$.*

If an algorithm A breaks the original D-CRP, then the D-CRP for the $G_{M\text{-}Paillier}$ can be solved using this algorithm A. It is an open problem to investigate the opposite direction.

5   Power of Generating the Key g

In this section we investigate the computational ability of generating the public key g. The public key g for the original Paillier cryptosystem can be chosen as random from $g \in \mathbb{Z}/n^2\mathbb{Z}$ or as $g = 1 + n$ using only the public information n. Therefore anyone can generate the key g for the original Paillier cryptosystem. On the contrary, we prove that the power to generate the public key g for the M-Paillier cryptosystem can factor the RSA modulus. We cannot generate the key g for the M-Paillier without factoring n.

Let $\mathcal{O}_n$ be the oracle, which answers b such that $g = a + bn \in G_{M\text{-}Paillier}$ for given RSA modulus n and a random integer $a \in \mathbb{Z}/n\mathbb{Z}$. In the real world, the oracle is an algorithm, which computes the public key g for a given public key n. As we reviewed in section 3, the key g is represented as two integers $g = a + bn$, where $0 \le a, b < n$. The integer b can be computed by $b = (1 - L(a^{\lambda}))a\lambda^{-1} \bmod n$ for a given integer a if the secret key λ is known. Then we have the following theorem.

Theorem 3. *The RSA modulus n can be factored using the oracle $\mathcal{O}_n$.*

Proof. We will construct an algorithm A, which computes λ using the oracle $\mathcal{O}_n$. It is known that, once the secret key λ is obtained, the modulus can be easily factored. The algorithm A works as follows:

1. A generates a random a_1 in $\mathbb{Z}/n\mathbb{Z}$, runs $\mathcal{O}_n(a_1)$ and obtains b_1 such that $g_1 = a_1 + b_1n \in G_{M\text{-}Paillier}$.
2. A generates a random a_2 in $\mathbb{Z}/n\mathbb{Z}$, runs $\mathcal{O}_n(a_2)$ and obtains b_2 such that $g_2 = a_2 + b_2n \in G_{M\text{-}Paillier}$.
3. A computes $a_3 = a_1a_2 \bmod n$, runs $\mathcal{O}_n(a_3)$ and obtains b_3 such that $g_3 = a_3 + b_3n \in G_{M\text{-}Paillier}$.
4. Output $\lambda = (a_1^{-1}b_1 + a_2^{-1}b_2 - (a_1a_2)^{-1}b_3)^{-1} \bmod n$.

In step 1 and step 2 we know the relationships: $L(a_1^{\lambda}) + \lambda a_1^{-1}b_1 = 1 \bmod n$ and $L(a_2^{\lambda}) + \lambda a_2^{-1}b_2 = 1 \bmod n$. From $L(a_1^{\lambda}a_2^{\lambda}) = L(a_1^{\lambda}) + L(a_2^{\lambda}) \bmod n$, we have $L(a_1^{\lambda}) + L(a_2^{\lambda}) + \lambda(a_1a_2)^{-1}b_3 = 1 \bmod n$ in step 3. Thus we obtain the following equation:

$$\lambda a_1^{-1}b_1 + \lambda a_2^{-1}b_2 - \lambda(a_1a_2)^{-1}b_3 = 1 \bmod n. \tag{4}$$

If we know λ, the modulus n can be factored with at least probability $1/2$. Let t, ε be the time and the advantage of the oracle $\mathcal{O}_n$. The time and the advantage of the algorithm A is $t + \mathcal{O}((\log n)^2)$ and ε^3, respectively.

From this theorem, it is as intractable as factoring n to generate the public key g for a given public key n. The information obtained from the public key g for the M-Paillier cryptosystem is essentially different from that for the original Paillier cryptosystem. The C-CRP/D-CRP for the $G_{M-Paillier}$ differs from the original C-CPR/D-CRP. Thus the one-wayness or semantic security for the M-Paillier cryptosystem are generally not same as those for the original Paillier cryptosystem.

We often proof the correctness of key generation during the key generation in order to convince of it to other parties. There are several researches for the modulus n, namely proving that the modulus is a square free Blum integer [BFL91], the product of quasi-safe primes [GMR98], or the product of safe primes [CM99], etc. In this case, the public key of the Paillier/M-Paillier cryptosystem is not only the modulus n but also the key g. We have to develop a proof system that the public key g is correctly generated, e.g., g is random in $\mathbb{Z}/n^2\mathbb{Z}$, or g is in the set $G_{M-Paillier}$. It is an open problem to investigate the relationship between the proof system and theorem 3.

6   Chosen Ciphertext Attack

We describe the chosen ciphertext attack against the M-Paillier cryptosystem. An attacker is allowed to ask queries to the decryption oracle. The proposed chosen ciphertext attack against the M-Paillier cryptosystem factors the modulus n. If we use the technique used in section 4, the chosen ciphertext attack can be constructed. In the real attack we do not have to generate a ciphertext, which is randomly distributed in $(\mathbb{Z}/n^2\mathbb{Z})^\times$ and therefore the attack is easier.

Our chosen ciphertext attack works as follows: At first we change the public key g to $g + n$, and we encrypt a message m and the public key $g + n$ using a random $h \in \mathbb{Z}/n\mathbb{Z}$. The decryption oracle decrypts the ciphertext based on the secret key λ, which computes $L((g+n)^\lambda \bmod n^2)$. Then the attacker can recover the secret key λ based on the answer $L((g+n)^\lambda \bmod n^2)$ from the decryption oracle. Thus the modulus n is factored. We summarize the chosen ciphertext attack as follows:

- Generation of a ciphertext:
    1. Choose a random integer $h \in \mathbb{Z}/n\mathbb{Z}$.
    2. Change the public key g to $g + n$.
    3. Compute $c = (g + n)^m h^n \bmod n^2$.
    4. Return the ciphertext c of the message m.
- Decryption oracle:
    1. Return $m' = L(c^\lambda)$.
- Factorization of n:
    1. Compute $\lambda = g(m'm^{-1} - 1) \bmod n$.
    2. Factor n using the λ.

We can prove the correctness of the chosen ciphertext. We have the following theorem.

Theorem 4. *The above chosen ciphertext attack factors the modulus n.*

Proof. Let $g = a + bn \in G_{M\text{-}Paillier}$, then we have the following relationships:

$$(g + n)^\lambda = g^\lambda + \lambda g^{\lambda-1} n \bmod n^2$$
$$= (a + bn)^\lambda + \lambda g^{\lambda-1} n \bmod n^2$$
$$= 1 + (L(a^\lambda) + \lambda a^{-1} b + \lambda a^{-1}) n \bmod n^2$$
$$= 1 + (1 + \lambda a^{-1}) n \bmod n^2.$$

Here the decryption oracle decrypts the ciphertext c as follows: $c^\lambda = ((g + n)^\lambda)^m h^{\lambda n} \bmod n^2 = 1 + (1 + \lambda a^{-1}) mn$, and $L(c^\lambda) = (1 + \lambda a^{-1}) m$. We thus obtain the message $m' = (1 + \lambda a^{-1}) m$ from the decryption oracle. The λ can be recovered by $\lambda = a(m'm^{-1} - 1) \bmod n = g(m'm^{-1} - 1) \bmod n$.

The chosen ciphertext attack against the M-Paillier cryptosystem is effective because the public key is chosen from a special distribution $G_{M\text{-}Paillier}$. The attacker knows that the key g satisfies the condition $g^\lambda = 1 + n \bmod n^2$. On the contrary, the public key g from the original Paillier cryptosystem does not satisfy such a condition, but it satisfies $g^\lambda = 1 + rn \bmod n^2$ for an unknown random integer $r \in \mathbb{Z}/n\mathbb{Z}$. Attackers have to guess the random integer r in addition with the secret key λ. The chosen ciphertext attack does not work for the original Paillier cryptosystem. There is a security gap in the M-Paillier scheme and the original Paillier scheme.

The above chosen ciphertext attack aims at the cryptographic primitive of the M-Paillier cryptosystem. As we discussed in section 5, we can enhance a cryptographic primitive of a public-key cryptosystem to be semantically secure against the chosen ciphertext attack [FO99a], [FO99b], [OP01b], [Poi00]. Especially, Paillier and Pointcheval proposed a conversion technique, which makes the Paillier public-key primitive to be an IND-CCA2 scheme [PP99]. If we use these techniques, we can make the M-Paillier cryptosystem secure against the chosen ciphertext. However, the M-Paillier cryptosystem is used as a cryptographic primitive without the conversions for security protocols, and we should take care of its security.

7   Okamoto-Uchiyama Scheme

In this section we discuss the relationship between the Okamoto-Uchiyama scheme [OU98] and the M-Paillier cryptosystem. We call the Okamoto-Uchiyama scheme as the OU scheme in the following. The OU scheme is constructed over the ring $\mathbb{Z}/n\mathbb{Z}$, where $n = p^2 q$ and p, q are primes. The one-wayness and the semantic security of the OU scheme are as intractable as factoring the modulus n and solving the p subgroup problem, respectively [OU98].

The public key of the OU scheme is the modulus n and an element $g \in (\mathbb{Z}/n\mathbb{Z})^\times$ whose order in the subgroup $(\mathbb{Z}/p^2\mathbb{Z})^\times$ is divisible by p. If we choose a random g from $(\mathbb{Z}/n\mathbb{Z})^\times$, the probability that the order of g in $(\mathbb{Z}/p^2\mathbb{Z})^\times$

is divisible by p is $1 - 1/p$. The secret key is the primes p and $g_p = g^{p-1} \bmod p^2$. A message $m \in \{0, 1, ..., 2^{k-2}\}$ is encrypted by $c = g^{m+rn} \bmod n$ for a random integer $r \in \mathbb{Z}/n\mathbb{Z}$, where k is the bit-length of p. The ciphertext c is decrypted by $m = L(c^{p-1} \bmod p^2)L(g^{p-1} \bmod p^2)^{-1} \bmod n$ using the secret key p, where $L(a \bmod n^2) = (a - 1)/n$ for an integer a such that $a = 1 \bmod n$.

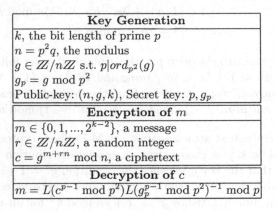

Key Generation
k, the bit length of prime p
$n = p^2 q$, the modulus
$g \in \mathbb{Z}/n\mathbb{Z}$ s.t. $p \vert ord_{p^2}(g)$
$g_p = g \bmod p^2$
Public-key: (n, g, k), Secret key: p, g_p

Encryption of m
$m \in \{0, 1, ..., 2^{k-2}\}$, a message
$r \in \mathbb{Z}/n\mathbb{Z}$, a random integer
$c = g^{m+rn} \bmod n$, a ciphertext

Decryption of c
$m = L(c^{p-1} \bmod p^2)L(g_p^{p-1} \bmod p^2)^{-1} \bmod p$

Fig. 3. Okamoto-Uchiyama Cryptosystem

Fujisaki and Okamoto enhanced the security of the OU scheme using the random oracle model [FO99a]. We call it as the FO scheme in the following. The IND-CCA2 security of the FO scheme can be proved as hard as factoring the modulus n with a tight security reduction. They modified the generation of the keys n, g in order to match their security proof. The primes p, q of the key $n = p^2 q$ are safe primes, i.e., $(p - 1)/2, (q - 1)/2$ are also primes. The key g is the integer g of $(\mathbb{Z}/n\mathbb{Z})^{\times}$ whose order in the group $(\mathbb{Z}/p^2\mathbb{Z})^{\times}$ is $p(p - 1)$. The probability that the order of g in $(\mathbb{Z}/p^2\mathbb{Z})^{\times}$ is $p(p - 1)$, which is at least $2^{-1}(1 - 2^{-k+1})$, where k is the bit-length of prime p.

Coi et al. proposed a modified version of the Okamoto-Uchiyama scheme [CCW01]. We call it the modified OU (M-OU) scheme in the following. The M-OU scheme uses a key contained in the following the set

$$G_{M\text{-}OU} = \{g \in (\mathbb{Z}/n^2\mathbb{Z})^{\times} \ s.t. \ g^{p-1} = 1 + p \bmod p^2\}. \tag{5}$$

There are at most p elements which satisfy $a^{p-1} = 1 + p \bmod p^2$ for $a \in (\mathbb{Z}/p^2\mathbb{Z})^{\times}$. Then the probability that a random g from $(\mathbb{Z}/n\mathbb{Z})^{\times}$ is contained in the set of keys is at most $1/\varphi(p)$, which is negligible in the bit length of p. It is an open problem to prove the one-wayness of the Okamoto-Uchiyama scheme for $g \in G_{M\text{-}OU}$.

In table 1, we summarize the probability on the distribution for the public key g for different schemes described in this paper. The probabilities for the M-Paillier cryptosystem and the M-OU cryptosystem are negligible in the bit length of the public key.

Table 1. Comparison of the probability on the distribution for public key g

Paillier[Pai99]	M-Paillier[CCW01]	OU[OU98]	FO[FO99a]	M-OU[CCW01]
$1 - 1/n$	$1/\varphi(n)$	$1 - 1/p$	$> 2^{-1}(1 - 2^{-k+1})$	$1/\varphi(p)$
overwhelming	**negligible**	overwhelming	$\approx 1/2$	**negligible**

8 Conclusion

We analyzed the modified Paillier (M-Paillier) cryptosystem proposed by Choi et al [CCW01]. Firstly, we proved the one-wayness of the M-Paillier cryptosystem is as intractable as factoring the modulus n, if the public key g can be generated only by the public information n. Secondly, we proved that the oracle that can generate the public-key can factor the modulus n. Thus the public keys cannot be generated without knowing the factoring n, although the public key of the original Paillier cryptosystem can be generated from only the public modulus information. Thirdly, we proposed a chosen ciphertext attack against the M-Paillier cryptosystem. Our attack can factor the modulus n by only one query to the decryption oracle. This type of total breaking attack has not been reported for the original Paillier cryptosystem. Finally, we discussed the relationship between the M-Paillier cryptosystem and the Okamoto-Uchiyama scheme.

The Paillier cryptosystem has been extended to the schemes over elliptic curves [Gal01] or other types of modulus [DJ01]. It is an interesting open problem to enhance the results in this paper to these schemes. Coi et al. also proposed a modification of the Okamoto-Uchiyama scheme, which uses the key $g \in (\mathbb{Z}/n\mathbb{Z})^{\times}$ such that $g^{p-1} = p + 1 \bmod p^2$ [CCW01]. It is also an open problem to investigate the security of the modified Okamoto-Uchiyama scheme.

References

[BDPR98] M. Bellare, A. Desai, D. Pointcheval, and P. Rogaway, "Relations among notions of security for public-key encryption schemes," CRYPTO'98, LNCS 1462, pp.26-45, 1998.

[BFL91] J. Boyar, K. Friedl, and C. Lund, "Practical zero-knowledge proofs: Giving hits and using deficiencies," Journal of Cryptology, 4(3), pp.185-206, 1991.

[CM99] J. Camenish and M. Michels, "Proving that a number is the product of two safe primes," Eurocrypt '99, LNCS 1592, pp.107-122, 1999.

[CGH01] D. Catalano, R. Gennaro, and N. Howgraw-Graham, "The bit security of Paillier's encryption scheme and its applications," Eurocrypt 2001, LNCS 2045, pp.229-243, 2001.

[CGHN01] D. Catalano, R. Gennaro, N. Howgrave-Graham, and P. Nguyen, "Paillier's cryptosystem revisited," to appear in the ACM conference on Computer and Communication Security, 2001. (available from
http://www.di.ens.fr/~pnguyen/)

[CCW01]   D. -H. Choi, S. Choi, and D. Won, "Improvement of probabilistic public key cryptosystem using discrete logarithm," The 4th International Conference on Information Security and Cryptology, ICISC 2001, LNCS 2288, pp.72-80, 2002.

[DJ01]   I. Damgård and M. Jurik, "A generalization, a simplification and some applications of Paillier's probabilistic public-key system, " PKC 2001, LNCS 1992, pp.119-136, 2001.

[FO99a]   E. Fujisaki and T. Okamoto, "How to enhance the security of public-key encryption at minimum cost," 1999 International Workshop on Practice and Theory in Public Key Cryptography, LNCS 1560, pp.53-68, 1999.

[FO99b]   E. Fujisaki and T. Okamoto, "Secure integration of asymmetric and symmetric encryption schemes," Advances in Cryptology – CRYPTO'99, LNCS 1666, pp.537-554, 1999.

[Gal01]   S. Galbraith, "Elliptic curve Paillier schemes," to appear in Journal of Cryptology, 2001. (available from http://www.isg.rhul.ac.uk/~sdg/)

[GMMV02]   D. Galindo, S. Martín, P. Morillo, and J. Villar, "An efficient semantically secure elliptic curve cryptosystem based on KMOV scheme," Cryptology ePrint Archive, Report 2002/037, 2002. (available from http://eprint.iacr.org/)

[GMR98]   R. Gennaro, D. Micciancio, and T. Rabin, "An efficient non-interactive statistical zero-knowledge proof system for quasi-safe prime products," ACM Conference on Computer and Communications Security, pp.67-72, 1998.

[OP01a]   T. Okamoto and D. Pointcheval, "The Gap-Problems: a new class of problems fro the security of cryptographic schemes," 2001 International Workshop on Practice and Theory in Public Key Cryptography, LNCS 1992, pp.104-118, 2001.

[OP01b]   T. Okamoto and D. Pointcheval, "REACT: Rapid Enhanced-security Asymmetric Cryptosystem Transform," In Proceedings of the Cryptographers' Track at RSA Conference '2001, LNCS 2020, pp.159-175, 2001.

[OU98]   T. Okamoto and S. Uchiyama, "A new public-key cryptosystem as secure as factoring," Eurocrypt'98, LNCS 1403, pp.308-318, 1998.

[Pai99]   P. Paillier, "Public-key cryptosystems based on composite degree residuosity classes," Eurocrypt'99, LNCS 1592, pp.223-238, 1999.

[PP99]   P. Paillier and D. Pointcheval, "Efficient public key cryptosystems provably secure against active adversaries," Asiacrypt'99, LNCS 1716, pp.165-179, 1999.

[Poi00]   D. Pointcheval, "Chosen-ciphertext security for any one-way cryptosystem," 2000 International Workshop on Practice and Theory in Public Key Cryptography, LNCS 1751, pp.129-146, 2000.

[Rab79]   M. Rabin, "Digitalized signatures and public-key functions as intractable as factorization", Technical Report No.212, MIT, Laboratory of Computer Science, Cambridge, pp.1-16, 1979.

[ST02]   K. Sakurai and T. Takagi, "New semantically secure public-key cryptosystems from the RSA-primitive," PKC 2002, LNCS 2274, pp.1-16, 2002.

How to Play Sherlock Holmes in the World of Mobile Agents

Biljana Cubaleska[1], Weidong Qiu[1], and Markus Schneider[2]

[1] University of Hagen, Fachgebiet Kommunikationssysteme,
D-58084 Hagen, Germany
{biljana.cubaleska|weidong.qiu}@fernuni-hagen.de
[2] Fraunhofergesellschaft, Institute for Secure Telecooperation,
D-64293 Darmstadt, Germany
markus.schneider@sit.fraunhofer.de

Abstract. In the world of mobile agents, security aspects are extensively being discussed. In this context, denial of service (DoS) attacks are of considerable interest where the focus is on malicious hosts that either delete received agents or prevent them from continuing their route. This paper discusses a detection method for *a posteriori* identification of such malicious hosts to build a trust policy useful for future agent journeys. Depending on how much the agent owner trusts the hosts, he can either define an appropriate order in which selected hosts should be visited, or he can decide which hosts he does not want to contact again. Additionally, we show how the sequence of hosts to be visited should be determined in order to minimize some costs. Moreover, our proposal ensures that hosts originally intended to be visited cannot be skipped as a result of one malicious host's misbehavior. Our method is achieved by a new protocol that combines the application of well-known cryptographic primitives and a set of rules. The proposed protocol also works in the case of colluding hosts.

1 Introduction

Mobile agents are assumed to have a great potential for Internet based electronic markets. Agents are autonomous programs, which, following a route, migrate through a network of sites to accomplish tasks or take orders on behalf of their owners. The owner of an agent can instruct it to visit many hosts in a network, and thereby execute some desired tasks for him. After having carried out all instructions the agent returns to its home and delivers the results it collected during its journey to its owner. On the one hand, one of the advantages for using mobile agents technology is that interaction cost for the agent owner is remarkably reduced since after leaving its owner the agent migrates from one host to the next autonomously. On the other hand, the paradigm of mobile agents creates many security threats for all involved parties.

In this paper, our concern focuses on potential denial of service attacks by malicious hosts. In such a denial of service attack, the malicious host can prevent an agent from continuing to migrate to another host or may even delete the agent. As a consequence, all results the agent has collected so far are lost. This may happen every time the agent passes through this malicious host, and the agent owner has no possibility to identify the source of the attack.

L. Batten and J. Seberry (Eds.): ACISP 2002, LNCS 2384, pp. 449–463, 2002.
© Springer-Verlag Berlin Heidelberg 2002

Unfortunately, there is no practical solution for the general prevention of *killing* visiting agents. Thus, agent owners need a mechanism which can be used for identifying the culprit host. The knowledge obtained by such a mechanism can be used by the agent owner to exclude the corresponding host from future migration routes. Therefore, the agent owner builds a trust policy based on his own experience he made with other hosts. In this context, trust is not only binary being either all or nothing. Instead, the trust to a host can range from 0% to 100% with all intermediate values. This trust policy is usable for more than just deciding if a host should be included in a route or not. It can also be exploited for the creation of agent routes with an appropriate sequence of hosts that allows minimization of relevant costs, e.g., the average effort for the investigation procedure. This is closely related to the fact that a clever selection of the host order leads to minimization of the average number for agent migrations.

In this paper, we present a protocol that allows an agent owner to identify malicious hosts executing denial of service attacks as previously described. The method also enables the agent owner to circumvent the activities of a collusion when malicious parties try to skip a host that should be visited. This works if the number of colluding hosts does not exceed a given system parameter. Improper protocol execution from some host can also be detected. This functionality is achieved by applying cryptographic primitives such as digital signatures and a fixed set of rules. Furthermore, we give a neccessary and sufficient condition of how some minima of costs can be achieved.

The remainder of this paper is organized as follows. In section 2 we introduce the components of a mobile agent system needed for our solution. Section 3 deals with different ways to perform denial of service attacks against mobile agents. A simplified solution for the identification of parties that perform denial of service attacks is given in section 4. In section 5 protocols are presented which solve the problems arising in the simplified solution. Furthermore, we explain the investigation procedure whose outcome is necessary for the trust policy. In section 6 we analyze the implications of the host trustworthiness on the costs and show how the costs can be minimized. Some related works in the area of protecting mobile agents against malicious hosts are discussed in section 7, and section 8 concludes the paper.

2   Some Basics for Mobile Agent Systems

Presently, there is a variety of mobile agent systems available, e.g., Aglets [3]. In the following, we will not focus on a specific mobile agent system. We will consider mobile agents in a rather abstract way. This means that exclusively those components of mobile agents will be considered which are of special relevance for the solution presented in this paper. So, in our level of abstraction, a mobile agent consists of the following components:

$$agent^j = (bc, md^j, uid, r, vc^{\#(c_j)}).   \tag{1}$$

Here, the parameter j refers to the agent residing at host c_j after being executed. Furthermore, bc denotes the *binary code* of the agent to be executed, and md^j denotes the *mobile data* contained in the agent *after* its execution at c_j. This means that for $j = 1, \ldots, n$, the mobile data md^{j-1} coming from host c_{j-1} are contained in md^j after the agent's execution at host c_j. These data can be thought of as being the results of the agent's previous executions or control data prescribed by the agent owner. These control data are then contained in md^0. Furthermore, r describes the mobile agent's *route* as an n-tuple (with $n \geq 1$) consisting of host addresses that have to be visited on the agent's journey:

$$r = (c_1, \ldots, c_j, \ldots, c_n) . \tag{2}$$

This route is given by the agent owner but the hosts do not necessarily have to be visited in the given order. The parameter uid is a *unique identifier* for the agent. This identifier is created by the agent owner in such a way that all his agents have distinct identifiers. We will use uid later to trace the agent in order to identify an attacker in case the agent does not return to its home host. The last component $vc^{\#(c_j)}$ describes the sequence of already *visited hosts* also including the host c_j when the agent resides at host c_j. Here, $\#(c_j)$ denotes the number of hosts that have been visited so far. Thus, $vc^{\#(c_j)}$ is a sequence with $\#(c_j)$ elements, i.e.,

$$vc^{\#(c_j)} = \underbrace{c_{i_1}, \ldots, c_j}_{\#(c_j) \text{ elements}} \tag{3}$$

where $i_1 \in \{1, \ldots, n\}$. Before the agent starts its first migration residing at its home h, the sequence of visited hosts $vc^{\#(h)} = vc^0$ is empty. When the first host c_1 on the agent's journey is visited, then c_1 creates $vc^{\#(c_1)} = vc^1 = c_1$ before it releases the agent. If we assume that the following visited host is c_3 —host c_2 as intended in the route r could be offline— then c_3 creates the sequence $vc^{\#(c_3)} = vc^2 = c_1, c_3$. In general, for $1 \leq j \leq n$ we have $vc^{\#(c_j)} = vc^{\#(c_j)-1}, c_j$. The components r and $vc^{\#(c_j)}$ are used in order to determine the next host to which the agent should migrate.

In general, agent systems allow hosts to extend the route prespecified by the agent owner. But in the following we assume that agents will exclusively visit hosts which are contained in r, i.e., dynamic route extensions are not considered. This will be done in future work. Furthermore, we assume that an agent computation at any host does not require the results produced at any other host. As a consequence, the hosts contained in the prescribed route r can be visited in any arbitrary order.

3 On Denial of Service Attacks

The agent owner can have benefits of using the agent system only if it works properly and if the visited hosts are willing to serve the agents, i.e., these hosts make their services available. However, it can happen that there are malicious hosts in the network which deny to provide their services. The goal of this section is to describe the distinct kinds of denial of service in order to point out the different properties of their consequences for the agent owner, and thus to give a more precise motivation for our approach.

We use the term *denial of service* when a host is not willing to let an agent continue its route. Two different categories of such behavior can be identified. In the first case the host is honest, i.e., after having been contacted by its predecessor it somehow expresses its intent not to provide its services to the agent. A motivation for this kind of denial of service can be, e.g., when the host is either too busy or is not willing to cooperate with the agent owner. In this case, the predecessor could skip the denying host by sending the agent to the next host. This behavior implies that the agent owner does not get results from the refusing host, but the results from all other visited hosts will be obtained in the end. In the second case, the host behaves in a malicious way, i.e., it receives the agent and makes its predecessor believe that it will do its job properly, but in fact it deletes the agent or interrupts its migration. As a consequence, the agent cannot return to its home. This is unacceptable for the agent owner since all results collected by the agent so far will be lost. Thus, from all considered cases this kind of denial of service is the most dramatic. Therefore, a mechanism that tackles these problems is required.

Having a mechanism dealing with the problem of malicious hosts performing denial of service attacks would be very useful for the agent owner. The solution presented in this paper enables the agent owner to identify malicous hosts *a posteriori*. The information an agent owner can get by using our solution can help him to obtain better knowledge about the hosts he is dealing with. This allows him to build a personal trust policy potentially containing a list of unstrusted hosts. He can use such a trust policy for future composition of his agent's routes.

4   Towards the Protection Method

In the following, we will present a simplified and rather naive solution of the described problem. Later, we will point out the shortcomings of this simple approach which will be tackled in the next section.

The underlying idea of our mechanism is based on the usage of undeniable proofs such as digital signatures: When an agent owner does not receive his agent after some waiting time, there arouses suspicion that the agent suffered a denial of service by a malicious host. In order to identify the attacking host, the agent owner asks all hosts which were contained in the original agent route r to show him a proof that they correctly dispatched the agent. The attacking host is surely not able to show such a proof.

We assume now —more or less naively— that all hosts in the system carry out the following rule: upon receiving an agent, each host c_{j+1} must send a confirmation to its predecessor c_j, where $1 \leq j < n$. This confirmation is actually a digital signature $sig_{c_{j+1}}(uid)$ created by host c_{j+1} on the unique identifier uid. One can understand uid as a unique name for the agent that remains valid for the agent's whole journey. The uniqueness of the uid is necessary in order to trace the agent in case of denial of service. Loosely speaking, it can be used later for the agent owner's investigations to find out who was the last party that saw *this* specific agent alive. Each host that has received such a confirmation should store it locally in a database. When the agent owner does not receive his agent and starts his investigations, a host c_j having such a confirmation can show it to the owner as an evidence that it properly dispatched the agent to the next host c_{j+1}. This evidence also gives the agent owner information which host was visited after c_j. This principle works as long as the host being considered did not perform denial of service.

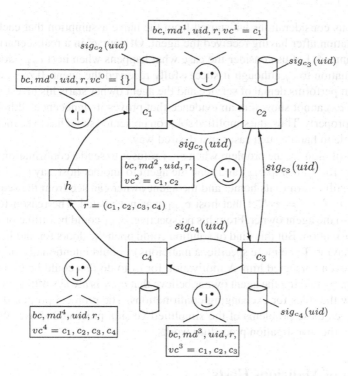

Fig. 1. An agent journey without denial of service

Without loss of generality, we now consider the case where we have $n = 4$ hosts on the agent's journey, as shown in figure 1. There, we see an agent journey on the route $r = (c_1, c_2, c_3, c_4)$ where after each migration an evidence is sent to the predecessor with two exceptions. These happen in the migrations where the agent owner is involved himself. These two cases need some further explanation. The original goal of our approach was to identify the party that did not send the agent to another host. Therefore, the succeeding host must provide the sending host with an evidence to be shown later to the agent owner to convince him about what happened. But in the first migration $h \rightarrow c_1$ the agent owner sends the agent himself, and thus does not need such an evidence from his succeeding host. Requiring confirmation in this step would mean that the agent owner has an evidence to convince himself that he sent the agent —which does not make any sense. The last migration $c_n \rightarrow h$ only takes place when no denial of service attack has occured. Thus, there is no necessity for the agent owner to start an investigation. In figure 1, we see that the evidences are only stored in the databases of the hosts c_1, c_2, and c_3.

The decisions of the agent owner when composing the future routes of his agents should be influenced by his experiences made in the past. According to these experiences the agent owner can create a list containing hosts and the trust values associated with them. These trust values can range between no trust (0%) and full trust (100%).

In all previous considerations we started from the naive assumption that each host sends a confirmation after having received the agent. Of course, in a real scenario this cannot be guaranteed. Let us consider the case what happens when host c_{j+1} does not send the confirmation to c_j although it successfully received the agent. If c_{j+1} or any other host after it performs denial of service and the agent owner starts his investigation procedure, then c_j cannot show him an evidence that proves its innocence, although it has done its job properly. Thus, the simplified solution presented so far has to be modified in order to be able to handle such cases in a desired way.

An obvious solution for the problem when c_{j+1} refuses to send a confirmation could be the possibility for c_j to skip c_{j+1} and send the agent to another host, say c_{j+2}. Then, the agent could still return to its home, and the agent owner can see from the sequence of visited hosts $vc^{\#(c_n)} = vc^{n-1}$ that host c_{j+1} was not visited. The reason for this remains hidden to the agent owner. From his perspective, c_{j+1} could be offline or refuse to send the confirmation. But this kind of solution could open the doors for another kind of dishonest behavior. To be more specific, a malicious c_j could intentionally skip c_{j+1} without having even contacted him. A motivation for c_j to do this could be to damage c_{j+1}'s reputation by making the agent owner believe that c_{j+1} is always offline or is not willing to follow the rules for exchanging confirmations. The protocol proposed in the next section solves these problems of the simplified version presented above. We will also explain how the investigation procedure works.

5   Detection of Malicious Hosts

The detection of malicious hosts requires two parts. The first part is the execution of a sender and a receiver protocol which is presented in subsection 5.1. The second part is an investigation procedure which is executed by the agent owner when the agent does not return to its home. It is presented in subsection 5.2.

5.1   The Protocol for Sending and Receiving Agents

For the protocol to be presented here, we require that the agent route $\tilde{r} = (r, sig_h(r)) = ((c_1, \ldots, c_n), sig_h(c_1, \ldots, c_n))$ contains a digital signature of the agent owner h on the addresses of hosts to be visited. With this signature visited hosts are assured that the route addresses are really created by the agent owner and have not been manipulated by others. Furthermore, we also assume that the unique agent identifier uid is signed by h. We also modify the list of already visited hosts introduced in section 2. Here, we will have some additional signatures in the list. Assume that on its journey the mobile agent migrates from host c_k to host c_l, $k \in \{1, \ldots, n-1\}$, $l \in \{2, \ldots, n\}$, and $k \neq l$. Then $vc^{\#(c_l)}$ will be derived from $vc^{\#(c_k)}$ in the following way

$$vc^{\#(c_l)} = vc^{\#(c_k)}, c_l, sig_{c_l}(vc^{\#(c_k)}, c_l). \tag{4}$$

We will explain this modification after the presentation of the algorithm *SelectNextHost* and the protocols. Furthermore, we introduce an agent system parameter $m \in \mathbb{Z}^+$. This parameter determines the maximum number of hosts that should try to contact another host which is not answering properly or not answering at all. This parameter is contained in the agent as a further component $\tilde{m} = (m, sig_h(m))$. For security reasons, m is signed by h. The agent to be forwarded by c_j is

$$agent^j = (bc, md^j, uid, \tilde{r}, vc^{\#(c_j)}, \tilde{m}). \qquad (5)$$

Visited hosts will always verify the validity of the signatures in $\tilde{r}$, uid, $vc^{\#(c_j)}$, and $\tilde{m}$. The signature verification is done before the host starts the execution of the protocols presented below. If a host detects an agent with corrupted route elements it will forward the agent directly to the agent owner. This will be done before any of the sender protocols presented below starts.

Our solution basically consists of a sender and a receiver protocol. The sender uses the algorithm *SelectNextHost* as a subroutine. In the algorithm, we use the predicate $in(e, S)$. For a given element e and set S the predicate returns *true* if $e \in S$, else *false*. The function $card(S)$ returns the number of the elements contained in S. For each agent to be processed, a host has a buffer buf to store addresses of hosts that are unreachable, or hosts that did not send a valid confirmation. After forwarding an agent properly, the host can delete the content of buf. The operator $\neg$ in the following algorithm represents the negation operator for a given boolean argument.

Algorithm *SelectNextHost* (at c_j).

```
i = 1
while (i < j)
    if (¬in(cᵢ, {vc^#(cⱼ)}) ∧ ¬in(cᵢ, buf))
        if (card({cᵢ₊₁, .., cⱼ} ∩ {vc^#(cⱼ)}) < m)
            append cᵢ to buf
            NextHost = cᵢ
            i = n + 2
        else
            i = i + 1
        endif
    else
        i = i + 1
    endif
endwhile
if (i == j)
    i = i + 1
    while (i ≤ n + 1)
        if (i == n + 1)
            NextHost = h
            i = n + 2
        else
            if (¬in(cᵢ, {vc^#(cⱼ)}) ∧ ¬in(cᵢ, buf))
                append cᵢ to buf
                NextHost = cᵢ
                i = n + 2
            else
                i = i + 1
            endif
        endif
    endwhile
endif
```

In the first `while` structure, the host checks if there are still some hosts that should have been visited before itself. If there is such a host that has potentially not been contacted by m other hosts before, it will be selected as $NextHost$. The following outer if structure describes the case in which a host selects hosts that are contained in the route after itself.

In the following, we will present the sender protocol and the receiver protocol. The confirmation needed here is different compared with the one introduced in section 4. If the mobile agent is forwarded from host c_k to host c_l then the confirmation to be created and replied by c_l is

$$sig_{c_l}(uid, vc^{\#(c_k)}).\tag{6}$$

We will explain the reason for this modification after the presentation of the protocols and the illustrating example.

Sender Protocol. Assume that the agent resides at host c_j. The protocol will be started at host c_j after the agent execution has terminated. The steps of the sender protocol are described in pseudo-code. Note that the sender protocol is not executed in the agent's first migration when it leaves h. If the result of $SelectNextHost$ is $NextHost = h$ then the agent is immediately sent to h and the sender protocol can be stopped. In this case, no receiver confirmation is required (see section 4).

```
1 Execute algorithm SelectNextHost
2 If (NextHost == h) stop
3 Store a copy of the agent
4 Send agent to NextHost found by SelectNextHost
5 Until (no confirmation received and no time-out)
     wait for confirmation
6 If (confirmation received and valid)
     store confirmation in local database
  else
     go to step 1
7 Delete agent copy
8 End.
```

Receiver Protocol. The receiver protocol is the reaction to the sender protocol. This protocol starts when the sender contacts the receiver to transfer the agent. When the sender protocol terminates in step 2, the execution of the receiver protocol is not required.

```
1 Receive agent
2 Create confirmation
3 Send confirmation
4 End.
```

After protocol termination, the receiver can do whatever it wants. It can execute the agent and then execute the sender protocol, or it can be malicious and kill the agent. But if it behaves in such a malicious way, then its confirmation stored by its predecessor can be used to identify it as an attacker in the investigation procedure.

The copy of the agent at the sender side is stored in order to conserve the agent with its results. Thus, the mobile data md^j collected so far will not be lost regardless of how the receiver will behave later. The value of *time-out* can be specified by each host itself and denotes the maximum waiting time for confirmations. The sender is required to verify the validity of the confirmation, i.e., to check that the digital signature is not forged and the receiver's certificate is valid. If the confirmation is valid it must be stored for an adequate period in the sender's database. The length of this period can vary depending on the specific properties of the system. Before we discuss the achievements of the presented protocols and of the *SelectNextHost* algorithm, we will illustrate both with an example.

Example. Consider an agent owner h that creates an agent with the following parameters: $\tilde{r} = (r, sig_h(r))$ with $r = (c_1, c_2, c_3, c_4, c_5)$, $\tilde{m} = (m, sig_h(m))$ with $m = 3$, and $vc^0 = \{\}$. For the sake of the example we assume that c_2 is offline. In the first migration, h sends the agent to c_1. Here, no confirmation from c_1 is required. Now c_1 updates the list of visited hosts by creating $vc^1 = c_1, sig_{c_1}(c_1)$ and inserts this result in the agent. Then, c_1 starts the sender protocol. With $j = 1$, *SelectNextHost* determines $NextHost = c_2$. But since c_2 is offline, *SelectNextHost* has to be executed for a second time. With c_2 contained in c_1's buffer it yields $NextHost = c_3$. Assume that c_3 is online, but for some reason it does not respond before time-out, then further execution of *SelectNextHost* yields $NextHost = c_4$. Now, c_4 starts the receiver protocol, creates the confirmation $sig_{c_4}(uid, vc^1)$, and replies with this confirmation to c_1. Then c_4 excutes the agent, updates the list of visited hosts by generating $vc^{\#(c_4)} = vc^2 = vc^1, c_4, sig_{c_4}(vc^1, c_4)$. The start of the sender protocol leads to the execution of *SelectNextHost* for $j = 4$. There, we have again $NextHost = c_2$ because c_2 is neither contained in vc^2 nor in c_4's buffer. Furthermore, $card(\{c_3, c_4\} \cap \{c_1, c_4\}) = 1 < 3$. But since c_2 is not reachable, *SelectNextHost* yields $NextHost = c_3$. Now, c_3 will react in time. It receives the agent, creates the confirmation $sig_{c_3}(uid, vc^2)$, and replies with this confirmation to c_4. The update of the list of visited hosts yields $vc^{\#(c_3)} = vc^3 = vc^2, c_3, sig_{c_3}(vc^2, c_3)$. After the execution of the agent, c_3 obtains $NextHost = c_2$. Without having received an answer from c_2, the next execution of *SelectNextHost* yields $NextHost = c_5$. After having sent $sig_{c_5}(uid, vc^3)$, c_5 creates $vc^{\#(c_5)} = vc^4 = vc^3, c_5, sig_{c_5}(vc^3, c_5)$. For $j = 5$, the application of *SelectNextHost* obtains in iteration step $i = 2$, that c_2 is neither contained in the list of visited hosts nor in c_5's buffer, but $card(\{c_3, c_4, c_5\} \cap \{c_1, c_3, c_4, c_5\}) = 3 \not< 3$. Thus, c_2 will not be contacted by c_5. Finally, c_5 obtains $NextHost = h$ and sends the agent to its owner. To conclude the example, we note that c_2 was contacted by $m = 3$ parties altogether, i.e., for the first time by c_1, second by c_4, and third by c_3. □

Now, we will discuss the achievements of the protocols and the algorithm *SelectNextHost*. In the protocol, each sending host checks the confirmation, and stores it persistently in its local database when the verification process was positive. The confirmation is used for potential investigation procedures when a denial of service has occured. If the next host in the route is not reachable, a new destination for the agent is determined by using *SelectNextHost*. According to the algorithm and the protocols, the agent is sent to its home if either all hosts in the route have been visited or all unvisited hosts have not given a proper answer. So, it is possible that one or more hosts contained in the original route have not been visited when the agent has returned to its home. Then, from the agent owner's perspective it is not clear if the hosts not visited were offline, or refused to handle the agent, or were replying with invalid signatures.

If the protocol and the algorithm are executed correctly then the hosts given in the route can be visited in many orders. If c_j does not forward the agent even though it received it and confirmed this, then it can be identified via the confirmation that is stored at c_j's predecessor. The confirmation consists of a signature on both uid and the list of visited hosts $vc^{\#(c_j)-1}$. The reason for this is described in the following.

The fact that the solution allows skipping of hosts could be exploited by a malicious host. E.g., such a host could possibly have the intention to exclude a competitor that is also contained in the route. To do this, it could register the address of the competitor in the list of visited hosts, so that this host will not be contacted again on the agent's journey, and thus is excluded from the interaction with the agent. Therefore, the integrity of the list of visited hosts has to be protected so that this attack is not possible. Thus, in our solution, each host obtains a signature also depending on the list of visited hosts from its successor that can be used as evidence in order to detect if the list was manipulated.

It is possible that a host c_j intends to skip another host which is the next host to be visited according to *SelectNextHost*. It could claim that this host was not reachable. In such a case it could forward the agent to another host selected by itself out of the set of potential candidates contained in the route. But then this successor of c_j would send the agent to the skipped host after having executed it. The only way for c_j to exclude a host is to initiate a collusion, e.g., by bribing. In the context of our solution, this would mean for c_j to convince the next $m - 1$ consecutive hosts to collude. If only one of these hosts is not willing to collude then the attack does not work. The only possibility would be to skip also the host which refuses to collude. But then, the story starts all over again, i.e., the attacker requires a new $m - 1$ hosts following the refusing host so that it can be skipped. Thus, besides a special case to be explained shortly, attacks can only have success if the size of a collusion is at least m —one initiator and $m - 1$ partners.

Of course, all this reasoning about collusion size only holds as far as there are at least $m - 1$ hosts that can be visited. E.g., consider the case in which we have n route entries and a host c_{n-2} that decides to skip c_{n-1}. In this case, c_{n-2} only has to collude with c_n if all other hosts have been visited before. This means, that here the collusion size is 2 which can be smaller than m. In the case of a malicious c_{n-1}, the skipping of c_n works even without initiating a collusion. Thus, if some hosts are contained near to the end of the route which have not been visited, the agent owner can decide to contact these hosts in a new agent journey. As a first conclusion, we point out that it is preferable for the agent owner to place such hosts at the end of the route which fulfill a higher level of trust. We can also conclude that a manipulation of $NextHost$ does not lead to denial of service (step 1).

In the discussion above we have considered the case in which a host does not properly execute step 1 of the sender protocol, e.g., via skipping. In the remaining considerations we will briefly discuss the implications of improper execution of the other steps.

If the host c_j playing the sender role in the protocol does not store the agent (step 3) or deletes the agent copy too early (step 7), then it can be identified as an attacker. E.g., this is possible when c_j does not have the agent copy anymore when it receives a forged signature from c_{j+1}. Then, c_{j+1} could delete the agent but the investigation procedure will identify c_j as an attacker. Thus, c_j is interested on having an agent copy for the required time. Therefore, we can assume that the host is not interested in violating the rule of this step.

If a host does not fulfill step 4, then it performs denial of service which can be detected provided that the earlier protocols have been executed properly. This attack can be detected using c_j's confirmation stored in c_{j-1}'s database.

A host is also interested in verifying the received confirmation carefully and in storing it persistently (step 6). If the signature is not valid then it has no proof that it forwarded the agent correctly. This would mean that, e.g., c_{j+1} could perform denial of service but c_j would be identified as the attacker since it cannot prove that it sent the agent to its successor even though it did. Thus, c_j has a natural interest to verify received signatures. The same argument holds for the case when c_j does not store the received confirmation in its database.

Let us consider the receiver protocol. Here, it can be also detected if the receiver c_{j+1} did not follow the rules. The case when c_{j+1} does not send a valid confirmation to c_j is already included in the sender protocol and discussed above. Even if c_{j+1} decides to forward the received agent without having given a valid confirmation to c_j, it would have no benefit. The situation is also clear if c_{j+1} sends a valid confirmation to c_j, and then performs denial of service.

5.2 Investigation Procedure

Now, it remains to show how the investigation procedure works. Let us assume that the agent owner is waiting for one of his agents that probably should have already returned. When the owner becomes suspicious that some malicious party has deleted his agent, he starts an investigation procedure. The investigation procedure basically consists of the consecutive application of an investigation protocol. This protocol consists of two steps: first, the agent owner's request, and second the answer in which a host shows its evidence —as far it is able to do that.

In the investigation procedure the hosts must not be queried necessarily in the same order as they are given in the route $\tilde{r} = ((c_1, \ldots, c_n), sigh(c_1, \ldots, c_n))$, because the real order of visiting hosts can differ from that one given in the initial route. But since all hosts —except the attacker— can provide the agent owner with the identity of their successor by presenting the confirmation, the agent owner can easily derive the real route step by step. Thus, the agent owner knows to which party he has to send the next request.

The agent owner starts his investigation procedure by requesting the first host in the agent route, which is here host c_1 according to the route shown above. This is the host to which the agent owner sent the agent himself. If c_1 has done its job properly, then it can present its successor's confirmation which includes the signature on uid and vc^2. Thus, after positive check of the confirmation presented by c_1, the agent owner is convinced that c_1 has dispatched the agent properly. Furthermore, he knows c_1's successor to which the agent owner will send his next request. Then, the sending of requests and collecting confirmations is repeated according to the same known principle: If the confirmation presented by a host c_i is valid, send the next request to the host found in $vc^{\#(c_i)+1}$. If the contacted host cannot present a valid confirmation, then the attacker is identified. The agent owner continues this procedure until he finds a host not able to show a valid evidence for forwarding the agent.

The outcome of investigation procedures can be used to build a trust policy. This policy can be understood as a list containing all hosts the agent owner was in contact with combined with the owner's trust values that the hosts will not perform denial of service. These trust values can be defined via probabilities. In this context, we consider the behavior of a visited host as the outcome of a *Bernoulli* trial dealing with a binary sample space. A host c_i can either follow the rules and forward the agent correctly with probability $P(c_i)$ on an agent journey, or perform denial of service with probability $1 - P(c_i)$.

Definition 1 *The agent owner's trust value* $trust(c_i)$ *that host* c_i *will not perform denial of service when visited by one of his agents is given by* $trust(c_i) = P(c_i)$.

The collection of all trust values for each host represents its trust policy. The agent owner's initial trust value for a host depends on the agent owner's personal estimation. Then, based upon the experience with this host, the trust value can be increased or decreased. If a host's trust value is below the personal threshold of the agent owner, he will not consider it for future agent journeys.

The trust policy can be used to compose the initial route in a way that the most trusted hosts should be contained at the end of the initial route (as already mentioned in subsection 5.1 because of decreasing collusion size).

6   Trust Policy Exploitation for Cost Reduction

The order of the hosts contained in the initial route can have some implications on the security level regarding collusion size. Besides this, there are some other properties worth considering that follow from the visit order. In this context, we consider the average number of migrations an agent really requires when its route contains n entries. This number of migrations can be understood as a cost parameter. Furthermore, it has a direct relationship to the effort required by the agent owner in the investigation procedure. Another interpretation is related to the average traffic an agent causes in the network during its journey. Obviously, it is advantageous if the average number of migrations can be minimized.

In the following, we assume that the agent route contains n addresses of hosts $c_1, \ldots, c_n$ that are associated with trust values $trust(c_i) = P(c_i) = p_i$, for $i = 1, \ldots, n$. Assume that the hosts will be visited in the given order. Furthermore, let X be a discrete random variable that specifies the number of migrations that have been made during an agent journey. This means that the sample space can consist of all values from $X = 1$ to $X = n + 1$. Then, $P(X = i)$ for $i = 1, \ldots, n$ gives the probability that the agent migrates until host c_i, but not further. $P(X = n + 1)$ gives the probability that the agent returns home after the complete journey assuming that h receives the agent with probability 1 when it is forwarded by c_n. These probabilities are given by the following terms:

$$P(X = 1) = 1 - p_1,$$
$$P(X = i) = p_1 \cdot \ldots \cdot p_{i-1}(1 - p_i) \text{ for } 1 < i \leq n,$$
$$P(X = n + 1) = p_1 \cdot \ldots \cdot p_n. \tag{7}$$

With these probabilities, we are able to present the expected value $E[X]$. It is given by

$$E[X] = \sum_{i=1}^{n+1} i \cdot P(X = i) = 1 \cdot (1 - p_1) + 2 \cdot p_1(1 - p_2) + \ldots + \tag{8}$$

$$n \cdot p_1 \ldots p_{n-1}(1 - p_n) + (n + 1) \cdot p_1 \ldots p_n$$

The value of $E[X]$ depends on the trust values of the hosts and also the ordering of the hosts in the route. Assume that an agent owner intends to send an agent to n distinct hosts, say $c_1, \ldots, c_n$. In general, there are $n!$ possibilities to do this. Note that all these possibilities have the same probability that the agent will not suffer on a denial of service attack according to equation (7). But which of these possibilities allows the agent owner to get minimum $E[X]$? In the following we provide a necessary and sufficient condition for minimum $E[X]$. The theorem shows how the order of hosts has to be selected in order to achieve minimum $E[X]$.

Theorem 1 *Let $c_1, \ldots, c_n$ be hosts that are contained in an agent route in order to be visited in the given order. Assume that the hosts have trust values $trust(c_i) = p_i$ with $0 < p_i \leq 1$ for $i = 1, \ldots, n$. Then, the expected value $E[X]$ is minimum if and only if $p_1 \leq p_2 \leq \ldots \leq p_n$.*

Proof: Let i, j be arbitrary selected with $1 \leq i < j \leq n$. Consider the expected value $E[X]_1$ according to equation (8) for which we assume that $p_i = \alpha$ and $p_j = \beta$. Now, consider $E[X]_2$ also according to equation (8) where we just change the order of c_i and c_j, replacing p_i by p_j, and vice versa. Assume that $E[X]_1 < E[X]_2$. Then, we have

$$\begin{aligned}
E[X]_1 = {}& 1(1 - p_1) + \ldots + \\
& ip_1 \ldots p_{i-1}(1 - \alpha) + \ldots + \\
& jp_1 \ldots p_{i-1}\alpha p_{i+1} \ldots p_{j-1}(1 - \beta) + \ldots + \\
& np_1 \ldots p_{i-1}\alpha p_{i+1} \ldots p_{j-1}\beta p_{j+1} \ldots p_{n-1}(1 - p_n) + \\
& (n + 1)p_1 \ldots p_n \\
< {}& 1(1 - p_1) + \ldots + \\
& ip_1 \ldots p_{i-1}(1 - \beta) + \ldots + \\
& jp_1 \ldots p_{i-1}\beta p_{i+1} \ldots p_{j-1}(1 - \alpha) + \ldots + \\
& np_1 \ldots p_{i-1}\beta p_{i+1} \ldots p_{j-1}\alpha p_{j+1} \ldots p_{n-1}(1 - p_n) + \\
& (n + 1)p_1 \ldots p_n \\
= {}& E[X]_2
\end{aligned}$$

After some steps of simplification, this term can be converted to $\alpha < \beta$. The relation holds for all i, j with $1 \leq i < j \leq n$. This argument can now be used to proof both directions of the theorem assertion. If $E[X]$ is minimum, then p_i cannot be greater than p_j. Having $p_i > p_j$ would mean that $E[X]$ is not minimum. Thus, we can derive $p_1 \leq p_2 \leq \ldots \leq p_n$. If $p_1 \leq p_2 \leq \ldots \leq p_n$, then no smaller $E[X]$ can exist for another ordering of the given trust values. This finishes the proof. $\square$

With the result of theorem 1, the agent owner has a recipe of how to create the agent route based on the trust values in his policy. Increasing trust values ensures a reduction of the costs consisting of the average number of actions required in the investigation procedure, or the number of migrations necessary for the agent journey. Of course, the desired value for migrations on one agent journey is $n + 1$. This means that the $P(X = n + 1)$ should be high enough. But this probability is not affected by changing the order of hosts in the route as can be seen in equation (7). So, the agent owner is interested in a high $P(X = n + 1)$ combined with a low expected value $E[X]$.

The requirement resulting from theorem 1 can be fulfilled simultaneously with the requirement of section 5 where we recommended to visit more trusted hosts at the end of the journey because of the decreasing collusion size.

On the other hand, there are cases in which the optimum of $E[X]$ cannot be reached even though the agent route was created by following theorem 1. If the initial route is composed according to the rules of theorem 1, the actual route can be different. This can happen, e.g., if a host is offline. In these cases, it is impossible for the agent to follow the initial route as given by the agent owner. But if the route has increasing trust values, then *SelectNextHost* always tries to follow the strategy of increasing trust values for the remaining part of the route once a violation of the initial order has occured.

7   Related Work

Many of the problems concerning the security of mobile agent systems, both protecting a host from malicious agents and protecting agents from malicious hosts, have been discussed in the literature. While countermeasures directed toward host protection are a direct evolution of traditional mechanisms employed by hosts, those for agent protection are often totally new concepts. Karjoth *et al.* [2] devised a technique for encapsulating partial results which reformulates and improves the technique of Yee [7], also offering a forward integrity and confidentiality. In [4], Kim *et al.* presented an adaptive migration strategy that can be used to avoid mobile agents from blocking or crashing. This is achieved by a route reordering algorithm and a backward recovery algorithm. In [6], Westhoff *et al.* describe methods for the protection of the agent's route against hosts spying out route information. One technique for ensuring that a mobile agent arrives safely at its destination is the use of replication and voting [5]. The problem of detecting the *black hole* —a stationary process destroying visiting agents— in an anonymous ring is addressed in [1].

8   Conclusion and Future Work

In this paper we treated the problem of denial of service attacks in mobile agent systems performed by a malicious host, i.e., when a host kills an agent or is not willing to let it continue its route. In order to convict the guilty party we have proposed a method that allows the agent owner to become a perfect detective, i.e., it enables the agent owner to identify the host who performed an attack. Furthermore, our proposal ensures that a host cannot be excluded from the agent's journey. The proposed protocol does not strongly prevent the deletion of mobile agents, but it can be assumed that it has some preventive power to a certain extent. This stems from the fact that an attacker can be uniquely identified in an investigation procedure. The outcome of the investigation procedure can then be used for the adaptation of the agent owner's trust policy. Furthermore, we have shown how the trust policy can be exploited in order to minimize some costs that are of interest for the agent owner. This was achieved by giving a necessary and sufficient condition for minimum expected value $E[X]$.

A problem to be solved in the future is given in the case in which the agent route contains entries for the collection of both dependent and independent results. So far, we have only considered routes with exclusively independent agent computations. Another problem to be handled is the question of dynamic routes where hosts or agents initiate migrations to hosts which were not contained in the route once composed by the agent owner. Other work to be done in the future focuses on formal proofs for our solution. Further aspects of interest are analysis of practicability and performance of our system.

Acknowledgement. This work was supported by the Ministry for Education, Science, and Research of Northrhine Westfalia, project *Research Alliance Data Security NRW*, and by the European Commission under contract IST-1999-10288, project *OPELIX*. We are grateful to Firoz Kaderali for his support. Also thanks to Brian Hunter for giving us useful comments.

References

1. Stefan Dobrev, Paola Flocchini, Guiseppe Prencipe, and Nicola Santoro. Mobile search for a black hole in an anonymous ring. In *Distributed Computing (DISC 2001), 15th International Conference, Proceedings*, number 2180 in LNCS. Springer Verlag, 2001.
2. G. Karjoth, N. Asokan, and C. Gülcü. Protecting the computation results of free-roaming agents. In *Mobile Agents (MA'98), Second International Workshop*, number 1477 in LNCS. Springer Verlag, 1998.
3. Danny B. Lange and Mitsuru Oshima. *Programming and Deploying Java Mobile Agents with Aglets*. Addison-Wesley, 1998.
4. Dong Chun Lee and Jeom Goo Kim. Adaptive migration strategy for mobile agents on internet. In *Technologies for E-Services (TES 2001), Second International Workshop, Proceedings*, number 2193 in LNCS. Springer Verlag, 2001.
5. Fred B. Schneider. Towards fault-tolerant and secure agentry. In *Distributed Algorithms, 11th International Workshop (WDAG'97), Proceedings*, number 1320 in LNCS. Springer Verlag, 1997.
6. Dirk Westhoff, Markus Schneider, Claus Unger, and Firoz Kaderali. Protecting a mobile agent's route against collusions. In *Selected Areas in Cryptography, 6th Annual International Workshop (SAC'99)*, number 1758 in LNCS. Springer Verlag, 2000.
7. Bennet S. Yee. A sanctuary for mobile agents. In J. Vitek and C.D. Jensen, editors, *Secure Internet Programming*, number 1603 in LNCS. Springer Verlag, 1999.

A Practical Approach Defeating Blackmailing

Dong-Guk Han[1]*, Hye-Young Park[1], Young-Ho Park[2], Sangjin Lee[1]
, Dong Hoon Lee[1], and Hyung-Jin Yang[1]

[1] Center for Information and Security Technologies(CIST),
Korea University, Anam Dong, Sungbuk Gu,
Seoul, KOREA
christa,hypark@cist.korea.ac.kr,
sangjin,donghlee@korea.ac.kr,
yangh@tiger.korea.ac.kr
[2] Dept. of Information Security & System, Sejong Cyber Univ., Seoul, KOREA
youngho@cist.korea.ac.kr

Abstract. To simulate the functionalities of the real cash, one of the important requirements of electronic cash systems is the anonymity of users. Unconditional anonymity, however, is also very well suited to support criminals in blackmailing. Recently Kügler and Vogt [6] proposed a payment system based on the blind undeniable signature that protects the privacy of the users and defeats blackmailing with the assumption that the victim of a blackmailing can inform the Bank of a blackmailing before delivering the money and transfer the decryption key(i.e. the secret key of the victim) used in confirmation protocol without being detected by a blackmailer. But the assumption that the victim is always able to inform the bank of blackmailing is very impractical in such cases as kidnapping and special impersonation. In this paper, we propose two practical methods that gives the Bank the information about blackmailing and decryption key without any unpractical assumptions.

1 Introduction

Anonymity in electronic cash systems is considered useful with the argument that real cash is also anonymous and users of the systems prefer to keep their everyday payment activities private. But anonymity could be used for blackmailing or money laundering by criminals without revealing their identies, as pointed out by von Solms and Naccache in [9]. For instance, if a blackmailer receives blackmailed coins from his victim, then neither the victim nor the Bank is able to recognize the blackmailed coins later. Furthermore, blackmailed coins can be transferred anonymously via an unobservable broadcasting channel. This attack is called the perfect crime, as it is impossible to identify or trace the blackmailer.

To control anonymity of users, payment systems with revokable anonymity have been proposed [1,3,4,5,10]. In these payment systems trusted third parties

---

* This work was supported by both Ministry of Information and Communication and Korea Information Security Agency, Korea, under project 2002-130

L. Batten and J. Seberry (Eds.): ACISP 2002, LNCS 2384, pp. 464–481, 2002.

are able to revoke the anonymity of the users in case of suspicious transactions. When illegal acts like blackmailing are disclosed, the trusted third parties can block various attacks on payment systems by tracing the coins or the user. If those trusted third parties use their power improperly, however, the privacy of honest users can be violated. To defeat blackmailing without trusted third parties, Kügler and Vogt [6] proposed online payment system providing the anonymity of users and anonymity revocation of the blackmailed coins. Generally depending on the power of the blackmailer, blackmailing can be categorized as follows.

▶ **Perfect crime**

The blackmailer contacts the victim via an anonymous channel and threatens him to withdraw some coins which are chosen and blinded by the blackmailer. The blackmailer communicates only with the victim.

▶ **Impersonation**

The blackmailer gains access to the victim's bank account and withdraws coins by himself. The blackmailer communicates with the Bank directly.

▶ **Kidnapping**

The blackmailer has physical control over the blackmailed victim and withdraws the coins in a way similar to the impersonation scenario. The blackmailer communicates with the Bank directly.

The main idea of the payment system in [6] is that it gives the marked coins in case of blackmailing. And it is impossible for the blackmailer to distinguish the marked coins from valid coins. And all spent marked coins can efficiently be detected at deposit. This enables to trace of the blackmailer. But, if the Bank issues the marked coins to an honest user intentionally, then the privacy of the user can be violated. Thus during normal withdrawal the Bank proves to the user that the coins are unmarked with a designated verifier style proof in confirmation protocol. In case of blackmailing, however, the blackmailer can also verify the validity of the coins through the confirmation protocol. For this reason, the process that generates a faked confirmation protocol is needed. To convince the blackmailer, who has kidnapped the user or disguised as the user, during a withdrawal that coins are unmarked(although in fact the bank has marked them) the Bank needs to obtain decryption key used in the confirmation protocol from the user. But the system is impracticable unless the victim informs the bank of blackmailing before coins are withdrawn. To meet such preconditions, it was assumed in [6] that the victim can inform the bank of blackmailing without the blackmailer's noticing in case of perfect crime and impersonation. But in case of impersonation, if the blackmailer accidentally obtains the information to access the victim's bank account not threatening the victim, then the victim can't know even the fact that he is blackmailed. In this case, even though there exists a covert channel between the Bank and the victim, the information about blackmailing can't be transferred to the Bank. We'll call this case a special impersonation. And, in case of kidnapping, the victim cannot let the Bank know about blackmailing because the blackmailer has physical control over the blackmailed victim. So they assumed the existence of a covert channel and then applied the idea of distress cash system using secure hardware for authentication at the beginning of the withdrawal[2] to give the Bank the information about blackmailing and decryption key. The main idea is that the hardware offers two different PINs, where one is used to indicate a blackmailing and deliver the decryption key. But this solution can give the Bank those informations only with the probability of 1/2.

In this paper we propose two methods defeating blackmailing. First we present Modified XTR-version Schnorr identification protocol and a practical method that informs the Bank of blackmailing ahead of withdrawal and transfers the decryption key. Our method does not need such above assumptions in order to give the information about blackmailing to the Bank. It exploits the fact that Modified XTR-version Schnorr identification scheme has three distinct and valid responses with respect to a single challenge. This enables the user to construct a covert channel to inform the Bank of blackmailing. Hence the victim can always inform the Bank of the crime and cheat the blackmailer into obtaining the marked coins in case of perfect crime, and with the probability of 2/3 in case of impersonation or kidnapping attack without unpractical assumption. But in case of impersonation and kidnapping, secure hardware is needed to transfer the decryption key like as [6]. Especially, our method is more useful than the method proposed in [6] in case of kidnapping and special impersonation. In special impersonation, if the method presented in [6] is used, then there is no way of informing the information of blackmailing and giving the decryption key to the Bank. But in this paper, we can give the Bank the information about blackmailing and transfer the decryption key with the probability of 2/3. And in kidnapping, PINs are not used in secure hardware for authentication unlike the method proposed in [6] and the probability that gives the Bank the information about blackmailing and decryption key is improved from 1/2 to 2/3.

Secondly, we present Modified-Schnorr identification protocol and present a practical method that informs the Bank of blackmailing ahead of withdrawal and transfer the decryption key. As in the first method, we don't need the assumption in order to give the information about blackmailing to the Bank. The basis of our method is as follows. We append a random value $t \in [1, n]$ to Alice's response in order to give the Bank the information about blackmailing. Thus, in this method n's different responses can be generated and only one of them is a proper value used in normal operations. Hence the victim can always inform the bank of the crime and fake the blackmailer in case of perfect crime, and with probability of $\frac{n-1}{n}$ in case of impersonation or kidnapping attack without unpractical assumption. As in the first method, in case of impersonation and kidnapping, secure hardware is needed to transfer the decryption key like as [6]. Controlling the size of n, we have our scheme defeated blackmailing as a probability that we want. Thus, we can give the Bank those two informations with more higher probability than that of above the first scheme.

The remainders of this paper are structured as follows. In Section 2 we discuss briefly the XTR public key system, and in section 3 we propose two schemes, the Modified XTR-version Schnorr identification scheme and the Modified-Schnorr identification scheme. A practical method of defeating blackmailing is given in Section 4. Finally, we draw our conclusion in Section 5.

2   XTR Public Key Cryptosystems

2.1   Preliminaries

In this subsection we review some of the results from [7] and the XTR-Schnorr Identification scheme. First we observe several terms in the finite fields $GF(p^2)$, $GF(p^6)$ prior to review XTR public key systems.

- **Conjugate :** The conjugates over $GF(p^2)$ of $h \in GF(p^6)$ are h, h^{p^2}, h^{p^4}.

- **Trace :** The trace $Tr(h)$ over $GF(p^2)$ of $h \in GF(p^6)$ is the sum of the conjugates over $GF(p^2)$ of h, i.e., $Tr(h) = h + h^{p^2} + h^{p^4} \in GF(p^2)$.

XTR is a method that makes use of traces to represent and calculate powers of elements of a subgroup of a finite field. XTR is the first method that uses $GF(p^2)$ arithmetic to achieve $GF(p^6)$ security, without requiring explicit construction of $GF(p^6)$. Let us look around the system parameters for XTR.

Let $p \equiv 2 \bmod 3$ be a prime of length 170 bits such that the sixth cyclotomic polynomial evaluated in p, i.e., $\phi_6(p) = p^2 - p + 1$ has a prime factor q of length 160 bits. Let $g \in GF(p^6)$ be an element with order q. We use $Tr(g)$ as an XTR subgroup generator.

For efficiency of operations of elements of $GF(p^2)$, we represent elements of $GF(p^2)$ with optimal normal basis for $GF(p^2)$ over $GF(p)$. Let $\{\alpha, \alpha^2\}$ be an optimal normal basis for $GF(p^2)$ over $GF(p)$, where α and α^2 are roots of the polynomial $(X^3 - 1)/(X - 1) = X^2 + X + 1$. With $\alpha^i = \alpha^{i \bmod 3}$ it follows that $GF(p^2) \cong \{x_1\alpha + x_2\alpha^2 : x_1, x_2 \in GF(p)\}$.

XTR has several properties as follows.

Fact 1. For $g \in GF(p^6)$ of order q, $Tr(g^i) = Tr(g^j)$ if and only if g^i and g^j are conjugates over $GF(p^2)$.

Proof. The proof is described in Appendix.

Fact 2 [7]. Let p and q be primes with $q \mid p^2 - p + 1$. If $g \in GF(p^6)$ of order q then the subgroup $< g >$ cannot be embedded in any proper subfield of $GF(p^6)$ such as $GF(p)$, $GF(p^2)$, $GF(p^3)$.

The application of XTR in cryptographic protocols leads to substantial savings both in communication and computational overhead without compromising security. XTR can be used in any cryptosystem that relies on the subgroup discrete logarithm problem.

2.2   XTR-Schnorr Identification Scheme

In this subsection, we apply XTR to Schnorr identification scheme. We call it as XTR-Schnorr identification scheme. First, we review Schnorr identification scheme.

■ **System Setup**

1. A suitable prime p is selected such that $p - 1$ is divisible by another prime q.
2. An element g is chosen, $1 \leq g \leq p - 1$, having multiplicative order q.
3. A parameter t(e.g., $t \geq 40$), $2^t < q$, is chosen.

■ **Selection of per-user parameters**.

Alice's secret key : $s \in [0, q - 1]$
Alice's public key : v such that $v = g^{-s} \bmod p$

■ **Protocol.**

1. Alice chooses a random k, $1 \leq k \leq q - 1$, computes $x = g^k \bmod p$, and sends x to Bob.
2. Bob sends to Alice a random e, $1 \leq e \leq 2^t$.
3. Alice checks $1 \leq e \leq 2^t$, computes $y = se + k \bmod q$ and sends Bob y.
4. Bob computes $z = g^y v^e \bmod p$ and accepts Alice's identity provided $z = x$.

Now, we describe XTR-Schnorr identification scheme shown in Fig.1. This scheme is just an application of XTR to Schnorr identification scheme.

■ **System Setup**

In XTR-Schnorr identification scheme, the system parameters are prime numbers p and q with $q \mid p^2 - p + 1$, $Tr(g)$ and t.

1. p is about 170 bits prime with $p \equiv 2 \bmod 3$ and q is about 160 bits prime
2. Find a proper $Tr(g)$ for an element $g \in GF(p^6)$ of order q.
3. Find $t > 40$ such that $2^t < q$

■ **Selection of per-user parameters**.

Alice's secret key : $s \in [0, q - 1]$
Alice's public key : v such that $v = Tr(g^{-s})$

■ **XTR-Schnorr identification protocol'**

1. Alice chooses a random k, $1 \leq k \leq q - 1$, computes $x = Tr(g^k)$, and sends x to the Bob.
2. Bob sends to Alice a random e, $1 \leq e \leq 2^t$.

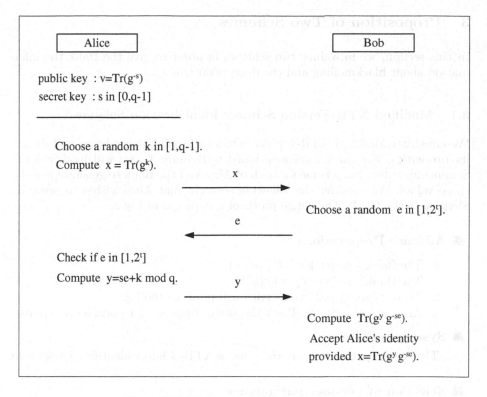

Fig. 1. XTR-Schnorr identification protocol

3. Alice checks if $1 \leq e \leq 2^t$, computes $y = (se + k) \ mod \ q$ and sends Bob y.
4. Bob computes $z = Tr(g^y g^{-se})$ and accepts Alice's identity provided $z = x$.

Theorem 1. *In Step 3. Alice's another responses,* $y' = (se + kp^2) \ mod \ q$ *and* $y'' = (se + kp^4) \ mod \ q$ *can pass this protocol completely.*

Proof. The proof is described in Appendix.

Remark 1. Alice's responses $y_1 = (se + k) \ mod \ q$, $y_2 = (se + kp^2) \ mod \ q$ and $y_3 = (se + kp^4) \ mod \ q$ are different values mutually, but only Alice can generate these three values and Bob cannot extract the others from given one response. Bob cannot obtain any information about the other two responses.

Remark 2. $Tr(g^y g^{-se})$ is computed by Algorithm 2.4.8 [7,8] based on $Tr(g), v = Tr(g^{-s})$ and y, e. Note that Bob dose not know the Alice's secret key s.

3   Proposition of Two Schemes

In this section, we introduce two schemes in order to give the Bank the information about blackmailing and the decryption key.

3.1   Modified XTR-Version Schnorr Identification Scheme

We construct Modified XTR-version Schnorr identification scheme and discuss its properties. For the reason mentioned in Remark 1., we will modify XTR-Schnorr identification scheme for both of Alice and the Bank to generate possible three values. We consider the following scenario that Alice wishes to prove his identity to the Bank. The entire protocol is depicted in Fig.2.

■ **Advance Preparations**

1. The Bank's secret key : b ($< q$)
   The Bank's public key : $Tr(g^b)$
2. There is an agreed symmetric encryption method E.
3. Alice agrees with the Bank the size of response for normal operations.

■ **System Setup**

The system parameters are the same as XTR-Schnorr identification scheme.

■ **Selection of per-user parameters.**

Alice's secret key : $s \in [0, q-1]$
Alice's public key : v such that $v = Tr(g^{-s})$

■ **Modified XTR-version Schnorr identification protocol**

1. Alice chooses a random k, $1 \le k \le q-1$, computes $x = Tr(g^k)$, and sends x to the Bank. Alice computes $Tr(g^{kb})$, and determines a symmetric encryption key K based on $Tr(g^{kb})$.
2. The Bank computes $Tr(g^{kb})$, and determines a symmetric encryption key K based on $Tr(g^{kb})$. The Bank sends to Alice a random e, $1 \le e \le 2^t$.
3. Alice checks if $1 \le e \le 2^t$. Alice computes $y_1 = (se + k) \bmod q$, $y_2 = y_1 \cdot p^2 \bmod q$ and $y_3 = y_1 \cdot p^4 \bmod q$. If $y_1 = 0$ then Alice terminates this protocol and begins this protocol again from step 1. If not, for $1 \le i \le 3$, Alice selects y_i among $\{y_i | 1 \le i \le 3\}$.
   Following substep 3.1 and 3.2 are implemented by a secure hardware.

   3.1. If y_i is the value of agreed size, then DATA is random value k' where the length of k' is the same as that of a decryption key used in confirmation protocol. Otherwise, DATA is the decryption key.
   3.2. Alice encrypts $y_i || DATA$ by using an agreed symmetric encryption algorithm E with the shared secret key K and sends $E_K(y_i || DATA)$ to the Bank. Note that $||$ means a concatenation.

4. The Bank decrypts $E_K(y_i \| DATA)$ with the shared secret key K and find y_i. For $1 \le i \le 3$, the Bank verifies $x \stackrel{?}{=} Tr(g^{y_i} g^{-sep^{2(j-1)}})$: if not, it is rejected. The Bank checks if y_i is the agreed size with Alice for normal operations. If y_i is not the size for normal operations, Alice is under the blackmailing and DATA is Alice's decryption key used in confirmation protocol.

Remark 3. In substep 3.1, confirmation protocol is the same thing as used in [6].

Modified XTR-version Schnorr Identification scheme has following properties.

Theorem 2. *Let* $y_1 = (se+k) \bmod q$, $y_2 = y_1 \cdot p^2 \bmod q$ *and* $y_3 = y_1 \cdot p^4 \bmod q$. *Then* y_i *for* $1 \le i \le 3$ *passes the verification step 4.*

Proof. The proof is described in Appendix.

Corollary 1. *If* $y_1 \neq 0$, *then* y_1, y_2, y_3 *are pair-wise distinct.*

Proof. The proof is described in Appendix.

Remark 4. Actually, 9 different responses, $y_{1i} = (se + k) \cdot p^{2i} \bmod q$, $y_{2i} = (se + kp^2) \cdot p^{2i} \bmod q$, $y_{3i} = (se + kp^4) \cdot p^{2i} \bmod q$ for $1 \le i \le 3$, can pass the verification step 4. But, the Bank can generate only three different values $\{y_{1i} \mid y_{1i} = (se + k) \cdot p^{2i} \bmod q$ for $1 \le i \le 3\}$ from given y_{1i} for $1 \le i \le 3$.

3.2 Modified-Schnorr Identification Scheme

We construct Modified-Schnorr identification scheme for the purpose of giving the information of blackmailing and the decryption key to the Bank and discuss its properties. The following scenarios are the same as above subsection. The entire protocol is depicted in Fig.3.

■ **Advance Preparations**
  1. The Bank's secret key : b ($< q$)
     The Bank's public key : $v = g^b$
  2. There is an agreed symmetric encryption method E.
  3. Alice agrees with Bank the value $a \in [1, n]$ for normal operations and $t \in [1, n], t \neq a$ for blackmailing.

■ **System Setup**
  The system parameters are the same as Schnorr-identification protocol.

■ **Selection of per-user parameters.**
  Alice's secret key : $s \in [0, q-1]$
  Alice's public key : v such that $v = g^{-s}$

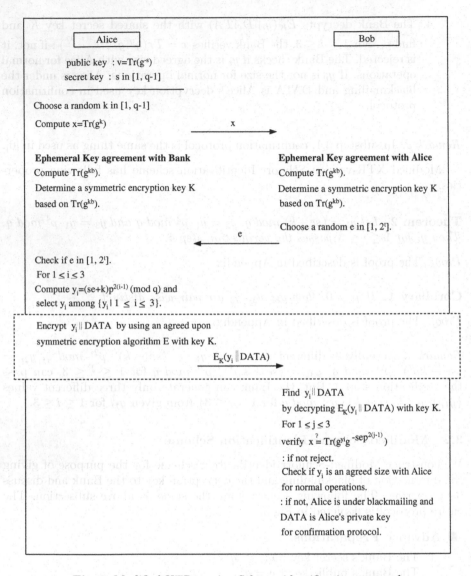

Fig. 2. Modified XTR-version Schnorr identification protocol

■ New XTR-version Schnorr identification protocol

1. Alice chooses a random k, $1 \le k \le q - 1$, computes $x = g^k \bmod q$, and sends x to the Bank. Alice computes g^{kb}, and determines a symmetric encryption key K based on g^{kb}.

2. The Bank computes g^{kb}, and determines a symmetric encryption key K based on g^{kb}. The Bank sends to Alice a random e, $1 \le e \le 2^t$.

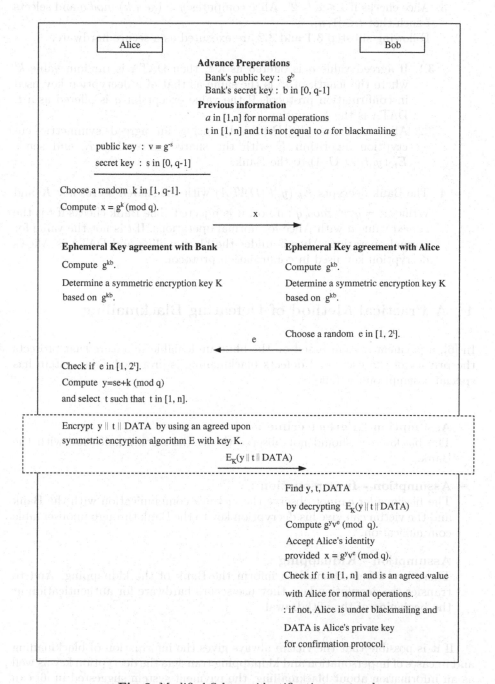

Alice		Bob
	Advance Preperations	
	Bank's public key : g^b	
	Bank's secret key : b in [0, q-1]	
	Previous information	
	a in [1,n] for normal operations	
	t in [1,n] and t is not equal to a for blackmailing	
public key : v = g^-s		
secret key : s in [0, q-1]		

Choose a random k in [1, q-1].

Compute $x = g^k \pmod q$.

$$x \longrightarrow$$

Ephemeral Key agreement with Bank

Compute g^{kb}.

Determine a symmetric encryption key K
based on g^{kb}.

Ephemeral Key agreement with Alice

Compute g^{kb}.

Determine a symmetric encryption key K
based on g^{kb}.

$$\longleftarrow e$$

Choose a random e in $[1, 2^t]$.

Check if e in $[1, 2^t]$.

Compute $y = se + k \pmod q$

and select t such that t in [1, n].

Encrypt y ‖ t ‖ DATA by using an agreed upon
symmetric encryption algorithm E with key K.

$$E_K(y \| t \| DATA)$$

Find y, t, DATA

by decrypting $E_K(y \| t \| DATA)$

Compute $g^y v^e \pmod q$.

Accept Alice's identity

provided $x = g^y v^e \pmod q$.

Check if t in [1, n] and is an agreed value

with Alice for normal operations.

: if not, Alice is under blackmailing and

DATA is Alice's private key

for confirmation protocol.

Fig. 3. Modified-Schnorr identification protocol

3. Alice checks if $1 \leq e \leq 2^t$. Alice computes $y = (se + k) \bmod q$ and selects t such that $t \in [1, n]$.
   Following substep 3.1 and 3.2 are executed as a secure hardware.

   3.1. If agreed value a is offered as a t, then DATA is random value k' where the length of k' is the same as that of a decryption key used in confirmation protocol. If the value except for a is offered as a t, DATA is the decryption key.
   3.2. Alice encrypts $y||t||DATA$ by using an agreed symmetric encryption algorithm E with the shared secret key K and sends $E_K(y||t||DATA)$ to the Bank.

4. The Bank decrypts $E_K(y||t||DATA)$ with the shared secret key K and verifies $x \stackrel{?}{=} g^y v^e \bmod q$: if not, it is rejected. The Bank checks if t is the agreed value a with Alice for normal operations. If t is not the value for normal operation, Alice is under the blackmailing and DATA is Alice's decryption key used in confirmation protocol.

4   A Practical Method of Defeating Blackmailing

In [6], a payment system based on the blind undeniable signature that protects the privacy of the users and defeats blackmailing is proposed. The system has special assumptions as follows.

– **Assumption - Perfect crime :**
  The blackmailer should not observe the victim's communication with the Bank.

– **Assumption - Impersonation :**
  The blackmailer cannot observe the victim's communication with the Bank and the victim can give his decryption key to the Bank through unobservable communication.

– **Assumption - Kidnapping :**
  There is a covert channel to inform the Bank of the kidnapping. And to transfer the decryption key, they use secure hardware for authentication at the beginning of the withdrawal

If it is possible that the victim always gives the information of blackmailing and in cases of impersonation and kidnapping transfers the decryption key as well as an information about blackmailing, the payment system suggested in [6] can be put into practice. But if not, it is unpractical. In the following subsection, we introduce a practical method of defeating blackmailing using two schemes proposed in previous section.

4.1 Using Modified XTR-Version Schnorr Identification Scheme

In this subsection, we introduce a practical method of defeating blackmailing although the victim cannot communicate to the Bank in other ways. The main idea of our method is as follows. In the electronic cash system, customers should go through identification protocol before withdrawal. To this process, we add a technique that the customer under blackmailing can inform his state without other ways of communicating with the Bank. Our method doesn't need any additional assumptions because identification protocol is a fundamental process of electronic cash systems. For this proposal, we use the following characteristic of Modified XTR-version Schnorr Identification Scheme that there are three distinct responses of $\{y_i \mid 1 \leq i \leq 3\}$ that satisfy the identification, as shown in Theorem 2. In order to apply this characteristic, a user need to choose one size among three distinct responses for normal operations when he opens an account with the Bank. The other two sizes are supposed to be used in case of blackmailing. When the user transfers the response, he encrypts $y_i \| DATA$ by using an agreed upon symmetric encryption algorithm E with key K and sends $E_K(y_i \| DATA)$ to the Bank. Then we can inform the bank of blackmailing before delivering coins and fake a confirmation protocol in cases of three scenarios prescribed. Thus we can block blackmailing without the special assumptions [6].

As we have referred in the main idea, encrypted $y_i \| DATA$ must be sent to the bank. Because, if $y_i \| DATA$ dose not be encrypted, then the blackmailer first observes $y_i \| DATA$ transmitted in normal operations by the targeted victim. And then he calculates y_i, $y_i \cdot p^2 \ mod \ q$, $y_i \cdot p^4 \ mod \ q$ to compare their sizes. By computing of three values, he can find out the size of y_i used for normal operations. The proof of this is shown in the Appendix.

Method of defeating blackmailing. We'll observe how to send the information of blackmailing and decryption key to the Bank in case of three blackmailing scenarios.

Note that, for instance, the smallest size is supposed to be used for normal operations, and the middle or largest one for blackmailing.

1. **Perfect crime**

   In this case, the blackmailer communicates only with the victim. When the blackmailer contacts the victim via an anonymous channel and threatens him to withdraw some coins, the victim must convince he Bank of his identification to withdraw coins. At this time, by using the middle or largest size y_i the victim can send the information of perfect crime. Since the victim can generate a faked confirmation protocol for himself, he don't have to transfer the decryption key to the Bank and secure hardware is not needed. Therefore, the victim always can inform the Bank of the crime ahead of the cash withdrawal and cheat the blackmailer into obtaining the marked coins.

2. **Impersonation**

The blackmailer comes in direct contact with the Bank in the identification protocol as well as withdrawal process by disguising his identity. The blackmailer obtains the information to access the victim's bank account but cannot know the size of response for normal operations. Thus the blackmailer can't help choosing one y_i among three. If the y_i's of a wrong size are chosen, then the decryption key is appended as a DATA through secure hardware. With the decryption key the Bank can fake a confirmation protocol. Since the probability of choosing the smallest size among three sizes is $1/3$, the blackmailer has more risk of sending the information of blackmailing to the Bank. That is, with the probability of $2/3$ the information about blackmailing is transferred to the bank. As a result, with the same probability the bank can issue the marked coins to the blackmailer and convince the blackmailer that the coins are unmarked. Especially, our method can give the information and decryption key even in special impersonation with the probability of $2/3$, but on the other hand the method proposed in [6] cannot even though there exists a covert channel between the bank and the victim.

3. **Kidnapping**

In case of kidnapping, the blackmailer comes in direct contact with the Bank like impersonation. In this case, the victim's secret key s can be easily known to the blackmailer. If the victim tells the blackmailer a wrong secret key, the blackmailer comes to know the consequence immediately during the identification protocol. It is not easy to give a false key because it can cause physically fatal effect on him. But, blackmailer must choose one y_i among three and cannot determine the validity of chosen y_i. If the wrong y_i are chosen, then the decryption key is appended as a DATA through secure hardware like above case. With the decryption key the Bank can fake a confirmation protocol. In [6] two PINs are used in secure hardware for authentication, but in our method PINs are not used and the probability that informs the bank of blackmailing is improved from $1/2$ to $2/3$. Of course, in [6] the probability is improved like our method but the burden that the user has to remember three different PINs becomes larger. Since the probability of choosing the smallest size among three is $1/3$, the blackmailer has more risk of sending the information of blackmailing to the Bank. So, it's hard to attack successfully, which means that the blackmailer is likely to avoid such an attack. As a result, in spite of revealed user's secret key s, the attack can be defeated with the probability of $2/3$.

The Security of Modified XTR-version Schnorr identification. It can be shown that the protocol is a proof of knowledge of s and the size of response y_i which is used for normal operations, i.e., any attacker completing the protocol as Alice must be capable of computing s and know the size of y_i. But since y_i is encrypted by using symmetric encryption algorithm with K, the attacker never comes to know y_i and its size without knowing K. Also, although the attacker knows the secret key s, he could not find out the shared secret key K because he does not know the random number k used in each identification protocol. Hence, in our scheme the stability of security on the size of y_i depends on the symmetric encryption algorithm. To know $K = Tr(g^{bk})$, the attacker tries to know b or k. But to find k or b from $Tr(g^k)$ or $Tr(g^b)$, respectively, is as difficult as solving the discrete logarithm problem. Therefore, calculating the size of y_i for normal operations is as difficult as solving the discrete logarithm problem.

4.2   Using Modified-Schnorr Identification Scheme

Now, we introduce a practical method of defeating blackmailing by using Modified-Schnorr identification scheme although the victim cannot communicate to the Bank in other ways. The main idea is similar as in the Modified XTR-version Schnorr identification scheme. We can inform about blackmailing before delivering coins and cheat the blackmailer into obtaining the marked coins in cases of three scenarios prescribed. Thus we can block blackmailing without the special assumptions [6]. In this case encrypted $y||t||DATA$ must be sent to the Bank also.

Method of defeating blackmailing. We'll observe how to send the information of blackmailing and decryption key to the Bank by using Modified-Schnorr identification protocol in case of three blackmailing scenarios. Note that $a \in [1, n]$ is supposed to be used for normal operations and $t \in [1, n]$ such that $t \neq a$ for blackmailing.

1. **Perfect crime**

   Since the victim communicate with the Bank directly, by using $t \in [1, n]$ such that $t \neq a$ he can send the information of perfect crime to the Bank. Also, the victim can generate a faked confirmation protocol for himself, he don't have to transfer the decryption key to the Bank and secure hardware is not needed. Therefore, the victim always can inform the Bank of the crime ahead of cash withdrawal and cheat the blackmailer into obtaining the marked coins.

2. **Impersonation**

   The blackmailer comes in direct contact with the Bank in the identification protocol as well as withdrawal process by disguising his identity. In the process that the blackmailer transfer the response corresponding to the challenge, he has to choose one value among $[1, n]$. But there is no way for the blackmailer to find out the accurate value. The blackmailer must choose one t among $[1, n]$. If the values except for a are chosen, then the decryption key is appended as a DATA through secure hardware. With the decryption key the Bank can fake a confirmation protocol. Since the probability of choosing the exact value a is $1/n$, the blackmailer has relatively much risk of sending the information of blackmailing to the Bank. That is, with the probability of $\frac{n-1}{n}$ the Bank issues the marked coins to the blackmailer. Like in Modified

XTR-version Schnorr identification, our method can give the information and decryption key even in special impersonation with the probability of $\frac{n-1}{n}$, but on the other hand the method of [6] cannot.

3. Kidnapping

In case of kidnapping, the blackmailer comes in direct contact with the Bank like impersonation. In this case, the victim's secret key s can be easily known to the blackmailer also. When it comes to t, there is no way for the blackmailer to find out the accurate value even though the victim gives a false information. The blackmailer must choose one t among $[1, n]$. If the values except for a are chosen, then the decryption key is appended as a DATA through secure hardware. With the decryption key the Bank can fake a confirmation protocol. Since the probability of choosing the exact value a is $1/n$, the blackmailer has relatively much risk of sending the information of blackmailing to the Bank. Also, PINs are not used in secure hardware for authentication and the probability that informs the Bank of blackmailing is improved to $\frac{n-1}{n}$. So, it's very hard to attack successfully, which means that the blackmailer is likely to avoid such an attack. As a result, with the probability of $\frac{n-1}{n}$ the Bank issues the marked coins to the blackmailer. In [6], the probability is improved like our method but the burden that the user has to learn by heart the n's different PINs becomes much larger. Therefore this attack is actually impractical.

The Security of Modified-Schnorr identification. The security of Modified-Schnorr identification depends on the Schnorr identification scheme. Thus the security of our scheme is guaranteed by original Schnorr identification scheme.

5   Conclusion

We have so far observed a practical method to block blackmailing attacks with Modified XTR-version Schnorr identification scheme and Modified-Schnorr identification scheme. The proposed schemes enable us to use a payment system [6] which is proposed to protect the privacy of users and to defeat blackmailing without impractical assumptions. Specially, in the most serious drawback of the known payment system, kidnapping, we can defeat the blackmailing with relatively higher probability than that of the method proposed in [6]. And, because the response value generated naturally or a random value among $[1, n]$ are used instead of the PINs, the convenience of the user is improved. Also, in special impersonation case we can defeat the blackmailing with the probability of 2/3 or $\frac{n-1}{n}$ but the method proposed in [6] cannot. Therefore, using Modified XTR-version Schnorr identification scheme and Modified-Schnorr identification scheme in payment system proposed in [6] can remarkably decrease blackmailing occurred in electronic cash systems without unpractical assumptions.

References

1. J. Camenisch, U. Mauer, and M. Stadler. *Digital payment systems with passive anonymity-revoking trustees.*, In Computer Security-ESORICS '96, volume 1146 of Lecture Notes in Computer Scienc, pages 31-43. Springer-Verlag, 1996.
2. G. Davide, Y, Tsiounis, and M. Young. *Anonymity control in e-cash systems.*, In Financial Cryptography '97, volume 1318 of Lecture Notes in Computer Science, pages 1-16. Springer- Verlag, 1997.
3. Y. Frankel, Y. Tsiounis, and M. Young. *"Indirect discourse proofs"; Achieving efficient fair off-line e-cash.*, In Advances in Cryptology - ASIACRYPT '96, volume 1163 of Lecture Notes in Computer Science, pages 286-300. Springer-Verlag, 1996.
4. M. Jakobsson and M. Yung. *Revokable and versatile electronic money.* In 3rd ACM Conference on Computer Communication Security (CCCS '96), pages 76-87. ACM Press, 1996.
5. M. Jakobsson and M. Yung. *Distributed "magic ink" signatures.* In Advances in Cryptology - EUROCRYPT '97, volume 1233 of Lecture Notes in Computer Science, pages 450-464. Springer-Verlag, 1997.
6. D.Kügler and H. Vogt. *Marking: A Privacy Protecting Approach Against Blackmailing.*, Proceedings PKC 2001, LNCS 1992, Springer-Verlag, 2001, 137-152.
7. A.K. Lenstra, E.R. Verheul, *The XTR public key system.*, Proceedings of Crypto 2000, LNCS 1880,Springer-Verlag, 2000,1-19; available from www.ecstr.com.
8. A.K. Lenstra, E.R. Verheul, *Key improvements to XTR* Proceedings of Asiacrypt 2000, LNCS 1976, Springer-Verlag, 2000,220-233; available from www.ecstr.com.
9. B. von Solms and D.Naccache. *On blind signatures and perfect crimes.*, Computers and Security, 11(6):581-583,1992.
10. M. Stadler. *Cryptographic Protocols for Revokable Privacy.* PhD Thesis, ETH No. 11651, Swiss Federal Institute of Technology, Zurich, 1996.

Appendix : Proof of Theorems

Fact 1. For $g \in GF(p^6)$ of order q, $Tr(g^i) = Tr(g^j)$ if and only if g^i and g^j are conjugates over $GF(p^2)$.

Proof. ($\Rightarrow$) For $g \in GF(p^6)$ of order q, $F(X) = X^3 - Tr(g^i)X^2 + Tr(g^i)^p X - 1 \in GF(p^2)[X]$ is an irreducible polynomial over $GF(p^2)$ and its roots are conjugates of g^i over $GF(p^2)$, i.e., g^i, g^{ip^2}, g^{ip^4} are roots of $F(X)$. As $Tr(g^i) = Tr(g^j)$, $F(X) = X^3 - Tr(g^i)X^2 + Tr(g^i)^p X - 1 = X^3 - Tr(g^j)X^2 + Tr(g^j)^p X - 1 \in GF(p^2)[X]$. So g^j is also a root of $F(X)$. Therefore, g^i and g^j are conjugates over $GF(p^2)$. ($\Leftarrow$) As g^i and g^j are conjugates over $GF(p^2)$, we have $g^i = g^j$, $g^i = g^{jp^2}$ or $g^i = g^{jp^4}$. Since $h^{p^6} = h$ for $h \in GF(p^6)$, we have $Tr(g^i) = Tr(g^j)$.

Theorem 1. In Step 3. Alice's another responses, $y' = (se + kp^2) \bmod q$ and $y'' = (se + kp^4) \bmod q$.

Proof. If $y' = (se + kp^2) \bmod q$ is sent to the bank, then $x = Tr(g^{y'}g^{-se})$. Since $Tr(g^{y'}g^{-se \bmod q}) = Tr(g^{(se+kp^2) \bmod q}g^{-se \bmod q}) = Tr(g^{kp^2}) = Tr(g^k) = x$. If $y'' = (se + kp^4) \bmod q$ is sent to the bank, then $x = Tr(g^{y''}g^{-se})$. Since $Tr(g^{y''}g^{-se \bmod q}) = Tr(g^{(se+kp^4) \bmod q}g^{-se \bmod q}) = Tr(g^{kp^4}) = Tr(g^k) = x$.

Theorem 2. Let $y_1 = (se + k) \bmod q$, $y_2 = y_1 \cdot p^2 \bmod q$ and $y_3 = y_1 \cdot p^4 \bmod q$. Then y_i for $1 \leq i \leq 3$ passes the verification step 4.

Proof. If $y_1 = (se + k) \bmod q$ is sent to the bank, then $x = Tr(g^{y_1}g^{-se})$ since $Tr(g^{y_1}g^{-se \bmod q}) = Tr(g^{(se+k) \bmod q}g^{-se \bmod q}) = Tr(g^k) = x$. If $y_2 = (se + k)p^2 \bmod q$ is sent to the bank, then $x = Tr(g^{y_2}g^{-sep^2})$ since $Tr(g^{y_2}g^{-sep^2}) = Tr(g^{(se+k)p^2 \bmod q}g^{-sep^2 \bmod q}) = Tr(g^{kp^2})$. By Fact 1, $Tr(g^{kp^2}) = Tr(g^k) = x$. If $y_3 = (se + k)p^4 \bmod q$ is sent to the bank, then $x = Tr(g^{y_3}g^{-sep^4})$ since $Tr(g^{y_3}g^{-sep^4}) = Tr(g^{(se+k)p^4 \bmod q}g^{-sep^4 \bmod q}) = Tr(g^{kp^4})$. By Fact 1, $Tr(g^{kp^4}) = Tr(g^k) = x$.

Corollary 1. If $y_1 \neq 0$, then y_1, y_2, y_3 are pair-wise distinct.

Proof. We consider the following three cases.

Case 1.

If $y_1 = y_2$, then $se + k \equiv (se + k) \cdot p^2 \bmod q$. So $(se + k) \cdot (p^2 - 1) \equiv 0 \bmod q$. This implies that $se + k \equiv 0 \bmod q$ or $p^2 - 1 \equiv 0 \bmod q$. Thus $p^2 - 1 \equiv 0 \bmod q$, as $y_1 \neq 0$ by assumption. Therefore $g \in GF(p^2)$. This is a contradiction to Fact 2. Thus $y_1 \neq y_2$.

Case 2.

If $y_1 = y_3$, then $se + k \equiv (se + k) \cdot p^4 \bmod q$. So $(se + k) \cdot (p^4 - 1) \equiv 0 \bmod q$ and thus $(se + k) \cdot (p^2 - 1) \cdot (p^2 + 1) \equiv 0 \bmod q$. This implies that $se + k \equiv 0 \bmod q$ or $p^2 - 1 \equiv 0 \bmod q$ or $p^2 + 1 \equiv 0 \bmod q$. Because $q \nmid p^2 - 1$ as shown in case 1 and $y_1 \neq 0$, $p^2 + 1 \equiv 0 \bmod q$. However as $p^2 - p + 1 \equiv 0 \bmod q$, $(p^2 - p + 1) - (p^2 + 1) = -p \equiv 0 \bmod q$. So $q \mid p$. But this is again a contradiction to $q < p$. Thus $y_1 \neq y_3$.

Case 3.

If $y_2 = y_3$, then $(se + k) \cdot p^2 \equiv (se + k) \cdot p^4 \bmod q$. So $(se + k) \cdot (p^4 - p^2) \equiv 0 \bmod q$ and thus $(se + k) \cdot p^2 \cdot (p^2 - 1) \equiv 0 \bmod q$. This implies that $se + k \equiv 0 \bmod q$ or $p^2 \equiv 0 \bmod q$ or $p^2 - 1 \equiv 0 \bmod q$. Because $q \nmid p^2 - 1$ as shown in case 1 and $y_1 \neq 0$, $p^2 \equiv 0 \bmod q$. Since p and q are primes, this is impossible. Thus $y_2 \neq y_3$.

Proof of subsection 4.1 :

We consider the following three cases.

1. When y_1 is sent to the Bank

In this case we compare the sizes of y_1, $y_1 \cdot p^2 \bmod q$ and $y_1 \cdot p^4 \bmod q$ then we can know the accurate size of y_1 which is used in the normal operation.

2. **When $y_2 = y_1 \cdot p^2 \bmod q$ is sent to the Bank**

In this case compute $y_1 \cdot p^2 \bmod q$, $y_1 \cdot p^4 \bmod q$ and $y_1 \cdot p^6 \bmod q$. As $p^2 - p + 1 \equiv 0 \bmod q$ and $p^6 - 1 \equiv 0 \bmod q$, $y_1 \cdot p^6 \bmod q = y_1$. Therefore $\{y_1 \cdot p^2 \bmod q, y_1 \cdot p^4 \bmod q, y_1 \cdot p^6 \bmod q\} = \{y_1 \cdot p^2 \bmod q, y_1 \cdot p^4 \bmod q, y_1\}$. Hence we can know the accurate size of y_2 which is used in the normal operation by comparing the sizes of $\{y_1 \cdot p^2 \bmod q, y_1 \cdot p^4 \bmod q, y_1 \cdot p^6 \bmod q\}$.

3. **When $y_3 = y_1 \cdot p^4 \bmod q$ is sent to the Bank**

In this case compute $y_1 \cdot p^4 \bmod q$, $y_1 \cdot p^6 \bmod q$ and $y_1 \cdot p^8 \bmod q$. As $p^6 \equiv 1$ and $p^8 \equiv p^2 \bmod q$, $y_1 \cdot p^6 \bmod q = y_1$ and $y_1 \cdot p^8 \bmod q = y_1 \cdot p^2 \bmod q$. Therefore $\{y_1 \cdot p^4 \bmod q, y_1 \cdot p^6 \bmod q, y_1 \cdot p^8 \bmod q\} = \{y_1 \cdot p^4 \bmod q, y_1, y_1 \cdot p^2 \bmod q\}$. Hence we can know the accurate size of y_3 which is used in the normal operation by comparing the sizes of $\{y_1 \cdot p^4 \bmod q, y_1 \cdot p^6 \bmod q, y_1 \cdot p^8 \bmod q\}$.

Privacy against Piracy: Protecting Two-Level Revocable P-K Traitor Tracing

Hyun-Jeong Kim[1], Dong Hoon Lee[1], and Moti Yung[2]

[1] CIST,Korea University, Seoul, KOREA,
khj@cist.korea.ac.kr[***], donghlee@korea.ac.kr
[2] CertCo, New York, NY, USA. moti@cs.columbia.edu

Abstract. In known traitor tracing schemes, an enabling block is used for both secure broadcast of a session key and tracing traitors in pirate boxes. This paper suggests a new traitor tracing scheme that has two-levels for efficiency. In the more frequent level an enabling block is used only for a very efficient session key distribution, and a new block, less frequently used, called a *renewal block* is used for the renewal of the group key and for the detection and revocation of traitors. This organization increases efficiency: the computational complexity of encryption/decryption of the often employed enabling block is constant, while only that of the sporadically employed renewal block depends on the allowed revocations (as in earlier schemes). However, our saving has a price: in a two-level broadcasting scheme, the new danger is that rather than performing piracy by leaking the keys of the renewal block, the individual traitors may leak to pirates the means to decode the enabling blocks at the sessions. For example, if the enabling block is naively implemented as a single key-encrypting-key that is known to all– and this key is used to encrypt session keys, then any participant can leak this key without being detected. (Note that leaking the session keys themselves, constantly all the time, is typically considered in the literature not to be an economically viable option). In order to prevent this new potential leakage, a novel idea of personal enabling keys (used throughout) is suggested. In order to get a session key, a user will need access to the enabling block with his own personal key. To discourage leakage of the personal key (which would violate the service), a novel self-enforcement method is employed that ties "privacy" to "leakage". The self-enforcement of personal keys uses the fact that if the key is leaked then the party which leaks may lose its private data to the party it leaks to (i.e. it is a privacy-based protection mechanism). In our self-enforcement, a subscriber's private information is not embedded into his personal key directly (as was done earlier). Thus, if a subscriber's important data is altered, his personal key needs not to be regenerated. The separation into two-level broadcast (for efficiency) together with the novel flexible self-enforcement (privacy-based protection of the enabling-block keys) is the central contribution of this work.

[***] This work was supported by grant No. R012-00100-0537-0 from the Korea Science & Engineering Foundation.

L. Batten and J. Seberry (Eds.): ACISP 2002, LNCS 2384, pp. 482–496, 2002.
© Springer-Verlag Berlin Heidelberg 2002

1   Introduction

This paper deals with a novel improved revocable public-key traitor tracing schemes that are methods to control digital rights (discourage piracy) by protection mechanisms that trace traitors who have collaborated with a pirate. We use a privacy-based-protection in a novel fashion to enable the schemes to remain protected after the improvement. This demonstrates a novel way and area where privacy of sensitive data (treated as an important resource) is employed to discourage piracy.

Recently, broadcast encryption schemes are applied to distribution of digital contents −multimedia, software, or pay TV− on the network. In the broadcast encryption schemes it is important that only authorized subscribers can access digital contents and any malicious user should not obtain digital contents from broadcast encryption messages. In general a broadcast encryption message consists of pairs of (*enabling block, cipher block*). A cipher block is a symmetric encryption of a cleartext by using a session key s and an enabling block is an encryption data of the session key. When a broadcast message is published, only authorized subscribers who receive their personal keys from a data supplier (DS) can obtain a session key.

Another important requirement in the broadcast encryption schemes is *traitor tracing*. It was introduced by Chor et al. [6] and enables to trace authorized subscribers, called *traitors*, who collude for manufacturing a pirate decoder. Since a pirate decoder always has to decrypt a session key in an enabling block for obtaining a cleartext, traitor tracing to detect illegal subscribers is achieved by using enabling blocks. Note that leaking session keys individually is considered impractical (economically non viable) piracy.

In the traitor tracing schemes proposed in [6,14,8], the complexity of encryption/decryption of an enabling block is dependent on the size of subscribers and the thresholds of coalition. Boneh and Franklin then (based on a preliminary suggestion of [8]) initiated the study of public key traitor tracing schemes [3], where DS encrypts a session key using only one public encryption key and each subscriber decrypts the session key using a distinct personal key. In view of applicability, a public-key scheme allows content to be sent by many content providers. This gives a scalable design of content distribution schemes with many content sources. The complexity of encryption/decryption of an enabling block of the public key traitor tracing schemes in [3,11,17] is independent of the number of subscribers, but dependent on the thresholds of coalition.

In [11,17] efficient revocation schemes were proposed using the method in [1], where session keys were encrypted using Shamir's polynomial based secret sharing scheme [15]. In [11], two type of schemes for revocation were proposed: schemes for a single revocation and schemes for many revocations. These schemes are secure against coalition of size up to k and revoke up to z traitors' personal keys where $z (\geq k - 1)$ is the degree of the polynomial. The size of an enabling block and the computational overhead in the decryption algorithms in [11,17] are dependent on the degree z.

In the existing schemes, DS embeds information into the enabling block to trace and revoke traitors. This causes an inefficiency in a computation of decryption of an enabling block since the size of an enabling block is always dependent on the coalition thresholds even if the enabling block is to be used only for distribution of a session key.

1.1   Our Work

Two-Level Scheme: Revocable Enabling/Renewal Traitor Tracing. We propose a new improved type of a traitor tracing scheme in which broadcast encryption messages consist of triples of (*enabling block, renewal block, cipher block*). In our scheme an enabling block is used only for secure broadcast of a session key and a renewal block is used for detecting and revoking traitors' rights and regenerating the group key. This separation of functionalities is based on the simple idea that most operations performed by subscribers are decryption, while revocation and tracing are performed less often. Thus, this gives a two-level scheme which is typically more efficient.

To obtain a session key, subscribers decrypt an enabling block containing only the encrypted data of the session key. Each subscriber must use a renewal block when it is changed. In these cases, DS sets a time check flag $\mathcal{N}_{\mathcal{E}W}\mathcal{C}_{\mathcal{H}\mathcal{G}} = CurrentDate\|CurrentTime$ and inserts into the renewal block the encryption data of the regenerated group key. Given a broadcast encryption message, each subscriber checks whether $\mathcal{O}_{\mathcal{L}\mathcal{D}}\mathcal{C}_{\mathcal{H}\mathcal{G}} = \mathcal{N}_{\mathcal{E}W}\mathcal{C}_{\mathcal{H}\mathcal{G}}$ where $\mathcal{O}_{\mathcal{L}\mathcal{D}}\mathcal{C}_{\mathcal{H}\mathcal{G}}$ has been saved by himself. If $\mathcal{O}_{\mathcal{L}\mathcal{D}}\mathcal{C}_{\mathcal{H}\mathcal{G}}$ differs from $\mathcal{N}_{\mathcal{E}W}\mathcal{C}_{\mathcal{H}\mathcal{G}}$, a subscriber decrypts the renewal block and changes the value of $\mathcal{O}_{\mathcal{L}\mathcal{D}}\mathcal{C}_{\mathcal{H}\mathcal{G}}$ into the value of $\mathcal{N}_{\mathcal{E}W}\mathcal{C}_{\mathcal{H}\mathcal{G}}$. When DS finds a pirate decoder, DS feeds a broadcast encryption message containing a renewal block for tracing traitors to the pirate decoder. Since the pirate decoder cannot decide whether the renewal block is for tracing or for renewal of the group key, the pirate decoder tries to decrypt the renewal block. If a pirate decoder does not use renewal blocks, it can't decrypt session keys in enabling blocks after the group key is regenerated. That is, a pirate decoder has to decrypt a renewal block when it is changed, and hence traitors can be traced by using the renewal block. Through this process DS finds at least one traitor of m-coalition with $m \leq (threshold\ k)$. Most existing traitor tracing schemes can be adapted to design a renewal block in our scheme. In this paper, we follow the structure proposed in [17] for renewal, tracing and revocation algorithms. For the revocation of traitors' rights, a renewal block is used in such a way that each subscriber except the traitors can obtain the new group key. Thereafter the revoked traitors cannot obtain session keys from broadcast encryption messages. The complexity of decrypting a renewal block is dependent on the coalition thresholds, but DS needs not perform a renewal process very often. Therefore our scheme is more efficient and practical than the schemes proposed in the literature, though the length of a broadcast encryption message is increased a little.

Efficiency: Comparison to Previous Work. The two-level idea is to allow better efficiency. We compare our scheme and other schemes in the *Table* 1 in view of the followings : the length of a personal key, the data redundancy, the complexity of an encryption, the complexity of an decryption, and the thresholds of revocation.

Table 1. Comparison of the different schemes. The parameters include n–the number of subscribers, k–the maximum number of coalition of traitors, H–The hash function, p, q–primes s.t $|p| \geq 1024$, $|q| \geq 160$ and $q|(p-1)$, z–the degree of a polynomial s.t $z \geq (k-1)$

Scheme	Personal Key	Data Redundancy	Encryption	Decryption	Revocation Thresholds
[6] (open one-level)	$O(k^2 \|n\|)$ $\times\|H\|$	$O(k^4 \|n\|)$ $\times\|H\|$	$O(k^4 \|n\|)$ XORs	$O(k^2 \|n\|)$ XORs	-
[3]	$\|q\|$	$(2k+1) \times \|p\|$	$\approx (2k+1)$ Exps. (mod p)	$\approx (2k+1)$ Exps. + $(2k+1)$ Mults. (mod p)	-
[11] (many revocations)	$\|q\|$	$O(z)$ $\times(\|p\|+\|q\|)$	$O(z)$ Exps. (mod p)	$O(z)$ Exps. +$O(z)$ Mults. (mod p)	$\leq z$
[17]	$\|q\|$	$O(z)$ $\times(\|p\|+\|q\|)$	$O(z)$ Exps. (mod p)	$O(z)$ Exps. +$O(z)$ Mults. (mod p)	$\leq z$
Our Scheme	$2\|p\|+\|q\|$	$(2+O(z))$ $\times(\|p\|+\|q\|)$	3 Exp.+3 Mults. (mod p) + $O(z)$ Exps. (mod p)	1 Exps.+3 Mults. (mod p) + $O(z)$ Exps. + $O(z)$ Mults. (mod p)	$\leq z$

Usually, the complexities of our scheme are those in the first line of *Our Scheme* in the *Table* 1. In case of a changed renewal block, the results of (*the first line + the second line*) of *Our Scheme* in the *Table* 1 are the total complexities of our scheme.

Protecting Enabling keys: Self-Enforcement Property. Since we employ the two-level scheme for efficiency, and since renewal blocks change infrequently, it may become a viable option to leak the group key from the renewal phase to allow decoding of the enabling blocks (which will be useful, until the renewal block is changed). Thus, we need to protect against this and enforce non-leakage. The basic central idea here is to employ personal keys which are good throughout many renewal blocks and are needed as part of the decoding of the enabling blocks, and to use self-enforcement to protect these personal keys. Self-enforcement can be viewed as extending the basic ideas of off-line digital cash, where double spending was tied to lose of privacy (anonymity). The concept of self-enforcement is that a subscriber's sensitive information is embedded into his personal key [7,11]. This will discourage leakage of the personal key. If a subscriber leaks his personal key, his sensitive data such as a credit card number or an account number is revealed simultaneously. Hence subscribers can not easily hand over their keys to a designer of a pirate decoder. This is a classical way to employ the need for privacy as a security or protection mechanism (it was used, as mentioned above, in digital cash [5] and recently in preventing leakage of public keys via the use of proprietary certificates [10]). This property is important for making schemes more efficient because it can lower values for the coalition thresholds. One property is not desirable in this method of embedding privacy in keys as was done in the past: if a subscriber's important data is changed, his personal key must be modified using the new data. For example, whenever a subscriber opens and closes bank accounts, his personal key should be updated accordingly.

In our scheme, we propose a novel variant: a subscriber's sensitive information is not embedded into his personal key directly. Instead, we use a subscriber's personal key for encryption/decryption of his sensitive data such as settlements of an account (which can be put in encrypted form in public bulletin boards). This provides a self-enforcement property since one who knows a subscriber's personal key can obtain his important data. Simultaneously our method is flexible in the sense that it can easily accommodate changes in sensitive data.

Organization: This paper is organized as follows. Section 2 describes the model of our scheme. Section 3 constructs our traitor tracing scheme and explains our self-enforcement property. The security of proposed scheme is analyzed in Section 4. In Section 5, we introduce a variant of the scheme which is secure against adaptive chosen ciphertext attacks. Finally, we conclude in Section 6.

2   The Model of Our Scheme

In our scheme there are two parties, a data supplier DS and n subscribers. Each subscriber has a personal key to decrypt a session key embedded in an enabling block and a renewal key to obtain the regenerated group key. Usually DS broadcasts encrypted messages with an unchanged renewal block. Only when renewal, tracing, or revocation is required, a renewal block is altered.

Our traitor tracing scheme consists of the following procedures:

SYSTEM SETUP : an algorithm to set up system parameters. Using this algorithm, DS estimates the number of possible subscribers in advance and then pre-computes the group key and system parameters for the encryption of session keys. If the number of subscribers exceeds the expected number, each subscriber can regenerate his personal key using public data with two modular multiplications.

REGISTRATION : an interactive protocol between DS and a subscriber who wants to register. As a result, a subscriber receives a personal key, a renewal key and the group key from DS securely.

ENCRYPTION OF ENABLING BLOCK : an algorithm which generates enabling blocks. This encryption algorithm is semantically secure against passive adversaries with assuming the hardness of the decision Diffie-Hellman problem.

DECRYPTION OF ENABLING BLOCK : an algorithm which, on input an enabling block and a personal key, returns a session key.

ENCRYPTION OF RENEWAL BLOCK : an algorithm which generates renewal blocks. This algorithm is based on Shamir's polynomial based secret sharing scheme.

DECRYPTION OF RENEWAL BLOCK : an algorithm which, on input a renewal block and a renewal key, returns the regenerated group key. Traitor tracing, revocation and regeneration of the group key are done by using this algorithm. When DS finds a black-box of a pirate decoder, he feeds a changed renewal block to the pirate decoder, which will try to obtain a new group key by decrypting the renewal block. By comparing the input and output from the decoder, DS detects traitors and then changes the group key using a renewal block. In this time, traitors are to fail to correctly decrypt the renewal block and can not obtain the changed group key from the renewal block. So their access authorizations are revoked. The legitimate subscribers obtain the changed group key by correctly decrypting the renewal block.

The following security goals in our model must hold:

Security of Encryption of Enabling Block/Renewal Block : It should be infeasible that adversaries obtain plaintexts from ciphertexts.

Soundness of Self-Enforcement : It should be hard that traitors who don't reveal their personal keys produce a pirate decoder.

Validity of Tracing using Renewal Block : When a renewal block is changed, a pirate decoder should not determine the role of the renewal block and have to decrypt it.

3   Our Proposed Scheme

In this section we construct our traitor tracing scheme and describe a new self-enforcement. Our scheme concerning renewal, traitor tracing and revocation is based on the method proposed in [17].

3.1   Our Scheme

First DS estimates the number of subscribers in advance and then starts the system setup. Let n be the estimated number of subscribers.

System Setup. Let $\mathcal{G}$ be a pseudo random number generator and $\mathcal{H}$ be a hash function based on modulus arithmetic [9]. DS setups the system as follows:

1. Choose prime numbers p and q such that $q|p-1$.
2. Choose a random value $g \in \mathbb{Z}_p$ with order q.
3. Choose randomly $h \in \mathbb{Z}_q^*$.
4. Perform the following steps for $1 \le i \le n$.
   a) Generate the ith random number v_i using the pseudo random number generator $\mathcal{G}$ on an input random seed value s_v.
   b) Obtain an output a_{i1} from $\mathcal{H}$ based on modulus q on input value v_i. In this time, a_{i1} must contain in $\mathbb{Z}_q^*$. Otherwise, go to Step (a).
   c) Compute $a_{i2} \equiv h - a_{i1}$. If $a_{i2} \notin \mathbb{Z}_q^*$, go to Step (a).
5. Compute $A_1 \equiv a_{11}a_{21}\cdots a_{n1}a_{r1}$ (mod q) and $A_2 \equiv a_{12}a_{22}\cdots a_{n2}a_{r2}$ (mod q) with values $a_{r1}, a_{r2} \in_R \mathbb{Z}_q^*$.
6. Select a degree $z(\ge k-1)$ polynomial $f(x) = \sum_{l=0}^{z} a_l x^l$ with $a_l \in \mathbb{Z}_q^*$.
7. Select random values $K_1, K_2 \in_R \mathbb{Z}_q^*$ as the group key $\mathcal{K} = (K_1^{-1}, K_2^{-1})$.

DS saves the values (h, A_1, A_2), a seed s_v and the polynomial $f(x)$ secretly, and publishes (g, g^h, p, q) and the key set $\langle g^{a_0}, g^{f(1)}, \cdots, g^{f(z)} \rangle$. Finally DS publishes $g^{x_{DS}}$ with $x_{DS} \in_R \mathbb{Z}_q^*$ for the self-enforcement property.

Registration. When a new subscriber S_i wants to obtain the authorization of digital contents, DS generates a personal key using values (h, A_1, A_2), a seed s_v and $(\mathcal{G}, \mathcal{H})$, and a renewal key using the polynomial $f(x)$. First DS identifies S_i and then sends the keys to him.

1. Generate (a_{i1}, a_{i2}) using the value h, s_v, $\mathcal{G}$ and $\mathcal{H}$.
2. Compute $\sigma_{i1} = (A_1/a_{i1})$ and $\sigma_{i2} = (A_2/a_{i2})$, i.e.,

$$\sigma_{i1} = a_{11}a_{21}\cdots a_{(i-1)1}a_{(i+1)1}\cdots a_{n1}a_{r1} \text{ and}$$
$$\sigma_{i2} = a_{12}a_{22}\cdots a_{(i-1)2}a_{(i+1)2}\cdots a_{n2}a_{r2}.$$

3. Compute $f(i)$.
4. Send the pair of personal key $(\sigma_{i1}^{-1}, \sigma_{i2}^{-1})$, the pair of renewal key $(i, f(i))$ and the group key $\mathcal{K}$ to S_i.

When the number of subscribers exceeds the expected number in the setup, DS regenerates the values A_1 and A_2 using the pseudo random number generator $\mathcal{G}$ and the hash function $\mathcal{H}$. After A_1 and A_2 are changed from $(a_{11}\cdots a_{n1}a_{r1})$ and $(a_{12}\cdots a_{n2}a_{r2})$ to $(a_{11}\cdots a_{n1}a_{(n+1)1}\cdots a_{(n+\alpha)1}a_{r'1})$ and $(a_{12}\cdots a_{n2}a_{(n+1)2}$ $\cdots a_{(n+\alpha)2}a_{r'2})$ respectively, DS publishes $\theta_1 = a_{r1}(a_{(n+1)1}\cdots a_{(n+\alpha)1}a_{r'1})^{-1}$ and $\theta_2 = a_{r2}(a_{(n+1)2}\cdots a_{(n+\alpha)2}a_{r'2})^{-1}$. Each subscriber can change his personal key by computing $\sigma_{ib}^{-1} := \theta_b \cdot \sigma_{ib}^{-1}$ where $b \in \{1, 2\}$.

Encryption of Enabling Block. Let s be a session key such that $s \in \mathbb{Z}_p$. An enabling block E is constructed as follows.

Let $r, w \in_R \mathbb{Z}$ be one-time random numbers.

$$E = \left\langle s \cdot g^{rh}, g^r, g^{rw^{-1}}, A_1 K_1 w, A_2 K_2 w \right\rangle.$$

DS broadcasts a cipher block and an enabling block containing an encryption message of the session key. Encryption data of digital contents in a cipher block is a symmetric encryption with the session key.

Decryption of Enabling Block. When each subscriber S_i receives a broadcast encryption message, S_i obtains a session key from the enabling block with his personal key $(\sigma_{i1}^{-1}, \sigma_{i2}^{-1})$ and the group key $\mathcal{K}$ as follows.

$$s = s \cdot g^{rh}/g^{rw^{-1}\{A_1K_1w\cdot(\sigma_{i1}K_1)^{-1} + A_2K_2w\cdot(\sigma_{i2}K_2)^{-1}\}}$$

To get digital contents, subscribers decrypt a cipher block using the session key s.

Encryption of Renewal Block. Suppose that DS wants to change the group key $\mathcal{K}$ into $\mathcal{K}' = ((K_1')^{-1}, (K_2')^{-1}) \in_R \mathbb{Z}_q^* \times \mathbb{Z}_q^*$. DS first sets a time check flag $\mathcal{N}_{\mathcal{E}\mathcal{W}}\mathcal{C}_{\mathcal{H}\mathcal{G}} = CurrentDate\|CurrentTime$ and encrypts the values K_1' and K_2' using the encryption algorithm in [17].

Decryption of Renewal Block. When a renewal block is changed (i.e., $\mathcal{O}_{\mathcal{L}\mathcal{D}}\mathcal{C}_{\mathcal{H}\mathcal{G}} < \mathcal{N}_{\mathcal{E}\mathcal{W}}\mathcal{C}_{\mathcal{H}\mathcal{G}}$), each subscriber decrypts the renewal block with his renewal key and obtains the new group key $\mathcal{K}'$.

Traitor Tracing. There are two tracing traitor methods in [17]. These methods perform traitor tracing after a set of suspected traitors is constructed. We explain them briefly in view of our scheme.

   Method 1. First, DS constructs a set of the suspected traitors $\{c_1, c_2, \cdots, c_m\}$, $(m \leq k)$. For tracing traitors, DS sets the time check flag $\mathcal{N}_{\mathcal{E}\mathcal{W}}\mathcal{C}_{\mathcal{H}\mathcal{G}} = CurrentDate$
$\|CurrentTime$ and regenerates a renewal block which contains the encryption data of the new group key $\mathcal{K}'$, traitors' m-renewal keys $\{(c_1, f(c_1)), \cdots, (c_m, f(c_m))\}$, and $(z - m)$ unused pairs.

   If the pirate decoder has renewal keys contained in the set $\{(c_1, f(c_1)), \cdots, (c_m, f(c_m))\}$, it cannot correctly decrypt the renewal block. If the pirate decoder does not output the correct contents, DS confirms the set $\{c_1, c_2, \cdots, c_m\}$ as a potential set of traitors.

   Method 2. In this method, only a pirate decoder can obtain the correct digital contents. Let a set $\{c_1, c_2, \cdots, c_m\}$ for $m \leq k$ be a set of the suspected traitors. DS first constructs a degree-z polynomial $t(x) = \sum_{l=0}^{z} b_l x^l$ which has $(c_1, f(c_1)), \ldots, (c_m, f(c_m))$ as roots and is different from $f(x)$, i.e., $\{the\ roots\ of\ f(x)\} \cap \{the\ roots\ of\ t(x)\} = \{(c_1, f(c_1)), \ldots, (c_m, f(c_m))\}$. Next, DS creates a renewal block using $t(x)$ and z unused pairs and then sets the time check flag. In this method, if the pirate decoder outputs the correct contents, DS confirms the set $\{c_1, c_2, \ldots, c_m\}$ as a potential set of traitors.

In [17] the following is shown:

Fact 1 *For degree-z polynomials $f(x)$ and $t(x)$, the distributions of the renewal blocks constructed by $f(x)$ and $t(x)$ are computationally indistinguishable assuming that the DDH problem is hard.*

Fact 2 *Let $C = \{c_1, c_2, \cdots, c_k\}$ and $D = \{d_1, d_2, \cdots, d_k\}$ be two disjoint subscriber sets. All linear combination of shares of C and those of D are different except the zero point.*

Fact 3 *Assume that the DDH problem is hard. The encryption algorithm of a renewal block is semantically secure against the passive adversary.*

Fact 4 *Assume that computing the discrete logarithm over G_q is hard. No coalition of z or less legal subscribers can compute the renewal key of another legal subscriber with a non-negligible probability.*

Fact 5 *Assume that the DDH problem is hard. The encryption algorithm of a renewal block is semantically secure against the adaptive chosen ciphertext attack.*

By *Fact* 1 renewal blocks created using $f(x)$ and $t(x)$ are computationally indistinguishable.

Revocation. Let a set of subscribers $\{c_1, \cdots, c_m\}$, $(m \leq z)$ be confirmed traitors whose personal keys are to be revoked. DS first constructs a renewal block containing traitors' renewal keys $\mathcal{I} = \{(c_1, f(c_1)), \cdots, (c_m, f(c_m))\}$ as follows.

1. Generate a renewal block with m-renewal keys $\mathcal{I}$ and $(z - m)$ unused pairs such that
$$\langle (K_1')^{-1} g^{\mu a_0}, (K_2')^{-1} g^{\mu a_0}, (c_1, g^{\mu f(c_1)}), \cdots, (c_m, g^{\mu f(c_m)}), (j_1, g^{\mu f(j_1)}),$$
$$\cdots, (j_{z-m}, g^{\mu f(j_{z-m})}) \rangle$$
   where $\{(j_1, g^{\mu f(j_1)}), \cdots, (j_{z-m}, g^{\mu f(j_{z-m})})\}$ are unused pairs and $\mu \in_R \mathbb{Z}_q^*$.
2. Set the time check flag.

The renewal block is broadcasted with an enabling block. The traitors $\{c_1, \cdots, c_m\}$ cannot decrypt the value $\mathcal{K}'$.

3.2   The Self-Enforcement Property

Now we propose a simple and efficient way to implement the self-enforcement property. We don't directly embed a subscriber's sensitive information into his personal key. We use a value σ_{i1}^{-1} of the personal key and $f(i)$ of the renewal key for the self-enforcement property. In our self-enforcement, it is the idea that only DS and a subscriber S_i can compute the values $(g^{x_{DS}})^{\sigma_{i1}^{-1}}$ and $(g^{x_{DS}})^{f(i)}$ where $g^{x_{DS}}$ is a public value in setup.

In the registration, DS identifies a subscriber S_i and receives the important subscriber's information such as the account number or the credit card number. After sending the keys to S_i, DS performs the followings.

1. Compute values $(g^{x_{DS}})^{\sigma_{i1}^{-1}}$ and $(g^{x_{DS}})^{f(i)}$.
2. Encrypt the subscriber's personal key $P = (\sigma_{i1}^{-1}, \sigma_{i2}^{-1})$ using $(g^{x_{DS}})^{f(i)}$.
3. Encrypt the subscriber's sensitive data M using $(g^{x_{DS}})^{\sigma_{i1}^{-1}}$.
4. Publish the encryption data $E_{(g^{x_{DS}})^{f(i)}}(P)$ and $E_{(g^{x_{DS}})^{\sigma_{i1}^{-1}}}(M)$ in a public directory. The data in the public directory must be able to be changed by DS only.

Afterward DS continuously regenerates the encryption data of new sensitive information such as settlement of accounts of subscribers in the public directory. Each subscriber can confirm the decryption data M using his key σ_{i1}^{-1}. Also, if a subscriber wants to change his information, he sends the encryption data $E_{(g^{x_{DS}})^{\sigma_{i1}^{-1}}}(M')$ to DS.

Therefore, in our system, one who knows the key σ_{i1}^{-1} or $f(i)$ of a subscriber S_i can not only obtain the sensitive data of S_i but also alter it. Our method easily accommodates changes in a subscriber's sensitive data. Ultimately our goal is the protection of collusion by this self-enforcement property. To protect the important data of revoked subscribers, DS can delete their encryption data. Furthermore, using this method DS can easily alter personal keys of subscribers in a special subgroup.

4   Security Analysis

In this section we analyze the security in our scheme. To prove the security of our scheme, we review the decision Diffie-Hellman(DDH) assumption. First, define two sets for a group G $=< g >$ as following.

$$\mathcal{D} := \{ (g_1, g_2, y_1, y_2) \in \mathrm{G}^4 \mid ord(g_1) = ord(g_2) = q, \ log_{g_1} y_1 = log_{g_2} y_2 \},$$
$$\mathcal{R} := \{ (g_1, g_2, y_1, y_2) \in \mathrm{G}^4 \mid ord(g_1) = ord(g_2) = ord(y_1) = ord(y_2) = q \}.$$

Definition 1. *The group* G *satisfies the DDH assumption if there is no DDH algorithm $\mathcal{A}$ for* G *satisfying, for some fixed $c > 0$ and sufficiently large k*

$$\mid Pr[\ \mathcal{A}(\rho) = 1 \mid \rho \in_R \mathcal{D}\ ] - Pr[\ \mathcal{A}(\rho) = 1 \mid \rho \in_R \mathcal{R}\ ] \mid > \frac{1}{k^c}.$$

The assumption above about our group G is mentioned in [4]. Now, we explain the security of our scheme based on the preceding assumptions.

Theorem 1. *If the decision Diffie-Hellman problem is hard, our encryption algorithm of an enabling block is semantically secure against a passive adversary.*

Proof. Suppose to the contrary that there exists an adversary $\mathcal{A}$ that successfully breaks the encryption algorithm E in terms of semantic security. That is, on the public key (g, g^h, p, q) as an input, there exist a probabilistic polynomial-time algorithm $\mathcal{A}$ and two session keys s_0, $s_1 \in_R \mathbb{Z}_p$ such that $|\Pr[\mathcal{A}(E(s_0)) = 1] - \Pr[\mathcal{A}(E(s_1)) = 1]| > \varepsilon$ with non-negligible advantage ε. We show that there is a probabilistic polynomial-time algorithm $\mathcal{B}$ that can decide DDH problem using $\mathcal{A}$ as a subroutine with non-negligible advantage ε.

Given (g, g^a, g^b, y) as an input $\mathcal{B}$ can decide whether the input value is contained in $\mathcal{D}$ or $\mathcal{R}$ with $\mathcal{A}$ as follows.

1. Choose random values $A_1, A_2 \in \mathbb{Z}_q^*$ and $K_1, K_2 \in \mathbb{Z}_q^*$.
2. Send (g, g^b, p, q) as public keys to $\mathcal{A}$, and receive the values s_0 and s_1 from $\mathcal{A}$.
3. Uniformly choose $s \in_R \mathbb{Z}_p$ and estimate the value $\Pr[\mathcal{A}(E(s)) = 1]$.

Then $\mathcal{B}$ can calculate the difference $|\Pr[\mathcal{A}(E(s_b)) = 1] - \Pr[\mathcal{A}(E(s)) = 1]|$ where $b \in_R \{0, 1\}$. Now, from the following inequality we know that if $\mathcal{A}$ does not distinguish between s_0 and random values, it must distinguish between s_1 and random values with accuracy better than $\frac{\varepsilon}{2}$.

$$
\begin{aligned}
\varepsilon &< |\Pr[\mathcal{A}(E(s_0)) = 1] - \Pr[\mathcal{A}(E(s_1)) = 1]| \\
&= |\Pr[\mathcal{A}(E(s_0)) = 1] - \Pr[\mathcal{A}(E(s)) = 1] + \\
&\quad \Pr[\mathcal{A}(E(s)) = 1] - \Pr[\mathcal{A}(E(s_1)) = 1]| \\
&\leq |\Pr[\mathcal{A}(E(s_0)) = 1] - \Pr[\mathcal{A}(E(s)) = 1]| + \\
&\quad |\Pr[\mathcal{A}(E(s)) = 1] - \Pr[\mathcal{A}(E(s_1)) = 1]|.
\end{aligned}
$$

Without loss of generality we assume that $\mathcal{A}$ can distinguish between s_0 and a random value. Then $\mathcal{B}$ randomizes s_0 to s_0' based on the given (g, g^a, g^b, y) and uses $\mathcal{A}$ on (s_0, s_0'). If $(g, g^a, g^b, y) \in \mathcal{D}$, then $s_0 = s_0'$. Otherwise, s_0' is an uniformly chosen random value. When $\mathcal{A}$ distinguishes between s_0 and s_0' with accuracy better than $\frac{\varepsilon}{2}$, $\mathcal{B}$ outputs a result as $(g, g^a, g^b, y) \in \mathcal{R}$.

$\mathcal{B}$ randomizes s_0 to s_0' using (g, g^a, g^b, y) and generates enabling blocks with s_0 and s_0' as follows.

1. Uniformly select $c, r, u, v, w \in_R \mathbb{Z}_q^*$.
2. Compute the enabling blocks

$$
\begin{aligned}
E(s_0) &= \left\langle s_0 \cdot (g^b)^u,\ g^u,\ g^{ur^{-1}},\ A_1 K_1 r,\ A_2 K_2 r \right\rangle, \\
E(s_0') &= \left\langle s_0 \cdot (g^b)^v y^r,\ g^{ar} g^v,\ (g^{ar} g^v)^{c^{-1}},\ A_1 K_1 c,\ A_2 K_2 c \right\rangle.
\end{aligned}
$$

If $y = g^{ab}$ then $s_0 = s_0'$. But if $x \neq ab$ for $y = g^x$ then $s_0' = s_0 \cdot g^{(x-ab)r}$. Hence, $\mathcal{B}$ can decide DDH with a non-negligible advantage $\frac{\varepsilon}{2}$. $\square$

To obtain session keys, a subscriber needs to know the proper group key in our scheme. When the group key is regenerated, each subscriber must decrypt a renewal block to obtain the new group key. However it is still feasible, as mentioned in Section 1, for pirates to decode the enabling block using information leaked by the traitors until the group key is changed. The proposed idea of personal enabling keys is used to prevent the new potential leakage.

We discuss the security goals of our traitor tracing scheme:

Security of Encryption of Enabling Block/Renewal Block : Due to *Theorem* 1 the encryption algorithm of an enabling block is semantically secure against a passive adversary. Additionally we show that the variant of the algorithm is secure against CCA in Section 5. The security of the encryption algorithm of a renewal block is based on *Fact* 3 and *Fact* 5.

Soundness of Self-Enforcement : We have explained the self-enforcement property in Section 3.2. A pirate decoder must use legitimate renewal keys when the group key is changed. A designer of the pirate decoder with the renewal keys of traitors can know their personal keys and sensitive data. Finally it is hard for traitors to produce a pirate decoder without revealing their personal keys.

Validity of Tracing using Renewal Block : From *Remark* 1, we know that a pirate decoder has to decrypt renewal blocks. A pirate decoder cannot determine the role of the renewal blocks by *Fact* 1 and will try to decrypt them. Our traitor tracing using a renewal block can detect at least one traitor by *Fact* 2 and *Fact* 4.

5   A Secure Variation against an Adaptive Chosen Ciphertext Attack

The algorithm for renewal, tracing and revocation is secure against an adaptive chosen ciphertext attack (CCA) by *Fact* 5. Now we propose a variation of the encryption algorithm of an enabling block using the hybrid conversion of REACT by [13], which is secure against an adaptive chosen ciphertext attack under the random oracle model. Note that OAEP conversion[2] cannot be applied since our scheme is not a one-way permutation.

First, we explain the REACT briefly. For this conversion, Okamoto and Pointcheval defined a new kind of attacks, where given a message m and a ciphertext c, an adversary can check whether or not $E(m) = c$ is valid. This attack is called the *Plaintext-Checking Attack*. For the description of the hybrid conversion, REACT[13], we explain Plaintext-Checking Attack and several notations.

Definition 2. (Plaintext-Checking Attack). *The attacker has access to a Plaintext-Checking Oracle, PCO, without any restriction. PCO outputs 1 if and only if $E(m) = c$ on input values, a plaintext m and a ciphertext c. Otherwise PCO outputs 0.*

An OW-PCA-secure encryption scheme denotes an one-wayness secure encryption scheme against the plaintext-checking attack. This hybrid scheme $(\mathcal{K}^{hyb}, \mathcal{E}^{hyb}, \mathcal{D}^{hyb})$ is secure against adaptive chosen ciphertext attacks under the random oracle model, if the asymmetric encryption scheme is OW-PCA-secure and the symmetric encryption scheme is IND-secure [13].

Let $(\mathcal{K}^{asym}, \mathcal{E}^{asym}, \mathcal{D}^{asym})$ be an OW-PCA-secure asymmetric scheme and let a symmetric scheme $(\mathcal{E}^{sym}, \mathcal{D}^{sym})$ be semantically secure(IND-secure) against passive attacks. Let G and H be two hash functions. Then the hybrid scheme $(\mathcal{K}^{hyb}, \mathcal{E}^{hyb}, \mathcal{D}^{hyb})$ is constructed as follows.

The Hybrid Conversion

- $\mathcal{K}^{hyb}(1^k)$: Run $\mathcal{K}^{asym}(1^k)$ and output a pair of keys $(\mathsf{sk}, \mathsf{pk})$.
- $\mathcal{E}^{hyb}_{\mathsf{pk}}(m, R, r)$: Output an encryption message (c_1, c_2, c_3) of message m with random values R and r where

$$c_1 = \mathcal{E}^{asym}_{\mathsf{pk}}(R; r) \text{ and } c_2 = \mathcal{E}^{sym}_{\mathsf{s}}(m) \text{ where a session key } \mathsf{s} = G(R)$$
$$c_3 = H(R||m||c_1||c_2).$$

- $\mathcal{D}^{hyb}_{\mathsf{sk}}(c_1, c_2, c_3)$: Extract $R = \mathcal{D}^{asym}_{\mathsf{sk}}(c_1)$ and then compute the session key $\mathsf{s} = G(R)$. Return the message $m = \mathcal{D}^{sym}_{\mathsf{s}}(c_2)$ if and only if $c_3 = H(R||m||c_1||c_2)$. Otherwise, output "Reject".

Now, we convert our scheme using this hybrid conversion. For the conversion, it is sufficient that we prove our encryption scheme of an enabling block is OW-PCA secure. OW-PCA-security of our scheme is based on the Gap-Diffie-Hellman Problem(GDH) [12,13].

Problem 1. **(GDH Problem).** Solve the Computational Diffie-Hellman Problem with the help of a Decision Diffie-Hellman Oracle.

Theorem 2. *Our encryption scheme is* OW-PCA-*secure relative to the* GDH *problem.*

Proof. Given public keys (g, g^h, p, q), an enabling block $\langle s \cdot g^{rh}, g^r, g^{rw^{-1}},$ $A_1 K_1 w, A_2 K_2 w \rangle$ and a message s', a Plainext-Checking Oracle(PCO) checks if $s = s'$. Then PCO simply checks if $(g, g^h, g^r, s \cdot g^{rh}/s')$ is contained in $\mathcal{D}$. $(g, g^h, g^r, s \cdot g^{rh}/s') \in \mathcal{D}$ if and only if PCO outputs 1. Therefore PCO is exactly a DDH Oracle. $\qquad\square$

Finally, we choose two hash functions G and H and a symmetric encryption $(\mathcal{E}^{sym}, \mathcal{D}^{sym})$ which is IND-secure against passive attacks. For a content m, a broadcast encryption message (c_1, c_2, c_3) in the variant of our scheme is as follows:

$$c_1 = \left\langle s \cdot g^{rh}, g^r, g^{rw^{-1}}, A_1 K_1 w, A_2 K_2 w \right\rangle$$
$$c_2 = \mathcal{E}^{sym}_{\mathsf{K}}(m) \text{ where } \mathsf{K} = G(s)$$
$$c_3 = H(s||m||c_1||c_2)$$

6   Conclusion

In this paper we have proposed a new type of a traitor tracing scheme. By separating tracing and revocation capability from that of broadcast session-key distribution and session key extraction we have suggested a two-level broadcast scheme. We have constructed an efficient scheme with constant decrypting of the enabling block where session keys are extracted. This gives efficiency compared to earlier schemes. Though the length of broadcast encryption messages is increased a little (by the enabling information), from a point of view of computational overhead, our scheme is significantly more efficient. (Note that in addition we can improve even further: the value g^h needs not be published and a value g^r in an enabling block may be eliminated. The length of an enabling block is shortened and this doesn't affect the security.)

The added efficiency (namely the two-level idea) introduces the danger of leakage in the session key decryption procedure (enabling block level). To cope with this we have employed "privacy-based-protection" idea and introduced a flexible self-enforcement property with personal keys that are used throughout. This is, perhaps, the central contribution of our work. We have also presented a variant which is secure against CCA (in the random oracle model) using REACT. (We note that in this paper, the traitor tracing scheme by [17] is applied to construct a renewal block, but other schemes can be used as well, since no special property of this scheme was employed.)

References

1. J. Anzai, N. Matsuzaki and T. Matsumoto, "A Quick Group Key Distribution Scheme with Entity Revocation", In *Proc. Advances in Cryptology - Asiacrypt '99*, Vol. 1716 of Lecture Notes in Computer Science, pp. 333-347, Springer Verlag, 1999.
2. M. Bellare and P. Rogaway, "Optimal Asymmetric Encryption — How to Encrypt with RSA.", In *Eurocypt '94*, LNCS 950, pages 92-111. Springer Verlag, 1999.
3. D. Boneh and M. Franklin, "An Efficient Public Key Traitor Tracing Scheme", In *Proc. Advances in Cryptology - Crypto '99*, Vol. 1666 of Lecture Notes in Computer Science, pp. 338-353. Springer Verlag, 1999.
4. D. Boneh, "The Decision Diffie-Hellman Problem", In *Proc. the Third Algorithmic Number Theory Symposium*, Vol. 1423 of Lecture Notes in Computer Science, pp. 48-63. Springer Verlag, 1998.
5. D. Chaum , A. Fiat, and M. Naor. "Untraceable electronic cash", In *Advances in Cryptology - Crypto'88*, Lecture Notes in Computer Science, pp. 319-327. Springer-Verlag, 1990.
6. B. Chor, A. Fiat and M. Naor, "Tracing Traitors", In *Proc. Advances in Cryptology - Crypto '94*, Vol. 839 of Lecture Notes in Computer Science, pp. 257-270, Springer Verlag, 1994.
7. C. Dwork, J. Lotspiech and M. Naor, "Digital Signets: Self-Enforcing Protection of Digital Information", In *28th Symposium on the Theory of Computation '96*, pp. 489-498, 1996.

8. K. Kurosawa and Y. Desmedt, "Optimum Traitor Tracing and Asymmetric Schemes", In *Proc. Advances in Cryptology - Eurocrypt '98*, Vol. 1403 of Lecture Notes in Computer Science, pp. 145-157, Springer Verlag, 1998.
9. A. J. Menezes, P. C. van Oorschot and S. A. Vanstone, "Handbook of Applied Cryptography", *CRC Press*, pp. 351-352, 1996.
10. M. Jakobsson, A. Juels and P. Nguyen, "Proprietary Certificates", to appear in *Topics in Cryptography CT-RSA 2002*, 2002.
11. M. Naor and B. Pinkas, "Efficient Trace and Revoke Schemes", In *Proc. Financial Cryptography '00*, Anguilla, February 2000.
12. T. Okamoto and D. Pointcheval, "The Gap-Problems: a New Class of Problems for the Security of Cryptographic Schemes", In *International Workshop on Practice and Theory in Public-Key Cryptography - PKC '01*, Vol. 1992 of Lecture Notes in Computer Science, pp. 104-118, Springer Verlag, 2001.
13. T. Okamoto and D. Pointcheval, "REACT: Rapid Enhanced-security Asymmetric Cryptosystem Transform", In *The Cryptographers' Track of the RSA Conference '2001*, Vol. 2020 of Lecture Notes in Computer Science, pp. 159-175, Springer Verlag, 2001.
14. B. Pfitzmann, "Trials of Traced Traitors", In *Proc. Workshop in Information Hiding*, Vol. 1174 of Lecture Notes in Computer Science, pp. 49-64, Springer Verlag, 1996.
15. A. Shamir, "How to Share a Secret", In *Comm. ACM*, Vol. 22, No. 11, pp. 612-613, 1979.
16. D. R. Stinson, "Cryptography Theory and Practice", *CRC Press*, pp. 330-331, 1995.
17. W. Tzeng and Z. J. Tzeng, "A Public-Key Traitor Tracing Scheme with Revocation using Dynamic Shares", In *International Workshop on Practice and Theory in Public-Key Cryptography - PKC '01* , Vol. 1992 of Lecture Notes in Computer Science, pp. 207-224, Springer Verlag, 2001.

Asynchronous Perfectly Secure Computation Tolerating Generalized Adversaries

M.V.N. Ashwin Kumar, K. Srinathan*, and C. Pandu Rangan

Department of Computer Science and Engineering
Indian Institute of Technology, Madras
Chennai - 600036, India
{mvnak,ksrinath}@cs.iitm.ernet.in, rangan@iitm.ernet.in

Abstract. We initiate the study of perfectly secure multiparty computation over asynchronous networks tolerating generalized adversaries. The classical results in information-theoretically secure asynchronous multiparty computation among n players state that less than $\frac{n}{4}$ active adversaries can be tolerated in the perfect setting [4]. Strictly generalizing these results to the non-threshold setting, we show that perfectly secure asynchronous multiparty computation among n players tolerating the adversary structure $\mathcal{A}$ is possible if and only if the union of no *four* sets in the adversary structure cover the full set of players. The computation and communication complexities of the presented protocols are polynomial in the size of the maximal basis of the adversary structure. Our results generalize the results of [16,10] to the asynchronous setting. Furthermore, when restricted to the threshold setting, the protocols of this paper result in solutions as good as the best known asynchronous threshold protocols for the perfect setting. Incidentally, the problems of designing efficient asynchronous secure protocols and adapting the efficiency improvement techniques of the threshold setting to the non-threshold setting were mentioned as open in [18,17].

1 Introduction

Consider the scenario where there are n players (or processors) $\mathcal{P} = \{P_1, P_2, \ldots P_n\}$, each P_i with a local input x_i. These players do not trust each other. Nevertheless, they wish to correctly compute a function $f(x_1, \ldots, x_n)$ of their local inputs, whilst keeping their local data as private as possible. This is the well-known problem of *secure multiparty computation*. This problem takes many different forms depending on the underlying network, the function to be computed, and on the amount of distrust the players have in each other and the network. The problem of secure multiparty computation has been extensively studied in several models of computation. The *communication* facilities assumed in the underlying network differ with respect to whether secure communication channels are available [5,9] or not available [14], whether or not broadcast channels are available [23,1,11] and whether the communication channels are

---

* Financial support from Infosys Technologies Limited, India, is acknowledged.

L. Batten and J. Seberry (Eds.): ACISP 2002, LNCS 2384, pp. 497–511, 2002.

synchronous or asynchronous [4,6]. The *correctness* requirements of the protocol differ with respect to whether exponentially small probability of error is allowed (*unconditional*) or not allowed (*perfect*). The corrupted players are usually modeled via a central *adversary* that can corrupt up to t players. The adversary may be computationally bounded (*computational setting*) or unbounded (*secure channels setting*). One also generally distinguishes between actively corrupted players (*Byzantine*), passively corrupted players (*eavesdropping*).

We consider the problem of perfect asynchronous secure multiparty computation over a fully connected network of n players (processors) in which a non-trivial subset of the players may be corrupted by a Byzantine adversary, where every two players are connected via a secure and reliable communication channel (secure channels setting). The network is *asynchronous*, meaning that any message sent on these channels can have arbitrary (finite) delay.

To model the faulty players' behavior, we postulate a computationally unbounded generalized Byzantine adversary characterized by an adversary structure. An adversary structure is a monotone set of subsets of the player set. The adversary may choose to corrupt the players in any *one* of the sets in the adversary structure. Once a player is corrupted by the adversary, the player hands over all his private data to the adversary, and gives the adversary the control on all his subsequent moves. To model the network's asynchrony, we further assume that the adversary can schedule the communication channel, i.e. he can determine the time delays of all the messages (however, he can neither read nor change those messages). Note that the threshold adversary is a special case of our setting where the adversary structure consists of all the subsets of t or less players.

It was shown in [4] that perfect asynchronous secure multiparty computation is possible in the threshold setting if and only if $t < \frac{n}{4}$. In [6] an $\left(\lceil \frac{n}{3} \rceil - 1\right)$-resilient protocol is described that securely computes any function f when exponentially small probability of error is allowed.

Our investigations are motivated by the following observations.

1. The complicated exchanges of messages and zero-knowledge proofs in protocols like [4,6] might render them impractical.
2. The threshold adversarial model is insufficient to model all types of mutual (dis)trust [15,16].

In the synchronous secure multiparty computation setting there have been many attempts to reduce the communication/round complexity of multiparty protocols [3,2,12,13,18,10]. More recently, the results in [10] and [17] significantly improve the message complexity of non-threshold and threshold secure synchronous multiparty computation respectively. The problem of reducing the communication complexity of secure multiparty computation over an asynchronous network was left open in [18,17]. In this work, we initiate an investigation of perfectly secure multiparty computation over asynchronous networks tolerating generalized adversaries. We generalize the results of [4] to the generalized adversary model. We prove the necessary and sufficient conditions for the existence of asynchronous secure protocols tolerating generalized adversaries. Furthermore, whenever such protocols exist, we design fast protocols for the same. Our solutions heavily draw on the techniques of [8,4,10,18].

2   Definitions and Model

We consider n players $\mathcal{P} = \{P_1, P_2, \ldots, P_n\}$ connected by a complete asynchronous network. We assume that the players in $\mathcal{P}$ have (polynomially) bounded computational power[1] and can communicate with their neighbours. We assume that randomization is achieved through random coins. A computationally unbounded *Byzantine adversary* $\mathcal{B}$ is a probabilistic strategy that controls/corrupts a subset of players and endeavors to violate the security of the system. We assume that the adversary can corrupt only the players and not the links connecting them.[2]

The adversary $\mathcal{B}$ is characterized by a generalized adversary structure $\mathcal{A} \subset 2^{\mathcal{P}}$, a monotone set of subsets of the player set, where the adversary $\mathcal{B}$ may corrupt the players of any one set in the structure. To characterize necessary and sufficient conditions for secure multiparty computation, we define the $\mathcal{Q}^{(k)}$ predicate.

Definition 1. *Let $\mathcal{Y}$ be a finite non-empty set and k be an integer, $k > 0$. A structure $\mathcal{Z} \subseteq 2^{\mathcal{Y}}$ satisfies the predicate $\mathcal{Q}^{(k)}$ if no k sets in $\mathcal{Z}$ cover the full set $\mathcal{Y}$. $\mathcal{Q}^{(k)} \iff \forall Z_{i_1}, \ldots, Z_{i_k} \in \mathcal{Z} : \bigcup_{j=1}^{k} Z_{i_j} \neq \mathcal{Y}$*

Since the underlying network is asynchronous, we "overload" the adversary with the power to schedule all the sent messages (over all channels) as it wishes and hence the order in which the communicated messages are received is totally under the adversarial control.

Defining security for secure multiparty computation is subtle and has been a field of research on its own [21,1,22,7]. In essence, any protocol Π for secure multiparty computation is defined to be *secure* if Π "emulates" what is called an "ideal" protocol $\mathcal{I}$. In $\mathcal{I}$, all the players hand their inputs to an *incorruptible* "trusted" player, who locally computes the desired output and hands it back to the players (there is no communication among the players). Therefore, in $\mathcal{I}$, the adversary, essentially, learns/modifies the inputs and outputs of only the corrupted players. Now, Π is said to "emulate" $\mathcal{I}$ if *for all* adversaries attacking Π in the given setting, *there exists* a comparable (in complexity) adversary attacking $\mathcal{I}$ that induces an *identical* "output" in $\mathcal{I}$, where the "output" is the concatenation of the local outputs of all the honest players and the VIEW of adversary.

---

[1] The players can be modeled as Probabilistic Polynomial Time Turing Machines (PPT).

[2] Our techniques can be easily adapted to provide a solution even when the adversary corrupts only the links or both links and channels. Such an adversary on network $\mathcal{N}$ can be simulated by an adversary corrupting nodes alone on a new network $\mathcal{N}'$ got by replacing each insecure link $e = (u, v)$ by a node w and two links $e_1 = (u, w)$ and $e_2 = (w, v)$.

In the case of the *asynchronous* setting, unlike the *synchronous* counterpart where there is no "functional" approximation, the local output of the honest players is only an approximation of the pre-specified function f over a subset S of the local inputs, the rest taken to be 0, where $S \supseteq (\mathcal{P} \setminus D) | D \in \mathcal{A}$, for the given generalized adversary structure $\mathcal{A}$ (this is analogous to the definitions of [4] regarding the threshold model). Furthermore, Π is *perfectly* secure if the local outputs of the honest players are *correct*, Π *terminates* with certainty and the "output" of Π is identically distributed with respect to the "output" of ideal model (which involves a trusted party that approximates f).

Tackling generalized adversaries requires new paradigms and tools. In response, we introduce the concept of GMSPs (see Definition 3).

Definition 2 (MSP). *A Monotone Span Program [20] is defined as the triple* $(\mathcal{F}, M, \Im)$ *where $\mathcal{F}$ represents a finite field, M is a $d \times e$ matrix with entries in $\mathcal{F}$, and $\Im : \{1 \dots d\} \to \{P_1 \dots P_n\}$ is a function. Each row of the matrix M is labeled by players in the sense that $\Im$ assigns the label $\Im(k)$ to the k-th row of M, $1 \le k \le d$. For $A \subset \{P_1 \dots P_n\}$, M_A denotes the matrix that consists of all rows in M labeled by players in A. Let $\boldsymbol{T} \in \mathcal{F}^e$ be the target vector. A MSP is said to accept (or reject) a structure $\mathcal{Z}$ if $\forall Z \in \mathcal{Z}$, there exists (does not exist, respectively) a linear combination of the rows of M_Z which equals $\boldsymbol{T}$. An MSP is said to correspond to an adversary structure $\mathcal{A}_{adv}$ if it rejects exactly $\mathcal{A}_{adv}$ and accepts exactly $2^{\{P_1,\dots,P_n\}} \setminus \mathcal{A}_{adv}$. By the size of an MSP, we mean the number of rows in M.*

Let $\mathcal{A} = \{D_1, D_2, \dots, D_{|\mathcal{A}|}\}$, be a generalized adversary structure satisfying the predicate $\mathcal{Q}^{(k)}$, over the player set $\mathcal{P}$. Trivially, the *corresponding access structure* can be defined as $2^{\mathcal{P}} \setminus \mathcal{A}$. However, the size of the smallest MSP corresponding to $\mathcal{A}$ may not be the best since there may exist a structure $W \supset \mathcal{A}$ such that the MSP corresponding to W is *smaller* (see [10]). Therefore, we define the corresponding access structure $\mathcal{A}_{acc}$ so that the *best* corresponding MSP is not ruled out by the definition itself!

Let $\mathcal{I}$ denote the set of all combinations of $(k-1)$ classes from $\mathcal{A}$.[3] Define $\mathcal{A}_{acc} = \{\mathcal{P} \setminus \alpha, \forall \alpha \in \mathcal{I}\}$. Finally, define the set of "don't care" sets[4] $\mathcal{A}_x = 2^{\mathcal{P}} \setminus (\mathcal{A}_{acc} \cup \mathcal{A})$.

Definition 3 (Generalized MSP). *A GMSP is an MSP (see Definition 2) which corresponds to the generalized adversary structure $\mathcal{A}$ if it rejects exactly $\mathcal{A}$, accepts exactly its corresponding access structure $\mathcal{A}_{acc}$ and either accepts or rejects the corresponding "don't care" structure $\mathcal{A}_x$.*

---

[3] Note that for all $\alpha \in \mathcal{I}$, $\alpha \subset \mathcal{A}$, $|\alpha| = (k-1)$ and that $|\mathcal{I}| = \binom{|\mathcal{A}|}{k-1}$.

[4] These are the sets that can be freely appended to the adversary structure to reduce the corresponding MSP size to a minimum.

3   Characterization of Tolerable Adversaries

Theorem 1. *Asynchronous perfectly secure multiparty computation tolerating $\mathcal{A}$ is possible if and only $\mathcal{A}$ satisfies $\mathcal{Q}^{(4)}$, i.e. if no four sets in the adversary structure cover the full player set.*

PROOF:
Necessary: For the sake of contradiction assume that asynchronous perfectly secure multiparty computation tolerating $\mathcal{A}$ is possible even when $\mathcal{A}$ does *not* satisfy $\mathcal{Q}^{(4)}$. This implies the existence of four sets D_1, D_2, D_3 and D_4 such that[5] $D_1 \cup D_2 \cup D_3 \cup D_4 = \mathcal{P}$. Consider four players p_1, p_2, p_3 and p_4 where p_1 plays for all the players in D_1, p_2 plays for those in D_2, p_3 plays for those in D_3, and p_4 for those in D_4. By our hypothesis, we can construct a protocol that tolerates an adversary that corrupts *one* of p_1, p_2, p_3 or p_4. However, we know that no such protocol exists [4].
Sufficiency: See Section 4 for a protocol for perfectly secure asynchronous multiparty computation tolerating $\mathcal{A}$, which satisfies $\mathcal{Q}^{(4)}$.   □

4   Asynchronous Perfectly Secure Multiparty Computation

Each player P_i holds a private input x_i, and the players wish to securely compute the exact value of a function $f(x_1, \cdots, x_n)$. However, since the network is asynchronous, and the players in some set $D \in \mathcal{A}$ may be faulty, the players can never ever wait for more than $|\mathcal{P} \setminus D|$ of the inputs to be entered to the computation. Furthermore, the missing inputs (treated as 0) are not necessarily of the faulty players (as already mentioned earlier).

Efficient protocols for non-threshold perfect asynchronous secure computation can be constructed based on sub-protocols for *Agreement on a Common Subset, Input Sharing, Multiplication, Segment Fault Localization and Output Reconstruction.* We deal with the primitives, viz. *Non-Threshold Broadcast* and *Non-Threshold Asynchronous Byzantine Agreement* separately (see [19]).

In a nutshell, an agreed function is computed as follows: Let x_i be the input of P_i. Let $\mathcal{F}$ be a finite field known to all players, and let $f : \mathcal{F}^n \to \mathcal{F}$ be the computed function. We assume that the players have an arithmetic circuit computing f; the circuit consists of addition gates and multiplication gates of in-degree 2. All the computations in the sequel are done in $\mathcal{F}$.

First each player "shares" his input among the n players using the sub-protocol for *InputShare* (see Section 4.3). This sub-protocol runs in two phases. In the first phase it uses a technique similar to the commitment technique of [10], modified to the asynchronous setting ($NAVSS$-SHARE, see Section 4.2). In the second phase, the players agree, using the protocol for *Agreement on a Common Subset*, on a core set $\mathcal{G}$ of players that have successfully shared their input. Once

---

[5] From the monotonicity of $\mathcal{A}$, the D_i's can be made pair-wise disjoint.

$\mathcal{G}$ is computed, the players proceed to compute the function in the following way. First, the input values of the players not in $\mathcal{G}$ are set to a default value, say 0. Note that in the process of the above sharing, in order to tolerate the adversary structure $\mathcal{A}$ it may be necessary for some of the players to "act" for more than one similar players, i.e., they may receive more than one share etc; hereafter, we use the notation $\mathcal{P}_{phy}$ to mean the physical set of players and $\mathcal{P}_{log}$ to denote the logical set of players (wherein two players simulated by the same physical player are considered different). Next, the players evaluate the given circuit gate by gate as follows. If the gate is an *addition* gate, then simply adding the secret-shares of the input lines would suffice (due to the linearity of the *NAVSS*-SHARE scheme). Multiplication gates are evaluated using the sub-protocol *MUL* (see Section 4.4) which applies the player-elimination technique [18] (by dividing the circuit into segments); either the outcome is a proper sharing of the correct product, or a fault is detected. In the latter case, the sub-protocol for *Segment Fault Localization* (see Section 4.5) is applied (at the end of that segment) to determine a localization $\mathcal{D}$. Then the (logical) players in $\mathcal{D}$ are eliminated from the further protocol, and the shared values are re-shared for this new setting involving fewer (logical) players using the sub-protocol for *Re-*SHARING (see Section 4.4). Finally, after all gates have been evaluated, the output value is reconstructed from the shares of the output line toward each of the (physical) players using the sub-protocol *NAVSS*-REC. The top-level protocol is described in Section 5.

4.1   Agreement on a Common Subset

In a perfect asynchronous resilient computation, very often the players in $\mathcal{P}_{phy}$ need to decide on a subset $\mathcal{G}$ of players, that satisfy some property, such that $\mathcal{G} \supseteq (\mathcal{P}_{phy} \setminus D)$, for some $D \in \mathcal{A}$. It is known that all the honest players will eventually satisfy this property, but some faulty players may satisfy it as well. In our context, we need to agree on the set $\mathcal{G}$ of players who have completed correctly sharing their input. For implementing this primitive, we adapt the protocol presented in [6] to the non-threshold setting. The idea is to execute a *BA* (Byzantine Agreement) protocol for each player, to determine whether it will be in the agreed set. Notice that if some P_j knows that P_i satisfies the required property, then eventually all the players will know the same. Thus, we can suppose the existence of a predicate $\mathcal{J}$ that assigns a binary value to each player P_i, denoted $\mathcal{J}(i)$, based on whether P_i has satisfied the property as yet. The protocol is denoted by $AgreeSet[\mathcal{J}, \mathcal{P}_{phy}, \mathcal{A}]$ and given in Fig. 1.

Theorem 2. *Using the protocol $AgreeSet[\mathcal{J}, \mathcal{P}_{phy}, \mathcal{A}]$ the players indeed agree on a common subset of players, denoted by $\mathcal{G}$ such that $\mathcal{G} \supseteq (\mathcal{P}_{phy} \setminus D)$, for some $D \in \mathcal{A}$. Moreover, for every P_j in $\mathcal{G}$, we have $\mathcal{J}(j) = 1$.*

Proof. Similar in lines with [6]. We omit it due to space constraints.   □

4.2   NAVSS Protocol

Definition 4 (NAVSS). *Let* (SHARE,REC) *be a pair of protocols in which a dealer* P_D, *shares a secret* s. *We say that* (SHARE,REC) *is a NAVSS scheme tolerating the adversary structure* $\mathcal{A}$ *if the following hold for every adversary* $\mathcal{B}$ *characterized by* $\mathcal{A}$, *and every input.*

* Termination: *With certainty, the following conditions hold:*
  1. *If the dealer is honest, then each honest player will eventually will complete protocol* SHARE.
  2. *If some honest player has completed protocol* SHARE, *then each honest player will eventually complete protocol* SHARE.
  3. *If an honest player has completed protocol* SHARE, *and all the honest players invoke protocol* REC, *then each honest player will complete protocol* REC.
* Correctness: *Once an honest player has completed protocol* SHARE, *then there exists a unique value,* r, *such that certainly the following holds:*
  1. *If the dealer is honest, then* r *is the shared secret, i.e,* $r = s$.
  2. *If all the honest players invoke protocol* REC, *then each honest player outputs* r. *(Namely,* r *is the reconstructed secret).*
* Secrecy:[6] *If the dealer is honest and no honest player has begun executing protocol* REC, *then the faulty players have no information about the shared secret.*

Our construction of the *NAVSS* protocol is given in Fig. 2.

Theorem 3. *The pair* NAVSS-(SHARE, REC) *is a* NAVSS *scheme tolerating the adversary structure* $\mathcal{A}$, *provided* $\mathcal{A}$ *satisfies* $\mathcal{Q}^{(4)}$.

Proof. We assert the Termination, Correctness and Secrecy requirements of the above scheme. As per the definition, if the dealer is honest, an *NAVSS* scheme has to terminate with certainty for all uncorrupted players. In case of a corrupted dealer no requirements are posed on the termination. The protocol *NAVSS*-SHARE terminates with probability 1 for an honest dealer (this follows quite easily from the proof of the V-Share protocol given in [4]). The protocol *NAVSS*-REC terminates with certainty since P will eventually receive messages from at least the players $\mathcal{P}_{log} \setminus D_{log}$, for some $D_{log} \in \mathcal{A}_{log}$. The correctness of the *NAVSS*-SHARE protocol follows from the results of [4,10]. The correctness of the protocol *NAVSS*-REC can be proven as follows: Assume that a player hands a bad vector $u_i' \neq u_i$. Of the $\mathcal{P}_{log} \setminus D_{log}$ messages received, this vector is inconsistent with that of at least $(\mathcal{P} \setminus (D_1 \cup D_2))$ logical players. At least $(\mathcal{P} \setminus (D_1 \cup D_2))$ logical players gave their correct vectors to P. Player P will detect inconsistencies for every set in the access structure and ignore this vector. On the other hand, if u_i is the correct vector, at most the vectors of $D \in \mathcal{A}_{log}$ for some D, will be inconsistent. Hence P interpolates only correct vectors and computes the correct

---

[6] An honest player is not required to complete protocol SHARE in case the dealer is faulty.

AgreeSet$[\mathcal{J}, \mathcal{P}_{phy}, \mathcal{A}]$

1. For each P_j for whom P_i knows that $\mathcal{J}(j) = 1$, participate in BA_j (Byzantine Agreement) with input 1.
2. Upon completing BA_j protocols for all $P_j \in (\mathcal{P}_{phy} \setminus D)$, for some $D \in \mathcal{A}$ with output 1, enter input 0 to all BA protocols for which P_i has not entered a value yet.
3. Upon completing all n BA protocols, let the $AgreeSet_i$ be the set of all indices j for which BA_j had output 1. Output $AgreeSet_i$.

Fig. 1. Agreement on a Common Subset

SHARE **Protocol**

Publicly known Inputs: Player set $\mathcal{P}_{log}$, adversary structure $\mathcal{A}$, (corresponding) access structure $\mathcal{A}_{acc}$ and the GMSP $\mathcal{M} = (\mathcal{F}, M_{d \times e}, \Im)$ that corresponds to $\mathcal{A}$.
Code for the Dealer P_D (on input s):

1. Choose a symmetric $e \times e$ matrix R at random, with $R[0][0] = s$. Let v_i be a row in M assigned to P_i and let $v_i{}^T$ be its transpose (column vector). Then P_D sends to P_i the vector $u_i = R \cdot v_i{}^T$. A share s_i of s given to P_i is defined to be the first entry of u_i. Hence, the product $\langle v_j, u_i \rangle = s_{ij}$ can be thought of as a share of s_i given to P_j. Note that we have $\langle v_j, u_i \rangle = \langle v_j \cdot R, v_i{}^T \rangle = \langle v_i, R \cdot v_j{}^T \rangle = \langle v_i, u_j \rangle$.

Code for player P_i:

1. Upon receiving u_i from P_D, send to each logical player P_j, $\langle v_j, u_i \rangle$.
2. Upon receiving x_{ji} from P_j, if $s_{ij} = x_{ji}$, then Broadcast (OK,i,j).
3. Upon receiving a broadcast (OK,j,k), check for the existence of a $\mathcal{A}$-clique in $\mathbf{OK}_i$ graph (The *undirected* $\mathbf{OK}_i$ graph = $(\mathcal{P}_{log}, \mathcal{E})$ where edge $(P_j, P_k) \in \mathcal{E}$ if P_i has received broadcasts (OK,j,k) & (OK,k,j)). If an $\mathcal{A}$-clique is found (all players in $D_i = (\mathcal{P}_{log} \setminus D), D \in \mathcal{A}$ form a clique in the $\mathbf{OK}_i$ graph), go to Step 5 and send D_i to all physical players.
4. Upon receiving D_j add D_j to the set of 'SUGGESTED CLIQUES'. As long as a clique is not yet found, then whenever an (OK,k,ℓ) broadcast is received, check whether D_j forms an $\mathcal{A}$-clique in the $\mathbf{OK}_i$ graph.
5. Upon finding an $\mathcal{A}$-clique, and if $i \notin D_i$, correct u_i as follows: For each $D \in \mathcal{A}, D \subseteq D_i$, check if there exists a linear combination of the rows in $M_{D_i \setminus D}$ resulting in the target vector (i.e., $(D_i \setminus D) \supseteq A$ for some $A \in \mathcal{A}_{acc}$). Use that $D^* = D_i \setminus D$ to construct u_i. (This is surely possible since the number of linearly independent rows in M_{D^*} is greater than the number of linearly independent columns, i.e. $|u_i| = e$.)
6. Once u_i is correct, (locally) output u_i.

REC **Protocol** (Toward Player P)

Code for player P_i:

1. Send u_i to player P.

Code for player P:

1. Wait for receipt of u_i's from all the players in $D' = (\mathcal{P}_{log} \setminus D)$.
2. Reconstruct secret as follows: Find $D^* \subseteq D'$ such that $\forall P_i, P_j \in D^*, \langle v_j, u_i \rangle = \langle v_i, u_j \rangle$. Let s be the first elements in each of the u_i's in D^*. Now find λ_{D^*} such that $\lambda_{D^*} \times M_{D^*} = T$. The required secret is $\lambda_{D^*} \times s^T$.

Fig. 2. Error-free NAVSS protocol.

secret s. The secrecy of protocol $NAVSS$-SHARE follows from the definitions of an MSP. The privacy of the $NAVSS$-REC protocol is obvious as no player but P receives any information. □

4.3   Input Sharing

The protocol for Input Sharing has two phases: first, each party shares its input using $NAVSS$-SHARE) scheme; next, the parties use the AgreeSet protocol to agree on a set $\mathcal{G}$ of at least $|\mathcal{P}_{phy} \setminus D|$, for some $D \in \mathcal{A}$ players who have shared their inputs properly. The protocol $InputShare$ is formally specified in Fig. 3.

4.4   Multiplication

A protocol for multiplication starts with sharing of x, y and ends with a sharing of $z = x.y$ (if there are no inconsistencies) or with a partial fault detection (if there exist inconsistencies). The adversary's view of the computation is distributed independent of the initial sharing for any adversary characterized by $\mathcal{A}$. Our implementation of the multiplication protocol is given in Fig. 3.

Re-SHARING **Protocol.** We begin by defining a multiplicative MSP (MMSP).

Definition 5 (MMSP[10]). *A multiplicative MSP is an MSP $\mathcal{M}$ for which there exists an vector r called a* recombination vector, *such that for any two secrets s and s', and any ρ, ρ', it holds that*

$$s \cdot s' = \langle r, M(s, \rho) \diamond M(s', \rho') \rangle$$

where $x \diamond y$ is defined as the vector containing all the entries of the form $x_i \cdot y_j$, where $x = (x_1, \ldots, x_d)$, $y = (y_1, \ldots, y_d)$ and $\Im(i) = \Im(j)$. We say that $\mathcal{M}$ is strongly multiplicative *if for any player subset A that is rejected by $\mathcal{M}$, $\mathcal{M}_{\overline{A}}$ is multiplicative.*

Assume that s is shared with a strongly MMSP $\mathcal{M} = (\mathcal{F}, M_{d \times e}, \Im)$ and random $R'_{e' \times e'}$ matrix, with player P_i holding $u_{i_k} = R' \cdot v_{i_k}{}^T, \forall i_k \ni \Im(i_k) = P_i, 1 \leq i \leq n$. The goal of Re-SHARING protocol is to transform this sharing into a proper sharing of s resulting from the use of the random sharing matrix $R_{e \times e}$, $e' < 2e$. A protocol for Re-SHARING starts with a R'-sharing of s and ends with either a R-sharing of s (if there are no inconsistencies) or with a partial fault detection (if there exist inconsistencies). Also, the adversary view of the protocol is distributed independent of the initial sharing for any adversary characterized by $\mathcal{A}$. We implement the Re-SHARING protocol as follows: first, every logical player P_i R-shares $s_i = u_i[0]$ using the protocol $EfficientAVShare$(see Fig. 3) and proves that the value shared is in fact s_i using the protocol $ACheckShare$(see Fig. 3). For this, since the secret s_i has already been shared using u_i (represented as u' in Fig. 3), sharing it again with u as the first row of $R_{e \times e}$, implies that the player P_i has to prove $u[0] = u'[0]$, which is what is accomplished by our protocol $ACheckShare$. Now, every logical player locally computes the linear combination using the known recombination vector of the MMSP which results in a R-sharing of s [10]. The formal description of the implementation of the protocol Re-SHARING is given in Fig. 3.

Protocol InputShare[$\mathcal{P}_{phy}, \mathcal{A}$]

Code for party P_i with secret s_i

1. Initiate $NAVSS\text{-}\text{SHARE}_i[\mathcal{P}_{log}, \mathcal{A}, P_i, s_i]$. For $1 \leq j \leq |\mathcal{P}_{log}|$, participate in $NAVSS\text{-}\text{SHARE}_j$. Let $\boldsymbol{u}_i^{(j)}$ be the output of $NAVSS\text{-}\text{SHARE}_j$.
2. Execute protocol $AgreeSet[\mathcal{J}, \mathcal{P}_{phy}, \mathcal{A}]$ with the boolean predicate : $\mathcal{J}(j) = 1$ if all the logical players associated with the physical P_j have completed their respective $NAVSS\text{-}\text{SHARE}$ successfully. Let $\mathcal{G}$ be the output of the protocol.
3. Output $\mathcal{G}, \boldsymbol{u}_i^{(j)}, P_j \in \mathcal{G}$.

Protocol EfficientAVShare[$\mathcal{P}_{log}, \mathcal{A}, P, s$]

The dealer P chooses a symmetric random matrix $R_{e \times e}$ such that $R[0, 0] = s$ and sends the vector $\boldsymbol{u}_i = R \cdot \boldsymbol{v}_i^T$ to logical player P_i.

1. Upon receiving $\boldsymbol{u}_i$, send $\langle \boldsymbol{v}_j, \boldsymbol{u}_i \rangle$ to logical player P_j.
2. Upon receiving messages m_{ji} from all logical players in $\mathcal{P}_{log} \setminus D$ for some $D \in \mathcal{A}_{log}$ (we use $\mathcal{A}_{log}$ to denote the adversary structure over logical players) check if $m_{ji} = \langle \boldsymbol{v}_i, \boldsymbol{u}_j \rangle$. If equality holds for all m_{ji}, and for all the logical players that P_i is acting for, then, send a $CheckMessage_i := "OK"$, else, send $CheckMessage_i := j$, where j denotes the smallest index such that the value received from P_j was not equal to $\langle \boldsymbol{v}_j, \boldsymbol{u}_i \rangle$, to all logical players.
3. Execute protocol $AgreeSet[\mathcal{J}, \mathcal{P}_{phy}, \mathcal{A}]$ with the boolean predicate: $\mathcal{J}(j) = 1$ if all the $CheckMessage$'s corresponding to physical player P_j has been received. Let $\mathcal{G}$ be the output of this protocol. If $CheckMessage_j = "OK" \; \forall \, j$ such that $P_j \in \mathcal{G}$, then the protocol succeeds with output $\boldsymbol{u}_i$. Else, set $FaultDetected_i := TRUE$.

Protocol ACheckShare[$\mathcal{P}_{log}, e', \mathcal{A}, P, s$]

1. The dealer sets $(0, \boldsymbol{g}) := \boldsymbol{u} - \boldsymbol{u}'$ and distributes shares using $(\boldsymbol{g}, 0)$ as the first row of R_{new}, to every logical player P_j using the protocol $EfficientAVShare$. If this fails, then the whole verification protocol fails.
2. Every logical player P_i checks that $\left(R' \cdot \boldsymbol{v}_i^{\;T} \right)[0] + \frac{\boldsymbol{v}_i[k+1]}{\boldsymbol{v}_i[k]} \left(R_{new} \cdot \boldsymbol{v}_i^{\;T} \right)[0] = \left(R \cdot \boldsymbol{v}_i^{\;T} \right)[0]$. If consistent for all the logical players that P_i is acting for, the physical player P_i sends $CheckBit_i := 1$, else he sends $CheckBit_i := 0$, to all (physical) players.
3. Every physical player executes protocol $AgreeSet[\mathcal{J}, \mathcal{P}_{phy}, \mathcal{A}]$ with $\mathcal{J}(j) = 1$ if all $CheckBit$'s related to physical player P_j has been received. Let $\mathcal{G}$ be the output of this protocol. If $CheckBit_j = 1$ for all $j \mid P_j \in \mathcal{G}$, then the verification was successful. Else, set $FaultDetected_i := TRUE$.

Protocol Re-SHARING[$\mathcal{P}_{log}, e', \mathcal{A}, s$]

1. Initiate $EfficientAVShare_i[\mathcal{P}_{log}, \mathcal{A}, P_i, s_i]$. Participate in $EfficientAVShare_j$ for all logical players P_j. If $FaultDetected_i = FALSE$ then let $\boldsymbol{u}_j$ be the output of $EfficientAVShare_j$. Else terminate with output 'NULL'.
2. Run $ACheckShare_i[\mathcal{P}_{log}, e', \mathcal{A}, s_i]$. Participate in $ACheckShare_j$ for all logical players P_j. If $FaultDetected_i = TRUE$ then terminate with output 'NULL'.
3. Execute protocol $AgreeSet[\mathcal{J}, \mathcal{P}_{phy}, \mathcal{A}]$ with the boolean predicate: $\mathcal{J}(j) = 1$ if P_j has completed $EfficientAVShare$'s for all the logical players that he is acting for, successfully to get the output say $\mathcal{G}$.
4. Locally compute the linear combination of the shares received from players in $\mathcal{G}$, to result in an $R_{e \times e}$-sharing, as in [10].

MUL[$\mathcal{P}_{log}, \mathcal{A}, x, y$]

Each logical player P_i does the following:

- Evaluates $\boldsymbol{z}_i[j] = \boldsymbol{x}_i[j] \cdot \boldsymbol{y}_i[j]$, for $j = 0, \ldots, e - 1$.
- Calls $Re - Sharing[P, 2e - 2, e, z]$ which starts with a $2t$-sharing of z.
- If the above Re-SHARING call outputs 'NULL' then terminates with output 'FAIL', else ends with the $R_{e \times e}$-sharing of z.

Fig. 3. Input Sharing with Fault Detection, Re-SHARING and Multiplication

Theorem 4. *The protocol Re-*SHARING *is a* $\mathcal{A}$-*resilient protocol for the re-sharing functionality.*

Proof. (sketch) The protocol *EfficientAVShare* terminates because the players of at most one set $D \in \mathcal{A}_{log}$, for some set D, is corrupted and hence at least $(\mathcal{P}_{log} \setminus D)$ players will distribute consistent vectors and so the set $\mathcal{G}$ is well defined. On similar lines, we can see that the protocol *ACheckShare* terminates as well. The correctness of the Re-SHARING protocol follows: If the protocol *EfficientAVShare* succeeds, then it implies that there exists a set of players $\mathcal{G} \supseteq (\mathcal{P} \setminus D)$ such that each player $P_i \in \mathcal{G}$ is consistent with the vectors of at least players in $(\mathcal{P} \setminus D)$ of which at least $(\mathcal{P} \setminus (D_1 \cup D_2))$ are honest. Since $\mathcal{A}$ satisfies $\mathcal{Q}^{(4)}$, the players in $\mathcal{G}$ have verifiable vectors and the $(\mathcal{P} \setminus (D_1 \cup D_2))$ honest players in $\mathcal{G}$ define a unique sharing of s. Also, if the sharing phase of the protocol *ACheckShare* succeeds, then indeed the vectors of all players are as per R'-sharing. Hence, if there exists a set of players $\mathcal{G} \supseteq (\mathcal{P} \setminus D)$ such that each honest player $P_i \in \mathcal{G}$ is consistent with $(R' \cdot v_i{}^T)[0] + \frac{v_i[k+1]}{v_i[k]}(R_{new} \cdot v_i{}^T)[0] = (R \cdot v_i{}^T)[0]$, then the vectors u, u' and $(0, g)$ are uniquely defined which implies that $u[0] = u'[0]$ (i.e. *same* secrets!). The secrecy of this protocol is due to the independence of the the sharings.   □

4.5   Segment Fault Localization

The purpose of fault localization is to find out which players are corrupted or, because agreement about this can usually not be reached, at least to narrow down the set of players containing the cheaters. The output of an (r, p)-localization is a set $\mathcal{D}_{log}$ with $|\mathcal{D}_{log}| = p$ logical players, guaranteed to contain at least r corrupted logical players.

For our lazy re-sharing procedure, to preserve the ability for continuing the computation, it is required that after a (sequence of) (r, p)-localizations and logical player eliminations (without Re-SHARING), still $\mathcal{A}$ satisfies $\mathcal{Q}^{(4)}$ holds, and each R' sharing still satisfies $e' < 2e$. As will be evident in the sequel, the localizations used in our protocol indeed satisfy these requirements.

In our protocol, if a segment has detected a fault, the first faulty sub-protocol is found and we invoke the corresponding fault localization procedure. In what follows, we outline the fault localization methodology for the various sub-protocols that are allowed to fail with a partial fault detection, viz. *EfficientAVShare*, *ACheckShare* and *Re-*SHARING.

1. **Sharing Protocol (*EfficientAVShare*):** From the corresponding common set $\mathcal{G}$, among all the physical players who complained about an inconsistency, each of the uncorrupted players can agree on the physical player P_i with the smallest index i. From P_i's *CheckMessage$_i$* all the players know some P_j that P_i complained about. The physical players execute a BA protocol (with their *CheckMessage$_i$*, that P_i sent to them, as input) to agree on a single P_j. Then every physical player sets $\mathcal{D}_{phy} := \{P, P_i, P_j\}$, where P is the corresponding dealer. It is obvious that all players find the same set $\mathcal{D}_{phy}$, and at least one physical player in $\mathcal{D}_{phy}$ must be corrupted. Define the

weight[7] of a physical player P_i to be $w(P_i) = |\{k|\Im(k) = P_i, 1 \le k \le d\}|$.
Let $w_{min} = \min(w(P), w(P_i), w(P_j))$ where $\mathcal{D}_{phy} := \{P, P_i, P_j\}$. Define the
localization $\mathcal{D}_{log} = w_{min}$ *rows of each of* P, P_i *and* P_j. Clearly, $\mathcal{D}_{log}$ is a
$(w_{min}, 3w_{min})$-localization.

2. **Verifying Shares Protocol ($ACheckShare$):** Let P_i be the physical
   player with the smallest index in the common set $\mathcal{G}$ who complained. Then
   the set $\mathcal{D}_{phy} := \{P, P_i\}$, and $\mathcal{D}_{log}$ is constructed similarly.

3. **Re-SHARING Protocol:** Failure of Re-SHARING protocol is due to the failure of either or both of the above sub-protocols. Then the same $\mathcal{D}_{log}$ is
   determined as in the first failed sub-protocol.

5   The Top-Level Protocol

Let $f : \mathcal{F}^n \to \mathcal{F}$ be given by an arithmetic circuit $\mathcal{C}$. Our protocol for securely
computing $f(x_1, x_2, \dots, x_n)$ is described in Fig. 4.

6   Complexity Analysis of Our Protocol

In this section, MC stands for message complexity, BC denotes Broadcast complexity, BAC denotes Byzantine Agreement complexity and d denotes the size
of the minimum monotone span program correpondinng to the $\mathcal{A}$.

Complexity Analysis of Initial Sharing : In the $NAVSS$-$\text{SHARE}_i[\mathcal{P}_{phy}, \mathcal{A}, P]$ pro-
tocol the distribution phase communicates $MC = ne \lg |\mathcal{F}| + d^2 \lg |\mathcal{F}|$ bits. In
the verification phase each party needs to send a clique in the graph which
requires $O(d)$ bits. So, this phase has $MC = O(d^2)$ and $BC = O(n \lg n)$.
The $InputShare[\mathcal{P}, \mathcal{A}]$ protocol runs $NAVSS$-SHARE_i n times followed by an
$AgreeSet$ protocol. Hence, $MC = O(nd^2 \lg |\mathcal{F}|)$ bits and $BC = O(n^2 \lg n)$ bits.
Complexity Analysis of Receiving Output : The $NAVSS$-$\text{REC}[\mathcal{P}_{log}, \mathcal{A}, P]$ protocol requires each logical player to send e field elements to P. This requires
$MC = O(ed \lg \mathcal{F})$ bits.
Complexity Analysis of our Efficient VSS: In the $EfficientAVShare_i$ protocol
the distribution phase communicates $MC = ne \lg |\mathcal{F}| + d^2 \lg |\mathcal{F}|$ bits. The pair-
wise consistency checks need another $MC = O(d^2 \lg |\mathcal{F}|)$ bits to be sent. The
agreement on $\mathcal{G}$ has $BAC = O(n)$ bits. The $ACheckShare$ protocol runs an
$EfficientAVShare_i$ followed by n^2 bits of communication and an $AgreeSet$ pro-
tocol. Hence, $MC = O(d^2 \lg |\mathcal{F}|)$ and $BAC = O(n)$ bits.
Complexity Analysis of Re-SHARING : The Re-SHARING protocol amounts
to running each of the above two protocols, namely $EfficientAVShare$ and
$ACheckShare$ d times followed by an $AgreeSet$ protocol. This requires $MC =$
$O(d^3 \lg |\mathcal{F}|)$ bits and $BAC = O(dn)$ bits.
VSS with Fault Localization uses $BAC = O(\lg n)$.
Analysis of a Segment with ℓ Multiplications: Every multiplication gate takes up
to three Re-SHARING (re-sharing of arguments and the actual multiplication),

---

[7] Informally, the weight of a player is the number of rows in the MSP assigned to him;
i.e. the number of logical players that he acts for.

Protocol AsyncPerfectSecureCompute[$n, \mathcal{C}, x_1, \ldots, x_n$]

1. **Initialization:** Set $\mathcal{P}_{phy} := \{P_1, P_2, \ldots, P_n\}$ and $\mathcal{P}_{log} := \{P_1, \ldots, P_d\}$ and the adversary structure $\mathcal{A}$ satisfies $\mathcal{Q}^{(4)}$.

2. **Input Sharing:** Set $(\mathcal{G}, u_i^{(j)}) := InputShare[\mathcal{P}_{log}, \mathcal{A}], j \in \mathcal{G}_{log}$ (we use $\mathcal{G}_{log}$ to denote all the logical players enacted by the physical players in $\mathcal{G}$).
   The secret s_i of a physical player P_i in the above sub-protocol is x_i. For a line l in the circuit, let $l^{(i)}$ denote the share of logical player P_i in the value of this line. If l is the jth input line of the circuit, then: Set $l^{(i)} := u_i^{(j)}[0]$ if $j \in \mathcal{G}$ and $l^{(i)} := 0$ otherwise.

3. **Computation:**

   For each segment of the circuit :
     Repeat
       For each physical P_i: Set $FaultDetected_i := FALSE$.
       For each gate g in the segment:
         Each logical player P_i does the following:
           Wait until the ith shares of all input lines of g are computed.
           If g is an addition gate with output line l and input lines l_1, l_2:
             Set $l^{(i)} := l_1^{(i)} + l_2^{(i)}$.
             Logical players P_i with $FaultDetected_i = TRUE$ use random shares.
           If g is a multiplication gate with output line l and input lines l_1, l_2:
             If l_k, $k = 1$ or 2 is shared with $R_{e' \times e'}$, with $e' > e$:
               Call $Re - Sharing[\mathcal{P}_{log}, e', \mathcal{A}, l_k]$
               Every physical player P_i with $FaultDetected_i = TRUE$ uses
               random shares in the sub-protocol. If the sub-protocol
               outputs 'NULL', then P_i sets $FaultDetected_i := TRUE$
             Set $l := MUL[\mathcal{P}_{log}, \mathcal{A}, l_1, l_2]$
             Every physical player P_i with $FaultDetected_i = TRUE$ uses
             random shares in the sub-protocol. If the sub-protocol
             outputs 'FAIL', then P_i sets $FaultDetected_i := TRUE$
       For each physical P_i, broadcast $FaultDetected_i$.
       Set $\mathcal{G} := AgreeSet[\mathcal{J}, \mathcal{P}_{phy}, \mathcal{A}], \mathcal{J}(j) = 1$ for P_j if it received the broadcast
       from P_j.
       If at least one physical player in $\mathcal{G}$ has $FaultDetected_i = TRUE$:
         Each P_i broadcasts the index of the first sub-protocol that failed.
         Agree on the smallest sub-protocol that failed.
         Invoke the fault localization procedure for that sub-protocol
           to get $\mathcal{D}_{log}$ from $\mathcal{D}_{phy}$.
         Set the logical player set $\mathcal{P}_{log} := \mathcal{P}_{log} \setminus \mathcal{D}_{log}$
         and $\mathcal{A} := \mathcal{A} \setminus \{D | D \in \mathcal{A}, \mathcal{D}_{phy} \cap D = \emptyset\}$.
     Until $((FaultDetected_i = FALSE)$ for all $P_i \in \mathcal{G})$.
   For each physical player P needing output:
     Call $OutputReconstruction[\mathcal{P}_{log}, \mathcal{A}, P]$.

Fig. 4. Protocol for Asynchronous Secure Computation

where the re-sharings can be performed in parallel. In every Re-SHARING only the actual computation with partial fault detection is performed. At the end of the segment, during (strict) fault detection, n bits are broadcast as well as an *AgreeSet* is run. If there are faults, extended fault localization is performed. There are at most $O(n\ell)$ partial fault detections, hence to localize the first one which reported some failures $O(n \lg(n\ell))$ bits are broadcast. The total complexities are $MC = O(\ell d^3 \lg |\mathcal{F}|)$ and $BAC = O(\ell n d)$.

Cumulative Complexity Analysis: The protocol *AsyncPerfectSecureCompute* $[n, \mathcal{C}, x_1, \ldots, x_n]$ uses *InputShare*$[\mathcal{P}, \mathcal{A}]$ sub-protocol followed by the computation of $\frac{m}{\ell}$ segments, each of which has ℓ multiplications. In all, at most n segments may fail and require repetition. Finally the protocol *NAVSS*-REC$[\mathcal{P}, \mathcal{A}, P]$ is performed $O(n)$ times, possibly in parallel. The overall complexity is as follows. $MC = \{O(d^3 \lg |\mathcal{F}|)\} + \{(\frac{m}{l} + n) O(\ell d^3 \lg |\mathcal{F}|)\}$ and $BAC = \{(\frac{m}{l} + n) O(\ell n d)\}$. When setting $l = \frac{m}{n}$, we have $MC = O(m d^3 \lg |\mathcal{F}|)$ bits and $BAC = O(mnd)$ bits. When restricted to the threshold case $(d = n)$, the protocol broadcasts $O(mn^2)$ bits which substantially improves over the protocol of [4] that broadcasts $O(mn^4)$ bits.

7   Conclusions

In this work we have initiated the study of perfectly secure multiparty computation over asynchronous networks in the non-threshold adversarial model – we show that perfectly secure asynchronous multiparty computation is possible if and only if no *four* sets in the adversary structure cover the full player set. We provide efficient constructions whenever possible and remark that these constructions are as good as the *best* known asynchronous protocols when restricted to the threshold setting. We remark that drawing upon ideas in [8,6,17] and those in this paper, one can give similar constructions for unconditionally secure asynchronous multiparty computation with less stringent constraints on the adversary structure and much smaller communication complexities – unconditionally secure (i.e., with a non-zero but negligible error probability) asynchronous multiparty computation is possible if and only if no *three* sets in the adversary structure cover the full player set. Furthermore, we remark that by using techniques in [17], a much more efficient protocol is achievable.

References

1. Donald Beaver. Secure multiparty protocols and zero-knowledge proof systems tolerating a faulty minority. *Journal of Cryptology*, pages 75–122, 1991.
2. Donald Beaver, Joan Feigenbaum, Joe Kilian, and Phillip Rogaway. Security with low communication overhead. In *CRYPTO '90*, pages 62–76, 1990.
3. Donald Beaver, Silvio Micali, and Phillip Rogaway. The round complexity of secure protocols. In *Proceedings of 22nd ACM STOC*, pages 503–513, 1990.
4. M. Ben-Or, R. Canetti, and O. Goldreich. Asynchronous secure computations. In *Proceedings of 25th ACM STOC*, pages 52–61, 1993.

5. M. Ben-Or, S. Goldwasser, and A. Wigderson. Completeness theorems for non-cryptographic fault-tolerant distributed computation. In *Proceedings of 20th ACM STOC*, pages 1–10, 1988.

6. M. Ben-Or, B. Kelmer, and T. Rabin. Asynchronous secure computation with optimal resilience. In *Proceedings of 13th ACM PODC*, pages 183–192, 1994.

7. R. Canetti. Security and composition of multiparty cryptographic protocols. *Journal of Cryptology*, 13(1):143–202, 2000.

8. R. Canetti and T. Rabin. Optimal asynchronous byzantine agreement. In *Proceedings of 25th ACM STOC*, pages 42–51, 1993.

9. D. Chaum, C. Crepeau, and I. Damgard. Multiparty unconditionally secure protocols. In *Proceedings of 20th ACM STOC*, pages 11–19, 1988.

10. R. Cramer, I. Damgard, and U. Maurer. Efficient general secure multiparty computation from any linear secret sharing scheme. In *EUROCRYPT2000*, LNCS, Springer-Verlag, 2000.

1. Ronald Cramer, Ivan Damgard, Stefan Dziembowski, Martin Hirt, and Tal Rabin. Efficient multiparty computations secure against an adaptive adversary. In *EUROCRYPT '99*, volume 1592 of LNCS, pages 311–326, 1999.

Matthew K. Franklin and Moti Yung. Communication complexity of secure computation. In *Proceedings of 24th ACM STOC*, pages 699–710, 1992.

Rosario Gennaro, Micheal O. Rabin, and Tal Rabin. Simplified VSS and fast-track multiparty computations with applications to threshold cryptography. In *Proceedings of 17th ACM PODC*, 1998.

O. Goldreich, S. Micali, and A. Wigderson. How to play any mental game. In *19th ACM STOC*, pages 218–229. ACM Press, 1987.

15. M. Hirt and U. Maurer. Complete characterization of adversaries tolerable in secure multiparty computation. In *16th ACM PODC*, pages 25–34, August 1997.

16. M. Hirt and U. Maurer. Player simulation and general adversary structures in perfect multiparty computation. *Journal of Cryptology*, 13(1):31–60, April 2000.

17. Martin Hirt and Ueli Maurer. Robustness for free in unconditional multi-party computation. In *CRYPTO '01*, LNCS. Springer-Verlag, 2001.

18. Martin Hirt, Ueli Maurer, and Bartosz Przydatek. Efficient multi-party computation. In *ASIACRYPT 2000*, LNCS. Springer-Verlag, December 2000.

19. M. V. N. Ashwin Kumar, K. Srinathan, and C. Pandu Rangan Asynchronous Perfectly Secure Computation tolerating Generalized Adversaries Technical Report, IITM, Chennai, February 2002.

20. M. Karchmer and A. Wigderson. On span programs. In *Proceedings of the 8th Annual IEEE Structure in Complexity Theory*, pages 102–111, 1993.

21. S. Micali and P. Rogaway. Secure computation. In *CRYPTO'91*, volume 576 of LNCS, pages 392–404. Springer-Verlag, 1991.

22. S. Micali and P. Rogaway. *Secure Computation: The information theoretic case.*, 1998. Former version: Secure Computation, In *CRYPTO '91*, volume 576 of LNCS, pages 392-404, Springer-Verlag, 1991.

23. T. Rabin and M. Ben-Or. Verifiable secret sharing and multiparty protocols with honest majority. In *Proceedings of 21st ACM STOC*, pages 73–85, 1989.

Author Index